MILESTONES

A Chronology of
American Women's History

Doris Weatherford

Facts On File, Inc.

Milestones: A Chronology of American Women's History

Copyright © 1997 by Doris Weatherford

Facts On File, Inc.
11 Penn Plaza
New York NY 10001

Library of Congress-in-Publication Data

Weatherford, Doris.
    Milestones : a chronology of American women's history / Doris L.
Weatherford.
       p.   cm.
    Includes bibliographical references and index.
    ISBN 0-8160-3200-9 (alk. paper)
    1. Women—History. 2. Women—Social conditions. I. Title.
HQ1121.W34 1997
304.5'09—dc20   96-18359

Facts On File books are available at special discounts when purchased in bulk quantites for businesses, associations, institutions or sales promotions. Please call our Special Sales Department in New York at (212) 967-8800 or (800) 322-8755.

Text design by Cathy Rincon
Cover design by Molly Herron

Printed in the United States of America

RRD FOF 10 9 8 7 6 5 4 3 2 1

This book is printed on acid-free paper

For my sisters

and brothers,

Norman Barge,

Elaine Byrnside,

Warren Barge,

Ralph Barge,

and Margaret Motley

Contents

I

Women in the
Age of Exploration

1492–1699

1492 Christopher Columbus uses maps obtained from his mother-in-law in his historic voyage. A widow, Doña Isabel Moniz carefully preserved maps, logs, and other useful items that had belonged to her husband.

Columbus also benefits from the experience of his late wife, Filipa Perestrello e Moniz. She not only explored dangerous waters with her father, but she also made valuable geographical drawings that her husband now uses.

1504 Queen Isabella, who funded the initial Columbus voyage, dies in Spain. Her scientific curiosity, especially in supporting the risky idea of sailing west to go east, is directly responsible for European exploration of the Americas.

1513 Following up on Columbus's explorations, Ponce de Léon's ship reaches land that will become part of the United States; this expedition on Florida's east coast includes at least one woman from the Caribbean.

1527 Although no women are on board, the first English ship to explore North America's East Coast is named for a woman: the *Mary Guildford* sails from Labrador to Florida and on to the Caribbean.

1528 Panfilo de Narvaez lands on Florida's west coast and greets a Timucuan chief, Hirrihigua, by cutting off his nose. When Hirrihigua's mother objects, Spanish dogs eat her alive.

1539 Ana Mendez and Francisca Hinestrosa sail with Hernando de Soto from Cuba to Florida. Hinestrosa is killed at the battle of Chicaga in 1541, but Mendez, who had been Doña Isabel de Soto's servant, survives and testifies on her experience before a Spanish commission in 1560.

1549 Dominican Father Luis Cancer is guided by a native woman called Magdalena from Vera Cruz, Mexico, to Tampa Bay.

1558 Elizabeth I succeeds her half sister Mary I and begins the long and successful reign that makes her known as Good Queen Bess. A strong monarch of England, she will support numerous voyages of American exploration.

1564 Fort Caroline on the St. Johns River near the modern Florida-Georgia border is settled by French Protestants. Many of these Huguenots will be killed by Spanish soldiers the following year, but some escape and are protected by natives.

This predicts future patterns, for the French will build better relations with natives than other Europeans do. Often women are the crucial link between the natives and the newcomers. In contrast to European values, some American natives have no word for virginity and most tribes are matrilineal, so that children are never seen as bastards and women have more sexual freedom.

1565 Spanish St. Augustine, the nation's oldest city, is founded in Florida. Soon it will have some 100 women among 1,200 men. On September 8, the settlers hold the first celebratory mass of thanksgiving at a permanent North American community. Several other Thanksgivings were conducted at impermanent sites as early as 1513—and all of them, of course, predate the Pilgrims' famous 1621 Thanksgiving.

Not until the year 2055 will the American flag have flown over Florida for as long as the Spanish flag did.

1567 When Don Pedro Menendez de Aviles and his party of soldiers and Jesuit priests arrive in Florida, they find, to their surprise, three Christian women living with the west coast Calusa tribe. The women may have been victims of a shipwreck or pirate captives from the Caribbean.

No nuns come with these Spanish priests. Although the Spanish develop permanent cities in both Florida and the Southwest, Spanish sisterhoods are not included in either place. The schools, hospitals, and other humanitarian institutions that they might have established will remain undeveloped for more than a century, until French nuns finally arrive in New Orleans in

This 1564 illustration of indigenous women in Florida planting corn was done by Jacques LeMoyne, one of the French Huguenots at Fort Caroline on the St. John's River, near the modern Florida-Georgia border. Library of Congress; LeMoynes' engraving originally published by Theodore DeBry in *Grandes Voyages,* 1591

1727. No sisters are sponsored by the Spanish until well into the 19th century.

1568 Planned family colonization begins, and some 225 Spanish settlers go as far as north Santa Elena, in modern South Carolina. Among other crops, this colony grows sassafras for curing syphillis.

1571 Menendez de Aviles moves to the Santa Elena colony with his wife and daughters; their dower contracts eventually transfer power to his sons-in-law.

1587 The English attempt colonization. Only days after arrival on Roanoke Island in what will become North Carolina, Elenor White Dare delivers the first English child born in North America, Virginia Dare.

Elenor White Dare, who sailed in the advanced stages of pregnancy, is one of 17 women among 116 settlers. After Virginia Dare is christened on August 24, her grandfather John White, the ship's captain, goes to Europe for supplies and is delayed; when he returns three years later, no trace can be found of anyone in this "Lost Colony."

1593 Maria Menendez y Posada marries Juan Menendez Marquez, establishing a family dynasty that holds power in Spanish Florida through five generations. Maria is the 12-year-old niece of Don Pedro Menendez de Aviles, and her dowry brings Juan the title of royal treasurer.

1598 Spanish settlement of the Southwest begins when Juan de Ornate leads some 400 men, women, and children north from Mexico. Some settle at what is now El Paso, Texas, while others move on into modern New Mexico.

Ornate pays for this expedition himself, but most Spanish expansion is characterized by government-sponsored soldiers and priests—as opposed to the family-based settlements that the English will establish in the East. Although Spanish soldiers cohabit with native women, the failure to bring more women from Spain eventually is a factor in the loss of the Spanish empire to the English, whose colonies see quick population increases because of the presence of many more women.

1602 Martha's Vineyard, an island off the coast of Cape Cod, is named by English explorer Bartholomew Gosnold for his child, who had died recently. Death during infancy and childhood will continue to be common until well into the 20th century; often it is a reflection of the poor health of women who cannot limit their pregnancies.

1607 One of the first Englishmen to arrive in Virginia writes of the high status accorded a native woman of Powhattan's tribe:

> Wee sawe the queene of this country cominge in self-same fashion of state as Powhattan; yea, rather, with more majesty. She is a fat, lusty, manly woman. She had much copper about her neck: a crownet of copper upon her hed. She had long black haire, which hanged loose downe her back to her middle; which only part was covered with a deare's skyn, and ells all naked. Our captain presented her with guyfits liberally; whereupon she cheered somewhat, and requested him to shoote off a peece [gun]. She had much corne in the ground. . . .

Pocahontas, a daughter of Powhattan, saves the life of Captain John Smith, who led the founding expedition to Jamestown earlier in the year. Smith is captured by Powhattan's warriors, and he later writes that "at the minute of my execution," the chief responded to the pleas of his daughter, then about 12 years old. As a result, Pocahontas becomes a mediator between the two groups; she will save the Englishmen from ambush again in 1609.

1608 Virginia—named for Elizabeth, the Virgin Queen who ruled over a Golden Age of English history until her death five years ago—receives the first English-speaking women who settle in America's first permanent colony of Jamestown. Anne Forrest, a married woman, and her 13-year-old maid, Anne Burras, join some 400 men.

Two months after Anne Burras marries she turns 14. Her husband is John Laydon, and their wedding is the first in English America. She bears a child named Virginia and at least three more daughters, surviving the starvation and sickness that plagues others.

1609 In August, seven ships arrive at Virginia's Jamestown, with more than 100 women aboard. The colony's financiers initially offer women free land, but when it is discovered that such independence limits female willingness to wed, the practice ends.

Thereafter, about one of every three newcomers in the Southern colonies is a woman. Many are indentured (bound to a slavelike status until their fare is repaid), and men greet ships to buy these women as brides, thereby repaying their fares. Although a "boundwoman" could repay her indenture by working (usually for seven years), few suitable jobs are available, and the women encounter a great deal of pressure to wed and reproduce.

✦ Santa Fe is founded, with Don Pedro de Peralta as governor; the new city is initially called La Villa Real de Santa Fe de San Francisco de Assisi.

1610 Most of Jamestown's colonists die in the "starving tyme," for the colony's men did not plan sufficient supplies to feed the new arrivals through winter. Approximately 450 of the colony's 500 settlers starve during the winter of

1609–10, and some resort to cannibalism: Jamestown's Captain John Smith records that a man "did kill his wife . . . and had eaten part of her before it was known, for which he was executed."

1614 Pocahontas weds Englishman John Rolfe, and the marriage signals an alliance for peace between her people and the newcomers. She adopts English dress and, calling herself Rebecca Rolfe, travels to England with her husband, where she bears a son named Thomas.

Captain John Smith sends a letter of introduction to the queen, praising the "relief . . . brought us by this Lady Pocahontas." She lives near Kew Gardens, has her portrait painted, attends balls, and is received at the court of James I.

1617 After visiting her husband's family in Norfolk, Pocahontas is preparing to return to Virginia when she falls ill. The ship is already headed down the Thames, and she dies soon after being taken ashore. She is buried on March 21 at St. George's Church in the parish of Gravesend. When her husband returns without her, hope for peaceful coexistence between natives and newcomers quickly wanes.

1619 The first black women and men arrive in North America when a Dutch ship brings about 20 to Jamestown. They are treated much like white indentured servants, with limitations on working conditions and hope of eventual freedom, until chattel slavery is codified into Virginia law three decades later.

Titled "The Beginning of New England," this illustration accurately represents the bleak living conditions of the Pilgrim women who arrived in Massachusetts in December 1620. No preparations had been made for their arrival; this poor planning on the part of the colony's leadership proved fatal. Library of Congress

1620 Of the 104 Pilgrims who arrive at Cape Cod's Provincetown in November on the *Mayflower*, 18 are adult women; by the end of that terrible winter, 14 of them will be dead. This 78% death rate indicates suffering greatly disproportionate to that of the Pilgrim men, whose death rate is 40%. Because 16% of children die—at a time when childhood death rates are often much higher—Pilgrim mothers are probably starving themselves so that their children can eat.

At least three of the *Mayflower* women are pregnant when they venture into the unknown: Elizabeth Hopkins bears a son at sea, whom she names Oceanus; Susanna White delivers a boy, Peregrine, soon after arrival; and Mary Norris Allerton's child is born dead in dark December, while she herself will die in February.

While the ship is anchored in Cape Cod Bay, Dorothy Bradford, the governor's wife, either falls or jumps to her icy death.

✦ Mary Chilton is the first woman to set foot on Plymouth Rock when the *Mayflower* arrives there from its temporary anchorage at Provincetown. The Pilgrims land at Plymouth on December 25, but the date is not significant, for they disapprove of England's Christmas celebrations.

Too sick to begin building in the wintry wilderness, the Pilgrims continue to live on the ship until January 27. Burials are conducted at night so that the natives will not see their weakened state.

1621 When spring comes to Plymouth, four adult women and 11 girls remain alive. Greatly outnumbered by males eager for the girls to reach "marriageable age," this tiny remnant of females "went willingly into the fields and took their little ones with them to set corn."

✦ The first wedding of the Plymouth colony is held in May. Susanna White, who was widowed only 11 weeks earlier, marries Edward Winslow, whose wife died during the tragic winter.

A more famous wedding is held later. It is the first between never-married partners, and the courtship of Priscilla Mullins by John Alden becomes legendary when a poem is written about it

more than two centuries later. The legend's romanticism ignores the harsh circumstances of Priscilla Alden's life: she was orphaned, bore at least 11 children, and died in such obscurity that the date is unknown.

1623 Thirty families—110 men, women, and children—arrive in May on the *New Netherland* to settle New Amsterdam, which later becomes New York City. It is an international community from the beginning, for these first colonists are sponsored by Dutch financiers but are mostly Walloons—Protestant, French-speaking refugees from what is now Belgium. Another Dutch ship arrives at New Amsterdam three months later, and the colonists form settlements from Albany to Delaware.

✦ Mistress Elizabeth Poole, of Taunton in England's Somerset area, joins the stockholders of the Dorchester Company of Adventures; later she is considered the founder of Taunton, Massachusetts.

"Mistress" is the title given women of genteel but not noble rank; women of lower rank are called "Goodwife," which is often shortened to "Goody."

1624 Catelina de Trice is the only woman with eight men who settle at Fort Orange, now Albany, New York. After delivering New Netherland's first baby in the fort, she returns to Manhattan and eventually becomes known as "the Mother of New York." Twice widowed, she bears at least eight children by three husbands; her second husband is a Norwegian from Bergen —from which that New Jersey place-name derives.

1626 A second Massachusetts colony begins at Salem; about 50 English colonists arrive two years later and some 300 in 1629. Thirty families organize a Puritan church on July 20, 1629, but, unlike Plymouth, Salem and its Charlestown branch attract colonists whose motivations are at least as much economic as religious.

◆ About 30 Dutch families settle on Manhattan Island. Expanding from there, some become extremely wealthy, at least in part because of the exceptional enterprise of the women. Urban Dutch women will engage in business from the earliest days of what eventually becomes New York, while those who settle in rural areas soon run manors that are the equivalent of grand European estates. Albany's Van Rensselaer family alone will own some 700,000 acres of land.

1630 Pregnant Margaret Winthrop says good-bye to her husband John, who leads the settlement of Massachusetts Bay. She will bear the baby, manage Groton Manor, their English estate, and preserve his letters—from which a detailed knowledge of this Puritan colony can be gained. She will join him two years later and, as the first lady of Massachusetts, will share her home with governing officials.

They arrange a mental telepathy upon his departure: "mundayes and frydayes at 5: of the clocke at night, we shall meet in spiritt."

Winthrop's *Arabella*, the flagship for three other ships of English settlers, arrives to colonize Boston and other Massachusetts towns. The flagship is named for young Lady Arabella Fiennes, who is aboard with her husband, Isaac Johnson, and her sister, Lady Sarah Fiennes. This group of about 1,000 is by far the wealthiest of any colonists; they settle between the two existing colonies at Salem and Plymouth.

◆ Dutch Tryntje Jonas becomes the first woman to practice medicine in what will become New York; a widow, she earned credentials in the Netherlands in midwifery and nursing.

1631 Despite their affluence, winter proves severe for the Boston settlers. Once again those in charge fail to plan: Although they had arrived in June, they planted no crops to carry them through. Lady Arabella dies, and 120 indentured servants are freed to forage for their own food.

◆ Thirty-four people from the Netherlands settle on the eastern shore of modern Delaware. When another Dutch ship arrives to check on them the following year, only skulls and bones are found.

1633 Among the first buildings constructed by New Amsterdam's new governor is a house for the colony's midwife, Tryntje Jonas.

1634 Maryland is founded by Catholic families, who are often persecuted in England. Its name is said to be in honor of Queen Henrietta Maria, wife of English king Charles I, who granted the colony's charter. The colonists, however, name their first settlement St. Mary's—a clear reference to the biblical mother of Jesus. The Catholic settlers may also be honoring Queen Mary I, whose five-year reign and tragic life was profoundly affected by her devotion to Catholicism.

◆ In the Boston colony, it is recorded that a daughter of the Humfry family went mad and that two others, both under 10, were found to have been "often abused by divers lewd persons, and filthiness in [t]his family." The scandal, and especially a decision on appropriate punishment, is a source of deep intellectual difficulty for the society's patriarchs.

1635 Penelope Van Princes is the only survivor when her Dutch shipmates are ambushed by natives as they disembark near what is now Monmouth, New Jersey. Left for dead with her intestines spilling out, she is rescued by a native woman who nurses her back to health and sells her to the Dutch at New Amsterdam.

1637 The church and state are synonymous in Massachusetts, and Anne Hutchinson is tried for sedition by Boston clergy who resent the popularity of religious gatherings in her home. Hutchinson, who had come to Boston from England three years earlier, is a midwife and a natural leader. Her emphasis on inner faith over outward piety is appealing to both men and women, but no dissent on religious ideas is allowed in this theocracy.

The clergy are especially upset that men respect Hutchinson, and she is charged with "all promiscuous and filthy coming together of men and women." When some of her male supporters refuse to join the militia in pursuit of Pequot natives, Hutchinson is tried and banished, but allowed to remain under house arrest until the end of winter.

1638   In March, Anne Hutchinson endures a second traumatic trial. At 47, she is pregnant and so ill that she is unable to defend herself. She is excommunicated from the church and banished from Massachusetts, and when the pregnancy ends disastrously, her suffering is taken as proof of God's disfavor. She moves to Rhode Island, where her supportive husband has prepared a home.

When Hutchinson is excommunicated, the only person to exit the church with her is Mary Dyer, a young married woman who had come from England three years earlier. Excommunication charges are then filed against Dyer, and she and her family also are exiled to Rhode Island.

✦ Swedish families arrive in Delaware on two ships, whose names translate to *Key of Calmar* and *Bird Grip*; they introduce the log cabin, which will become the most frequent type of frontier home. Their initial settlement, at modern Wilmington, is named Fort Christina for the reigning Swedish monarch.

✦ Prenuptial agreements are written in New Amsterdam: Annetje Jans assures her property rights prior to marriage, and later she will do the same for her daughters. All Dutch women retain their names at marriage; a baby girl takes her father's first name as her surname, with the result that there are no generational family names.

✦ Catholic Margaret Brent is given a large proprietary grant by Lord Baltimore as an incentive for her to emigrate from England with a shipload of siblings and servants. In Maryland, she is akin to a princess of a feudal state: She owns all of the land for miles and everyone who lives there works for her. Perhaps influenced by the recently dead

Queen Elizabeth, Mistress Brent turns down all suitors.

1639   Mistress Eaton, wife of the head of three-year-old Harvard College, confesses that she has done a poor job of administration. She blames the most egregious food failures on servants but acknowledges other faults, including "I must confess, that I have denied them [students] cheese, when they have sent for it, and it have been in the house; for which I shall humbly beg pardon." The Eatons are dismissed.

✦ Lady Deborah Moody, a widow in her 50s, leaves England for the religious freedom of America. She settles first on a large estate near Salem, where she soon finds that Massachusetts Puritans also expect more orthodoxy than she is willing to accept. In 1643, she will move to the greater freedom of Dutch New Amsterdam.

✦ Although Ursuline nuns begin work in Quebec this year, nearly a century will pass before nuns arrive in French New Orleans in 1727—and most of the 18th century will go by before the first convent is established within the boundaries of the almost wholly Protestant United States.

✦ In December, the first divorce decree in North America is granted by the Massachusetts Bay Colony. When Mrs. James Luxford discovers that her husband is a bigamist, the court not only grants a divorce but also awards his property to her and banishes him to England.

1641   The Body of Liberties is adopted as legal code in Massachusetts. Article 80 reads, "Eveire marryed woeman shall be free from bodilie correction or stripes by her husband, unlesse it be in his own defense upon her assault."

✦ From England, Lady Mary Armine endows a fund for spreading the gospel to Massachusetts natives. For the next 25 years, she contributes £20 sterling annually for humanitarian causes in the Bay Colony.

1642   Anne Hutchinson's husband dies, and the 51-year-old widow leads her family to a remote area near Long Island Sound. The Dutch who sell the land to her tell her that they have bought it from the natives, but that may not be the case. The following year, she and several of her 14 children will be killed by Algonquin.

Exiled from the security of Boston because of her desire to speak the truth as she saw it, Anne Hutchinson, a timeless martyr to freedom of thought, lived in America just nine years.

1643 With "good & pious intention," Ann Radcliffe, whose title is Lady Mowlson, donates £100 sterling to Harvard College, beginning "a p[er]petuall stipend" that will move "from one poore scholler to another." It is the nation's first scholarship fund—an endowment that will remain exclusively available to male students for more than two centuries.

✦ Without provocation, Dutch soldiers kill approximately 120 sleeping Algonquin camped on Manhattan Island; the natives retaliate, and Dutch women are killed along with children and men. After reinforcements arrive from Europe and other colonies, several hundred native women are among those killed in what is now Westchester County.

✦ In Massachusetts, Goody Armitage receives a license to "keepe an ordinary but not to draw wine." In other words, she was licensed as an innkeeper but was prohibited from bartending.

Other colonial women work in occupations that later became unconventional: they are barbers for both male and female customers, make rope and eyeglasses, and run slaughterhouses.

1644 When Lady Deborah Moody is attacked by Indians, she considers returning to Boston—until Governor John Winthrop calls her "a dangerous woeman" and insists that she must "leave her opinions behinde." Instead, she stays on Long Island—where her land includes modern Coney Island—and builds a colony dedicated to freedom of ideas.

✦ A woman and man are executed in Boston for adultery. The woman had recently married an

"old man," but according to a Boston chronicler, she continued to "receive the attentions of a young man of eighteen." They both are hanged.

1645 A fire that probably is set by disgruntled indentured servants destroys communal log structures at what is known as New Gothenburg in Delaware's Swedish colony, and the loss causes "great hardships" in winter.

Two years earlier, after Finns were recruited to the colony, the "whole white population of New Sweden consisted of 90 men, besides women and children." One of the Swedish settlers is the daughter of Governor Johan Printz; she married immigrant Johan Papegeja around 1644, and when Papegaja disappeared after a military controversy, she "obtained from the Council permission to take possession of Printzdorp and Tinnakonk."

1647 Lord Baltimore's younger brother, who is governor of Maryland, dies after naming Margaret Brent executor of his will. This makes her the effective governor of Maryland during a time of great unrest, and when colony's unpaid soldiers threaten armed rebellion, she uses her power-of-attorney to sell some of Lord Baltimore's property and raise the revenue needed to pay them.

Lord Baltimore, comfortably back in England, is outraged by her temerity, but Maryland's legislators defend her: Without Mistress Brent, they say, "All would have gone to ruin."

✦ On May 26, Alse Young is hanged in Windsor, Connecticut, on a charge of witchcraft. The following year—after delivering the baby she carries—Mary Johnson is executed for the same reason.

1648 America's first paved street is constructed when New Amsterdam's Annetje Lockermans Van Courtlandt tires of the mud and dust that comes from the road in front of her home and supervises her servants in paving it with cobblestone. Called Stone Street, it will survive for more than three centuries.

✦ A woman in Charleston, Massachusetts, is executed for witchcraft on vague charges. According to a clergyman's summary, she is "suspected partly because that after some angry words passing between her and her Neighbors, some mischief befell such Neighbors . . . or the like."

1649 The Maryland Toleration Act uses gender-neutral language in assuring civil rights to all Christian sects: "No person or persons . . . professing to believe in Jesus Christ, shall from henceforth be in any way troubled . . . for . . . his or her religion . . . nor in any way compelled . . . against his or her consent."

✦ Catholic Maryland welcomes a group of Puritans, including women, who flee political and religious strife in Virginia. In England, the same factors bring civil war, and pregnant Queen Henrietta Maria, daughter of the king of France and wife of England's Charles I, is forced into hiding. After delivery, she leaves her newborn behind and escapes to France, and thus avoids being beheaded like her husband.

✦ Massachusetts law refers to midwives in the same category as physicians and surgeons.

1650 Anne Dudley Bradstreet, a Massachusetts mother of eight, becomes America's first published poet. Without her knowledge, her sister's husband takes copies of her work to London, where it is published as *The Tenth Muse Lately Sprung Up in America*.

Her husband's family has more traditional views, however, for she rhymes, "I am obnoxious to each carping tongue; Who say my hand a needle better fits . . . For such despite they cast on Female wits."

✦ Maryland's Anne Arundell County, which will be the site of Annapolis, is named in honor of the recently dead wife of the current Lord Baltimore. Born in 1615, Anne Arundell had married at 13. Her Catholic family's fortune kept Lord Baltimore afloat financially, and she bore nine children before her death at age 34.

1651 Maryland founder Margaret Brent moves to Virginia. Although she is Catholic and Maryland is a Catholic haven, she presumably prefers to remove herself from controversy over her role as Lord Baltimore's executor. She lives prosperously in Virginia with a sister and brother until her death approximately 20 years later.

✦ In the frontier settlement of Springfield, Massachusetts, Widow Horton is charged with selling a gun to a native. She argues that she merely lent the gun, and is admonished to "speedily get it home againe or else it would cost her dere for no commonwealth would allow of such a misdemenor."

At the same time, an English boy is fined for hitting a native woman with a stick.

1652 A meeting of the newly formed Society of Friends, commonly called Quakers, goes on record against the American institution of slavery. The first members of this English sect start arriving in America during this decade; 30 years later, a major movement begins with the founding of Pennsylvania.

Unlike any other of the era's religions, Quakers feature nearly equal roles for women. They follow the model of true friendship created by English founders George Fox and Margaret Fell.

✦ Mary Dyer, who has borne at least five sons after her banishment to Rhode Island, accompanies Roger Williams and other of the colony's leaders to England, where she and her husband stay five years. During this time, she converts to the new Society of Friends. The high status that Quakers grant women naturally appeals to her, and when she returns to America in 1657, she will act as a missionary for the faith. Meanwhile, both Massachusetts and Connecticut will have banned Quakers.

1653 Eleven women are brought to court in Massachusetts for dressing above their station in life, in violation of Bay Colony law that does not allow a woman to wear silk scarves or hoods unless her husband is worth more than £200 sterling. Two pay fines; others prove their husbands have sufficient net worth, and one man who cannot meet the standard writes a defiant letter to the court defending his wife's right to dress as she chooses.

1654 The first Jewish families arrive in New Amsterdam from Brazil, where their ancestors had gone when Jews were expelled from Spain in 1492. Even in this relatively tolerant Dutch city, Jews lack full civil rights; they do not worship publicly until 1673.

✦ When Queen Christina abdicates the Swedish throne to devote herself to the study of philosophy and religion in Rome, the colony of New Sweden responds by abdicating its sovereignty: Knowing they will be overwhelmed by superior Dutch forces, they abdicate to New Amsterdam without warfare. Another 130 Swedes will arrive in Delaware in 1656, unaware of the surrender to the Dutch.

1655 A New Amsterdam man kills an Algonquin woman who was picking fruit from his tree, and a three-day "Peach War" results when the natives retaliate. About 100 whites are killed, including at least one woman who is tortured to death. Some 250 other whites are taken as hostages and held for ransom.

1656 The first Quakers to arrive in Boston are Mary Fisher and Ann Austin, Englishwomen who come via Barbados. Austin is the mother of five. Fisher, who is younger, becomes the better known: she has suffered severely for her belief in the Society of Friends, having been flogged naked and imprisoned in England. Their stay in Boston is brief, for the colony's theocrats soon banish them back to the West Indies.

1657 Two Quaker women are jailed and then expelled from New Amsterdam. Soon two other Quaker women—one of whom is a nursing mother—are arrested, roped to a cart, and taken to a dungeon. Governor Peter Stuyvesant alleviates this persecution after arguments from his sister, Annake Verlett.

✦ Spanish friars at Apalachee, Florida, complain to the governor, "Sir, these Indians are very jealous and they are excited beyond measure when someone approaches their wives, daughters, or sisters. And the lieutenant and the soldiers who are there are men and by that fact are weak. . . ."

1658 Quaker missionary Mary Dyer is banished from New Haven, Connecticut; she had been jailed in Boston and banished from the Bay Colony a year earlier for preaching heresy.

1659 Mary Parsons, a western Massachusetts woman, accuses her husband of causing their baby's death through witchcraft; when he is convicted, she confesses to infanticide but is found dead in her jail cell before she can be hanged.

✦ When Mary Dyer defies her exile and returns to Boston to visit two male Quakers who are jailed there, she is imprisoned. Again banished to Rhode Island, she returns a few weeks later, insistent on preaching the gospel as she believes it.

Her friends are hanged, and she is marched to the gallows with them—but her son and others (including the governor of Nova Scotia) have arranged a last-minute reprieve without her knowledge. She spends the winter with family in Rhode Island and Long Island, during which time they try to dissuade her from preaching.

1660 On the first day of June, Mary Barrett Dyer is hanged in Boston for heresy. Her family could not succeed in keeping her from the dangerous theocracy, and she returns there from Long Island in the spring. Her husband, who does not share her religious beliefs, pleads for her life, while her last speech is for freedom of expression.

1661 Anne Wolsley (Lady Calvert) is first lady of Maryland, where she immigrated last year with her husband, Governor Philip Calvert, to carry out Lord Baltimore's intention of firming up Catholicism. She is a good choice for this mission, for her English grandmother was burned at the stake for the faith.

When the couple dies about 20 years later, they are buried in lead coffins that protect their bones from decay. In 1994, more than 300 years later, scientists at the Smithsonian Institution open the coffins and announce that Lady Calvert was "very malnourished," despite her wealth. She has only five teeth; a low level of iron shows persistent bleeding; and her body also contains arsenic, which she may have taken in a vain attempt to treat the "permanent limp and painful abscess" that resulted from an improperly healed broken leg.

1662 Virginia law declares: "Whereas some doubts have arisen whether children got by any Englishman upon a Negro woman should be slave or free, be it therefore enacted . . . that all children . . . shall be held bond or free according to the condition of the mother."

◆ When Margaret Hardenbrook (or Hardenbroeck) marries merchant Frederick Phillipse, they combine two Dutch commercial enterprises, for they meet when Phillipse sails on a packet line owned by Hardenbrook. After the wedding, she continues to be an exporter of furs and importer of mercantile goods, and she frequently travels between the Netherlands and America. Like other Dutch women, she uses her maiden name and apparently continues in business all of her life —despite bearing five children by two husbands.

1664 New Netherlands becomes New York when Dutch colonists refuse to engage superior British military forces. About three-fourths of the current civilian population is composed of natives of the Netherlands; the remaining one-quarter includes not only the English but also French, Finns, Swedes, Portuguese, and Africans—most of whom were brought to North America from Brazil.

One of the Dutch majoriy is Sara Roeloef, the daughter of pioneer Annetje Jans. She speaks English, Dutch, and Algonquian fluently and is employed several times as an interpreter.

1665 Mary Hall, a resident of an island in Long Island Sound, is accused of murder through witchcraft. The court releases her to the custody of her husband, who had been charged with complicity.

This New York case is unusual, for most witchcraft charges are brought in the New England colonies. Between 1647 and 1662, 14 alleged witches are executed in Connecticut and Massachusetts; no one is ever executed for this crime in the southern colonies.

1666 *A Brief Description . . . of Carolina* promises, "If any maid or single woman have a desire to go over, they will think themselves in the Golden Age, when men paid a dowry for their wives; for if they be but civil, and under fifty years of age, some honest man or other will purchase them for their wives."

1667 Neighbors of Katherine Harrison, a wealthy widow, suspect her of witchcraft and try to have her banished from Westchester County, New York, but the court upholds her freedom.

1668 The English governor of New York marvels that "three Dutch girls, using books imported from Holland, became fine Latin scholars."

1669 Approximately 100 women and men sail from London to settle Charles Town, which later becomes Charleston, South Carolina. Soon English colonists from Barbados join them, for Carolina's expansive land is preferable to the limited space of Caribbean islands.

1671 Plymouth Colony signs a peace agreement with the Wamponoags, and one of the signatories is a woman, Awashonks. The widow of a chief, she heads the Sogonate band of these Rhode Island-based natives. Although she is a cousin to Wamponaoag King Philip, she keeps her people out of the worst of the warfare he leads during the next decade.

1672 Poet Anne Bradstreet dies at 60. She has continued to hone her ability as a wordsmith but remained too modest to publish in her lifetime. Other poems probably were destroyed when her home burned six years prior to her death. "To My Dear and Loving Husband" will be the best remembered of her work; it belies Puritan stereotypes and testifies to a lifetime of romance.

Among Anne Bradstreet's descendants will be abolitionist Wendell Phillips and two famous men who are both named Oliver Wendell Holmes.

1674 Maria Van Rensselaer, the daughter of New Amsterdam businesswoman Annetje Lockermans Van Courtland, administers her husband's vast estate after he dies, leaving her with six minor children. She holds the best property parcel in the colony—a fiefdom near Albany that is 24 miles square and includes gristmills, sawmills, and other enterprises as well as thousands of acres of farmland. She fights and wins several legal challenges, including one by her husband's brother.

1675 Violence erupts when a Spanish priest forces an elderly Chacato leader in western Florida to separate from three of his four wives. During the next two years, the Spanish, in nighttime raids on the Chacato villages, kidnap women and children to sell into slavery in the newly established English colony of Carolina.

✦ In New England's Plymouth Colony, Mehitabel Woodsworth accuses Mary Ingham of bewitchment. Ingham is tried and acquitted of witchcraft charges.

✦ When Thomas Walley of rural Massachusetts writes of his upcoming marriage, he—like other Puritans—emphasizes the practical over the romantic and gives all credit to God: "As for my Journey to Boston it is spoiled. God hath sent me a wife . . . and saved me the labor of a tediouse Journey. Mrs. Clark of the I[s]land was come to our Towne . . . we are agreed to become one."

1676 Early on a February morning, Wampanoags attack Lancaster, Massachusetts, killing 12 and capturing two dozen others, including Mary Rowlandson, who later writes of her expe-

rience. She is the mother of four children and, like many frontier women, smokes a pipe. Along with others, she is taken prisoner and held for ransom until May.

About the time that she is released, what the colonists call King Philip's War breaks out on Massachusetts' South Shore. Mrs. Henry Ewell of Scituate is baking bread on a May morning when she hears Narragansett war whoops; she runs to the garrison and alerts soldiers. When she returns, her baby is still asleep and the house is undisturbed—except that the bread is missing. Later in the day, however, her home is burned.

✦ The Pocasset band of Wamponoag is led during this year-long war by a woman named Wetamoo, who replaced her husband as sachem after his 1661 death. Only 26 of her 300 warriors survive the conflict, and her own head is displayed in Taunton, Massachusetts.

Over 50 New England towns are attacked and more than dozen completely destroyed, but ultimately the war is a disaster for the natives. It ends in August, when Philip—whose true name is Metacomet—is captured. His head will be exhibited in Plymouth for the next quarter-century, while his wife and child are sold into slavery in the West Indies. Ironically, Metacomet's father was Massasoit, the Indian who showed the Pilgrims how to plant corn and shared their first Thanksgiving.

✦ Kateri Tekakwitha, a young Mohawk, canoes at night to Sault St. Louis on the St. Lawrence River, where there is a village of Christian Indians. She is escaping from her tribe, for her Catholic baptism has met with disapproval so strong that she has been stoned.

At baptism, she took the Christian name of Catherine, which translates to Kateri. She also soon becomes known as the Lily of the Mohawks, for when she dies at age 24, she is quickly seen as a godly figure. Christian Indians in the Portage River area will pray to her and attribute miracles to her, and in 1932, she will be proposed for beautification by the Catholic church.

Tekakwitha's mother was an Algonquin captured by Mohawk prior to 1656. Like most young female captives, a warrior took her; she bore two children. Except for little Tekakwitha, the entire family died in a 1660 smallpox epidemic.

1677 Officials of the Virginia colony present a medal to Cockacoeske, a member of the Pamunkey tribe who has been influential in preserving peace. She has borne a child by an Englishman and is a vital link between the two groups; the widow of a chief, she signed a treaty with the English last year.

1680 In the far Southwest, Pueblo Indians revolt against their colonial rulers, and more than 400 Spanish settlers, including women, are killed in the Santa Fe area. Almost 2,000 others flee from New Mexico. More than a decade will pass before the Spanish return.

✦ French Huguenots arrive in southern Carolina, where women join men in an unsuccessful attempt to build an economy based on growing silkworms and making wine.

1681 Maria, a slave owned by Joshua Lamb of Roxbury, Massachusetts, is burned at the stake for arson. According to Boston newspapers, she "willfully set fire to her master's house."

1682 Pennsylvania is founded by Quakers, who differ from all other of the era's religions in their view of women as nearly the equal of men. Women are ordained as ministers and preach publicly. Female church leaders are involved in the decision making of female members, including such decisions as whether to marry.

Tens of thousands of Quaker women will provide future leadership in national efforts to end slavery, establish justice for minorities, and end war. Countless women in the 19th-century suffrage movement will have Quaker backgrounds, and the visionary members of this small religious sect ultimately have an impact on American history vastly disproportionate to their numbers.

✦ Unconnected to the Quaker migration to Philadelphia, Mary Fisher Cross—who was banished from Boston for her Quaker beliefs in 1656—returns to America from England. She has done missionary work throughout Europe, apparently including even an attempt to convert a Turkish sultan. In the time since her first trip to America, she has been married, widowed, and remarried. She now settles with her husband and children in Charleston, South Carolina, where a small Society of Friends exists.

Her remarriage is not unusual. In fact, widows —especially propertied ones—are so popular with single men that New England's Reverend Cotton Mather warns widows to beware of "such a pretended lover [who] may court *hers* more than *her.*"

✦ Mary Rowlandson's account of her 1676 experience with the Wampanoag is published as *The Soveraignty and Goodness of God . . . A Narrative of the Captivity and Restauration of Mrs. Mary Rowlandson.* It becomes a standard of American literature and will be reissued in at least 30 editions.

1683 Thirteen Mennonite and Quaker families from Krefeld, in western Germany near the Netherlands, settle Germantown, Pennsylvania. As much Dutch as German in origin, they keep their native language and conservative ways, but immediately protest against American slavery: "What thing in the world can be worse . . . than [to sell] slaves to strange countries, separating husbands from their wives and children."

1684 British authorities annul the charter of the Massachusetts Bay Colony, in part because colonial theocrats have executed British subjects for religious dissent. Among those is Mary Dyer, an English-born Quaker hanged in Boston 24 years earlier.

1687 Three black women, eight men, and one child escape from slavery by sailing from British Georgia to Spanish Florida. When Georgians demand their return the following year, Governor Quirogea of St. Augustine refuses, saying their work makes them assets to the community and they have converted to Catholicism. During the next decades, many other slaves will follow this example, some with Indian help.

1688 A group of French Huguenots, including women, arrives in New York to settle land purchased from an English lord; they name their community New Rochelle.

1689 The governance of the English colonies changes as Queen Mary II, daughter of deposed King James II, takes the throne. Unlike the reigns of Queens Elizabeth I and Mary I, however, this reign will be known as that of William and Mary, for she shares power with her Dutch husband.

✦ Antonia Basalia de Leon, the daughter of a widow who owns a large amount of land near modern Jacksonville, marries Francisco Tomas, an heir of the Menendez dynasty. Together their families own tens of thousands of acres in central Florida; some 7,000 head of cattle are raised on La Chua ranch alone.

✦ Boston's Cotton Mather publishes *Memorable Providences Relating to Witchcraft and Possessions*, which forms the basis of much of the witchcraft hysteria that arises within a few years. Mather, a minister, is perhaps the era's leading intellectual, and his voluminous writings reveal much about early colonial life, including that of the women. He does not consider his family of 16 children to be unusual, for he cites cases of women who bore 22 and 23 babies, as well as men who fathered more than 25 children by two or more wives.

1690 Boston officials authorize a consortium of 30 women to saw lumber and manufacture potash, a fertilizer.

1692 In January, girls in Salem, Massachusetts, amuse themselves by listening to tales of witchcraft told by Tituba, a young Caribbean-born slave in the home of Reverend Samuel Parrish. When Parrish's nine-year-old daughter Betsy shows signs of mental illness, the diagnosis is bewitchment. Several of her young friends also claim to be "afflicted," and they begin naming Salem citizens, especially women, as their bewitchers.

Sarah Good, Sarah Osborne, and Tituba are the first to be arrested in February, but only Tituba confesses. She is imprisoned and will be sold for the price of her prison fees next year; Salem, like other colonial towns, charges prisoners for their food and housing.

The witchcraft hysteria continues to grow, and three sisters whose maiden names were Towne are arrested in March and April. Rebecca Nurse, a property-owing matriarch, is the first. Accused by young Ann Putnam and Abigail Williams as well as by adult neighbors, there is such an uproar when the jury finds her innocent that the judge orders the men to reconsider. Her sisters, Mary Esty and Sarah Cloyce, are tried in April; Esty will be hanged in September, but Cloyce manages to avoid execution.

Meanwhile, Bridget Bishop is the first to be hanged. She has less family support than the Towne sisters, and she angers the court by arguing defiantly for herself. Perhaps most incriminating of all, she owns a red bodice. She dies for this on June 10. Five women, including Rebecca Nurse, follow her to Gallows Hill on July 19.

As the uproar continues through the summer, a total of 141 people are charged as witches, three of whom die in jail. After bizarre trials in which most save themselves by "confessing," the final mass execution is on September 22. In the end, 19 people—six men and 13 women—choose death over dishonesty and are hanged.

Giles Corey, an 80-year-old man who testified against his wife, is pressed to death on September 19 for refusing to be tried himself. In the last mass hanging, three days later, Martha Corey follows him to eternity.

1693 The Salem witchcraft trials continue in January, and eight people see their death warrants signed—but on the last day of the month, the Massachusetts governor reprieves them and forces the judge from his bench. In May, the governor frees those still imprisoned.

✦ North America's second college, the College of William and Mary, is founded in Virginia. Al-

This drawing of the Salem witch trials portrays women in two distinctive ways: while the one near the bench is making a strong argument in her defense, the other on the floor demonstrates the hysteria that seemed to possess accusers. Library of Congress

though named for a woman, it will be open—like all colleges—only to men.

◆ King Charles II of Spain establishes policy on runaway slaves in Florida, granting "liberty to all . . . the men as well as the women." His motivation probably is not so much humanitarian as the economic loss that such a policy can mean for the British colonies to the north.

1695 Dinah Nuthead carries on the Annapolis printing business that her husband began after he dies. She is the first of a number of female printers who will be active in the colonial era.

1697 The Massachusetts General Assembly grants Hannah Dustin (or Duston) of Haverhill £25 sterling as a reward for tomahawking nine Indians.

She and midwife Mary Neff were taken captive on March 15, just a week after Dustin's 12th-child was born. During a 100-mile march into New Hampshire, she had seen her infant daughter dashed against a tree until the brain came out of the baby's skull.

On the night of March 30, when their captors were asleep, Dustin retaliated. With a Worcester boy captured the previous year, she deftly slayed an Indian family of four adults and six children. They bring the scalps to Boston and are rewarded; Neff and the boy, who each killed one Indian, each receive half what Dustin gets.

◆ Five years after the Salem witch trials, Judge Samuel Sewall confesses what he now sees as his sinful role to the congregation of Boston's Old South Church. The other nine judges who joined in the executions remain silent.

1699 As the century ends, church and court records indicate that many brides are pregnant on their wedding day. This is especially true in the southern colonies and among indentured servants. In one Maryland county, illegitimate pregnancy is so common that 20% of all female indentured servants—who are forbidden to marry under the terms of their contracts—bear a child out of wedlock.

2

From Puritanism to Revolution

1700–1775

1700 The French build a fort at Detroit and later expand to Illinois and the Mississippi Valley. French settlements are made up of soldiers, fur traders, and priests; their relations with natives are the most humane of any European group, and their men often cohabit with native women. A lack of French women prevents them from establishing their culture and language in the way that English families do; instead, French men tend to adopt the ways of the native women with whom they live.

1701 Domestic workers are in such short supply in Boston that the city government takes steps to encourage the immigration of white servants, especially women, whose labor is most needed in an urban areas.

1702 Queen Anne takes over the English throne and the governance of its colonies. Although she bears 17 children, all will die before she does. When she dies without an heir in 1714, German-speaking George I is imported from Hanover, Germany. (It is against his grandson, George III, that the American colonies will revolt.)

1704 Women and men fight through the February night as French soldiers and Abenaki natives attack the English settlement of Deerfield, in western Massachusetts. The majority of the town's 268 residents are either slain or taken as prisoners for slave labor or ransom. Many women see their infants killed by the common method of smashing the skull against a hard object.

Survivors tell of at least two pregnant women who are killed because their physical condition could slow the captives' 300-mile march to Canada. Eunice Williams, who had given birth to her 11th child only weeks before, falls while wading a river, and a hatchet blow sends her drowning.

Her body is recovered, and she is buried with 48 other victims of the raid. The grave is marked: "Here lies The Body of Mrs. Eunice Williams the Virtuos & desirable Consort of the Revrd. Mr. John Williams . . . She was Born Aug: 2, 1664,

and fell by the rage of ye Barbarous Enemy . . . Her Children arise up and Call her Blessed."

1705 Sarah Kemble Knight, a 38-year-old Boston mother, returns from riding horseback on an unaccompanied six-month business trip to New York. Her record of this winter sojourn, *The Journal of Madam Knight,* will not be published until a century later. It reveals a bright, optimistic personality. Knight, who rarely mentioned husband or home, uses humor to describe crossing icy rivers on horseback and sleeping in vermin-filled taverns, and her observations on the area's differing economies and cultures are astute. She will continue as a shopkeeper after widowhood, invest in land, and die quite wealthy.

1706 The survivors of the Deerfield Massacre are ransomed and returned to Massachusetts—except for the little daughter of Eunice Williams. Some Quebec Macqua Indians are so fond of her that they "would not give her up at any price." She lives the rest of her life with them, adopting their ways and marrying within the tribe. When she visits a brother much later, her choice of cultures is clear: she refuses stay in his house, builds a wigwam of her own, and remains dressed in blankets.

1707 The end of violence against women in the name of religion is signaled when the family of accused witch Rebecca Nurse—an elderly, deaf mother of eight—succeeds in vindicating her with the Salem church. Ann Putnam—who at age 12 was Nurse's chief accuser—confesses the wrongness of her behavior.

1708 The first group of Germans arrive in New York. Called Palatines, they have fled from war in the Rhineland. Queen Anne pays the fares of 40 of these refugees.

✦ The Spanish governor of Florida reports that some 10,000 natives have been sold into slavery in the Carolinas. Likely disproportionately more women have been sold than men, for male warriors are more apt to be killed, while there is profit in selling women.

1709 Thinly populated Charleston, South Carolina, cannot support the Anglican rector of St. Philip's Church, so Henrietta Johnston draws portraits to supplement her husband's meager income. Born in Ireland, she had taken her children alone to the New World two years earlier, when the Reverend Johnston missed his ship.

Even more remarkably, Henrietta Johnston uses a newly developed technique to do pastels. Although she probably had little if any formal training, her portraiture looks professional, and the area's notable men sit for her. While she will disappear from the historical record after her husband's 1716 drowning, Henrietta Johnston may be America's first female commercial artist.

✦ A map in the Colonial Office of London tersely reports of the Tampa Bay, Florida, area: "Tocobaga Indians, Destroyed 1709."

1711 Slavery has grown much faster in New York City under the British than it had under the Dutch, and this year a slave market opens on Wall Street. The Africans are often badly treated, and one woman grows so resentful that she murders her master, mistress, and five children, for which she is burned at the stake.

✦ "Madame Montour" interprets at an Albany conference between the governor of New York and the chiefs of the five Iroquois nations. Her origins are obscure, but she presumably had an Indian mother and French father and has learned to speak English; she is currently married to an Oneida chief. Her skills as an interpreter will become so valuable that she attends similar councils for the next three decades, while the French try to outbid the English for her services. Several places in western New York and Pennsylvania will be named for her and for her female descendants, who carry on her leadership tradition.

✦ Massachusetts allocates £578 sterling to victims of the Salem witch trials, many of whom lost their property two decades ago. Samuel Sewall, whose remorse is greater than that of other judges who participated in the trials, oversees the distribution to survivors and the families of those executed.

1712 A slave revolt in New York kills nine whites; the rebels, including at least one pregnant woman, are caught, tortured, and executed.

✦ Eighteen-year-old Sarah Wells (later Bull) moves alone to stake out a claim in the New York State wilderness that will become known as Land O' Goshen. This is due west of West Point; her journey back to civilization requires two days and includes rowing across the Hudson.

In the 20th century, she will be commemorated in the area with the Sarah Wells Trail.

1713 Queen Anne's War, which began with her accession in 1702, ends with the French signing a treaty highly favorable to the English. Frenchmen and their native allies are pushed farther west, and the vital importance of including women and children in colonial settlement begins to be clear.

1715 The Maryland legislature details exactly what emoluments must be granted an indentured woman at the end of her servitude: "A waistcoat and petticoat of new half-thick or pennistone, a new shift of white linen, shoes and stockings, a blue apron, two caps of white linen, and three barrels of Indian corn."

✦ When the fourth Lord Baltimore dies this year, his longtime mistress, a Mrs. Grove, continues in the same role with the fifth Lord Baltimore. Meanwhile, her friends say that Lady Baltimore has been treated with "barbarous cruelty."

1716 Licenses are issued to New York midwives. Other New York women also engage in business, and Polly Provoost, a young widow in the import trade, lays America's first sidewalk on her property at Broad and Marketfield. The rationality of a mud-and-dust-free entrance is soon so obvious that other businesspeople lay their own sidewalks.

◆ In the kitchen of her Rehoboth, Massachusetts, home, Mary Peck Butterworth perfects a method of making counterfeit money that she and her relatives use for years. Both Rhode Island and Massachusetts arrest various passers of the money—including, in 1723, Butterworth herself. None of those involved will confess, however, and because her ingenious method leaves no incriminating evidence to be found in searches of her home, Butterworth is never convicted.

1718 In an attempt to forestall Spanish expansion from Pensacola, New Orleans is settled at the mouth of the Mississippi by the French. The settlement grows quickly; by 1731, Louisiana will be home to some 5,000 whites and 2,000 blacks.

1721 Anne Bonney and Mary Reed are among the "Calico Jack" pirates who are defeated in battle with an English vessel. They are taken to Jamaica, where Bonney escapes hanging only because she is pregnant with her second child.

1727 The first convent is begun in New Orleans by Ursaline nuns, whose mother convent is in Italy. They will operate a hospital, orphanage, and school in New Orleans, and the order will continue throughout the 20th century.

The sisters also serve as guardians for young women who come to Louisiana from France to marry lonely Frenchmen. These brides are called "casket girls" (*filles à les cassettes*) for the dowry-like hope chests they bring to the marriage and their new household.

The presence of these women will give Louisiana a permanent French influence that is never the case with their Upper Mississippi settlements in places such as Detroit.

◆ When George II ascends to the British throne, colonists refer to his wife as Caroline the Good. Although the king continues the downward slide that culminates in revolt against George III, Queen Caroline is revered for not only for her kindness but also for her exceptional ability. Appointed regent, she virtually reigns while her husband returns to their German homeland. The

queen supports Handel, Newton, and other intellectual forces of her era and sets an example by having her daughters inoculated against smallpox.

1730 Benjamin Franklin and Deborah Read Rogers formalize a common-law marital arrangement when they are unable to wed legally. Rogers cannot terminate her marriage because her husband has disappeared; rumors that he has a second wife and that he died in the West Indies are not sufficient grounds for divorce. Known as Deborah Franklin, she will mother Franklin's children and run his businesses during his frequent travels.

◆ As settlers move into western Carolina and northern Georgia, a treaty is negotiated with the Cherokee who live there. Most white observers of the Cherokee lifestyle are not sufficiently astute to notice that the women use an herb that has a striking similarity to modern birth control pills; they chew the roots of the spotted cowbane plant for four consecutive days when they wish to prevent conception.

1732 Cree women live with the Frenchmen who found Fort Charles, at modern Lake of the Woods, Minnesota—so far north that its waters flow into Hudson Bay.

1735 When New York newspaper publisher Peter Zenger goes to prison for criticizing the governor, Anna Maulin Zenger publishes the paper for a year. After her husband's death in 1746, she resumes the role of publisher.

1736 Ann Smith Franklin, the sister-in-law of Benjamin Franklin, is named official printer for the colony of Rhode Island. Widowed young, Franklin will survive all five of her children and earn great respect as a Newport printer.

1738 Gracia Real de Santa Theresa, a community near St. Augustine that includes women as well as men, becomes the first legally sanctioned settlement of free blacks in North America. Also

The quilting bee is an excellent example of sociability combined with practicality. Although rising affluence is clear in this colonial drawing, women did not feel justified in merely visiting each other. Work was so fundamental that even wealthy colonial women were seldom without a needle, even in "leisure." Library of Congress

known as Fort Mose, it has about 70 inhabitants in 1763; when Spain cedes Florida to Britain that year, they will leave for Matanzas, Cuba.

1739   Teenage Eliza Lucas—who will become famous as Eliza Pinckney after her 1744 marriage —runs three South Carolina plantations. With her mother dead and her father assigned to the West Indies for the British military, she not only rears younger siblings but also begins the botanical experiments that entitle her to be considered the nation's first agriculturist.

By age 22, she succeeds in hybridizing an ideal strain of indigo and sells its seeds to English textile manufacturers eager for the clear blue dye it provides. Her achievement makes an astonishing difference in the colonial southern economy: in 1745–46, a mere 5,000 pounds of indigo was exported; two years later, more than 130,000 pounds sail out of Charleston.

1740   The Delaware Assembly makes it more difficult to emancipate slaves—but not necessarily because Delaware is more undemocratic than other colonies. Instead, the law is designed to prevent masters from "freeing" slaves who are too old or ill to work.

1742   When her husband dies, Philadelphian Cornelia Bradford becomes publisher of their *American Weekly Mercury*. She does both the editing and printing, most of it without assistance, and she will continue to do bookbinding and business printing even after she sells the paper. Her will frees the two slaves she owned.

1746   Three-year-old Sarah (Sally) Franklin is inoculated against smallpox by her progressive parents, Deborah and Benjamin Franklin. They had lost a four-year-old son to the disease a decade earlier. For more than a century, however, vaccination will continue to be controversial.

◆ Teenage Lucy Terry, who was kidnapped in Africa and sold into slavery as a child, writes what probably is the first poem by an African American —predating the more famous Phillis Wheatley by two decades.

Terry lives in Deerfield, Massachusetts, and her 28-line poem is devoted to what locals call the Deerfield Massacre, a 1704 ambush by natives. How she became literate is not known, but in 1756, she will marry Abijah Prince, who may have purchased her. She moves with him to a farm near Sunderland, Vermont, where they become quite affluent.

1747 "The Speech of Polly Baker" appears in a London paper this year and will soon be reprinted as authentic in both Europe and America, but it was actually written by Benjamin Franklin. "Polly Baker" supposedly is a Connecticut woman "dragg'd before your Court" for the fifth time "because I have had Children without being married." She makes reasoned arguments that she is obeying the biblical injunction to "Encrease and Multiply" and that "instead of a Whipping," she ought "to have a statue erected to my Memory." In the Victorian era of the next century, the speech will be considered too scandalous to be mailed.

1749 Twenty-two ships carrying 7,000 immigrants from the Rhineland area of Germany arrive in Philadelphia, enhancing Pennsylvania's reputation as a haven for the non-English speaking and religiously unconventional.

1751 The country's first hospital begins in Philadelphia, but it is thought of as an asylum or poorhouse. Not until well into the next century will hospitals be seen as reputable institutions, and nursing takes even longer to professionalize.

1753 The records of a Newport, Rhode Island, midwife indicate that she has delivered 2,498 babies since 1746—or almost a delivery a day.

1755 Mary Draper Ingles becomes the first white woman to see the Ohio River when she is taken captive during the French and Indian War. Her family had settled in the mountains of western Virginia in 1747, and she was days away from giving birth when captured. Her sister-in-law, Betty Draper, is also taken prisoner; they are separated and Draper is never heard of again. Ingles' two young sons are sent north to Detroit; one dies on the way and the other eventually is ransomed.

After bearing her baby, Ingles makes the painful decision to leave the child with the Shawnese women, while she and an elderly Dutch woman escape. They forage for food in the wilderness and have managed most of the 700-mile journey back when the Dutch woman goes insane, and Mary Ingles has to flee from her.

◆ French families known as Acadians (or Cajuns) are expelled from Nova Scotia, where the British have taken power from the French. Several thousand move to North America's other major French settlement, New Orleans, but the long voyage is so difficult that many die along the way.

1756 Warfare with natives breaks out in settlements on the Pennsylvania frontier, and among those orphaned is five-year-old Margaret Cochran —who, as Margaret Corbin, will be a hero of the American Revolution. Her father is killed and her mother taken captive, never to return.

1757 When Cherokee chief Attacullaculla negotiates trade with whites in South Carolina, he is surprised to see that no women are present and says: "Since the white man as well as the red is born of woman, does not the white man admit women to their councils?"

Matrilineal descent is important to most native tribes. Ancestry is traced through the mother; property passes from mother to daughter; and when couples marry, the man goes to live with the woman's family. Both women and men are shamans who hold medical knowledge and spiritual power.

1758 Virginia's governor Robert Dinwiddle ends his service this year, and among the reports he has sent home is one to the Bishop of London on a colonial clergyman, who had "very near" murdered his wife by "ty'g her up by the Leggs to the Bed Post and cut'g her in a cruel Man'r with Knives."

1759 Colonel George Washington marries Martha Dandridge Custis, an extremely wealthy 27-year-old widow with two children. There are indications that Washington, who is slightly younger than she, is more emotionally attached to Sally Fairfax, but he recognizes how much Custis' property can mean to his career. Nonetheless, he proves to be a devoted husband and stepfather.

◆ A native Mohawk known as Mary (Molly) Brant bears the first of nine children that she has with widower Sir William Johnson, Superintendent of Indian Affairs for the Northern Colonies. Although they never marry in English law, she will serve as hostess at the palatial estate Sir William builds in 1763 near Johnstown, New York, in what visitors describe as "an Absolute Forest," 14 miles from the river that is the era's main highway. Travelers report that the estate is "generally crowded with Indians," and when Sir William dies during a stressful 1774 council with quarreling Shawnee and Mohawk, 600 are camped on the grounds. In accordance with the English system of primogeniture, Molly Brant is then displaced from the mansion by the oldest Johnson son, but she and her children inherit other property.

◆ Streetwalkers have become so common in Philadelphia during this decade that Benjamin Franklin jokes about their disproportionate use of shoe leather.

1761 At age 17, Princess Charlotte of Mecklenburg in modern Germany marries the recently crowned King George III of England. A number of newly settled American places will be named for her in the years prior to the colonies' separation from England. Queen Charlotte will reign for 57 years, during which time her husband becomes insane. She has 15 children and never permits any of her daughters to wed.

1762 Sarah Updike Goddard finances Rhode Island's *Providence Gazette.* Her son William is the ostensible editor, but he travels much of the time and it is Goddard and her daughter Katherine who truly run the newspaper. The women add entertainment items to the local and foreign news, which prove popular and profitable. In 1768, they will sell it and move to Philadelphia, where they publish the *Pennsylvania Chronicle.*

1765 Mary Jemison marries a Seneca leader, having chosen the Seneca way of wife over that of the English. Known as "the white woman of the Genese," she had been captured in warfare at 14, married a man of the Delaware tribe, and then was widowed at 18. Her adopted name is Dehhe-wa-mis, and her stature with the Seneca, along with her ability to speak English, gives her power as a mediator in the Lake Erie area.

◆ The Sons of Liberty begin to agitate against British rule, and the Daughters of Liberty soon join them. These women will be vital to the effectiveness of boycotts against goods imported from Britain, and they inconvenience themselves by readopting old ways: they make homespun cloth rather than buy fabric from the new British textile mills, and they grow herbs and other plants to provide substitutes for tea. The Daughters of Liberty will become the nation's first female political association, holding meetings, marches, and even physically attacking Loyalists.

1766 To support herself after widowhood, Philadelphian Quaker Margaret Hill Morris becomes a physician. Like the men of her era, she studies medicine as an apprentice—in this case, her physician father teaches her medical skills.

1767 Anne Catherine Hoff Green, mother of 14, becomes the official printer for the colony of Maryland. She inherits both the governmental contract and the *Maryland Gazette* when her husband dies, and she is paid at the same rate as her late husband had been. Green also will demonstrate courage in risking her state business to publish *Gazette* stories on the Boston Tea Party, John Dickinson's anti-British *Letters*, and other items supportive of the nascent American Revolution.

✦ A petition to the South Carolina Assembly complains that a shortage of clergy has resulted in sexual liaisons outside of marriage, with some men "Swapping away their Wives and Children, as they would Horses or Cattle." An Anglican missionary in North Carolina agrees that polygamy is "common, bastardy no disrepute, and concubinage general."

1768   The sixth Lord Baltimore sets a low standard of morality in his personal behavior, and newspapers write openly this year on his premeditated rape of a young woman from a good family. When he dies in 1771, he designates an illegitimate son as Maryland's proprietor.

✦ Connecticut's last execution for witchcraft takes place; since that of Alse Young in 1647, 37 people in this colony have been hanged as witches. The vast majority of them have been women.

1769   Advertisements for runaway wives in southern newspapers are "almost as numerous" as advertisements for runaway slaves. The ostensible reason that men give for placing these ads is to publicly disavow their wives' debts, but many describe the fugitive—"she has a mark over one of her eyes"—as if to invite capture. Others include humiliating details on what the husband sees as the reason for the marital breakup: one in the *Maryland Gazette* this year is not unusual in accusing the wife of having an affair with a black man.

1770   Margaret Wake Tryon presides over North Carolina's Tryon Palace, which is called "the most beautiful public building in North America." As the home of the colonial governor, however, it is not exactly a public building, and resentment of the near-royal lifestyle there is a factor in the growing spirit of rebellion against the English crown.

1772   Recent widow Patience Lovell Wright leaves America for London, where she sculpts with wax—decades prior to the more famous Madame Tussaud. Her sales are sufficient to support her five children, and among her admirers is Benjamin Franklin, who introduces Wright to European society. Her wax figure of William Pitt, a hero to American revolutionaries, will be Westminster Abbey's first piece by an American.

✦ Mercy Otis Warren anonymously publishes the first of three plays that stir the revolutionary pot. *The Adulateur* casts the British governor of Massachusetts in the role of "Rapatio," a villain who returns next year with *The Defeat* (1773). *The Group* (1775) comes out as the Revolution builds to violence; all are thinly veiled satires of British governance.

Warren uses male imagery for the British rulers and female allusions for America, the innocent victim, but this device also necessarily makes some feminist views obvious. In tavern talk with other men, for example, her character Hateall says: "When young indeed I wedded . . . But all I wish'd was to secure her dower. I broke her skirts when I'd won her purse . . . The green Hick'ry or the willow twig will prove a curse for each rebellious dame."

1773   Phillis Wheatley, who is about 20, goes from Boston to London, where *Poems on Various Subjects, Religious and Moral* is published. She had come to Boston as a child on a slave ship, probably from Gambia, in 1761. She so charmed the family that bought her that they did not treat her as a slave, and by her teens, Phillis Wheatley was celebrated as the nation's first African-American poet, praised by such prominent men as John Hancock.

✦ Sarah Bradlee Fulton becomes known as "the Mother of the Boston Tea Party" when she and her sister-in-law, Mrs. Nathaniel Bradlee, handle the makeup and clothing of the men who disguise themselves as Mohawk to destroy tea in ships docked in Boston Harbor.

Later in the war, Fulton will dare a British officer to shoot her when she claims ownership of wood that he confiscated—and he surrenders it to her. She also will serve as a courier for the rebels, walking approximately 20 miles to Boston alone after midnight and earning George Washington's personal thanks.

- Although she is the mother of five young children, Clementina Rind takes over editing and publishing the *Virginia Gazette* when her husband dies. Her Williamsburg-based paper exhibits Rind's interest in science and especially features news from the College of William and Mary. The following year, the House of Burgesses makes her their official printer over male competitors but she is not able to enjoy her success, for she dies just a few months later at 34.

1774 After twice being imprisoned in England for her disruptive preaching, 38-year-old Ann Lee emigrates with a group of mostly male disciples to New York. They believe she is a prophet, based on a mystical experience she had after the death of her four children. Her message emphasizes the feminine side of the dual gender attributed to God and believers become known as Shakers because of their incorporation of movement into worship.

- Margaret Green Draper inherits the *Boston News-Letter* along with her husband's contract as printer for the colony of Massachusetts when he dies. Draper will vocally support the British as the American Revolution begins; she drives six competitors out of business and has the last newspaper operating in Boston when the British evacuate in 1776. Like other Loyalists, she then flees to England, where she lives the rest of her life.

- The quartering of soldiers in homes becomes an important factor in bringing on the Revolution. The British government often provides no barracks, and soldiers are assigned to American homes—whether or not the usually overburdened housewife wishes to feed them, launder their clothes, and make their bed. Invasion of privacy is inevitable, and sexual harassment also occurs frequently, for these intimate living arrangements invite soldiers to prey upon women and girls.

- When the First Continental Congress meets in Philadelphia in September, delegates are welcomed by the Daughters of Liberty, who open their homes to them. Among the delegates is John Adams of Massachusetts, who saves the interesting letters that his wife sends: Abigail Adams' voluminous correspondence with her husband and other prominent men will eventually provide historians with much detail on the new nation.

She manages to find time to write while bearing five children and running the farm. She buys land and animals, and over the years, it is Abigail who thus builds the family estate while John travels to endless meetings.

- In October, Maryland hosts an even more destructive version of the Boston Tea Party. The *Peggy Stewart*, a ship just arrived from England, is burned to the water because there is tea on board. Some say that its owner, Anthony Stewart, bows to the Annapolis rebels who destroy his property because he is concerned with the safety of his wife, who gave birth to a daughter just two days earlier.

- A New York newspaper advertises: "Servants just arrived from Scotland, to be sold on board the *Commerce* . . . among which are a number of weavers, tailors, . . . hatters, and spinsters, 14 to 35 years of age . . ."

1775 The boycott of British goods results in the nation's first industrialization, and women are employed from the beginning. Some 1,200 women and children become textile workers in Boston, while another 400 are employed in Philadelphia.

- When the British retreat from the battle of Concord, Betsy Hagar recovers six damaged cannon they leave behind. Called Handy Betty, she had been "bound out" as a nine-year-old orphan to a machinist and learned mechanics from him. Now 25, she repairs the cannon and turns them over to the rebels. She will spend the rest of the war making ammunition—as she had spent the earlier portion of the rebellion refitting muskets and matchlocks that dated back to Queen Anne's War.

◆ Like other Mohawk, Molly Brant—who has borne nine children by a recently deceased British official—remains loyal to the crown. Tory commanders view her as so valuable an ally that they supply a house for her near the Canadian border, and she assists them in maintaining their alliance with the Cayuga and Seneca nations. At war's end, she will move with other Loyalists to Ontario, and the grateful British reward her with a sizable annual pension.

◆ Only weeks before Patrick Henry delivers his famed "liberty or death" speech, his wife dies in

Women in Edenton, North Carolina, signing a pledge not to drink British-taxed tea. Although such revolutionary activity has been more commonly attributed to women in northern cities, it also took place in rural southern communities. Library of Congress

the basement of their Scotchtown plantation, where he has kept the allegedly insane woman confined for at least the previous year.

Sarah Shelton was pregnant when she married Patrick Henry in 1754; her father supplied the young couple—both still in their teens—with 300 acres of land and six slaves. Patrick was elected to the Virginia House of Burgesses a decade after their marriage, but even though Sarah bore him six children, few of his political colleagues ever met her. For the rest of his life he refuses to discuss her death; he marries again in 1777 and fathers 10 more children by his second wife.

It will be another century before most states offer any legal protection to women whose husbands decide that they are insane.

◆ Quaker women and men in Philadelphia form the Society for the Relief of Free Negroes Unlawfully Held in Bondage.

◆ In December, Martha Washington travels from Virginia for the first time to join her husband, who commands the rebel forces based in Cambridge, Massachusetts. In future winters—when her agricultural management duties at Mount Vernon are at their seasonal lull—she will live with Washington and his troops. Other commanders' wives join her, providing inspiration and comfort in winters at Morristown, New Jersey; Valley Forge, Pennsylvania; and Newburgh, New York.

◆ Rebecca Bryan Boone joins her husband, Daniel, in frontier Kentucky. She has maintained their family alone during much of their 20-year marriage while he explored to the west of their North Carolina home.

The following year, their daughter Jemina and her friends Betsey and Frances Calloway are canoeing across a river when Shawnee ambush and capture them. Daniel Boone leads a rescue party, greatly enhancing his reputation; the story receives far more publicity than many other similar cases.

After two decades in Boonesborough, Kentucky, the family will move still farther west, going to the wilds of Spanish-held Missouri in 1798.

3

The Beginnings of an American Woman

1776–1827

1776 In March—well before the signing of the Declaration of Independence in July—Abigail Adams writes to her husband:

> I long to hear you have declared an independency, and, by the way, in the new code of laws which I suppose it will be necessary for you to make, I desire you would remember the ladies and be more favorable to them than your ancestors. Do not put such unlimited power into the hands of husbands. Remember all men would be tyrants if they could. If particular care and attention are not paid to the ladies, we are determined to foment a rebellion and will not hold ourselves bound to obey any laws in which we have no voice or representation.

✦ Gang rapes by British soldiers in the Philadelphia-New York area are so frequent during this first full year of warfare that the Continental Congress collects documentation of such attacks. Among the most egregious cases are two in New Jersey: Sixteen young women are held several days in a British camp, during which time they are repeatedly raped, and a 13-year-old girl is assaulted by three soldiers while her family is held at bay.

That soldiers would consider such behavior acceptable is not surprising, for one Staten Island commander says that court-martials for rape occur "every day," and he characterizes the testimony as "most entertaining."

✦ Lorenda Holmes spies for the British invading New York in the summer. When she is caught, she is "stripped naked and exposed" to a rebel mob.

The humiliating experience does not end her work as a Loyalist activist, however, and when the Americans again find her aiding the British, they burn her foot with hot coals.

✦ As the war moves South, some 3,000 slaves —about 40% of them female—are believed to escape to British camps, where they are welcomed as allies. Slaves belonging to Loyalists are returned to their masters, however, and when the Americans win the war, many of these erstwhile British allies are forced back into slavery. Others take advantage of wartime disruptions to flee west or south to Florida, where they join native tribes.

✦ While the war rages, pacifist Mother Ann Lee establishes the first Shaker colony in New York's Albany County. The members begin building a farm and orchard in swampland called Niskayuna by the natives and Watervliet by the Dutch; eventually it is known as Wisdom's Valley because of the thoughtful philosophy spread by Ann Lee.

✦ On November 16, Pennsylvanian Margaret Corbin, who accompanied her husband to war, fights at Fort Washington on Manhattan Island. When her artillery-gunner husband is killed almost as soon as combat begins, she takes up his battle station and fires the cannon until the battle ends, even after she is wounded by grapeshot. She permanently loses the use of an arm, and three years later, the Continental Congress recognizes her "distinguished bravery." Margaret Corbin is the first woman to earn a soldier's pension.

✦ One of the women who suffers through the winter at Valley Forge is newlywed Catherine Littlefield Greene. Like a number of officers' wives, she moves with her husband throughout the war—as can be seen in the record of her pregnancies, for she bears five children in the nine years between 1775 and 1784. The oldest boy is named George Washington and the oldest girl for Martha Washington.

✦ Mary Bartlett, mother of 12, suffers the consequences when her husband, a New Hampshire delegate to the Continental Congress, is the first to answer the roll call on the Declaration of Independence. Tories burn her Kingston home, and she is forced to resettle on rural land.

✦ In New York, Tories loot the home of wealthy Catherine Beeker and "every article of furniture" is stolen. Mary Lindley Murray aids Americans retreating from Long Island by deceptively inviting a British general for a leisurely breakfast, which allows the rebels time to get away.

✦ Deborah Scudder Hart, wife of New Jersey Congressman Richard Hart, dies alone with her home in ruins and her husband hunted "like a criminal" by the British. Annis Stockton, another general's wife managing alone during the war, bravely retrieves and hides seditious papers from British troops attacking Princeton.

Meanwhile, New Jersey's Margaret Vliet Warne, who practices as a physician, rides "through the country ministering to . . . soldiers and their families without price."

✦ A Philadelphia newspaper advertisement reads "Wants a place, as Wet Nurse, a young woman with a good breast of milk."

1777 Katherine Goddard, who is listed equally with her brother William as editor and publisher of the *Maryland Journal*, makes publishing history by issuing the first copy of the Declaration of Independence that includes the signers' names.

Goddard also serves as postmistress of Baltimore from 1775 to 1789; when she is replaced by a man, widespread objection will be heard from residents pleased with her performance.

✦ All through the night of April 26, 16-year-old Sybil Ludington rides 40 miles through Putnam County, New York, alerting members of her father's regiment of the need to assemble. The British are burning Danbury, Connecticut, but the messenger who brings the news is too tired to continue. Her father must prepare for battle, and young Sybil therefore calls his men to action.

Her ride, which is longer than Paul Revere's famous one, is dangerous because Tories easily could have captured the lone night rider. After the battle at Danbury, George Washington and French General Rochambeau come to the Ludington home to thank Sybil.

In May, Philadelphian Betsy Ross, a 25-year-old widow, is paid for the manufacture of "ship's colours, etc." by the State of Pennsylvania. In June, Congress adopts a flag of "thirteen stripes in alternate red and white . . . and thirteen stars, white in a field of blue," without mention of Ross. More than a year earlier, General Washington had recorded in his Cambridge camp, "we hoisted the union flag in compliment to the United States," again without mention of Ross or any Philadelphia trip for flag design.

The great American myth associating Betsy Ross with the flag will not arise until almost a century later, when her grandson tells the family legend to an 1870 local historical society meeting. Meanwhile, Ross goes on to marry twice more, bear seven children, and again be widowed by the war; she conducts a successful upholstery business and invests in land. When she dies at age 84—leaving no record of ever meeting Washington or making a flag for him—she wills her business to a daughter.

✦ The scalped body of Jane McCrea is found on July 27 in the upper Hudson Valley. A young woman planning to marry, she had refused to evacuate the wartorn area because she was expecting her fiance. News of her death shocks people as far away as London, where a speaker in Parliament uses it to argue against British alliance with Indians.

Soon after McCrea's death shakes the Hudson Valley, Catherine Van Rensselaer Schuyler, the wife of an American general and mother of 14, decides to leave the relative safety of Albany to check on the family's property at Saratoga Springs. When she learns that the British army is approaching, she sets fire to her ripening wheat crop rather than allow the enemy to capture it.

✦ In accordance with their religious beliefs, Quakers refuse to fight on either side during the war. In Philadelphia, Sally Fisher bears a child while husband is imprisoned as a conscientious objector; she notes later that she gained financial experience in his absence.

✦ When the British advance on Philadelphia, Sarah Franklin Bache is forced to flee—four days after childbirth and for the second time in less than a year. The daughter of Benjamin Franklin and the wife of Postmaster General Richard Bache, she writes, "I shall never forget nor forgive them for turning me out of house and home in midwinter."

✦ Philadelphian Lydia Darrah, who practices as a mortician, overcomes both fear and the qualms of her Quaker conscience to warn Washington of

General Howe's attack plans, which she learns by eavesdropping on troops quartered in her home.

The reverse situation occurs in Charlestown, Massachusetts, where shopkeeper Elizabeth Thompson spies on Americans for the British.

✦ An observer of cultural behavior writes that the colonial New England practice of bundling is "in some measure abolished along the sea coast," but still common inland. Bundling is a courtship ritual in which a fully clothed man and woman share the same bed, sometimes with a board separating them.

1778 One of the most violent episodes of the Revolution—particularly in its effects on civilians—takes place this year when Loyalists, including British men and their Dutch and Indian allies, attack settlers in the remote Wyoming Valley of western Pennsylvania. Several hundred are killed, including women and children. After refugees in a fort near Wilkes-Barre surrender, they are tortured and killed.

✦ Pennsylvanian Mary Hayes, who had accompanied her husband to war, becomes legendary at the battle of Monmouth, New Jersey. Already known as Moll of the Pitcher because she carried water to soldiers during fighting, she takes over her husband's artillery gun when he is wounded at the beginning of the battle. She holds her position all day, and General Washington personally thanks "Molly Pitcher" for her bravery. He goes on to send Congress a recommendation, which they accept, that she be commissioned as a sergeant and granted half pay for the rest of her life.

✦ A century prior to the era that historians designate for the "women's club movement," Hannah Mather Crocker begins a study club in Boston. She presides over the meetings of women who study languages together while their men socialize at lodge meetings that include both the pageantry of Masonic ritual and a good deal of heavy drinking.

The granddaughter of colonial leader and key thinker Cotton Mather, Crocker is a young bride

Pennsylvanian Mary Hayes, legendary as "Moll of the Pitcher." Although the era's illustration emphasizes her serving role, she nonetheless fired her gun all day. Women in Military Service Memorial

at this point; her intellectual interests will have to be set aside while she bears 10 children during the next 15 years.

✦ Poet Phillis Wheatley's fortunes begin to decline. Her white family has been broken up by deaths and financial reversals during the Revolution, and she marries John Peters, a free black man in April. Peters will desert her periodically, and although she still writes poetry, Wheatley's life is increasingly tragic. She bears three babies, all of whom die, before she dies from malnutrition in a freezing room in 1784. She will be largely forgotten until 1834, when Boston abolitionists republish her work.

✦ At age 43, Martha Moore Ballard begins practice as a midwife in rural Maine; when she dies in 1812 at 77, she is still delivering babies. She leaves a diary detailing her experience as the mother of nine and the midwife for 816 babies.

1779 With the British no longer capable of enforcing laws that forbade whites from moving into native territory west of the Appalachians, some Americans begin moving far into the interior. A Virginia group that makes the perilous journey down the Tennessee and Cumberland rivers includes 12-year-old Rachel Donelson, who later will marry Andrew Jackson. When they are attacked by Indians while their boat is snagged by rocks, Mrs. Peyton jumps into the icy water to free the boat, Mrs. Jennings tosses cargo to lighten the load, and Charlotte Robertson beats the assailants into the river with her oar.

The natives track them along the shores, and eventually the group endures near starvation because, during much of the four-month journey, no one can go ashore for game. Much like Plymouth's Pilgrims, they arrive at their Nashville destination on Christmas Day of an extremely cold winter.

✦ When the American revolutionaries raid the Lake Erie area where Mary Jemison lives, this "White Woman of the Genese" sees the warfare from the point of view of her adopted Iroquois. She will recall.

> At that time I had three children who went with me on foot, one who rode on horseback, and one whom I carried on my back. . . . [Whites] destroyed every article of food. . . . They burnt our houses, killed what few cattle and horses they could find, destroyed our fruit trees, and left nothing but the bare soil. . . . The weather had become cold and stormy; and as we were destitute . . . I immediately resolved to take my children and look out for myself.

✦ In Gloucester, Massachusetts, Judith Sargent Stevens, a childless sea captain's wife, spends her days writing essays that include strikingly original feminist theory. This year Stevens writes, but does not yet publish, "Essay on the Equality of the Sexes." She argues that males and females have equal mental abilities, but girls are prevented from using their capabilities.

When she does begin publishing, it is under pseudonyms, including Honora and Constantia. The first of her published works, entitled "Encouraging a Degree of Self-Complacency, Especially in Female Bosoms," will appear in a 1784 issue of *Gentlemen and Lady's Town and Country Magazine*. When the magazine collapses, however, there will be a five-year hiatus before her thoughts are offered to the public again.

After her husband dies in the West Indies, she remarries, becoming Judith Sargent Murray, bears two children although in her late 30s, and eventually adopts a more public persona. In additions to essays, she writes poems and plays; some credit her with the first production by an American playwright.

1780 Esther DeBerdt Reed—who had come to Philadelphia from England only a decade before leads the city's women in a fund raising campaign to support the Revolutionary army. About 40 women conduct a door-to-door canvass of other women, raising some $300,000 in Continental dollars from over 1,600 donors.

They are inspired by Reed's publication, *The Sentiments of an American Woman*, in which she details women's contributions to world history and argues for the right of women to participate in public affairs. In September, Reed dies suddenly at 33—leaving five children under ten.

Sarah Franklin Bache takes over Reed's leadership role. By Christmas, she informs General Washington that the women have provided the army with 2,005 linen shirts, most of which were cut in Bache's home.

✦ American soldiers briefly arrest and detain Shaker leader Ann Lee. She is a pacifist, but they assume that her failure to support the rebel cause means that she is a Loyalist. In fact, she has no reason to be loyal to English authorities who, prior to her emigration, twice imprisoned her.

✦ At age 20, Anne Kennedy runs a South Carolina farm when the four males of her family go to war. She fights with British troops who burn her crops, throws a soldier down a staircase, and saves her home—an act of bravery for which she will bear the scars for the rest of her life.

Catherine Sherrill, who lives in the wilderness of eastern Tennessee, is besieged by Cherokee allied with the British. Like many other frontier women, she leaves her home and lives in a stockade for the duration of the war.

✦ Sculptor Patience Lovell Wright is loyal to America, although her business demands the more lucrative customer base that she has established in London. She passes on to Americans whatever military information she can garner and this year goes to France, where she also promotes revolution. More than once, Wright insults King George III and Queen Charlotte, who seem amused by her unconventional behavior.

1781 Guerrilla warfare continues in South Carolina, where Emily Geiger, who is "scarcely out of her teens," volunteers to deliver a crucial message from General Nathanael Greene to General Thomas Sumter. She rides horseback for two days in May to cross a British-occupied wilderness; she is taken prisoner briefly, but manages to bluff her way out and complete the assignment. Perhaps because she is a member of a small community of Dutch immigrants in Orangeburg County, Emily Geiger's feat is little noted—but her 50-mile ride is far longer than that of the famed Paul Revere.

Also in South Carolina, Mary Gill Mills heads "a band of 11 women" who go from farm to farm harvesting crops for families whose men are gone to war. When the British occupy her plantation mansion, Rebecca Motte sets her home on fire to drive the soldiers into the ranks of attacking Americans.

In North Carolina, British-born Margaret Gaston is forced to watch while her physician husband is shot to death for treating rebels. In Georgia, elderly Nancy Morgan Hart placidly fixes a meal for demanding Tories—and then draws a gun as they began to eat and holds them captive for hanging.

◆ Because neither Congress nor the states have ever adequately supported the revolution's soldiers, North Carolinian Elizabeth Maxwell Steele insists on giving her horde of gold and silver coins to General Greene. In a famous engraving of the scene that is circulated after victory, Steele is depicted as saying "Take it, you need it, and I can do without the money."

New Jersey's Rachel Wells is another who supported her government financially. An artisan who crafts wax models, she loaned £300 sterling to New Jersey at the beginning of the war, but after victory, the state does not repay her. "I have don as much to Carrey on the Warr," she will plead in 1783, "as maney that Sett now at ye healm of government."

◆ Prostitution is common during the war, with little indication of disapproval by either British or American authorities. Some prostitutes openly state their business in filing claims for monetary losses caused by the war, and British officers testify to the truthfulness of at least one such claim.

◆ A Cherokee leader who has taken the English name Nancy Ward negotiates with whites on a Tennessee treaty this year; unlike most Indians, she supported the Americans during the Revolution. In 1755, she replaced her dying husband during battle with another tribe, but as Indians become more familiar with white ways women's powers lessen. Iroquois women back East especially begin to lose their strong traditional property rights during this era.

◆ In Virginia, Mary Willing Byrd is tried, but not convicted, of treason for her presumed role as a Loyalist and a relative of well-known traitor Benedict Arnold.

◆ In this last year of significant warfare, Martha Washington loses the last of the four children she bore during her first marriage. Two died in infancy, one at 17, and the last at 27. She will rear the youngest two of her four grandchildren, and her cheerful personality is remarkably unaffected by this sorrow.

◆ The British lose what will turn out to be the last major battle of the war, at Yorktown, Virginia, on October 19. Lord Cornwallis surrenders the army of the world's most powerful nation, perhaps thinking of what one of his officers had written to him earlier in the war: "We may destroy all the men in America and we shall still have all we can do to defeat the women."

1782 At age 21, Deborah Sampson is mustered into the 4th Massachusetts Regiment in

May, disguised as a man named Robert Shurtleff. Her church excommunicates Sampson for "dressing in men's clothes, and enlisting as a soldier in the Army," but she will serve until October of 1783, when the unit is disbanded after the peace treaty with England is signed. She marches as far as Philadelphia and participates in several skirmishes with the enemy, including one at Tarrytown, New York, in which she is wounded.

✦ Even though she remarries this year, Pennsylvania soldier Margaret Corbin will continue to be carried on regimental muster lists until the war formally ends next year. She is also granted the full ration of rum or whiskey that is included with soldiers' compensation.

✦ Conflict continues at western outposts, where the British ally with Indians who naturally resent the encroachment of American settlers. When Bryant's Station, Kentucky, is attacked this summer, the women are immortalized in a drawing that credits them with "supplying the garrison with water . . . and defeating the stratagem of the Indians led on by Simon Girty the renegade."

Similarly, when the western Pennsylvania home of Ann Newport (later Royall) is destroyed by Indians on July 13, she is one of about 60 women and children forced to march north. Even without warfare, life is hard; Royall would later recall: "We were half of the time without salt or bread. We pinned our scanty clothing with thorns. We lived on bear's meat and dried venison."

✦ A September attack on Fort Henry, at Wheeling in western Virginia, makes a hero of young Betty Zane. She is credited with dodging bullets while running between the fort and her home to resupply ammunition. Much later, she will serve as inspiration for the first book of a descendant, Zane Grey—but Betty Zane (1903) must be published at the author's expense. When he switches to more conventional male heroes for his frontier adventure stories, Zane Grey will become one of the 20th century's best-selling writers.

1783 The war finally, formally ends when the Treaty of Paris is signed in September; Washington says farewell to his last troops in early December. Independence has been won at great cost, and even families that saw no combat suffer from economic hardships imposed by the long years of fighting. Seaport towns especially endured a decade or more of lost business, as American boycotts and the British fleet made trade impossible. In Gloucester, Massachusetts, for example, one in every six residents is on charity at the war's end.

✦ Over 450 Loyalist women will submit claims for the wartime loss of their homes. More are likely to be eligible, but they are—in the words of some who file after the deadline—"destitute of advice or Assistance" and they do not know "how to proceed."

Many Loyalists are forced into exile when the new United States wins the war: they go to Canada, England, or British islands in the Caribbean, losing both their property and their lifelong support systems. One woman writes that her new home in Scotland is "not like Virginia. Poverty there would have been much more tolerable to us, we sincerely wish we had never left that Country."

✦ When the former colonies reincorporate as states and legal codes are rewritten, some rights afforded to certain women are lost. The new codifications tighten up previously permissive language, and women in the post-Revolution era suffer a gradual lost of property rights. Fewer will conduct independent businesses in the way that their grandmothers did.

✦ The Revolution virtually ends the importation of indentured servants, a practice that already had begun to fade because of greater labor availability due to population increases in the North and the growth of race-based slavery in the South. During the colonial era, however, as many as one-half to two-thirds of all arriving Europeans, both men and women, came bound in the semislave status of indenture.

✦ As the new nation begins, few Americans are aware of the existence of New Spain in other parts of what eventually becomes the United States. Nevertheless, a map analysis at this time shows a line of southern cities that stretches across the continent from east to west: St. Augustine, Pensacola, San Antonio, El Paso, Santa Fe, Tucson, San Diego, Los Angeles, and San Francisco all reveal the Spanish nature of this other culture. The fact that few women in these cities are natives of Spain is a major reason for the eventual dominance of the English language and lifestyle.

1784 Elizabeth Hunter Holt is named the official printer for the State of New York after her printer husband dies. She takes over the publication of the *Independent Gazette*, running it for more than a year before turning it over to her daughter, also named Elizabeth, and her son-in-law, Eleazar Oswald. Elizabeth Oswald will repeat her mother's history and continue in the newspaper business after she also is widowed.

✦ Hannah Adams becomes known as the first professional writer among American women when she publishes *An Alphabetical Compendium of the Various Sects*. She had worked on the manuscript because of her own intellectual curiosity and now publishes it to meet family needs after her father's bankruptcy. This useful reference of religious ideas will be reissued in a half-dozen editions published as late as 1823.

✦ Shaker founder Mother Ann Lee dies just a decade after her arrival in America. In an era when most women did not even speak in public, she has founded a religion. Her original group of eight disciples expanded to several thousand; while touring New England, she converted entire Baptist congregations.

The sect's growth depends on such conversions, for celibacy is one of its ideals. Shakers live in communal groups and strive for peace and equality, beliefs that hold special appeal for women. After Ann Lee's death, her followers organize themselves as the United Society of Believers in Christ's Second Coming; they are also known as the Millennial Church and, most commonly, as Shakers.

1786 One of the nation's first novels, *Victoria*, is published by Susanna Haswell. After becoming Susanna Haswell Rowson through marriage the following year, she will continue to write books and plays that convey distinctly feminist ideas while also acting on stages in Philadelphia and Baltimore and playing the trumpet in Boston.

Her most famous novel, *Charlotte Temple: A Tale of Truth*, will be published in England in 1791; after its 1794 release in America, it becomes the nation's first best-seller. *Charlotte Temple* will be reprinted at least 200 times during its first 100 years; it has never gone out of print.

1787 The Philadelphia Young Ladies Academy begins. It will evolve into a significant educational opportunity for women during the next decade, with students from all over the nation and even the Caribbean. Its founder and faculty, however, are men, who discourage their students from venturing outside the "proper sphere" for young ladies.

✦ Seventeen-year-old Maria del Carmen Hill, daughter of a wealthy South Carolina family, marries Francisco Xavier Sanchez, who owns 10 Florida *haciendas*. In marrying her, Sanchez abandons his common-law wife, Maria Beatriz Stone, a free black born in Charleston. He recognizes their eight mulatto children, however, and they share his estate (including slaves) with 10 children from his second marriage—the last of whom is born only days before he dies at age 71.

✦ The end of the war with the British does not mean the end of conflict with their Indian allies, and frontier settlement inevitably brings periodic violence. In Bourbon County, Kentucky, "the Widow Scraggs" defends her home from Indian attack this year and receives appreciable national publicity for her valor.

1788 Jemima Wilkinson, who calls herself the "Publick Universal Friend," leads a group of nearly 300 in a Seneca Lake settlement on western New York's frontier. Her religious philosophy is based on loving kindness; she advocates peaceful relationships with the area's natives, experiments with faith healing, and prophesies. Treated as genderless by her followers, she advocates celibacy but does not insist upon it.

✦ Abigail Adams returns from four years in France and England, where she has set social precedents as the wife of the ambassador of world's first democracy. She is comfortable in English society but glad to leave France in the age of Marie Antoinette and violent revolution.

✦ While ice forms in the Ohio River, the first families begin to build homes in what will become Cincinnati but is, for the first two years, called Losantiville. Like the Plymouth women, they accompany men who plan so poorly that the families arrive without shelter or resources in December.

1789 When George Washington takes the oath of office on April 30 at Federal Hall in New York City, Martha Washington sets up a temporary presidential home on Broadway. Called Lady Washington by many, she holds state dinners on Thursdays and issues open invitations for "respectable" visitors to Friday evening receptions.

Abigail Adams, wife of the vice president, cohosts, and they introduce a similar, though slightly grander, system the following year when the capital moves to Philadelphia. Lady Washington makes it a firm rule to return her social calls within three days.

✦ *The Power of Sympathy*, which some call the nation's first novel, is published this year. Many

This illustration of a Bourbon County, Kentucky, widow defending her home against an attack by local Indians is typical of the genuine dangers of life on the frontier. Her experience in 18th-century Kentucky was the same as that faced by women on the Atlantic coast in the seventeenth century, and it represents the future for 19th-century women farther west. Library of Congress believe the anonymous author is Sarah Wentworth Morton, who is developing a reputation as a Boston poet and literary salon leader. Decades later, a male neighbor is deemed the author, but the plot is based on the facts of Morton's life: her husband and her sister had an affair that ended in the sister's suicide.

♦ Independence from Britain means American industrialization, and a sailcloth factory in Boston employs some 30 women and girls. Their work is good enough to impress visitor George Washington.

♦ In a letter to her friend Thomas Jefferson, Lucy Ludwell Paradise hints broadly of spouse abuse: "*I am not the object of Mr. P's affections.* Pray my dear sir, remember my sex when you go to Virginia, and introduce [the] Marriage Settlement for to preserve my Sex from want in case of Bad behavior of their husbands. . . ."

1790 Inspired by the ideas of liberty expressed in the Declaration of Independence, New Jersey implicitly enfranchised women in 1776, when the new state constitution granted the vote to "all free inhabitants." Because women are accustomed to gender-neutral language that nonetheless is intended to exclude them, however, no women attempted to cast ballots. In a recodification of election this year, remarkably enough, the legislature makes it clear that women may vote.

The new law spells out the inclusion of New Jersey women by adding the phrase "he or she." Only three men vote against the amendment, which is sponsored by Joseph Cooper, a Quaker who is accustomed to women with decision-making authority. Most women remain unaware of their new right, however, and few cast ballots.

♦ At Port Tobacco in Carroll County, Maryland, four Carmelite nuns establish the first convent within boundaries of the United States. (The New Orleans one begun by Ursuline nuns in 1727 is in French Louisiana.) The leader is Maryland-born Ann Teresa Mathews, who took the name of Bernadina Teresa Xavier when she took vows in Belgium in 1754.

She is assisted by Englishwoman Frances Dickinson and by her two nieces, Susanna and Ann Teresa Mathews, all of whom also have been educated in Belgium. When Mother Bernadina dies a decade later, the convent has 14 nuns. They will move to Baltimore in 1831, and many other sisterhoods grow from these roots.

♦ Author Judith Sargent Murray makes her first trip out of New England; she visits New York, where she meets Martha Washington and observes Congress. She writes: "Shall I own a truth? Let it be in a whisper . . . A question of most importance [was being debated] while gentlemen . . . were picking their nails, examing the beauty of their boots, ogling the galleries, etc."

♦ The chances of widowhood—and resultant poverty—remain high for women in seafaring areas: In one Massachusetts town, for instance, almost 500 widows of sailors are on the pauper rolls. Some of these women, of course, may have been deserted instead of widowed, for a disappearing sailor's final fate is seldom known.

♦ Rachel Donelson Robards, who pioneered with her Virginia family in the wilderness of modern Tennessee and Kentucky, flees from her abusive husband to Natchez, Mississippi. When she hears the following year that he has divorced her, she marries Andrew Jackson—but divorce is a rare and complex procedure involving both the legislature and the courts, and Robards has completed only half of the process. As a result, Rachel is guilty of bigamy, and the Jacksons will suffer for this the rest of their lives.

1791 Women are employed as soon as the first water-powered textile mill begins running in Pawtucket, Rhode Island. Other manufacturers will soon emulate Samuel Slater in hiring women and children for factory work. Among the rationales typically offered for this new employment outside of the home are: women are more docile than men and less likely to disobey their bosses; men are naturally attracted to the nation's free or cheap land and cannot be persuaded to leave their farms; and "idle" women not only are a burden to society but also risk immorality. Many textile employers soon add that men are incapable of doing the detailed work of making cloth, and women's "nimble fingers" become a national asset.

◆ The First Day Society begins in Philadelphia; its intention is to use the first day of the week for Sunday school. These are not the church-connected Sunday schools of the future, however, but instead are intended to offer basic literacy and moral training to children who are expected to work during the week. The philanthropists who found the society are all male, but they educate both girls and boys. The teachers also are exclusively male—and, unlike the female Sunday school teachers of the future, they are paid.

◆ While the city of Knoxville on the Tennessee frontier is first established this year, eastern life is sufficiently refined that Albany builds an arts institute. Among the paintings that will be exhibited is one of Ariaantje Coeymans, a Dutchwoman prosperous enough to have her portrait painted in oils in 1722.

1792 Louisa St. Clair, daughter of General Arthur St. Clair, is so respected by Indians for her wilderness skills that she goes alone to negotiate a treaty with Ohio natives who trust her.

◆ English Mary Woolstonecraft publishes her famous *Vindication of the Rights of Women*—but Judith Sargent Murray had published similar ideas earlier. She also has a record of moral courage: in 1788, as a widow between her marriages, she was among dissidents expelled from First Parish Church in Gloucester, Massachusetts, for "error in sentiment and practice."

The Massachusetts Magazine begins to feature her essays regularly this year with a series called "The Gleaner." After she moves into Boston next year, Murray takes advantage of the state's repeal of its ban on plays: her comedy, *The Medium, or Happy Tea-Party*, is performed at the Federal State Theater in 1795, and it is followed by a drama at the same theater in 1796.

◆ Two years after the arrival of nuns and before the District of Columbia exists, Holy Trinity Church is built in Georgetown. It will remain a solace to Catholics, especially black Catholics, for two centuries.

◆ In Litchfield, Connecticut, Sarah Pierce begins teaching in her home, and her instruction proves so popular that by 1798, the town builds her a school. Miss Pierce's Academy will expand into Litchfield Female Academy in 1827, drawing students from all over the United States and Canada. Like other female educators, Pierce also writes her own textbooks and publishes four of them in the early 1800s. Among her most famous students are Catharine Beecher—who will become an innovative educator in her own right—and her sister, Harriet Beecher Stowe.

1793 Williams College begins classes in western Massachusetts, and former slave Lucy Terry Prince again demonstrates her exceptional abilities: she presents her son's case for admission to the board of trustees. After a long discussion, they vote against accepting a black man, but they are impressed by his mother's argument. No blacks or women will be admitted to an American college until 1833.

◆ Free black women form the Philadelphia Benevolent Society to provide mutual aid and charity in their community. It may be the nation's first organization of African-American women.

◆ George Washington serves as a pallbearer for South Carolina agriculturist Eliza Pinckney. Despite marriage, motherhood, and living in England for part of her life, Pinckney managed as many as seven plantations simultaneously and continued to experiment with diverse crops.

◆ The invention of the cotton gin this year is credited to Eli Whitney, a Yale graduate who recently arrived in Georgia, but the idea is suggested to him by his landlady, Catherine Littlefield Greene.

A native of Rhode Island and the widow of General Nathanael Greene, she has supported five young children on a Savannah River plantation since her husband's death just two years after the

Revolution's end. She explains to Whitney the need for a mechanism to comb cotton seeds from fiber, and after he fabricates the machine, she supports him in lawsuits against neighbors who copy the idea.

The machine ultimately brings tragic historic change, for it makes slavery far more profitable and vastly increases the pressure to harvest ever-increasing cotton crops.

1795   Twelve-year-old Betsey Metcalf of Dedham, Massachusetts, creates an entire American industry when she develops a new method of hand-weaving straw into hats. She demonstrates her work to hundreds of women, and by the 1830s, literally thousands of New Englanders earn money by making straw hats.

1797   Lucy Terry Prince, who wrote the nation's first poem by an African American and who argued for her son's admission to college, brings a lawsuit before the U.S. Supreme Court. It is the culmination of litigation over property boundaries, and in this era when the Court rides a circuit and plaintiffs may argue their own cases, Prince appears before the nation's highest bench.

She wins, and Justice Samuel Chase is said to have commented that this ex-slave, born in Africa, did a better job than any Vermont lawyer could have. In fact, one of the lawyers hired by the opposition was Harvard's 1766 valedictorian.

+ Just 12 years after immigrating to New York from Scotland, Isabella Graham and her daughter, Joanna Graham Bethune, begin the Society for the Relief of Poor Widows and Small Children. It is the first of several charitable organizations they build: after the turn of the century, they will found an orphanage, and during economic troubles caused by the War of 1812, they organize the Society for the Promotion of Industry Among the Poor. Most of all, however, the women will be known for their role in the Sunday school movement.

+ *The Coquette* is published by "A Lady of Massachusetts." The author is Hannah Webster Foster, but her name does not appear on the book until 1866, over a quarter-century after her death. The novel, based on a true case of a woman who rejected societal standards, becomes a long-term best-seller. More than a dozen editions will be published during Foster's life, and the book is reprinted for decades.

+ Settlers move deep into the mountains of Kentucky, where Elizabethtown, near Mammoth Cave, is named for pioneer Elizabeth Hynes.

+ Women in Elizabethtown, New Jersey, march together to cast ballots. They nearly defeat the candidate whom local powers have agreed upon for the state legislature, and agitation begins to repeal the state's suffrage law.

Editorial scorn for the Elizabethtown voters is so strong that women in other localities are discouraged from voting. Among the calumnies is this poem fragment: "Men of rank, who played this prank/beat up the widow's quarters/Their hands they laid on every maid/and scarce spar'd wives, or daughters!"

1798   Susan Black Winchester and her husband, General James Winchester, begin building Cragfont, a mansion in central Tennessee on mountainous land that he has received as compensation for his Revolutionary War service. They bring laborers and materials over 600 miles of rough terrain from their native Maryland and build a palatial home large enough for distinguished visitors—and for the 14 children that she bears.

+ In need of income as her husband's health declines, Judith Sargent Murray publishes the many essays she has written. George Washington endorses her, subscription sales for three volumes are guaranteed, and her work is compared favorably with that of Noah Webster.

After writing her last book in 1816, she will move from her lifelong Boston home to join her newly married daughter in the wilderness of Mississippi. When she dies there in 1820, this unacknowledged mental giant of colonial days is buried on a bluff overlooking the river near Natchez.

1799 Visitation nuns from France begin a convent in Washington, D.C. In 1848 they will establish a second home in Wheeling, West Virginia.

✦ Hannah Adams publishes *A Summary History of New-England*, firmly establishing herself as a professional writer and as an early American historian. Her work is praised by Boston's male establishment, and she goes on to further achievement, including an internationally published *History of the Jews* (1812).

✦ A traveler in western New York reports on his visit to the Seneca Lake settlement of religious leader Jemima Wilkinson:

> Her disciples were a very orderly, sober, industrious, and some of them well educated set of people; and many of them possessed of handsome properties. She called herself the 'Universal Friend,' and would not permit herself to be designated by any other appellation. . . . Her disciples placed the most unbounded confidence in her, and yielded, in all things, the most implicit obedience. . . . For [an] offense committed by one of her people, she banished him to Nova Scotia for three years, where he went, and from whence he returned only after the expiration of his sentence.

✦ As the century ends, so ends the life of George Washington. "The Father of His Country" dies without fathering children, although Martha Custis Washington had children by her first marriage and was young enough to bear more by Washington when they married. Similarly, James Madison, who is known as "the father of the Constitution," has no children, although Dolley Payne Todd was a young widow with children when she married him.

1800 Abigail Adams moves to Washington in November, where she becomes the first woman to preside over the still-incomplete mansion that is later called the White House. Because her husband loses that month's election, the first lady lives in the presidential home only until March—when she is glad to leave the cold, drafty house. Thomas Jefferson, who defeats her husband, is a widower; his niece will lead the city's nascent social life.

1801 The Female Association for the Relief of Women and Children in Reduced Circumstances is founded in Philadelphia. It includes both Christian and Jewish women.

1802 Author and playwright Susanna Haswell Rowson becomes editor of the *Boston Weekly Magazine*. She also operates an academy for "young ladies," which she opened in 1797, and has written some of the textbooks her students use. Her institution proves tremendously popular and becomes a model for the "finishing schools" that educate upper-class women in the next century.

1803 The mother-daughter team of Isabella Graham and Joanna Graham Bethune organize the first Sunday school in New York. Like the founders of the First Day Society in Philadelphia, they hire teachers for secular instruction—but, unlike the men who organized the 1791 model, the Graham women personally teach classes in religion.

From these roots, many other similar projects arise. Girls, who have less educational opportunity than boys, attend Sunday school eagerly. Many adult women also learn to read and write at Sunday school before the institutional emphasis shifts from literacy to evangelism. As the schools become increasingly church-based, male dominance at the executive level is inevitable, but the unpaid position of Sunday school teacher will provide one of very few outlets for leadership allowed to countless women in the future.

✦ Baltimore belle Elizabeth Patterson marries Jerome Bonaparte, the younger brother of Emperor Napoleon, in a Catholic ceremony on Christmas Eve. The French ruler refuses to recognize his brother's marriage, and when the young couple arrives in Europe in 1805, the pregnant bride is immediately exiled to England, while the groom gives in to Napoleon's command for a politically profitable marriage.

✦ A bill to abolish slavery in Delaware fails on a tie vote. Abolitionists continue to petition the legislature for many years into the future; among their leaders is Mary Parker Welch. When moral arguments fail to bring change, they appeal to economics and argue that Delaware is so far north that maintaining slaves through the winter is not financially advantageous.

✦ West Africans on their way to Georgia resolve not to submit to slavery and drown themselves instead. When their ship begins disembarking on a remote tributary of the Frederica River, these Igbo people sing to their god, Chukwu, as they march into the water rather than onto the land.

1804   Paul Revere writes to Congress on behalf of soldier Deborah Sampson, now a married woman with three children. Congress responds with a federal pension for Deborah Sampson Gannett, which is paid because of her service in a Massachusetts regiment during the Revolutionary War.

✦ In the frontier near Nashville, Andrew and Rachel Jackson build a magnificent home that she aptly calls The Hermitage, for she remains there while he pursues his military career. She will later write that less than one-fourth of their 30-year marriage was spent together, and she manages their plantation so successfully that they become quite wealthy.

She avoids society, for when her abusive first husband belatedly divorced her in 1793, it was on the grounds of adultery; legally helpless to do anything to change her marital status or to clear herself of this slur, she remarried Jackson as soon as that was possible.

✦ Similarly, Anna Symmes Harrison and her husband, Indiana territorial governor William Henry Harrison, begin construction of a mansion in the wilderness of Vincennes. The mother of nine, she oversees the family business while he travels. She will remain in Indiana all of her life, for she will not yet have moved to Washington when her

husband dies soon after his 1841 presidential inauguration.

1805   Sacajawea, a Shoshoni who has given birth only weeks before, leads the Lewis and Clark exploration party; while breast-feeding her baby, she shows them the way across hundreds of miles of Dakota prairie and into the Rocky Mountains. The only woman in the group, she introduces the men to native plants for food and medicine, while her interpretation abilities are vital in preventing potential warfare.

✦ At age 77, Mercy Otis Warren of Plymouth, Massachusetts, publishes the three-volume *History of the Rise, Progress and Termination of the American Revolution*. Decades earlier, her anti-British plays and essays were a factor in creating the Revolution.

Her insider's view is heightened by the fact that Warren's husband, brother, and other close friends and family were revolutionary leaders. She begins volume 1 by writing of events that "stimulated to observation a mind that had not yielded to the assertion that all political attentions lay out of the reach of female life."

In fact, Warren has a highly astute political mind, and along with Judith Sargent Murray and Hannah Adams, she carves out a place for women as nonfiction writers who sell their words for money in the way that men do. Her history emphasizes the military and political aspects of the Revolution, to the virtual exclusion of any social or economic (much less women's) history. A professional to the core, Warren's handwritten manuscript of more than 1,200 pages also includes an index and appendixes. The work will long be valued by historians of the Revolution.

✦ In Lexington, Kentucky, Mary Menessier Beck opens an academy for girls; among her students will be future first lady Mary Todd. Beck is French and emigrated a decade earlier, after marrying an American artist in France.

✦ Also in Kentucky, Shakers establish a village at Pleasant Hill. Within a few decades, these followers of Ann Lee's religious philosophy attract some

500 women and men who communally farm more than 4,000 acres of land.

1806   After spending the winter with her tribe in modern Idaho, Sacajawea escorts the Lewis and Clark party through the Big Hole and Bozeman passes of the Bitterroot Mountain Range in modern Montana, where elevations top 7,000 feet.

Clearly influenced by this experience with outsiders, she will settle in St. Louis with her French husband and their child in 1810; before returning to the Dakota country, she briefly adopts the dress of white women. Meanwhile, the journals of the Lewis and Clark Expedition will testify to the esteem that the explorers have for her.

1807   New Jersey removes the language in its constitution that has allowed women and free blacks to vote since 1790. The repeal is a direct result of a corrupt election the previous year: Newark and Elizabethtown got into a heated contest over the location of a new courthouse, and according to one observer, "Women and girls, black and white, married and single, with and without qualifications, voted again and again. And finally men and boys disguised as women voted once more. . . ."

The incident provides a perfect excuse to the incumbent legislator who was nearly defeated by Elizabethtown women in 1797, and he successfully pushes a bill that repeals the right to vote for all New Jersey minorities. Because few women had exercised their franchise anyway, no one petitions against this loss.

1808   The importation of slaves becomes illegal this year, as the compromise written into the Constitution at the time of its passage goes into effect. No effort is made to patrol the long Atlantic and Gulf coastlines, however, and as many as 250,000 more Africans, including women, will come to America in chains after the official end of slave importation.

Also this year, the American Anti-Slavery Society holds its first annual convention, which will continue until slavery is abolished throughout the United States. Women, especially Quaker women, are continually involved in the society.

1809   First lady Dolley Madison becomes the nation's most beloved person in this unofficial position and remains so for decades into the future. Her wit and charm are well known in part because of her astute use of public relations: she is a good friend of the wife of the publisher of the *Intelligencer*, America's first national newspaper.

✦ Elizabeth Ann Seton, a widowed mother of five still-young children, takes vows as a nun and begins the Sisters of Charity of St. Joseph in western Maryland. The order will expand to Philadelphia and New York, operating schools and serving the poor. Some 20 other convents will evolve from this mother house.

Although she dies at age 46, so powerful is Mother Seton's influence that she will be canonized in 1975, thus becoming the first American-born saint of either gender.

✦ Connecticut's Mary Dixon Kies patents a weaving machine, but lacks the capital to refine it and does not become successful.

1810   The "female department" of Raleigh Academy is sufficiently prestigious that the president of the University of North Carolina speaks to the young women—although "maidenly delicacy" is the focus of his attention.

Young women who attend such mixed-gender schools are strictly segregated into a separate curriculum; they study language and arts, while young men learn mathematics and sciences. Nevertheless, many parents consider even this much contact with the opposite sex dangerous and send their daughters to finishing schools for girls only. Both types of institutions are limited, of course, to the upper class.

1811   Six years after Sacajawea did similar work, Madame Marie Dorian, a native of the Iowa tribe who is married to a man of Sioux/French parentage, guides explorers going to the Pacific on behalf of fur-trading magnate John Jacob Astor.

Also known as Marie Iowa and by several French variations of that name, she travels farther and suffers greater hardships than Sacajawea: she has two young children and bears a third while on a 3,500-mile trek from St. Louis up the Missouri River to the Black Hills of South Dakota and on through the Rockies to modern Astoria, Oregon. She interprets for the men, gives birth in midwinter, endures starvation, and sees her infant die before the expedition reaches the coast almost a year later.

✦ When the Philadelphia Academy of Fine Arts opens, one of the paintings on display is by Anna Claypool Peale, who is just 20. A specialist in miniatures, she will be elected to the academy in 1824; some critics call her portraits warmer and more natural than that of her famous father, James Peale. Among the people who will pose for her are two presidents, James Monroe and Andrew Jackson.

1812 Using the alias of George Baker, Lucy Brewer serves in the War of 1812 as a Marine on the frigate *Constitution*.

Her story begins three years earlier, when, pregnant and unwed, she fled from her prosperous rural Massachusetts home to Boston. Using the pseudonym Louisa Baker, she unsuccessfully sought work as a servant until seemingly kind women entrapped her in a house of prostitution.

After the birth of her baby, a sailor in the brothel tells her of Deborah Sampson's enlistment during the Revolutionary War, and she determines to do the same. Dressed in sailor's clothing, she escapes from the house and enlists as a Marine.

For the next three years, her gender will go undetected as she sails the northeast Atlantic. This year she is involved in August and December battles that result in the capture of British ships; at one point, she falls overboard and is nearly drowned.

✦ During the War of 1812, Indians once again ally with the British. On the far western edge of the war, Mrs. Heald, whose husband commands the U.S. Army at Chicago, rides a horse, wields a sword, and battles the Powtawatami like a man. Nonetheless, virtually all the civilians who live near Fort Dearborn are killed.

✦ Despite disapproval from her Massachusetts family and friends, Ann Hasseltine Judson has met and quickly married a recent graduate of Andover Theological School because she wants to leave with him for the missionary fields of Asia. They depart in February, but when they arrive in Calcutta in June, the United States is at war with Britain, and the Judsons are forced go to Burma to evade deportation by British authorities in India. Ann Judson learns Burmese and writes Christian tracts in that language while also teaching women's classes and bearing two children, both of whom die young.

Harriet Atwood Newell and her newly ordained husband also sail with the Judsons, but Newell will have no opportunity to develop her missionary career. The Newells go from Calcutta to Mauritius, an island in the Indian Ocean off the coast of southern Africa. There she dies from a pregnancy complicated by tuberculosis. Her premature child, born at sea, lives just five days, and Harriet Newell dies shortly after her 19th birthday.

✦ Two orders of nuns establish convents in the Kentucky wilderness: the Sisters of Charity begin missionary work at Nazareth, while the Sisters of Loretto at the Foot of the Cross are pioneers in Saint Charles, Kentucky.

✦ Russian men establish Fort Ross (meaning Russia) near San Francisco; it is the southernmost post of the Russian-American Company. They engage in fur trading and marry native and Spanish women on the West Coast. Records from the 1820s will show many divorces, with some of the suits brought by women who are abandoned when their husbands return to Russia.

1813 The commander of Baltimore's Fort McHenry wants a flag so big "that the British will have no trouble seeing it." He calls on a well-established manufacturer of insignia for ships, 36-year-old widow Mary Pickersgill. With her daughter and two nieces, she spends weeks weaving 1,200 square feet of wool into a seamless flag and then presents the military with a bill that reads: "One American Ensign From First Rate Bunting, $405.90."

The flag is finished in August, and in September, it inspires Francis Scott Key's "Star Spangled Banner" when Baltimore is bombarded by the British. Pickersgill's work not only survives the battle but is of such quality that almost two centuries later, it will still hang in the Smithsonian Institution, where it reaches a height equivalent to that of a three-story building. Yet while all Americans know the name of Betsy Ross—who may not have made any significant flag—almost no one will remember the work of Mary Pickersgill.

✦ Sarah Grimké uses her position as a South Carolina Sunday school teacher to defy laws against teaching black children to read.

1814 First lady Dolley Madison rescues state documents and important art acquisitions when the British set fire to the capitol on August 24 and 25. James Madison and other officials have fled with the army and the presidential home is badly burned, but Dolley Madison exhibits cool judgment. After repainting, the mansion becomes known as the White House.

✦ The war has demonstrated the need for American factories that are independent of British suppliers, and the nascent industrialization that began in the Revolution booms during this war. When a textile mill opens in Waltham, Massachusetts, women become its main employees, and Deborah Skinner is credited with being the first woman to run a power loom.

✦ In the far Pacific Northwest, the husband of explorer Marie Dorian is killed by natives. She escapes with her children and, by eating her horse, survives until spring, when she hikes through the mountains to safety among the Walla Walla.

✦ At the same time, the first white woman in the Pacific is Jane Barnes, a barmaid from Portsmouth, England, who sailed to Oregon on the *Isaac Todd* on April 22. After turning down several marriage proposals from both white and native men, she will return to England.

1815 When Napoleon falls, Elizabeth Patterson Bonaparte goes back to Europe with her son, who is Napoleon's nephew. Although she has lost the $12,000 annual pension that the emperor granted when he terminated her marriage, she enters society and tries to find a place for her son; her former husband, meanwhile, has married a German princess.

1816 At age 14, Dorothea Dix opens a school in Worcester, Massachusetts, that she runs successfully for three years before returning to her grandparents in Boston. She had left her dysfunctional Maine family at 12, and before she is famous as a mental health reformer, she will have a long career in education. Dix publishes five textbooks in the 1820s, one of which—on science—is reprinted 60 times during the next 45 years.

✦ When Lucy Brewer publishes her experiences during the War of 1812, she uses a pseudonym to protect her family's reputation from the scandal of her earlier life as a prostitute. The title page by a Portsmouth, New Hamsphire, publisher reads: *An Affecting Narrative of LOUISA BAKER, A NATIVE OF MASSACHUSETTS, Who, in Early Life Having Been Shamefully Seduced, Abandoned Her Parents, and Enlisted, in Disguise, on Board an AMERICAN FRIGATE AS A MARINE, Where in Two or Three Engagements, She Displayed the Most Heroic Fortitude, and Was Honorably Discharged Therefrom, a Few Months Since, Without a Discovery of Her Sex Being Made.*

1817 From a mother house established in Emmitsburg, Maryland, in 1809, the Daughters of Charity of Saint Vincent de Paul expand to New

This drawing from the 1820s is the earliest available view of the innovative school that Emma Willard began in 1818. The big building to the left is the school; the rest depicts the town of Troy, New York, which financed this rare educational opportunity for young women. Archives, the Emma Willard School

York. The following year, Sacred Heart nuns settle in the wilderness of Saint Charles, Missouri.

✦ The examples of Ann Lee and Jemima Wilkinson continue to promote women as religious leaders in rural New York state: in Oneida County, Deborah Pierce publishes *A Scriptural Vindication of Female Preaching, Prophesying, or Exhortation.*

✦ An ice-covered ship carrying over 300 German men, women, and children arrives in Annapolis during frigid February weather. After 15 weeks at sea, the passengers are in very poor condition from hunger and cold.

1818 Emma Willard presents *An Address . . . Proposing a Plan for Improving Female Education* to the New York legislature. Her suggested curriculum—especially the teaching of anatomy —shocks the lawmakers, who do not consider her petition.

Influential people in nearby Troy, New York, however, hear about Willard's plan, and the town will raise taxes to open Troy Female Seminary in 1821. Within a decade, some 300 women enroll to study subjects as trigonometry and geology. Although Willard does not dare to call her school a college, it is in fact the first institution of higher education for women. So many young women from affluent families are eager for this opportunity that the school is financially sound from the beginning, and it will endure through the 20th century.

Unlike most of the era's educators, Willard is a married woman who had opened a school in 1814 after her husband's bankruptcy. While rearing five children, she educated herself by reading her nephew's college textbooks. She will go on to write more than 20 books, especially geography and history textbooks that she illustrates with complex drawings.

✦ At the same time, Bostonian Hannah Mather Crocker publishes *Observations on the Real Rights of Women.* Despite being the mother of 10, she has found time to read the works of Mary Woolstonecraft and another English feminist, Hannah More, to whom she dedicates her book. Her "observations" are just that: the book is the experiential writing of a woman who has seen that girls and boys have similar natural abilities until societal training and legal barriers create inequality.

◆ Fifteen-year-old Maria Becraft, a free African American, opens a school for black girls in Washington, even though both law and strong taboos make most blacks illiterate.

◆ Just a few years after the opening of the first weaving mills, approximately 12,000 people—most of them women and children—work in textile factories; within a decade, that figure will rise to 55,000.

◆ When former first lady Abigail Smith Adams dies, her minister reflects on her uncommonly egalitarian 54 year marriage. Her relationship to her husband, the clergyman writes, was that of "an equal and friend," for John Adams "had lived himself into one with the wife of his bosom." The former president survives his wife; both he and Thomas Jefferson will die on July 4, 1825—the 50th anniversary of the Declaration of Independence.

1819 The Female Hebrew Benevolent Society begins in Philadelphia under the leadership of Rebecca Gratz, a well-established, unmarried philanthropist. When Sir Walter Scott publishes *Ivanhoe* the following year, many believe that the model for his Rebecca—a brave, beautiful, kind Jewish woman—is Rebecca Gratz.

◆ Settlement of the upper Midwest begins this year at St. Anthony's Falls when the U.S. Army opens Fort Snelling, which will lead to the development of Minneapolis. Women, including black women who go as household slaves, are part of the settlement from its primitive beginnings. The diary of Pennsylvanian Eliza Taliferro, who moves to the fort in 1828, will give a 10-year account of life in this frigid frontier.

◆ Religious leader Jemima Wilkinson, "the Publick Universal Friend," dies in her home at Seneca Lake, New York, on July 1. Her supporters continue to practice the faith, but their ideal of celibacy necessarily decreases their numbers. The communal settlement does continue for more than a decade, however, for an 1832 traveler will record that "the present head of the society, Esther Plant," lacks Wilkinson's "tact."

◆ When Hawaiian king Kamehameha dies, his favorite wife, Kaahumanu, who stands six feet tall and weighs 300 pounds, essentially reigns until her 1832 death. One of her first acts is to break the taboo on men and women eating together. During the next decade, she will establish the islands' first legal code, which includes trial by jury.

1820 When the first missionaries arrive in Hawaii, they discover that women there are powerful. One of them is Kapiolani, a noble and a religious leader who enjoys several husbands; she soon converts to Christianity, divorces all but one of the men, becomes literate, and adopts Western ways.

In 1824, Kapiolani will withstand the power of her old religion and take on the volcano goddess of Pele. She climbs some 500 feet into Kilauea, confronts molten lava, and, observed by terrified onlookers, offers a demonstration of the superiority of her new god over the old ones.

◆ Elizabeth Yates of Charleston, South Carolina, denounces slavery in a letter to a Massachusetts senator. She urges him to take up the issue in Congress and says that she and her husband are freeing their slaves, despite the loss of $25,000.

Hers is a minority opinion, however, and two years later, Charleston is rocked by the discovery of plans for a major slave rebellion. Thirty-seven men, led by free black Denmark Vesey, are executed.

1821 In Scotland, Frances Wright publishes *Views of Society and Manners in America*; based on her 1818 trip, it becomes the first important American travelogue. She will return to the United States in 1824, and after touring in the East with the famed marquis de LaFayette, she sails around the Gulf of Mexico and up the Mississippi River approximately to Memphis. There Wright establishes a colony for freed slaves in 1825—decades before abolitionists propose such plans.

In this remote wilderness, however, successful enterprise is unlikely. When the colony fails, Wright finances the move of approximately 30 blacks, personally escorting them to Haiti in 1830.

◆ Philadelphia Quaker Lucretia Mott, who has preached both in and out of the meetinghouse while also bearing six children, is named an official minister of the Society of Friends. She will go

A slave woman plummets onto a Boston street when captors surround the house in which she hides. Library of Congress, from an engraving in Torrey, *American Slave Trade, 1822*

on to be considered one of the founders of both the abolitionist and women's rights movements.

◆ Rachel Jackson leaves her Tennessee Hermitage for the only time in her life, when she spends four months in Pensacola as first lady of Florida. Andrew Jackson goes from the territorial governorship to win the presidential election of 1828, but Rachel will die during the stress of preparing to move to Washington. Although her husband writes more than 100 words to be chiseled on her tombstone, he mandates that only his name appear on his tombstone.

◆ From Wethersfield, Connecticut, Sophia Woodhouse Wells patents a method of making bonnets from dried meadow grasses. She turns down an offer from London manufacturers and, with her husband, begins her own business.

◆ The Spanish governor of Texas permits some 300 families to settle near the Gulf of Mexico; led by Moses Austin, they are the first Anglo Americans officially allowed there.

1822   Kentucky receives its third convent: Dominican Sisters begin work at Saint Catherine, joining nuns of other orders who are already established at Nazareth and Saint Charles.

◆ Catharine Sedgwick publishes her first book and is immediately successful. Somewhat daringly for the time, when most novels are set in Europe, *A New-England Tale* is set in her native area, and it becomes the historical fiction standard far into the future. Sedgwick goes on to write similar works that sell well; she lives in the Berkshires in the summer and New York in the winter, becoming so well respected that some pre–Civil War literati "rank her with James Fenimore Cooper."

1823   Catharine and Mary Beecher open a Hartford, Connecticut, school for girls. It is unusual in its stress on high academic standards rather than the needlework often assigned in dame schools, and especially in that the girls perform calisthenics. Catharine Beecher will go on to a career as an educational reformer, with particular emphasis on the importance of diet, exercise, and clothing less restrictive than that mandated by the era's fashion.

✦ Ann Judson publishes *A Particular Relation of the American Baptist Mission to the Burman Empire* while in the United States for medical treatment. When she returns to Burma, the natives are in revolt against the British, and her husband is arrested as a spy. Despite pregnancy, she argues his case with whatever authority will listen, and when the area is afflicted with famine, she starves herself to bring food to her imprisoned husband. The strain is too much, and she and her child die soon after his 1825 release. Baptists will long revere Ann Judson as an early American martyr.

1824 The nation's infant industrial scene sees its first strike, as women and men go on strike in the textile mills of Pawtucket, Rhode Island.

✦ Lydia Francis, who is later famous as Lydia Maria Child, publishes *Hobomok*, the story of love between a white woman and a Native American man in early New England. Her book sells surprisingly well, and the 22-year-old author is admitted to the prestigious Boston Athenaeum. The next year, she follows this success up with another piece of historical fiction, *The Rebels, or Boston before the Revolution.*

✦ Southern aristocrat Mary Randolph publishes the first "truly American cookbook," *The Virginia House-wife.* Although a woman of Randolph's status does not toil in the kitchen, the book reflects the knowledge a successful hostess has to acquire, especially if her servants are illiterate.

✦ *The Life of Mary Jemison* is published in Canandaigua, New York. It begins with the 1755 raid of Jemison's home by six Senecas and four Frenchmen, when 11-year-old Mary was one of the few in her frontier Pennsylvania settlement to survive. Her tale especially emphasizes her adoption ceremony into the tribe, where she chose to live the rest of her life.

The ceremony was conducted entirely by women, and she was adopted specifically to replace the dead brother of two Seneca sisters: "From mourning," she recalls, "they became se-

rene—joy sparkled over their countenances, and they seemed to rejoice over me as over a lost child. I was made welcome . . . and was called Dickewamis, which [means] pretty girl . . . I was ever considered and treated by them as a real sister." She draws a philosophical point from her experience: "It is family, and not national sacrifices among Indians, that . . . has given them their character."

1825 Although she may not have the legal right to do so, Pennsylvanian Rebecca Pennock Lukens assumes that she inherits the ironworks her husband and father have run when both men die. While nursing a newborn, she manages the foundry, pays off the debts from its recent expansion, and successfully carries on through the 1837 financial depression. Her business builds an outstanding reputation for quality and has national contracts, including the hull of the nation's first metal ship.

✦ Massachusetts schoolteacher Mary Lyons is so interested in laboratory science that she manages to get permission to attend classes at the all-male Amherst College and at New York's new Rensselaer Institute.

She and her friend Zilpah (Polly) Grant also establish a precedent at Adams Academy in New Hampshire by issuing diplomas to young women. They later resign when the male board of trustees insists that they teach "music and dancing" rather than the innovative curriculum in science and geography that Lyon has created.

✦ America's first families from Norway arrive on the *Restaurationen*, but it will be another 40 years before major Norwegian immigration occurs. Almost invariably Lutherans, their women are better educated and have a higher legal status than most other European Women.

✦ When white explorers negotiate a treaty with the Kansa in what will become modern Kansas, they note that this tribe, like many others, accords a high status to women. It is matrilineal, which means that because women hold the family name, no child endures the stigma of bastardy, and women have greater sexual freedom. Women also own the family property and perform sacred ceremonies.

1826 The nation's first magazine for children is begun by popular author Lydia Francis. The bimonthly publication is called *Juvenile Miscellany.*

◆ At age 57, widowed, and in need of money, Anne Newport Royall leaves her western Virginia mountain home to support herself by traveling throughout the nation and writing books based on her experience. She will publish 10 travelogues between 1826 and 1831 that deal with all facets of American life.

   The observations she makes on women include these: "The ladies of New York do not read. This is perhaps owing to their numerous sources of amusement such as theaters, gardens, etc." In contrast, "the excellence of the Boston ladies is found in the improvement of their minds . . . a striking contrast to the vacant stare of many of the ladies of New York."

◆ Thomas Jefferson dies, on July 4, after using his legal skills to see that his inheritance bypasses his son-in-law and goes to his daughter, in contradiction of current law that allows married women no independent property rights.

◆ Following up on the work of their founder, Mother Ann Lee, Shakers build colonies as far west as Indiana and Ohio. They now have eight colonies in 18 states, each dedicated to egalitarianism, celibacy, and work-sharing.

◆ Women are the sole strikers when the United Tailoresses declare a strike in New York City. The women's move comes just three years after the nation's first industrial strike, and it requires more organizing skill because most of these women work at home rather than in a unified, easily identified locale. Not surprisingly, little long-term success is gained—although the women

show their awareness of the importance of language in terming themselves "tailoresses" rather than the more conventional "seamstresses." By definition, a woman is never a tailor, and tailors, of course, earn more.

1827 A slave called Isabella, later known as Sojourner Truth, flees her upstate New York master to join a Quaker household, where she is protected. The Quakers help her file suit to recover her son Peter from Alabama, where he has been sold in violation of New York's 1810 law that provided for gradual emancipation. The court agrees, and Peter is returned.

◆ At a time when women refrain from speaking in public, Elizabeth Peabody delivers lectures on America history in Massachusetts homes—and charges significant fees for them. During the next decade, she will produce a three-volume question-and-answer series designed to teach history.

◆ A black woman who calls herself Matilda writes a letter to the editor of the abolitionist *Freedom's Journal*, saying in part: "I don't know that . . . you have said sufficient upon the education of females. I hope you are not to be classed with those who think that our mathematical knowledge should be limited to 'fathoming the dish-kettle. . . .'"

◆ Eliza McCardle marries Tennessee tailor Andrew Johnson, and as he sews, she instructs him in reading and writing. He goes on to a career in politics and becomes president in 1865 when Abraham Lincoln is assassinated; he continues to respect her mental capability in the White House, when she prepares his daily summary of newspaper coverage.

◆ Seven-year-old Louisa Lane, who has been on the London stage since infancy, thrills Baltimore audiences when she plays the boy's role in *William Tell*. As an adult, she will establish the Drew dynasty of American actors.

4

Jacksonian Justice, Abolition,
and Agitation for
Women's Rights

1828–1860

1828 The election of Tennessee's Andrew Jackson as president this year signals an end to the power of the seacoast aristocracy. When frontiersmen assert themselves at the ballot box, women of all classes also begin to adopt democratic goals.

✦ Sarah Buell Hale, a New Hampshire widow with five young children to support, takes a Boston job as editor of the new *Ladies' Magazine*. She also is the author of almost everything in the magazine during its early days, and in 1830 she writes a little poem that becomes immortal: "Mary Had a Little Lamb." Because publications aimed at women are virtually unknown, Hale will develop the basic magazine format and exert a tremendous influence during the next 50 years. Her words will be read monthly by almost every female community leader in America.

✦ The entire work force of Paterson, New Jersey, goes on strike briefly. The causes of discontent are not local, for more than 300 female textile workers in Dover, New Hampshire, also strike.

✦ Maria Weston—later famous as abolitionist Maria Weston Chapman—becomes the "lady principal" of a private high school for young women in Boston.

✦ Young Clarina Howard graduates from the public school at West Townshend, Vermont, and delivers a speech that she calls a "comparative of a scientific and an ornamental education for females." As Clarina Howard Nichols, she will become a well-known journalist and women's rights leader.

1829 President Andrew Jackson spends much of his first year in office defending the reputation of Peggy Eaton, the wife of his secretary of war. Cabinet meetings are seriously disrupted by this "Petticoat War," as the wives of other cabinet members socially ostracize the Eatons for their presumed relationship prior to the death of Peggy Eaton's first husband.

Because Jackson's recently dead wife, Rachel, was also the object of hurtful gossip, the president feels strongly about this issue, and although John Eaton insists on resigning from the cabinet, Jack-

son will punish Vice President John C. Calhoun —whose South Carolina wife leads the opposition to Peggy Eaton—by dropping him from the presidential ticket at reelection time.

✦ Successful travel writer Anne Newport Royall is convicted on a charge of being a "common scold," after confronting an obstreperous group of Christians who gather day and night near her Washington home. Because Royall is an outspoken opponent of organized religion, several clergymen push the case to conviction; the witnesses on her behalf consist of "a few ladies and Secretary Eaton," the husband of controversial Peggy Eaton.

When the jury finds Royall guilty, there is discussion of the traditional punishment of dunking—but the prospect of seeing a 60-year-old widow immersed in the Potomac is too much even for her Calvinist enemies, and Eaton pays the $10 fine imposed on Royall.

✦ Female workers in Taunton, Massachusetts, are led out on strike by 15-year-old Salome Lincoln. The women are especially concerned about the long days required in summer, for in this pre-electric era, they are expected to toil from dawn to dark.

✦ The first order of African-American nuns, the Oblate Sisters of Providence, is founded in Baltimore. The sisters operate a school for girls that attracts students from Philadelphia and other cities; their work will expand dramatically after the Civil War, when they build orphanages for black children as far away as Kansas.

✦ At the same time, American-born nuns of the Sisters of Charity of Our Lady of Mercy establish themselves at Charleston. For a long time theirs remains the only southern convent outside of Louisiana.

✦ Angelina Grimké writes a letter to an abolitionist newspaper about her personal experience as a member of a South Carolina slaveowning family. Publisher William Lloyd Garrison contacts her and her sister Sarah, who have recently moved to Philadelphia, and the two women become the only southern whites who will be highly visible in the abolitionist movement. Hostility against them at home becomes so strong that they can never return to visit the large family they leave behind in Charleston.

◆ Defying the convention that women do not speak in public, Frances Wright conducts a lecture tour that attracts large audiences of both women and men. She uses the Declaration of Independence to argue for women's rights and criticizes organized religion for assigning a secondary place to women. A socialist and abolitionist active in the development of several utopian communities, Wright also argues for birth control and divorce —positions that will remain controversial a century later.

◆ Almira Lincoln publishes *Familiar Lectures on Botany*, which, with revisions, will sell over 275,000 copies. The youngest sister of Emma Willard, she is a widow with young children to support and teaches at Willard's Troy Female Seminary.

Later, as Almira Lincoln Phelps, she will head other innovative schools for young women in New Jersey and Maryland; her husband—and their children from three marriages—will move with her as her career advances.

◆ The title of Lydia Maria (Francis) Child's third book demonstrates the change in her life since marriage: Unlike the historical fiction she wrote earlier, this book is called *The Frugal Housewife*. Such practical books for women are new and sales are excellent—there will be 21 editions during the next decade.

Copyright protection is so poor, however, and her idealistic husband is such an unreliable source of income that the author must remain frugal. When David Child decides to experiment with growing sugar beets a few years later, they live in near poverty on a western Massachusetts farm.

1830 Congress passes the Indian Removal Act, and the Cherokee begin a forced march under military supervision from their homelands in the western Carolinas and northern Geor-

gia/Alabama to the Indian Territory—which, 60 years later, will be taken from them to become the State of Oklahoma. Some 4,000 Cherokee— including, of course, women and children—die along the Trail of Tears that displaces them from their homes.

In western New York—where radical religious ideas have been standard since Jemima Wilkinson opened this frontier in 1788—Joseph Smith publishes *The Book of Mormon*. He lives with his wife's family while working on it and then organizes the Church of Jesus Christ of the Latter-Day Saints, which adopts the communal style of property ownership that a number of other utopian societies in this era also accept. More than this communism, however, it is polygamy, in emulation of the Old Testament, that will make Mormons controversial.

◆ Educator Emma Willard, who was widowed five years earlier, travels to Greece. She sets up a school there based on the model she has developed at Troy, New York, and when she returns home, publishes a book on her experience.

◆ Women in the textile mills of Lowell, Massachusetts, sing a lengthy description of their work: "Come all ye ladies of Lowell," the song invites. "The factory bell begins to ring." More than 20 verses detail the complexities of their work, and it concludes with "This corporation now is good . . . May friendship reign throughout the whole."

1831 Abolitionist William Lloyd Garrison publishes work by Bostonian Maria Stewart, an African American who was born free. Stewart continues to write and, even more unconventionally, to make speeches against slavery. That there are other literate black women in Boston at the time is clear from the fact that Stewart belongs to the Afric-American Female Intelligence Society— and when she moves to New York the following year, she joins the Female Literary Society there.

◆ Educator Catharine Beecher begins the Western Female Institute in Cincinnati. She struggles to keep it open in what is still a frontier but succumbs to bankruptcy in the Panic of 1837. A few years later she will assist famous William McGuffey on his fourth elementary reader.

+ The New York Female Moral Reform Society begins efforts to prevent prostitution. Among its most devoted workers is Margaret Prior, a wealthy woman who goes into the city's worst slums trying to rehabilitate lives.

+ Delia Bacon, who was educated at Catharine Beecher's Hartford school, achieves success before her friend Harriet Beecher Stowe does: Bacon wins a $100 prize from the Philadelphia *Saturday Courier* for a story based on the 1777 killing of Jane McCrea by Indians allied with the British during the Revolution.

Two years later Bacon breaks taboos on public speaking to begin a series on historical and literary themes. She delivers these lectures in Hartford, New Haven, and even Boston and New York, speaking to large audiences composed primarily, but not exclusively, of women.

+ Travelogue author Anne Newport Royall, who has settled permanently in Washington, begins a newspaper, *Paul Pry*; after it is confused with other papers that use the term "pry," she calls her paper the *Huntress*. A strong Jacksonian Democrat, she specializes in exposing corruption, including fraud against Indians. She will publish until age 85, with editorials that are said to have "shot terror into evil-acting public men."

+ Sarah Miriam Peale, the youngest of the famous Philadelphia family of painters, moves to Baltimore and becomes that city's most popular artist—until St. Louis patrons recruit her away in 1846. Never marrying, Sally Peale supports herself well; her portrait customers include such men as Daniel Webster and Lafayette.

1832 The Boston Lying-In Hospital is founded. The nation's first obstetric hospital, it will be used as a training ground for physicians. The patients are women too poor to pay for private treatment; more affluent women will continue to have their babies delivered at home throughout the century.

+ Maria Weston Chapman founds the Boston Female Anti-Slavery Society. It publishes an annual report titled *Right and Wrong in Boston* and attempts to provide educational opportunity for the city's free blacks. Most Bostonians greet the society's circulation of petitions against slavery with great hostility.

+ When a white North Carolina man attempts to divorce his white wife because she has given birth to a suspiciously dark baby, the court rules that "the birth of a mulatto child is not always sufficient cause for divorce."

Miscegenation is in fact far more common than polite society would admit: an analysis of the state's divorce petitions shows the third most common reason is "cohabitation with a Negro." Meanwhile, South Carolina court records include several cases of slaves who gain their freedom by proving that their mothers were white.

+ English Fanny Kemble is perhaps the first actor to develop nationwide fans when she tours the country as Shakespeare's Juliet. She marries two years later and lives unhappily on her husband's South Carolina plantation, where she keeps a diary that, when published in the midst of the Civil War, is very helpful to the antislavery cause.

+ Young Elizabeth Cady, who has taught herself Greek and Latin from books bought for her brother, travels from western to eastern New York state to attend Emma Willard's Troy State Academy. Willard's influence on the brilliant young woman is profound, and Elizabeth Cady Stanton will maintain the life of the mind even while mothering seven children.

+ The town of Troy—which taxed itself two decades ago to build Willard's school—inspires independent young women, and this year a 25-year-old Troy resident, Jane Maria Eliza McManus, makes the first move in what will be a vast behind-the-scenes political career. Because her family is in financial difficulty, her father sends her to see their old friend Aaron Burr, a former vice president of the United States and longtime national expansionist, about moving to "some new Country." Acting on Burr's recommendation, she leads the McManus family to Texas, which is still a part of Mexico.

She also exhibits exceptional independence in her personal life, for, although she is the mother of an infant son, she obtained one of the era's rare divorces last year. Her historical achievements will be obscured in part because she vacillates between using her maiden and married names: She is both "Mrs. McManus" and "Mrs. Storms" in this era; later marriages will change her name twice more.

✦ "Just Published," an advertisement reads. "An Interesting Narrative of the Captivity of Misses Francis and Almira Hall, two respectable young females (sisters) of the ages of 16 and 18, who were taken prisoners by the Savages at a Frontier Settlement near Indian Creek, in May last, when fifteen of the inhabitants were barbarously murdered, among whom were the parents of the unfortunate female. . . ." The story sells for 12 cents.

✦ Catharine and Harriet Beecher belong to the Semi-Colon Club of Cincinnati, a reading and discussion group that is unusual in its inclusion of both men and women.

1833 Quaker educator Prudence Crandell opens a school in Canterbury, Connecticut, for "young ladies and little misses of color." When prosperous black families throughout the Northeast send their daughters, Crandell's big boardinghouse on the town square becomes a target for those who oppose educating blacks.

Within a month, the legislature has passed a specifically tailored law that bans schools from teaching "any colored person . . . not an inhabitant . . . in this state" without permission of the local government. When Crandell refuses to close her school, she is arrested and jailed; the trial results in a hung jury, but the second jury convicts her. Juries, of course, are exclusively male in this era.

✦ Popular author Lydia Maria Child publishes *An Appeal in Favor of That Class of Americans Called Africans*. It is the first abolitionist classic: her work not only details the history of slavery but also explores many aspects of the issue, from current proposals for colonization of slaves to laws against miscegenation to the integration of public facilities. Boston society is shocked by her radical ideas, and Child is socially ostracized; her book sales collapse and the children's magazine she has published since 1826 goes bankrupt.

✦ Massachusetts Protestants attack a Charlestown convent, and the occupants barely escape with their lives. At the same time, women of the French-based Congregation of Our Lady of Mt. Carmel start the second convent in New Orleans —the first was founded, more than a century ago in 1727, by Ursuline nuns.

✦ The Philadelphia Anti-Slavery Society is founded by both women and men. Ordained Quaker minister Lucretia Mott will serve as its president— decades before most American women join even single-sex organizations, to say nothing of presiding over an audience that includes men.

Mott also personally boycotts all Southern goods, which means finding alternatives for such staples as cotton, sugar, and rice. Her political action predates that of famous male abolitionists; according to black leader Robert Purvis, Mott spoke in "colored churches as early as 1829"— prior to William Lloyd Garrison.

✦ Female shoemakers in Saugus, Massachusetts, win a pay increase; their counterparts in nearby Lynn go on strike and organize a boycott until they win a similar pay scale.

✦ Grieving after the death of her daughter, Washington's Mary G. Wilkinson accepts two young women who are new to the city and alone into her Capitol Hill home, which eventually becomes the Young Woman's Christian Home—a Washington, D.C., institution for two centuries.

✦ As the nation's oldest college, Harvard, nears its 200th birthday, the first college that is willing to admit both blacks and women opens: Oberlin College in frontier Oberlin, Ohio, is coeducational from the beginning. On December 3, classes begin for 29 men and 15 women, and although the women are initially restricted to a "Ladies Course," they will enroll for the "full course"—with a curriculum modeled on Yale's— within four years.

All faculty is, of course, male; their wives serve on the Ladies' Board of Managers that oversees female students. Life at Oberlin is not privileged: all students rise at dawn and perform manual labor in addition to studying. Most are vegetarians, and an extra fee is charged those who insist on meat. No caffeine or spices are served.

1834 Mary Lyon travels alone in western Massachusetts, collecting money to build her dream of a quality institution for the higher education of women. She canvasses 60 towns and literally thousands of farms, receiving donations of as little as 6 cents from women. When she is criticized for this unladylike behavior, she replies, "I am doing a great work; I cannot come down."

An amazingly effective fund raiser, Lyon garners half of her $30,000 goal within two years. At the same time, she cleverly establishes a male board of trustees for her school: "The plan," she writes to a female friend, "should not seem to originate with us, but with benevolent gentlemen."

◆ In July, a higher court overturns the ruling against Prudence Crandell, who has continued to operate her Connecticut boarding school for black girls—despite the refusal of merchants to sell to her, being forced to carry water for two miles after her well is deliberately contaminated, and other property destruction and personal attacks.

In September, however, the school (which is also her home) is attacked at night, and the recently married Crandell gives up and moves away. She will work for suffrage and temperance in Illinois and Kansas, and in 1886—four years prior to her death—the Connecticut legislature finally will offer her a modest monetary compensation.

◆ Eliza Bowen Jumel Burr sues for divorce from 77-year-old Aaron Burr, a former U.S. vice president. They have been married just a year, and she alleges that her grounds are his infidelity with Jane McManus Storms.

Eliza Burr's past, however, does not conform to the era's standards for women. As a young prostitute, she bore an illegitimate child in 1794 and then spent years as mistress to Frenchman Stephen Jumel in New York prior to their 1804 marriage. Jumel provided her with a luxurious lifestyle in both France and New York but, using the power of attorney he granted her when he went to Paris, she cashed in his New York properties, leaving him to die virtually indigent in 1832. The following year, she married Burr, whom she now seeks to divorce. The decree will be granted on the day Burr dies.

1835 The *American Protestant Vindicator*, a New York anti-Catholic paper, serializes the salacious story of Maria Monk, an unwed teenage mother, supposedly based on her experience in a Montreal convent. Her male associates do the actual writing, alleging that nuns are forced to submit to lascivious priests and that the unwilling are murdered, as are the infants born from the unwanted pregnancies. Published the next year as *Awful Disclosures of Maria Monk*, it becomes a longtime best-seller and does great harm to the image of Catholicism.

◆ The national gullibility that enables Maria Monk's tales to be accepted as truth is also responsible for building P.T. Barnum's belief that "there's a sucker born every minute." At 25, he sees an aged black woman, Joice Heth, who is being exhibited in Philadelphia as George Washington's 160-year-old nurse. Barnum buys Heth, creates authentic-looking documents alleging her historic role, and uses the proceeds to build the fortune that eventually supports the Barnum & Bailey Circus. When Heth dies, he buries her in his family's plot with great publicity—and then, to keep his name in print, he writes anonymous letters attacking her credibility.

◆ A Female Moral Reform Society begins at Oberlin College; it is an offshoot of the New York Female Reform Society, whose "directress," Lydia Andrews Finney, has recently moved to Oberlin. With an organizational goal of battling "the sin of licentiousness, in all its forms and horrors," the group will grow to 380 members by 1840, including student Lucy Stone.

A further indication of the college town's unusual interest in women's issues is the formation of the Maternal Association of Oberlin this year; that organization will endure until 1866.

♦ After two years of studying medical books, Bostonians Sarah and Harriot Hunt, with encouragement from their mother, begin to practice medicine—without, of course, any licenses. They are motivated primarily by Sarah's recovery from chronic pulmonary disease, which comes only after they abandon physicians whose treatments have included such dangerous interventions as leeches, calomel, and prussic acid.

The sisters emphasize sanitation, diet, and exercise, and they slowly establish a practice consisting mostly of women and children, many of whom have been written off as incurable by traditional physicians. After they notice that much disease seems to be based in "concealed sorrows," the sisters also begin to recognize the reality of psychosomatic illness.

♦ At age 11, Lucy Larcom begins work in the textile mills of Lowell, Massachusetts, where her widowed mother runs a boardinghouse for female workers. Her older sisters are founders of *Operative Magazine*, and young Lucy publishes her first writing there. Much later, she will write a classic memoir of this era, *A New England Girlhood* (1889).

Lowell women also organize evening classes and study everything from botany to music. They hire a German professor to teach them that language, and for several years these unusual factory workers fulfill their self-expression and communication needs with regular publications.

♦ Female Anti-Slavery Society branches begin to spread beyond the founding cities of Philadelphia and Boston. In Lynn, Massachusetts, women begin door-to-door political canvassing. Society members speak to other women about slavery, urging them to sign petitions and donate to the cause.

♦ A mob gathers as abolitionist William Lloyd Garrison appears at a meeting of the Boston Female Anti-Slavery Society attended by both black and white women. The mayor orders the women to leave the meeting, but their leader, Maria Weston Chapman, replies, "If this is the last bulwark of freedom, we may as well die here as anywhere." When they finally do leave, Chapman tells each white woman to take the hand of a black woman, and they meet the mob. Garrison is assaulted, but the women are not.

♦ Paulina Kellogg Wright and her husband organize an anti-slavery meeting in Utica, New York, and a mob attacks their home.

♦ In Washington, D.C., an English visitor writes of slave pens within sight of the Capitol: "In this wretched hovel all colors except white, both sexes, all ages, are confined. . . ."

♦ Lydia Maria Child expands her writing from the status of blacks to that of women, publishing a two-volume work titled *The History and Condition of Women, in Various Ages and Nations.*

1836 Missionaries Narcissa Whitman and Eliza Spaulding, traveling with their husbands, become the first white women to cross the Continental Divide, settling in what will become Washington State. Their trip is complicated by the fact that Spaulding's husband once proposed to Whitman, who rejected his offer, and the men become increasingly jealous and hostile toward each other along the way.

The couples separate in Oregon, and Narcissa Whitman joins her physician husband in delivering health care to both the native Cayuse and to the Oregon Trail pioneers who will follow them in the 1840s. She spends a good deal of time alone while her husband goes back East, and she endures the drowning of her little daughter and her own near blindness while still in her 30s.

♦ In the frontier of Limestone County, Texas, nine-year-old Cynthia Ann Parker is taken prisoner by

Comanche on May 19. She will grow up, marry, and bear three children; when Texas Rangers recapture her in 1860, the only English word that she remembers is her name. She wants no part of white culture and dies soon after going to live with her brother.

In 1875, one of her sons, Quanah, will be the last Comanche chief to surrender. In 1957—more than a century after her capture—her body and his are reburied at Fort Sill, Oklahoma.

+ Georgia Female College is established in Macon. Construction is slowed by the financial panic of the next year, but classes will begin in 1839 on a four-acre campus, with one large building that includes classrooms, a chapel, and dining room, as well as sleeping space for the young women. They study advanced mathematics and science; both Latin and French are required.

+ Women in the shoe manufacturing business in the Philadelphia area strike for several months; their counterparts in local cotton mills have been involved in long strikes over the last two years.

+ Ernestine Rose, who changed her name from Siismund Potowski after emigrating from Poland, sends the New York Legislature a petition "to give a married woman the right to hold real estate in her own name." It has just five signatures, which she obtained "after a good deal of trouble." Although happily married, Rose is undeterred in her work for this principle, and by the time of the first Women's Rights Convention in 1848, she has already achieved a record surpassing that of any other feminist. "During the 11 years from 1837 to 1848," she writes later, "I addressed the New York Legislature five times."

+ When Sarah Grimké attempts to discuss slavery during the annual meeting of the Philadelphia Society of Friends, she is officially rebuked. Although Quakers have no objections to public speaking by women and though they oppose slavery, many Friends are beginning to discover that their abolitionism clashes with their pacifism.

Women such as Lucretia Mott, of course, have spoken against slavery for years—but the Grimké sisters are newcomers, unlike the wealthy, well-

established, and married Mott. Moreover, as it appears less likely that Southern states will end slavery voluntarily, as Northern states are doing, there is a greater possibility that this clash of ideas will become deadly. To speak against slavery is to risk war, and Sarah Grimké is silenced.

+ Angelina Grimké writes *An Appeal to the Christian Women of the South.* Her plea is not merely on behalf of slaves: She also argues that slavery harms white women by encouraging the sexual misbehavior of their men. When she points out that many black children clearly resemble their white fathers, her candor is too shocking for most readers. Postmasters confiscate any copies that appear in Southern states.

+ Less than a decade after she was the city's "lady principal," Bostonian Maria Weston Chapman writes that she is afraid to be on the streets because of the hostility toward her Female Anti-Slavery Society. Both the town's rabble and its upper class object to this unconventional activity by women; in addition, the wealth of many of Chapman's former friends is based on trade with slaveowners.

+ Thirteen-year-old Virginia Clemm marries her cousin, Edgar Allan Poe; they live in Richmond, Virginia.

1837 The nation's first serious economic depression occurs. The Panic of 1837 creates ironic opportunity for a number of women: Susan Anthony, Elizabeth Blackwell, Anna Ella Carrol, and others are forced to become income providers when their fathers go bankrupt. The experience gives them habits of independence that will be fundamental to their later leadership.

The Panic ends the barely begun Factory Girls Association, a nascent union of the textile mill women centered in Lowell, Massachusetts.

+ Unemployment in New York City causes widespread hunger, and on a February night, women join men in breaking into a warehouse where food is being held for higher prices. They steal or destroy some 500 barrels of flour and 1,000 barrels of wheat. One woman stabs a policeman attempting to quell the riot, while another woman is credited for saving the life of an officer assaulted by the mob.

+ *Three Experiments in Living* by Hannah Farnham Lee is a tremendous sales success despite—or perhaps because of—the economic crisis. Lee presents three scenarios of living under, with, and beyond one's means. Her book will go through 30 editions in the United States and Europe, showing that the public will accept advice from a woman on money management.

+ Caroline Healey opens a child nursery for the working-class women of Boston's North End and keeps it operating successfully for five years, even though her father will suffer financially during the depression and even though the concept of profit-making child care is unknown in this era.

　　When she finally closes the nursery, Healey moves on to Washington, D.C.; there she will be an administrator at Georgetown's prestigious Miss English's School for Young Ladies while also attempting to provide education for the city's free blacks.

+ The depression does not deter visionary educator Mary Lyon, who persuades the town of South Hadley, Massachusetts, to donate $8,000 in exchange for becoming the site of her Mount Holyoke Female Seminary. Classes begin in November, and an innovative work/study program not only enables poorer students to enroll but also eases the class distinctions that will long characterize other colleges.

　　The 80 students must pass entrance examinations, and the curriculum includes botany, physiology, chemistry, geology, algebra, history, politics, and several areas of philosophy and theology. Women's desire for this sort of serious education is so great that some 400 applicants have to be turned down the following year.

　　Many Mount Holyoke graduates will enter the missionary field by marrying ordained ministers (especially from nearby Amherst and Yale), thus fulfilling the intent of a "female seminary." So eager are women to enroll that Mount Holyoke is fiscally secure from the beginning; it will

go on to become the oldest of the women's colleges known as the Seven Sisters.

+ *Ladies' Magazine* is merged with *Godey's Lady's Book* when it is bought by the Philadelphia publisher who is the magazine's namesake. Editor Sarah Buell Hale moves to Philadelphia and continues to expand her national audience; *Godey's* becomes the century's most important periodical for women. Hale editorially crusades for female opportunity, especially in education and medicine, and she is influential in other successful ideas, including the regular observance of Thanksgiving Day. Within two decades, over 150,000 women will subscribe to *Godey's*.

+ Two hundred women from nine states attend the first Women's Anti-Slavery Convention in New York. White abolitionist Abby Kelly of Lynn, Massachusetts, makes her first major speech, and a number of free black women also participate, including members of Philadelphia's affluent Forten and Purvis families. It is arguably the first national political gathering of women; it violates the era's taboo on public speaking by women as well as codes on integration.

+ Even liberal Quakers assume the correctness of racial segregation, and the Grimké sisters are rebuked for sitting in their Philadelphia meetinghouse on the same bench as Sarah Douglass, a free black female teacher.

+ Congregational clergy in Massachusetts issue a Pastoral Letter against "unnatural" public speaking by women, saying that "the power of woman is in her dependence." The specific targets of the ministers' admonition doubtless are Sarah and Angelina Grimké, who continue to speak against slavery. Because the sisters know slavery's reality from living on a South Carolina plantation, their message is particularly disturbing to those who want no change in the status quo. Many Massachusetts people ignore the pastoral advice, however, and a lecture series that the Grimké sisters present the next year attracts thousands.

+ The German Widows and Orphans Society is organized under the aegis of St. Matthew's Lutheran Church on New York City's Mott Street. Similar benevolent societies in mainstream Protestant churches will become increasingly common; they give many women their only organizational experience.

◆ *Further Disclosures by Maria Monk* keeps the anti-Catholic controversy alive with repetitions of the allegations in the first book. The "author," however, does not share in the profits. After bearing a second illegitimate child, she is imprisoned for prostitution in 1849 and dies in New York's notorious Blackwell Island poorhouse at age 33.

◆ Without any special ceremony or controversy, the first women matriculate in a coeducational college curriculum. On September 6, four women pay the fees to enroll as freshmen at Ohio's Oberlin College: Mary Hosford of Oberlin, Mary Kellogg of Jamestown, New York, Elizabeth Prall of New York City, and Caroline Rudd of Huntington, Connecticut.

Mary Kellogg will be forced to drop out when her family moves to Louisiana the following year, but in 1841, the three others earn bachelor of arts degrees—even though some think that terms such as "bachelor" and "freshmen" in itself means that women cannot be counted as full college students. Indeed, throughout the century, some coeducational colleges will distinguish degrees granted to women by such terms as "Maid of Arts" or "Mistress of Philosophy"—the terminology that currently prevails at female seminaries.

1838 Kentucky women gain the first voting rights that women have had since New Jersey took away women's vote in 1807. Kentucky widows with no children currently in school are allowed to vote in school elections.

◆ Congress passes a special act granting the children of Revolutionary War soldier Deborah Sampson a retroactive pension payment for their mother's military service.

◆ Richmond women form a stock company; they sell shares at $25 and raise $5,000 in capital, which they use to buy materials for indigent dressmakers—thus providing employment to poor women, while earning a profit on the sales of the completed garments.

◆ At a time when public speaking by women is condemned, Mary Gove not only lectures but speaks on the forbidden subject of women's anatomy. An unhappily married woman whose five pregnancies produced only one healthy baby, she has secretly read medical books to teach herself the fundamentals of female physiology. She goes to Boston at the invitation of women interested in learning what she has learned. Except for the fact that her husband confiscates her earnings, she successfully launches a career as a health educator.

◆ Although she never becomes as famous as other abolitionist writers, Rhode Islander Frances Green publishes *Elleanor Eldridge*, which is based on the actual case of a mistreated black woman. It is popular enough that the sequel follows next year, and Green continues to write fiction empathetic to the poor as well as nonfiction, including a botany textbook.

◆ Former president John Quincy Adams, now a member of the House of Representatives, exhibits the empathy toward blacks that his mother, Abigail Adams, had taught him. In a speech to the House, he tells of a woman imprisoned in nearby Alexandria, Virginia, who, with her four children, was about to be sold away from the children's father. The distraught woman preferred to see her little ones die rather than suffer this fate, and she strangled two of her children before jailors stopped her.

◆ In May, the second Anti-Slavery Convention of American Women meets in Philadelphia, but the women are greeted with even more hostility than they were last year in New York. While a threatening mob gathers in the City of Brotherly Love, Bostonian Maria Weston Chapman calmly continues to preside and then leads the women from the hall with blacks and whites holding hands. Afterward rioters burn the hall.

The mob may have been incited when Harriet Forten Purvis arrived at the meeting and her light-skinned husband helped her from their carriage. Robert Purvis is a wealthy Philadelphian who was technically born into slavery in South Carolina; although his white father never married his mulatto mother, they lived together openly and Purvis inherited a large estate. Apparently the sight of this light-skinned man with his darker wife was more than white Philadelphian males could bear.

✦ Sarah Grimké writes *Letters on the Equality of the Sexes and the Condition of Women*, which spells out the similarity of legal codes that define blacks and women as inferior. Angelina Grimké sets a precedent for women by testifying to a committee of the Massachusetts legislature—five years prior to Dorothea Dix's better known written "memorial" to that legislature.

Later in the year, Angelina Grimké marries abolitionist Theodore Weld in a wedding that includes black guests. Philadelphians angry at this integration again riot: two days after the wedding, a mob burns down not only the new office of the antislavery society but even the Shelter for Colored Orphans.

1839 Massachusetts teacher Abby Kelly leaves her job and sets out to earn a precarious living by lecturing against slavery. Not only is it unconventional for a woman to speak in public, her topic is also incendiary: Kelly will be physically attacked, slandered, and refused hotel rooms on the grounds that respectable women do not travel without male escort.

✦ Margaret Fuller, a genius who at age seven read the classics in Latin, delivers lectures in her Boston home. Although she does not defy the conventions against speaking in public, she nevertheless earns money when both women and men pay to attend her "Conversations." The next year, philosophers Ralph Waldo Emerson and Henry David Thoreau are among those who invite her to edit their new publication, *The Dial*.

✦ Sarah Grimké and her brother-in-law Theodore Weld publish *American Slavery as It Is: Testimony of a Thousand Witnesses.* Irrefutable proof of slavery's harsh reality, the book reprints the most revealing of news stories culled from Southern papers.

1840 Elizabeth Cady and Henry Stanton set a milestone when they agree that she should omit "obey" from her wedding vows. He recognizes that to persuade this unusual woman to marry, he must allow her an unusual degree of independence.

They go to London on their honeymoon, where she attempts to join him at the World Anti-Slavery Conference—but she and other women, including longtime Philadelphia abolitionist leader Lucretia Mott, are not allowed entrance. They listen to the discussion of their presence from behind curtain and Stanton writes: "Would there have been no unpleasant feelings had [black men] been refused their seats, and had *they* listened one entire day to debates on their peculiar fitness for plantation life?"

✦ Despite Abby Kelly's personal sacrifice as a lecturer against slavery, men in the American Anti-Slavery Society refuse to accept William Lloyd Garrison's appointment of her to the business committee. Turmoil erupts at the convention, and almost half the male delegates are so insulted that they leave the organization and form a rival group.

Next March, Abby Kelly will resign from the Society of Friends because of the growing reluctance of many Quakers to risk war for black freedom.

✦ After the split in the American Anti-Slavery Society makes Garrison's group more hospitable to women, Lydia Maria Child joins the society's executive committee. The following year she will move to New York to edit the weekly *National Anti-Slavery Standard*. For part of her tenure as editor, Child has what is later called a commuter marriage: she lives in New York, while her husband works as a journalist in Washington, D.C.

✦ Georgia Female College in Macon grants its first degree, "the very first traditional A.B. degree to women." The school will change its name to Wesleyan Female College in 1843 to emphasize the support that it receives from Methodist churches. By then it has approximately 200 students who study under male professors.

✦ Bostonian Elizabeth Peabody establishes an extremely influential bookstore/publishing house, which becomes a regular gathering place for Ralph Waldo Emerson and others of the nation's literati.

Peabody publishes some of the first works by her brother-in-law, Nathaniel Hawthorne. She also takes genuine risks in publishing abolitionist materials, including Henry David Thoreau's "Civil Disobedience," an essay that is controversial during the debate on slavery and later becomes an oft-cited document in favor of nonviolent resistance during the 20th century.

✦ Publishers in the United States and Europe follow up Hannah Farnham Lee's success with her 1837 money management book by publishing several manuscripts that Lee—a widow with children to support—had been unable to publish earlier. In this decade, she averages more than a book a year.

Lee writes both fiction and nonfiction, eventually specializing in history and biography. The range of her subjects is astonishing; they include histories on the Huguenots, sculpture and painting, and biographies of German Martin Luther, English Thomas Crammer, and Haitian Pierre Toussaint. Even the books on such obscure figures as Crammer and Toussaint go through more than one edition.

✦ Teacher Amelia Jenks marries liberal lawyer and newspaper editor Daniel Bloomer. Thus his name will be memorialized a few years later when the term "bloomers" enters the language.

✦ Famine drives a million immigrants from Ireland to American shores during this decade, while another million starve to death at home. Most arrive in the extreme Northeast, which is closest to Ireland; many drift down from Canadian ports to the towns surrounding Boston, where they displace Yankee women from their textile mill jobs.

1841 When Oberlin College grants three women the first bachelor degrees earned by women at a coeducational institution, one initially skeptical man summarizes: "The experiment is unequivocally successful. We consider it now fully established, that the sexes may be educated together. This discovery is one of the most important ever made. The benefits which are likely to flow from it are immense."

One of the three graduates, Elizabeth Prall, has become controversial by raising the issue of restrictions on female speech that are customary even at Oberlin. Speaking of Queen Elizabeth, she says, "Strange that woman in monarchial England should be permitted to address . . . any audience, while in liberty-loving America she is not permitted to speak." According to a classmate, "all the men came out so 'ungallantly against Miss Prall's sentiments that the poor girl cried sadly.'"

✦ In the frontier city of Bloomington, Indiana, women form a club for their intellectual improvement. They call themselves the Edgeworthalean Society, a combination of the names of Maria Edgeworth, a currently popular British author, and Thalia, the Greek muse of comedy. They meet once a week for three years at the Monroe County Female Seminary, discussing papers presented by members. The women's attempts at mental stimulation meet with criticism and ridicule by many of their neighbors.

✦ The frontier town of Marietta, Ohio, is the scene of an exhibition of paintings by young Lilly Martin. She raises enough money to go to Cincinnati, where her reputation soon grows enough that her work is exhibited at the National Academy of Design.

Her 1844 marriage will not deter a move to New York in 1848, and for the rest of her life, Lilly Martin Spencer is the only woman of her era to have a significant career as an artist. Not only does she provide the primary income for the family, but she also bears 13 children.

✦ The Brook Farm Institute for Agriculture and Education begins near Roxbury, on the outskirts of Boston, when 20 utopians move into the large farmhouse of Sophia and George Ripley. Before the colony formally disbands six years later, it will grow to some 120 members, including transcendentalist Margaret Fuller and other notable thinkers. Young Louisa May Alcott, however, will remember her family's time there as a horror of hunger and exhaustion, especially for her mother.

◆ Dorothea Dix who has taught school, worked as a governess, and published textbooks during the last quarter century—goes to teach Sunday school at the Cambridge, Massachusetts, jail and finds her life changed. She discovers hungry women freezing in a filthy room and realizes that most are not guilty of any crime but are mentally ill. She takes the story to the newspapers and, defying the era's taboo against women traveling alone, begins a two-year study of the places where the state's mentally ill are locked away.

◆ Catharine Beecher publishes *A Treatise on Domestic Economy* and follows it up in 1846 with *The Domestic Receipt Book*. Although the field of home economics does not yet formally exist, both books are popular and go through several editions. After her sister Harriet Beecher Stowe becomes famous, they will co-author *The American Woman's Home* (1869).

◆ Hawaiian magistrate Kapiolani again demonstrates her courage by having a malignant breast removed without anesthetic. She survives the trauma and is about to leave for a legislative gathering in Maui when massive infection sets in and she dies.

1842 *Peterson's Ladies' Magazine* is founded in Philadelphia. Although the publisher names it for himself, he hires Ann S. Stephens as editor. She has been associate editor of *Ladies' Companion* since 1837 and is a model of modern careerism: Stephens maintains a happy marriage in which she provides the major share of family income, and her husband will tend their two children when she does a European tour a few years later.

The new magazine is intended to tap into the market of female readers that was uncovered by *Godey's Lady's Book*, which was also named for its male publisher. *Peterson's* circulation figures soon outpace those of the more prestigious *Godey's*, which is still edited by Sarah Buell Hale.

◆ The Lowell Female Labor Reform Association unites women who work in several factories in Lowell, Massachusetts. Some 500 women join this early union; with Sarah Bagley as their president, between 1842 and 1844 they collect several thousand petition signatures supporting a 10-hour day. When management in one textile mill tries to increase the standard workload from three looms to four, almost every woman signs a pledge refusing to do more work without more pay, and management concedes.

◆ These enterprising women also publish the *Lowell Offering*, in which Caroline Bean writes this year: "From whence originated the idea, that it was derogatory to a lady's dignity, or a blot upon the female character, to labor? and who was the first to say, sneeringly, 'Oh, she *works* for a living'?"

◆ What will become the largest order of African-American nuns begins in New Orleans. The Sisters of the Holy Family operate a hospice for the sick and needy, and after the Civil War makes education possible for black children, they will run about 50 schools.

◆ The first wagon heads out on the route that will be called the Oregon Trail; some 500,000 people will follow before the first transcontinental railroad makes the trail obsolete in 1869. Tens of thousands of women and men walk much of the 2,000-mile trek from Independence, Missouri, to Portland, Oregon. Along the way, they cross mountains that—at their most accessible points—are higher than 8,000 feet.

Elvina Apperson's father dies on the trail, and because she is one of 10 children, her mother arranges a marriage between 14-year-old Elvina and a 44-year-old man, who turns out to be an abusive alcoholic. "At that point in time," she will write later, "we had slavery of Negroes in the South and slavery of wives all over the country."

◆ Among the sights that Charles Dickens wants to see when he visits America is 12-year-old Laura Bridgman, whose triumph over disabilities has made her an international celebrity: deaf and blind since she had scarlet fever at age two, Laura has learned to read and communicate by touch.

She has lived the last five years at Boston's Perkins School for the Blind, where visitors line up to see her. The school is headed by Dr. Samuel Gridley Howe—whose wife, Julia Ward Howe, will one day be more famous than he. Dr. Howe's instruction of Laura Bridgman sets the precedent for Helen Keller's similar success story in the 20th century, but unlike Keller's experience, Bridgman's celebrity is relatively short. Her adulthood is spent quietly at the school and at her parents' New Hampshire home.

1843   In what is later called "the first piece of social research ever conducted in America," Dorothea Dix presents a "memorial" to the Massachusetts legislature that outlines the conditions in which she found 958 "insane paupers." Many are chained in attics and cellars, where they are beaten and starved.

While some are sympathetic to Dix's concern, others deem her a busybody who invades the privacy of families burdened by these hopeless cases. Undaunted, Dix moves on to other New England states where she does similar documentation. Her work sees some quick success, as the Medical Superintendents of American Institutions for the Insane organizes the following year.

◆ New York educator and author Emma Willard finally obtains a divorce from the man she married in Massachusetts in 1838. Her second husband had proven to be interested only in her money, and when she left him after less than a year of marriage, he stooped to writing nasty letters to the editor about her and her goal of education for young women.

◆ That divorce rights depend to a great extent on the political influence of the individuals affected is clear in the case of Clarina Howard Carpenter: her Vermont family is prominent, and she manages quietly to divorce her husband, retain cus-

tody of their three children, and marry her employer—the publisher of a Brattleboro newspaper—the following month. As Clarina Howard Nichols, she will have a long career in the women's rights movement.

◆ Teacher and governess Mary Peabody marries Horace Mann; her background in education will play a major role in the development of Antioch College, the nation's second coeducational college, during the 1850s. In this she continues the unpaid roles that wives of male heads of many institutions hold.

After Horace Mann's death, she will join her more famous sister, Elizabeth Peabody, in working for the new kindergarten movement and will write several books, including a three-volume biography of her husband. Her sister-in-law, Lydia Mann, is also an educator who will teach free blacks in Washington, D.C., prior to the Civil War.

◆ In Farmington, Connecticut, Sarah Porter begins a school that will become the most elite finishing school through the 20th century. Porter is a well-educated woman, having derived her learning via male relatives associated with Yale University. In time, Miss Porter's School will attract the daughters of the nation's wealthiest families; it gives them a thorough education, including languages, science, and math—but the school philosophy is careful to avoid any implication that these sheltered young women might consider careers.

◆ Dr. Oliver Wendell Holmes causes great controversy within the medical profession for an essay that blames maternal deaths from puerperal fever on physicians who fail to wash their hands well and spread contagion. His argument is scorned, but a study in Vienna three years later confirms that the view: a maternity ward run by male medical students—who also do autopsies—has a death rate that is 437% higher than that of the midwives' ward.

◆ Convinced that much of women's illness is due to ignorance of their bodies, Harriot K. Hunt organizes a Ladies Physiological Society in Charlestown, Massachusetts. She has been in solo practice since her sister Sarah's 1840 marriage, and so many patients recommend her to their friends that she builds a lucrative income.

✦ The first nuns from Ireland arrive. The Sisters of Charity of the Blessed Virgin Mary establish the first Catholic convent in Philadelphia, a city known for its religious diversity. The following year, nuns from Switzerland's Sisters of the Precious Blood will pioneer at Peru, Ohio.

1844 Jewish immigrant Ernestine Rose lectures "in the backwoods of Ohio" and the next year she lobbies the legislature of frontier Michigan for women's rights. She is especially concerned with property rights for American women. As a teenager in Poland in 1826, she successfully sued to inherit her mother's estate and to cancel marriage plans that her father arranged without her consent.

✦ Margaret Fuller becomes the nation's first professional book reviewer when Horace Greeley asks her to join his *New York Tribune*. The paper has a national audience, and she is in a powerful position to influence public reading tastes. She uses that position to develop an appreciation for American, rather than British, authors, thereby promoting the careers of her friends, Nathaniel Hawthorne, Ralph Waldo Emerson, and others who later are seen as the founders of American literature.

✦ In December, three single women sail to China after the Episcopal church drops its insistence that female missionaries be married. One is Eliza Gillet, whom Dr. Elijah Bridgman, America's first missionary to China, sees as the literal answer to his prayers. They marry, and Eliza Bridgman builds schools for women in Shanghai and Peking that she will run until her 1871 death.

✦ Cornelia Connelly, a 31-year-old married Louisiana mother of three, enters a convent at the request of her husband, who finds this course of action the only possible way that he can fulfill his desire to become a Catholic priest. Her spiritual advisers quickly promote her, and after she

founds a new order in England, her jealous husband will renounce the church, sue to reestablish the marriage, and spend the rest of his life slandering her. In 1959, Mother Connelly will be proposed for beatification as a saint.

1845 Six women testify before a committee of the Massachusetts legislature on working conditions in the Lowell textile mills. The public hearing is the first government investigation of labor needs in the nation's history, and the women's testimony sets a public speaking precedent for women. They present a petition signed by 2,139 people, "a very large proportion" of whom are women. Eliza Hemmingway tells the legislators of 14-hour summer days, for in a time prior to electricity, women are expected to take advantage of the daylight and work from five in the morning to seven in the evening. Judith Payne and Olive Clark echo her testimony and ask for a 10-hour day.

Their leader is Sarah Bagley, who goes on to expand her Female Labor Reform Association to mills throughout Massachusetts and New Hampshire. In May, she is elected to office in the New England Working Men's Association, and in November, the unionists demonstrate amazing political ability by successfully organizing to defeat an antilabor Lowell legislator.

✦ When abolitionists Abby Kelly and Stephen Symonds Foster wed, they establish an uncommon marriage in which Abby Kelly Foster continues to go on lecture tours while her husband tends their daughter. When the Fosters jointly speak at Oberlin College, young Lucy Stone is inspired by their example. Others object to their egalitarianism and especially to female public speech; this is one of the points at issue when Stephen Foster engages Oberlin's president in a "12-hour tongue-lashing debate."

✦ After teaching unhappily in Kentucky, Elizabeth Blackwell—who was born in England and grew up in New York and Cincinnati—determines that she wishes to earn her living as a physician. She is motivated in part by a female friend dying of "a painful disease" who tells Blackwell, "If I could have been treated by a lady doctor, my worst sufferings would have been spared me."

Blackwell reads medicine and then goes South, where she continues to support herself by teaching while studying under two physicians in North and South Carolina. Because the idea of a woman practicing medicine seems less improbable in the Quaker tradition, she then goes to Philadelphia (the home of both Quakers and of the nation's first medical school, in 1765) and seeks an institution that will admit a woman. She will be turned down by every school in Pennsylvania and New York as well as by several others in neighboring states.

◆ After her husband dies and Paulina Kellogg Wright becomes an independently wealthy widow, she begins traveling and lecturing on female anatomy, which she has taught herself by reading. She imports an instructional mannequin from Paris, and although some audience members are traumatized by the sight of this naked female facsimile, she uses it to teach women the basics of their bodies.

To some extent, Wright is emulating the work of health educator Mary Gove, but Gove's personal life continues to be far less rewarding. She has been separated from her tyrannical husband for several years, but Massachusetts law does not grant women either divorce or custody rights. Her husband forcibly takes their child this year, and only after months of futile legal efforts do Gove's friends surreptitiously return the girl to her mother.

When her husband finally divorces her because he wishes to marry another woman, Gove remarries and goes on to appreciable prominence as Mary Gove Nichols; her second husband shares her alternative health and spiritualistic interests.

◆ Massachusetts teachers organize a professional association of both men and women—but men dominate such organizations to the point that young Susan Anthony will be denied permission to speak at a meeting of the similar New York State Teachers' Association in 1853.

◆ Twenty-one ships arrive at Galveston from Bremen and Antwerp; they carry 3,084 German families recruited by promoters of a Germanic state in Texas, which is not yet part of the United States. They will be joined by over 5,000 more the following year and by some 8,000 in 1847. These German women and men will be more likely to learn Spanish than English as their second language.

◆ New York seamstresses earn $1.25 to $1.50 a week for work days that average 14 to 16 hours each.

◆ Charlotte Cushman—who has worked American stages from New Orleans to New York in opera, drama, and even management—debuts in London. Cushman will go on to true international stardom, specializing in Shakespeare and playing both male and female roles. She is one of the first to benefit from fan clubs, and some Charlotte Cushman clubs will endure long after her 1893 death.

◆ Margaret Fuller publishes *Woman in the Nineteenth Century*, which becomes the chief classic of feminist thought for decades. The book is a factor in bringing about the first Women's Rights Convention and is especially ahead of its time in discussing the sexual liberation that the era termed "free love."

1846 Maria Mitchell, a Nantucket librarian who studies the stars from the roof of her local bank, is paid $300 annually by the U.S. Coastal Survey to report her celestial observations for their effects on navigation. Except for employment in such traditionally feminine occupations as cooking or sewing, this may be the first case of a woman being hired by the federal government.

◆ Three women are elected to serve with five men on the board of directors of the New England Labor Reform League. All are themselves workers —but as unionism grows, such gender equity will become increasingly rare.

◆ Union organizer and political activist Sarah Bagley sets another precedent by becoming the nation's first female telegraph operator. Unwelcome in the textile mills because of her union leadership, she accepts a job as "superintendent" of the newly opened telegraph office in Lowell, Massachusetts.

✦ Lydia Maria Child again demonstrates her wide-ranging, prescient mind: in the midst of voluminous other work to pay the bills, she also publishes *Fact and Fiction; A Collection of Stories*, which offers an empathetic view of women who engage in illicit sex.

A few years later, she will write *The Progress of Religious Ideas* (1855), a three-volume study of comparative religion. Child argues against revealed truth and shows that the evolution of religious ideas is similar to other progressive human change. Neither work is expected from the stereotypes associated with the author of *The Frugal Housewife*.

✦ Amelia Bloomer sets an important milestone with the *Lily*, a temperance newspaper published for women by a woman. Based in Seneca Falls, New York, initially Bloomer is much more concerned with alcoholism than with women's rights. When she finally begins appearing with women's rights leaders, she is still ambivalent on the question of suffrage—although she advocates the right of divorce, which is usually seen as a more radical position. The *Lily* will continue to operate even after the couple moves to Ohio in 1853. In Seneca Falls, Bloomer also served as deputy postmaster to her husband.

✦ Susan B. Anthony is headmistress of the Female Department of Canajoharie Academy of Rochester, New York. After working several years to help pay debts from her father's bankruptcy, she spends some money on herself: abandoning Quaker dress codes, Anthony indulges her lifelong enjoyment of clothing, and among her purchases is a $22.50 shawl—on a $125 annual salary.

✦ Twenty-three-year-old Jessie Benton Frémont, the daughter of popular Missouri senator Thomas Hart Benton, begins to develop the controversial reputation that plays a part in her husband's failed 1856 presidential campaign.

Her husband, army officer John Charles Frémont, serves in the Far West, and in his absence, she furthers his career by withholding damaging orders from the War Department and by using information that she gains from translating confidential letters for the secretary of state. She lobbies President Polk on Frémont's behalf, and even feminists criticize her as excessively ambitious.

✦ Sisters of Charity from Baltimore arrive to teach girls in the frontier town of Milwaukee. Two years later, they will begin the area's first hospital.

✦ *Woman as She Was, Is, and Should Be* is early feminist thought published by Ohio's Hannah Tracy. While she was pregnant with her third child two years earlier, her husband died as a result of injury suffered as he helped slaves escape. She had wished to attend Oberlin College when she was single, but her father wouldn't allow it; now, as a widow, she will enroll, and in 1850, she is named principal of the female department of the new high school in Columbus, Ohio.

✦ In far-off Brownsville, Texas, Sarah Borginnis is called the Heroine of Fort Brown. She resupplies soldiers under siege during the Mexican War, and General Zachary Taylor grants her the rank of brevet colonel. Taylor is accustomed to the presence of women in military camps; when he commanded at Florida's Fort Brooke (now Tampa), his wife and daughter did crucial medical work, saving his life and those of others during an epidemic.

✦ Abolitionist author Lydia Maria Child opposes the Mexican War because she fears that it will lead to the expansion of slavery in the new territory of Texas. She leads a campaign that collects some 45,000 signatures on petitions arguing against Texas statehood. She also urges the State Department to recognize Haiti, the only New World country governed by blacks.

Jane McManus Storms, who frequently travels between her New York home and her Texas land during this decade, takes the opposite side of the Texas annexation and later, the Haitian issue. Next January, she will go to Mexico City to translate for President Polk's special agent, Moses Yale Beach. In fact, she may well be responsible for Beach's appointment, for she knows the president and was at the White House prior to Beach's assignment. To appoint a woman as a diplomat, of course, is unthinkable.

✦ Winter comes early in California's Sierra Nevada and the women and men of the Donner party starve when deep snow halts their journey from Illinois. They are stranded in early November, and 41 of the 87 travelers die of starvation or exposure. Those who live do so only by resorting to cannibalism of the dead.

Their ordeal warns other Easterners of the seriousness of making this transcontinental trip: wagons headed to California must be well equipped; they must stick to known routes; and they must depart early in the spring and travel as many miles a day as possible. Although this pace often causes tremendous physical demands, especially of pregnant and nursing women, delay can be deadly.

1847   The war with Mexico continues, and Jane McManus Storms is the only correspondent to report from behind enemy lines. She writes more than 30 pieces from Mexico City for the *New York Sun*, with additional items for the *New York Tribune* and the *Philadelphia Public Ledger*.

When the male emissary for whom she translates is forced to flee in March, Storms travels alone through enemy territory to inform General Winfield Scott. Thus she is familiar with the current conditions on the 200-mile route from Mexico City to Veracruz, and Scott accepts her detailed analysis of the best strategy for his march on the capital city, which will prove successful. Storms then sails from Veracruz to Washington, where she briefs President James K. Polk in May.

✦ In Brattleboro, Vermont, newspaper editor Clarina Howard Nichols writes on women's lack of property rights, and her articles inspire the passage of legislation granting women the right to own, inherit, and bequeath their property. Vermont's legislation predates that of many presumably more progressive states, and these issues

will remain fundamental to the nascent women's rights movement.

✦ Emily Frances Fairchild receives a master's degree from Oberlin College. She is the sister of the college's third president, and it is probably the first master's degree granted any woman in the world.

✦ Even progressive Oberlin College does not allow women to engage in public speaking, and Lucy

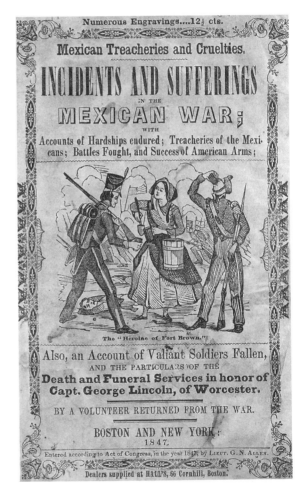

"The Heroine of Fort Brown" apparently needed no explanation to potential readers in 1847. It referred to Sarah Borginnis, who supplied soldiers under siege during the Mexican War in Brownsville, Texas. She was granted the rank of brevet colonel by General Zachary Taylor.

Stone rejects the "honor" of writing a commencement speech that would be read by a man. She is almost 30 at graduation because she supported herself through college when her affluent father refused to pay her tuition. Stone is Massachusetts' first female college graduate—although she had to go to Ohio to earn that distinction and although Massachusetts has had a college for more than 200 years.

+ Antoinette Brown graduates along with Lucy Stone, but even Stone thinks that Nettie Brown's desire to enter Oberlin's theology department is absurd. College authorities finally decide to allow her and another woman, Lettice Smith, to enroll, but not even liberal Oberlin will give women full status in a theology department. On the college's 50th anniversary, Stone will write: "The Oberlin catalogue has never yet honored itself by putting in the names of these women as theological students."

At the end of the three-year course, Brown is neither granted the degree nor licensed to preach. She nevertheless begins traveling the lecture circuit, preaching to whomever will listen. In 1893, in the last speech of her life, Stone will recall the hostility that greeted women like Brown: one congregation assaulted a female speaker with stones and rotten eggs.

+ The Boston Lying-In Hospital is the nation's first to use anesthesia to ease the pain of delivery. Many people, especially clergymen, will continue to object to anesthesia, on the grounds that the biblical story of Eve mandates pain for women in childbirth.

+ The first group of German nuns arrives in the United States. The School Sisters of Notre Dame come from Bavaria and establish themselves at Saint Marys, Pennsylvania. The nation now has 28 Catholic convents, most of which originated in either France or the United States. They are located in just 12 states, with disproportionate numbers in Maryland, Missouri, and Kentucky. None are in New England.

+ Dorothea Dix, whose four years of lobbying for the mentally ill has been in written form, breaks the era's taboo on public speaking by women and addresses the Tennessee legislature.

+ Cartoonist and humor writer Frances Berry Whitcher is published in *Godey's Lady's Book*. Although she will continue to work, she never completely recovers her health after giving birth in 1849 and dies just five years after publication. Her sketches focus on women in small town situations, especially mocking the pretentious. A posthumous collection reportedly sells more than 100,000 copies.

+ Despite their lack of educational opportunity, so many women learn to write on their own that Rufus W. Griswold issues a directory, *Female Poets of America*.

+ Margaret Fuller continues to write from Europe, where she has fallen in love with a young Roman nobleman who is a leader in Italy's revolution. She bears his child at 38 and marries him a year later.

+ Elizabeth Blackwell arrives in November at Geneva Medical College in western New York, which—as she learns later—accepted one of the many applications that she sent out at least partly because some of the male student body, to whom the question of a female applicant was posed by the faculty, thought it was a joke.

Although she is older and better prepared than most students, initially she is treated with skepticism and excluded from routine work. After "a second operation at which I was not allowed to be present," Blackwell writes a letter that is read to the students, and within a few weeks, the "annoying" harassment ends. By graduation, she will declare that the "behaviour of the medical class . . . was that of true Christian gentlemen."

Much later, one of her classmates will argue for coeducation on the grounds of his experience at Geneva College. Prior to Blackwell's admission, he says, his classmates "were rude, boisterous, and riotous beyond comparison. . . . During lectures it was often impossible to hear the professors." Her entrance "acted like magic . . . The sudden transformation of this class from a band of lawless desperadoes to gentlemen, by the mere presence of a lady, proved to be permanent in its effects."

✦ When Harriot K. Hunt, who has successfully practiced as an unlicensed Boston physician since 1835, hears of Blackwell's admission, she asks Dr. Oliver Wendell Holmes, dean of Harvard Medical School, about enrolling. He sees this as an intriguing experiment, but the Harvard Corporation forbids it.

After three black men are admitted to the medical school in 1850, Hunt will renew her application and receive permission to attend lectures—but the male students display such anger that the 45-year-old Hunt decides the effort is not worthwhile.

✦ Dr. Holmes, incidentally, also enjoys considerable literary fame, and in that parallel career, he will write that he opposes the vote for women because "Hannah already has enough power in the kitchen." Fear of immigrant women will become an increasingly strong factor for many who oppose suffrage: most immigrants at this time are Catholics driven out of Ireland by famine, and Americans will be candid about their fear that the women are apt to vote the way that their priests dictate.

✦ In late November near Walla Walla, Washington, Narcissa Whitman is among 14 whites killed by Cayuse warriors. They blame her and her physician husband for failing to cure their children in a measles epidemic. Because white children easily survive this sickness while Cayuse children die, the warriors conclude that the missionaries' medicine is poison.

Narcissa Whitman, one of the first two American women to pioneer the West Coast, had lived there only a little more than a decade before her violent death.

1848 A two-day meeting on July 19 and 20 in the little town of Seneca Falls, New York, later will be acknowledged as the birthplace of the international women's movement. Organized primarily by Elizabeth Cady Stanton, the meeting is prompted by the visit of Philadelphian Lucretia Mott. In 1840, these women had promised to follow up on the conversations about women's roles that they had begun when they were both banned from the World Anti-Slavery Convention in London.

Stanton has recently moved from Boston, where she was part of the most intellectually lively city in America, to tiny Seneca Falls, a rural area close to the Canadian border. Lonely and frustrated, she finds soulmates at a tea party hosted by Jane Hunt. With the two other guests, Mary Ann McClintock and Martha Wright, Stanton and Mott plan a meeting to explore the issues troubling them.

A simple newspaper announcement of a meeting on "the social, civil and religious rights of women" draws some 300 women and men to Seneca Falls from as far as 50 miles away. Surprised at the turnout and inexperienced in parliamentary procedure, the women call upon James Mott to preside, but they soon find their voices and adopt a strong Declaration of Rights for Women. Stanton models it on the nation's Declaration of Independence and declares:

> We hold these truths to be self-evident; that all men and women are created equal. . . . The history of mankind is a history of repeated injuries . . . toward woman. . . . He has never permitted her to exercise her inalienable right to the elective franchise. He has compelled her to submit to laws, in the formation of which she had no voice. He has withheld from her rights which are given to the most ignorant and degraded men—both natives and foreigners. . . . He has made her, if married, in the eye of the law, civilly dead. He has taken from her all right in property, even to the wages she earns. . . . He has so framed the laws of divorce . . . and guardianship . . . giving all power into his hands. He has monopolized nearly all the profitable employments. . . . He has denied her the facilities for obtaining a thorough education, all colleges being closed against her.

The only area of intense debate is on the right to vote, which Stanton includes in the declaration over Mott's objection. After it passes by a close margin, 68 women and 32 men sign the final document. Amelia Bloomer reports on the meeting for her temperance newspaper, and the story is quickly distributed to the mainstream press.

◆ Two weeks after the Seneca Falls meeting, a follow-up gathering on women's rights is held in Rochester, New York. This time a woman, Abigail Bush, is chosen president. She will later recall:

> The party had with them a fine-looking man to preside . . . James Mott, who had presided at Seneca Falls. . . . [My] old friends, Amy Post, Rhoda de Garmo and Sarah Fish, at once commenced to prove that the hour had come when a woman should preside, and led me into the church. Amy proposed my name as president; I was accepted at once, and from that hour I seemed endowed as from on high to serve.

The meeting attracts immigrant Ernestine Rose and the family of Susan Anthony, although Anthony herself does not attend. She is interested in the ideas that her family shares from this meeting, but for several years temperance will be a higher priority for her.

◆ Elizabeth Cady Stanton responds to newspaper criticism of the Seneca Falls convention with a letter to the editor. So carefully reasoned are her views that editor Horace Greeley makes note of this unusual writer and begins to publish Stanton's thoughts in the pages of his *New York Tribune*. The women's rights movement thus begins to reach a national audience almost immediately.

◆ Martha Wright, one of the five planners of the Seneca Falls meeting, lives in nearby Auburn and is Lucretia Mott's sister. She typifies the status of these women, for she is pregnant with her seventh child. At the same time, she has an unusual commitment to gender equity, for she teaches her sons to knit: one, she says, "has knit a bag to put his marbles in."

◆ The New England Female Medical College begins in Boston, but the name does not accurately reflect its nature. Instead of being a true medical college, it is primarily a training school for midwives—which has as its motivation the male founder's belief that it is indecent for men to be present at childbirth.

Within a decade, however, advertising for the school says that it is incorporated by the Massachusetts Legislature and has "a full Board of Professors, and gives complete Medical Education, including the usual branches, Anatomy, Surgery, Physiology and Hygiene, Medical Jurisprudence" and more.

◆ During the summer between her studies at Geneva Medical College, Elizabeth Blackwell works in the "women's syphilitic department" of a Philadelphia almshouse. Much later, she will write that she was not taught the nature of her patients' illness, for syphilis was "an unknown problem to me." Moreover, she would remain "strangely ignorant" for another 20 years: "It was not until 1869, when attending the Social Science Congress in Bristol, that my mind at last fully comprehended . . ."

◆ The New York legislature passes a bill that addresses married women's lack of property rights, but it is sponsored by wealthy men interested in only narrow application to their daughters' inheritance rights.

◆ Political revolution in Europe this year brings immigrants from German and Austro-Hungarian principalities. Most are young families of educated men and women, and they bring both ethnic diversity and leftist ideas to American political thought. Some of the women join the nascent suffrage movement, while almost all support the antislavery societies in which American women play leadership roles.

One of the most visible of these women is Mathilde Annecke, who—after riding with her husband into unsuccessful combat against Prussian military forces—will settle in Milwaukee next year. The mother of six, Annecke supports herself by teaching, lecturing, and writing in German and English, especially after permanent separation from her husband in 1861. She has published a German treatise that translates as *Woman in Conflict with Social Conditions* (1847), and she will publish a feminist newspaper beginning in 1852, first in Milwaukee and later in Newark.

✦ These Germans are the smaller portion of the nation's first major influx of immigrants that occurs during this decade. More are Irish who flee famine; many are in such poor health that they die on the voyage, and the almshouses of coastal cities are crowded far beyond their capacity with sickly arrivals. Although "famine fever" is usually considered the cause of death, many are infested with typhus—a disease that is not yet known to be due to shipboard vermin. The dying Irish who arrive in Philadelphia motivate Elizabeth Blackwell to write her medical school thesis on typhus.

✦ Ten years before Minnesota becomes a state, enterprising Sarah Judd establishes a daguerreotype business in Stillwater. The nation's immigrants are particularly eager to have themselves depicted with this early form of photography, for there is little probability that grandparents in Europe will ever see their grandchildren.

✦ Thousands of women manage alone when their men take off for California when gold is discovered there. An Oregon woman will remember, "If it had not been for our Indian neighbors, not many of us women could have survived. . . . They could be counted on to do whatever they were paid for . . . except for one thing. No Indian would ever milk a cow."

Jane Caufield is one who makes more money during the gold rush than her prospector husband. She runs the store they opened the previous year, buys wheat and sells the flour to new arrivals in California, and turns a tremendous profit in his absence.

✦ Elizabeth Lummis Ellet, who has been publishing poetry and light pieces since 1834, issues two volumes of carefully researched history with *The Women of the American Revolution*. She uses previously unpublished letters and other documents to detail the roles of more than 160 women

in the nation's birth; two years later, she adds more information with *Domestic History of the American Revolution*. Ellet will continue to develop this expertise, publishing her last book of women's history in 1869. She is the nation's first writer to recognize the breadth of women's contributions to America.

✦ Some of Ellet's work is illustrated by Lilly Martin Spencer, who continues to build her artistic reputation. Last year, the Western Art Union commissioned her to make an engraving that the artists' group used as the first prize in a lottery of their works. Spencer's art is also so regularly published in magazines that by the end of her career, more than a million colored lithographs by her will have been published. She acknowledges that much of this work is quickly done to support her seven living children, but Spencer is also capable of careful craftsmanship. She twice turns down $20,000 for a painting that is lost.

✦ At age 30, astronomer Maria Mitchell becomes the first woman elected to the American Academy of Arts and Sciences; almost a century will pass before a second woman is added. She receives this honor and other international accolades for her discovery the previous year of a new comet, which will be named for her. Proud Boston women buy her a new telescope, and she continues her work on Nantucket until 1865, when the opening of Vassar College finally provides her with a better laboratory.

✦ At Christmas, Ellen and William Craft use their holiday passes to escape from slavery in Macon, Georgia. She disguises herself as his master, for she has so many white ancestors that her skin is light; she also pretends to be old, male, and ill, so that no one questions the need for a manservant. William is a skilled carpenter who has been permitted to keep some of the wages he earns, and they use this money for train and boat fares to Philadelphia, where they become part of the abolitionist network. They will spend the next two years in Boston, telling their story at abolitionist fund raisers, until passage of the 1850 Fugitive

Slave Law makes it necessary for them to flee to England.

1849 Elizabeth Blackwell proves herself and graduates at the top of her medical school class. She is the first woman in the modern world to earn such a degree, and at graduation, she writes, "all the ladies" of the area arrive "*en masse* to see a lady receive a medical diploma." Although the school's officials are "very anxious" to have her march with the procession and send two messages requesting her to join the other graduates, Blackwell believes that this would not be "ladylike" and turns them down. Her brother proudly writes that the college president extols her as "the *leader* of her class."

Eager to be exceptionally well credentialed, Blackwell goes to Europe for postgraduate work. She finds stereotypes so profound that when she registers with the Paris police as an *etudiante*, the official objects, "*Mon enfant*, you must not put yourself down as a student!" She is limited to classes for midwives and nurses in France, but this experience, plus a close friendship that she forms with Florence Nightingale, gives Blackwell a greater appreciation for nurses than most physicians have, and she will emphasize sanitation and other nursing principles throughout her career.

English attitudes are somewhat broader, and in London she writes, "Every department was cordially opened to me, *except the department for female diseases*"—the area that initially drew her to medicine. She encounters as much prejudice among women as men, but writes with confidence of the future: "A hundred years hence women will not be what they are now."

◆ Successful in her aims for Texan independence from Mexico, newspaper correspondent Jane McManus Storms turns her attention to other territorial expansion possibilities, including Cuba, which she visited last year. She argues for annexation of Cuba to the United States in *Queen of the Islands and King of the Rivers* (1850); the book will be issued under the pseudonym Cora Montgomery, and that becomes her publishing name for the rest of her life.

She creates the final variation of her name this year when she marries and becomes Jane Cazneau. She moves with her husband to a New Mexico settlement near El Paso, where—despite being 150 miles from a mail route—she still manages to correspond with major Washington officials and to file reports for the *New York Tribune* and other papers. Not surprisingly, her activist personality will not be content for long in such remoteness.

◆ Elizabeth Smith Miller appears in "turkish trousers" on the streets of Seneca Falls, New York. She is emulating famous actress Fanny Kemble, who has adopted the Middle Eastern style because it offers women far greater freedom of movement. Miller is also encouraged by her well-known abolitionist father, Gerritt Smith, who believes that the strikingly different appearance of men and women reinforces gender stereotypes.

When Seneca Falls resident Elizabeth Cady Stanton also briefly adopts what is touted as the "American Costume," editor Amelia Bloomer writes of the new style in her temperance newspaper, the *Lily*. Readers seem more interested in fashion than in temperance, and subscriptions quickly double. Newspapers throughout the country pick up on the idea—and use Bloomer's name for the new garment. Bloomer herself tries wearing pants under a short skirt, and although she writes of the style's practicality, she and her feminist friends give it up within a few years. Arguments over clothing, they decide, are not worth the distraction from their more important work on legal rights.

◆ A "widow by fate, but not by fact," Mrs. E.D.E.N. Southworth separates from her husband, teaches to support her two children, and publishes her first novel. A Washington, D.C., resident, she sells *Retribution* to a local newspaper for $15, which, she will later say, "gave me more enjoyment than any thousand dollars I received later in life." *Harper's* publishes it in book form this year, and Southworth goes on to great success. One of the best-known women of her era, she will write more than 60 books that are best-sellers both in America and in several European languages.

Although scorned by critics, her stories are serialized in such magazines as *Saturday Evening Post*, where fiction serves to introduce millions of readers to the facts of women's lives; Southworth's marital experience enables her to write especially tellingly about divorce and about women's dependence on men for money. She earns enough to support her children in style, and her Washington home becomes a longtime gathering place for writers and for the suffrage movement, which she strongly supports.

Her unusual first name, incidentally, is a combination of Emma Dorothy Eliza Nevitte—the names given her at christening. A second curiosity is that she was born in the only house that George Washington ever owned in Washington.

✦ The Massachusetts Historical Society—the oldest and most prestigious institution of its sort—admits its first female member: Frances Caulkins, who is actually a historian of Connecticut, not Massachusetts. She is especially noted for her *History of New London*, and she will remain the only woman elected to the society for more than a century.

Caulkins also is active in the Ladies' Seaman's Friend Society that ministers to New London's sailors and has written numerous evangelical works for the American Tract Society.

✦ Some Washingtonians fear the stinging editorials published by Anne Newport Royall, and several congressmen make a cruel point of blocking her legitimate claim to a pension as the widow of a soldier in the Revolution. Decades after it was due, Illinois congressman Abraham Lincoln sponsors her bill, and at age 80, she finally receives a small lump sum.

Royal will write her last words in 1854, and although she does not expect to die, they turn out to be prescient: her final editorial opinion is a hope "that the union of these states will be eternal."

✦ Hearing rumors that she is about to be sold, Harriet Tubman escapes from Maryland to Phila-

delphia. She later explains: "I had reasoned this out in my mind. There was one of two things I had a right to—liberty or death. If I could not have one, I could have the other, for no man shall take me alive." The next year she will risk her freedom by returning to Baltimore to lead out her sister's family, but Tubman's husband is unwilling to take the risk and refuses her offer of escort. By the end of the decade, she will have made 19 such daring trips, leading more than 300 people to freedom.

No other person—black or white, male or female—will display as much sheer courage as she, for Tubman repeatedly risks her own life on behalf of others. She overcomes the handicap of illiteracy that makes her unable to read maps or signs; even more significantly, she suffers from a childhood brain injury (inflicted when her angry master threw an object at another slave) that can cause her to drop into a deep sleep without warning.

Tubman operates by memorizing landmarks and develops an uncanny sense of direction. Although slaveowners become aware of her activities and she is trailed by detectives, she will display her keen intelligence in a number of ways. In one case, for example, she will mislead her pursuers into thinking that they are trailing the wrong group of blacks by spending precious money to buy train tickets south—for runaway slaves would not be going south.

✦ More than 50 years after founder Ann Lee's death, her idea of peaceful, communal utopianism reaches its peak. Some 6,000 Shaker women and men live in 23 colonies from Maine to Florida. They farm during the summer and work through the winter at making furniture and brooms. Their products develop a reputation for sturdy value, with the result that many Shaker-made items will outlast the sect itself. Their commitment to celibacy means that the faith depends on conversions, but few of her followers are as charismatic as Ann Lee.

✦ Some 40 utopian communities have developed in the first half of the century, but none will become more controversial than the community of

Oneida in upper New York State. The men and women who founded this colony the previous year practice "complex marriage," in which they accept each other as spouses. Although they also continue to view themselves as Christians, Oneidans engage in sexual liaisons that outsiders would view as criminal incest and/or juvenile exploitation. Nor is there as much individual freedom as it would appear, for relationships are often mandated by the community's leader, John Humphery Noyes.

Women nonetheless have a high status in the community: their views are considered as seriously as those of men; they wear short hair and short skirts with long pants; their sporting activities include swimming, fishing, skating, and camping; and they share equitably in both the community's labor and its property—which eventually is considerable. Perhaps most significantly, the sexuality of older women is not neglected, and men are required to practice Noyes' withdrawal technique of birth control unless a woman chooses to become pregnant.

1850 The Women's Rights Conventions held earlier at Seneca Falls and Rochester in New York now develop nationally with meetings at Salem, Ohio, in April and at Worcester, Massachusetts, in October.

Salem, an eastern Ohio town between Pittsburgh and Akron, is a center of abolitionist activity. The *Anti-Slavery Bugle* is published there; among its writers is Josephine Griffing, who also shelters fugitive slaves in her home. At the Salem meeting, men are forbidden to speak—in contrast to the Seneca Falls meeting, where the timorous women asked a man to preside.

The Worcester meeting is organized from Providence, Rhode Island, by Paulina Wright Davis (whose name changed with her second marriage last year), and because women come from several states, it is termed the first National Woman's Rights Convention. Among those attending are Philadelphia abolitionist Lucretia Mott, Boston physician Harriot K. Hunt, and Vermont newspaper editor Clarina Howard Nichols, who recently succeeded in lobbying her

legislature for a married women's property rights act. Lucy Stone of Massachusetts is perhaps the convention's biggest star: since her Oberlin graduation three years earlier, Stone has endured much heckling to establish herself on the lecture circuit as a speaker on abolition and women's rights.

✦ The passage of the Fugitive Slave Law creates great turmoil, for it soon results in slave traders kidnapping free blacks in the North and selling them South under the guise of law. Quaker women organize networks of safe houses that become called the "Underground Railroad," where black women and men know that they will be hidden from law enforcers by day and helped on their way to Canada at night.

Courageous Harriet Tubman begins escorting those whom she helps to escape all the way to her home in St. Catherine's, Ontario. Although the general public remains unaware of Tubman's existence until after the Civil War, slave traders offer as much as $40,000 in rewards for the capture of this woman whom her people call Moses.

✦ With eight women enrolled, Philadelphia Quakers begin the Female Medical College of Pennsylvania. Male Quakers provide the initial faculty, and they lobby the legislature to approve a charter. The school will withstand both an 1858 challenge from the local medical society and noisy disruptions by male medical students. Closed briefly when the Civil War begins, it will reopen in 1862 as Woman's Medical College of Pennsylvania.

✦ When Zachary Taylor dies in July, Millard Fillmore becomes president—and Abigail Fillmore is the first first lady who can be considered a working woman. She and her husband met as schoolmates from poor families in rural New York, and she not only worked while he went to law school, but she even defied convention by continuing to teach after their 1826 marriage.

✦ Margaret Fuller Ossoli is returning to America with her Italian husband and child when their ship wrecks off the coast of Fire Island, and all are drowned. Thoreau and others of her Massachusetts friends come to New York to search for her body but cannot find it. They later erect a monument to her in Cambridge's Mt. Auburn Cemetery, which says in part: "IN MEMORY OF MARGARET FULLER OSSOLI . . . BY BIRTH, A CHILD OF NEW ENGLAND; BY ADOPTION, A CITIZEN OF ROME; BY GENIUS, BELONGING TO THE WORLD."

✦ Defeated after three wars in the first half of the century, Florida Seminoles are transported to Indian Territory in the Midwest. When their ship stops for fuel at San Marcos, in the Florida Panhandle, Polly Parker reportedly escapes and walks approximately 500 miles back to the Everglades, where remnants of her people had fled.

✦ Oregon's Land Donation Act predates the national Homestead Act by 12 years. Unlike most similar land grants in the past, women are eligible receipients: the act offers an unmarried woman 320 acres of free land, while a married couple is entitled to 640, with the wife eligible to hold her half in a separate title. With four men to every woman in the state, the men are eager to attract female settlers.

✦ Women in the textile mills of Holyoke, Massachusetts, many of them Irish immigrants, go on strike.

✦ At midcentury, women account for 90% of all domestic workers. Footmen, gardeners, and handymen who did a variety of chores in colonial households disappear from all but the most wealthy urban homes. Women remain as servants, while the tasks that men traditionally performed are done by independent businessmen.

The live-in "hired man" will remain vital to the rural economy far into the future, but he is not considered a domestic worker—even though the "hired girl" falls into that category.

✦ The Ladies Union Benevolent and Employment Society of Washington, D.C., is a sophisticated organization. It has divided the city into six districts, with two managers per district who report to the administrative decision makers. At the top is Eliza Barnwell Mills, whose architect husband

designed the Washington Monument. The society finds jobs for women, especially "poor widows with small children," and assists them in obtaining "the common necessities of life"—though preferably with goods, not cash.

1851 Susan Bogert Warner publishes *The Wide, Wide World*, the first American book to sell 1 million copies. So popular is this "feminist Huck Finn" that it outsells *David Copperfield* in England. Warner will write many more books during the next 30 years, but copyright law is such that she is never financially secure. She lives most of her life on a Hudson River island near West Point; she shares her home with her sister, Anna Bartlett, the author of "Jesus Loves Me, This I Know" and other songs and stories. Whenever they need something not available on their island, the two women must row a boat to the mainland.

✦ Akron, Ohio, is the site of a women's rights convention in May, and ex-slave Sojourner Truth makes her famous "Ain't I a Woman?" speech. She electrifies the audience; one in the attendance will write, "I have never in my life seen anything like the magical influence" of that oration.

Freed of the dialect that her contemporaries use to record it, part of the speech says: "That man over there says women need to be helped into carriages and lifted over ditches, and to have the best place everywhere. Nobody never helps me into carriages or over puddles, or gives me the best place—and ain't I a woman? . . . I could work as much and eat as much as a man—when I could get it—and bear the lash as well! And ain't I a woman?"

✦ Indiana women also hold a convention in the town of Dublin, in Wayne County, and organize themselves into the Indiana Women's Rights Society. Until she moves to Kansas after the Civil War, their chief leader will be Amanda Way, a woman who invites comparison to Susan Anthony: she is single, has ties to the temperance and abolitionist movements, and remains active well into the 20th century. Perhaps because she is based in the Midwest, she remains less well-known than Easterners with similar achievements.

✦ The "Second National Women's Rights Convention" is held at Worcester, Massachusetts, in October. Jewish Ernestine Rose argues against a resolution offered by Protestant theologian Antoinette Brown, which states that "the Bible recognizes the rights . . . of women." Rose's argument that "we require no written authority from Moses or Paul" carries the day, and Brown's resolution fails. The two will tangle again at the 1860 convention over a resolution on divorce.

✦ In the seemingly unlikely location of Winchester, Tennessee, Mary Sharp College begins. It requires both Latin and Greek and therefore can be considered a true college, predating the more famous women's colleges that begin after the Civil War.

✦ The second woman to graduate from medical school is Lydia Folger Fowler, a happily married woman without children who grew up on Nantucket Island at the same time as astronomer Maria Mitchell. Almost 30 when she graduates in June, Dr. Fowler has already established herself as a lecturer on women's health and published *Familiar Lessons on Physiology* (1847).

She graduates from Central Medical College of Rochester, a previously all-male institution of "eclectic" medicine that admitted several women along with her in November 1849. After graduation, she is hired to teach obstetrics and gynecology—making Dr. Fowler the world's first female medical professor.

When the school runs into financial problems, she will establish a practice in New York City that she maintains until the Fowlers move permanently to England in 1863. Fowler probably encounters less discrimination than Elizabeth Blackwell both because she is married and because she practices among colleagues whose medical views are less traditional.

✦ Myrtilla Miner, a white woman, courageously opens a school for black girls in Washington, D.C., defying even the advice of abolitionist Fredrick Douglass. Although threatened by ruffians and often short of funds, she will operate it successfully until the beginning of the Civil War. At least six of her black students will conduct their own schools. One of her white teachers, Emily Howland of western New York, will endow some 30 schools for blacks after the Civil War.

✦ In August, educator and writer Hannah Tracy is one of the delegates to the World's Peace Congress in London. The widowed mother of three, she finances her trip by serving as a correspondent for the *Ohio Statesman* and by lecturing to sizable British audiences on women's rights.

As Hannah Tracy Cutler after the Civil War, she will earn a medical degree and practice in Illinois and California.

✦ With collaboration from Harriet Taylor, a married woman who later becomes his wife, famed English philosopher John Stuart Mill publishes "The Enfranchisement of Women." His thoughts are based on a Lucy Stone speech that was reprinted in the international press.

✦ Sisters Alice and Phoebe Cary move from Cincinnati to New York City, where their home serves as a salon for writers during the next decades, while both are published in popular magazines such as *Harper's* and *Atlantic Monthly*. Alice will publish numerous volumes of poetry and fiction, in addition to serving as the first president of New York's first professional women's club, Sorosis. Phoebe writes less, but her work earns greater critical praise.

✦ At age 19, Louisa May Alcott publishes her first story. She has been tutored by her progressive educator father, Bronson Alcott, and by famous neighbor Henry David Thoreau. By the end of her life, Alcott will have published some 300 works—many of which she writes for boys under male pseudonyms. Her first decade of work is motivated by a family need for money, and the stories and plays are often lurid adventures reflecting the era's violence.

✦ The long history of Catholicism in the Far West has been one of Spanish priests, but not nuns. When California's first convent begins this year, it is staffed by Frenchwomen. The Sisters of the Third Order of Saint Dominic establish themselves at Monteray, while in the Oregon wilderness, the Sisters of Notre Dame de Namur also begin work.

◆ The Graham Institution for Aged and Indigent Females begins in Brooklyn. It will evolve into an institution that differs somewhat from its name, for instead of a poorhouse, it becomes an early model for retirement homes. By 1870, its residents—who must be over 60—will be required to show evidence of their "respectability" and to endow the institution with $100. It will attract women from middle-class families (including the famed Beecher family), who live in what is essentially a condominium with meal service.

◆ On the last day of the year, police guard commencement exercises at Female Medical College of Pennsylvania because they fear disruption by male medical students. The graduates are Ann Preston and Hannah Longshore; both have previous medical experience and graduate on an accelerated basis.

Dr. Longshore—whose sister-in-law Anna Longshore is also a student—sets a precedent in being the married mother of two; her Quaker physician husband is one of the school's founders and faculty members. She will practice in Philadelphia for 40 years and builds a larger clientele than most male physicians—many of whom secretly refer their female relatives to her.

Dr. Preston, who has taught physiology to Quaker women for a decade, remains with the school and becomes its first female dean in 1866.

1852 In April, the last of 40 installments of *Uncle Tom's Cabin* is published in a Washington-based abolitionist newspaper; when the book is released, tens of thousands are waiting to purchase it. Author Harriet Beecher Stowe, the mother of six young children, has written from her Maine kitchen what becomes perhaps the single most influential novel in American history.

It is banned in many Southern states, where dozens of writers respond with tales casting slavery in a positive light; many point out that Stowe

has never been south of northern Kentucky. In the North, however, it captures public attention like no other previous story, with plays, songs, and even card games based on it.

Stowe gives $1,000 of its profits to the school for blacks that Myrtilla Miner established in Washington last year—but more important to her is that millions of readers are moved to end slavery.

◆ Newspaper editor Clarina Howard Nichols speaks to the Vermont legislature. Only one vote is cast in opposition to her appearance, and she follows up her successful married women's property rights act with a bill to allow women to vote in school elections. Although the state's politicians clearly respect her, they do not pass this bill—despite, as she will write in her 1881 reminiscences, a "petition signed by more than 200 of the most substantial business men, including the stauchiest conservatives, and tax-paying widows."

The women who watch her speech from the galleries greet her afterward: "We did not know before what Woman's Rights were, Mrs. Nichols, but we are for Woman's Rights."

◆ Antioch College is founded near Dayton, Ohio. It is the nation's second major coeducational college, following Oberlin by two decades. Like Oberlin, Antioch will host controversial speakers and become an incubator for ideas too radical for the older, all-male institutions on the East Coast.

Its president is Horace Mann; his wife, Mary Peabody Mann, is an educator in her own right. The Manns attract a progressive faculty to Antioch, including young mathematics and astronomy professor Lucretia Crocker. Influenced by naturalists Louis and Elizabeth Agassiz, Crocker will go on to a national reputation as a science educator.

◆ The University of Michigan rejects several applications from Augusta Chapin on the grounds of gender—even though she is so gifted and self-disciplined that she has been employed as a teacher since age 14. An application from Olympia

Brown is rejected on the same grounds the following year.

✦ The American Woman's Educational Association is formed under the leadership of Catharine Beecher. Its goals are to expand the educational opportunities open to women and to send teachers to western frontier towns.

✦ Dr. Elizabeth Blackwell publishes *The Laws of Life with Special Reference to the Physical Education of Girls*. Her initial attempt to establish a practice in New York has been frustrating, for every hospital in the city denies her privileges, and she even finds it difficult to rent space because "female physician" is a common code for abortionist. Quaker friends begin to bring her patients, but Blackwell is so lonely that she adopts an orphaned girl—who finds it odd when she discovers than men are also doctors.

✦ Emily Blackwell seeks admission to an established medical school. Geneva College turns her down, despite her sister's Elizabeth's top position at graduation. Emily goes to Rush Medical School in Chicago—but after she endures the expense of moving and successfully completes a year, the school bows to pressure from Illinois physicians and refuses to accept her a second year. She finally is accepted at Cleveland Medical College (later Western Reserve), from which she will graduate in 1854.

✦ Clemence S.H. Baker (later Lozier) graduates with highest honors from Syracuse Medical College, the successor to the medical school that granted Lydia Fowler's degree last year. She is 40 and a mother; her first husband died, and she is separated from her second. When she finally manages to get a divorce in 1861, she will resume her first husband's name of Lozier and become well known in the women's rights movement. Dr. Lozier eventually builds a successful practice in New York City, becomes quite wealthy, and donates generously to liberal causes.

✦ Although she still lacks a medical degree, Harriot K. Hunt is sufficiently confident of her status that she calls herself a physician when she addresses "the authorities of the city of Boston." Her lengthy statement protests "against the injustice and inequality of levying taxes upon women, and at the same time refusing them any voice or vote."

✦ The August issue of Amelia Bloomer's publication, the *Lily*, includes an article titled "The Duty of Drunkards' Wives—Divorce." It follows up on the uproar that Elizabeth Cady Stanton created at a state meeting of the women's temperance society, where she argued that women have a right to divorce drunken husbands. Most temperance advocates feel that such radicalism jeopardizes their cause, but Bloomer uses her paper to defend women's separate agenda within the temperance movement. A one-sentence story used as a filler in her eight-page paper dramatically highlights the need. "A young man named Dow, while intoxicated, cut the throat of his wife at Seabrook, New Hampshire on last Friday."

✦ Women from eight states and Canada attend the Third National Women's Rights Convention, held in Syracuse, New York, in September. "Immense audiences" attend the three-day session, "notwithstanding an admission fee of one shilling." Because Quakers do not preside at meetings where admission is charged, Lucretia Mott initially turns the gavel over to Paulina Wright Davis. Dr. Lydia Folger Fowler serves as a secretary, along with Reverend Samuel May.

As has been the case in the past, the gathering is well reported in the press. The *New York Herald* begins its long editorial: "The farce at Syracuse has been played out" and continues with "Who are these women? What do they want?" —thus unwittingly devoting hundreds of words to publicizing the women's issues.

This is the first convention attended by Quaker temperance leader Susan Anthony, and Elizabeth Cady Stanton becomes her mentor and close friend. For the rest of the century, Anthony will be a frequent visitor to Stanton's home; because Stanton's travel is limited by her seven children, Anthony will go there, and the two plot strategy. Their relationship evolves into one in which Stanton thinks and writes, while Anthony speaks and organizes. Others in the women's movement will say Stanton "makes the thunderbolts, while Susan Anthony throws them."

✦ Clara Barton, who has been teaching for two decades, gets enough political support to found one of the first cost-free public schools in New Jersey. It is such a success that the school board decides she must be supervised by a man—and two years later, she leaves teaching forever. That she is going on to much greater fame, of course, cannot be known when the unemployed schoolmarm moves to Washington, D.C.

✦ Frances Wright slips on ice and dies in Cincinnati at age 57. One of the nation's first internationalists, she crossed the Atlantic five times in the 1840s alone and presciently proposed a world government in an 1848 book. But because she bore a child before marrying the father—and then had to give up her daughter to obtain an 1842 divorce—Fanny Wright's brilliance is overlooked by those eager to ridicule her controversial life.

✦ Napoleon III assumes the French throne, and after almost a half-century, Elizabeth Patterson Bonaparte (called "Madame Patterson" in Europe) succeeds in having her son, Jerome Bonaparte, declared legitimate. He is less interested in royalty than she, however, and long ago returned to America and married an American.

✦ The Italian-based Benedictine Sisters of Pontifical Jurisdiction join three groups of German nuns affiliated with the School Sisters of Notre Dame in St. Marys, Pennsylvania. This small town in rural northwestern Pennsylvania will become the mother lode of Catholic sisterhood. Prior to World War I, it will send out more than 20 groups of nuns who establish new projects in places from Fort Smith, Arkansas, to Mount Angel, Oregon.

✦ Brigham Young, successor to Mormon founder Joseph Smith, publicly proclaims the church's acceptance of polygamy, which Smith has been rumored to have supported since an 1831 vision. Driven out of the East and the Midwest, Mormons pioneer the Utah desert in 1847, and Young becomes a true patriarchal model. When he dies in 1877, he will leave 17 widows and 47 children and has married at least 70 women, although some do not involve a physical relationship.

This introduction of Old Testament practice into modern society will make Mormonism a key factor in debates on the status of women for the rest of the century. Mormons, incidentally, avoid using the term "polygamy" and refer to their family structure as "plural marriage"—but, because women are not free to have more than one husband, "polygamy" is the more accurate term. It is not akin to the "complex marriage" of the Oneida community, in which both men and women have multiple spouses.

✦ In northern Ohio, between 50 and 60 women and children are among the "Christian Indians" who are "massacred" by "backwoodsmen."

1853 In February, Paulina Wright Davis begins publishing *Una*; it is arguably the first newspaper devoted to women's rights, given that Amelia Bloomer's *Lily* was originally motivated by temperance issues. With assistance from Caroline Healey Dall, a former educator who is now married to a Unitarian minister—and occasionally takes his pulpit—*Una* exists almost three years. It is published first from Davis' home in Providence, Rhode Island, and then from Dall's Boston base. A factor in its decline may be competition from a similar paper that will begin in early 1855.

✦ The annual women's rights convention held in New York City becomes known as the "mob convention" because it is repeatedly disrupted by jeering men. Sojourner Truth, who continues to identify herself as much with women's rights as with abolition, admonishes the male gangs: "I see that some of you have got the spirit of a goose and some of you have got the spirit of a snake."

It is particularly ironic that mob violence suppresses free speech on this occasion, for German freedom fighter Mathilde Annecke comes to this convention to praise American liberty. Ernestine Rose translates her speech above the roar of the crowd; more than 2,000 pack the hall, with most intent on disrupting the women's agenda. Lucretia Mott attempts to preside and, consistent with her Quaker principals, refuses to call police.

✦ At a calmer convention in Cleveland, the speakers include Lucy Stone, Lucretia Mott, and Ernestine Rose. It is presided over by Frances Dana Gage, who is affectionately known as "Aunt Fanny," the pen name she uses for her frequent writing in Ohio newspapers. After the 1850 convention in Salem, Ohio, Gage circulated a petition asking that the words "white" and "male" be omitted from the state's new constitution.

✦ Rev. Asa Mahan, president of Ohio's Oberlin College, is present at the Cleveland meeting—which makes this observation of Oberlin graduate Antoinette Brown all the more surprising: though she loves Oberlin, "much and deeply," Brown says she "must declare that it has more credit for liberality to woman than it deserves. Girls are not allowed equal privileges . . . The only college in the country that places all students on an equal footing, without distinction of sex or color, is McGrawville College in Central New York." Not even *The History of Woman Suffrage*, however, will feature any information on this college, which is presumably too progressive for its times.

✦ Women delegates to a World's Temperance Convention in New York City are refused seats. When divinity school graduate and unlicensed preacher Antoinette Brown attempts to speak, she is shouted down by male preachers.

✦ Susan Anthony also is refused permission to speak there, as she had been at an Albany temperance rally the previous year. These experiences solidify her growing commitment to women's rights over temperance, for as a Quaker, she is accustomed to participating in meetings. Most Americans, however, consider this taboo, and presiding officers routinely refuse to recognize women. Indeed, women in some Southern churches are said to be so reluctant to use their voices that they "wait until at least two lines" of a hymn are sung by men before they join the singing.

✦ Later in the year, two small Congregational churches in rural Wayne County, New York, ask Antoinette Brown to be their pastor. On September 15 she becomes the first woman ordained by a church belonging to a mainstream religion—although the Congregationalist denomination withholds its approval.

✦ Iron manufacturer Rebecca Pennock Lukens finally has a clear title to the Pennsylvania foundry that she has run since 1825. Although women lack legal standing in court, Lukens has been repeatedly sued throughout her business career. Besides her right to inherit, she has fought off other complex lawsuits—one of which was brought when her water-power dam on the Brandywine River flooded a competitor. She enjoys ownership of the Brandywine Iron Works only briefly, however, for she dies the following a year, leaving an estate of over $100,000.

✦ On a hill high above Nashville, Adelicia Acklen begins building Belmont (or Belle Monte) Mansion. She is an excellent example of the frequent contradiction between what laws decree and what women actually do, for her amazingly successful lifelong pursuit of wealth does not depend on any of her three husbands.

Belmont will be so grand a place that it includes such luxuries as a bowling alley and a $16,000 Italianate tower to furnish running water. Probably the richest Southern woman of her era, Acklen's chief assests are not in Tennessee. Winters are spent on one of her six Louisiana plantations, and she holds 50,000 acres of land in Texas. None of this, however, can spare her from human tragedy. In addition to losing her husbands, she also will bury six of her 10 children.

✦ Harriet Beecher Stowe publishes *A Key to Uncle Tom's Cabin*, which hotly refutes the slurs cast upon her and her book. Although Stowe claims that the book wrote itself as a divine power guided her, she also had done considerable research in abolitionist files. Other scenes are based on her experience living in Cincinnati, a haven for slaves who crossed the Ohio River into freedom.

Stowe's character of Lucy, a woman who drowns herself when her baby is sold away from her, for example, resembles the actual case of Margaret Garner, who escaped with her four children but was soon captured and sent back South. When the ship in which she was being transported wrecked, Garner drowned her infant and refused rescue for herself. She also killed her three-year-old while jailed.

♦ Sarah Remond, a black woman born free in Massachusetts, tries to integrate a Boston opera audience. When a policeman pushes her down the stairs, Remond goes to court and wins a $500 judgment.

♦ Mary Ann Shadd, a free Philadelphia black who fled to Canada after the Fugitive Slave Act, begins editing *Provincial Freeman*, a Toronto weekly for refugees in the Canadian provinces. The world's first black female newspaper editor, she endures criticism from other blacks as well as from whites, but keeps her paper alive.

♦ In recognition of the validity of Harriot K. Hunt's two decades of practice as a Boston physician, the Female Medical College of Pennsylvania grants her a degree.

♦ *Godey's Lady's Book* editor Sarah Buell Hale manages to find time to publish *Woman's Record, or Sketches of Distinguished Women*. She will update this early "Who's Who" with further volumes during this decade and the next. Her name recognition is so confidently assumed by Harper & Brothers that the title page of an 1872 printing says merely "By Mrs. Hale."

♦ Senate Document 59, *Report of an Expedition Down the Zuni and Colorado Rivers*, details the lives of Pueblo Zuni women. Among other routine tasks, they stand on raised platforms in cornfields with drums to scare away birds; in the winter, they spear fish through holes in the ice.

♦ In the fall, Vermont newspaper editor Clarina Howard Nichols and New York physician Lydia Folger Fowler travel some 900 miles throughout Wisconsin, speaking on women's rights and temperance.

♦ The peripatetic Jane Cazneau moves in December from New Mexico to the Caribbean, which will be the focus of the rest of her life. Her husband has a State Department appointment to Santo Domingo, but the *New York Post* asserts that it is she who is the "real" commissioner. She is soon in the thick of Caribbean politics, not only as a reporter for U.S. newspapers but also as a frequent correspondent with Washington's most powerful men, including three presidents. Her object is the opposite of that of abolitionists: She urges the United States to crush the black-run government of Haiti, while promoting trade with other Caribbean states.

1854 Southern women demonstrate their networking and funding ability when the Mount Vernon Ladies' Association begins. It is headed by Ann Pamela Cunningham, who organizes hundreds of women in 30 states to raise money for restoration of George Washington's plantation home, which is in danger of destruction. The women's project is the nation's first successful preservation effort, and it provides a model for similar endeavors later undertaken by men. The Ladies' Association will become the nation's oldest such organization; it continues to manage Mount Vernon at the end of the 20th century.

♦ Mental health reformer Dorothea Dix finally sees passage of the congressional bill for which she has lobbied since 1848—only to have it vetoed by President Franklin Pierce.

Her bill would have established a trust fund for the treatment of the mentally ill from the sale of land in the West. Pierce's veto is based on his limited view of permissible federal activity: he argues that the government cannot adopt such humanitarian causes, while Dix points out that at the same time, the government is giving land to private railroad companies.

After the veto, Dix goes to Europe and inspects asylums from Scotland to Turkey; she succeeds in getting the pope to begin reforms in Italy.

♦ Clara Barton, who has resigned her New Jersey educational position, sets the first of her national precedents by becoming a federal employee with the Patent Office in Washington, D.C. She uses a congressional contact to get the job, for women do not generally hold these positions.

The Patent Office, however, has a great deal of tedious copying work, and it is in this area that women begin to get civil service jobs. Most of the copyists that the Patent Office hires do their work at home, for their presence in the office is unwanted; their paychecks are mailed, with those to married women made out to their husbands.

Barton works in the office, where she endures much hostility from her colleagues, only to lose the job when her congressional supporter loses his 1856 election. She has no choice but to return to her family in Massachusetts—but in 1860, the Patent Office will belatedly recognize her ability and call her back to work.

◆ In March, Ohio's Frances Dana Gage speaks on women's rights in faraway New Orleans. Although she could expect a hostile audience because she is also an abolitionist, Gage's "Aunt Fanny" demeanor wins over her listeners.

◆ In May, Caroline Severance presents a memorial on behalf of the Ohio Women's Rights Association, petitioning the state senate to pass a bill granting married women the right to control their own wages and inheritance. No such bill is taken up, however.

◆ Elizabeth Cady Stanton makes her first major speech, addressing the New York legislature on behalf of a bill granting married women the right to control their inheritance and earnings. Current laws in most states give husbands absolute power over their wives' property—including even clothing. Susan Anthony begins organizing women in every county of New York State to gather signatures on petitions to change these laws, and women canvass door to door for signatures.

◆ The Massachusetts legislature is the first to respond to this issue, and it passes a historic Married Women's Property Act this year. The victory is largely the result of hard work by Mary Upton Ferrin, who collected petition signatures for six years after she realized that her husband had legal title to the property she owned prior to marriage as well as the right to all earnings from her labor.

◆ On May 10, African American Elizabeth Greenfield sings before Queen Victoria. Born in slavery in Mississippi, she grew up in Philadelphia—where her mistress moved, converted to Quakerism, and freed her slaves. Greenfield has been singing professionally for the past three years, and with support from Harriet Beecher Stowe, her British tour is a success. Unfortunately, her manager cheats her of her earnings, and she lives in relative obscurity in Philadelphia until her 1876 death.

◆ The Maine Anti-Slavery Society hires Frances Watkins (later Harper) as a speaker. A black woman born free in Baltimore, she taught herself to read and write and, by age 20, produced a volume of poetry. She will become sufficiently popular as an orator that she supports herself this way until the Civil War begins. In 1859, she also publishes "The Two Offers," which will be cited as the first short story by an African-American woman.

◆ Educated, affluent Matilda Joselyn Gage is vacationing at a fashionable Saratoga Springs resort when Susan Anthony introduces herself. Anthony's purse has been stolen, and she is in debt for flyers that promote a meeting for which she has no speakers. The stylish young Gage helps out, even overcoming her fear of speaking to join the agenda, and the women's rights movement makes important contacts. Gage becomes a lifelong leader.

Saratoga Springs, incidentally, draws visitors from great distances, including South Carolinian Mary Chesnut, who vacations here more than a decade prior to beginning her important Civil War diary. Like others of her era, she explains her vacation from plantation heat in terms of the health-restoring powers of the springs.

◆ A first novel by Maria Susanna Cummins of Massachusetts is an amazing success. *The Lamplighter* sells an unprecedented 40,000 copies in the first few weeks after publication; translated into French and German, it also sells well abroad.

Nathaniel Hawthorne has Cummins in mind when he complains, "America is now wholly given over to a damned mob of scribbling women, and I should have no chance of success." Hawthorne does have recent success, however: His best-sellers of 1850 and 1851 fall midway between the Brontë sisters in the late 1840s and Harriet Beecher Stowe in 1852.

✦ After less than a year in the pastorate that she had worked so hard to achieve, the Reverend Antoinette Brown asks to be released. Her faith is evolving from Congregationalist theology to that of Unitarianism, and she moves to New York City, where she performs a volunteer ministry in slums, jails, and asylums. She earns some income by writing of this for the *New York Tribune* and its liberal editor, Horace Greeley.

✦ The *New York Tribune* also publishes work by "Jennie June," a pseudonym that Jane Cunningham Croly will use for the next 40 years. She marries a journalist and continues to work, despite bearing five children. Croly will be considered the first female reporter to work for a major newspaper at a desk—as opposed to the "correspondent" style of working from home that prevails for women.

✦ Eight nuns from Kinsale, Ireland, arrive in the rough frontier town of San Francisco. The Sisters of the Presentation of the Blessed Virgin Mary will remain there through the 20th century, with the eventual total number of convent members reaching 358.

1855 In January, Anne McDowell begins publishing the *Woman's Advocate* from Philadelphia. Both the newspaper's investors and its employees are women, and it lasts for the rest of the decade, despite a somewhat timorous editorial policy that deemphasizes politics. Its pages are a forum for various views, and McDowell's main emphasis is on employment opportunity.

✦ Lucy Stone adds to her growing reputation by retaining her maiden name when she marries Henry Blackwell—something that the groom, who is appreciably younger, suggests to persuade Stone to marry him. Henry is the feminist brother of Drs. Elizabeth and Emily Blackwell.

The maiden name innovation, however, will be tempered by the era's insistence on an honorific, so that almost all contemporary documents—even those written by feminists—refer to her as "Mrs." Stone.

✦ Cordelia Greene follows Emily Blackwell as the second graduate of Western Reserve's medical school. Dr. Greene returns to Castile, New York, where she practices with her physician father and becomes a mentor for future India missionary Dr. Clara Swain. Also this year, Emeline Horton Cleveland graduates from Female Medical College of Pennsylvania; she will develop one of the century's best reputations during a lifelong medical practice as a married woman.

✦ The New York Infirmary for Women and Children opens in March in the city's Eleventh Ward, which, in the words of Dr. Elizabeth Blackwell, is "destitute of medical charity, while possessing a densely crowded poor population . . . chiefly, emigrants, mostly Germans." (These immigrants, incidentally, begin arriving this year at the nation's first systematic immigrant receiving station, New York's Castle Garden.)

The infirmary will have an all-woman staff, when Drs. Elizabeth and Emily Blackwell are joined by Dr. Marie Zakrzewska. They form a fine medical team: Emily Blackwell has two years of postgraduate work under European experts, and Dr. Zakrzewska, an 1856 Cleveland Medical School graduate, earlier earned credentials in midwifery in Berlin. She was mentored by Elizabeth Blackwell after her 1853 immigration. Emily Blackwell will perform the infirmary's surgery; although Elizabeth's lifelong dream had been to specialize in surgery, she was forced to give that up when she caught a contagious eye disease from a patient during her medical residency in Paris.

The women are astute enough to collect a male board of trustees for their venture, including editor Horace Greeley—who also befriended the Blackwells' new sister-in-law, the Reverend Antoinette Brown Blackwell.

- The importance of personal networks in the spread of ideas is further reinforced with the formation of the first women's rights organization in Illinois. Established in the town of Earlville, its founder is Susan Hoxie Richardson—a cousin of Susan Anthony.

- Congress passes legislation that grants citizenship to foreign women who marry American men. The reverse, however, is not true: Because she lacks full legal rights herself, an American woman cannot confer citizenship upon her husband. Both situations reinforce the common-law principle that marriage makes a man and woman one, and that one is the man.

- As the abolitionist cause grows, Maria Weston Chapman, who endured great abuse for her abolitionist views in the 1830s and 1840s, fades into the movement's background. Although she will live another 30 years, *How Can I Help to Abolish Slavery?* (1855) is her last major publication on the subject.

  In contrast, Ohio's Josephine Griffing becomes a paid agent of the Western Anti-Slavery Society, and the welfare of black people will be the focus of the rest of her life, even after the Civil War. Even though her children are still young, Griffing tours the Midwest speaking against slavery and singing abolitionist songs.

- The era's most popular singers are the Hutchinson Family, a group of four brothers and a sister, Abby Hutchinson, who continues to be known by this name despite her 1849 marriage. They have been a great hit at abolitionist and other reform gatherings for a decade, and this year they make their first appearance at a women's rights convention in Rochester, New York. They continue to sing on such occasions throughout the century, and their sweet songs, often religious, are capable of hushing rowdy crowds that no speaker can quiet.

- In September, a state women's rights convention in Boston features an "exhaustive" report on women's legal status in Massachusetts by Caroline Healey Dall.

- The national convention is held in Cincinnati, Ohio, in October; it is presided over by Martha C. Wright, Lucretia Mott's sister and one of the five organizers of the first women's rights convention in Seneca Falls. To draw attention to the artificial distinctions created by dress, some of the women who attend wear bloomers, while their "gentlemen" friends are courageous enough to make the point by wearing shawls.

- *Female Prose Writers of America* is an acknowledgment by a Philadelphia publisher of the success of women authors.

- Mobile's Octavia Le Vert, who raised $1,000 in one day for the Mount Vernon Ladies Association, is appointed by the governor to be Alabama's commissioner at the Paris Exposition.

- Calling herself Fanny Fern, Sara Farrington joins the *New York Ledger* and is paid a fabulous $100 per weekly column. The first of three book collections of her short pieces was published just two years earlier and has already sold more than 200,000 copies.

  Both widowed and divorced in the past, she has three children; her third marriage is to a man appreciably younger than herself, and she is known thereafter as Sara Parton. The public, however, knows her as Fanny Fern, and she attracts a half-million readers every week until her 1872 death.

  Her subjects appear to be routine domesticity, but she subtly raises the issues of injustice toward women that she knows so well from widowhood and divorce. Unlike most other writers of her era, Fanny Fern is an early suffrage supporter.

1856   The Reverend Antoinette Brown marries Samuel Blackwell, the brother of Lucy Stone's husband, Henry Blackwell. Both Blackwell men are strong supporters of women's rights, and Samuel long ago asked for an introduction to the unconventional theology student and then courted her persistently. Unlike her former Oberlin classmate, Brown takes her husband's name, and, with only occasional preaching, she will spend the next two decades as the mother of seven.

◆ Ohio's new Antioch College invites the Reverend Antoinette Brown Blackwell to preach, largely at the urging of student Olympia Brown—who is no relation, but who is inspired by the woman who shares her name. Olympia Brown will go on to graduate study in theology.

Antioch's first female graduate is Ada Shepard. She accepts one of the most likely sources of employment for genteel women of her era and becomes governess for the children of Sophia and Nathaniel Hawthorne.

◆ Lucy Stone presides over the annual Women's Rights Convention in New York, while philosopher Ralph Waldo Emerson speaks to a similar gathering in Boston.

◆ In Salem, Massachusetts, Charlotte Forten may be the first African-American woman to teach white students. She is a member of a Philadelphia family of blacks who have enjoyed generations of freedom and economic success. Nevertheless, Philadelphia's schools are segregated, so the Forten family sent her to Salem, where she graduated from the state teachers' training school last year.

◆ Mother Mary Joseph of the Sisters of Charity of Providence is assigned to the Pacific Northwest, where she will use the carpentry skills that she learned from her father literally to build 29 institutions. They range from hospitals to schools to homes for the needy, and she wears a hammer next to her rosary. After her death in 1902, Sister Mary Joseph—who was born Esther Pariseau —will be honored by the American Institute of Architects. The State of Washington makes her its second honoree in Statuary Hall of the national capitol.

◆ When American William Walker's unauthorized invasion of Nicaragua becomes successful, Jane and William Cazneau sail from Santo Domingo to Nicaragua to support his revolution. They then go on to New York, where they recruit soldiers. When Walker begins to lose battles, Jane Cazneau

goes to Washington and personally lobbies both the attorney general and President Buchanan on behalf of the imperialists.

◆ English theatrical producer Laura Keene opens a New York theater named for herself. Her experience includes theater management from Baltimore to San Francisco as well as acting in England and Australia. She develops a highly successful career and initiates both the regular matinee and the long run of a well-promoted play. Keene can be creditably called the nation's first successful businesswoman in the entertainment industry.

◆ Dancer Lola Montez—a pseudonym for Ireland-born Dolores Gilbert—settles in New York. She has performed throughout Europe during the last decade but is known primarily as the mistress of the Bavarian king. After the political revolutions of 1848, she toured Australia and America, where she was granted her third divorce—for reasons far less substantial than those of most other women who are unsuccessful in their fight for divorce.

◆ The presidential election sets precedents for women: it is the first to feature a potential first lady, as the smiling face of 32-year-old Jessie Benton Frémont appears on posters and a song, "Frémont and Our Jessie," becomes popular. The strategy is considered successful when John Charles Frémont, the first nominee of the new Republican Party, makes a strong showing—despite the fact that his father-in-law, Senator Thomas Hart Benton of Missouri, does not endorse him.

At the same time, Anna Ella Carroll writes publicity for Millard Fillmore and his American ("Know Nothing") Party. A member of a prominent Maryland family fallen on hard times, Carroll has earned a living in Washington politics since 1845; she specializes in using her social connections to help men who seek government jobs.

1857 New Englander Delia Bacon—who claims no relation to Sir Francis Bacon—publishes a 700-page book arguing that Shakespeare's work was actually written by Sir Francis and others. She is not greeted as a crackpot, for Ralph Waldo Emerson has helped fund her research trip to England and Nathaniel Hawthorne writes an introduction for the book. Future scholars repeatedly put down the theory, only to see it arise again—but seldom attributed to Delia Bacon.

♦ Popular novelist Catharine Sedgwick doubtless has personal intent with her last book, for *Married or Single?* is a defense of the unmarried state, and she has turned down several offers of marriage during her successful career.

♦ Belva Ann McNall, later famous as attorney Belva Lockwood, is elected superintendent of Lockport, New York's Union School. She is uncommonly hardworking and bright: As a young widow with a child to support, she recently earned a bachelor of science degree from the forerunner to Syracuse University.

♦ After more than 20 years of a bad marriage, Jane Grey Swisshelm leaves her husband and gives up the Pittsburgh newspaper that she has published for almost a decade. She moves out to Minnesota and begins publishing the *St. Cloud Visiter* [*sic*], but her abolitionist editorials outrage locals, who destroy her press. Forced to change the paper's name because of a libel suit, she calls her new one the *St. Cloud Democrat*, but she supports Republican Abraham Lincoln in the election of 1860 and spends the first two years of the Civil War urging him to move on abolition.

♦ Coincidentally, Democrats rewriting Minnesota's constitution this year briefly consider granting suffrage to married women. Perhaps because the unmarried female taxpayer may instead have the best claim for the vote, the idea is quickly dropped.

♦ The Ohio legislature passes a bill requiring a married man to obtain his wife's consent before disposing of property, and a woman "whose husband shall desert her or neglect to provide for his family" is also empowered to file suit for his wages.

The Ohio senate almost moves beyond this to a position that would be considered radical in the future: in response to a petition signed by 10,000, a committee favorably reports amending the state constitution to give women the vote. The proposal fails in a tie vote on the floor, 44 to 44.

♦ "The plan and policy of this school," writes Charles Lewis Cocke, president of Virginia's Hollins Institute, "recognizes the principle that in the present state of society young women require the same thorough and rigid training as that afforded young men."

He and his wife, Susanna Pleasants Cocke, spent $1,500 in 1846 to acquire a bankrupt school for boys and and girls begun in 1842 in Roanoke, Virginia. The name changed in 1855, when "Mrs. John Hollins induced her husband" to donate $5,000. Hollins will grow into one of the most prestigious women's schools in the South. When Cocke dies in 1901, his daughter, Matty L. Cocke, serves as president of Hollins College for the rest of her life.

♦ The first southern woman to earn a medical degree is Orianna Moon of Virginia, who graduates from Female Medical College of Pennsylvania. She practices all her life, including after her marriage. She will wed Dr. John S. Andrews when both work in a Confederate hospital during the Civil War, and they practice together in Charlottesville.

♦ Boston society leader Julia Ward Howe, who has published an anonymous book of poetry, uses her name on two plays—and her friends are bewildered, because these are dark tales of murder and suicide. Her husband, the father of her six children, is angry and embarrassed, for he knows that her thoughts are based in the unhappiness of their marriage.

♦ On September 7, a horrifying event occurs that, as the story slowly unravels, causes controversy for years into the future. A wagon train of hungry, thirsty pioneers is lured into a defenseless position in remote southwestern Utah Territory, and when the day is over, 134 women, children, and men are dead. Their bodies lay unburied for two months, while wolves chew on them.

Who is responsible for the Mountain Meadow Massacre becomes a subject of great dispute, but the Indians involved insist that they were hired and directed by Mormons. The Latter-Day Saints argue that this is still more calumny against their religion, but some children who survive say that Mormon women are wearing their mothers' dresses. Twenty years later, one man—a dissident Mormon—is executed for the crime; his testimony includes an acknowledgment that many women were raped before they were killed.

1858 Last year, for the first time since 1848, no national women's rights convention was held. This year, the women meet in New York, and the 10th anniversary of the Seneca Falls meeting attracts large crowds. In addition to familiar speakers such as Lucy Stone, Susan Anthony, and Lucretia Mott, the platform features new attendees such as Eliza W. Farnham and African American Sarah Remond.

Farnham's career has included service as a progressive matron at Sing Sing prison and as the leader of a group of women bound for the California gold rush. She believes that women are actually superior to men, rather than vice versa, and says: "Woman should recognize man as John the Baptist, going before to prepare the world of her coming . . . as heavenly mother as well as father."

Many New Yorkers are not willing to hear such innovative thought, and the convention is repeatedly "interrupted by the rowdyism of a number of men occupying the rear part of the hall."

✦ Iowa becomes the first state to admit women to its public university. At the same time, young Sarah Burger, who had attended a 1853 women's rights convention, organizes a dozen applications to the University of Michigan from women like herself. Although they draw attention to the issue, women will not be admitted to Michigan until 1870.

✦ Boston's Reverend William Hosmer publishes *Appeal to Husbands and Wives in Favor of Female Physicians*. He includes helpful information on Female Medical College of Pennsylvania and on New England Female Medical College. Students at the latter pay tuition directly to their teachers: "To each of the seven Professors, $10; to the Demonstrator of Anatomy, $5," etc.

✦ During the year between her pregnancies at ages 39 and 41, Lucy Stone sets another precedent by refusing to pay property taxes. Her demonstration of the principle of "no taxation without representation" is met with the publicized impoundment and sale of her household goods.

✦ When blind teacher Fanny Crosby marries another blind teacher at the New York City school where they live, she retains her maiden name because she is already a well-known songwriter. Prior to her death at age 95, Crosby will be the lyricist for an amazing body of hymns: she is credited with between 5,000 and 9,000 hymns written under more than 100 different pseudonyms.

✦ The first white woman climbs Pike's Peak. Abolitionist Julia Archibald Holmes of Massachusetts had gone to Kansas as a newlywed in 1854 to promote the "free state" cause, and when she and her husband move—by foot—to New Mexico, she takes a week for the adventure of climbing the 14,000-foot Colorado mountain. Even in July, snowstorms endanger them. After settling in Taos, Holmes will become a correspondent for the *New York Tribune*.

✦ Irish Margaret Gaffney Haughery becomes known as the Bread Lady of New Orleans after she opens a modern, steam-powered bakery. While she grew up poor, she has already demonstrated her executive ability by successfully operating a dairy; she will introduce other innovations such as crackers packaged to endure New Orleans' humidity. Haughery uses her profits to endow several Catholic orphanages.

✦ When cooper Patrick Kennedy dies, Bridget Murphy Kennedy becomes a widow at age 36. They had met on the *Washington Irving*, when both sailed from County Wexford to escape Ireland's potato famine in April 1849. They married in

Boston in September, and she bore five babies in less than a decade.

Now she must support her four living children: The oldest is a seven-year-old girl, while the youngest (and the only boy) is ten-month-old Patrick Joseph. Kennedy works briefly as a domestic and then clerks at a sewing notions store that she eventually manages to buy. Clearly a very bright and determined woman, she lives over the store, rents rooms, and when her son reaches adulthood, she will help him buy the tavern on which the Kennedy family fortune is based.

She will die in 1881, just a month after the birth of grandson Joseph Kennedy—on November 22, the same date on which her great-grandson, President John F. Kennedy, is assassinated in 1963. Bridget Murphy Kennedy founds the greatest American political dynasty since Abigail Adams' day, with only the resources of a poor Irish Catholic widow.

✦ After years of being hunted by bounty seekers who wish to collect the $200 that the federal government offers for the capture of Seminole women (as opposed to $500 for men), 124 Seminoles are deported from Tampa Bay to the Indian Territory of Oklahoma. Their ship is aptly called *Gray Cloud.*

The few hundred Florida natives who remain hidden in the Everglades have a breathing spell during the next decade, as the Civil War absorbs the military.

✦ *Captivity of the Oatman Girls . . . Among the Apaches and Mohave Indians* sells widely. It details the experience of two girls taken captive after witnessing the deaths of their mother, father, and four siblings in Arizona in 1851. The father, dissatisfied with the speed of their wagon train to Yuma, had separated their wagon from the train and taken his family into the desert alone. Mary Ann, who was seven when captured, starved to death during an 1853 drought—along with many Mohave—but Olive survives and tells their tale.

1859 Elizabeth Cary Agassiz publishes *Acetaea: A First Lesson in Natural History.* She will follow it up with two other science and nature books in the next decade, one of which is based on her travels in Brazil.

✦ The first thorough history of New York is published; its author is Mary Louise Booth, who is not primarily a historian, but instead a translator whose publisher asked her to write an appealing history of the city. Her specialty is French, and she translates all kinds of writing, from fiction to instruction books on watch repair and marble work. She also serves as secretary at women's rights conventions.

✦ Macon's Wesleyan Female College, formerly Georgia Female College, has enough graduates that it forms the world's first alumnae organization. Known as a liberal institution, it struggles financially as the South becomes increasingly conservative, but the college will survive the Civil War and Reconstruction.

✦ Sarah Remond goes to Britain as a lecturer for the Anti-Slavery Society. She draws large crowds, for she is the first black woman that many Europeans have seen. Her well-received speeches become a factor in preventing England from joining the American South in the coming war, and except for a brief postwar return, Remond lives in Europe the rest of her life.

Escaped Georgia slaves Ellen and William Craft are also active in English abolitionist circles. Their story will be published in London next year; *Running a Thousand Miles for Freedom* is written by an English friend while the Crafts work at learning to read and write. After the war, they return to the United States with their five children, buy a farm, and provide leadership to blacks in Georgia and South Carolina.

✦ Dr. Elizabeth Blackwell makes another trip to England and writes excitedly to her sister Emily: "I have only one piece of information to send, but that is of the highest importance—the Medical Council has registered me as a physician! . . . This will be of immeasurable value to the future of medical women in England," where there are not yet any female doctors.

Jane and William Cazneau return to the Caribbean, where they will wait out the Civil War. Using her Cora Montgomery pseudonym, she writes *In the Tropics; by a Settler in Santo Domingo* (1863). Spanish officials who fear the Cazneaus may be subverting them will raid their Santo Domingo estate in 1863, and the couple flees to Jamaica. Once again Jane Cazneau lobbies both Washington officials and the press from her distant post, and within two years, the couple is are able to return to Santo Domingo. She not only continues to write for the *New York Herald* but also is deeply involved in a number of commercial schemes.

In Michigan, Augusta Chapin preaches her first sermon. For the next several years, she will "ride circuit," enduring all the hardships and uncertainties of an itinerant preacher. The Universalist Church will grant her credentials in 1862, and in December 1863, the Reverend Chapin will be ordained in Lansing.

The *Women's Tribune* begins publication in Indianapolis under the editorship of Amanda Way and Sarah E. Underhill.

The Ninth Women's Rights Convention, held in New York on May 12, proves to be "another turbulent meeting." The recording secretary reports that Mozart Hall "at an early hour, was crowded to overflowing, every seat being occupied, and crowds standing in the aisle." This is not a sign of success, however, for most of those in attendance have come to mock the women. Even such experienced speakers as Antoinette Brown Blackwell and Ernestine Rose give up on trying to make themselves heard above the roar of the jeering men.

Women still are not hired for government clerical jobs, and the attitude of men in the Patent Office has not improved since Clara Barton left Washington. Lucy Coues' work experience there this year is unhappy—even though her father has a high-ranking position in the office. A New Hampshire native with connections to President Franklin Pierce, she will marry a Chicagoan and, as Lucy Flowers, become a force for civic improvements in Illinois.

"Miss Lotta, the San Francisco favorite," is 12-year-old Lotta Crabtree, who will become a national stage celebrity in the next few years. Talented at singing, dancing, and banjo-playing, she will also smoke and show her legs on stage—while somehow maintaining an image as an ingenue. In her 40s, she will still play children's roles, especially Charles Dickens' characters.

South Carolinian Mary Chesnut, the daughter of a U.S. senator, accompanies her husband to Washington when he is appointed to the Senate —but to her great disappointment, South Carolina soon will secede from the nation and she must return to isolated plantation life. As the Civil War approaches, however, she begins to keep her diaries more faithfully; unlike most others, she began recording her opposition to slavery while still a schoolgirl. Her feelings are motivated in part by a nascent feminism, for she is unwilling to turn a blind eye to the number of slave children who resemble their white masters.

On December 2, white abolitionist John Brown is executed for his October takeover of a federal arsenal at Harper's Ferry, in the mountains of western Virginia. Brown had intended to establish a free state for rebelling slaves there, and his plans included a leadership role for Harriet Tubman, whom Brown called General Tubman.

Sixteen other men, both black and white, also die; they are either killed in battle with federal troops or, like Brown, are captured and hanged. Supported by Lucy Stone and others, Rebecca Spring of Perth Amboy, New Jersey, attempts to arrange decent funerals for these men, but because the takeover of a federal arsenal is treason, much of the public disapproves of Spring's self-appointed task. A decade will pass before some of the men are properly buried.

Ex-slave Frances Ellen Watkins sends Brown a letter while he is awaiting his death. Writing from Indiana, she expresses her profound thanks for his effort, telling him that, as a girl, she had been taken from "the warm clasp of a mother's arms to the clutches of a libertine."

Watkins also raises money to support Brown's family. Mary Brown—who almost loses the family's midstate New York farm because she cannot pay the annual taxes—is too poor even to visit her husband prior to his execution. Among those who respond to Watkins' appeal for Mary Brown are black women in Detroit, who send $20, "not as as an act of charity but as a heartfelt offering of gratitude from those for whose cause you are now so sadly bereaved."

1860   As the decade begins, a reasonably scientific survey of New York City estimates that there is one prostitute for every 64 adult males. The study also indicates the dangers of venereal disease and violence: these women live only an average of four years after entering the trade.

✦ Despite blizzard conditions, about a thousand female shoemakers in Lynn, Massachusetts, join men for a March 7 demonstration. They carry a banner proclaiming that "American Ladies Will Not Be Slaves," and some 20,000 other New England shoemakers follow them out on strike.

✦ In response to petition drives and lobbying by women over the past several years, the New York legislature passes a bill granting married women rights in the guardianship of their children and the right to sue in court and to retain their own wages. This is a very significant victory, but later legislatures will reverse some of the gains.

✦ Susan Anthony is involved in passing New York's guardianship reform—but guardian law has not yet changed in Massachusetts, and Anthony's life is seriously disrupted when the wife and daughter of a Massachusetts state senator plead with her to help them flee from abuse.

The woman begs for Anthony's help after she is released from an insane asylum, where her husband committed her when she confronted him with evidence of his mistress. In disguise, Anthony leads the woman and her daughter into hiding and then resists threats of arrest from the senator's lawyers for over a year.

Because they fear damage to their cause, Anthony's male abolitionist friends pressure her to turn the fugitives in—while at the same time, they pride themselves on their resistance to the fugitive slave law. Finally, detectives locate the fugitives and kidnap the girl from Sunday school. Because guardianship routinely goes to the father, the wife must return home if she is to see her daughter.

✦ Harriet Tubman leads a group in Troy, New York, that successfully assaults officers guarding a fugitive slave, enabling him to escape to Canada.

✦ As the Civil War begins, there are approximately 200 "female seminaries" scattered throughout the nation. Their curriculum is often more serious and less secular than that found in finishing schools, and many are located in the South and Midwest. Their numbers will shrink after the war, due to economic decline in the South and increased coeducation in the Midwest, while in the East, prestigious women's colleges begin.

✦ Massachusetts finishing school graduate Harriet Hosmer had to learn sculpting with private male tutors, but this year she is the first woman to receive a major public commission for artwork: The State of Missouri hires her to carve a huge statue of its longtime senator, Thomas Hart Benton.

✦ Ann S. Stephens writes *Malaeska*, which is later included on a list published by New York City's Grolier Club of "The 100 Most Influential American Books." It is the story of the marriage of a white man and an Indian woman, and is but one of some 25 novels that Stephens writes while also maintaining a lifelong career as a magazine editor.

✦ Eliza Winston, a Mississippi slave who has accompanied her owner to Minneapolis, sues for her freedom on the grounds that Minnesota is a free state. She is supported by abolitionists, and in contradiction of the Supreme Court's *Dred Scott* decision and of Congress's Fugitive Slave Law, Minnesota grants her emancipation.

Not everyone in the state is an abolitionist, however, and the house in which Winston hides is attacked. Journalist Jane Grey Swisshelm writes that a "howling mob" threatens the Babbitt home from "midnight til morning." While Mr. Babbitt and his sister-in-law, Mrs. Messer, defend the house with pistol and club, Mrs. Babbitt escapes "through a back cellar" and runs for the sheriff—despite being seven months' pregnant.

"Eliza Winston," Swisshelm adds, goes "by underground railroad to Canada, because Minnesota . . . could not or would not defend the freedom of one declared free by decision of her own courts."

✦ In the never-ending quest to restore women's rightful place in history, Caroline Healey Dall publishes *Historical Pictures Retouched*.

5

The National Fabric
Ripped and Mended

1861–1876

1861 What will turn out to be the last Women's Rights Convention for several years is held in Albany in February; when Abraham Lincoln takes office as president the following month, the Civil War begins, and no feminist convention will be called until 1866, after the war is well over.

✦ When Lincoln's assumption of the presidency brings talk of secession in Maryland, political insider Anna Ella Carroll uses her influence with the governor. It is vital that Maryland stay part of the Union, for Washington, D.C., would be isolated from the rest of the United States if Maryland were to join the Confederacy, and Lincoln is grateful for Carroll's successful efforts.

Although Carroll is a member of a slaveowning family, she is an ardent supporter of the Union. She drops any feminine artifice from her writing, publishes several strong pieces that use legal precedents to argue for Lincoln, and the administration distributes her essay *The War Powers* to all members of Congress. During the next few years, the War Department will pay Carroll some $2,500 for writing and consulting services.

✦ Socialite Rose Greenhow, a beautiful widow in her 40s, uses her Washington connections to spy for the Confederacy in one of the earliest battles of the war, Bull Run. In the hairdo of a young associate, she hides coded intelligence on the number of Union troops and the route they will take. With this advance knowledge, the Confederates send the U.S. Army fleeing back to Washington, and many predict the South will win the war.

✦ Jefferson Davis, president of the Confederate States of America, commissions Sally Tompkins as a captain in the Confederate Army, thus enabling her to commandeer supplies for the hospital she runs in her Richmond mansion. At the war's end, Captain Tompkins' hospital will have the lowest death rate of any similar facility in the North or South, even though physicians send their worst cases there. Her staff of six—four of whom are still enslaved black women—treats more than 1,300 men and loses only 73.

✦ Elizabeth Van Lew is one of the few Richmond residents who openly supports the Union; educated by Philadelphia Quakers, she long ago had freed the slaves she inherited. When the Union loses the first battles, she begins visiting prisoners of war and insisting that they be treated humanely. As the war goes on, Van Lew expands into spying: she works out codes so that prisoners can pass on military information that she, in turn, conveys to Union generals.

✦ Iowan Annie Wittenmyer leads women in supplying the needs of soldiers camped on the Mississippi River. Several months prior to Clara Barton's similar work in the East, they are formally named State Sanitary Agents. Unlike most similar cases, Iowa pays these women for their work. They travel the Mississippi on hospital ships and serve under fire at Vicksburg and in other battle sites.

✦ The U.S. Sanitary Commission unites local relief efforts and evolves into a quasi-military institution. While men hold many governing positions, tens of thousands of Sanitary Commission women provide Union soldiers with food, medicine, surgical dressings, and other essentials that the military fails to supply. By the war's end, the Sanitary Commission will have some 7,000 local units across the Northern states, which raise a total of $50 million, a huge sum for the time. According to a postwar writer, "Nothing connected with the war so astonished foreign nations as the work of the Sanitary Commission."

✦ When Mary Ann Bickerdyke travels several hundred miles to deliver money from her Galesberg, Illinois, church to needy soldiers in the Mississippi River town of Cairo, she is shocked to find dying men untended in filthy surroundings. A 43-year-old widow, she leaves her young sons in Illinois and begins what is perhaps the longest, most difficult nursing career of the war. She works on Sanitary Commission ships that carry wounded men from the South for the rest of this year, then moves with Grant's army through the battles of Mississippi and Tennessee the next year.

- Back East, Clara Barton observes the military's inefficiency during the first battles around Washington. She advertises for supplies in the newspapers of her Massachusetts hometown, and when people begin sending them, she quits the Patent Office job that she worked so hard to secure, transforms her Washington home into a warehouse, and in the summer, begins delivering food, medicine, and other goods to troops in Maryland and Virginia. She is at the scene of bloody battles the rest of the year, but as the Sanitation Commission becomes better organized, Barton will be relatively inactive during the middle of the war.

- Confederate Ella K. Trader's work parallels that of Clara Barton. During the next four years, Trader establishes hospitals in Tennessee, Kentucky, Mississippi, and Georgia. She displays tremendous executive ability in procuring goods that the army lacks, often spending her own money or raising the funds to buy a railroad car of food or blankets.

- The first formal military position granted to a woman occurs on June 10, when the Secretary of War appoints Dorothea Dix as Superintendent of the United States Army Nurses.

  This will be, however, the least successful of Dix's three careers. The days when she was a beautiful teenage teacher and an innovative mental health reformer are over, and nurses will rebel against her demands that they be "plain looking" and over 30. After an accumulation of complaints, the War Department limits her authority in 1863, but she continues to work—while refusing any pay—until a year after the war's end.

- Canada-born Sarah Edmonds enlists in the Army of the Potomac under the pseudonym of Frank Thompson in June. She will serve in the first battle of Bull Run and the Peninsular campaign of 1862, and more than once volunteers to spy "disguised" as a woman. Her postwar book on her experience sells 175,000 copies.

  The most famous similar Confederate woman is Loreta Janeta Velazquez, who accompanies her husband to war and continues to fight after he is killed. She has a New Orleans tailor conceal her figure with a wired chemise and enlists under the name Harry T. Buford. When her gender is discovered eventually, Confederate officials are not grateful for her enthusiasm; she is fined $10 and sentenced to 10 days in jail. Velazquez will also publish a postwar book.

- Nearly 800 nuns of a dozen or more orders will volunteer as nurses in military hospitals during the war. It is the first experience that many American men have had with Catholics, and the women's valor and spirit of sacrifice effectively counters the anti-Catholic arguments of prewar Know Nothings and other xenophobes.

  This year, the Sisters of Providence are placed in charge of a large military hospital in Indianapolis; next year, the Sisters of the Holy Cross will operate the huge U.S. General Hospital at Mound City, Illinois. Nursing nuns also work on the hospital ships that carry men back up the Mississippi from Southern battlefields.

- Belgium-born Adele Parmentier Bayer works in much the same way as nuns, although her status as a married woman prevents her from taking vows. Fluent in several languages, she specializes in sailors at the Brooklyn Navy Yard, to whom she distributes rosaries, holy water, and prayer books. More unconventionally, she also begins acting as a banker for many of these men: Bayer encourages them to deposit their money with her instead of spending their pay in bars and brothels, and she sends regular allotments to hundreds of sailors' families throughout the world.

- When Emily Edson Briggs sends a letter to the editor of the *Washington Chronicle* defending the right of women to hold civil service jobs, the editor is so impressed that he offers her a daily column. Using the pseudonym of Olivia, she will write on politics for both the *Chronicle* and its co-owned newspaper, the *Philadelphia Press*. Mary Todd Lincoln becomes one of Brigg's contacts, and Briggs is the first woman to report from inside the White House; she also is one of the first women to be admitted to the congressional press gallery.

✦ Although men retain the vast majority of secretarial and clerical jobs, a few women begin to be hired in federal civil service positions when it becomes impossible to find enough qualified men during the war. The Patent Office expands from its Clara Barton precedent of hiring women, and at age 19, Anna Dickinson gets a job as a copyist at the U.S. Mint in Philadelphia—but loses it when she makes the same criticisms of military strategy that President Lincoln is making.

The Confederacy hires fewer women in these positions, but one is Julia Duckett Waring, who moves from Maryland to Richmond to work for the Treasury Department—where a number of women sign currency as part of their jobs. Women are also employed by that office in the North, and still another manager makes the "nimble finger" observation first cited of female textile workers decades ago: women prove better than men at separating sheets of paper money.

✦ After losing her civil service job, Anna Dickinson begins what will become an astonishingly successful career as an orator. She and Lucretia Mott share the Quaker tradition of female speakers, and Mott sells 800 tickets to Dickinson's first major speech, "The Rights and Wrongs of Women." Dickinson joins the abolitionist lecture tour, and some 5,000 people crowd Cooper Union for her first New York appearance. Because she is so remarkably successful at urging men into battle, she is termed "the American Joan of Arc."

✦ The first ladies of the North and the South both admire the dressmaking skills of Elizabeth Keckley, a former slave so talented that she has managed to buy both her own freedom and that of her half-white son—who dies in battle this year. Although Keckley sewed for Confederate first lady Varina Howell Davis before the war began, she becomes a traveling companion and confidante of Mary Todd Lincoln; she exerts an abolitionist influence on the Southern-born Lincoln, who has brothers fighting for the Confederacy. When Keckley founds the Contraband Relief Association to aid ex-slaves flowing into Washington the following year, the first lady donates generously.

✦ As the year goes on, Rose Greenhow continues to use her beauty and seeming innocence to pry valuable information from Washington men—apparently even including the chairman of the Senate Military Affairs Committee.

She sends to the South copious intelligence on the defenses that surround Washington; her details on each fort include such information as the number and caliber of its weapons and the experience of the commanding officers. Records captured later reveal that she conspires with men in the headquarters of both the U.S. Navy and the Army, and her network also includes as many as 50 women in five states who have additional contacts.

She is placed under house arrest, but the secretary of war acknowledges in December that Greenhow somehow still maintains "correspondence with the commanding general of the army besieging the capitol."

✦ Author Lydia Maria Child helps ex-slave Harriet Jacobs publish her autobiographical *Incidents in the Life of a Slave Girl*. The book helps feed the abolitionist fire, which is in some danger of being lost in the Union/secession debate.

Moreover, even though she is famous and even though her writing is a direct cause of the war, Child does not consider herself above doing the tasks necessary to improve the lives of the slaves who are escaping to the Union lines. She sends this descriptive letter with "a big box":

People are so busy giving and working for the soldiers that few think of the poor fugitives . . . I bought $15 worth of flannel and calico, and for a fortnight worked as hard as I could drive, repairing second-hand garments . . . I restitched many of the books, and . . . I gathered up all the Biographies of runaway slaves that I could find. I bound them anew . . . and pasted on the covers, as nicely as if I were doing it for Queen Victoria.

✦ The medical abilities of Drs. Elizabeth and Emily Blackwell are underutilized: Under the aegis of the War Department and the Woman's Central

Association of Relief, they spend the war selecting and training nurses.

✦ Dr. Emeline Cleveland of Philadelphia does post-graduate work at the School of Obstetrics in Paris and is awarded five prizes along with her diploma, two of them first place.

✦ Albermarle Institute in Charlottesville, Virginia, is a Baptist-sponsored female higher educational facility that yields to tradition by excluding "college" from its name—but nonetheless grants master's degrees to five women.

✦ In August, Louisa Lane Drew opens a theater in Philadelphia that she operates for the next three decades. Supported by stockholders who soon build a new facility, it is called Mrs. John Drew's Arch Street Theatre—but actor John Drew has far less to do with it than his wife. Her third husband, he is on tour when the theater opens and will die suddenly the following spring.

Louisa Drew never remarries, but devotes the rest of her life to such strenuous activity as producing 42 plays in one season—and acting in each. Meanwhile, she also rears four children, who will join a family tradition of theater that extends through the next century.

✦ Kansas women—many of whom moved there as part of the abolitionist effort to keep this territory from adding to the number of slave states—set an important precedent this year when they secure the right to vote in school elections.

✦ During the first winter of the war, Lillie Devereux Umsted (later Blake) becomes a Washington correspondent for two New York papers, the *World* and the *Evening Post*, even though she has two children under five. After the recent suicide of her husband, she discovered that her inheritance had been spent.

1862 When President Abraham Lincoln's State of the Union speech is leaked to the *New York Herald* before he delivers it, Mary Todd Lincoln is suspected of having sold an advance copy to pay her clothing bills. A congressional committee assigns itself the task of looking into

the matter, even jailing a White House aide whose testimony they find less than candid. The president defends his wife, fires two staffers, and pressures the committee to drop its inquiries. The accusation against the first lady is not proven.

Meanwhile, the Lincolns are frantic about their 11-year-old son Willie, who sickens and dies in February. Mary Todd Lincoln becomes profoundly depressed: Willie is the second of her four children to die, and she refuses to allow the eldest—the only one eligible for the draft—to go to war.

For this and for numerous other things, including her spending habits and her supposed sympathy with the South, Kentuckian Mary Todd Lincoln is criticized in the press as no other first lady has been. "From the moment she entered the White House," a Boston newspaper will conclude after her husband's assassination, "she has been the subject of open or covert attacks." Indeed, it is very nearly impossible for her to satisfy the contradictory demands of Washington pundits, for they alternate between ridiculing the Lincolns as frontier rubes incapable of leading polite society and complaining that they host social events despite the war.

✦ In the spring, Union General James Shields writes to Secretary of War Edwin M. Stanton that Southern female civilians make reinforcements necessary: "I can retake the [Shenandoah] Valley . . . but you must send men to keep it. The women will take it if we don't."

✦ New Orleans, the South's largest city, surrenders on April 25, long before the war in the East will end. Despite the surrender, the spirit of the rebellion lives on in New Orleans, and General Benjamin Butler imposes martial law that he finds difficult to enforce, especially among women. So many Confederate women display their distaste for the Yankee occupation force in such venomous ways that Butler imposes what becomes known as the "Woman's Order." It proclaims that "when any female shall, by word, gesture, or movement, insult or show contempt for any officer or soldier of the United States, she shall be . . .

Women nursed in the rotunda of the U.S. Capitol, which is clearly visible in this photograph. Wartime Washington was extremely crowded with not only soldiers but also "contraband" black people who escaped to the freedom of the nation's capital.
Women in Military Service Memorial; American Civil War

treated as a woman of the town plying her avocation."

The order does not end the problem, however, and a number of women are arrested, including Mrs. Philip Philips, whose husband had been a member of the Cabinet under President Buchanan. She is confined to the penal colony at Ship's Island for several months as punishment for laughing at the funeral procession of a Union soldier. A Baton Rouge Irish-American woman, Mrs. William Kirby, dies on Ship's Island, where she was confined for stealing federal supplies and running them through the lines of rebels. Caught with two cavalry rifles under her dress, she was sentenced to close confinement, and she dies at least partly because of poor prison food.

When Rose Greenhow's Washington, D.C., spy ring continues to be effective, she and her young daughter are confined to Old Capitol Prison (a notorious place directly behind the Capitol, where the 20th-century Supreme Court building will be located). Greenhow refuses to cooperate, and because a number of highly placed men plead for her release—quite possibly because they fear she will reveal their treasonous behav-

ior—she is freed after six months and exiled to the South. On June 4, Confederate President Jefferson Davis leads Richmond in welcoming her.

✦ While Greenhow spies for the South in the U.S. capital, Elizabeth Van Lew continues to spy for the North in the rebel capital. She persuades Mary Elizabeth Bowser, a slave whom Van Lew had freed years earlier, to give up the safety of Philadelphia and return to Richmond, where they implement an audacious plan: Bowser risks her freedom and gets a job in the dining room of the Confederate White House, where she eavesdrops on President Jefferson Davis.

✦ Teenage Virginian Belle Boyd—who fatally shot a Union soldier early in the war—is arrested for spying and detained in Baltimore for a week. Upon her release, she returns South and, with her mother, checks into a hotel hosting Union officers and again begins eliciting military information. She makes a famous ride on her horse Fleeter on the night of May 23, delivering to General Stonewell Jackson intelligence that he terms of "immense service." The secretary of war issues an arrest warrant for her on July 29, but she continues her covert activities.

✦ Mary Jane Patterson becomes the first black, female college graduate in America. She was born in North Carolina, and after the passage of the 1850 Fugitive Slave Law, her family escaped to the progressive town of Oberlin, Ohio. After graduation from Oberlin College, Patterson will serve a lifetime in education, virtually all of it in Washington, D.C., where her sisters also teach. She will be principal of Washington's elite high school for blacks from 1871 to 1884, although she is briefly displaced by the man who was Harvard's first black graduate.

✦ Despite its tradition of liberalism, even Oberlin College is affected by tense wartime race relations. Edmonia Lewis, a student who has a black father and a Chippewa mother, is accused of poisoning two white students. A court dismisses the case for lack of evidence, but Lewis leaves Oberlin anyway. She will go on to a successful career as a Boston sculptor.

In the midst of a war-filled summer, Congress passes two monumental pieces of legislation that will profoundly affect the nation's future. It fulfills one of President Lincoln's campaign promises by passing the Homestead Act—a radical idea that has been blocked by Southern plantation owners and many Northern land speculators. The act promises 160 acres of free land to anyone who lives on it for five years.

Unprecedented anywhere in the world, the program grants extraordinary opportunity for Americans and immigrants equally. While most settle as families, single women also "prove up claims." Teachers are the most likely to take advantage of the act; many move West, work their land in summer, and then supplement their income by teaching in winter.

Congress also passes the Morrill Act, which creates land-grant colleges in rural areas. These institutions—unlike older, Eastern colleges—will be coeducational, with an emphasis on practical, rather than classical, education. Millions of women will earn low-cost degrees in these colleges because they often include work/study programs. Male students grow crops and tend cows, for example, while female students work in kitchens and laundries. Land-grant colleges will sometimes require that men study military science or agriculture, while women are likely to be directed into home economics and teaching.

The head of the Army's Sanitary Commission in the Midwest is Mary Livermore of Illinois, who has been an active abolitionist since her experience as a Virginia governess in the 1840s. She is responsible for military hospitals in Illinois, Kentucky, and Missouri. Like her colleagues in the East, she finds an appalling lack of preparation on the part of the military.

Ohio women's rights leader Frances Dana Gage works for the Sanitary Commission in sites ranging from South Carolina to Mississippi.

With sponsorship from the governor of Massachusetts, Harriet Tubman joins Union soldiers on South Carolina sea islands, where she is authorized to use military transportation and act as a scout and spy. She does provide valuable information, for she easily passes among black informants behind rebel lines, but military leaders fail to take full advantage of this. Because Tubman has more experience in Southern covert activity than anyone—black or white, male or female—her abilities may surpass those of almost any intelligence officer, but Tubman spends most of the war years doing the same nursing chores assigned to other women. She is even reduced to selling chickens and eggs to support herself.

At the second battle of Bull Run, an "Irish washerwoman," who has gone to war with a regiment of friends from New York, stands "tall and unafraid."

In late August, Dakota Sioux in western Minnesota take advantage of the military's absence during the Civil War to wipe out settlers encroaching on the prairie. In the first day alone, some 200 white civilians are killed. The uprising continues for several weeks into the fall, and when it ends, some 40,000 are homeless. Hundreds of people, many of whom are recent immigrants from Germany and Norway, are brutally killed. Many women are taken prisoner and held for ransom; their captivity includes rape and forced labor. Near St. Peter, 30 women are herding cattle when their captors learn that the cavalry is coming. "They crowded the women into a house, set it on fire, and let them burn to death alive."

Several survivors later earn income by lecturing and writing on their experience: Sarah Wakefield's *Six Weeks in Sioux Tepees: A Narrative of Indian Captivity* is typical in that while the writer is clearly appalled by the "savages," she also points out that other Dakota assisted her. Indeed, many Indians, especially Ojibway, protect whites, and a Dakota woman, Aza-ya-man-ka-wan (Berry Picker), is later honored for her humanitarianism. Also called "Old Bets" or "Old Betz," her testimony is especially helpful in convicting the 38 Dakota warriors who are hanged in Mankato in the fall. Other women, of course, mourn these men, whose execution stands as the largest in the nation's history.

+ When her husband is taken prisoner of war in October, Betsy Sullivan goes with him and, known as "Mother Sullivan," nurses wounded prisoners. She had joined his First Tennessee Regiment when he did, and while they served in northern Virginia, "she marched on foot [and] slept on the frozen ground." She has a parallel in Bettie Taylor Philips of Kentucky, who also accompanied her husband to war and nursed at Shiloh, Donelson, and other battlefields.

+ Dr. Esther Hill Hawks arrives in Beaufort, South Carolina, where she lives in a mansion deserted by fleeing rebels and serves the recently liberated blacks. She will spend not merely the remainder of the war but also most of the Reconstruction era at work among the African Americans of coastal South Carolina, Georgia, and northern Florida.

  Dr. Hawks writes of the shocking behavior of Union men toward South Carolina's black women: "No colored woman or girl was safe from the brutal lusts of the soldiers—and by soldiers I mean both officers and men. . . . Mothers were brutally treated for trying to protect their daughters, and there are now several women in our little hospital who have been shot by soldiers for resisting their vile demands."

+ New Hampshire nurse Carrie Cutter is buried in the national cemetery created when Union forces capture New Bern, North Carolina. Age 20, she lies next to her fiancé; he died in battle and she of fever caught from sick soldiers.

+ Newspaper publisher Jane Swisshelm addresses the Minnesota senate on abolition and women's rights; she had spoken in the house two years earlier. In both cases, "the hall was packed and the lecture received with profound attention, interrupted by hearty audience."

  In Michigan, Quaker abolitionist Elizabeth Comstock similarly addresses the state senate. Nationally active for the goals of the Society of Friends, she will go on to meet with two presidents: she prays with Abraham Lincoln and lobbies James Garfield for aid to postwar black migrants in Kansas.

+ The publication of the "Battle Hymn of the Republic" in the *Atlantic* makes author Julia Ward Howe instantly famous. She writes the poem during a sleepless night in a Washington hotel, and set to the tune of "John Brown's Body," the song will be sung in virtually every Northern church and school. It becomes a standard of American life, and the literary reputation Howe has in Boston expands throughout the nation.

+ Undistracted by the war, 32-year-old Emily Dickinson spends long hours in the western Massachusetts home that she shares with her parents and an unmarried sister, writing poetry that no one reads. In this year alone, she produces more than 350 poems. Her work grows increasingly better, even though she is self-taught; Dickinson dropped out of Mount Holyoke College because she disliked its religiosity. She has also defied her family by refusing to affirm the Christian faith.

+ The New England Hospital for Women and Children opens under Dr. Marie Zakrzewska. After practicing medicine in New York with Drs. Elizabeth and Emily Blackwell, she moved to Boston in 1859, where she introduced reforms at the New England Female Medical College, a somewhat inferior institution begun in 1848. Under Dr. Zakrzewski, the school becomes so eminent that by 1881, she will limit her resident students to women who already have an M.D.

  One of the first students to enroll under Dr. Zakrzewska is Lucy Sewall. After postgraduate study in London and Paris, Dr. Sewall will hold leadership positions with the New England Hospital the rest of her life.

+ Mary Glover Patterson—who will be known as Mary Baker Eddy after her third marriage—enjoys a miraculous recovery from a lifetime of invalidism complicated by morphine addiction. Maine mesmerist Phineas Quimby convinces her that illness is a "false belief," thereby planting the ideas that she will expand into Christian Science.

+ In November, young Georgia widow Phoebe Pember takes charge of Richmond's Chimborazo Hospital. By the end of the war, she will have supervised the care of more than 15,000 men, as Chimborazo develops into the largest hospital ever known. She carries a gun that she uses to threaten drunken physicians and others who resent her control over the hospital's supply of alcohol, then used as a painkiller.

Pember is somewhat atypical of Confederate nurses: Her maiden name is Levy, and her parents were Jewish immigrants from Poland and England. The war is the high point of her life; she will publish a book on her experiences in 1879 and die in Pittsburgh in 1913, having never remarried or established any career comparable to the abilities she demonstrates in the war.

1863 William Truesdail, chief of the army police, hires several women to spy for the Union. Among them is actress Pauline Cushman, who "searches" for a brother in Confederate prisoner-of-war camps while gathering information on Southern defenses in the Tennessee Valley. When Cushman attempts to return to Nashville, she is searched. Maps and drawings are found concealed in her boots, and she is arrested; although she escapes her guard, she is recaptured.

In a military trial at the Shelbyville, Tennessee, headquarters of General Braxton Bragg, Cushman is sentenced to death. A few days later, however, a successful Union assault brings her freedom, and the *New York Herald* lauds Cushman as the "gallant Scout of the Cumberland who did such noble work for the Union." She is granted the honorary rank of major and the right to wear military attire.

✦ Elizabeth Waring Duckett, who lives in coastal Maryland, is jailed for a month in Washington's Old Capitol Prison because the aid she renders to rebels is presumed treasonous. The experience does nothing to change her attitudes, however, and after she is released, she carries a revolver and continues to visit the area's prisoners-of-war camps. Both her father and brother are prisoners, and she twice personally lobbies President Lincoln on behalf of the rebels.

✦ The Loyal League begins when hundreds of women attend a New York meeting convened by

Susan Anthony, Elizabeth Cady Stanton, and others. The group's name denotes loyalty to the Union, but another goal is to keep women's rights issues alive during the war. The league will attract some 5,000 members who gather almost 400,000 petition signatures, and because they charge a penny per signature, the women are able to maintain a New York office, where Susan Anthony earns a dependable salary. Meanwhile, Josephine Griffing serves the League in the Midwest.

✦ A May issue of *Frank Leslie's Illustrated Newspaper* shows Confederate women smashing the windows of a bakery to steal bread. One is barefoot and holds a pistol, while others wield clubs. In Vicksburg, hunger becomes extremely serious; while the city is under continuous bombardment for seven weeks, some women live in caves.

✦ In July, as many as 70,000 New Yorkers—women and men—riot over the draft. Most are Irish Catholics, and they object to an inequitable draft that forces poor men to go to a war that they do not necessarily support, while wealthy men can hire a replacement. Women are among the casualties when soldiers fire on the rioters, but the mob overpowers the police and takes control of the city.

Blaming blacks for the war, the rioters burn the Colored Orphan Asylum—an institution so big that its primarily female staff numbers about 50. Some 200 children are evacuated before the torching, but one little girl, who is hiding under a bed, is beaten to death by the mob.

The riot continues for several days. Liberal newspaper editor Horace Greeley—longtime friend to feminists—is a particular target, and late one night "every whorehouse" in the city is attacked. Women are the wrongdoers in other cases; several are seen desecrating the bodies of lynched black men.

Some 10,000 soldiers are called from Gettysburg to aid police, but the effective end comes when the Catholic archbishop finally denounces the mob's activities five days after it began. More than 1,000 New Yorkers die, most of them white rioters and policemen.

◆ Anna Dickinson is so effective a speaker that the Republican Party hires her to work the tough audiences of Northerners who sympathize with the South. She is sent to speak to men who have rioted against the war and its draft, and she successfully faces down heckling from blue-collar crowds. Coalminers in Pennsylvania literally take shots at her.

◆ In the midst of Tennessee battles, Confederate general Earl Van Dorn is murdered in a love triangle. Dr. George Peters summons Van Dorn to his medical office, demanding that he sign a confession of his guilt in seducing Mrs. Peters and exonerating her of blame for the affair. When the general refuses to sign, the doctor kills him with a bullet through the head.

◆ Over the objections of men on his staff, General George "Pap" Thomas commissions Dr. Mary Walker, the second woman to graduate from Syracuse Medical School, as an "assistant surgeon." She wears the uniform of a first lieutenant and is the highest-ranking woman in the Union Army. While waiting to be allowed to use her medical degree, she had worked—for no salary—in the Patent Office, where Clara Barton established the precedent for women. Dr. Walker retained her maiden name when she married in 1855; she is separated from her husband and unsuccessfully seeking a divorce in Iowa.

◆ After an internship with Drs. Elizabeth and Emily Blackwell in New York, Mary Harris Thompson graduates from the New England Female Medical College in Boston. Because female physicians are now well established in the Northeast, Dr. Thompson goes to Chicago to practice. There she becomes the first and ultimately the best-known woman doctor in the Midwest; she works with the Sanitary Commission until the war ends and then, in May of 1865, opens the Chicago Hospital for Women and Children.

◆ Women become so successful as fund-raisers in supplying military needs that a single Chicago event organized by Mary Livermore nets $70,000. As head of the Army's Sanitary Commission in the Midwest, Livermore forms some 3,000 local units that also procure supplies.

In the East, Louisa Lee Schuyler, the wealthy descendant of original Dutch settlers, systematizes the work of the Sanitary Commission's New York affiliate, the Women's Central Association of Relief. She develops management principles in coordinating the work of local committees and, after the war, goes on to a lifetime of bringing efficiency to charitable organizations; in 1915, Columbia University will reward her with a honorary doctorate.

Unlike Mary Livermore, who will become active in women's causes, Schuyler's privileged status as an unmarried heiress makes her indifferent to feminism.

◆ Confederate spy Rose Greenhow goes to Europe as an unofficial emissary to Southern allies there. After placing her daughter in a French school, she meets with Queen Victoria and Napoleon III; she also publishes selected information on her wartime activity in *My Imprisonment and the First Year of Abolition Rule at Washington*.

◆ Unknown to others, diarist Mary Chesnut continues to record the inside activities of Confederate government. A close friend of Confederate first lady Varina Howell Davis, she knows military and political strategies firsthand and candidly records her views on policy that she believes will lead to the South's defeat.

◆ Louisa May Alcott publishes *Hospital Sketches*, based on her experience as a nurse for the Union. Alcott nearly died of typhoid fever during her time in Washington's war hospitals.

Meanwhile, her mother's cousin, Abby W. May, heads the New England Women's Auxiliary of the Sanitary Commission and disburses almost $1 million in aid to soldiers. Last year May went from Boston to Virginia on a hospital ship to gain direct knowledge of the need for these funds.

◆ Jane Swisshelm sells her Minnesota newspaper and moves to Washington, D.C., to nurse the Union's wounded. At the war's end, she twice attempts to reestablish herself as a publisher, but she does not have the resources to compete in the nation's most news-conscious area.

+ Washington feels the effects of war far more than any other Northern city and is so crowded with wounded men that even the Capitol Rotunda holds hospital beds. Much later, a woman will recall that even crossing the street became difficult, and ladies tipped boys to help them: "The streets ran with liquid mud . . . so cut up were they by the vast numbers of army wagons and ambulances. . . . It was impossible to cross the street until the sweeper had swept a clean spot to rest the sole of your foot, then another spot was swept, and so on until the other side was reached."

+ With wartime inflation straining their low wages, hundreds of women come together in New York City to form the Working Women's Protective Union. The meeting is a result of a *New York Sun* editorial and thus gets national publicity; women in other cities soon emulate it.

+ Olympia Brown becomes the first woman to be ordained a minister without enduring major injustice. She has a four-year bachelor's degree from coeducational Antioch College, and, in June, she graduates from a two-year theological program at St. Lawrence University of Canton, New York. The Reverend Brown is ordained the same month, and after a year with a Universalist congregation in Malone, New York, she will be called by a Weymouth, Massachusetts, church, where she stays six years.

+ More than a decade after most feminists have abandoned the experiment of wearing pants, Lydia Sayer Hasbrouck continues the cause. She takes on the presidency of the somewhat pretentiously named National Dress Reform Association this year, while also publishing the *Sybil*, a dress reform and health journal that she keeps alive for almost a decade—during which she bears three children. Her exceptionally supportive husband established the paper for her when she married him; they live in Middletown, a small town north of New York City.

+ The October issue of *Atlantic Monthly* contains a poem by John Greenleaf Whittier that immediately becomes national lore. It is based on an idea suggested to him by novelist Mrs. E.D.E.N. Southworth, who has heard a story current in her Washington area: an elderly woman, it is said, defiantly flew the Union flag when rebel troops marched past her Fredrick, Maryland, home. Whittier writes:

> Shoot, if you must, this old gray head
> But spare your country's flag, she said.

The subject is 96-year-old Barbara Frietschie (also spelled Frietchie). No evidence exists that the incident actually occurred, and Frietschie died a few months earlier. A demonstration of ostentatious loyalty, however, is particularly plausible because she was a second-generation German and her husband's family had supported Britain in the Revolution. So much isolationist feeling has been aroused by the Know Nothings and other xenophobes that many whose names sound foreign feel obliged to appear especially patriotic.

+ Confederate General Sterling Price writes to Belle Edmondson, who lives in Holly Springs, Mississippi, near Memphis, and has a reputation for smuggling supplies to rebel troops. He tells her that her contributions will "make your name a household word to the Army of the West."

+ While the cold November rain creates seas of blood and mud, "Mother" Mary Ann Bickerdyke is the only woman to nurse almost 2,000 Union casualties in the battles of Lookout Mountain and Missionary Ridge.

1864   Only a few years after women began speaking in public, Anna Dickinson is invited to address the U.S. House, with President Abraham Lincoln in the audience. She is 21 years old.

+ Dr. Mary Walker is captured by Confederates and held as a prisoner of war in Richmond. She remains in prison from April to August, when she is part of a prisoner exchange between the two enemies. Upon her release, she contracts with the army as an "acting assistant surgeon," and goes from Washington to Kentucky and Tennessee.

✦ After three years of repeated arrests, Confederate spy Belle Boyd is finally deported to Canada under pain of death should she return to the United States. A national celebrity at 18, approximately 100 cavalrymen escorted her to her first major prison sentence in 1862. Since then, she has been confined in Boston, New York, and two Washington prisons—and in each, she charmed guards and newspapermen into aiding her.

She will go from Canada to England, where her August wedding, which is attended by high-ranking Confederate officials, makes world news. The groom is a former officer of the U.S. Navy—who was dismissed for his role in one of her earlier escapes.

Doubtless, a man who committed a series of offenses similar to Boyd's would have been executed for treason.

✦ African-American newspaper editor Mary Ann Shadd Cary (whose name changed with an 1856 marriage) leaves the safety of Canada to join the Civil War effort. She is commissioned by the governor of Indiana to recruit black soldiers and also travels for this purpose in Ohio, Pennsylvania, and Michigan. When the war ends, she takes her daughter to Washington, establishes a school, and becomes a leader of Washington blacks.

✦ Some women work as sutlers during the war—itinerant merchants who sell goods to soldiers. Mary Tippee, for example, moves with the 114th Pennsylvania Regiment and keeps the men supplied with tobacco, reading material, and even musical instruments that she scouts on the local market.

✦ The businesswoman most successful at exploiting the war is doubtless Adelicia Acklen, who deceives both Confederate and Union officials to transport 2,000 bales of cotton from her Louisiana plantations to the cotton-hungry mills of Liverpool, England. With her cousin, Sarah Ewing Carter, she sails past embargo barricades and returns to New York with $960,000.

✦ Dr. Clemence S. H. Lozier, an 1852 graduate of Syracuse Medical School, begins her own institution, New York Medical College for Women. The state legislature grants a charter after lobbying that includes Elizabeth Cady Stanton, and the school begins with seven students and eight faculty.

By the time Dr. Lozier dies in 1888, the school will have trained more than 200 physicians; it continues until 1918. This New York school, Dr. Marie Zakrzewska's Boston school, and Woman's College of Pennsylvania, which was begun by Philadelphia Quakers, all predate the medical college of the more famous Drs. Elizabeth and Emily Blackwell.

Meanwhile, African American Rebecca Lee graduates from New England Female Medical School, becoming the first black female physician. She will establish her practice in Richmond, Virginia.

✦ Sojourner Truth, who for the last decade has been based in the Midwest, travels from her home in Battle Creek, Michigan, to be honored by President Lincoln in Washington.

✦ In June, Clara Barton is appointed by General Benjamin Butler as head nurse of his Army of the James. She is officially a nurse for less than a year, for she resigns the following February to begin work on locating missing soldiers.

Instead of the nursing for which she has been stereotypically remembered, Barton's genius is in military bureaucracy. She makes her greatest wartime contributions in supply procurement and in tracing prisoners of war. In the postwar years, Barton will often point out that hundreds of women did more nursing than she did.

✦ Although hopeful of a Southern victory a few months earlier, young Mississippi smuggler Belle Edmondson is more downcast when she writes in her diary on June 30: "We heard the sad fate of two of our friends in Henderson's Scouts, the Yankees hung them . . . Oh! heavenly Father we pray and beseech thee to . . . drive the Enemy from our Soile and give us peace."

✦ Union spy Elizabeth Van Lew is called "Crazy Bet" by her Richmond neighbors; she adopts the mannerisms of insanity so her activities are less questioned. Under this guise, she obtains information that she passes on to Union officials, including advance notice when prisoners of war are scheduled to be moved farther south. She also hides escaped prisoners and helps some of the 109 men who dig a 54-foot tunnel out of captivity. She even digs up the desecrated body of a young Union soldier and ships the boy's corpse home for proper burial.

✦ Lavina Eastlick, one of the survivors of the Minnesota warfare two years ago, publishes *A Personal Narrative of Indian Massacres*. When her band of 34 whites was attacked by 200 warriors, her husband was quickly shot, while she was forced to watch two of her five children brutally beaten to death—by a woman. A third child also died, but her 11-year-old son managed to carry her baby 50 miles to safety, going without food all the while.

Although wounded in four places—including a bullet between her scalp and her skull that she carries the rest of her life—Eastlick shows tremendous fortitude, and a reissue of her saga decades later will describe how she supported her remaining children by farming alone.

✦ Pennsylvania Quakers found Swarthmore College, which is coeducational from the beginning. The indefatigable Lucretia Mott is among the fund-raisers.

✦ The Reverend Augusta Chapin, who has been preaching for five years, finally obtains her first regular pastorate. She will continue as a minister until 1901, ordained by congregations in five midwestern and rural eastern states. The Reverend Chapin remains single and often gives the invocation and benediction at suffrage meetings.

✦ Sculptor Harriet Hosmer sues two London periodicals for libel when they credit her work to a man, and both retract their statements. After the Prince of Wales buys one of her whimsical "Puck" pieces, Hosmer's work becomes sufficiently popular that she maintains homes in Italy and England and remains abroad most of her working life.

✦ In the fall, Rose Greenhow sails home from Scotland—but the ship encounters both a federal gunboat and a furious storm in North Carolina's Cape Fear River and crashes in the night. She demands a rowboat, but that too capsizes in the storm. The men with her swim ashore, but she is weighted down by $2,000 in gold coins under her heavy skirts, and she drowns. Her body is recovered, and on October 1, 1864, Rose Greenhow is given as close to a state funeral as the besieged rebels can manage. They bury her in Wilmington.

✦ Another incident that takes place at sea is never reported except in the feminist press after the war is over: a woman whose name goes unrecorded—probably because she was raped—recaptures a "Union ship" when it is taken by pirates.

The *J.P. Ellicott*, a merchant marine brigantine out of Maine, is sailing in the South Atlantic when pirates overtake it and capture the crew. The mate's wife is aboard, but rather than accept her status as a prize of war, she "succeeded in getting the officers intoxicated, handcuffed them and took possession of the vessel, persuading the crew, who were mostly colored men from St. Thomas, to aid her."

"Having studied navigation with her husband," she reaches St. Thomas, where she turns the men over the U.S. consul, who holds them as prisoners of war. Her name is not released, but feminists conclude: "Had this bold feat been accomplished by a man or boy, the country would have rung with praises of the daring deed."

✦ The *Atlantic Monthly* publishes "Life on the Sea Islands" by African-American educator Charlotte Forten. It is about her wartime experience as a teacher, nurse, and role model for newly freed slaves near Charleston, South Carolina.

✦ *The Gates Ajar*, a first book by 20-year-old Elizabeth Stuart Phelps of Massachusetts, is a bestseller both in the United States and abroad, where it is translated into four languages. Its American popularity may be based its unusual subject matter during this era of wartime grief: in barely novelistic form, Phelps explicates a view of death and afterlife that departs from traditional theology and offers a more comforting humanism. Doubtless her exceptionally mature thoughts are based on the loss of her own lover as he battled for the Union in 1862.

Phelps will never have another similar bestseller, but she supports herself by writing most of the rest of her life. Her second book also has an unconventional topic: *Hedged In* is a sympathetic view of prostitution.

1865 Sarah Palmer, a widow with two daughters, defied community disapproval when she joined her brothers and went South with New York's 109th Regiment in 1862. A Washington-area nurse ever since, she writes: "My work is hard, but the little I can do seems so inefficient. . . . We have twenty-five hundred wounded men in now, some . . . with the most frightful

Pennsylvanian Mother Mary of St. Angela supervises the loading of U.S. Navy hospital ship Red Rover. *Especially on the Mississippi River, such ships carried thousands of wounded men back to the North from Southern battlegrounds. Those staffed by religious sisterhoods not only offered a high standard of nursing, but also brought a new empathy for Catholicism from men who had never before met a nun.* Women in Military Service Memorial; original photograph from the Congregation of the Sisters of the Holy Cross, Saint Mary's, Notre Dame, Indiana

multilations. . . . How our grave-yard fills up!" She makes this diary entry on April 6, and the war ends three days later—but Palmer will stay on until June, nursing these men to a condition in which they are capable of making the trip home.

When the Confederacy surrenders, Mary Ann Bickerdyke is in North Carolina, having just returned South after taking a trainload of wounded men North. The only woman permitted in General Sherman's camps, she spent 1864 caring for the casualties of Chattanooga and Atlanta, and she will be part of Sherman's victorious march into Washington a month later. Respected by Grant and other Union generals, Mother Bickerdyke has seen more major battles than virtually any soldier.

✦ Once again Clara Barton charts new ground, for the military has no systems for dealing with its missing and dead. With President Lincoln's endorsement but with only halfhearted support from the War Department, Barton uses her supply procurement methodology to determine the fates of missing men. She draws up lists, advertises in newspapers, and acts as a clearinghouse for responses—while raising the project's funds, which requires her to make some 300 speeches.

In July, she goes to the notorious prisoner-of-war camp at Andersonville, Georgia, where she supervises the marking of almost 13,000 graves. She then works from an Annapolis office for another three years before the mournful job is over.

✦ When President Lincoln is assassinated a few days after the war ends, he is watching *Our American Cousin,* which is staged by producer Laura Keene. She is in the audience and recognizes actor/assassin John Wilkes Booth.

✦ On July 7, widowed boardinghouse keeper Mary Surratt, age 48, is hanged for complicity in the April assassination of President Lincoln, even though the evidence against her is highly circumstantial. The military tribunal that convicted her repeatedly violated her civil rights, and the defense was so inadequate that her legal counsel read of the guilty verdict in the newspapers. Although the guilty men swear that she is innocent, Surratt is executed along with three of the eight men tried with her.

✦ Four years of warfare have devastated the Southern economy, and many formerly wealthy women find themselves penniless. Even if their homes and crops managed to escape destruction, their investments in Confederate money and bonds are worthless, and, of course, millions of dollars in assets evaporate with the end of slavery. Women whose husbands were military and political leaders not only have no income but also initially are forced into hiding. Their men are guilty of treason, and it will be years before they can resume a normal business life.

Diarist Mary Chesnut is one who finds life shockingly different: Before the war, she was the mistress of five plantations; after it, she is reduced to selling butter that she makes with the help of a black woman. Chesnut's problems are more complicated than those of most other women, for she is childless, and under South Carolina law, her husband's estate will revert to his family when he dies. In this harsh new economy, she works desperately to secure some independent financial means for her inevitable widowhood.

✦ Chesnut's friend Varina Howell Davis, first lady of the defeated Confederate States of America, is in a much worse situation. She flees Richmond in March—along with her four children, two of whom were born during the war. Her husband joins her in Georgia after the rebel surrender, but both are captured in June; initially she is imprisoned alone in Savannah, but next year she will be allowed to join him in prison at Fort Monroe, Virginia.

Like her counterpart Mary Todd Lincoln, Varina Howell Davis suffered the death of a young child during her husband's presidency. Both women also endured hostility from a public that held contradictory views of the proper role of wartime first ladies. Both were criticized no matter what they did: if they did not host traditional entertainments, they were accused of neglecting their duties; if they did, others lambasted them for dancing while men died.

✦ The only woman to have ever received the Congressional Medal of Honor is Dr. Mary Walker, who is awarded the medal late this year for her wartime service and imprisonment. She joins the postwar lecture circuit but soon becomes controversial because of her masculine dress and apparent lesbianism. Although a graduate of a medical school that produced other successful female physicians, she does not practice her profession and eventually alienates even other feminists.

✦ Hundreds of white women go South to teach ex-slaves after the war ends. The largest school that develops is the Abraham Lincoln School in New Orleans; it is conducted in an imposing three-story brick building, but most schools are much smaller.

While some schools operate under the aegis of the Freedmen's Bureau that is created by Congress, many others are run with funds that female educators raise themselves. They teach black men and women the reading, writing, and arithmetic that was illegal for them to know in most slave states.

✦ The Freedmen's Bureau owes its existence in part to the vision of white Ohioan Josephine Griffing, who from Underground Railroad days has been dedicated to the cause of black liberty. She moves to Washington, D.C., when the end of the war is near and lobbies for federal aid to help slaves adjust to freedom; she favors a thoughtful program of locating new jobs and homes for them throughout the North rather than the focus on the South that is the ultimate Reconstruction policy.

The Freedmen's Bureau also becomes more militaristic and bureaucratic than she envisioned, and—despite support from several congressmen who urge a higher rank for her—Griffing is ultimately hired as an assistant to an assistant for the District of Columbia. She works hard there, and when agency aid fades in 1869, she will continue to assist hundreds of ex-slaves who flock to Washington. She raises funds privately and personally escorts groups of blacks to new homes and jobs that she locates in the North.

◆ Vermont's Anna M. Kidder teaches 89 black students of all ages and both genders in Hampton, Virginia, where the freedman school eventually develops into a famous college. She writes home in November that the Confederate woman who owns the mansion where the school is housed is demanding its return: "Mrs. Tyler has sent in for her house and land. She's a roaring Secesh [secessionist] . . . We'll probably go into the Mission or into one of the Hospitals. Mrs. T. has set her foot down that she'll not live in a house contaminated by Yankee schoolmarms. . . . I'm enjoying myself first rate."

◆ An 1857 graduate of New England Female Medical College, Dr. Esther Hill Hawks practices medicine only secondarily; she spends most of the war and Reconstruction years as a teacher and administrator of freedman schools in several towns along the Atlantic coast from South Carolina to northern Florida. Her husband, an army physician husband during the war, resigns his commission at the end and begins developing a colony for freed blacks in southern Florida. The Hawks thus live apart from each other for months at a time—a pattern that will continue until their 20th-century deaths.

More than most, Dr. Esther Hawks uses her position as a freedman school supervisor to work for an integrated society. While visiting her Charleston school months after the end of the war, she writes of a rare success. She hosts a tea for white and black teachers, and says: "I confess to feeling a little *nervous* as to how the thing would go on, but it was unnecessary—for *one* evening, at least, a company of ladies and gentlemen treated each as such without regard to color."

◆ Despite being the author of dozens of books and hundreds of articles, Lydia Maria Child is forced to spend her own money to publish *The Freedman's Book*. Publishers apparently think that newly freed slaves will not buy books and that the abolitionist market is gone now that the war is over. The book is intended as both a teaching tool and an inspiration for ex-slaves who are learning to read, and Child includes many pieces by unknown black writers.

◆ Three years after Mary Jane Patterson set the precedent, Fanny Jackson becomes the nation's second African-American woman to graduate from college. Like Patterson, she was born a slave but grew up free. A Philadelphia aunt purchased her freedom, and after supporting herself as a domestic servant, she studied at Rhode Island Normal School before her admission to Oberlin College.

After a distinguished career as a Philadelphia school administrator, she will marry a minister in 1881. Then, as Fanny Coppin, her educational interests will expand into the foreign missionary field, and she will spend most of the decade prior to her 1913 death in Africa.

◆ Vassar College, which was chartered in 1861 when the war began, opens for classes in Poughkeepsie, New York, with some 300 women enrolled. Founder Matthew Vassar respects women's mental abilities, and he endows a college for women that is intended to recruit those who want a curriculum comparable to that offered at the best male colleges.

During the war, coeducational Bates College in Maine became the first East Coast institution to grant degrees to women, but Vassar quickly becomes the model for eastern women's colleges. Its most eminent faculty mentor is internationally recognized, but self-educated, astronomer Maria Mitchell. She expects her students to be excited about science, and she refuses to enforce traditional rules of feminine behavior—especially the night curfew that is incompatible with studying the stars. Several of Mitchell's students go on to become noted scientists.

◆ Susan and Cyrus Mills—missionaries in Ceylon and Hawaii since 1848—buy Mary Atkins' Benicia Seminary in San Francisco. It eventually will become Mills College, which remains the oldest women's college on the West Coast through the 20th century. Susan Tolman Mills, who was educated under Mary Lyon, will serve as the school's president from 1890 to 1909, when she is 84.

◆ After enduring the death of her entire family— her husband and two children—Helen Hunt

Jackson begins to write in a conscious effort to retain her sanity. Her work appears in national magazines, and Ralph Waldo Emerson soon calls her poetry the best by an American woman. At the same time, her sense of modesty means that she also writes under male pseudonyms for some work.

✦ Mary Mapes Dodge publishes *Hans Brinker; or The Silver Skates*. It becomes a classic of children's literature and goes through more than 100 editions in her lifetime. Dodge moves to New York to join Harriet Beecher Stowe and other women associated with *Hearth and Home* magazine.

✦ When the Iowa State Dental Society has its founding meeting, Lucy Hobbs, who has practiced dentistry there for several years, is included. Though the Ohio College of Dental Surgery rejected her 1861 application, she learned her craft by apprenticing with well-credentialed Ohio men.

Perhaps because her Iowa colleagues treat her as a peer, the school reconsiders, and next year Hobbs will become the first woman to graduate from dental school. After her 1867 marriage, Lucy Hobbs Taylor teaches dentistry to her husband and the two enjoy a lifelong practice in Kansas.

✦ On December 18, the secretary of state announces that the 13th Amendment to the Constitution is officially ratified. The two-sentence amendment abolishes slavery.

1866 With the end of slavery, jubilant abolitionists disband their organizations. The American Anti-Slavery Society unanimously votes to merge with the Women's Rights Society, and the leaders of both organizations now transfer their activism into the formation of the American Equal Rights Association. The group aims to secure civil rights for ex-slaves and for women of both races.

The election of Lucretia Mott as president of the new organization initially reassures Susan Anthony and others who fear that women's legal status will not be treated as seriously as that of black men, but tension between these two priorities exists from the beginning. Anthony does not hide her disdain for those in the movement who wish to concentrate on granting the vote to illiterate male ex-slaves while denying it to educated women.

Wendell Phillips, who loses his position as president of the Anti-Slavery Society with the merger, argues that "this is the Negro's hour" and is distinctly cool to the women. Tension between the two factions will increase after Congress passes the 14th Amendment and sends it to the states for ratification.

✦ On May 2, black women are among the targets of white men during a Memphis riot. The title of an illustration in *Harper's Weekly* is "Shooting down negroes."

✦ In June, a Congress that does not yet include representation from the Confederate states adopts the 14th Amendment, a five-part amendment that Southern states will be required to ratify before they are readmitted to the Union. Intended to grant civil rights to ex-slaves, the amendment's first section is gender-neutral: it says that, except for Indians, "All persons born or naturalized in the United States . . . are citizens" and that states may not deprive any "person" of rights without "due process" and must offer "equal protection of the laws."

The next section, however, details the way in which states may be punished by losing representation in Congress if they deny the vote to "any of the male inhabitants," and the fine print of the amendment thus excludes women. Most people never notice either of these subtleties, for public discussion centers on other provisions punishing Southerners for the rebellion.

During the next two years, several border states reject the amendment and Southern states accept it only under duress—so abolitionists insist that the ratification drive requires support from women, even if they are excluded from its benefits.

✦ Frank Moore publishes *Women of the War*, in which he asserts that "hundreds" of graves marked "unknown" were actually "those of women obliged by army regulations to fight in disguise." He describes female soldiers who served for both the North and the South. Other contemporary writers also record many cases of female soldiers: upon the discovery of her gender, a woman in Iowa's 14th Regiment "placed the muzzle of her revolver to her head, fired, and fell dead on open parade-ground." Her true identity was never learned.

✦ The Young Women's Christian Association is formally organized in Boston, bringing together disparate efforts that had existed in major cities since 1855. The YWCA's origin was directly related to the need for women to travel during the Civil War, for its primary purpose is to provide safe and hospitable accommodations at a time when many hotel operators believe that any woman without male escort is a prostitute.

✦ In San Francisco, Mary Ellen Pleasant successfully sues for the right of African Americans to ride the city's streetcars. A boardinghouse keeper who knows some of the city's most powerful men, she will be in and out of the public eye for 50 years.

✦ Fisk University begins in Nashville, setting a model for higher education among African Americans. Unlike most white colleges, those for blacks are almost always coeducational.

✦ After studying at the Pennsylvania Academy of Fine Arts, young Philadelphian Mary Cassatt obtains parental permission to go to Paris. Except for short visits back home, she will remain in France the rest of her life. Cassatt studies painting in Italy, the Netherlands, and Spain; with Edgar Degas as her advocate, she is considered one of the pioneers of the impressionist school of art.

✦ Although some think the honor should go to established sculptor Harriet Hosmer, 18-year-old Vinnie Ream wins the first federal art commission granted a woman. Ream, who worked as a Washington postal clerk during the Civil War, has been sculpting only a few years, but was fortunate enough to have Abraham Lincoln pose for her prior to his death.

Mary Todd Lincoln is among those who regard Ream as too inexperienced for the job. The former first lady—always likely to be jealous of other women—predicts that the work will be "nothing but a mortifying failure," but Ream soon proves her critics wrong. Armed with a $10,000 commission to turn her clay model into marble, she goes to Italy to work; five years later, her full-size statue is unveiled in the Capitol Rotunda, where it remains through the 20th century.

✦ Harriet Beecher Stowe publishes a series of articles and books under the pseudonym Christopher Crowfield. Assuming this male anonymity gives her the freedom to write without reader prejudice based on her gender or on her previous work—and she needs the money.

Despite the huge sales of *Uncle Tom's Cabin*, copyright law is so poorly enforced that, only five years after building a Hartford, Connecticut, mansion, Stowe will have to sell it at a loss. She writes furiously for the rest of her life to earn enough to support her retired husband, unmarried daughters, and a son whose wartime experience drives him to alcoholism.

✦ The literary world takes little notice of war, and women continue to write best-sellers. Between that of Charles Dickens in 1861 and Lewis Carroll in 1866 are books by Mrs. E.D.E.N. Southworth and Mary Mapes Dodge, the best-selling authors of 1863 and 1865. Carroll and Dickens, of course, go on to classical fame, while Southworth and Dodge are assigned to future obscurity; presumably the reading public somehow lost its discernment after *A Tale of Two Cities* but recovered it for *Alice's Adventures in Wonderland*.

✦ Despite the presence of Catholicism in Florida since the founding of St. Augustine in 1565, the state gets its first convent only now: the Sisters of Saint Joseph, a French-based order, establish themselves at St. Augustine.

✦ In an attempt to draw attention to the exclusion of women from the proposed 14th Amendment that will grant civil rights to black men, Elizabeth Cady Stanton runs for Congress in the fall elections as an Independent. Running from New York City, where the Stantons have recently moved, she receives just 24 of approximately 12,000 votes.

✦ While the Stanton household establishes itself in Manhattan, Susan Anthony moves into a brick house at 17 Madison Street in Rochester, New York. It will remain her home for 40 years, until she dies in a second-floor bedroom in 1906. Visitors are more likely to find her sister, Mary S. Anthony, at home, for Susan Anthony travels much of the year; in particular, she spends winters in Washington when Congress is in session.

1867 In January, the House votes on enfranchisement of women in the District of Columbia; there are 49 positive votes and 74 negative ones, while 68 congressmen do not bother to record their views.

✦ Women's rights leaders converge on Kansas, where a referendum on suffrage is being held. Lucy Stone and her husband, Henry Blackwell, are the first to go west to work for equal voting rights for women and blacks; they are followed by the Reverend Olympia Brown, Susan Anthony, and Elizabeth Cady Stanton, who is taking her first long trip away from her seven children. They endure primitive conditions traveling to small audiences, and Anthony finds bedbugs so prevalent that she tries sleeping in her carriage— where fleas keep her awake.

Although they work hard and although Kansas women have been voting in school elections for six years, the effort to extend that right to all elections is not successful. The women's plank wins about 9,000 of 30,000 votes, and the freedmen do only slightly better. Elizabeth Cady Stanton will nonetheless term 9,000 votes a "victory," for she sees it as a herald of better times.

✦ When Mary Surratt's son John returns from hiding in Canada and is tried for complicity in the assassination of President Lincoln, his mother's innocence is clear. The prosecution drops its case against John Surratt after a majority of the jury votes for his acquittal, even though the evidence against him is far stronger than that which sent his mother to the gallows.

✦ Bostonian Ednah Cheney endows educational projects for freed slaves, sponsoring teachers who go South and later making major contributions to Hampton and Tuskegee institutes, despite her hesitation about thus encouraging racial segregation. Cheney is also one of the "lady managers" of the New England Hospital for Women, and she will be a founder of the Association for the Advancement of Women.

During the next decades, Cheney will make still another important contribution by publishing biographical memoirs of women who might otherwise be forgotten. Among the contemporaries whom she honors this way are Boston physician Susan Dimock and school board officials Lucretia Crocker and Abby W. May.

✦ At the same time that women go to the South to teach in freedman schools, thousands of others go west to the new schools of pioneer towns. Eliza Stewart is one of many possible examples. The valedictorian of her class at Pennsylvania's Washington Female Seminary, she travels alone to Laramie, Wyoming, where she and one other teacher will open the city's first public school in 1869.

The influence of these numerous but anonymous women is tremendous: in both the South and the West, they educate millions of children— but they also teach a view of American history that emphasizes the Pilgrim heritage and diminishes the importance of other cultures.

✦ Rebecca Cole becomes the second credentialed African-American female physician. After her graduation this year from Woman's Medical College of Pennsylvania, she will work with Drs. Elizabeth and Emily Blackwell in New York. Elizabeth Blackwell will recollect: "We established a sanitary visitor. This post was filled by one of our assistant physicians, whose special duty it was to give simple, practical instruction to poor mothers. . . . An intelligent young coloured physician, Dr. Cole, who was one of our resident assistants, carried on this work with tact and care."

After this training, Dr. Cole goes south to serve the medical needs of newly freed slaves in Columbia, South Carolina. She returns to Philadelphia to practice and her long career finally ends in Washington, D.C., where prior to her 1922 death, she is employed by the federal government to work with indigents.

+ Dr. Marie Zakrzewska, who heads the New England Female Medical College, manages to get clinical practice for some of her students at the prestigious Massachusetts General Hospital. One of them, Susan Dimock, is so obviously talented that Swiss physicians admit her for further study at the University of Zurich next year.

+ Mary Harris Jones loses her entire family—her husband and four children—in a Memphis yellow fever epidemic. Influenced by the links that her ironworker husband had to the nascent labor movement, after a decade of struggling to eke out a living as a Chicago seamstress, "Mother Jones" will dedicate her life to labor reform. She will work almost entirely with men, especially miners, and disdains suffrage as an upper-class cause.

+ Decades prior to any other state, Wisconsin passes a maximum hours law for women; the legislative intent is to protect mothers and potential mothers from overwork.

Germans who settled in Milwaukee after their unsuccessful 1848 revolution doubtless are a factor in creating the atmosphere for such progressive legislation. Mathilde Annecke continues to write for liberal German newspapers, and two years from now, she will be a founder of the Wisconsin branch of Susan Anthony's National Woman Suffrage Association.

+ Congress establishes Howard University in Washington. Named for the head of the Freedmen's Bureau, it is intended to make college accessible to blacks—but a number of white women enroll because they also are barred from other colleges.

A few years later, however, Howard officials will refuse to admit Belva McNall Lockwood to the law school, on the grounds that this white, middle-age school administrator will be distracting to young men. She has moved to Washington from western New York and runs a coeducational school, still an uncommon position for a woman.

+ More than two centuries after her death, a complete collection of work by colonial poet Anne Bradstreet is finally published. Even so, it is impossible to know her mature ability, for a house fire when she was 54 doubtless destroyed many poems. Although a 1650 volume that was printed without her knowledge was deemed an international success, Bradstreet was too modest to allow anything more to be published in her lifetime, and thus few Americans realize that she is the nation's first published poet of either gender.

+ When Harper & Brothers begin their long-running magazine, *Harper's Bazaar*, they hire translator and author Mary Louise Booth as editor. They are so pleased with her that, during her 22 years in this top position, Booth eventually earns the fabulous sum of $4,000 annually.

+ Louisa May Alcott works as an editor for *Merry Museum*, a magazine for girls. She prefers to write for boys and reluctantly tackles a girls' book at the urging of her publisher.

+ Civil War nurse Sarah Palmer is one of the first to publish her wartime memoirs. Called *Aunt Beckey's Army Life*, it ends by detailing her experience collecting 10 months of overdue pay (at $12 per month). She says that she "found it necessary to sit all day in the Department of the Treasury waiting for the cashier to decide to release the wages."

+ Sarah Brock Putnam publishes *Richmond During the War*, the first of a slowly expanding stream of diaries and recollections by Confederate women. Most such works will not be published until the 20th century, when the Southern economy is more financially sound; throughout that century, similar books will add to national knowledge of life during this troubled time.

+ The invention of the typewriter this year will hugely affect women's lives—but not for a decade or two. Like most major innovations, men control the machine until the novelty wears off.

◆ The 1846 patent that Elias Howe had obtained for his still-imperfect sewing machine expires; with further ideas contributed by Isaac Singer and others, the sewing machine becomes common in the postwar era. It not only alleviates the drugery of this endless household task, but it also will create millions of jobs for women in the mass production of garments.

◆ Tensions between the women and men of the Equal Rights Society continue to build at this year's convention. Ex-slave Fredrick Douglass argues that the organizational priorities should be "first negro suffrage, then temperance, then the eight-hour movement, then woman suffrage."

1868 In January, Elizabeth Cady Stanton and Susan Anthony begin publishing a weekly paper from New York called *The Revolution*. Its slogan is "Men, Their Rights, and Nothing More: Women, Their Rights and Nothing Less." Other goals are outlined on the masthead: The paper supports "educated suffrage, irrespective of color or sex," as well as an eight-hour day and equal pay for equal work. At least a dozen other positions are taken on nonfeminist issues, and a subscription is $2 annually.

The publication quickly succeeds in getting the attention of the established press—and even though most of the response is negative, mainstream papers spread the women's ideas even as they ridicule them. The *New York Independent* is one of the more complimentary when it says, "*The Revolution* will arouse, thrill, edify, amuse, vex, and nonplus its friends. But it will compel attention; it will conquer a hearing."

Stanton does much of the writing, while Anthony serves as publisher. They receive financing from George Francis Train and are thus obligated to publish his eccentric writing on issues unrelated to women's rights—ideas that are often so unconventional that they do great harm to the women's issues. Harriet Beecher Stowe offers to write for the *The Revolution* if Stanton and Anthony will change its name, but they refuse.

◆ Stanton is also vice president of the Equal Rights Society, and she presides over this year's convention. The meeting is again a tense one, and Anthony and Stanton are bitterly attacked by former abolitionists when they refuse to give civil rights for black men priority over women's issues.

Several old friendships are torn in debates on the society's priorities during its brief existence. Mary Livermore, for example, will accuse Stanton of acting in an undemocratic fashion while presiding: "It certainly requires a great amount of nerve to talk before you," Livermore says, "for you have such a frankness in expressing yourself that I am afraid of you."

◆ Typesetting for *The Revolution* is done by Augusta Lewis (later Troup), who lost her job the previous year in a conflict between management and the all-male typographers union. In September, Anthony and Stanton aid her in organizing the Working Women's Association, and women from this new group are included as delegates to the convention of the nascent National Labor Union. The convention accepts their resolutions for an eight-hour day and—more surprisingly—equal pay for equal work by women. It rejects a resolution on behalf of the vote for women.

◆ The Working Women's Association is not merely a union, but also a feminist social action group. It intervenes this year in the case of Hester Vaughn, who had been sentenced to die for infanticide. A recent immigrant from England, Vaughn had been raped, and she alleges that the baby died while she was alone and sick after delivery. The association brings in Dr. Clemence Lozier to provide medical proof, and the governor quietly pardons Vaughn—despite the sentencing judge's admonition that because "infanticide is increasing, some women must be made an example of."

◆ Former Civil War nurse Myra Bradwell begins publishing the *Chicago Legal News*. Her attorney husband is supportive, but she handles both the editorial and business aspects of publishing this court-record newspaper, which becomes vital to practicing lawyers throughout the nation. The following year, Bradwell will pass the Illinois bar exam, but the state's Supreme Court refuses to admit a woman—especially a married woman, whose legal rights are limited—to the practice of law. She appeals.

At the same time in nearby Missouri, men associated with prestigious Washington University in St. Louis are looking for a woman capable of setting the precedent for a coeducational law school. Encouraged by a family friend who is a judge, Phoebe Couzins successfully applies for admission.

Couzins will be joined by a second woman, Lemma Barkeloo of Brooklyn, New York. Like Couzins, she is unmarried and wealthy, and she moves to St. Louis for the law school opportunity. Barkeloo will be admitted to the bar in 1870—a few months prior to her death.

♦ New York City women form Sorosis, the nation's first club for professional women, after journalist Jane Cunningham Croly is excluded from a press club function for author Charles Dickens.

Because women's opportunities for personal growth and intellectual stimulation are rare, the response is enthusiastic, and by the end of the year, 83 women have paid the $5 annual dues—an amount equivalent to average female weekly wages. Meetings are held at famous Delmonico's Restaurant, but female presence in restaurants without male escort is unconventional and the group is widely criticized.

♦ The New England Women's Club begins in Boston. Its founders include Julia Ward Howe and other women who have both literary and political credentials. With the initial meeting hosted by Dr. Harriot K. Hunt, the club will provide a forum for women who were excluded from colleges in their youth. They present papers and share ideas, and several club members are publicly praised by the era's eminent male Bostonians. The president until 1871 will be Caroline Severance, and under her leadership, the club works for the establishment of Girls Latin School and the election of women to the Boston school board. Howe in particular launches a career of national lectures on the importance of female association via clubs.

♦ As head of the Civil War's Sanitary Commission for the Midwest, Mary Livermore has seen the need of political equality for women. She founds the Illinois Suffrage Association, serves as its president, and publishes a newspaper called *The Agitator*. The following year, she will join Julia Ward Howe and Lucy Stone in forming the American Woman Suffrage Association; they offer her the editorship of the AWSA's news organ, and she moves to Boston, bringing along much of her midwestern readership.

♦ Lydia Maria Child returns to the theme of her first book, written almost a half century earlier, when she publishes *An Appeal for the Indians*. Once again her cause is not popular, for the nation will remain actively at war with several tribes for decades.

♦ Sisters Victoria Woodhull and Tennessee (sometimes spelled Tennie C.) Claflin move to New York and begin a decade that makes them nationally notorious. Their past lives include divorce and arrest, but they are beautiful and very intelligent, and they successfully attach themselves to railroad magnate Cornelius Vanderbilt. With his mentorship, they establish a brokerage that soon makes them the envy of Wall Street males.

♦ Dressmaker and former slave Elizabeth Keckley publishes *Behind the Scenes* about her experience as Mary Todd Lincoln's maid and confidante. The book is actually ghostwritten (some say by one of two men, but others believe it was by Jane Swisshelm), and the semiliterate Keckley cannot control its content. Although she later says that she intended to portray the Lincolns sympathetically, it has the opposite effect. Most blacks believe she has betrayed the dead president, whom they idolize, while her white clientele fears she can no longer be trusted. Her business drops dramatically and she lives the rest of her long life in poverty, dying in a Washington home for the destitute in 1907.

♦ "Patience on a Monument" is the title of a *Harper's Weekly* drawing that depicts a black woman and her children dead at the monument's base. Indeed, the end of slavery means that racism is perhaps even more bold, as white mobs attack the homes of blacks in Memphis and New Orleans. Newspapers speak in violent terms against the freed slaves, warning them that, "like the Indians," they could be "exterminated." Another aspect of the *Harper's* drawing alludes to dangers particular to women: "Daughters, Mothers, Wives, and Sisters Ruined."

♦ Anna Dickinson continues to be so popular a lecturer that she earns as much as $20,000 annually—a tremendous income for the era. Some of her topics border on salacious, as she speaks on subjects such as polygamy and venereal disease. She also writes a novel on interracial marriage and will be a vice president of Susan Anthony's National Woman Suffrage Association.

Her correspondence with Anthony uses the "thee" and "thou" of their mutual Quakerism, and they become such good friends that Anthony calls the young woman "Chicky Dicky."

♦ Drs. Elizabeth and Emily Blackwell open a medical school for women in conjunction with their New York Infirmary. Its uncommonly high standards include entrance exams and graduate exams that are administered by nonfaculty; the result is that women training there receive a better education than most male physicians.

The school will soon be run solely by Emily Blackwell, for Elizabeth moves aboard permanently to teach at the new London School of Medicine for Women. As early as 1851, America's first female physician had expressed her desire to further medical education for women in England.

♦ White abolitionists Sarah Grimké and Angelina Grimké Weld discover that two young men studying at a Pennsylvania school for blacks are their nephews: their South Carolina brother has fathered two sons with a slave woman, and the boys use the Grimké name. The sisters welcome them into their home and assist with their educa-tions; both go on to be well-known professionals and civil rights leaders.

♦ Zion's Co-operative Mercantile Institution begins in Salt Lake City. Unlike the usual practice, Mormon leader Brigham Young insists that women work as clerks; men, he argues, should be "producers" or farmers, while women are natural "traders." When ZCMI celebrates its 100th birthday in 1968, it will term itself America's oldest department store.

♦ In the November election, 172 women, including four blacks, cast ballots in Vineland, New Jersey; they are placed in a separate box because it is assumed that they will not be counted. The women believe they have a right to vote under the language of the recently passed 14th Amendment, which says that "all persons born or naturalized in the United States . . . are citizens" entitled to "equal protection of the laws." Officials point to the word "male" in the second section, a section that the women argue applies only to those states that rebelled.

♦ The first women organize in opposition to suffrage this year; 200 women from Lancaster, Massachusetts, send a petition to their legislature. They do not want the vote, they say, because "it would diminish the purity, the dignity, and the moral influence of women."

1869 In February, Congress passes the 15th Amendment, a two-sentence provision that spells out voting rights for ex-slaves, and thus brings to a head the divisions within the Equal Rights Society. As Susan Anthony and Elizabeth Cady Stanton feared, the group prioritizes black men and endorses the amendment without concern for its apparent exclusion of women. After a stormy argument with the male leadership, Anthony and Stanton form the National Woman Suffrage Association (NWSA) in May.

They do not invite the more moderate women in the Equal Rights Association to join them, however, and conspiratorial rumors circulate for months about this internecine conflict. In November, Lucy Stone, Julia Ward Howe, Harriet

Beecher Stowe, and other moderates of the Equal Rights Society respond by creating the American Woman Suffrage Association (AWSA). Until the groups merge again in 1890, there will be two major women's organizations, and they will engage in destructive rivalry.

With Howe as its first president, the AWSA is centered in Boston; it includes men, publishes the literary-quality *Woman's Journal*, and emphasizes state campaigns for the vote instead of an amendment to the federal constitution. It focuses on the vote and is careful to avoid divorce reform and other issues that distract from the political possibility of getting the vote.

Stanton presides over the NWSA, which is centered in New York and Washington; it has little place for men and publishes the controversial and debt-ridden *Revolution*, which includes such distracting issues as vegetarianism and "free love." The NWSA makes a point of holding its conventions in Washington, D.C., thus demonstrating its federal strategy. It also takes the radical position of opposing the 15th Amendment, thus splitting from former abolitionist friends.

The ever-popular, serene Philadelphia Quaker Lucretia Mott is one of the few who remains esteemed by both factions.

✦ At the last meeting before the Equal Rights Association disbands, Mathilde Annecke speaks in German and Jeanne de Hericourt speaks in French. Madame de Hericourt submits a far-sighted resolution to the body, which calls for "a League of all women claiming their rights, both in America and Europe." Her six-point platform includes a proposal for annual meetings to help end the prejudices that cause war and thoughtfully foreshadows modern cultural exchanges by proposing international exhibits of art by women. Her innovative resolution is lost amid the dissolution of the organization.

✦ One of those attending the first convention of the American Woman Suffrage Association is Olive Logan, who has been on international stages since infancy. At age 30, she realizes that she does not particularly enjoy acting and spends the next decades as a successful lecturer and translator of French plays; she also writes a half-dozen novels that explicate women's issues. The new organization welcomes her celebrity.

✦ In San Francisco, Emily Pitt Stevens is an avid reader of the NWSA's *Revolution*. The holder of a "propriety interest in the *San Francisco Mercury*," she becomes the sole proprietor this year, changes its name to *The Pioneer*, and begins editorial support of the suffrage movement. She serves as a founder of California's suffrage organization this year, which she calls "the first association for this purpose on the Pacific coast."

The membership of the new organizations includes admirers of both NWSA and AWSA leaders, and when they cannot agree on which of the two national groups to affiliate with, they resolve to remain independent. The action presages a trend, for western women will continue to be markedly independent of national movements.

The California women begin lobbying their legislature for the vote and other causes. Some of the leadership even crosses the border to Nevada, where Laura de Force Gordon will speak to the legislature in 1871. The men assembled in Carson City defeat her proposed suffrage amendment by just two votes.

✦ The war has opened enough government jobs to women that the Spencerian Business College in Washington establishes a "ladies department." It is headed by Ellen Spencer, a sister of the owner, who has been educated in various midwestern schools, including the historic Oberlin College. As Ellen Spencer Mussey, she will begin a law school for Washington women in 1898.

✦ When Union General Ulysses S. Grant becomes president in March, one of his first acts is to reward Elizabeth Van Lew for the sacrifice of wealth and social status that she made for the Union. He appoints her postmistress of Richmond, Virginia.

✦ Also in March, periodicals from *The Revolution* to *Harper's* cover the story of expert rower Ida Lewis' rescue of two drowning sailors during a blustering storm in Newport, Rhode Island. This feat, however, is far from new: Lewis has saved at least eight victims of boating accidents during the last decade, after taking over her invalid father's duties as the keeper of the Lime Rock lighthouse.

Yet it will be another decade (and seven years after her father's death) before the federal government acknowledges her work and officially grants Lewis the position. Two year later, she is honored with a gold medal by Congress after she saves more men—when she is almost 40.

✦ Myra Bradwell's appeal to the Illinois Supreme Court for admission to the bar is denied, although the court must use painfully tortured reasoning to reach its lengthy conclusion. The opinion immediately concedes that Bradwell "earnestly and ably maintained" her argument in her written appeal, and even adds that "of the qualifications of the applicant we have no doubt." Bradwell's overriding disability, in the court's view, is that she has had the bad sense to marry.

✦ Shoemakers organize the first national labor union exclusive to women. They call themselves the Daughters of St. Crispin, the patron saint of shoemakers; by the end of the year, they have 24 chapters, including three in Canada. Delegates to the first convention in Lynn, Massachusetts, come from as far as San Francisco.

✦ About 400 women strike the laundries centered in Troy, New York, while some 800 women who work in the textile mills of Dover, New Hampshire, also strike.

✦ While Susan Anthony was admitted to last year's convention of the National Labor Union, this year she is refused credentials by the Working Women's Association. She and her typesetter friends have quarreled over the primacy of union activity vs. suffrage activity, and the New York women block her admittance when the union meets in Philadelphia.

The women, meanwhile, transform themselves to Women's Typographical Union No. 1, with Augusta Lewis as president. The following year, Lewis will be elected corresponding secretary of the International Typographical Union;

for many years that is one of the highest positions granted a woman in the mostly male craft unions.

✦ Dr. Clara Swain graduates from Woman's Medical College of Pennsylvania and sails for India under the aegis of the Woman's Foreign Missionary Society of the Methodist Episcopal Church. She will build public health services in northern India near the borders of Nepal and China, riding an elephant to remote villages. For the rest of the century, she will work against the religious seclusion of women that limits their mobility, and she particularly speaks out against the common practice of killing baby girls.

✦ Hannah Tracy Cutler, who has been an active midwestern feminist from 1846, earns a degree from Cleveland Medical School. Dr. Cutler will practice medicine for the next two decades in Cobden, Illinois, and Brentwood, California. Like Caroline Severance, Amanda Way, and other women's rights leaders, she moves to California late in life to join her adult children.

✦ Amateur architect Harriet Morrison Irwin of Charlotte, North Carolina, patents her design for a hexagonal house. She has read widely in architecture and believes that her design offers greater openness and better access to the outdoors, especially for invalids such as herself. Her house plans are offered for sale in magazine advertisements.

✦ Iowa is the first state to admit a woman to the bar. Arabella Mansfield's admission is arranged by a judge who believes in equal rights, even though Mansfield does not intend to practice law. Instead, she has a long career as a professor and administrator at colleges in Iowa and Indiana.

The judge interprets the masculine pronouns in the Iowa statutes on bar admission to be gender-inclusive, and the legislature soon follows up on the case by amending the law. The fact that Mansfield is married seems of no importance in Iowa, while in neighboring Illinois, Myra Bradwell's married state is a critical disability.

✦ "Good-bye woodsheds, good-bye ash-sifters, good-bye stove dust," enthuses the female editor of the Oneida colony's newsletter, as these imagi native utopians install a central heating system in their imposing three-story brick Mansion House. Among other ingenious devices that Oneida women enjoy are steam cookers, dumbwaiters, a washing machine, a mechanical potato peeler, and even "Turkish baths." The colony also becomes known for the first Lazy Susan, and the women wear what they call "the final shoe," which is designed for comfort instead of style.

✦ *Little Women* is published in two parts during this and the previous year. Although Louisa May Alcott's editors suspect that there is a market for a book about girls, they are astounded by its size: bookstores have trouble keeping it in stock, and the story quickly becomes a national classic.

✦ Harriet Beecher Stowe creates an international fracas when she writes in *Atlantic* magazine that long-dead poet Lord Byron had been guilty of incest. The literati of England and America respond furiously; her British sales are seriously hurt, while 15,000 readers cancel their *Atlantic* subscriptions. Although what she wrote was true, Stowe is condemned as both prurient and prudish, while her criticism of Byron's behavior is ignored.

✦ Mary Surratt's daughter receives permission to give her mother's bones a proper burial. Surratt had been executed four years earlier because boarders in the roominghouse that she kept were involved in a conspiracy to kidnap or kill not only President Lincoln but also members of his cabinet. Her body is returned from the infamy of Old Capitol Prison to internment in Washington's Mount Olivet Cemetery. Ironically, Surratt's initial gravesite will be the site of a new building for the Supreme Court in the 20th century.

✦ On December 10, the women of Wyoming Territory become the first in the nation to have an unqualified right to vote. Additional constitutional assurances include the rights to sue, own property, enter into contracts, and conduct business on the same terms as men. Territorial law even provides equal pay for women and men in public employment.

1870 The first issue of the *Woman's Journal* appears in January, sponsored by the American Woman Suffrage Association, and timed to coincide with the second anniversary of *The Revolution*, the publication of the rival National Woman Suffrage Association.

The *Woman's Journal* is a quality magazine that includes Harriet Beecher Stowe and Louisa May Alcott among its supporters, and it will continue until 1917. After Mary Livermore ends her initial editorship in 1872, it is edited primarily by Lucy Stone, her husband, Henry Blackwell, and their daughter, Alice Stone Blackwell. Long-time newspaper publisher Jane Swisshelm also contributes articles.

The Revolution, in contrast, goes bankrupt within the year, and Susan Anthony embarks on a lecture tour to pay its bills. That she is increasingly popular is clear from the fact that she charges a $75 speaking fee and pays the $10,000 debt within six years. While newspapers reviewing Anthony's speeches are usually scornful of her ideas, even that publicity promotes the cause. Thousands of women hear her and begin to form their own follow-up networks.

✦ On February 14, Esther Morris becomes the nation's first female government official when the governor of the Wyoming Territory appoints her justice of the peace for South Pass City. A gold-mining boom town, it is the largest in the territory and a challenge to any officer. Her six-foot height doubtless is helpful in making her an effective authority figure, and she draws national attention. Morris handles as many as 70 cases without a reversal by higher courts, but after issuing a warrant against her husband for assault in June 1871, she moves on to Laramie, where she turns down a nomination for the state legislature on the slate of a nascent women's party.

✦ The 15th Amendment receives final ratification on March 30. Now women can indisputably argue that their right to vote should be included in the language covering ex-slaves, for the amendment reads in its entirety: "The right of citizens of the United States to vote shall not be denied or abridged by the United States or by any State on account of race, color, or previous condition of servitude."

A number of women begin testing the gender-neutral "citizen." During the next two years, approximately 150 women will attempt to vote in almost a dozen different jurisdictions ranging from Delaware to California. The first this year is Marilla Ricker, a young and wealthy widow in Dover, New Hampshire. Her ballot is initially accepted but then rejected; she considers suing town officials but is dissuaded by their Republican friends. The case generates generally respectful press attention in New Hampshire.

Among the most famous of the women attempting to vote are early abolitionists Angelina Grimké Weld and her sister Sarah Grimké, who is nearly 80. They go to the polls with a group of their neighbors in the Hyde Park section of Boston, where they moved in 1863. While Massachusetts by this time is proud of its abolitionist history, women's rights are not seen as analogous, and the idealistic sisters meet with the same obduracy that greeted them 30 years earlier on the slavery issue. Many women are especially chagrined that illiterate men are entitled to vote, especially in the case of Irish immigrants who not only are ignorant of American history but also rioted against the Union during the Civil War.

Even in South Carolina, a few black women, protected by Reconstruction officials, cast ballots.

◆ In March, for the first time in the history of jurisprudence, women serve on juries in the Wyoming Territory—to the delight of cartoonists back East, who find the idea hilarious. The reaction in Wyoming is the opposite, for as recently as 1868, the West remained so wild that no jury of Laramie men was willing to convict "even those captured in the commission of their crimes."

The first grand jury called after the new legislation includes six women. The first to be summoned is an unmarried schoolteacher; the others are a young widow and four women who are respectively married to a physician, a merchant, and two government clerks. The oldest woman is

40 and the youngest 22. The grand jury meets for three weeks and hears cases ranging from murder to illegal branding. The judge assures the women on the first day, "You shall not be driven by sneers, jeers, and insults from the temple of justice, as your sisters have from some of the Medical Colleges of the land."

Despite the incredulity of newsmen, Laramie's law enforcement officials clearly consider the experiment a success, and seven women are included in the follow-up petit jury. The sheriff also appoints a female bailiff: Martha Boies is the first woman in the world to hold this position.

◆ Women in the Utah Territory, who were enfranchised a few months after Wyoming women, are the first to cast ballots when their territory holds municipal elections. Leaders note that this first election in which women vote is marked by a solemnity and respect for the process that had been missing in earlier elections, which were routinely disrupted by the all-male electorate.

In the fall, Eliza A. Swain is the first woman in the world to vote in a general election. Laramie men open the polls early for her, as an honor for this "white-haired housewife, Quakerish in appearance."

◆ Abigail Scott Duniway begins the Oregon Equal Rights Society. She had emigrated West in 1852, taught school, married, bore six children, and sold thousands of pounds of handmade butter annually; when her investment was beginning to pay off, her husband lost their farm by cosigning a loan for a friend without her knowledge. After he is disabled, she will earn the family income in various creative ways, including arranging lectures for Susan Anthony in return for "one-half the gross proceeds."

Duniway's primary occupation, however, will be as publisher of the *New Northwest*, a newspaper that she establishes in Portland next year. Although it competes with her brother's paper, Duniway is sufficiently skilled as an editor and publisher that the newspaper supports her family for 16 years. It will go bankrupt soon after she sells it.

+ Emulating New York's Vassar College, Wellesley College is founded in Wellesley, Massachusetts. It is endowed with a 400-acre, million-dollar campus by Henry Fowle Durant, and its matriculation requirements are similar to those of nearby Harvard. Some 300 women enroll in its first classes, but unlike Vassar, Wellesley has female presidents from its earliest years.

  At the same time, the midwestern universities of Michigan and Illinois, as well as Ohio State University, become coeducational. Medical schools at the universities of California, Iowa, and Michigan accept their first women.

  Much later, Dr. Elizabeth Mosher will write: "I well remember the day we read in the Boston papers that the University of Michigan had opened its doors to women in all departments. We five young women joined hands and danced around the table. We all went to that college and graduated from there with a degree of M.D."

+ Matilda Joselyn Gage, an officer in the National Woman Suffrage Association, publishes *Woman as Inventor*, which shows her expertise in women's history. The following year, she publishes *Woman's Rights Catechism*, and by the end of her life, she will have moved far beyond her feminist friends in her advanced thought, as *The Dangers of the Hour* (1890) presages modern feminist theory. All the while, Gage remains happily married to a freethinking merchant and is the mother of five.

+ Former textile mill worker Lucy Larcom does most of the editing of three anthologies that are published this decade under the name of her friend John Greenleaf Whittier. After leaving the mills at age 22, she educated herself in Illinois and has taught there and in Massachusetts.

+ Louisa May Alcott does not rest on the laurels of *Little Women*, but writes constantly during this decade. Among her best books for children are *An Old Fashioned Girl* (1870), *Little Men* (1871), *Eight Cousins* (1875), and *Rose in Bloom* (1876). She also writes two novels aimed at adults: *Work* (1873) and *A Modern Mephistopheles* (1877).

+ Kate Field is a London correspondent for the *New York Tribune*. She will follow a career in journalism and lecturing for the next three decades, including publishing her own highly personalized newspaper, *Kate Field's Washington*, from 1890 to 1895. A well-traveled social and political liberal, Field nonetheless will not endorse suffrage until three years prior to her 1896 death.

+ The federal Bureau of Education hires Pike's Peak climber Julia A. Holmes, who has been living in Taos, New Mexico, as a translator after she moves to Washington, D.C. When she resigns in 1887, she is chief of the Division of Spanish Correspondence.

+ Wells College drops the "female seminary" name that it used when it was chartered just two years ago. Located in the same Finger Lakes district of western New York that is home to Susan Anthony and other feminists, it will remain single-sex and educate many of the future's female leaders.

+ Freedman school teacher Anna M. Kidder has worked in Virginia and North Carolina during the past five years and now opens a school at Ocala, Florida. She finds the subtropical climate hard to bear, although she is encouraged that "I haven't heard any grumbling from the Whites about my school lately." Segregation, however, extends even to water: "I know of one colored well and two white ones that have been dug since Emancipation."

+ This decade sees the beginning of a huge influx of immigration that does not ebb until World War I again disrupts the flow. Increasing numbers of these newcomers will be from Catholic areas of eastern and southern Europe, which results in many more nuns. Almost 200 new sisterhoods will be established in this period. The greatest number have their mother house in France, with the United States, Italy, Germany, and Ireland following in order as countries of origin. There are even convents of nuns from the Netherlands, Poland, Romania, and Ukraine.

+ As the decade begins, there are 1,341 Catholic schools in America, many of them run by nuns.

Increasing immigration and the Civil War's cancellation of laws that prohibited teaching black children are probably responsible for enrollment increases, for only 200 such schools had existed prior to the war.

While many cities, especially in the East and South, still depend on private, single-sex schools for secondary education, the cost-free, coeducational high school begins to offer employment (as well as educational) opportunities for women. In 1874, for example, school officials in Saginaw, Michigan, hire Annie Peck of Rhode Island as "preceptress" for their high school; while holding this position, which is equivalent to principal, she simultaneously earns additional degrees at the University of Michigan.

✦ Two-thirds of all employed women are domestic workers, as most households with middle-class pretensions deem it necessary to have at least one servant. Young men who cannot afford to provide their wives with domestic help generally do not wed, and it is not unusual for a newly married couple to live in a hotel until they can meet this standard. In the North, virtually all domestic workers are single women, often immigrants; in the South, they are usually black women, often married.

1871 Phoebe Couzins' graduation from the law school of Washington University is heralded by feminists throughout the nation, as is her June 20 admission to the bar. Later this year, Arkansas also honors Couzins with the right to practice; Utah, Kansas, and the Dakota Territory also will grant admission to their bars.

Despite this gratifying acceptance of her credentials, Couzins never develops a career as an attorney. Like other women of her class who are accustomed to inherited wealth, she depends on her family for financial support—while spending so lavishly, especially on clothing, that she incurs criticism from feminist friends. Although Couzins initially befriends Susan Anthony, she will reject suffrage goals near the end of her life, and she dies in 1913 alone and in poverty.

✦ Among those testifying to the House Judiciary Committee for the inclusion of women under the 15th Amendment is Victoria Woodhull, who is well known for her advocacy of "free love." Washingtonians crowd the capitol and are surprised to see a beautiful, soft-spoken lady who makes reasoned arguments for the vote.

✦ Because no state government exists in Washington, D.C., to contradict the gender-neutral language of the 15th Amendment, women there feel they have a stronger legal case for voting rights. They march "in solid phalanx some 70 strong to the registrar's office," but he refuses to register them. They go on to the polls, where other officials also deny them ballots.

At the same time, however, Belva McNall Lockwood is among several women who take part in the caucuses that choose Washington's delegate to Congress. That her own candidacy receives some votes is not unusual to Lockwood, for she was elected school superintendent in a New York town more than two decades earlier.

✦ A Detroit voter registration official turns down a request from Catherine A. F. Stebbins, a married woman, but then decides to accept her friend, Nanette Gardner, on the grounds that Gardner is a widow and a taxpayer. She casts a ballot in an April election and, despite lengthy negative debates by city officials, goes on quietly voting for years.

✦ The Woman's Anti-Suffrage Association of Washington City is organized by the wives of two popular Civil War military men, Mrs. William Sherman and Mrs. James Dahlgren. They joined by Almira Lincoln Phelps, who is a sister of Emma Willard, the great founder of higher education for women: Phelps' visibility against suffrage attracts particular notice because when she taught at Willard's school 40 years ago, young Elizabeth Cady was a student there.

✦ The first woman to graduate from the University of Michigan is Amanda Sanford, who is already a graduate of New England Female Medical College. While a university official lauds this historic event, Dr. Sanford—whose grades are the highest of her 90 classmates—is pelted by young men in the gallery, who use hymnal pages to make "spit balls."

Their protests are in vain, however, and during the next two years, 18 women will graduate from the university's medical school. Dr. Sanford goes on to further study in Europe, and after her 1884 marriage, practices as Amanda Sanford Hickey in Auburn, New York; she is elected president of the county's medical society the year after joining.

✦ When Susan Anthony tours Oregon this year, she is assisted by Bethenia Owens, who understands the need for female independence: Married at 14, she managed in 1859 to get a divorce and the right to return to her maiden name. She works for Portland newspaper publisher Abigail Scott Duniway, and Duniway will take charge of Owen's son when Owen goes to Philadelphia to earn an 1874 medical degree.

She then practices in Portland, and after putting her son through medical school, earns a more prestigious degree from the University of Michigan in 1880. As Dr. Bethenia Owens-Adair after an 1884 marriage, she bears a second child at age 47 and practices medicine the rest of her life.

✦ Smith College is founded in Northhampton, Massachusetts, with a $400,000 donation from heiress Sophia Smith; it is the first of the prestigious women's colleges to be endowed by a woman.

The very first student admitted, Corinne Tuckerman Allen, will demonstrate its aim of educating women for the benefit of families more than for personal careers: She will be the mother of Florence Allen, the first female appellate judge in America.

✦ Anna Howard Shaw is licensed as a Methodist preacher in Michigan. In the next two decades, she will earn both divinity and medical degrees from Boston University. By the end of the century, the Reverend Dr. Shaw is Susan Anthony's protégé in the suffrage movement; one of Anthony's nieces, Lucy Anthony, will function as Shaw's secretary for three decades.

✦ Margaret Knight has her first device accepted by the Patent Office, even though a man challenges it. An element of luck is present in the decision in her favor: the patent commissioner happened to see Knight's work on paper-bag folding in Boston three years earlier, and he thus knows that, despite her lack of any engineering education, this 32-year-old woman is an authentic mechanical genius. Knight will go on to register at least 27 patents during the next 35 years, setting precedents for her work in heavy machinery and rotary engines, especially for the Knight-Davidson Motor Company.

✦ While in Europe during the Franco-Prussian War, Clara Barton establishes a Strasbourg sewing shop where women impoverished by the war can earn a living. She also goes to Geneva to study the International Committee of the Red Cross, which began in 1863, and discovers that the U.S. State Department refuses to participate.

✦ Julia Ward Howe and Caroline Severance of the New England Woman's Club begin a Women's International Peace Association, but both are busy with other causes and this one is short-lived. Howe does help organize a conference in London, however, as the women's movement begins to have global effect.

✦ Mary Todd Lincoln, who is living in Chicago, loses the third of her four children; Tad dies at age 18, just six years after her husband's assassination. She is also fearful of poverty and pained by stories in the press of Lincoln's alleged first love, Ann Rutledge—a growing legend that is completely without documentation. Mary Todd Lincoln's always precarious mental health collapses, and two years later, her remaining son will have her adjudicated insane. After treatment and a second hearing, the decision is reversed, and she lives much of the rest of her life abroad before dying in Springfield, Illinois, in 1882.

✦ Mrs. O'Leary's cow is blamed for kicking over a lantern and beginning the Great Chicago Fire, which kills 300 and leaves 90,000 homeless. It burns for two days in October and causes some $200 million in damage. The fire burns south from Catherine O'Leary's barn; she escapes un-harmed, but loses all of her property, including five cows that grazed in what will become the 20th century's downtown Chicago. Although she suffers equally with others, O'Leary will be vilified for the rest of her life by many who blame her for the devastation.

◆ The fire destroys the Woman's Hospital Medical College that Dr. Mary Thompson had begun only the previous year. She organizes donors to help her rebuild it and the associated medical school.

Her colleagues begin to view her with enough respect that a decade later, she will be elected vice president of the Chicago Medical Society. Like other female physicians, however, she is often referred to as "Miss" instead of "Dr."—a usage that will continue to be widespread, even among progressive people, far into the 20th century.

◆ The rebuilding of Chicago spurs the national economy—and while virgin forests in Wisconsin and Michigan are cut to furnish wood, many urban women manage alone when their men go to work as lumberjacks.

1872 Victoria Woodhull is a declared candi-date for president. Far too intelligent to expect to garner any significant number of votes, she uses her candidacy to bring attention to women's issues in *Woodhull & Claflin's Weekly*—which also makes publishing history by including the first English translation of Marx's *Communist Manifesto*. Her "nominating convention" names Frederick Douglass as her running mate, disre-garding his refusal to be associated with such radicalism.

Woodhull's scandalous sexual history alien-ates her from most suffragists, but she is sup-ported by some who admire her temerity. Her candidacy proves so disruptive to the annual meeting of the National Woman's Suffrage Asso-ciation that Susan Anthony gavels it to adjourn-ment and orders the janitor to close the building.

◆ Republican leadership acknowledges the change in the status of women caused by the Civil War.

While ducking the issue of suffrage, their party platform states that it is "mindful of its obliga-tions to the loyal women of America for their noble devotion to the cause of freedom; their admission to wider fields of usefulness is received with satisfaction; and the honest demands of any class of citizens for equal rights should be treated with respectful consideration."

Further indications of women's changing po-litical roles are seen in campaign hiring: both Susan Anthony and Anna Dickinson are offered impressive speaking fees by rival Republican can-didates.

◆ Mary Livermore stops editing the *Woman's Jour-nal* to launch what becomes a very successful career as a lecturer and author. She is a top attraction on the national speaking circuit for the next two decades, and one of her most popular talks is "What Shall We Do with Our Daughters?" Livermore's speaking fees and royalties earn her an uncommonly high income, while also demon-strating public interest in new roles for women.

◆ Responding to lobbying by Belva Lockwood and other Washington, D.C., women, Congress passes legislation that gives female employees of the federal government equal pay for equal work; previously no woman could be paid more than $75 a month for any government service.

While the legal principle is very significant, the practical result is much less so, for few women are hired for positions in the same civil service classi-fications as men.

◆ Charlotte E. Ray graduates from Howard Uni-versity Law School and is admitted to the bar in Washington, D.C. The first black female attorney in the United States, she achieves this goal only three years later than the first white woman.

Like Arabella Mansfield and Phoebe Couzins, however, Ray will not develop a career as a prac-ticing attorney, although she tries. The black community does not supply enough clients for her, and before the decade is over, she will be forced to return to teaching in New York.

◆ Illinois follows the precedent begun in Iowa in 1869: Its legislature deletes "male" from the statutes on bar admission, and Alta M. Hulett becomes a lawyer. Supported by the network created with Myra Bradwell's bar application, Hulett led the lobbying effort that resulted in the change—but it is still not enough to cover Bradwell's situation. Hulett is single, unlike Bradwell, and as long as married women are barred from entering into contracts without their husband's permission, the court is disinclined to admit married women to the bar.

Hulett's milestone cannot be fully developed, however, for she will die just five years after her bar admission. Because Missourian Lemma Barkaloo also died soon after her entry into the legal profession, some observers begin to believe that women lack the physical stamina to practice law.

◆ Howard University not only has its first female law school graduate in Charlotte Ray, but also its first female medical school graduate: Mary D. Sparkman sets this precedent, which will be followed by six other black women in this decade. By far the greatest number of African-American female physicians will be Howard alumnae until 1891, when Meharry Medical College in Tennessee graduates its first women.

◆ Margaret Cochrane Cooper earns a medical degree from Philadelphia's Penn College, one of the most prestigious American institutions to grant this degree to a woman. Born in Ireland, she was one of 11 children of a widowed mother; widowed herself, she supported two sons by nursing before the financial freedom of a second marriage allowed her to attend medical school. Dr. Cooper will practice medicine in Battle Creek and Saginaw, Michigan, for the rest of her life.

◆ The North Carolina Medical Society grants honorary membership to Dr. Susan Dimock, a native of that state who is practicing in Boston, where the Massachusetts Medical Society has refused her admission. After earning her medical degree with high honors from the University of Zurich last year, she is developing a surgical specialty with the New England Hospital for Women and Children. This promising career will be cut short after

less than three years of practice, however, when Dr. Dimock drowns in an 1875 shipwreck at age 28.

◆ Dr. Mary Putnam organizes the Association for the Advancement of the Medical Education of Women to encourage young women to become physicians. Her marriage next year to pediatrician and political emigre Dr. Abraham Jacobi will not deter the career of either, as both go on to national prominence. Dr. Mary Jacobi eventually publishes over 100 scientific papers and pioneers the field of industrial toxicology.

◆ Although women have nursed from the beginning of recorded time, this year marks the founding of the nation's first school for the formal training of professional nurses. It is based at Dr. Marie Zakrzewska's New England Hospital for Women and Children in Boston, and Dr. Susan Dimock is a motivating force during her short life. Both of these women are familiar with European credentialization of women as medical assistants in nursing and midwifery, and they begin the first nursing school class with five students this year.

One student is Linda Richards, who becomes known as America's first trained nurse. She will go on to establish her own precedent-setting educational programs as superintendent of nursing at New York's Bellevue Hospital and at Massachusetts General Hospital. In these settings, she leads the next generation of professional nurses.

◆ Mary Clemmer Ames becomes the highest-paid newswomen in history when she earns a $5,000 annual salary from the *Brooklyn Daily Union*. She began her career after separating from her husband, a Methodist minister, and from 1866, she wrote a "Woman's Letter from Washington" for the weekly *Independent*. Working from the ladies' galleries in Congress, Ames comments on the political news for most of two decades. When her divorce is finally granted in 1876, she will resume the use of her maiden name.

◆ Buffalo's Amanda Jones receives the first of a dozen patents she will earn by 1914. Most are associated with the canning of food, and in 1890, she will attempt to put her ideas into practice with the establishment of the Women's Canning and Preserving Company of Chicago. She also publishes on heating systems in engineering journals—but at the same time, most of her life centers around interests in spiritualism, not science. Indeed, she asserts that her furnace patents have a psychic source.

◆ At the same time, Jane Wells patents her baby-jumper. A hanging device with springs, it enables a child who cannot yet walk to amuse herself while exercising the leg muscles, leaving Mother a chance to do something other than entertain the baby.

◆ Southern Baptists break precedent by sponsoring two missionaries who are unmarried women. One of them is Edmonia Harris Moon; the following year, her sister Lottie Moon will join her in China. They are the sisters of Dr. Orianna Moon Andrews, a pre-Civil War Virginia physician.

◆ Women continue to test the 15th Amendment by attempting to vote in the fall elections. Pointing out that she owns "a little house" and that "taxes be taxes," Sojourner Truth tries unsuccessfully to cast a ballot in Battle Creek, Michigan. Matilda Joselyn Gage tries to vote in her home state of New York and then is the sole woman to join Susan Anthony in a lecture tour on the issue; despite Gage's distaste for oratory, she makes 16 speeches in less than a month.

◆ Anthony becomes the focus of public attention once more, however, when she leads 15 women to the polls in her hometown of Rochester. As expected, local officials not only are unwilling to count her vote but also have her arrested. She is tried in U.S. District Court and convicted without benefit of jury by a judge who writes his opinion before the trial ends. Anthony refuses to pay the $100 fine, but no enforcement action is taken against her—thus frustrating her plans for an appeal to a higher court.

1873   The nation's most serious depression to date brings an end to nascent labor unions, including the shoemakers in the Daughters of St.

Crispin. Prior to the depression, however, these women organized workers in shoe factories from coast to coast.

◆ Despite the depression, Scribner's begins a new magazine for children, choosing Mary Mapes Dodge as its editor. She names it *St. Nicholas*, buys articles from exceptionally good writers—including youngsters—and edits it until her 1905 death. *St. Nicholas* will publish Louisa May Alcott, Frances Hodgson Burnett, and the young Rachel Carson, along with men such as Alfred Lord Tennyson and Mark Twain.

◆ At the same time, *Home Companion* begins publication; its name will be altered to *Woman's Home Companion* in 1897. The market for women readers is clearly large, for although the new magazine sells well, it does little damage to the sales of rival *Godey's Lady's Book* or *Peterson's Ladies' Magazine*.

Two years ago, *Peterson's* launched the national career of humorist Marietta Holley with a story published under the pseudonym Josiah Allen's Wife. While writing from a married woman's viewpoint, Holley remains single; her chief character, Betsey Bobbet, holds low opinions of men and of women who find their identity in men. Holley—who lives in the same rural western New York area that spawned Susan Anthony and other feminists—issues her first book of humor this year. Her publisher is the same man who took a chance on Mark Twain, and her sales are similar.

◆ Like Harriot K. Hunt in 1852 and Lucy Stone in 1858, unmarried sisters Julia and Abigail Smith remind Americans of the principle of "no taxation without representation" by refusing to pay their property taxes. They attend the town meeting in Gastonbury, Connecticut, where Abby makes the point. She will be refused permission to speak at the next town meeting, but her outdoor protest draws widespread attention. The following January, seven of the Smiths' cows will be sold for taxes.

The "Gastonbury Cows" becomes a celebrated case, but less attention is paid to a more serious attachment of the Smiths' estate: a grasp-

The "Gastonbury Cows" becomes a cele-brated case, but less attention is paid to a more serious attachment of the Smiths' estate: a grasp-ing neighbor manages to buy 15 acres of their land for a fraction of its value because of their tax protest. The sale violates other aspects of law, however, and the sisters eventually get it back—but not without years of court battle that is rendered more difficult because of women's infe-rior legal status.

Pioneer abolitionist Abby Kelly Foster and her husband also refuse to pay their taxes to further demonstrate the principle. Their Connecticut farm is sold by tax authorities, but supporters buy it and return it to the Fosters.

◆ *Bradwell v. Illinois* is a solid defeat for women, as the U.S. Supreme Court rules that states may exclude a woman from the practice of law, even though—as in this suit by Chicagoan Myra Brad-well—she has passed the bar exam.

While the 14th Amendment explicitly says that all citizens are entitled to equal protection under the law, this does not apply to female citizens. Because of women's "timidity and deli-cacy," the Court says, the "law of the Creator" overrules the Constitution. States may exclude women from the bar.

◆ Belva McNall Lockwood encounters a similar struggle in her attempt to become an attorney. Several law schools had refused to admit this well-credentialed school administrator, but Lockwood graduates from Washington's new National University Law School in May—then has to appeal to President Ulysses S. Grant, who is a trustee of the school, to receive the degree she has earned. Another woman, Lydia S. Hull, also graduates from this law school in the same year, but neither woman's name appears on com-mencement lists.

Lockwood is admitted to the Washington, D.C., bar in September; it had set a precedent the previous year in admitting African American Charlotte Ray. Perhaps because Lockwood is a white activist supported by an affluent husband, she is treated as a greater threat to the profession. Even after admission to the bar, she is denied permission to argue before federal courts—essen-tial to successful practice in the District of Colum-bia, which lacks a state government.

◆ The Association for the Advancement of Women is convened by New Yorkers associated with Sorosis and by Bostonians led by Julia Ward Howe of the New England Women's Club. Their goal is to improve educational opportunities so that women can enter professions; Civil War hos-pital administrator and author Mary Livermore is AAW president.

That women are ardent about such opportu-nity is clear when 400 attend the first meeting, which is later referred to as the First Woman's Congress. Charter members Catharine Beecher, the Reverend Antoinette Brown Blackwell, and the Reverend Augusta Chapin deliver papers, while astronomer Maria Mitchell encourages young women to study science.

◆ Congress passes legislation that has the effect of defining information on contraception as ob-scene, and as such, banning its distribution in the mail. Moralist Anthony Comstock is given a spe-cial appointment as a postal inspector, and, using what becomes known as the Comstock Law, he single-handedly does much harm to the nascent birth control movement. Mail is seized and news-papers are shut down—even immigrant newspa-pers that unwittingly run advertising in a foreign language for products that only secondarily may have a contraceptive effect.

◆ Ellen Swallow Richards is the first woman to graduate from the newly established Massachu-setts Institute of Technology. She already has a bachelor's degree from Vassar, which also awards her master's degree this year. She will go on to complete her doctorate work, but MIT will never award the degree—although the school employs her (sometimes without pay) for the rest of her life. A true systems thinker, Richards makes sig-nificant scientific contributions in disciplines ranging from chemistry to metallurgy. Her pio-neer work on air and water pollution will set standards in the emerging field of environmental-ism.

marriage four years earlier, when she was 24 and he was 68. Although he treats her to more luxury than his other wives enjoy, she has abhorred polygamy ever since her father married women other than her mother.

She becomes a huge attraction on the national lecture circuit, with even President Grant attending a Washington appearance. The divorce suit languishes when Brigham Young refuses to pay anything beyond court costs, and it is still unsettled when he dies.

✦ Precedents for women in civil service jobs continue when Alice Mary Robertson is hired as a clerk for the Office of Indian Affairs in Washington, D.C. She is very well qualified: Robertson is a college graduate who has lived most of her life in the Indian Territory, having been born to missionary parents at the Tullahassee Mission of the Creek Nation. Almost 50 years later, she will be elected to Congress from Oklahoma.

✦ The Bellevue Hospital Training School for Nurses is begun in New York City, following standards designed by British Florence Nightingale. Its founders are women, and the Bellevue model will be adopted by hospital boards of "lady managers" throughout the nation.

✦ Charlotte Forten, a member of an old Philadelphia family of free blacks, moves from teaching in freedmen schools to a clerkship with the Treasury Department in Washington, D.C., making her an early African-American female federal employee.

In 1878, at age 41, she will marry Francis James Grimké, a graduate of Harvard Law School and the biracial nephew of the famous abolitionist Grimké sisters. As Charlotte Forten Grimké, she will long be a Washington leader of black women.

✦ After a decade as a Universalist minister, the Reverend Olympia Brown marries a merchant in Bridgeport, Connecticut. She retains her maiden name and her pastorate, bears children at ages 39 and 41, and then continues her ministerial career in Racine, Wisconsin.

✦ *Atlantic* critic Thomas Wentworth Higginson pays his second and last visit to the "half-cracked poetess" who lives in Amherst, Massachusetts. His attention is virtually all that Emily Dickinson receives from the literati of her era, and he advises her against publication.

✦ This election year brings a dramatic victory in Boston, where the New England Women's Club has targeted election of women to the city's school board. Four women, including educator Lucretia Crocker and Civil War Sanitary Commission executive Abby W. May, win their races, but the men on the board initially refuse to seat them. Next year, however, the women succeed in getting the legislature to pass an act declaring women eligible for such positions, and in December, six women join the board.

Crocker will serve for the rest of her life. She has written two textbooks and takes the lead in establishing modern science education, while author Lucretia Peabody Hale uses her elective office to promote kindergartens and summer school.

✦ In the winter, women in several midwestern states begin praying and singing hymns outside of saloons. Because women have little legal protection in property rights, guardianship of their children, or their physical safety from abusers, drunken men can literally destroy their lives.

They aim to make this point, and the prayer demonstrations continue. The following year, the Women's Christian Temperance Union will be formally organized in Cleveland. Its first president is Annie Wittenmyer, an Iowa widow who learned organizing skills in the wartime Sanitary Commission; she will attract more than 25,000 members to the WCTU during the next five years.

1874 In March, over 60 women in Washington, D.C., unsuccessfully attempt to register to vote. Among them is African American Mary Ann Shadd Cary, who justifiably argues that the leadership she provided during the Civil War by both recruiting soldiers and publishing an abolitionist newspaper should entitle her to the vote as much as any newly freed male slave.

Later in the year, even white males in the District of Columbia lose their right to vote when its territorial government is abolished; for a century into the future, District residents are disenfranchised.

♦ The Supreme Court settles the question of whether the recent constitutional amendments allow women to vote when it rules against Virginia Minor, a former president of the Missouri Woman Suffrage Association.

In *Minor v. Happersett*, she sued a St. Louis official named Happersett for refusing to register her to vote. Her attorney husband argues that the language of the Constitution entitles women to vote and that they need no further permission from state government. With the chief justice writing the opinion, the Court disagrees, ruling that the states alone define who may vote and the federal government may not overrule them. The Court even cites New Jersey's 1807 withdrawal of language that has permitted some of its female citizens to vote as proof of this principle—which conveniently ignores the fact that Southern states were recently required, as a condition of readmittance to the Union, to define ex-slaves as voters.

The decision is heartbreaking for suffragists, for it makes it clear that women have no choice except to conduct state-by-state campaigns or win the extraordinary majorities that are necessary for an amendment to the federal Constitution. The political struggle the suffragists are forced to begin will not be won in the lifetimes of most.

♦ Lavinia Goodell, an unmarried woman who recently moved from New York, is admitted to practice law in Janesville, Wisconsin—but when one of her cases goes to the state Supreme Court next year, she is not allowed to argue the case. The ruling against her goes further, declaring that female lawyers to be "departures from the order of nature"; it is so strongly negative that several newspapers are moved to support Goodell.

The Wisconsin legislature shows itself to be more liberal than its judiciary. It emulates other midwestern states in amending its bar qualification statutes to include women—who, as Goodell points out, are already eligible for admission to the state university's law school. Except for the District of Columbia, all of the early legal victories for female attorneys are in the Midwest.

Goodell's promising career, however, ends with her 1880 death, just six years after her local practice began. It adds to the credibility of many physicians who assert that women are not physically suited for the traditionally male professions.

♦ Saloon-front demonstrations continue, and women are arrested in Cincinnati. The caustic comment of one national publication is: "The police authorities that do not enforce the laws against liquor traffic, that do not suppress gambling or houses of ill repute, distinguish themselves by arresting 43 women who went on the streets to sing and pray."

♦ Michigan holds a referendum on women's suffrage, and Susan Anthony campaigns there. Despite evidences of feminism in the state, such as its early admission of women to college and to the clergy, the vote is lost.

Meanwhile, Illinois grants women the right to hold school offices—but they will have to be elected by men, for women have no right to vote, even in school elections.

One of the women chosen to the Boston school board this year is Kate Gannett Wells, a patrician whose lineage reaches back to Mary Chilton, reputedly the first woman to debark at Plymouth Rock. Although Wells holds elective office, she opposes suffrage, and a decade from now, she will be one of the signers of a "remonstrance" to the legislature against the vote for women. Her rationale is largely anti-immigrant: "Let the great mass of uneducated women be added to the . . . men," she says, "and the State will [face] demands . . . for bread, work, money."

♦ Cornell University inaugurates a branch for women, Sage College. This year's students include Anna Botsford, who, as Anna Comstock, will establish a national reputation as an entomologist, especially known for her many textbook illustrations of insects. In 1899, she will be the first woman appointed to the Cornell faculty, although jealous colleagues briefly succeed in reducing her rank from assistant professor to lecturer.

◆ New York socialite Jennie Jerome sets a pattern for the Gilded Age when she marries Lord Randolph Churchill, son of the duke of Marlborough. Elite families on both sides of the Atlantic will follow this trend. The grooms offer noble titles, social connections, and aristocratic homes that are in need of the brides' American money. Lady Churchill will become the mother of future British prime minister Winston Churchill, and after her husband dies of syphilis, she will twice marry men who are younger than her son.

◆ An October article in *Harper's Weekly* entitled "Louisiana and the Rule of Terror," begins: "Julia Hayden, the colored school teacher, one of the latest victims of the White Men's League, was but seventeen years of age." She had completed her education at Nashville's Central College; three days after arriving to teach in Hartsville, Louisiana, she was shot dead.

1875 The trial of the Reverend Henry Ward Beecher for adultery makes headlines throughout the nation, revealing a secret that suffragists had tried to keep quiet for five years. Beecher, an extremely popular preacher and a former president of the American Woman Suffrage Association, is the brother of author Harriet Beecher Stowe. She defends him, but his half sister, Isabella Beecher Hooker, a founder of the New England Suffrage Association, speaks candidly of his guilt. Writer/educator Catharine Beecher, the oldest and most conservative of the family, is deeply embarrassed, for she opposes suffrage and other liberal views held by her younger siblings.

Several of their friends, including Susan Anthony, are aware that the Reverend Beecher had an affair with Elizabeth Tilton, a married member of his fashionable Brooklyn congregation. She confessed the relationship to her husband and ended it in 1869, but then neither of the Tiltons seemed quite capable of allowing the matter to die. Theodore became obsessed with jealousy of Beecher; Lib sobbed out her sorrows to other women, including Anna Dickinson, who writes, "She is very lovely and quiet and beautiful, but she is insane."

Although Susan Anthony warns Theodore Tilton of the damage that public exposure will do to their shared causes, he sues Beecher for adultery and alienation of affection. When the Reverend Beecher vaguely proclaims his innocence on the witness stand, the all-male jury fails to reach a unanimous decision—but meanwhile, great harm is done by the gossip and internal division. The scandal widens the rift between the two suffrage organizations, for AWSA members generally support their former president, while NWSA members are more likely to see Lib Tilton as the hapless victim of a jealous husband and a charming preacher.

All of this is further complicated by the fact that it was the notorious Victoria Woodhull who first revealed the affair—but instead of drawing public attention to the Reverend Beecher's hypocrisy, as she intended, Woodhull and her sister, Tennessee Claflin, are jailed on obscenity charges for telling the story in their *Woodhull & Claflin's Weekly*.

Lib Tilton is excommunicated from the church and ends her days in lonely poverty; before he exiles himself in France, Theodore is so depressed that Elizabeth Cady Stanton writes him, "the least you can do is to *live.*" Only the Reverend Beecher, who retains his position as pastor, escapes relatively unscathed.

◆ Popular author and lecturer Mary Livermore serves as president of the American Woman Suffrage Association during this difficult time; her image as a happily married pastor's wife is helpful to the cause.

The National Woman Suffrage Association convention resolves "that the denial of Elizabeth B. Tilton's right to testify in the pending Brooklyn trial is but proof of women's need of the ballot in her own right for self-defence and self-protection." NASA members, including Matilda Joselyn Gage, also testify to a congressional committee on behalf of the vote this year.

Beret Olesdatter Hagebak sits in front of the sod house that she and her husband built in Lac qui Parle County, Minnesota, in 1872, after leaving Norway in 1867. Because few trees grew on midwestern plains, there was no construction alternative to sod. Such homes probably were a greater shock to Americans from the East than they were to Europeans, who were more familiar with earthen materials, especially the thatched roof. Photo by H.J. Chalmers; Minnesota Historical Society and Lac Qui Parle Historical Society of Madison, Wisconsin

Meanwhile, women in Minnesota and Michigan gain the vote in school elections. They mark smaller ballots that are deposited in separate boxes.

✦ The American Medical Association admits its first female member. Just five years ago, a motion to do so had been tabled without discussion. She is young Sarah Stevenson, who graduated at the top of her class at Woman's Medical College of Chicago last year. The Illinois Medical Society honors Dr. Stevenson by choosing her as a delegate to the national convention this year; she will go on to a lifetime of similar achievement, including the authorship of two books and positions on the Illinois State Board of Health and at Cook County Hospital.

✦ Dr. Emeline Cleveland becomes the first known female physician to perform major surgery. She has a 20-year record as a physician and has been the main source of income for her invalid husband and a son whom she bore while practicing.

✦ Sculptor Anne Whitney wins a commission for a statue of Massachusetts Senator Charles Sumner —but loses it when the judges discover that the winning model was done by a woman.

Whitney, incidentally, shares sculptor Harriet Hosmer's hometown of Watertown, Massachusetts. Her first exhibit was in 1860 at the National Academy of Design, and after studying in Rome over the next decade, Whitney has been building a successful Boston studio. At the end of a highly productive life, she will make her last work, at age

80: the carving of the Sumner statue that was rejected in her youth. It stands near Harvard Square.

✦ The Reverend Antoinette Brown Blackwell publishes *The Sexes Through Nature*, a feminist critique of Darwinism. With her children grown, she returns to the activism of her youth: she publishes other works, participates in the American Woman Suffrage Association headed by her sister-in-law Lucy Stone, and preaches occasionally, even ordaining two other women. When her husband goes bankrupt, she returns to the lecture circuit to earn income.

✦ While exceptional women have been creating organizations for several decades, the vast majority of middle-and lower-class women still have almost no socializing opportunities. The beginning of change in this area is clear when Eastern Star organizes this year; it is an auxiliary for women whose men are Masons—members of a fraternal lodge that has existed in America since colonial days.

✦ Female weavers in Fall River, Massachusetts, vote to strike in response to a pay cut that men accept.

This Chippewa home is not so different from the sod houses of immigrants, but—unlike European habits— women were the primary builders of Native American structures. The women pictured are Mary Bigwind, Maggie Ski-naway, and Mrs. John Mink; they planned to live here while tapping maple trees for syrup near Lake Superior. Although this photo could have been taken during any nineteenth-century winter, it is actually from 1925. Harry D. Ayer Estate and Minnesota Historical Society

+ New Jersey's Claytonia Dorticus invents a chemical bath for developing photographic prints. She goes on to patent other photography equipment as well as devices for dyeing leather.

+ In need of funds after her husband's business collapses in the depression of 1873, Lydia Pinkham applies her botanical knowledge of roots and herbs and begins to sell a health tonic out of her home in Lynn, Massachusetts. Her oldest son and her daughter, a teenage teacher, work to provide the necessary capital, while two younger sons develop sales.

  Lydia Pinkham's face on the bottle proves the key to success, and only a year later, the family rejects an offer of $100,000 for their trademark. Millions of women and men believe in the healthful efficacy of her tonic, and sales will peak long after her death.

+ From the same town at the same time, Mary Baker Eddy develops similar ideas on health. She publishes *Science and Health* and establishes the Christian Scientists' Home in Lynn, Massachusetts. Many women are attracted to her ideas, for they have great appeal in an era when the societal roles assigned to women often result in clinical depression that manifests itself as illness.

  Feminism is also revealed in her revision of the Lord's Prayer to read "Our Father/Mother." With almost 400 revisions in Eddy's lifetime, *Science and Health* will sell widely, and in 1879, she formally begins the Church of Christ (Scientist). It becomes the only major religion to be founded by a woman.

1876 A giant Centennial Exposition in Philadelphia commemorates the 100 years that have passed since the Declaration of Independence was signed in that city. Women determine to use the occasion to focus on their exclusion from a document that says "All men are created equal." The event's officials grant only a small space to the American Woman Suffrage Association, while the National Woman Suffrage Association finds it difficult to rent any location outside of the fairgrounds because state law forbids married women from signing contracts. Susan Anthony, who is single, finally rents a headquarters that the organization uses to gain visibility with the 10 million people who visit Philadelphia.

  Matilda Joselyn Gage writes a Declaration of the Rights of Women that is modeled on the 1776 Declaration, and on July 4, NWSA women distribute hundreds of copies. They take over an empty bandstand, and Anthony reads the document to a receptive crowd. The event marks a milestone in suffrage activity, and many networks grow out of it. The women learn the effectiveness of having a headquarters—where, at age 83, Lucretia Mott leaves $5 tips when she stops in for tea (at a time when $5 was a week's wages for most women).

+ Among the women exhibiting their work at the Centennial is Edmonia Lewis, who is usually called a Negro sculptress, despite the fact that she is half Chippewa. The fair adds to her already wide client list, but within a decade, she will largely disappear from public attention. She spends increasing amounts of time in Rome, where she studied in her youth, and presumably dies there after the turn of the century.

+ Annie Besant and Charles Bradlaugh are prosecuted in England for distributing a pamphlet on birth control. They are acquitted, and widespread publicity of the trial begins an international movement for the right to information on the prevention of pregnancy.

  At the same time, Dr. Elizabeth Blackwell's innocuous work on sex education, *Counsel to Parents on the Moral Education of Their Children*, is rejected by 12 English publishers. She prints it privately.

+ Graduation exercises at the University of Michigan for the first time include female speakers. Progressive Oberlin College featured its first commencement essays read by women only two years earlier.

+ A California Senate committee hears testimony on Chinese immigration. When a senator asks if it is not a fact "that a great many [Chinese] people are held in slavery here," the testifying clergyman replies, "Only the women. I don't think there is a man so held. The women as a general thing are held as slaves."

✦ Josephine Shaw Lowell is the first woman appointed to the New York State Board of Charities. Her charitable work began with the Civil War's Sanitary Commission and the Freedman's Bureau, for she lost both her husband and brother in the war. Her brother was Robert Gould Shaw, the famous leader of the first regiment of black soldiers, and when her husband was killed in 1864, she was 20 years old and pregnant.

Last year, Lowell conducted a study of able-bodied paupers that impressed Governor Samuel Tilden. She will go on to develop a strong view that job opportunity and adequate wages are the key to eliminating charity need.

✦ In Jersey City, New Jersey, women form the Aesthetic Society, but the topics they undertake to study are not limited to the genteel. Their foremost leader, geologist Erminnie Platt Smith, is a graduate of Germany's Freiberg School of Mines, and hundreds attend a demonstration of the new concept of sound recording.

✦ Encouraged by the feminist networks she has discovered after her refusal to pay taxes, Julia Smith publishes a translation of the Bible that she completed two decades earlier. The version is based on years of work, during which this Connecticut farmer taught herself Greek and Hebrew to do a word-by-word translation of the entire Bible. She realizes what other scholars later learn: the King James version, which will remain standard for most of another century, distorts many original meanings. Not surprisingly, Smith is forced to issue her publication at her own expense.

✦ As was the case in the 1872 election, political parties continue to recruit female leaders to support their candidates, even though most women still lack the vote. The November presidential election is unlike any other in American history, and many women work to influence male voters in a campaign that in some ways is the final chapter of the Civil War story.

Democratic nominee Samuel Tilden of New York is supported by Southerners and by enough Northerners that he wins the popular vote; through complex machinations, however, Republican Rutherford B. Hayes is awarded 185 electoral votes to Tilden's 184.

In return for the presidency, the Republicans agree to remove the federal troops that occupy rebel states. This allows former Confederates regain control of local governments, and they will begin moving newly free blacks back into a semi-slave status, often as sharecroppers. Federal protection of abolitionist women who run schools in the South also ends.

Many Republican women, including Susan Anthony and her followers, pin their hopes on the new first lady Lucy Hayes, who supports suffrage—but their wishes are in vain. Hayes does nothing to further their cause.

✦ The withdrawal of federal troops from the South brings down the final curtain of activism for virtually all of the thousands of Northern women who went South during and after the war to assist emancipated slaves. Unlike most of these women, Dr. Esther Hill Hawks will maintain some association with Florida for the rest of her life. Her husband lives primarily there, while she builds a medical practice in Lynn, Massachusetts; he visits her in the summer, and she visits him in the winter. Their roles also reverse in that she was primarily an educator during the war, while he worked as a physician; now she practices medicine full time, while he concentrates his efforts on Florida land development—but with the unusual twist of recruiting former slaves to Florida.

Dr. Hawks serves as a National Woman Suffrage Association vice president for Florida, and she also is a progressive activist in Lynn, the town in which nontraditional healers Mary Baker Eddy and Lydia Pinkham live. Moreover, at least part of the time, Dr. Hawks works in partnership with another female physician.

✦ Another result of the Republican electoral compromise and the consequent removal of federal troops from the South is that Elizabeth Van Lew loses her position as postmistress of Richmond,

Virginia. She accepts an inferior position with the post office in Washington, but she will resign in protest against still another demotion when President Hayes is succeeded by Grover Cleveland in 1885. Former president and Civil War general Ulysses S. Grant dies at the same time, and without him, no one in power remembers her Civil War sacrifice. She returns to Richmond and lives alone and poor, shunned by her Confederate neighbors.

6

Feminism in the Victorian Age

1877–1899

1877 The first American woman to earn a Ph.D. is Helen Magill, who completes a doctorate in Greek at Boston University. Her undergraduate degree is from Swarthmore, and she will do further work at England's Cambridge University—but she will never obtain a teaching position equivalent to her credentials.

As a girl, she was allowed to enroll at Boston Public Latin School—which, despite the "public" in its name, was limited to boys. The exception was made in her case because her father was on the faculty.

✦ Four years after their release from prison for violation of obscenity laws, sisters Victoria Woodhull and Tennessee Claflin move to England. Some say that the move is financed by Vanderbilt heirs in return for their promise not to contest the will of multimillionaire Cornelius Vanderbilt, with whom they had a close relationship. Their lives are far from over, however, for both marry wealthy men, and far into the 20th century, they will continue their radical politics with publications on the other side of the Atlantic.

✦ Women are among those killed by militia in Baltimore and Pittsburgh during a giant strike by male railroad employees. Mother Mary Jones comes to public attention during this strike, for her organizing abilities and especially her earthy oratory soon make her the most visible woman in the labor movement. She is not a feminist or suffragist, however; she will specialize in helping miners and is seldom involved in strikes by women.

✦ With the formation of Bell Telephone Company, thousands of women soon become telephone operators; many were previously telegraph operators. As telephone systems are built throughout the nation, literally millions of women will find a new source of independent income.

✦ The International Red Cross, which began in Switzerland more than a decade ago, carries out humanitarian activities during war between Russia and Turkey, and Clara Barton begins to make speeches educating Americans on the organization. She meets with little success, however, until she reshapes her message to speak to the agency's possibilities with natural disasters rather than war.

✦ Julia Constance Fletcher publisher the novel *Kismet* under the pseudonym George Fleming.

✦ Colorado conducts a referendum on suffrage; despite Susan Anthony's presence for the campaign, it loses.

1878 A California senator, A.A. Sargent, introduces a proposed amendment to the U.S. Constitution at the request of the National Woman Suffrage Association. Called the 16th Amendment at this point, its words are those that eventually grant women the vote when the 19th Amendment is adopted. It is also known as "the Susan B. Anthony Amendment," and women will lobby for it in each Congress that convenes until final passage in 1919. Its authors are long dead by then, and suffragists will have presented literally millions of signatures on petitions. No other constitutional amendment will have such a lengthy history or so many dedicated supporters.

✦ Women in the Utah Territory have the right to vote but not to hold office—something that confirms the nascent feminism of Emmaline B. Wells. Despite a unanimous endorsement at a county convention, she is not allowed to be a candidate for treasurer of Salt Lake City.

A Massachusetts native who moved with church pioneers to Illinois and then to Utah, Wells is the mother of five living children, all of whom are girls. She is the seventh wife of a prominent Mormon official and has been married twice before: her first husband deserted, and the next—who was appreciably older than she—died just five weeks after the birth of her second baby.

Because there is often great disparity in the ages of Mormon men and their later wives, young widowhood is a significant possibility. The result, some assert, is that a Mormon woman becomes "accustomed to acting for herself instead of leaning upon another."

✦ The Chautauqua Scientific and Literary Circle develops from study groups at a Methodist campground on Lake Chautauqua in western New

York. Within a decade, some 50 local groups study Chautauqua's correspondence courses in the winter and attend the lectures, concerts, and plays that "the traveling Chautauqua" presents in summer.

For women, this is of tremendous importance. Chautauqua speakers introduce feminist philosophy throughout the nation, and many suffrage leaders earn their living on its lecture circuit. Because the vast majority of women never had the opportunity to attend college, many take advantage of Chautauqua's learning system.

+ New York's new department store, Macy's, includes a ladies' lunchroom as well as a room in which women can rest, visit, or read newspapers provided by the store. In the Midwest, even small towns begin to attract female shoppers by building "comfort stations" or "rest rooms" where farm women can nurse their babies and change diapers. Some of these facilities will exist until the middle of the 20th century.

+ Isabella Bird travels in remote areas of Japan never before seen by Westerners; upon her return, she publishes *Offbeaten Tracks in Japan*.

As Isabella Bird Bishop in the 1890s, she will be the center of an international debate on whether women can be fellows of the Royal Geographic Society. A letter to the London *Times* proclaims: "The genus of professional female globe-trotters with which America has lately familiarized us is one of the horrors of . . . the century."

+ Jane Cazneau, who was widowed two years ago, publishes her last work. *Our Winter Eden: Pen Pictures of the Tropics* is not the romantic travelogue that its title implies; instead Cazneau continues her long tradition of foreign affairs activism. She argues for colonization and increased trade in the Caribbean and even for the establishment of a particular naval base. She is returning from New York to Santo Domingo when her ship sinks, and she drowns at age 71.

+ The suicide of Ann Trow Lohman makes headlines in New York, for, under the name of Madame Restall, she has practiced as an abortionist since the 1830s. Restall's notoriety as a "female physician" hampered the career of young Dr. Elizabeth Blackwell—but at the same time, Restall's long and successful practice would not have been possible unless she gave her patients competent care. The willingness of New Yorkers to go to her for abortions is clear from the fact that she leaves an estimated $1 million estate, including a Fifth Avenue home that she allegedly built near St. Patrick's Cathedral as a deliberate reminder of social hypocrisy.

It is the prevention of pregnancy, however, and not its termination that causes her undoing. She slits her throat on the day of her trial for selling contraceptive materials to undercover agent Anthony Comstock. Hers is one of the first of 15 suicides that Comstock will boast of causing, as he continues his moralist crusade until his 1915 death.

+ Caroline Still graduates from Woman's Medical College of Pennsylvania; she was the only black woman in Oberlin College's 1868 class. As Dr. Caroline Still Anderson, she will practice in Philadelphia, where her parents, William and Letetia Still, were Underground Railroad activists. The Presbyterian church in which her husband serves as pastor will support the clinic that she runs for almost four decades, and Dr. Anderson also founds the Philadelphia YWCA for Colored Women.

+ An epidemic of yellow fever, a disease largely caused by poor sanitation, kills approximately 20,000 people in the Mississippi Valley this year.

1879 On February 15, years of lobbying by attorney Belva Lockwood finally pays off, and Congress passes legislation permitting women to practice law in federal courts. She follows up by becoming the first woman credentialed to argue before the U.S. Supreme Court. During this decade, Lockwood also represents female journalists in their case for equitable news space and succeeds successfully lobbies for the hiring of female guards for female prisons.

✦ Under the leadership of Frances Willard, the first dean of women at Northwestern University, about 180,000 signatures are gathered on petitions to the Illinois legislature for the right of women to vote in referenda on liquor sales.

As a result of this work, Willard is elected president of the Women's Christian Temperance Union; she uses that position to combine the suffrage and temperance causes and to expand women's agenda with her "Do Everything" program. An uncommonly good organizer, she will develop global networks and influence a range of political forces, including male organizations.

Indeed, Willard arguably becomes the key factor in moving the suffragist image from radicalism and ridicule to mainstream respectability. She leads the WCTU in working for "Home Protection" legislation—a pro-family focus that makes more acceptable the fact that women are demanding the vote to pass laws against alcohol, domestic violence, and other forms of female exploitation. Willard becomes immensely popular, and her autobiography, *Glimpses of Fifty Years* (1889), will be a best-seller.

✦ That black women also have developed national networking systems is clear this year when so many former slaves leave the South for the "free soil" of Kansas that the state's resources are strained—and Josephine St. Pierre Ruffin organizes the Boston Kansas Relief Association to send supplies.

Like a number of others deemed African-American, Ruffin could pass for white: her father was a Frenchman from Martinque and her mother's ancestry included French and Indian as well as African forebears. Prior to the Civil War, she married a free black man from Richmond, and a decade ago, he graduated from Harvard Law School. Ruffin is one of the most prominent members of Boston's African-American community.

✦ Mary Mahoney graduates from Dr. Marie Zakrzewska's nursing school and is considered the world's first black professional nurse. She nurses in northeastern states until retirement in 1912, and African Americans will honor her by naming medical facilities for her.

✦ Young Susette La Flesche, a member of the Omaha tribe, interprets for Ponca chief Standing Bear as he tours the East; his object is to tell of the injurious treatment that the Ponca receive, which has resulted in the deaths of a third of the tribe. Known as "Bright Eyes," La Flesche proves a very popular speaker and influences the opinions of many previously apathetic people. Authors Louisa May Alcott, Helen Hunt Jackson, and Mary Mapes Dodge are among those who provide her with more publicity opportunities. She is honored with an invitation to speak in Boston's famed Faneuil Hall, a rare distinction for a woman and an Indian.

A decade later, after marriage to a supportive journalist changes her name to Tibbles, she and her husband will conduct a lecture tour abroad and repeatedly testify before Congress. She will win significant legislative victories for Plains Indians prior to her death at age 48.

✦ Many Americans see works of French impressionism for the first time when the new Society of American Artists exhibits the work of American Mary Cassatt, who continues to paint in Paris.

✦ Minnesota newspapers will be absorbed for years with *Muus v. Muus*, a divorce suit filed by the wife of a Norwegian Lutheran minister. When she alleges neglect and cruelty, not only the civil courts but also well-publicized church discipline proceedings cause a sensational discussion of parsonage life. Ultimately, Oline Muus moves to far-off Alabama, while the Reverend Muus returns to Norway.

✦ Poet Ethel Beers, whose Civil War poem "All Quiet Along the Potomac To-night" was sufficiently popular that its phrasing entered the language, always felt that if the poems she published in magazines were sold as a collection, she would die. Finally persuaded that her superstition is foolish, *All Quiet Along the Potomac and Other Poems* (1879) is issued on October 10; she dies the next day at age 52.

✦ On December 20, women not only vote in municipal elections in Boston and Cambridge but also campaign by canvassing voters at the polls.

1880   In January, Sarah Winnemucca, a Piute called "Shell Flower" in her native Nevada, meets with President Rutherford B. Hayes in Washington. In response to her effective argumentation, Interior Secretary Carl Schurz instructs agents in the Bureau of Indian Affairs to rectify their corrupt practices, but Hayes leaves office the following year and any long-term reform is slight.

Winnemucca, who speaks Spanish and English in addition to three Indian languages, proved herself a valued interpreter and brave warrior during 1878 tribal conflicts in Oregon and Idaho. Although some of her tribe believe that she has deserted them, when Winnemucca dies at 48 in Montana in 1891, she is generally deemed the most famous of western native women.

♦ New York women receive the right to vote in school elections in February, and Lydia Sayer Hasbrouck is elected to the school board of Middletown, New York—despite decades of avowed feminism that includes wearing pants and refusing to pay her taxes because she cannot vote.

♦ The American Woman Suffrage Association celebrates the 30th anniversary of the first National Woman's Rights Convention; like that meeting, this one is held in Worcester, Massachusetts. The featured speaker is pioneer feminist Abby Kelly Foster, age 70, who uses the platform to denounce the recent enfranchisement of New York women for school elections only. She believes that "half a vote" is worse than none.

♦ Miriam Leslie inherits the periodical publishing empire of Frank Leslie at his death; when she married him in 1872, she was the twice-divorced editor of *Frank Leslie's Ladies Journal*. She soon demonstrates business abilities even superior to his: after discovering far more debt than anyone realized, she sells six of the company's 12 publications and concentrates on the two lowest-priced items, *Frank Leslie's Popular Monthly* and *Frank Leslie's Illustrated Newspaper*. Legally changing her first name to his, she personally supervises 400 employees and soon has a sound financial base. Pundits dub her "the empress of journalism."

♦ With backing from Philadelphia Quaker women, Bryn Mawr College is chartered by the State of Pennsylvania; classes will start five years later. A year earlier, "Harvard Annex" for women began in Cambridge; it will be another 15 years before it is finalized into Radcliffe College.

♦ In San Diego, young Rosa Smith discovers a new species of fish and publishes a paper on it. Although she has no education beyond business school, she becomes the first woman recognized as an ichthyologist. She publishes some 20 scientific papers in her own name and, after her 1887 marriage to a German-born ichthyologist, co-authors another 15 with her husband—but in 1893, Rosa Smith Eigenmann will give up her career entirely to mother five children.

♦ Katherine Coman earns one of the most prestigious degrees yet granted to a woman, when she receives a doctorate in economics from the University of Michigan. Teaching at Wellesley College the rest of her life, Dr. Coman will be active in a number of feminist organizations, and her *Industrial History of the United States* (1905) becomes a standard of economic history.

♦ The University of Michigan grants a medical degree to Martha Hughes, a graduate of Utah's University of Deseret. Because she wants a stronger scientific background and oratorical training, she goes to Philadelphia and enrolls simultaneously in an elocution school and the University of Pennsylvania—which, in the reverse of the usual order, will grant Dr. Hughes a bachelor of science degree in 1882. All of this is excellent preparation for the next decade, when Martha Hughes Cannon becomes the nation's first female state senator.

♦ The annual meetings of the Association for the Advancement of Women receive respectful press coverage throughout the decade. Papers by the nation's most accomplished women are the main feature, with those by Julia Ward Howe especially drawing attention. Another important paper is that of Omaha leader Susette La Flesche, whose 1881 speech is entitled "The Position, Occupation, and Culture of Indian Women." As female college graduates become more common, however, interest in the organization declines, and eventually the American Association of University Women takes over many of the group's goals.

✦ Eight years after formal nursing education began at the New England Hospital for Women and Children, the Illinois Training School for Nurses opens in Chicago. The Chicago Woman's Club promotes it, while Dr. Sarah Stevenson is the chief medical advocate for professionalization of the city's nurses.

✦ Members of the National Woman Suffrage Association, including Matilda Joselyn Gage, attend the national conventions of the Democratic, Republican, and Greenback parties, where they unsuccessfully lobby the male delegates for a suffrage plank in the party platforms.

✦ Harriet Stone, using the pseudonym Margaret Sidney, publishes *The Five Little Peppers and How They Grew*. It and other stories about the fictional Pepper family will sell more than 2 million copies during the next three decades. A publisher as well as the author of 40 books, she lives in a Concord, Massachusetts, house occupied earlier by both Nathaniel and Sophia Peabody Hawthorne and Louisa May Alcott.

✦ Carrie Lane, who will be famous as Carrie Chapman Catt, graduates first in her class at Iowa State Agricultural College—despite working part time because her father refused to pay tuition for a girl. Within a few years, Miss Lane is the superintendent of schools for Mason City, Iowa.

✦ The previous decade has seen an 80% increase in the number of female teachers. Many are women who go west to teach in prairie and mountain schools, where they find little competition from men, who prefer to farm or ranch the free land. The "schoolmarm" becomes a leading fixture of western towns, replacing the "schoolmaster" of the East Coast.

As the decade begins, the nation has 800 high schools; at its end, there are more than 2,500. Most are coeducational, and this opportunity is a tremendously important factor in the improving status of women.

1881 The Dutch begin birth control clinics operated under the aegis of the government; decades later, Margaret Sanger and other Americans will use these clinics to educate themselves regarding contraception.

✦ Eight female physicians—including Dr. Emily Blackwell and Dr. Marie Zakrzewska, who run competing medical schools—offer Harvard $50,000 to open medical studies to women. Harvard turns them down.

✦ Harvard Observatory hires Williamina Fleming—a deserted wife and mother who was working as a maid—to do mathematical calculations. She is so successful that other women are hired as "computers," while Fleming goes on to serious astronomical research. During the next decade, she will use newly invented telescopic photography to observe and classify some 10,000 celestial bodies. Fleming's methodology becomes so successful that it is named for her.

✦ Alice Stone Blackwell, the daughter of Lucy Stone and Henry Blackwell, enters an all-male class at Boston University—and goes on to graduate Phi Beta Kappa and also to be elected class president. Much later she is appointed a university trustee.

✦ Women's colleges have now graduated a generation of students, and the Association of Collegiate Alumnae begins. With the name later changed to the American Association of University Women (AAUW), this national organization provides a mechanism for college-educated women—who are still a tiny minority—to find each other when they move to new communities.

✦ The Minnesota Woman Suffrage Association organizes in the small town of Hastings, near St. Paul. Fourteen women are present, but by the end of the year, membership will be 124. Minnesota women also present 31,228 names on petitions to the legislature for the vote in elections on alcohol prohibition.

◆ Conscious of the historical significance of their work, Susan Anthony, Elizabeth Cady Stanton, and Matilda Joselyn Gage publish the first volume of *The History of Woman Suffrage*. The history begins with the 1840 World Anti-Slavery Conference and ends with the beginning of the Civil War. Gage's introductory and summary chapters offer especially thoughtful feminist theory.

◆ *Century of Dishonor* by Helen Hunt Jackson is the first book to document the nation's wrongs toward its natives; Jackson was inspired by Susette La Flesche's Boston tour. The book is widely read and discussed, and Jackson's evidence of corruption in the Bureau of Indian Affairs results in some reform. She is commissioned by the Interior Department to do a study of California's Indians, and her book leads to the establishment of the Indian Rights Association.

◆ The Knights of Labor, a new semisecret labor coalition, opens to women; 192 women's units will be formed within five years.

1882 Political reporter Emily Edson Briggs, a married woman who has written her Washington column under the pseudonym "Olivia" for more than 20 years, is elected the first president of the Woman's National Press Association when that body begins. Although these Washington women exercise political power through their writing, most will be like Briggs in that they will never live to cast a ballot themselves.

◆ After living with the Omaha for a year, ethnologist Alice Cunningham Fletcher moves to Washington, D.C., where she lobbies on their behalf. The tribe hopes to lessen the power of the Bureau of Indian Affairs by dividing the Omahas' communal land into individual holdings, and Fletcher drafts and lobbies through the appropriate legislation. She administers the project in Nebraska and writes a Senate report on it, and then, at the request of the interior secretary, goes to Alaska to report on natives there.

◆ Emma Lazarus, whose Jewish family has lived in America since they emigrated from Portugal in the 1600s, publishes *Songs of a Semite*. She becomes internationally famous four years later, when her lines are used on the Statue of Liberty: "Give me your tired, you poor, your huddled masses yearning to breathe free . . ." She dies prematurely the following year.

◆ When New Orleans businesswoman Margaret Gaffney Haughery dies, the city closes its offices out of respect to this Irish self-made philanthropist. She has long endowed Catholic orphanages, and her will leaves money to Protestant and Jewish charities as well.

◆ The second volume of *The History of Woman Suffrage* comes out; its authors are again Susan Anthony, Elizabeth Cady Stanton, and Matilda Joselyn Gage. The book offers fascinating material detailing the history of women's roles in the Civil War and Reconstruction. When Stanton's daughter, Harriot Stanton Blatch, points out the omission of any reference to the American Woman Suffrage Association, she is authorized to write a chapter on the group that rivals her mother's.

◆ Although California women cannot vote, Marietta Stowe declares herself a candidate for governor in an attempt to bring women's issues to electoral attention. The experience will make her a mainstay of Belva Lockwood's new National Equal Rights Party.

◆ The Senate ratifies the International Red Cross treaty, and Clara Barton becomes president of this new public/private agency. Under her leadership, the American Red Cross begins successfully responding to natural disasters, including the 1889 Johnstown flood.

◆ The University of Zurich grants a Ph.D. to M. Carey Thomas of Baltimore; it is the first degree the institution has awarded to either a woman or a non-European. She will go on to become the first female president of Bryn Mawr in 1894, where she serves for the rest of her life. One of the few academic leaders to associate herself with the suffrage movement, Dr. Thomas will form the college-based Equal Suffrage League in 1908, two years after Susan Anthony's death.

✦ At age 27, academic superstar Alice Freeman becomes president of Wellesley College—but she will lose the position when she marries five years later. Wellesley is more liberal than many of the elite eastern women's colleges in having female presidents, but employing a married woman in this position seems unthinkable.

After a time as the wife of a Harvard professor, Alice Freeman Palmer will return to higher education and play a leading role at the new University of Chicago. Like other midwestern institutions, Chicago will be coeducational from its 1891 beginning, and as dean of women, Palmer ensures fairness for women students and faculty. While holding this position, she and her Harvard professor husband conduct an early commuter marriage.

1883 Like the women of Wyoming and Utah, those in the Washington Territory gain the right to vote. They will lose it within four years, however, when a court strikes down the territorial law that enfranchises them. Women do not regain the right to vote until 1910, more than two decades after statehood—but still a decade prior to the enfranchisement of most women in 1920.

✦ Louisa Knapp Curtis edits the women's supplement of a farm magazine, and when it has more readers than the "main" magazine, she and her husband Cyrus begin *Ladies' Home Journal.* Clearly a large audience of female readers exists, for there are 270,000 subscribers in the first three years. The magazine becomes the foundation of powerful Curtis Publishing and continues through the 20th century.

✦ Belle Starr, infamous as the "Bandit Queen" of the Indian Territory that will become Oklahoma, serves time for robbery in a federal prison in Michigan. She will return to run her criminal operation again before her 1889 death, and no one ever will be convicted for shooting her in the back two days before her 41st birthday.

✦ The Florence Crittendon Homes begin in New York City when evangelist and patent medicine salesman Charles Crittendon opens a New York mission for "fallen women" and names the project for his mother. By 1897, there are 53 Florence Crittendon Homes throughout the nation, with many receiving support from the Women's Christian Temperance Union. While they initially shelter drug addicts, prostitutes, and spousal abuse victims, eventually they specialize as homes for unwed mothers.

✦ Orator Mary Ellen Lease of Kansas is disdainfully called "Mary Yellin" by those who resent her speeches on behalf of farmers, which draw thousands to rallies. She will second the nomination of Populist Party presidential candidate James B. Weaver in 1892 and is remembered for admonishing farmers to "raise less corn and more hell."

✦ Nebraska men soundly defeat a referendum for which national suffrage leaders have worked for six weeks. The women had expected to do far better: "Every train brought some of the speakers to their headquarters in Omaha, with cheering news from the different localities they had canvassed. . . . Some of the ladies went in carriages to each of the polling booths and made earnest appeals. . . . Others stood dispensing refreshments and the tickets they wished to see voted."

✦ Young Ella Wheeler of rural Wisconsin publishes *Poems of Passion* and finds that some poems are too passionate for Victorian America. Her book is condemned as salacious, even though it sells well enough that she is famous for the rest of her life. She marries the next year and, as Ella Wheeler Wilcox, moves to suburban New York, where she enjoys literary prestige. One line from the book remains in the nation's collective memory: "Laugh, and the world laughs with you; Weep, and you weep alone."

✦ The graduating class of Washington's Howard University Law School is composed of three white women, one black woman, and one black man. The black woman is pre–Civil War newspaper editor Mary Ann Shadd Cary, now age 60.

✦ As Oberlin College celebrates its 50th anniversary, Lucy Stone, class of 1847, reminisces about her student days in the nation's first coeducational college: "Some of us worked for three cents an hour and boarded ourselves. Some took in washing at 37 1/2 cents per dozen. One, whose rich father would give her no money, but provided her with ample store of clothes, sold the silk that was for dresses and used the money to clothe her mind. . . ."

✦ On November 16, at a Liverpool reception in honor of Susan Anthony and Elizabeth Cady Stanton, the women's movement becomes global. Women from England, Scotland, Ireland, and France join the Americans in unanimously endorsing a resolution that begins: "Recognizing that union is strength and that the time has come when women all over the world should unite in the just demand for their political enfranchisement . . ."

They form committees of correspondence and plan for a giant meeting in the United States five years later, when the 40th anniversary of the Seneca Falls convention will occur.

1884   Congress retroactively awards a soldier's pension to Sarah Edmonds Seelye, who served in the Civil War under the name Frank Thompson. Her former comrades send written testimonials to her military worth and to the fact that they did not realize she was a woman. She has since become the mother of three, and in 1898, she will be honored as the only woman with full membership in the Grand Army of the Republic.

✦ Mary Lincoln—who has no connection to Mary Todd Lincoln—publishes *Mrs. Lincoln's Boston Cook Book*, which becomes a culinary classic. Not merely a cookbook, it includes virtually the entire curriculum of the innovative Boston Cooking School. The book goes through many reprintings and provides a model for cooking schools throughout the country.

✦ After 21 years in the ministry, the Reverend Olympia Brown retires so that she can devote more time to feminist causes. She is soon elected a vice president of the National Woman Suffrage Association, and, as president of the Wisconsin Woman Suffrage Association, she leads women to take advantage of the language of state law that allows them to vote in school elections. For many years, she will pursue a court case to expand this language to all elections.

✦ In Massachusetts, about 20 women—the wives of wealthy men—sign a "remonstrance" against suffrage when a resolution for it is presented to the legislature. These women also work to defeat a suffrage referendum held in Oregon this year, and they will continue to fund suffrage opponents in other western states in future elections.

✦ The National Equal Rights Party, a small group with membership primarily on the West Coast, nominates Washington, D.C., attorney Belva Lockwood for president of the United States. The vice presidential nominee is Marietta L. B. Stowe of San Francisco. The Californians' hope is to "get one elector elected on our ticket so that person will form one of the electoral college . . . and become the entering wedge."

Mainstream suffrage leadership is not enthusiastic about what they see as a rerun of Victoria Woodhull's quixotic 1872 campaign, and they suspect Lockwood is aggrandizing herself and her law practice at the expense of serious suffragists. In November, Lockwood receives some 4,000 votes in California and five northern states—of 10 million total. According to Lockwood, the Indiana electoral college also cast its votes for her after first voting for successful nominee Grover Cleveland.

Lockwood responds to suffragists' criticism of her effort with: "Why not nominate women for important places? Is not Victoria Empress of India? Is not history full of precedents of women rulers? We shall never have equal rights until we take them, nor respect until we command it."

✦ Republican presidential nominee Senator James G. Blaine uses the talents of Mary Abigail Dodge as a ghostwriter for his speeches. Dodge's essays have appeared in the same publications as those of Ralph Waldo Emerson, Nathaniel Hawthorne, and other giants of her era, and in 1877, she did a series of columns in the *New York Herald* on political topics. Although an expert on politics, her conservative views are so strong that she opposes women's right to vote.

1885 Calling herself Nellie Bly from a popular Stephen Foster song, Elizabeth Cochrane begins writing for the *Pittsburgh Dispatch* after her letter to the editor in favor of suffrage attracts attention from the antisuffrage editor. She pioneers investigative journalism by going into Pittsburgh's burgeoning immigrant slums and writing exposés. Repeatedly disguising herself as a potential victim for exploitation, she reveals the city's underside and becomes an extremely popular reporter.

✦ Sharpshooter Annie Oakley joins Buffalo Bill Cody's Wild West Show, where she will delight international audiences for the next 16 years with such feats as hitting a moving target while standing on a galloping horse. When the Crown Prince of Germany insists on participating in one of her tricks, she shoots the cigarette he holds in his lips.

✦ Utah's Emmeline B. Wells lobbies in Washington for the unique Mormon goals of polygamy and woman suffrage. Under the signature of "Aunt Em," Wells is also a longtime writer for Mormon publications. She fights against the work of another female lobbyist, Angela F. Newman, who represents Methodists: Wells will lose on one issue next year, when Newman succeeds in getting Congress to appropriate $40,000 to fund a rehabilitative center in Salt Lake for women who wish to leave their marriages. Annual operating expenses will also be appropriated until 1893, setting a precedent for federal funding of what is essentially a center for displaced homemakers.

✦ *Anna Ella Carroll v. The United States* is filed in Carroll's attempt to force the judiciary to do what the executive branch has failed to do: to compensate her for services she rendered during the Civil War. Feminists support Carroll's claim that she was responsible for successful military strategy— but in doing so, they disregard not only the fact that thousands of other women rendered similarly uncompensated services but also that Carroll does not support suffrage. A Washington insider who has earned her living by lobbying since 1845, Carroll is in a position to help the suffrage cause, but she uses her connections only for personal financial gain. Her time of influence is waning, and her claim—a source of controversy for two decades—is never successful.

✦ The Oregon legislature passes a bill enabling women to practice law. It is the result of intensive lobbying by Mary Gysin, whose interest in law began when she was tried for (and acquitted of) the murder of her husband. The state Supreme Court, however, will delay her admission to the bar with various excuses, even though she practices in nearby Washington state.

✦ The Southern Baptist Foreign Mission Board revokes the traditional right of female missionaries to vote in business meetings, presumably because the men resent the popularity of missionary Lottie Moon, who has served in the Shantung Province of China since 1873. When Moon resigns in protest, the board quickly reneges. From China, she organizes American women into a tradition of donations at Christmas, and the Lottie Moon Christmas Offering eventually becomes a multimillion-dollar source of mission revenue.

✦ Three years after Eliza Eddy's death, the probate court releases a $40,000 bequest that she wanted equally divided between Susan Anthony and Lucy Stone. Eddy's will "requested" that they use the funds "to further what is called the 'Woman's Rights Cause,'" adding that "neither of them is under any legal responsibility to any one or any court." The first of such bequests to benefit women's rights activists came from New York liberal Charles Hovey in 1859.

✦ The American Woman Suffrage Association meets in Minneapolis at the invitation of Dr. Martha Ripley, president of the state suffrage association. She knows AWSA leadership from her medical school days in Boston, and she understands the need for suffrage leadership to move beyond its East Coast base.

◆ The New York Academy of Sciences admits its first woman: she is Erminnie Platt Smith, who after attending Emma Willard's Troy Female Seminary and a German mining school, has switched from geology to the new field of ethnology. She specializes in the Iroquois and, among other achievements, has done the field research necessary to write a dictionary of their language. An active member of New York's Sorosis club, Smith's first academic paper, which she presented to the American Association for the Advancement of Science in 1879, was on jade.

◆ The Women's Anthropological Society of America begins with the blessings of the field's founder, Sir Edwin B. Tylor. He argues that female anthropologists are essential to success, for women's activities are central to any culture and the women of preliterate societies will more easily reveal information to other women. In fact, women are accepted in this field so quickly that the society disbands in 1899, when the American Anthropological Association begins as a mixed-gender organization.

◆ Woman's College of Baltimore is chartered by Methodist women concerned with Maryland's lack of educational opportunity for women. In honor of major donors, it is soon renamed Goucher College.

◆ The literary world is shocked by the suicide of Marian Hooper Adams, 42-year-old wife of famed author Henry Adams. Educated in Boston by Elizabeth Agassiz, Adams lives across the street from the White House and is seen as one of Washington's most sophisticated women. Novelist Henry James compares her mind to that of Voltaire.

She also is an experimental photographer, and she uses those chemicals to kill herself when she discovers that her husband is involved with another woman. Henry Adams will erect a monument to her in Washington's Rock Creek Park that is a modernist image of a tragic woman, aptly called "Grief."

1886 White House gossip reaches new heights when President Grover Cleveland, a lifelong bachelor, appears to be courting. Instead of visiting a widowed friend, however, he is seeing her daughter. Frances Folsom, a 22-year-old recent college graduate, weds the 49-year-old president. He calls her "Frank," the press calls her "Frankie," and she attracts more far more publicity than any other first lady. Despite the groom's age, the Clevelands will have five children.

◆ Future Nobel Prize winner Emily Balch goes to Bryn Mawr College instead of to the closer Radcliffe in order to accompany a friend whose Harvard professor father "was not willing to have it known among his Cambridge friends that he was disgraced by having a daughter at college."

◆ The Women's Christian Temperance Union, led by Angela F. Newman of Nebraska, presents Congress with 250,000 petition signatures against polygamy. Although many WCTU members support suffrage, the petition also urges Congress to rescind the right to vote that women in the Utah Territory have: the WCTU position is that the multiple votes of Mormon wives are being used by their powerful husbands against the best interests of women.

◆ The third volume of *The History of Woman Suffrage* is issued. It covers the decade from 1876 to the publication date and is the last that will be authored by the team of Susan Anthony, Elizabeth Cady Stanton, and Matilda Joselyn Gage.

Volume 3 addresses both the national and international status of women, with reports from each state and nations ranging to the Far East. It also covers important events, including the 1876 centennial activity and the conventions of the National Woman Suffrage Association. Each of the three volumes published thus far is approximately 1,000 pages, and more than 1,200 privately printed copies are distributed at suffragists' expense to libraries in America and Europe.

◆ The latest volume of *The History of Woman Suffrage* contains a report on Iowa women written by Amelia Bloomer, whose name is now synonymous with the wearing of pants by women—although she has not worn them for decades. Much more conventional than her image, the real Amelia Bloomer lives with her husband and two adopted children in Council Bluffs, Iowa; she served as the 1871 president of the Iowa Woman Suffrage Association and is also a gardener and gourmet cook.

✦ South Carolinian Mary Chesnut dies. She has managed to copy the 400,000 words of her diaries into a manuscript that offers a unique insider's view of the Civil War Confederacy—but she leaves publication to executors, who do a poor job. *A Diary from Dixie* will be not issued until 1905; it is expanded in 1949, but the 20th century is almost over before Chesnut's historical treasure is adequately published.

✦ Congress belatedly grants a $25 monthly pension to stellar Civil War nurse Mary Ann Bickerdyke. The money is both two decades overdue and an insufficient amount, because Bickerdyke—who has already demonstrated her physical stamina with battlefield nursing in her 40s—will live on to 1901.

✦ Leonora Barry is elected to head the women's department of the Knights of Labor. A widow who brought up her children on the meager wages of a seamstress, Barry creates her own models for organizing women; she travels the nation for four years, but her work is limited by both women's lack of political power and the Knights' reluctance to be publicly visible. After her 1890 marriage, she is known as Mother Lake or Mrs. Barry-Lake, and her views become increasingly conservative.

✦ The few Asian women who manage to immigrate find that life in America is dangerous: at least 40 Chinese are killed and as many as 600 are driven from their homes when white men demand their mining jobs in Rock Springs, Wyoming.

✦ After studying Florence Nightingale's methods in England, nursing educator Linda Richards goes to Japan for five years, where she sets up that nation's first school of nursing.

✦ Responding to popular demand for a sequel to *Little Women*, Louisa May Alcott publishes *Jo's Boys*, although she is busy caring for her senile father and a young niece. She is also active in the New England Woman's Club and, the previous year, sent a letter to the American Woman Suffrage Association to make it clear on which side of the debate she stood. "I should be a traitor to all I most love," she wrote, "if I did not covet a place among those who are giving their lives to the emancipation of the white slaves of America."

✦ *Little Lord Fauntleroy* is an instant classic for English-born Virginian Frances Hodgson Burnett. Made into a play, it is soon so popular that 400 acting troupes produce it simultaneously, while the title enters the language to denote a boy dressed in velvet and lace. Burnett overcomes her lifelong struggle against poverty while also demonstrating more business acumen than many writers: she sues copyright violators in British court and establishes important precedents for all authors.

✦ At age 55, Emily Dickinson dies in the western Massachusetts town where she was born, having traveled out of the state only once. She has traveled in her mind, though, and her sister eventually finds almost 1,800 poems, most of which are neatly dated and packaged for posterity. Just seven were published in Dickinson's lifetime—and those mostly because of the intervention of her friend, popular author Helen Hunt Jackson.

Thomas Wentworth Higginson, one of the era's most popular critics, continues to advise against posthumous publication. He calls Dickinson's work "too crude in form."

1887 For the first and only time in the 19th century, the U.S. Senate takes a vote on the Susan B. Anthony Amendment that enfranchises women. It fails, 34 to 16, and 25 senators do not bother to vote. Both houses of Congress have had Select Committees on Woman Suffrage since 1882, but although they issue favorable reports, floor action does not follow. The House never takes up the amendment named for Anthony until well into the 20th century, after she is dead.

♦ When Congress outlaws polygamy, women in Utah Territory lose the franchise that they have had since 1870. The bill contains a clause rescinding women's right to vote, and suffragists offer no organized objection to this revocation.

Emmeline B. Wells, who had lobbied in Washington during the two previous years, is not present this year. A vice president of the National Woman Suffrage Association already in 1874, she now organizes the Woman Suffrage Association of Utah to regain the vote.

A number of Mormons are so angered by what they see as governmental interference with their lifestyle that they move to Mexico. Women concerned about the legitimacy of their children are especially likely to take this step, but the migration also includes monogamists. They retain their U.S. citizenship, however, and many eventually return.

♦ Kansas women, who have voted in school elections since 1861, win enfranchisement for municipal elections. This is a great boon to the temperance movement, for the crucial "wet" or "dry" decision is made at the local level.

Rhode Island is the first eastern state to hold a referendum on suffrage; it fails, but getting the legislature to put the issue on the ballot in itself is something of a victory.

♦ Congress incorporates the Young Woman's Christian Home "to provide a temporary home for young women . . . in the District of Columbia, who shall, from any cause, be in want of and willing to accept temporary home, care, and assistance." It will make appropriations of $1,000 annually for almost two decades to care for these homeless women.

The University Settlement House begins to serve the needy of New York's Lower East Side. It is not well known nationally, however, and Jane Addams is unfamiliar with it when she begins the more famous Hull House in Chicago.

♦ When Pittsburgh reporter Nellie Bly goes to Mexico and writes of the exploitation of the poor by the aristocracy, the Mexican government is outraged and expels her. Joseph Pulitzer is so impressed with her work that he hires her to pose as insane to get into New York's notorious Blackwell Island asylum. Bly turns both experiences into best-selling books and continues to do exposés for Pulitzer, including entrapping men who take bribes and/or sexual favors.

♦ The nation's first female law school graduate, Phoebe Couzins, becomes its first female federal marshal. Couzins holds this position in eastern Missouri for two months after her father's death; she had served as his deputy since his 1884 presidential appointment.

♦ Members of the Women's Christian Temperance Union are active in a Tampa, Florida, election, though none publicly calls herself a suffragist. They campaign throughout the balloting, rewarding supportive men with lapel badges, lemonade, and a free dinner, while "prepared to brave any amount of indignity" from those who oppose them. More than 1,000 ballots are cast, and the WCTU loses the election by just 25 votes.

♦ Congress passes the Dawes Act, which is intended to reform mistreatment of American Indians. The lobbying effort for the act is due in large part to Helen Hunt Jackson's *Century of Dishonor*, which, in turn, was inspired by Omaha leader Susette La Flesche.

Ethnologist Alice Cunningham Fletcher, under contract with the Interior Department, administers the act for the Winnebago of Nebraska and the Nez Perce of Idaho. Fletcher finds a lifelong assistant in Francis La Flesche, the younger brother of famed "Bright Eyes." Fletcher had proved herself in her first contact with the Omaha by camping out during rainy days and nights, guided by Susette La Flesche.

Fletcher is associated with Harvard's Peabody Museum, and she will be recognized by her social science colleagues with the vice presidency of the American Association for the Advancement of Science in 1896. She will be a cofounder of the American Anthropological Association at the turn of the century.

♦ Luella Miner graduates from Oberlin and goes to China as a missionary; she will live there until her

1922 death. Initially she teaches only young men —for whom she writes textbooks in Chinese —but in 1905, she will organize Women's Union College in Peking. As its president, Miner confers the first degrees earned by Chinese women.

+ Oregon newspaper publisher Abigail Scott Duniway sells the *New Northwest*, a Portland weekly that she has successfully operated for 16 years. Having brought up her six children with the paper's profits, she semiretires. She edits other publications, serves as an officer in the suffrage movement and in the General Federation of Women's Clubs, and becomes the most visible representative of the West at national women's meetings.

+ Dorothea Dix dies and is buried in a Cambridge, Massachusetts, cemetery near the jail where she began her career as the nation's first advocate for the mentally ill. In the four decades since then, Dix traveled some 30,000 miles and played a role in building 32 institutions.

1888 The 40th anniversary of the Seneca Falls Women's Rights Convention is commemorated with the formation of the International Council of Women. Held in Washington, D.C., the meeting grew out of contacts Elizabeth Cady Stanton and Susan Anthony made during an 1883 visit to England. With additional sponsorship from Frances Willard of the Women's Christian Temperance Union, it attracts representatives from 49 nations and 53 American organizations.

The call for the convocation, issued last year, encourages women to go global: "It is impossible to overestimate the far-reaching influence of such a Council. An interchange of opinions on the great questions now agitating the world will rouse women to new thought . . . and give them a realizing sense of the power of combination."

The invitation is signed by Stanton as president and Anthony as vice president, along with five other officers. They have put a great deal of effort and $12,000 into planning; some 4,000 letters were mailed and the 16-page program was revised and reprinted so many times that a "low estimate" of the printing is 672,000 pages.

The convention goes on for eight days, and President and Mrs. Grover Cleveland attend some of it. Among the Americans featured as speakers are Frances Watkins Harper, a popular African-American orator employed by the WCTU, Leonora Barry of the new Knights of Labor, and Mary Livermore, whose new book, *My Story of the War* (1887), is a top seller.

The council resolves to hold national assemblies every three years and international ones every five years. Its platform includes many aims on behalf of women, but stops short of demanding suffrage, which is too radical for delegates from many foreign countries.

+ By this time, Susan Anthony's days of poverty and persecution are largely over. When not traveling, she spends much of the summer at her Rochester home; in the winter, she goes to Washington, D.C., where a suite is made available at the Riggs Hotel; the owners not only agree with her political views but also benefit from having this celebrity guest.

Anthony receives additional financial support from Rachel Foster Avery, who serves for more than two decades as the corresponding secretary of the National Woman Suffrage Association. Avery is a wealthy Philadelphian, who, like Anthony, grew up as a Quaker; she pays for European trips and even buys clothes for her "Aunt Susan."

+ The Young Women's Hebrew Association is formed in New York to offer the growing numbers of female Jewish immigrants the same services that are available from the Young Women's Christian Association.

+ Six Methodist women, including WCTU officials Frances Willard and Angela Newman, are elected as delegates to the church's governing General Conference, but the assembly of men refuses to seat women.

+ Mary Baird Bryan, the wife of future presidential nominee Willian Jennings Bryan, is admitted to the Nebraska bar. Not only is this unusual for a married woman, but Bryan is also a mother. Her daughter Ruth, a future congresswoman, is three.

◆ The new Department of Labor is headed by progressive Carroll D. Wright, and he appoints Clare de Graffenried as one of 20 special investigators. De Graffenried's reports on her native Georgia and elsewhere spell out the harsh working conditions that women face in the nation's factories. Although sympathetic, her studies are not sentimental, and her statistical analyses will be sufficiently good to win top prizes from the American Economic Association.

Born in 1849, she graduated at age 16 from Wesleyan Female College in Macon, which terms itself the oldest women's college in the world. Until she became a federal employee, de Graffenried taught mathematics at Georgetown Female Seminary.

◆ Louise Blanchard Bethune is the first woman elected to the American Institute of Architects. She began drafting blueprints in 1876 and has practiced jointly with her husband in Buffalo since 1881. During a 30-year career, she will design and supervise the construction of many western New York buildings.

◆ When the Marine Biological Institute opens at Woods Hole, Massachusetts, the first researcher assigned a project is zoologist Cornelia Clapp. Influenced by naturalists Louis and Elizabeth Agassiz a decade earlier, she studies at such prestigious institutions as MIT, Syracuse, and the University of Chicago. A lifelong professor at Mount Holyoke College, Dr. Clapp earns three doctorates, and, in 1906, she will be included in the first edition of *Men of Science*.

◆ After a decade of unpaid work for the Bureau of American Ethnology, Matilda Stevenson finally receives a salary when she becomes a widow. A specialist on the Zuni of New Mexico, she works with them for three decades; she publishes a number of reports and also brings hundreds of unclassified southwestern plants for further study at the Smithsonian Institute.

◆ Californian Gertrude Atherton begins moving her residence between Europe and America every two years, a practice that she will maintain until 1931, as she seeks new settings for her historical novels. The eventual author of some 40 books, including the 1923 best-seller *Black Oxen*, Atherton will be elected to the National Institute of Arts and Letters in 1937. She initially published anonymously because her Spanish in-laws disapprove of such activity—as a bride, she was even prevented from reading.

◆ Bryn Mawr offers one of the first courses in sociology, "Charities and Corrections." The college also buys a settlement house in nearby New Jersey, where its students can gain social work experience with immigrants who are arriving in unprecedented numbers.

◆ The United Methodist Church begins a deaconess program in Boston modeled on the Catholic church's training for nuns. The program is designed to allow Protestant women to adopt the church as a vocation without being ordained.

◆ The Equal Rights Party meets in Iowa and again nominates Belva Lockwood for president of the United States. This effort, however, receives less attention than it did four years ago.

◆ Illinois men who support the Progressive Party clearly indicate their willingness to vote for a woman: Mary Allen West is part of a four-candidate statewide slate, and her 21,614 vote total is only slightly less than the top candidate's 21,800. She outpolls one of the men.

◆ President Cleveland's recent marriage becomes an election issue—as, indeed, his sexuality had been when he was still single. In his losing 1884 election, Republican opponents focused on his youthful paternity of an illegitimate child. In this campaign, Frances Folsom Cleveland attempts to end persistent rumors that he beats her by issuing a press release in which she calls him "kind" and "considerate." Although few women can vote, propriety demands that her statement be addressed to "the women of our Country." In the end, Cleveland wins the popular vote but loses the electoral vote, and the newlyweds vacate the White House.

◆ President Cleveland's Republican opponent hires popular Civil War speaker Anna Dickinson, but this is the last profitable year of her career. Dickinson's partisanship against the Democrats is so intense that even her Republican bosses are embarrassed by her baseless attacks on the president. Within a few years, she exhibits signs of paranoia so serious that she is institutionalized; upon her release, she successfully sues several newspapers that have deemed her insane.

✦ Louisa May Alcott, age 55, dies on the day of her father's funeral. Like many other famous women, she had been strongly influenced—for good and for ill—by her father.

1889 In Chicago, Jane Addams and her friend Ellen Gates Starr begin Hull House. While on an European tour two years earlier, they were inspired by Toynbee Hall, a project for London's poor recently founded by Samuel and Henrietta Barnett. Back home, they persuade Charles J. Hull to donate his former summer mansion, which is now surrounded by the urban poor instead of pleasant countryside.

Hull House offers a range of services to Chicago's immigrants. While Starr emphasizes cultural education, Addams specializes in legal and financial problem-solving. They quickly attract other affluent young women eager to do something meaningful with their lives. These women live at the settlement house and provide 24-hour assistance to foreigners unable to cope with family emergencies.

Their model is soon replicated in all U.S. cities with a significant immigrant population. Hull House also becomes a laboratory for new social scientists, as Edith and Grace Abbott, Emily Balch, Sophonisba Breckinridge, Alice Hamilton, Florence Kelly, Julia Lathrop, and other pioneers in sociology affiliate themselves with it.

✦ Seven Italian nuns of the Missionary Sisters of the Sacred Heart of Jesus arrive in New York, where they begin a school and orphanage for Italians. Led by Mother Frances Xavier Cabrini—who is later declared a saint—their work will expand not only throughout the nation but as far as Argentina.

The year is a high point for the establishment of Catholic sisterhoods, as nine new ones begin, ranging from the Sisters of the Sorrowful Mother in Wichita, Kansas, to the Little Franciscan Sisters of Mary in Worcester, Massachusetts.

Also this year, the Founding Asylum of the Sisters of Charity in New York pays more than 1,100 women to serve as wet nurses for abandoned babies.

✦ On April 22, women join men in an unprecedented land rush when Oklahoma is opened to white settlement. Some 50,000 settlers claim 2 million acres of former Indian Territory in one 24-hour period. During the next few years, Congress will buy several million more acres of Indian land, and in 1893, there will be another even larger rush of incoming homesteaders.

✦ Susan La Flesche, younger sister of Indian activist Susette La Flesche, graduates from the venerable Woman's Medical College of Pennsylvania. She is the first Native American woman to become a physician, and she graduates at the top of her class. She will spend the rest of her life among the Omaha of Nebraska, where her father, Iron Eye, was chief.

He was exceptional not only in his belief in the need to enter the white world but also in sending his daughters to eastern boarding schools. Susette, Susan, and their sister Marguerite were educated in Elizabeth, New Jersey; Susan and Marguerite went on to Virginia's Hampton Institute, which was originally set up for black men. Iron Eye moved beyond his initial refusal to allow his daughters to go to school with men, and the La Flesche sisters were among the first women to break this gender bar.

Marguerite will teach on the reservation all of her life, and after Susette's death, Dr. Susan La Flesche becomes in effect, though not in title, chief of the Omaha. Her name changes to Picotte after her 1894 marriage, but she continues her leadership role, even leading a lobbying delegation to Washington.

✦ A Wyoming prostitute known as Cattle Kate is hanged from a cottonwood tree by ranchers an-

Jane Addams and Ellen Gates Starr founded Chicago's Hull House in 1889 after investigating a recently developed project for London's poor. Their work quickly became a model for similar settlement houses in other U.S. cities, especially those with large numbers of immigrants. Both men and women worked in these efforts, and the women were especially likely to also live at the settlement; in this Hull House photo, the residents are seen at dinner. Many of Addams' protégées went on to independent fame in the social sciences. University of Illinois at Chicago; The University Library; Jane Addams Memorial Collection

gry that she accepts stolen cattle as payment for her services. Although some men are arrested, no one ever goes to trial for her death.

✦ Barnard College, associated with Columbia University in New York, begins. Named for Columbia's current president, it is the last of the colleges that will be termed the Seven Sisters—northeastern women's colleges known for both their high academic standards and for their social links to the elite young men of the seven Ivy League colleges.

In chronological order by founding date, the Seven Sisters are: Mount Holyoke, Vassar, Wellesley, Smith, Radcliffe (still called "Harvard Annex"), Byrn Mawr, and Barnard.

✦ *Ladies' Home Journal* raises its annual subscription to $1, but sales climb nonetheless. Editor Louisa Knapp Curtis retires to spend more time with her children; Edward Bok, a Dutch immigrant and Curtis's future son-in-law, replaces her. Although he is scorned by other men in the magazine business, he has a feel for what women want to read. Among his innovations are the publication of music and of architectural drawings; even Mark Twain writes for *Ladies' Home Journal*.

✦ In November, *New York World* journalist Nellie Bly embarks on an all-time attention-getter—enacting Jules Verne's 1863 science fiction story, *Around the World in Eighty Days*, with currently available transportation.

After persuading editor Joseph Pulitzer to put up the money, she sails for France, interviews Verne, and then proceeds around the world using various methods, including camels. Her stories are telegraphed back, and Pulitzer's newspapers sell at unprecedented rates. She is welcomed in San Francisco and hurries on to New York, having beaten the 80-day requirement by more than a week.

✦ Joseph Pulitzer also hires former Confederate first lady Varina Howell Davis to write a weekly column after Jefferson Davis dies this year. The job is more nearly charity than a career move, for the former president had no business skills and the family never recovered after the Civil War devastated their fortune. Davis also wounded his wife with excessive attentions to other women, even though he was significantly older than she. After they returned from exile abroad in the 1870s, their relationship was so bad that she refused to live with him.

1890 After more than 20 years of divisive rivalry, the American Woman Suffrage Association and the National Woman Suffrage Association merge. Alice Stone Blackwell, daughter of Lucy Stone of the AWSA, and Harriot Stanton Blatch, daughter of Elizabeth Cady Stanton of the NWSA, play important roles in overcoming the bad feelings between their mothers' organizations. Although an AWSA founder, Mary Livermore has remained popular with NWSA women, and she also acts a conciliator.

The terms of the merger are worked out between Stone and Susan Anthony of the NWSA, and Anthony wins two concessions that she considers important: the word "National" comes first in the new name of the National American Woman Suffrage Association (NAWSA), and her ally Stanton is chosen president. Anthony will become president two years later and remain so

until the turn of the century. The new organization's publication is that of the AWSA, *Woman's Journal*. Alice Stone Blackwell continues to be its editor; also elected corresponding secretary, she will hold these positions more than two decades.

Not everyone is pleased with the merger, and former NWSA officer Matilda Joselyn Gage, who sees the mainstream movement becoming too social and insufficiently political, forms her own Woman's National Liberal Union. She retains the union's presidency until her death eight years later, but it never grows beyond a small membership. The Federal Suffrage Association, which will be led by the Reverend Olympia Brown, is similarly motivated. These women feel that NAWSA leadership is growing too comfortable with the status quo and losing its political edge.

✦ Two other major women's organizations begin this year:

The Daughters of the American Revolution is founded during an era of huge immigration, when descendants of American colonists fear a loss of early history and of their personal identity. Membership requires tracing one's genealogy to a soldier who served with the American forces during the Revolution; although many blacks participated in the war, no black women are included as DAR members. The DAR grows much larger and more powerful than the comparable Sons of the American Revolution.

Of significance to many more women is the founding of the General Federation of Women's Clubs. The federation combines the many newly established clubs throughout the country, most of which aim at local civic improvement and/or literary self-improvement for women who had no opportunity to attend college. Journalist Jane Cunningham Croly is the energetic president of the GFWC, and by 1915, it will represent some 2 million women in thousands of clubs.

During this same era, industrialist Andrew Carnegie begins providing grants for public libraries, and the GFWC works closely with that effort during the next decades. Some communities refuse to accept Carnegie money, and local women's clubs frequently bear the responsibility of funding city libraries. Ultimately, the GFWC claims a role in the creation of 75% of the nation's libraries.

✦ Wyoming Territory becomes a state with the enfranchisement of women as part of its constitution—although many congressmen object strongly to Wyoming's insistence on including women, and the vote on statehood is close in both houses.

Esther Morris, the nation's first woman to hold governmental office as an 1870 Wyoming justice of the peace, is honored in Cheyenne by the new state's governor. Some 10,000 people attend the celebration.

✦ The author of the suffrage provision in the Wyoming constitution is Grace Raymond Hebard, who went west in 1882 to work as a draftsman for the Surveyor-General's Office. She has degrees in civil engineering from the University of Iowa and later earns a doctorate in political economy. Hebard will write several books on western history, teach at the University of Wyoming, and allegedly dominate its board of trustees. In 1898, she will add to her credentials by being the first woman to pass the state's bar examination.

✦ Although Wyoming is the only state in which women currently have full voting rights, varieties of partial enfranchisement exist in 19 states. Such rights are dependent both on the individual's status and the type of election; the most common is to allow women to vote in school elections. Other variations require women to be unmarried and/or to own property in order to be able to vote in municipal elections or on tax referenda. Kansas women currently have the most liberal form of partial enfranchisement: all women are eligible, but they are limited to voting in school and municipal elections.

The NAWSA supports full voting rights, and in the summer, the newly united organization tests itself with a state suffrage campaign in South Dakota. It goes badly. Farmer and labor organizations do not keep their promises, and the women lose by a large margin.

✦ On its own initiative, the Illinois Supreme Court reconsiders the 1869 application of Myra Bradwell and admits her to the bar. She has continued to publish the *Chicago Legal News* for more than two decades and will pass it on to her daughter, who becomes an attorney without similar struggle. Through her husband, a state representative, Bradwell is also responsible for several successful bills for women, including the right to hold school offices and to be notary publics. In 1892, Myra Bradwell will be admitted to practice before the U.S. Supreme Court, which had soundly struck her down her right to be an attorney less than 20 years earlier. The victory comes two years before her death.

✦ Opponents of suffrage begin publishing *The Remonstrance*, which will appear quarterly until they finally lose the debate in 1920. Initially it is edited by a man; later, a woman will take over. Like the two-decade-old *Woman's Journal* in favor of suffrage, the new publication is based in Boston and addresses a national audience.

✦ Congress receives a petition asking that women be included on the board of managers for the 1892 celebration being planned to commemorate the 400th anniversary of Columbus' voyage. Susan Anthony, who is unwilling to see women blocked from this event as they had been from the nation's 1876 centennial, has quietly gathered signatures from some of Washington's elite.

Congressmen cannot ignore a request signed by their wives and the wives of Supreme Court and cabinet members, and they create a 150-member Board of Lady Managers. Its head is Chicagoan Bertha Honore Palmer, a wealthy socialite and businesswoman who supports women's rights. She develops planning committees in every state, which will offer women unprecedented networking opportunities.

Palmer's executive abilities even extend to successfully defending herself in a lawsuit filed by St. Louis attorney Phoebe Couzins next year. Couzins sues after Palmer removes her from a paid position as secretary of the board—but Couzins had proven to be inefficient, arrogant, and disruptive to the planning work, and the majority of the board concurs in her firing.

♦ The Isbella Association, a group of Chicago women intent on ensuring that the event recognizes the vital role of the Spanish queen who financed Columbus' voyage, also plans for the Columbian Exposition. The members meet at the office of Dr. Frances Dickinson, whose ophtalmology practice is successful enough to pay for an office on State Street.

♦ The marriage of businessman George Catt to 31-year-old-widow Carrie Lane Chapman, who supports herself as a journalist, includes a notarized promise that the bride is free to travel for the suffrage movement during four months of the year.

♦ Although an heir to a copper fortune, Grace Dodge devotes herself to full-time social work; unlike other women of her class, she takes only two weeks of vacation each year. She funds much of the activity of the working women's associations that began in 1885, and this year Dodge directs their first national convention. These groups are social organizations, not unions. They concentrate on recreation and classes in domestic arts for women who are often immigrants with little or no formal education.

♦ Mountaineer Fay Fuller is the first woman to reach the summit of Mount Ranier, an ice-covered, dormant volcano amid the glaciers of Washington State.

♦ Charlotte Smith founds the National Women's Industrial League to encourage inventions by women. The first organizational difficulty, however, is simply locating female inventors, for Smith believes that many "are hidden under the name of fathers, husbands, brothers, and sons."

In the league's news organ, *Woman Inventor*, Ellen F. Eglin provides an additional insight when she explains why she sold her wringer washer patent for $18: "If it was known that a Negro woman patented the invention, white ladies would not buy the wringer."

♦ Four decades after Elizabeth Blackwell set the precedent, the nation has 1,302 female medical students. They are enrolled in 64 of its 152 medical schools—still less than half.

♦ A study finds just 30 black women in the entire nation who have received any university degree—only slightly more than one for each of the 25 years since slavery ended.

♦ Several southern women's colleges begin this decade that offer a parallel to the Seven Sisters colleges of the Northeast. Agnes Scott College, named for a donor, begins in Decatur, Georgia, near Atlanta, this year; next year, Randolph-Macon Woman's College is chartered in Ashland, Virginia, near Richmond. It is associated with a much older college for men, and the same is true of New Orleans' Sophie Newcomb Memorial College, which opens under the aegis of Tulane University. None of these colleges admits blacks.

♦ Over 35,000 people, two-thirds of them women and children, are employed in newly built textile mills in the South. Centered in northern Georgia and the Carolinas where hills provide water power, almost all of the workers in these mills are white.

Census records for southern states also show that the region has 434 female physicians and 120 female "clergymen," but just 12 women are lawyers.

Another census analysis shows that some 40,000 women identify themselves as midwives and nurses, but nursing schools are still so new that only about 500 of these women are estimated to have professional training.

♦ New York's Caroline Schermerhorn Astor engages in a decade-long feud with her niece by marriage, Mrs. John Jacob Astor IV, over which is the true "Mrs. Astor." The older Mrs. Astor continues to rule the Gilded Age's elite: In 1888, she created the famous "Four Hundred" list of those who matter. Invitations to her parties are highly prized status symbols, although the events themselves are considered dull. She favors the old families of Dutch colonial New York, snubs the era's millionaires, and never invites a divorcee until her daughter is one.

✦ A few days after Christmas, army cavalry kill some 200 enfeebled Lakota at Wounded Knee, South Dakota. Women and children trapped in a ravine are shot to death; there are no survivors.

1891   The World Woman's Christian Temperance Union is formed in Boston. At the opening meeting, 7 million names are presented on "Polyglot Petitions" that appeal to governments throughout the world to curtail narcotics as well as alcohol

✦ Illinois women have two milestones this year: They win the right to vote in school elections, and the University of Chicago is chartered as a coeducational institution. It will offer women some of the best programs available, especially in the traditionally female fields of education and social work.

As coeducation becomes commonplace in the Midwest, the Woman's Medical College of Chicago, which was founded by Dr. Mary Thompson in 1870, is absorbed into Northwestern University. Dr. Thompson, who also invented an abdominal needle and performed pioneering major surgery, dies four years later.

✦ Although Meharry Medical College, a Nashville institution for blacks, has been in existence since 1876, only now does it begin to produce female physicians. The first is Osceola C. Queen; in 1893, the second will be Georgia Washington

The original caption on this photo read: "Soldiers standing over a pit; the bodies of victims of the Massacre of Wounded Knee, South Dakota, December 29, 1890." Lakota women and children, already sick and near starvation, were killed by U.S. Army trooops. Minnesota Historical Society; original photograph by Northwestern Photo Co. of Chadron, Nebraska

Patton, who spends the rest of her life as a medical missionary in Liberia.

The first black women are also licensed as physicians in the South this year. Dr. Halle T. Dillon, who will be affiliated with Tuskegee Institute, is the first woman of any race to pass Alabama's medical examination, a written test that she believes was made more difficult for her.

Other African-American women who are the first in their state to be licensed as physicians are Dr. Mildred A. Evans in South Carolina and Dr. Verina Morton-Jones in Mississippi, both graduates of Woman's Medical College of Pennsylvania, and Dr. Sarah G. Jones, a Howard graduate who practices in Virginia. These women must expect to work in a segregated world where they and their patients are barred from tax-funded hospitals.

◆ Mary Kenny O'Sullivan is the first woman hired by the American Federation of Labor to organize women. She has been employed since age 12, and during the previous decade in Chicago, she built the first local of women in the bookbinding trade.

She does not receive steady pay for her union work, and it is not until 1914 that she will find a stable place as an inspector for the Massachusetts Board of Labor.

◆ The American Economics Association honors author Helen Campbell with a prize for her writings on working women. Campbell—who has supported herself by writing in many different genres since her 1871 divorce—has methodically documented female wages.

She demonstrates in *Prisoners of Poverty* (1886) that regardless of the industry or skill level, women are almost invariably paid half as much as men. Beyond that, she points out that women's expenses are greater because society expects them to meet higher standards in housing and dress. Campbell concludes that the economic system thus forces women into patterns of trading sexuality for financial security.

◆ Philadelphia millionaire Katherine Drexel, who entered the sisterhood two years earlier at 31, begins a new Catholic order of nuns with the blessing of the pope. Her Sisters of the Blessed Sacrament for Indians and Colored People grows quickly; when she dies at age 98, the order has some 500 daughters who run 60 schools for these racial minorities.

◆ The Seneca Nation honors Harriet Maxwell Converse for the successful lobbying she led this year, which prevented the breakup of communal Seneca lands by the New York legislature. An adopted member of the Snipe Clan since 1885, she is now made an honorary Seneca chief and granted rare ceremonial privileges.

◆ The New York Botanical Garden is established in the Bronx, primarily because of efforts made by young Elizabeth and Nathaniel Britton after they were inspired by a visit to England's Kew Gardens. Initially a geologist, he follows her into botany. While she had published her first scientific paper prior to marriage and her knowledge of botany was sufficiently keen that she was hired to teach at the college level at age 17, she will never earn a salary during the three decades she works at the botanical gardens.

A specialist on mosses, Elizabeth Britton publishes more than 300 articles and functions as the primary dissertation advisor to a number of successful doctoral candidates—who seem to resent it when she devotes less time to unpaid scholarship and turns her attention to crusading for preservation of wildflowers and native plants.

◆ In Athens, Georgia—home to the all-male University of Georgia—12 women form what is later termed the nation's first garden club.

◆ After her husband dies this year, Cleveland's Julia Tuttle buys a square mile of land at the mouth of Florida's Miami River. A clever real estate developer, she sells or donates alternate lots to ensure growth, and she convinces rail executive Henry Flagler to bring train service south by sending him orange blossoms during a northern freeze. She will die in Miami at age 50, two years after the railroad arrives. "It is the dream of my life," Tuttle writes, "to see this wilderness turned into a prosperous country."

◆ Mary Cassatt holds a one-woman show in Paris. Her painting has moved from impressionism to a more linear style that often features the mother/child relationship. Next year, she will ship a mural to Chicago for the exposition honoring the 400th anniversary of Columbus' voyage, and in 1893, Cassatt will have a second exclusive show in Paris.

At the same time that Cassatt prepares art in Paris for the Columbian celebration, Harriet Hosmer is in Rome, carving a statue of Queen Isabella that is commissioned by the city of San Francisco.

◆ Young art student Janet Scudder is fired from her Chicago woodcarving job when the factory's union refuses to accept a woman. She goes on to far greater success than any of these jealous men, however: Scudder will exhibit at both the 1893 World's Fair and the 1915 Panama-Pacific Exposition, and among the customers for her whimsical garden sculptures are the Rockefellers and the Metropolitan Museum. Within a few years of her firing, she is successful enough to divide the rest of her life between homes in New York and France.

◆ Florence Barclay calls herself Brandon Roy when she publishes her first novel. Her work becomes an international best-seller under her own name after the turn of the century, as her stories are translated into several languages and published in such far-flung places as Chile, Iceland, and Romania. *The Rosary* will be the American best-seller of 1913 and goes through 20 editions; as late as 1940, her work is still being published in new translations.

1892 On February 7, the Boston Symphony Orchestra and the city's Handel and Haydn Society perform Mass in E Flat Major, Opus #5, by 25-year-old Amy Beach. It includes parts for individual vocalists as well as for the chorus, orchestra, and an organ. Both critics and the public applaud the work, which took Beach three years to compose. Later this year, her Festival Jubilate will open the Women's Building at the Columbian Exposition in Chicago.

Mrs. H.H.A. Beach, as she is known, goes on to write other works performed by the New York Symphony Orchestra and similar musical groups in other cities. After her husband's death in 1910, she will spend much of her time in Europe, where she is well received as both a composer and a concert pianist.

◆ Congress passes a bill providing pensions for nurses who served in the Civil War, three decades earlier. This belated response is largely due to lobbying by the Women's Relief Corps, a group dedicated to the needs of veterans.

In the same session, a House committee reports favorably on the proposed constitutional amendment granting women the vote, but it is not taken up on the floor.

◆ Lack of progress on the suffrage amendment prompts longtime leader the Reverend Olympia Brown to split with the National American Woman Suffrage Association. With others who attend the Columbian Exposition in Chicago later this year, she forms the Federal Suffrage Association. Although the group will remain small, it forms coalitions with other suffrage dissidents; Brown serves as president from 1903 until the federal amendment is finally ratified in 1920.

◆ Similar independence is shown by Lillie Deverux Blake, the New York State Woman Suffrage Association president for more than a decade. In 1886, she began the Society for Political Study to focus on a diversity of feminist legislative goals rather than merely suffrage. This year, she holds the first of a series of Pilgrim Mothers' Dinners, which will attract upper-class attendees for 15 years. Although Blake remains an NAWSA officer until shortly before Susan Anthony's death, there is tension: Anthony resents any organizational work that she sees as detracting from suffrage.

◆ After long debate on the admission of women—much of which again centers on nomenclature—one of the first "fellows" of Britain's Royal Geographic Society is American May French Sheldon. While her husband waited in Naples, she was the sole white member of a recent exploration party to Zanzibar, where she was attacked by a python and fell into a river when a bridge collapsed. She does not allow her guides to shoot their guns except in extreme danger, specializes in returning from Africa with artifacts made by women, and promotes her adventures as indicative of women's untapped abilities.

+ Teachers College of Columbia University begins operation this year, and the treasurer of its board of trustees is millionaire social worker Grace Dodge. She holds this position until 1911, and when the college runs a deficit, she personally pays the annual debt.

+ The nation's attention is riveted on the trial of Lizzie Borden, a genteel 32-year-old Massachusetts woman accused of the murder of her father and stepmother, who had cared for Lizzie since she was five. Strong evidence points to the probability that she killed them with an ax as they napped after lunch on a hot summer day. The male jurors, however, apparently cannot bring themselves to believe that a woman so like their own daughters could be capable of such a heinous crime, and she is acquitted. She moves to a more expensive home but spends the rest of her life as a recluse; when she dies in 1927, Lizzie Borden's will stipulates that she be buried secretly at night.

+ Entire congregations of black churches in Memphis move to live among the Oklahoma Cherokee after riots force them from their homes.

+ "The Yellow Wallpaper" is published by Charlotte Perkins Stetson, who is later famous as Charlotte Perkins Gilman. It is a fictionalization of the mental breakdown she suffered when marriage, motherhood, and especially the vacuousness of Victorian female life overwhelmed her. The thesis is radically feminist, and the story is written with a candid surrealism that is decades ahead of literary style.

Stetson is a member of the influential Beecher family through her father—but after his desertion, Charlotte's childhood was one of poverty complicated by pretension. This denial of women's economic needs and the class code that forbids them to solve their problems is at the heart of her writing. In this story, she shows how such constraints cause nervous disorders that the era's medical professionals reinforce by treating female patients as less than full adults.

+ Novelist Olive Logan, who was a founder of the American Woman Suffrage Association in 1869, marries her secretary; he is 20 years younger than she and takes her name at marriage. Their relationship sours after the turn of the century, however, and it is Tennessee Claflin of the Beecher/Woodhull scandal—now Lady Cook—who rescues Logan from poverty by bringing her to England to live out her life.

+ Wyoming Republicans elect Theresa A. Jenkins as a delegate to their national convention. The first woman to be so honored, she is a University of Wisconsin graduate who went west in 1877. Jenkins also will make hundreds of suffrage speeches during campaigns in Colorado and Kansas.

The Democratic national convention has its first female delegate in the next presidential year. Dr. Martha Hughes Cannon of Utah will annoy other Mormons by voting for a candidate who is an excommunicated Mormon.

+ The federal government takes over immigration from the states when a complex of buildings opens on Ellis Island in New York's harbor. The site will be important not only to millions of newly arrived women but also to the many female social workers and translators employed there.

+ Born in slavery in North Carolina, Washington educator Anna Julia Cooper publishes a collection of speeches and essays entitled *A Voice from the South*. She has a master's degree from Oberlin and is a popular orator; next year, she will be one of the black women featured at the Columbian Exposition. Perhaps her most compelling speeches are those in which she candidly poses the problems of sexism as well as racism.

Speaking of the African-American woman, Cooper says:

She is confronted by both a woman question and a race problem. . . . The colored woman too often finds herself hampered and shamed by a less liberal sentiment and a more conservative attitude on the part of those for whose opinion she cares most. . . . As far as my experience goes, the average man of our race is less frequently ready to admit the actual need . . . for woman's help or influence.

◆ In October, Chicago hosts a giant exposition in celebration of the 400th anniversary of Columbus' voyage. The expo that opens on Columbus Day will see 21 million visitors during the following year.

A beautiful Woman's Building is constructed under the supervision of 22-year-old Sophia Hayden, who is the first female graduate of the architecture department at the Massachusetts Institute of Technology. The Board of Lady Managers insists that not only the architect but also the sculptors and artists who decorate the building are all women, and even the music played is composed by women. The building will offer some 80,000 exhibits by women around the world, although the governments of several mideastern countries refuse to allow their women to participate.

African Americans have to fight for inclusion, and Ida Wells-Barnett leads those insisting on black speakers and exhibit space. The fair finally allots a small space for "Evidences of the Advancement of the Colored Women of the United States," and some African-American women speak, but Wells-Barnett is not included.

◆ In the November election, young Frances Folsom Cleveland is again an issue. The Democrats renominate her husband and decide to undercut the ugly rumors of the last race by creating a positive focus on her at the beginning. Unlike the usual practice, they include her photo on campaign materials, and this openness proves successful. Her husband becomes the only president elected to nonconsecutive terms.

◆ Some of the photographs of Frances Folsom Cleveland are taken by her relative, Frances Benjamin Johnston. A West Virginia native who grew up in New York, this connection to the first lady

enables Johnston to build a solid reputation for her Washington studio. She published her first magazine photographs in 1889, and next year, she will issue *The White House*, a book of interior pictures. In 1897, Johnston will write an article for *Ladies' Home Journal* encouraging girls to take up the camera as a new employment opportunity.

1893   Although many women intend to go to Chicago this year for the ongoing Columbian Exposition, the annual convention of the National American Woman Suffrage Association is held once again in January in Washington, D.C. —the location of every annual meeting since Susan Anthony and Elizabeth Cady Stanton formed the National Woman Suffrage Association in 1869. Anthony feels strongly that meeting in Washington is symbolic of a commitment to a federal suffrage amendment, but this year some leaders of the old American Woman Suffrage Association move to hold annual meetings elsewhere in alternate years.

Anthony's response to the motion, according to the meeting minutes, is "a forcible speech" in which she scolds delegates: "Our younger women naturally can not appreciate the vast amount of work done here in Washington by the National Association in the last twenty-five years. . . ." She loses the vote, 37–28, and future annual conventions alternate in and out of the capital.

◆ Also in January, Hawaii's Queen Liliuokalani is displaced from her throne by American sugar and pineapple interests who fund a rebellion when she tries to reassert powers that her brother, who died two years earlier, had surrendered. The Americans apply for annexation of Hawaii to the United States, but President Grover Cleveland refuses.

◆ After more than a century of operation, the U.S. Post Office finally issues a stamp depicting a woman—but she is not an American: Spanish Queen Isabella is honored as the Columbus anniversary year continues. The $4.00 denomination indicates that the stamp is not intended for general usage; only seven are printed and they quickly become collectors' items.

✦ The $4.00 Queen Isabella stamp, in fact, represents a week's wages for many women, as this year the nation suffers its most serious economic depression to date. There is widespread unemployment and hunger, especially among urban newcomers who have no support systems. In New York, Russian immigrant Emma Goldman is sentenced to a year in prison for telling an audience of jobless men that they have a right to steal if they cannot get food in any other way.

✦ Despite the depression, the Columbian Exposition draws millions of visitors to Chicago, especially in the spring and summer. The Chicago Woman's Club, under the presidency of physician Sarah Stevenson, is a major sponsor of the fair's events, but this is not merely a local or even national occasion. In May, the expo serves as the five-year international meeting that was pledged by the first International Council of Women in 1888.

A World's Congress of Representative Women, presided over by Indiana's May Wright Sewall, draws women from 27 countries who represent 126 organizations. Sewall traveled throughout Europe in 1891 and 1892 recruiting speakers, and space for 10,000 proves too small for the audiences attracted. There are a total of 330 speakers, and over 150,000 women attend a week of simultaneous seminars.

At the expo's end, six volumes are published to make the information presented widely available. Among the less well known American speakers are Sue Huffman Brady of Fort Worth, who is the first female superintendent of schools in Texas, and newswoman Jean Loughborough Douglass of Little Rock, who reports that many Arkansas women head post offices and libraries. Ellen Hayes of the International Council's Committee on Dress Reform creates a stir when she models a suit with ten pockets that emulates the better functionality of male clothing. The *Chicago Tribune* calls it "appallingly ugly" and predicts that "no woman with proper regard for her duty towards men will yield to it."

✦ Populist Party orator Mary Ellen Lease is the featured speaker for Kansas Day at the Columbian Exposition. She also runs for the U.S. Senate this year; although Kansas women have the vote for local elections, the state's men are not so progressive that they will vote for a woman at this high level. The *New York World* hires her as a political writer in 1896, and she spends the rest of her life on the East Coast, campaigning for Theodore Roosevelt's Progressive Party in 1912.

✦ The Reverend Augusta Chapin, who has been preaching since 1859, chairs the women's committee of the World Parliament of Religions, which is held in Chicago during the Columbian Exposition, and she speaks to the assembly of both men and women. Also this year, Chapin becomes the first American woman to receive an honorary doctor of divinity degree.

The Reverend Annis Ford Eastman also speaks to the World Parliament of Religions; an Oberlin graduate, she has been an ordained Congregational minister since 1889, when, as the mother of four young children, she assumed her invalid husband's ministry. After the turn of the century, she will study with several of Harvard's great philosophers.

✦ The founding of the National Council of Jewish Women is a direct outgrowth of the World Parliament of Religions. Its convener and first president is Hannah Greenebaum Solomon, an accomplished amateur pianist who broke precedent in 1877 when she was the first Jew admitted to the prestigious Chicago Women's Club. The Columbian Exposition provides Jewish women with their first opportunity to assemble nationally, and within three years, 50 local chapters will develop. These women, who are largely German Jews resident in America for several decades, will focus their charitable activities on the Jews from Russia and eastern Europe who pour into Ellis Island during this era.

✦ Another organization that evolves out of the expo is the American Society of Superintendents of Training Schools, a group for nurse administrators that, in turn, will become the organizational grandmother of the American Nurses Association.

The impetus comes from speeches by Lavinia Dock and Isabel Hampton (later Robb). Both are graduates of the nursing school that Linda Richards built at New York's Bellevue Hospital—the nation's first program to emulate Florence Nightingale's work abroad. Dock will be associated primarily with Lillian Wald's Henry Street Settlement in New York, while Hampton publishes two nursing textbooks and shapes curriculum at the new schools associated with Cook County Hospital in Chicago and Johns Hopkins Hospital in Baltimore.

✦ Many organizations use the fair as a global networking opportunity: ethnologist Matilda Stevenson, for example, reads papers on the Zuni culture at both the Congress of Women and at the International Congress of Anthropology. International news, such as the fact that women in New Zealand have won voting rights, also spreads rapidly.

✦ Among the spinoffs from the Chicago exposition is another book by humorist Marietta Holley, who is popular enough to get a $14,000 advance for *Samantha at the World's Fair* (1893). Like her colleague Mark Twain, Holley's writing has a progressive political edge. She not only makes feminist points with insightful wit, but also takes on other controversial topics—as is indicated by last year's title, *Samantha on the Race Problem* (1892).

✦ At age 75, Lucy Stone gives her last speech at the Columbian Exposition. Her friends commission sculptor Anne Whitney to make a statue of Stone that is displayed there, and she dies a few months later. Ever the innovator, Stone requests that she be cremated.

✦ The Stone piece is only one of several works exhibited by Anne Whitney. Despite being more than 70 years old, she carves a large work titled "Roma" and several smaller pieces for the expo. Her career also includes immortalization of Frances Willard, Harriet Beecher Stowe, and other of the era's most famous women, and her sculpture of Massachusetts' hero Samuel Adams is one of the two statues that each state is allowed to display in the U.S. Capitol's Statuary Hall. Although Whitney is white, several of her most important statues also feature blacks; the best-known is titled "Africa."

✦ Lucy Stone's death signals the beginning of a sense of futility that seems to afflict the National American Woman Suffrage Association, as younger members do not widely replicate the strong style of the original suffragists. This situation will be particularly apparent in Congress: this year sees the last favorable congressional committee report on suffrage for almost two decades. Feminists seem not to expect the proposed constitutional amendment to move from the committee to the floor, and they will increasingly go through the biannual legislative motions as if defeat is expected.

✦ Lillian Wald begins the Henry Street Settlement House in New York. Emphasizing public health, it will evolve into the nation's first visiting nurse association; by 1915, when she publishes her best-seller, *The House on Henry Street*, almost 100 nurses will have delivered services under Wald's aegis. Most such settlements will serve the era's largely Catholic and Jewish immigrants, and the women who run them are almost invariably Protestant—but Wald is an exception, for she is from a Jewish family that has long resided in America.

✦ A similar project is begun in Boston with the Denison House, which aims to assist Italians and other immigrants from southern and eastern Europe who are arriving in New England. Denison House will be guided for the next 20 years by Wellesley College's Vida Scudder and its longtime "headworker," Bryn Mawr graduate Helena Dudley.

Future Nobel Prize winner Emily Balch is the initial Denison House headworker, until she becomes disillusioned by the seeming hopelessness of charity in overcoming the poverty she sees there. She will go to the new University of Chicago and then to the University of Berlin to study economics.

+ Wellesley College English professor Katherine Bates climbs Pike's Peak and, inspired by the scene, writes "America the Beautiful." Published in 1911, it becomes an unofficial national anthem that many prefer to Francis Scott Key's more militaristic "Star-Spangled Banner."

+ Mount Holyoke College, now more than 50 years old, drops the "seminary" portion of its former name. Wesleyan Female College of Macon, Georgia, which was founded a year prior to Mount Holyoke, now has enrollment of 250—approximately the same number of students as at the all-male University of Georgia.

+ Florence Bascom earns what may be the first doctorate of science ever granted a woman; it is definitely the first at Johns Hopkins University, a leader in coeducational, graduate-level science. Next year, Dr. Bascom will become the first woman elected to membership in the Geological Society of America. She goes on to be credentialed by the U.S. Geological Survey and becomes an expert on the geology of the Mid-Atlantic states. Dr. Bascom is the daughter of the president of the University of Wisconsin, and she will teach at Bryn Mawr most of her life.

+ The precedent for doctorates in the liberal arts was set in 1877, and this year, the first woman earns a Ph.D. in history. Kate Ernest Levi is awarded the degree from the University of Wisconsin.

+ *Vogue* magazine begins publication. It draws away those subscribers of *Godey's Lady's Book* and *Ladies' Home Journal* who are primarily interested in fashion, and its most important role becomes that of liberating women from their confining clothing. One of its first issues shows a woman wearing a short skirt over high boots, dressed to go hunting.

+ Mary Livermore and Frances Willard publish *A Woman of the Century*, a large collection of biographical sketches of contemporary women.

+ Pauline Cushman—who 30 years earlier received military honors for her work as a Union spy—dies as a San Francisco scrubwoman so pained by arthritis that she is addicted to morphine. She never received a pension, and Cushman avoids a pauper's burial only after the newspapers publish her obituary; then veterans of the Grand Army of the Republic memorialize her.

+ At age 67, Matilda Joselyn Gage publishes *Woman, Church and State*, attacking Christianity as one of the chief sources of female oppression. She develops her tenets historically, moving from matriarchal societies to current culture, and arguing that because Christianity blames original sin on Eve and teaches that women are to submit themselves to men, it inexorably gives excessive power to men.

The book is widely read, but many, especially the thousands of suffragists who hold membership in the Women's Christian Temperance Union, are appalled by it. Gage is alienated from most of her friends—even from Elizabeth Cady Stanton, whose *Woman's Bible*, which will be published two years later, offers many of the same views.

Gage lives with her daughter's family in Chicago; after her death, her son-in-law, Frank Baum, will write *The Wizard of Oz*.

+ In November, Colorado grants women full voting rights. They join only Wyoming women as full voters, for both Utah and Washington women have lost the franchise they had, and female voters in other states lack full rights. Carrie Chapman Catt, later president of the National American Woman Suffrage Association, demonstrates her organizing abilities as campaign manager of the successful Colorado referendum.

1894 Wyoming Republicans elect Esther Morris as a delegate to their national convention, and at age 80, the nation's first female elected official goes to Cleveland to vote on platform issues. She attracts much media attention there, for many easterners still cannot quite fathom that Wyoming had a woman as an active law enforcement officer more than two decades ago.

+ The inadequate "Harvard Annex" is formalized into Radcliffe College and named for colonial philanthropist Ann Radcliffe, who had begun the first scholarship fund for Harvard men in 1643.

Cambridge educator and natural scientist Elizabeth Cary Agassiz plays the leading role in establishing Radcliffe, and she will serve as its president until 1903. The college thus has female presidents from the beginning, and they establish a precedent for long tenure: Radcliffe will have just seven presidents during its century-plus existence.

◆ Twenty-five years after Vassar College held its first graduation, a survey of alumnae finds that only 39% have married. Educated women are clearly suspicious of giving up their personal freedom, and the era's consensus of opinion is that marriage and careers are incompatible. Yet even though Vassar women lead very independent lives, suffragist activism is prohibited on its campus.

◆ Even though Illinois women do not yet have the vote, Lucy L. Flowers wins a statewide election for a seat on the University of Illinois Board of Trustees. Both political parties nominate a woman to this position—presumably to represent the 17% of the students who are female—and Flowers, a Republican who was appointed to the Chicago School Board in 1891, defeats the Democratic nominee, Julia Holmes Smith.

The joy with which women greet this breakthrough is clear in 1896, when 11 women will file as candidates for the board. Most receive only a handful of votes, but Mary Turner Carriel is second among the 18 candidates. Julia Holmes Smith, the 1894 Democratic nominee, places sixth in this extremely tight contest; she misses fifth place by just one vote, while Carriel misses first place by 5 votes—9,129 to 9,124.

◆ Mathematician Charlotte Scott, who earned her doctorate at the University of London in 1885 and is the only woman on the council of the new American Mathematical Society, publishes *An Introductory Account of Certain Modern Ideas in Plane Analytical Geometry*. When she nears retirement from a long career at Bryn Mawr, emi-

nent British scholar Alfred North Whitehead will come to speak at ceremonies in her honor.

◆ Young Dr. Anna Wessels Williams, an employee of the New York City Department of Health, isolates a strain of the diphtheria bacillus, and within months, the city's doctors use her antitoxin to stem this fatal disease. Williams remains with the Health Department another four decades, until she is forced to retire during the Great Depression. In addition to her pioneer research on diphtheria, she also makes progress on streptococcal infections, pneumonia, and trachoma, while her work on rabies is hailed by the American Public Health Association.

◆ Dr. Mary Putnam Jacobi publishes *"Common Sense" Applied to Woman Suffrage*, a refutation of physicians' arguments that female physique and voting are incompatible. Dr. Jacobi, who is the mother of three, is recognized as the nation's leading woman in medical research and is a member of a half-dozen prestigious medical societies—but although she treats primarily women, she is never admitted to the Obstetrical Society.

◆ Under the aegis of both Chautauqua and the World's Women's Christian Temperance Union, African American Hallie Q. Brown begins a long career on the British lecture circuit. While she also returns to the United States during this time, she will appear on British platforms through 1910 and is twice presented to Queen Victoria. An 1873 graduate of Ohio's Wilberforce University, Brown also will be part of the 1899 International Council of Women in London.

◆ Julia Ward Howe's wide range of interests is clear when she is elected the first president of the United Friends of Armenia. Alice Stone Blackwell also befriends Armenians, many of whom immigrate to Boston in this era because of genocide by Turks in their homeland. Blackwell publishes poetry by exiles translated from Armenian, Yiddish, Hungarian, and other languages.

◆ Emulating the Daughters of the American Revolution that formed four years earlier, the Daughters of the Confederacy begins with headquarters in Richmond, Virginia. Three decades have passed since the Civil War, and as its participants begin to die, these women attempt to preserve wartime memories with a historical library.

+ The Women's Municipal League is organized in New York City. Although its members lack the vote, their aim is to oppose the corrupt practices of Tammany Hall and to promote "humanitarian reform through political action."

   The primary founder is Josephine Shaw Lowell, who has been an active reformer since her Civil War youth. She was a founder of the progressive Consumers League in 1890, and despite being a member of an old and wealthy New England family, she supported workers in the violent Homestead strike two years ago.

+ The U.S. Department of Agriculture authorizes nutritional research, a boon to the growing field of home economics.

+ The fall election is historic: women are elected to a state legislature for the first time when Clara Clessingham, Carrie Holly, and Frances Klock win races for the Colorado House of Representatives. Like many westerners of the time, they are liberal Republicans. Both the Republican and Populist parties organized women's divisions for this election, and although "there was no chance of electing their ticket," even the state's Democratic women formed 12 clubs.

+ Wyoming elects Esther Reel as State Superintendent of Public Instruction. She receives more votes than any candidate in the state's past—which makes her the largest female vote-getter in the world.

   She will use her experience as Registrar of the Land Board to survey public lands for increased educational revenue. When she worked for the Land Board, Reel also held an appointment as secretary of the State Board of Charities and Reform.

+ Back East, Helen Jackson Gougar attempts to vote in the November election. The Indiana Supreme Court has recently admitted women to the practice of law, and Gougar decides to create a test case on suffrage. Election officials in Lafayette reject her ballot, and she sues them. Although she is admitted to the bar in January and allowed to argue her case, the state courts, not surprisingly, follow the federal precedent of the Supreme Court's 1874 ruling in *Minor v. Happersett*, which allowed states to define their voters.

1895   Elizabeth Cady Stanton shocks even feminists with the publication of *The Woman's Bible*, a carefully researched argument against women's subordinate position in religion that—like her earlier periodical, *The Revolution*—is more reasonable than its inflammatory title implies.

   She acknowledges her literary debt to an earlier work, *Men, Women, and Gods* (1884), by Helen Hamilton Gardener. Stanton had met Gardener (a pseudonym consistently used by Helen Chenowith Smart) when each spoke at the 1893 Columbian Exposition.

+ The New York State Association Opposed to Woman Suffrage begins in April. Similar groups are under way in Washington, D.C., and Massachusetts; eventually 19 other states will have organizations composed of women who do not wish to be entitled to vote. Not surprisingly, most of these women are the wives of wealthy, conservative men, and some clearly state that their primary motivation is to keep political power from working-class and black women.

+ The Women's Educational and Industrial Union of Boston, which operates under the aegis of Denison House, issues a report on the status of domestic servants, most of whom are immigrant women. It also establishes classes in the growing field of home economics, runs an employment agency, and makes proposals for easing women's domestic burdens through communal living.

+ Jane Addams has complained so often about the indifference of garbage collectors in the Hull House neighborhood—where even dead horses lay in the street until they rot—that city officials appoint her as garbage inspector for the 19th

Ward. Her annual salary of $1,000 is the only one she ever has.

✦ International media focuses on 45-year-old Annie Peck, who climbs the Matterhorn. After teaching school in the Midwest and Northeast, Peck went to Athens in 1885 as the first woman admitted to the American School of Classical Studies—but she fell in love with the Alps instead. Except for lecturing to raise money for expeditions, she spends the rest of her life mountaineering.

In her 50s, Peck will risk repeated dangers as she scales unexplored peaks in Argentina and Bolivia, climbing higher in the Western Hemisphere than any other man or woman. She is honored by the government of Peru, becomes a fellow of the Royal Geographic Society in 1917, and climbs her last mountain at age 82. A candid feminist, Peck placards Andean heights with "Votes for Women."

✦ Cornell University confers a doctorate of science on Caroline Willard Baldwin, who was born in California in 1869. A specialist in physics and mathematics, Baldwin earned an 1892 bachelor's degree at the University of California in Berkeley, and she will return to her home state to teach at the California School of Mechanical Arts.

Cornell's first president, Andrew Dickson White, is the husband of Helen Magill, who in 1877 became the first woman to earn a Ph.D. Magill and White married in 1890, soon after his retirement from Cornell.

✦ Alice and Edith Hamilton, sisters who have earned degrees from prestigious American institutions, go to Germany for further study in their respective fields of medicine and classical literature. No German university admits women, but Dr. Alice Hamilton is allowed to attend lectures in bacteriology provided that she remains "inconspicuous." Edith, in contrast, is put on display at the front of the lecture hall: "I had to take notes at a little desk on the platform. The head of the university used to stare at me, then shake his head. . . ."

✦ After operating a Philadelphia studio and studying in France, painter Cecelia Beaux is the first woman appointed to the faculty of the Pennsylvania Academy of Fine Arts. The following year, she will enjoy the unusual honor of being elected to the French *Societe Nationale des Beaux-Arts*.

✦ Mrs. Leslie Carter appears on the stage for the first time. Although charged with infidelity in her 1889 divorce from prominent Chicagoan Leslie Carter, she uses his name and is commonly called "Mrs. Carter" during a long stage and screen career.

✦ Headlines reflect New York society's shock when Alva Vanderbilt sues her husband William for divorce. During her 20 years of marriage, she has not only headed New York society but also drawn attention to herself by serving as the architect for their Fifth Avenue, Long Island, and Newport mansions.

Her charges of his adultery are doubtless true, but his behavior is not uncommon for men in his position; the headlines instead are prompted by the simultaneous suit of young banker Oliver Hazard Perry Belmont for a divorce from his wife. Suspicions prove true a year later, as Belmont and Vanderbilt marry in a civil ceremony; despite their prominence, a church wedding is not possible.

✦ New Jersey librarian Carolyn Wells writes the first of 170 books she will publish prior to her 1942 death. About half of them are mysteries, and she will be given much credit for defining that genre —but she also writes humor, light verse, and other works in such quantity that some believe Carolyn Wells is in fact a literary factory.

✦ Tekahionwake, whose English name is Emily Pauline Johnson, publishes her first book of poetry, *White Wampum*. She is the great-granddaughter of Mohawk leader Molly Brant and colonial governor Sir William Johnson.

✦ African American Mary McLeod of South Carolina graduates from the famous Moody Bible Institute in Chicago but finds no church willing to sponsor her as a missionary to Africa.

◆ One of the black women who was allowed to speak at the Columbian Exposition, Fannie Barrier Williams, is the center of a Chicago furor when some white women sponsor her for membership in the prestigious Chicago Woman's Club. Her reputation as the refined wife of a lawyer and a leader in the National League of Colored Women finally gains her admittance.

◆ When Cuba declares its independence from Spain, Kate Stewart of the Tampa, Florida, chapter of the Women's Christian Temperance Union goes to Havana and opens a "reading room," which is supplied with clothing, medicine, bedding, and books by WCTU women.

◆ Susan Anthony is honored on her 75th birthday with an $800 annuity from feminist friends. She travels all over California during the winter, working on a suffrage referendum that the liquor industry will defeat the following spring.

1896 Western women continue to far outpace eastern ones in gaining political power. Idaho is added to the list of states in which women can vote this year, when a referendum campaign run by Iowa's Carrie Chapman Catt, a National American Woman Suffrage Association newcomer, is successful.

Utah women regain the vote when the Mormon church renounces polygamy in order to become a state. At the same time, Democrat Martha Hughes Cannon becomes the nation's first woman in a state senate. A physician, Cannon is also the fourth wife of Mormon official Angus Cannon and had once exiled herself in England to prevent his arrest for polygamy. They both run in an at-large race, and Mr. Cannon, a Republican who is appreciably older than his wife, loses.

Colorado adds to the three women who joined its legislature in the previous election; three more women, all from minor parties, are voted in this year.

In contrast to these victories, women suffer a heartbreaking loss in California. The NAWSA organizes a huge effort there and appears on the edge of victory, but the male electorate rejects the suffrage amendment by a narrow margin after liquor interests pour big dollars into advertising against it.

◆ The California loss may be dispiriting enough to cause the NAWSA to back off of intense political action, for no more states are added to the suffrage column until 1910. NAWSA meetings will be increasingly marked by pageantry and social activity, and the minutes of some annual conventions reflect as much attention to decorations and decorum as to politics. Only six referenda will be held in the next 14 years; all except New Hampshire are in the West, and all lose.

◆ Susan Anthony hires Californian Ida Husted Harper, who has worked as a journalist all of her life, as a publicist for Anthony's tour during this year's election. She is so impressed by Harper's work that she asks her to move into her Rochester home, where Harper works in Anthony's attic sorting her numerous papers.

◆ Queen Liliuokalani, who has been under house arrest in Hawaii, goes to Washington, D.C., to plead her case against the American businessmen who wish to annex Hawaii. She meets with little success, however, for Democratic President Grover Cleveland, who has opposed annexation, leaves office this year. He is replaced by Republican William McKinley, who is more sympathetic to imperialism, and the Spanish-American War two years later will seal Hawaii's fate. Liliuokalani returns to Honolulu, where she is granted a modest pension and lives on until 1917.

◆ Delegates from 25 states, representing about 5,000 women, found the National Association of Colored Women in Washington. After a temporary chairmanship by Margaret Murray Washington, wife of Booker T. Washington, the president will be Mary Church Terrell. She has an 1888 master's degree from Oberlin College and along with Anna Julia Cooper, may be the best-educated black woman in the world. Terrell rejects the leisurely life that her inherited wealth would allow and will become increasingly active during her long life.

◆ Mary Calkins, who has studied psychology and philosophy with Harvard's famous William James, earns a doctorate—but the Harvard Corporation refuses to grant it to a woman. Five years earlier, Calkins established one of the world's first experimental laboratories in psychology at Wellesley College, where she specialized in dream theory. Her textbooks on psychology are widely used in colleges that adopt this new field of study.

◆ Fannie Farmer, a self-taught dietician and cooking teacher, publishes the *Boston Cooking School Cookbook*—and publisher Little, Brown & Company is so unaware of a women's market that they insist she cover the printing costs. With revisions that are called *The Fannie Farmer Cookbook*, it will sell more than 4 million copies.

◆ Sarah Orne Jewett publishes *The Country of the Pointed Firs*, which becomes a classic of regional literature. In 1901, Maine's Bowdoin College, an all-male institution, will give her the first honorary degree it grants a woman. A future critic credits Jewett with "inventing" the novel form in which setting takes priority over plot.

◆ Tufts University awards an honorary degree to feminist leader and Civil War Sanitary Commission chief Mary Livermore. The next year, she publishes *The Story of My Life*, which sells well enough to pay for her granddaughter's college education; Livermore herself grew up in an era when women were not admitted to college.

◆ Washington, D.C., attorney Belva Lockwood receives a federal appointment as a delegate to a Geneva conference on international charity. She will also serve on one of the first committees for Nobel Prize nominations.

◆ Rose Hawthorne Lathrop, the youngest daughter of Nathaniel and Sophia Peabody Hawthorne, has followed the writing path of her father and aunts, but her life changes dramatically this year. She separates from her alcoholic husband, takes a nursing course, and begins the Congregation of Saint Rose Lima. She had converted to Catholicism in 1891, and as Sister Mary Alphonsa, she will spend the rest of her life comforting the incurably ill among New York's poor.

◆ At the annual convention of the National American Woman Suffrage Association, the Reverend Anna Howard Shaw and others present a resolution disassociating it from *The Woman's Bible* published by their former president, Elizabeth Cady Stanton. Despite Susan Anthony's impassioned plea on behalf of her old friend, the motion passes.

◆ With statues of Susan Anthony and Elizabeth Cady Stanton serving as "bridesmaids," sculptor Adelaide Johnson weds Fredrick Jenkins in her Washington, D.C., studio. She has studied at the St. Louis School of Design and maintained studios in Chicago and several European cities.

In honor of what he terms her "genius," the groom changes his name to hers—but Johnson nevertheless will divorce him in 1908. She later quarrels irrevocably with Anthony, too, who does not attend the wedding, even though she is frequently in Washington and has known Johnson since both founded the International Council of Women.

◆ In November, the unsuccessful candidacy of Democrat William Jennings Bryan marks one of the most controversial presidential campaigns in American history. Both he and Republican campaign manager Mark Hanna have active support from teenage daughters named Ruth, and in 1928, both Ruth Hanna McCormick and Ruth Bryan Owen will be elected to Congress.

1897 Arguing that "for every kindergarten, there are a thousand prisons, jails, asylums, and hospitals," Alice McLellan Birney and Phoebe Apperson Hearst call a February 17 meeting in Washington. They hope that perhaps 500 women will attend their National Congress of Mothers, but more than 2,000 show up. They adopt goals to improve conditions for children, and the organization eventually becomes the Parent-Teacher Association, more commonly called PTA.

◆ *Home Companion* alters its name, with *Woman's Home Companion* intended to present a direct challenge to *Ladies' Home Journal*. Especially after 1911, when Gertrude Battles Lane assumes editorship, *Woman's Home Companion* will publish significant material on women's changing roles.

◆ Anna Katherine Green creates what may be the nation's first fictional female detective, a character named Amelia Butterworth. Green's first detective story, *The Leavenworth Case* (1878), sold a half-million copies, and Sir Arthur Conan Doyle, the creator of Sherlock Holmes, is a fan of her carefully laid plots.

◆ Beatrix Jones, who will be known as Beatrix Jones Farrand after her 1913 marriage, begins a career as a landscape architect. A niece of Edith Wharton, her social connections ease the development of an impressive client list, but she charges professional rates when she lays out estate gardens for the Rockefellers, Morgans, and other wealthy families. Along with America's giant of city planning, Fredrick Law Olmstead, Jones will be a cofounder of the American Society of Landscape Architects in 1899.

◆ On New York's fashionable Fifth Avenue, Gertrude Stanton Kasebier, married and a mother, opens a photography studio that she will maintain until 1926. Her artistry manages to be popular with the public, while it is sufficiently avant garde that she is featured in the first issue of Alfred Stieglitz's *Camera Work*. A native of Iowa, Kasebier will sell photographs—especially of Plains Indians—to such widely read magazines as *McClure's* and *Scribner's*. Her work is acquired by the Museum of Modern Art and the Smithsonian, and she is long considered the dean of female photographers.

◆ Antisuffragists widely publicize Phoebe Couzins' renouncement of her former views. Although she was a founder of the National Woman Suffrage Association in 1869—during her time as the nation's first female law school student—Couzins now has become embittered toward her feminist friends. Her new political position is quickly re-warded by the United Brewers Association, which hires her as a lobbyist against suffrage.

◆ The right of Minnesota women to vote in school elections and to hold school elective offices, which they have had since 1875, is slightly expanded to include library governance.

◆ Wellesley College seniors predict that senior class president Molly Dewson will become president of the United States. Although she does not, Dewson will go on to become a close advisor to President Franklin Delano Roosevelt.

◆ Freshmen at the University of South Carolina elect Laura Bateman as class president, but the administration insists that she resign, arguing that a woman cannot hold this position.

◆ One of the two women in the Utah House of Representatives, Eurithe K. LaBarthe, sponsors a bill imposing fines of $1 to $10 on women whose hats obstruct the view of others in a public audience. The bill passes.

◆ Like countless other women, 24-year-old Virginian Ellen Glasgow publishes her first novel anonymously.

1898 War with Spain over Cuba is threatened from January and declared in April, and Clara Barton and her Red Cross find many of the Civil War's problems repeated in the Spanish-American War. Barton goes to Cuba, where she tries to cope with a Medical Corps that, primarily because of bad sanitation and inadequate food, loses five times more men to disease than to battle.

But Barton is 77, and although she appears much younger, she earns almost as much criticism as acclaim in this war. As was the case with Dorothea Dix during the Civil War, Barton's detractors complain that her management style is outdated and autocratic. Instead of behaving as the chief executive of a major organization, she insists on trying to do everything personally, including field cooking and laundry.

Despite the criticism, Barton continues as president of the American Red Cross until 1904, when the board ousts her from leadership of the organization that she founded. She will die in 1912 at age 91.

- While they have no military status, some 1,600 civilian women contract with the U.S. Army to provide nursing services during the war. They staff hospitals in Cuba and Puerto Rico, and they serve on ships returning the wounded to mainland hospitals. In the Pacific, women nurse in the Philippines and Hawaii; one who works in the Philippines is Theresa Ericksen, a Minnesotan who emigrated from Norway.

   While the nurses' status with the military is ambiguous, they are encouraged by the example of Dr. Anita Newcomb McGee, a Washington physician whose leadership will prove vital in the postwar establishment of the Army Nurse Corps.

- Paulina Pedroso is the chief female revolutionary in exile. Born in Cuba in 1845, she supports herself as a Tampa cigarmaker while organizing La Sociedad Libres to promote Cuban independence from Spain. The great Latin American leader José Martí headquarters his U.S. activities in Pedroso's home, even though he is white and she is black.

- In the spring, 18-year-old Agnes Nestor leads Chicago glovemakers in a successful 10-day strike; these women, like others, are required to supply their own needles and to pay rent for the factory's sewing machines.

   Nestor will go on to a long union career: she will be a founder of the International Glove Workers Union in 1902 and, from 1913, serves as president of the Chicago branch of the Women's Trade Union League. When the eight-hour day is finally achieved in 1937, many credit her work as the most influential.

- Charlotte Perkins Stetson (later Gilman) writes *Women and Economics* after study at the London School of Economics. Its thesis of women's need for financial independence has broad appeal; it is translated into seven languages and brings her both international acclaim and enough money to help her ex-husband support their child, whose custody she had amiably given him—to great criticism from her friends.

- Ida Husted Harper publishes a two-volume *Life and Work of Susan B. Anthony*. At the same time, Anthony joins with other women of her generation, none of whom had the opportunity to attend college, in persuading the University of Rochester—near where she has lived her whole life—to admit women.

- The conservatism of women's elite academic role models is clear when a survey of Radcliffe students finds only 2 of 72 willing to support suffrage.

- Harvard rewards astronomer Williamina Fleming with the first official appointment given to a woman. Fleming, who had grown up in Scotland when colleges would not admit women, has no educational credentials, but her work is so outstanding that she is named curator of astronomical photographs.

- The corporate editors who replace Sarah Buell Hale of *Godey's Lady's Book* and Ann S. Stephens of *Peterson's Ladies' Magazine* cannot create the kind of magazines that interested millions of women for more than a half century, and they lose out to competitors *Vogue*, *Ladies' Home Journal*, and *Woman's Home Companion*. Within five years, *Ladies' Home Journal* will pass the million subscriber mark that Louisa and Cyrus Curtis set as their goal when they began the magazine in 1883.

- African-American journalist Ida Wells-Barnett goes to the White House to lobby President McKinley for an antilynching law. She has used her part ownership of a Memphis newspaper to editorialize for civil rights, and when her property was looted and her life threatened, she moved on to newspapers in Chicago and New York. In 1893, her lectures in England urging a boycott of southern cotton pressured Memphis civic leaders into apologizing for the violent behavior of the city's whites. She also writes two histories of lynching during this decade, but her effort for a national law against lynching is not successful.

- The coeducational Washington College of Law is opened by Ellen Spencer Mussey and Emma M. Gillett in the nation's capital. Mussey, who was a business school administrator prior to marriage, worked in her invalid husband's Washington law office for 16 years. She applied to law schools after his 1892 death, and after rejection on the grounds of gender, she passed the bar without benefit of classes. She has been admitted to practice before the Supreme Court, and the Swedish and Norwegian embassies are so pleased with her that they will retain her for 25 years—but when Columbian College (later George Washington University) rejects six young women who read law with her, she resolves to start her own school.

Gillett, also a former teacher and protégée of pioneer lawyer Belva Lockwood, avoided rejection by graduating from the mostly black Howard University in 1883. Together Gillet and Mussey make their school a genuine success; it will operate until it is absorbed into American University in 1949, long after both founders are dead.

♦ Kathryn Newell Adams, who was born in Prague of American missionary parents, graduates from Oberlin College and begins an international career in higher education. After further study at Radcliffe, Columbia, and Oxford, Adams serves at institutions ranging from Hawaii to Turkey; in 1924, she will become president of American College for Girls in Istanbul.

♦ President William McKinley appoints Wyoming's school superintendent, Esther Reel, as National Superintendent of Indian Schools. Her confirmation by the U.S. Senate is the first for a woman —and is unanimous. She promotes vocational education in the schools and, as a single woman, especially encourages the girls to be self-supporting.

♦ Educator, feminist, and temperance leader Frances Willard dies. Congress honors her with a statue in the Capitol Rotunda, and the inscription refers to her as "the first woman of the 19th Century, the most beloved character of her times."

♦ In Washington, the National American Woman Suffrage Association celebrates the 50th anniversary of the Seneca Falls convention. Among the speakers is the nation's first female state senator,

Dr. Martha Hughes Cannon of Utah. Abigail Bush, the first woman to preside over a Woman's Rights Convention, writes from her California retirement: "You will bear me witness that the state of society is very different from what it was fifty years ago . . ."

♦ On December 9, Ellen May Tower becomes the first American nurse to die on foreign soil. She is recovering from typhoid when overwork causes a heart attack, and at age 30, Ellen Tower dies in a tent in Puerto Rico. Two of her colleagues soon follow her to early graves.

Tower will be buried in Michigan with full military honors in January. Although other nurses died in similar circumstances during the Civil War, the publicity accorded a war on foreign soil causes the media to shower much more attention on what the public sees as a new type of military hero. A special train with armed escorts brings her flower-covered body home, and Ellen Tower is buried exactly five years after her graduation day. A village in Michigan will be named for her.

1899   One of the few stagecoaches still operating is robbed in the Arizona desert by 24-year-old Pearl Hart and a male accomplice. The oddly anachronistic crime draws national attention, which Hart uses to deliver a feminist message on women being punished by laws they can play no part in writing. The all-male jury is sympathetic and acquits her, despite undisputed evidence against her, while sentencing her partner to 30 years. The judge overrules the jury, and Hart is imprisoned until 1902; when reporters continue to flock to her cell, she is finally pardoned "on the grounds of the lack of accommodations for women prisoners."

♦ After publishing several travelogues of bicycle trips in remote areas surrounding the Mediterranean, Fanny Bullock Workman and her husband, Dr. William Workman, who are both more than 40 years old, begin exploring India's Himalayas and devote the next two decades to their exploration. Bullock Workman (as she prefers to be called) climbs higher than 23,000 feet—enduring oxygen deprivation and extreme cold in an era prior to radio communication, airplanes, or other safety equipment. She is rewarded with the highest medals of ten national geographic societies. She lectures at the Sorbonne and, like Annie Smith Peck, uses media opportunities to advocate the vote for women.

✦ The five-year meeting of the International Council of Women is held abroad for the first time. The London setting provides a great deal of international press, especially when Queen Victoria, who is close to the end of her 63-year reign, asks to meet Susan Anthony, the aging symbol of all things new and radical. The gathering is chaired by the countess of Aberdeen, and its favorable publicity does much to further women's causes. May Wright Sewall of Indiana will serve as council president from this year until 1904.

✦ St. Louis author Kate Chopin, who has published popular fiction set in the bayou country of Louisiana where she lived in the 1870s, writes her last book, although she is only 48. *The Awakening*, with its themes of female sexuality and miscegenation, is so bitterly criticized by her contemporaries that Chopin stops writing.

✦ Sociologist Florence Kelley, who also holds an 1894 law degree from Northwestern University, heads the newly founded National Consumers League, which will grow into a very influential organization of liberals who pursue the goals of workers as intently as those of consumers.

Kelley has already set a precedent with her 1893 gubernatorial appointment as chief factory inspector for Illinois, and she will summarize much of her life's work in the aptly titled *Some Ethical Gains Through Legislation* (1905).

✦ The General Federation of Women's Clubs establishes a national model for juvenile courts. Its platform also endorses the eight-hour day and an end to child labor.

✦ When the New York garment factory in which Rose Schneiderman works is destroyed by fire, she and other women who are required to buy their own sewing machines as a condition of employment lose their means of livelihood—even

These nurses assigned to the U.S. Army Hospital Ship Relief *served in Cuban waters during the Spanish-American War. Women's contributions in this war resulted in the authorization of the Army Nurse Corps, the nation's first female military unit, in 1901.* Women in Military Service Memorial; U.S. Naval Historical Center

though management's losses are covered by insurance. Schneiderman is galvanized into becoming a union leader.

✦ At age 18, Mary Antin publishes *From Plotzk to Boston*, a collection of letters she wrote during her emigration from Russia just five years earlier. Her achievement is possible because her poor but exceptionally supportive Jewish parents allow her to attend Girls Latin School, where the city's most prestigious teachers help publish the book.

✦ Two of three jurors for an exhibit by the Philadelphia Photography Society are women, Frances Benjamin Johnston and Gertrude Kasebier. Next year, Johnston will be the only American woman invited to participate in the Third International Photographic Congress in Paris.

✦ Musicologist Frances Densmore begins her study of the music of Native Americans. As the technology of sound recording develops, she becomes a rare expert in this field. For more than 50 years, she will document music ranging from the Ojibway of her Minnesota home to the Teton Sioux and Ute of the Pacific Northwest and the Arapaho and Zuni of the Southwest. With sponsorship from the Bureau of American Ethnology, she makes thousands of recordings and publishes numerous papers on native music.

✦ The virtually all-male American Federation of Labor enthusiastically listens to a speech by Susan Anthony and then unanimously adopts a resolution urging Congress to grant women the vote.

✦ As the century ends, the Patent Office has granted more than 8,000 patents to female inventors.

7

The Progressive Era and the Triumph of Suffrage

1900–1920

1900 At the turn of the century, almost three-quarters of the nation's teachers are female—a reversal from the beginning of the last century, when the "schoolmaster" was far more common.

◆ Another turn-of-the-century report says that at least half of all childbirths are still attended by midwives or lay women.

◆ A third study reveals that two-thirds of divorce cases are initiated by the wife; a century earlier, most women lacked the right to sue and were hopelessly locked into bad marriages. Many states, however, still punish women more than men for marital failure. In particular, women accused of adultery are subject not only to the loss of their children but even of property they owned prior to the marriage.

◆ Some 100 settlement houses for new immigrants are in operation as the century begins, all of them emulating the precedents set by Jane Addams and Lillian Wald only a decade earlier. They are operated largely by women, who do both the fund raising and the administration necessary to provide a wide variety of social and legal services vital to newcomers. The volunteer female staff of most settlement houses also live there, making themselves available day and night as nurses and social workers.

◆ Turn-of-the-century life expectancy in Lawrence, Massachusetts, is 15 years. Infants deaths are so common that they drastically lower the average in this and other towns with a large population of immigrant industrial workers. Unhealthy women give birth to malnourished babies, and textile mill women especially die of tuberculosis and other respiratory diseases caused by the inhalation of lint. Many lose their hearing from machinery noise.

◆ Women make up 21% of the turn-of-the-century labor force, or just over one in every five workers. Most are young and unmarried. The vast majority work in manufacturing, but almost 200,000 are employed in clerical jobs such as bookkeeping and stenography.

◆ As the century begins, 80-year-old Susan Anthony steps down from the presidency of the National American Woman Suffrage Association. She surprises the NAWSA with her choice of a successor: instead of the expected announcement of the Reverend Dr. Anna Howard Shaw, Anthony chooses relative newcomer Carrie Chapman Catt.

Since joining the Iowa Suffrage Association in 1887, Catt has demonstrated unusual organizational and networking abilities, and her experience in both the Midwest and the Far West gives the NAWSA a wider base and new perspective.

◆ Lillie Devereux Blake, an active suffragist since 1869, resigns from the NAWSA when her bid for the presidency is rejected. With support from Elizabeth Cady Stanton, who is embittered by the organization's resolution against her *Woman's Bible*, she founds the National Legislative League.

The league is intended to focus on women's issues other than enfranchisement, but both Stanton and Blake are aged and ailing, and they are not able to develop an organization strong enough to survive their deaths. Their league, however, is analogous to the League of Women Voters that will develop after the vote is finally obtained.

◆ While married women have been assured of their property rights in most states, a married Pennsylvania woman still cannot sign a business contract without her husband's permission—the same problem that prevented women from renting space during the nation's bicentennial in 1876. Women in southern states lack even more of these rights. In Louisiana, where the legal code is based on French law, even a woman's clothing belongs to her husband.

◆ In Kiowa, Kansas, Carry Nation takes aim at her first saloon. Armed with rocks and bricks, she breaks liquor bottles and then uses a hatchet—her symbol of female empowerment thereafter—to destroy furniture while an audience of shocked men look on. Her life and that of many of her Women's Christian Temperance Union associates have been ruined by alcoholism, for most women have no recourse from physically abusive husbands who also have sole authority over family income.

+ The International Ladies' Garment Workers' Union is founded. As indicated by the name, it is a union of people who work on ladies' garments rather than of female workers. Although women far outnumber men in the industry, the union's leadership will remain male throughout the 20th century. During this era, most members are Jewish women living in New York.

+ The *American Journal of Nursing* begins publication in October. Linda Richards, the most eminent graduate of Dr. Marie Zakrzewska's pioneer nursing school in Boston, is honored by being presented with the publication's first share of stock. Its editor is Sophia Palmer, an 1878 graduate of the nursing program established by Richards at Massachusetts General Hospital. Palmer has experience with a similar journal published by the nursing school of Rochester General Hospital, which she has headed since 1896.

New York City settlement house nurse Lavinia Dock will give the journal an international flavor by regularly reporting on the status of nursing abroad; she attended the International Council of Women last year, and she is a founder of the new International Council of Nurses. Dock also will show exceptional courage as the only nursing professional to candidly address venereal disease and birth control—positions that shock many of those who read her monthly pieces during the next two decades.

+ When the Boxer Rebellion breaks out in China, several female missionaries associated with Oberlin College are among those who die. Early in July, Mary Sanders Atwater and Ernestine Harriet Atwater are killed at Tai-Yuan; later Susan Rowena Bird, Mary Louise Partridge, and Mary Jane Clapp and her husband, Dwight, are killed at Taiku. On August 15, Elizabeth Graham Atwater and Eva Jane Price die along with their husbands and children at Fenchow-Fu.

+ The National Association of Colored Women sets its goals, which include "equality of pay," "care for the children of absentee mothers," and job training. In the words of NACW president Mary Church Terrell, this emphasis on employment opportunity is necessary because "so many families are supported entirely by our women."

+ When the first Pan-African Conference is held in London, men from the United States, the Caribbean, Europe, and Africa listen to a speech by Washington's Anna Julia Cooper.

+ Bostonian Josephine St. Pierre Ruffin finds that she is not welcome as a delegate of her club when the General Federation of Women's Clubs meets in Milwaukee, even though her Woman's Era Club, which is made up of black women, is a GFWC affiliate. Nervous GFWC officials offer to seat Ruffin with women from one of the integrated clubs to which she belongs (including the prestigious New England Woman's Club), but she refuses to accept this slight to her club and is not seated.

+ President William McKinley appoints Bertha Honore Palmer, who did a stellar job of chairing the board of lady managers for the 1893 Columbian Exposition, as a representative of the United States at the Paris Exposition of 1900. Although she has made a great deal of money in Chicago real estate, Palmer is supportive of women's causes. She will spend much of her future doing animal husbandry on some 100,000 acres of Florida land she owns.

+ Dr. Emily Blackwell, who has directed the education of more than 350 female physicians, closes her medical school because she is ready to retire and because Cornell University Medical School now accepts women. The New York Infirmary for Women and Children—which Emily and Elizabeth Blackwell began prior to the medical school—continues on through the century.

+ Lillian Moller becomes the first woman to speak at commencement ceremonies at the University of California at Berkeley. After her name changes to Gilbreth with her 1904 marriage, she will become a nationally known industrial engineer.

✦ Two sisters from Kentucky who live in New York City write the song "Happy Birthday." Mildred and Patty Hill include the tune in their *Song Stories for the Kindergarten*.

✦ The Springer Opera House in Columbus, Georgia, an opulent institution in a segregated city, nevertheless is the setting for the debut of African-American singer Gertrude Pridgett, who, as "Ma" Rainey, will be recognized later as the most important female jazz innovator of the era. For the next two decades, she will tour the South; national fame comes with a Paramount recording contract in 1923. Numerous future musicians will emulate her style.

✦ At age 30, Jessie Tarbox Beals persuades her husband to give up their Massachusetts home and see the world through itinerant photography; she argues that as a single woman, she made more money taking pictures on her front porch in summer than she did by teaching school all winter. In September, she becomes the world's first female news photographer when she sells pictures that are published in Vermont newspapers. After the couple winters in Florida, she is hired by a Buffalo paper as a staff news photographer.

✦ Confederate spy Belle Boyd dies in Wisconsin while on a lecture tour and, ironically, is buried by an honor guard of Union veterans. Boyd's life has been hard since her Civil War celebrity; she reared five children from three marriages, sometimes in great poverty. During the last year of the Civil War, her first husband died in a U.S. prison, to which he was sentenced for aiding in her escape.

✦ The year's best-selling book is *To Have and to Hold*, which is based on the men and women who starved in the 17th-century Jamestown settlement. Its author is Mary Johnston of Virginia, who will write 23 books of historical fiction, some of which are made into films.

Decades later, Margaret Mitchell will consciously emulate Johnston's carefully researched settings when she writes *Gone with the Wind* —but Mitchell does not feel her work meets Johnston's high standards.

1901 Carry Nation spends New Year's in jail, while women pray and sing outside. After six months of wrecking small-town saloons almost at will, this muscular woman was arrested when she broke up the bar of a Wichita hotel favored by politicos. Upon her release, she unsuccessfully calls on the governor to enforce the state's duly enacted prohibition law and then goes on a national tour. It is motivated in part by her need for money to pay court fines as well as to support a Kansas City shelter for the families of alcoholics —one of the nation's first such havens.

✦ Congress creates the Army Nurse Corps, the first formal military unit for women. The ANC is a direct result of experience in the Spanish-American War, during which the health care lessons of the Civil War had to be relearned. The legislation recognizes that nurses, like any military component, need an existing corps to be effective.

A woman rows on Newcomb Lake in New York's Adirondack Mountains in 1901. While only upper-class people enjoyed vacations in this era, many poorer women rowed. Waterways were more accessible than highways in the early stages of settlement throughout the nation's history, and it was not uncommon for women in underdeveloped areas to use boats for their marketing and social needs. Courtesy of the Adirondack Museum; Blue Mountain Lake, New York

Its first commander is Dita H. Kinney, who receives no rank and is addressed as "Miss." A graduate of the prestigious Massachusetts General Hospital Nursing School and an experienced army nurse, she is well qualified, but military bureaucracy makes her tenure difficult and she will be dismissed in 1909.

✦ The army follows up on the death rate from tropical yellow fever during the recent war. Young nurse Clara Maass earns $100 by allowing herself to be bitten by the suspected mosquito carrier and dies in Havana as a result.

The daughter of German immigrants, Maass is an 1895 graduate of the nursing school associated with a German hospital in Newark. She is the only woman involved in the experiments, and she gives her life to establish the crucial link between the insect and the disease. It will be physician Walter Reed, however, who is remembered as the hero of yellow fever.

✦ The University of Chicago awards the world's first political science Ph.D. granted a woman to Sophonisba Breckinridge. The men of her Kentucky family have a long history of political careers, and she became the state's first female attorney in 1895. Dr. Breckinridge will be affiliated with the University of Chicago for the rest of her life; she writes several books on legal issues pertaining to women and children while also serving as an officer in feminist organizations.

✦ A New Orleans columnist known as "Dorothy Dix" commands a huge $5,000 annual salary when she joins the Hearst syndicate as a crime reporter. Elizabeth Meriwether Gilmer never uses her real name as she covers several of the era's most sensational sex/murder trials.

✦ A Chicago teacher, Mary Murphy, is automatically dismissed when she marries; she sues and wins a court ruling that "marriage is not misconduct" and thus does not fit into the board's grounds for dismissal. Most school boards ignore the decision, however, and female teachers who marry will continue to be fired routinely until after World War II.

✦ Margaret A. Haley becomes business agent for the Chicago Teachers' Federation, a career that lasts more than three decades. A teacher since 1876, Haley uncovers funds for teachers' salaries that the school board has failed to collect; she will lobby successfully for a tenure law and a pension system.

When Ella Flagg Young becomes superintendent of Chicago's schools in 1909, she and Haley set an unprecedented example of women heading one of the nation's largest educational systems; yet, when Haley speaks on the floor of the National Education Association's convention this year, she believes that she is the first woman to do so.

✦ The women's auxiliary of the African-American National Baptist Convention hears a report from their energetic new organizer, Nannie Burroughs. During the previous year, she traveled 22,000 miles, made 215 speeches, and wrote over 9,000 letters. Burroughs is aware of gender as well as racial discrimination, for her maiden speech is titled "How the Sisters Are Hindered from Helping."

✦ In September, revolutionaries in Macedonia kidnap American missionary Ellen M. Stone. They hold her for ransom, which they want to finance warfare against the Turks. A 56-year-old Congregationalist, Stone remains a captive until the following February, when she is finally freed in exchange for $66,000 raised by public donations. President Theodore Roosevelt's "big stick" foreign policy seemingly plays little part in the release of this American citizen.

✦ At age 14, Ethel Barrymore performs in her first starring role. Born into a family of established actors, she goes on to great fame on London and New York stages—and as other media develop, she also stars in radio, movies, and finally television. The acknowledged queen of Broadway early in the century, she will wed at age 30, bear three children in three years, and—like her mother and grandmother before her—continue her career. She will give her last performance in 1957, after enjoying more than a half century of success.

+ Carrie Jacobs Bond of Janesville, Wisconsin, publishes what becomes a standard wedding song for the rest of the century, "I Love You Truly." She will achieve genuine fame as a songwriter. The sheet music for "The End of a Perfect Day," which is inspired by a 1909 California sunset, sells more than 5 million copies.

+ Witnessed by thousands, adventurer Anne Edson Taylor is the first person to go over Niagara Falls in a barrel and survive.

1902   The first American woman honored with a postage stamp is not remembered for her own achievements but rather as the wife of a man: Martha Washington is depicted this year on a 1-cent stamp, which will be reissued in 1923 and 1938.

+ Despite decades of women's rights activism centered in the Northeast, this year sees what is only the second state suffrage referendum east of the Mississippi. New Hampshire men vote the question down, just as Rhode Islanders did in 1887, when the first eastern election was held. In contrast, the first referendum in the West was held in 1867, and women have won voting rights in five western states.

+ Free public education is not standard in the Deep South, and Georgian Martha Berry turns her 35,000-acre plantation into a school that allows poor white students to earn their tuition by working. Coeducational Berry College is added in 1926, and in some years as many as 5,000 applicants have to be turned down. Berry will eventually receive honors for her educational innovation, and the school continues after her 1942 death.

+ Future first lady Lou Henry Hoover studies at the London School of Mines. She has an 1898 geology degree from Stanford and collaborates with her husband, civil engineer Herbert Hoover, on technical articles and the translation of a complex 16th-century mining textbook, for which they receive the Gold Medal of the Mining and Metallurgical Society. When the Hoovers lived in China during the Boxer Rebellion, she upset natives by defying their belief that a woman descending into mines means bad luck.

+ Dr. Ida Sophia Scudder supervises the construction of a hospital in the town of Vellore in southern India. For the next two decades, she will be the hospital's only surgeon, but she devotes even more of her time to building a nursing school and then a medical school to train native women as nurses and physicians.

A native of India, Dr. Scudder was born to medical missionaries in 1870 and graduated from Woman's Medical College of Pennsylvania in 1895. She decided to study medicine one night when she saw three Indian women die because their husbands refused to allow her father—or any male physician—handle their deliveries.

+ Susie King Taylor pays for the publication of *Reminiscences of My Life in Camp*, a memoir of her time as an escaped slave living in a Union Army camp on Georgia sea coast islands during the Civil War.

+ The fourth volume of *The History of Woman Suffrage* is printed in the same year that Elizabeth Cady Stanton dies. Previous authors have been Stanton, Susan Anthony, and Matilda Joselyn Gage, but Gage had quarreled with the others over the movement's increasing conservatism prior to her 1898 death, and this volume is written by Anthony with her biographer, Ida Husted Harper.

It covers the years from the last volume, in 1886, to 1900. Volume 4 is largely a chronicle of the annual meetings of the National American Woman Suffrage Association, with its emphasis on Anthony's side of any internal dissension.

+ While Elizabeth Cady Stanton is dying, one of her daughters, Harriot Stanton Blatch, returns to the United States from England, where she has been living with her merchant husband. Blatch is shocked by the growing conservatism and apathy in the American suffrage movement, and she introduces more militant British strategies.

Using the techniques that political scientists now call "visibility," she organizes parades, rallies, and poll watchers; she reaches out to working-class women and, by the end of the decade, she will have some 20,000 New Yorkers in her Equality League of Self-Supporting Women. One of the most visible members is nursing leader Lavinia Dock, who was arrested for voting in 1896.

✦ From her London base, Dr. Elizabeth Blackwell publishes her final book, *Essays in Medical Sociology*; her other works include two controversial books on sex education. The first accredited female physician in the world, she will die in England in 1910 at age 89—but at 86, she is still strong enough to cross the Atlantic for one last visit.

✦ In New York's theater district, playwright Rachel Crothers makes her debut. She will go on to write almost 40 plays, with at least a dozen as major Broadway successes that have longer-than-average runs. Several feature titles reflective of Crothers' witty feminism: *A Man's World* (1909), *He and She* (1911), *When Ladies Meet*, (1932), and *Susan and God* (1937).

1903 The Women's Trade Union League begins at a convention of the American Federation of Labor. It will develop as an unusual meld of working-class women supported by educated affluent women; the first president is Mary Morton Kehew, a Boston philanthropist who during the previous decade worked to get women into labor unions. Among the unions involved are those representing glove, cap, hat, and shoemakers; newer unions include waitresses, retail clerks, train ticket agents, and typographers.

✦ Mother Jones loses her job with the United Mine Workers when the national union disavows a wildcat strike in the Colorado coal mines where she is working. She remains in the West for a decade, however, organizing copper miners from Idaho to Arizona.

✦ As many as 75,000 workers, many of them women, participate in textile mill strikes in the Philadelphia area.

✦ In Richmond, Virginia, Maggie Mitchell Walker begins St. Luke's Penny Savings Bank, thereby becoming the nation's first female bank president. The bank is an outgrowth of a mutual aid insurance program for African Americans, which Walker turned from bankruptcy in 1899, when she became executive director, to long-term success. At the same time, she mothers three sons.

✦ Kate Wiggin publishes *Rebecca of Sunnybrook Farm*, which becomes one of the best-selling children's books of the century. Wiggin was already so well known as an author that she retained her first husband's name when she remarried in 1895.

✦ English Mrs. Humphry Ward is the best selling novelist in America both this year and in 1905. Her books are *Lady Rose's Daughter* and *The Marriage of William Ashe*.

✦ *The Land of Little Rain*, a first book by Californian Mary Austin, who lives on the edge of Death Valley, brings her lifelong fame. Sales of future books are sufficient to allow her to maintain homes in Manhattan and in the artist colonies of Carmel, California, and Santa Fe, New Mexico; her friend Willa Cather will write *Death Comes to the Archbishop* while living in Austin's adobe home. She is also welcomed in Europe, where literati such as William Butler Yeats and George Bernard Shaw read her books. While her writing is occasionally eccentric, her work on the Southwest, especially its native peoples, will be favorably compared to nature writers such as John Muir and Henry David Thoreau.

✦ The residents of Deadwood, South Dakota, bury local legend Calamity Jane next to her erstwhile lover, Wild Bill Hickok. Born Martha Jane Canarray, she had dressed like a man most of her life; she drank, smoked cigars, swore, worked as a mule skinner, and claimed to have been an Indian scout in the 1870s. Her unconventional ways brought her to the attention of national publicists in the 1890s, and Calamity Jane toured with two Wild West shows—but when she was unable to stay sober, "Buffalo Bill" Cody paid her way back to the West.

◆ After Carry Nation sells her hatchets in a Coney Island sideshow, the Women's Christian Temperance Union severs its ties with her. Despite tremendous personal problems—including the mental illness of her daughter—she will continue her national crusade until 1910, when a female saloon operator in Montana beats her so badly that she dies six months later.

1904 The five-year meeting of the International Council of Women, held in Berlin, is the last of the organization as such and the last international meeting for 84-year-old Susan Anthony. It includes many garden parties and similar events that her niece Katharine Anthony believes are intended to distract women from their work. Competition between English and German women presages the coming of World War I, and the result is that dissatisfied delegates have a follow-up meeting in which they found the International Woman Suffrage Alliance.

The key word is "suffrage," a goal to which many delegates of the old organization were unwilling to pledge themselves. The new group includes women from the United States and seven other nations: Australia, Britain, Denmark, Germany, the Netherlands, Norway, and Sweden. Carrie Chapman Catt of Iowa is elected president, replacing May Wright Sewall of Indiana; other officers are from Germany, Britain, and the Netherlands. A Declaration of Principles affirms the equality of men and women, lists unfair treatment of women under national laws, and calls for the ballot.

The most discussed event of the Berlin International Council of Women is a speech by Mary Church Terrell, the founding president of the National Association of Colored Women, which she gives in German, French, and English.

Terrell, who was born to wealth, compares the status of blacks in the United States to that of Jews in Germany. Her speech exhibits great courage, and African Americans take pride in her achievement: One periodical slyly comments, "Southern ladies will have to drop the Empress of Germany from their calling lists on account of her reception of this negress."

◆ Although Carrie Chapman Catt retains the presidency of the International Woman Suffrage Association, she is forced to give up the presidency of the National American Woman Suffrage Association to care for her dying husband. The Reverend Dr. Anna Howard Shaw is elected president and serves until 1914.

◆ The World's Fair in St. Louis offers many networking opportunities, and pictures taken by photographer Jessie Tarbox Beals, some of which are shot from a balloon, are published internationally. Beals also makes important contacts, but her husband refuses to allow her to accept a commission from Secretary of War William Howard Taft to photograph the Philippines.

When the couple compromises and settles in New York, she experiments with night photography, an as-yet undeveloped technique. A newspaper leaves her identity anonymous when it reports: "The explosion . . . of flashlight powder . . . caused tremendous excitement and considerable damage. . . . Scores of families . . . came scurrying into the street, some of them in their night clothes."

◆ Sculptor Gertrude Vanderbilt Whitney mounts her first major exhibit at the St. Louis fair—but because she fears that her work may be judged on the basis of her wealthy family names rather than on its merit, she uses an assumed name until 1910. When she wins an award from the National Academy of Design that year, she will go on to a lifetime of achievement. While also mothering three children, Whitney will fulfill many public commissions, including a statue of "Buffalo Bill" in Cody, Wyoming, and one of Columbus in Palos, Spain.

◆ Also at the St. Louis World's Fair, Annie Turbo Malone reaches a national audience with her hair products designed for black women. Two years later, she will copyright her business under the name of Poro, an African term for physical achievement. By 1917, she has a million-dollar complex in St. Louis; a decade later, as many as 75,000 women will work as Poro agents. Her enterprise begins to collapse during the Great

Depression, however, and by her death in 1957, she is virtually bankrupt.

✦ Chicago obstetrician and surgeon Bertha Van Hoosen begins experiments with "twilight sleep," an anesthetic that will become popular for relieving the pain of childbirth during much of the century. She safely delivers some 2,000 babies in the next four years and, in 1915, publishes the results of her work as *Scopolamine-Morphine Anaesthesia*. In that same year, she also becomes the founding president of the American Medical Women's Association, which is established because she and other female physicians feel excluded at medical conventions dominated by men. An 1888 University of Michigan graduate, Dr. Van Hoosen trains many other female surgeons, some of whom work overseas as medical missionaries.

✦ Helen Keller, who has been both deaf and blind since early childhood, graduates from Radcliffe. The achievement is possible partly because of the remarkable optimism and persistence of Keller's mother and especially that of her lifelong governess, Anne Sullivan, who expands on the system of teaching by touch that was developed for Laura Bridgman in the 1830s. Despite her inability to hear, Keller has learned to speak; she will travel the world inspiring millions and eventually is the author of a dozen books.

✦ Concern about "white slavery" prompts an Ellis Island rule that forbids the entry of young, single women unless they are accompanied by escorts the authorities deem "proper." A well-intended woman implementing this policy is proud to announce that "unprotected women and children are detained."

The result is that, to "guarantee the observance of all the proprieties," weddings occur at Ellis Island almost every day—and some women who do not understand English are unknowingly forced into marriages that they do not want.

✦ The Colony Club is founded in New York. It is the first private club for wealthy women, similar to the clubs with eating and sleeping facilities that long have been available to wealthy men.

✦ Journalist and historian Ida Tarbell publishes the two-volume *History of the Standard Oil Company*. Despite its seemingly academic nature, it becomes a huge success and draws public attention to corrupt business practices.

Tarbell's history of Napoleon, published in 1895, has already sold more than 100,000 copies, and she will go on to lecture and write on a number of other topics, including women's issues.

✦ Fannie Farmer publishes what she considers to be her most important work, *Food and Cookery for the Sick and Convalescent*. The connection beween diet and health is still new, and the book establishes sufficient credentials for her that she lectures at Harvard and other medical schools. Partially crippled most of her life, she will continue to teach after she can no longer walk.

✦ English Eva Booth assumes command of the American Salvation Army and changes her name to Evangeline Booth. A preacher in London slums since girlhood, she will demonstrate great organizing and fund-raising abilities during the next three decades in the United States.

✦ Mary McLeod Bethune separates from her husband and takes her young son with her when she opens the Daytona Beach Literary and Industrial School for Training Negro Girls in an old Florida house. She has no savings but soon develops extraordinary fund-raising skills, and by the time of World War II, Bethune-Cookman College is a coeducational institution with 14 buildings on a 32-acre campus.

✦ In Paris, American-born artist Mary Cassatt is made a Chevalier of the Legion d'Honneur. Although she lives until 1926, Cassatt's sight is beginning to fail and she stops painting with the outbreak of World War I.

✦ The liberated behavior of President Theodore Roosevelt's 20-year old daughter Alice—who blows cigarette smoke at photographers who catch her gambling at racetracks—causes so much scandal that his advisors fear she will cost him the election. Roosevelt's response is to say that he can govern the nation or he can govern Alice, but he cannot do both.

1905 Nettie Maria Stevens wins a $1,000 prize endowed by scientist Ellen Swallow Richards; it enables Stevens to continue what is a very productive, but brief, career as a biologist.

Stevens was 35 before she moved from her native New England to California, where she earned both her bachelor's and master's degrees from Stanford University. She joined the faculty of Bryn Mawr in 1900 after obtaining her doctorate there, and now does graduate work in Germany, using the prize money to conduct genetic experiments.

Before her 1912 death from breast cancer at age 50, Dr. Stevens will make the fundamental discovery that an embryo's sex is determined by the X or the Y chromosome in the sperm of the male parent. Her breakthrough will not be accepted until long after her death, and meanwhile, countless women continue to be blamed when the babies they bear are not of the desired sex.

◆ Because of the centennial of the Lewis & Clark Expedition, the annual meeting of the National American Woman Suffrage Association is held in Oregon and honors Sacajawea. Association leaders unveil a statue of her, while NAWSA historian Ida Husted Harper says that national attention to Sacajawea is "very significant of the changing sentiment toward women."

◆ Independently of Annie Turbo Malone, Sarah Breedlove Walker begins selling hair products designed for African Americans, which will make her the nation's first black female millionaire within the next decade.

She had been orphaned at six, married at 14, and widowed at 20, and her life was one of extreme poverty until, as she says, the hair formula came to her in a dream. Calling herself "Madame C.J. Walker," she builds an Indianapolis manufacturing plant, develops a nationwide network of "Walker agents," and contributes to artistic and educational causes prior to her death in 1919.

◆ In *Lochner v. the United States*, the Supreme Court strikes down a New York law limiting the hours of bakery employees as an unfair burden on employers. Progressives are undaunted by the ruling, however, and during the next two decades, almost all states will pass legislation declaring maximum work weeks for women that are between 48 and 60 hours.

Many states also include bans on night work for women—with exceptions for occupations such as nurses and telephone operators, which are considered natural to women and must be done at night.

◆ Florence Finch Kelly begins reviewing books for the *New York Times*. Although a journalist for 25 years, she understood that "a forthright application . . . from any woman held a very slight chance of success," and initially hid her identity—but with support from publisher Adolph Ochs, she will develop both the book review section and herself into real publishing powers.

By 1936, when she will retire at age 78, Kelly doubtless is one of the best-informed people in the United States, for the position requires her to read hundreds of books annually. When she includes her earlier years as a journalist, she will be able to summarize, "As far as I know, I had spent more years in newspaper offices than any other woman."

◆ The first women are elected to the Hall of Fame for Great Americans, a New York memorial hall built in 1899. They are educators Mary Lyon and Emma Willard and astronomer Maria Mitchell.

Author Harriet Beecher Stowe and temperance leader Frances Willard will be added in 1910; they will be joined by actress Charlotte Cushman and educator Alice Freeman Palmer in 1915 and 1920.

◆ Novelist Edith Wharton speaks profoundly to the changing roles of women in *The House of Mirth*. Educated by governesses as a girl, she never had any formal schooling.

◆ Nebraskan Edith Abbott earns a doctorate in economics at the University of Chicago and goes on to further study at the London School of

Economics. In 1908, she will return to Chicago, where she is associated with the university and with Jane Addams' Hull House. In 1910, she publishes *Women In Industry*, a study so comprehensive that it could be a lifetime achievement rather than a first book.

✦ San Franciscan Isadora Duncan, whose barefoot style of modern dance has made her a sensation on European stages, adds further to her liberated image by bearing a child out of wedlock. When an American tour a few years later is a failure, she returns to her successful Parisian scene and has a second child without marrying the father. Both children are killed in a 1913 accident, and a third, who is born soon after, also dies. Although Duncan will perform with the Metropolitan Opera in 1917, her lifestyle, dress, and dance techniques are too controversial in the United States, and she returns to Europe at the end of World War I.

✦ *Peter Pan* is written for the wistful face of Maude Adams, who performs the role some 1,500 times before retiring in middle age. She will return to the stage during the 1930s to play mature roles; considered a premier classical performer, she teaches drama into her 70s.

✦ In November, Susan Anthony goes to the White House to lobby Theodore Roosevelt. She presents him with a list of seven specific requests, ranging from an endorsement of the federal suffrage amendment to putting "experienced women on boards and commissions relating to such matters as they would be competent to pass upon." All of her suggestions are ignored—although Roosevelt does include her in social functions and has sent greetings on her birthday.

1906 In February, Susan Anthony attends her last suffrage convention in Baltimore. Her speech includes a line that becomes a motto for feminists: "Failure is impossible." She dies at age 86 a month later, back home in Rochester, and is eulogized throughout the world.

✦ Long-simmering divisions in the suffrage movement between women living in the East and West come to a head with Susan Anthony's death, and

former vice president Abigail Scott Duniway of Oregon resigns from the NAWSA.

The chief cause of this factionalism is the tendency of easterners to link suffrage with prohibition, in which many suffragists are also active. This causes great political harm to western women, where men have long demonstrated a greater willingness to grant women legal rights—but where they also cherish their saloons.

✦ The International Woman Suffrage Alliance meets in Copenhagen. In addition to women from the United States and the eight northern Europe countries who founded the group, others attend from Australia, Iceland, Canada, Hungary, Italy, and Russia. They congratulate the progress of Norwegian and Danish women, who receive partial enfranchisement this year; women in Australia won full rights in 1901, as do Finnish women this year.

✦ More than a decade before U.S. entrance into World War I, Bostonian Lucia Ames Mead presciently writes of the danger of excessive nationalism in *Patriotism and the New Internationalism*. Also a suffragist, she argues that women will never achieve equality in a world in which decisions are made through violence. She lectures on peace to thousands of people annually for three decades. Jane Addams will say of Mead: "No one in the United States has done more . . . [to] substitute law for peace than has Lucia Ames Mead."

✦ At the same time that these suffrage alliance women are international travelers, Wyoming educator Edith K.O. Clark must take a two-day stagecoach journey to reach the nearest railroad. As an elected county superintendent of schools during this decade, she rides horseback to visit remote mountain schoolhouses.

✦ Wealthy New Yorker Mary Drier becomes president of the Women's Trade Union League. Under her leadership, the WTUL becomes a true power, and she is arrested during the great garment strike of 1909–10. After the 1911 Triangle Fire, Drier is appointed to a special commission on factory safety.

The president of the Chicago branch is Mary McDowell, who heads the University of Chicago's settlement house—a position of great influence that she will retain until 1929.

+ Deaf and blind author Helen Keller writes an article for *Ladies' Home Journal* on the connection between neonatal blindness and venereal disease in the mother. Thousands find such candor inappropriate and cancel their subscriptions, but the magazine continues its editorial advocacy of sex education.

+ The Pure Food & Drug Act is a victory for many women, especially those of the General Federation of Women's Clubs, who have lobbied for its passage. The law's enforcement will make life easier for women, who must shop for food and milk knowing that many vendors sell contaminated goods.

+ After an eight-year search, public health authorities finally track down "Typhoid Mary," a cook who had worked in places where typhoid fever occurred. Although not ill herself, her condition as a carrier of the fatal disease cannot be cured, and Mary Mallon will live under quarantine the rest of her life.

+ One of those who works on the Typhoid Mary case is Dr. Josephine Baker, a young New York public health physician who will specialize in reducing the city's high rate of infant mortality. One important factor in this battle is seemingly simple: Dr. Baker encourages women to breast-feed rather than risk using the era's frequently contaminated milk. In this, however, she will have to battle many male physicians who deem bottle-feeding "more scientific."

+ Emma Goldman and her lover begin publishing a leftist monthly called *Mother Earth*; two years later Goldman is the sole author of *Anarchism and Other Essays*. A true intellectual as well as a leftist activist, Goldman will address *The Social Significance of Modern Drama* in 1914, in which she discusses the ideas of George Bernard Shaw, Henrik Ibsen, and others contemporary playwrights.

+ During a theatrical performance at Madison Square Garden, millionaire Harry Thaw pulls a gun and kills architect Stanford White, a former lover of Thaw's new bride, Evelyn Nesbit. Thaw is incarcerated as insane, and Nesbit uses the notoriety to build an acting career. The newspapers are filled with the story for years.

+ A group of women who consider themselves Socialists as well as suffragists, including Elizabeth Gurley Flynn, meet in New York's Lower East Side and begin developing the idea of an International Women's Day.

+ The nation's first successful female attorney, Belva Lockwood, wins a major case before the Supreme Court—at age 76. Lockwood obtains $5 million for Cherokees in North Carolina and eastern Tennessee. Her law practice has long consisted of clients whom other lawyers do not accept, and thus, despite successes on behalf of Indians, blacks, and women, Lockwood ends her days in poverty.

+ Decades after giving up her artistic career for conventional wifehood, Vinnie Ream Hoxie undertakes a commission for Iowa's sculpture in the nation's Capitol. Her husband, who years earlier insisted that she give up sculpting, has mellowed to the point that he builds rigging to enable her to chisel more easily, for she is now partially disabled. She will receive another commission from the State of Oklahoma, which she manages to largely complete prior to her 1914 death. Vinnie Ream, as she continues to be known, then is honored with burial in Arlington National Cemetery.

+ The social event of the year is the White House wedding of Alice Roosevelt to Congressman Nicholas Longworth. The previous year, President Theodore Roosevelt gave away the bride at the New York wedding of his niece Eleanor Roosevelt, who married her distant cousin of the same surname, Franklin Roosevelt.

+ Female photographers hold a show in New York. Their advertising proclaims the historic nature of the event, as 32 women exhibit some 200 prints.

1907 The post office issues its third stamp recognizing the historical roles of women, this one of the founding of Jamestown 300 years ago. The honor goes to Pocahontas, but the drawing of her is in English dress that looks decidedly masculine. Indeed, the image and the title, "Founding of Jamestown," gives the impression that the stamp is dedicated to Sir Walter Raleigh, not Pocahontas. An assumed birthdate of 1595 and her death date of 1617 also appear on the stamp.

Future post office publications will diminish the role of Pocahontas (or Rebecca Rolfe) by referring to her as "legendary." This ignores not only documentation on her life in America, but especially on her death in England, where written records are obtained comparatively easily.

✦ Unlike many immigrants on the East Coast, most of Minnesota's immigrants are well assimilated, and this year they begin the Scandinavian Woman Suffrage Association, influenced by the superior enfranchisement progress of their sisters back in Europe.

✦ Hull House, which Jane Addams and Ellen Gates Starr began as the nation's first immigrant settlement house in 1889, now has 13 buildings in its Chicago complex, including a coffeehouse that operates as a nighttime alternative to saloons. MIT's Ellen Richards has contributed to Hull House design, especially its kitchen facilities.

✦ Congress revises immigration rules, making an increasing number of people ineligible. The worst inequity for women is that the revised law contains provisions that cause a woman to lose her citizenship if she marries a noncitizen. Although this rule applies to women born in the United States as well as to those who are naturalized, few notice or object. Because most women cannot vote, the loss of citizenship does not seem tremendously important.

✦ The Industrial Workers of the World sponsor teenage orator Elizabeth Gurley Flynn when they organize in Minnesota's iron range. She goes on to Montana and Spokane, where she is twice arrested and jailed during violent strikes; in 1910,

she returns to the East Coast and plays major roles in several strikes.

✦ Margaret Drier Robins, sister of Women's Trade Union League president Mary Drier of New York, is active in the labor movement in Chicago. This year, Robins is named to the executive committee of the Chicago American Federation of Labor, where she will serve until 1916. In later years, women will be included less often at this level of union power.

✦ When astronomer Williamina Fleming publishes a study of the 222 variable stars she has discoverd, a British colleague comments: "Many astronomers are deservedly proud to have discovered one . . . the discovery of 222 . . . is an achievement bordering on the marvellous."

In the previous year, Fleming became the first American woman elected to the Royal Astronomical Society; she also receives major honors from the governments of France and Mexico. Nor is her life limited to science, for she actively supports suffrage.

✦ When her financier husband dies, Margaret Slocum Sage establishes the Russell Sage Foundation. Far more generous than he, she gives some $80 million to charitable, educational, and artistic causes.

The foundation will be of particular importance to the history of American women both because it funds women's organizations and because its records provide massive documentation on the lives of needy women. The total amount of her donations makes Margaret Sage the equivalent of Andrew Carnegie and other more famous philanthropists.

✦ The nation's first Mother's Day is celebrated in a Philadelphia church; with energetic organizing by Anna Jarvis, the "tradition" is observed in every state within four years. Father's Day follows with a 1910 observance in Spokane, and in 1914, Congress formalizes the second Sunday in May as Mother's Day.

✦ Emily P. Bissell, a founder of the Delaware Anti-Tuberculosis Society, emulates a Danish fund-raising method and begins what will become a highly successful tradition of selling Christmas seals.

✦ Adelaide Nutting, longtime superintendent of nurses at Baltimore's John Hopkins Hospital, moves to New York, where she is the first nurse to hold a university chair. Teachers College of Columbia University inaugurates a nursing program that ultimately will have global influence. Nutting has persistently crusaded against hospitals' exploitation of student nurses, who typically work long hours at menial tasks for no pay and little educational benefit.

With her colleague Lavinia Dock, she also coauthors the first two volumes of Dock's four-volume work, *History of Nursing* (1907–12). Johns Hopkins honors Nutting by hanging her portrait, which was painted by Philadelphia artist Cecelia Beaux.

✦ Maria Montessori opens her first preschool (*Casa dei Bambini*) in Italy, and her system of early childhood education is soon popularized by Dorothy Canfield Fisher in a 1912 book.

Fisher, who writes fiction as well as nonfiction, goes on to establish a literary reputation in the 1920s that is comparable to her friends Willa Cather and Pearl Buck. She will be the first woman to serve as a selector for the new Book-of-the-Month Club in 1926.

✦ The year's fiction best-seller is *The Lady of the Decoration* by Frances Little, a pseudonym of Fannie Caldwell Macaulay. Born in Kentucky in 1863, she will write many popular novels prior to her 1941 death. Next year, *Ladies' Home Journal* features an article about her travels in Japan.

1908 The International Woman Suffrage Alliance meets in Amsterdam, with 20 nations represented. The new militant strategy of the British suffrage movement is debated, for British women are beginning to attack their opponents with physical damage of personal and public property. A resolution passes that objects to any imprisonment of women as "common law breakers instead of political offenders."

✦ With Bryn Mawr president M. Carey Thomas as its leader, the Equal Suffrage League is formed on college campuses. This is the first such organization, and its formation 60 years after the 1848 women's rights convention is indicative of the tepid support that female academicians give suffrage. Most hold themselves separate from the middle-class housewives who form the backbone of the movement.

✦ The National American Woman Suffrage Association convention votes to obtain 1 million petition signatures on behalf of women's enfranchisement. Two years later, the group presents Congress with 404,000—an impressive number, but still less than half of the goal. The World Woman's Christian Temperance Union, in contrast, had gathered 7 million signatures for prohibition more than a decade ago.

✦ In *Muller v. Oregon*, the Supreme Court upholds an Oregon law establishing a maximum 10-hour day for women employed in laundries, thereby reversing its 1905 *Lochner v. the United States*.

Attorney Louis Brandeis (a future Supreme Court justice) argues the case, with materials prepared by the Consumers League's Josephine Goldmark and its attorney, Florence Kelley. Goldmark comes from a prominent Jewish family long resident in the United States and is Brandeis' sister-in-law.

They win the case by amassing a huge amount of data on women's deplorable employment conditions. The Court sets a significant precedent with its consideration of this sociological, contemporary evidence over the legalistic, case-history argumentation of the past.

✦ The Navy Nurse Corps is founded with Esther Voorhees Hanson as its director. Modeled on the Army Nurse Corps, it is the second military unit for women.

✦ Black women are not admitted to either the Army or Navy Nurse Corps or, indeed, any major organization, and so, with 25 founding members, the National Association of Colored Graduate Nurses begins this year. The American Nurse Association will not integrate until 1951.

The use of "National" and "American" in these groups' names, incidentally, is indicative of a wider phenomenon: the National Bar Association, for example, is the black counterpart to the American Bar Association, and the usage is repeated in other cases.

◆ The American Home Economics Association is formed after a series of educational conferences led by MIT scientist Ellen Richards. Richards, who has conducted research on toxic substances in homes and invented plumbing and heating systems for her own home, also endows the association's journal.

◆ Two years prior to her death, Mary Baker Eddy founds the *Christian Science Monitor*. Her motivation is the need to counter negative publicity generated by lawsuits against Christian Scientists, including one by her long-estranged son.

Since 1887, Eddy has secluded herself in her Boston mansion or her New Hampshire retreat and is seen only by a few of those who direct her religious corporate structure. When she dies at age 89, her estate is valued at over $2 million.

◆ The 60th anniversary of the Seneca Falls Women's Rights Convention features a speech by African American Mary Church Terrell, who reminds listeners of the historic links between the end of slavery for blacks and the end of subordination for women.

◆ The National Association of Colored Women, which has more than 15,000 members in 31 states, tackles its own internal color barrier. Mary Church Terrell and other NACW officers had slaveowner ancestors, and this year's convention features a candid movement to elect darker women. "We prefer a woman who is altogether Negro," a delegate explains, because the leadership's ability "is attributed to their white blood. We want to demonstrate that the African is as talented."

◆ Frances Kellor is named secretary of the New York State Immigration Commission. In a reversal of the usual order, Kellor earned her law degree from Cornell University and then obtained her bachelor's degree from the University of Chicago; not even a high school graduate, she was admitted to law school on the basis of her test scores.

As the immigration secretary, she will concentrate on policies that protect immigrant women from exploitation—although such efforts also sometimes limit female freedom of movement. With similar goals, Kellor had founded the National League for the Protection of Colored Women two years earlier; herself white, she is concerned about friendless black women moving to the urban North from an agricultural lifestyle in the South. In both organizations, she and those who support her aim to prevent forced entry into prostitution.

◆ Rose Knox ignores advice when her husband dies, and she takes over the rural New York gelatin business that they have run. She invests in research, uses creative publicity and innovative personnel policies, and triples corporate income in less than a decade. Knox Gelatine Company soon dominates the national market and will be one of very few business that does not lay off a single employee during the Great Depression.

◆ Authorized biographer Ida Husted Harper adds a third volume to *Life and Work of Susan B. Anthony*. Harper's work proves sufficiently popular that, in the following year, she will begin as a regular columnist for the widely read *Harper's Bazaar*.

◆ Almost 12% of Colorado homestead claims since 1887 have been filed by single women. As late as World War I, women will homestead land in remote sections of the state.

◆ The La Porte, Indiana, farm of Belle Gunness draws national notoriety when the dismembered bodies of at least seven men and three women are found buried there. In the charred remains of her home are those of her three children, along with a body that may or may not be hers. Many suspect that when authorities began inquiring about people who disappeared after answering her newspaper advertisements, she substituted a corpse from her garden, set the fire, and fled.

Gunness immigrated from Norway more than two decades ago, and all of the identifiable victims have Norwegian names. After collecting substantial insurance money on husbands who died in Chicago and in Indiana, she began advertising for companions, making it clear that they should bring cash.

A man hired to work on her farm confesses that he helped dispose of some of the bodies; he will die in prison in 1911. Some accounts say that Gunness is responsible for as many as 14 deaths and that she collected as much as $100,000 from her victims.

✦ Julia Ward Howe, who has published in almost every genre on a wide range of issues, is the first woman voted membership in the American Academy of Arts and Letters. When she dies two years later at age 91, her funeral at Symphony Hall will feature a 4,000-voice choir singing "The Battle Hymn of the Republic."

1909 Chicago is the nation's first city to have a woman at the head of its school system. She is Ella Flagg Young, an educational administrator since 1863. Her promotion to the top position is a logical—but nevertheless highly unusual—natural progression, for she has held the rank of assistant superintendent since 1887. Young earned a Ph.D. at the University of Chicago in 1900; she was also appointed to the faculty there and worked with famed educator John Dewey.

✦ Nora Stanton Blatch DeForest—daughter of Harriot Stanton Blatch and granddaughter of Elizabeth Cady Stanton—becomes the first woman admitted to the American Society of Engineers. A 1905 honors graduate of Cornell University, she works for the New York City water department. She is just establishing her career, so her admission is on a junior level; when she becomes eligible for full status in 1916, her membership is dropped because she is not working as an engineer but rather devoting her time to suffrage. Her lawsuit against the society fails, and the society does not admit another woman until 1927.

✦ The International Woman Suffrage Alliance meets in London in April; hundreds attend, including five delegates from South Africa. The women exchange information about the political progress of women worldwide, and there is considerable debate on the increasingly militant tactics of British suffragists. The meeting's minutes run 57 pages and end with a resolution to meet more frequently than every five years.

✦ Among the founders of the National Association for the Advancement of Colored People are Mary Church Terrell, who is well-known in black America, and Frances Blascoer, who assumes the infant organization's administrative work. The NAACP leadership, however, is dominated by black men and by whites, leaving little opportunity for black women.

One of the three white founders who will prove most important to the development of the civil rights organization is Mary White Ovington. A descendant of New York abolitionists, she is a settlement house worker who has futilely attempted to build such a project for blacks. Ovington will serve in a variety of official NAACP capacities until her 1940 retirement, working as a full-time volunteer in an era when lynchings and other manifestations of racism are on the rise.

Another prominent white leader is Fanny Garrison Villard, daughter of early abolitionist William Lloyd Garrison. Villard also endows several African-American educational institutions and is an active suffragist and pacifist.

✦ With the motto "We specialize in the wholly impossible," the National Training School for Women and Girls begins on six acres in suburban Washington, D.C., under Nannie Burroughs.

She aims at preparing young African-American women for the realities of the workplace, and the school teaches both the fundamentals of grammar and such unconventional courses as shoe repair and printing. Burroughs emphasizes "the Bible, the bath, the broom"—but also introduces a Department of Negro History.

Although she has never attended college, she proves a superior educational executive; she keeps her school in business until after World War II, graduates some 2,500 women, and is proud of the fact that it is funded solely by blacks.

◆ Charlotte Perkins Gilman creates "Herland," which becomes the most famous feature of *Forerunner*, a utopian magazine that she will publish until 1916. "Herland" is a futuristic setting in which women are full partners in developing a society based on peaceful cooperation. Gilman's vision for the future includes such pragmatic proposals as communal nurseries and kitchens to ease domestic burdens and allow women to live full lives.

◆ Popular authors Ellen Glasgow and Mary Johnston begin the Virginia Equal Suffrage League. At the same time, the *Woman's Journal* reports that four Massachusetts women are conducting a "trolley tour" around the state to speak for the vote.

◆ The International Brotherhood of Electrical Workers, which traditionally represents telegraph and telephone workers, finally admits women to membership—at a time when more than 75,000 women are employed as phone operators.

◆ Government investigator Elizabeth Beardsley Butler publishes *Women and the Trades*, a study of working women in Pittsburgh. She finds some 4,500 women working at coremaking in metal foundries, a job that requires lifting 60 pounds. Most are Hungarians, Poles, and other Slavs; fewer than one-fifth can speak English. The metal industry is the third-largest employer of women in Pittsburgh, exceeded only by laundries and cigarmaking.

◆ In the fall, New York sees the greatest strike by women workers in its history. Over 20,000 workers in the garment industry—most of them young immigrant women, especially Jewish women—strike for recognition of the International Ladies' Garment Workers' Union and for better wages and working conditions. Picketers are attacked, and over 700 women are arrested during November and December. The Women's Trade Union League spends an average of $1,000 a day for bail.

Women's Trade Union League president Mary Drier has carefully forged links between suffragists and unionists, and an uncommon number of upper-class women support the workers. Future ambassador Daisy Harriman is one of the wealthy women who boycotts nonunion clothing and donates to the league. Alva Belmont—Mrs. O.H.P. Belmont to the newspapers—goes in person to bail out jailed strikers. Affluent Mary Drier is also assaulted and arrested; when she shows her torn coat in court, the policeman says he would have never arrested her if he had known who she was.

1910   The garment strike continues through the winter, forcing the closure of almost 500 factories in New York City. Many of these are small sweatshops designed to exploit workers, and it is not unusual for owners to disappear without paying the wages owed. Women are also charged for necessary supplies, including the electricity to run their sewing machines—which they also often have to purchase. They are paid by the piece, not by the hour, which means they can be at work for hours without earning a dime. Finally, because they have to pay for the materials if they make a mistake, women can literally work for a week and end up owing money.

Most women support the strike, and as the owners see their solidarity, they are forced to bargain with the union. The strike ends February 15, with most of its objectives achieved; only 19 factories refuse to bargain.

From the experience, several garment makers move on to new careers as union leaders. Among them are Theresa Malkiel, who writes *Diary of a Shirtwaist Striker*; Rose Schneiderman, who eventually advises Franklin Roosevelt on labor issues; Pauline Newman, who joins the International Ladies' Garment Workers' Union during the strike and remains on its staff the rest of her life; and Swedish immigrant Mary Anderson, who has been an active union member since 1899, but now goes on to national prominence.

◆ In a campaign that attracts little attention from the national suffrage leadership, women in the

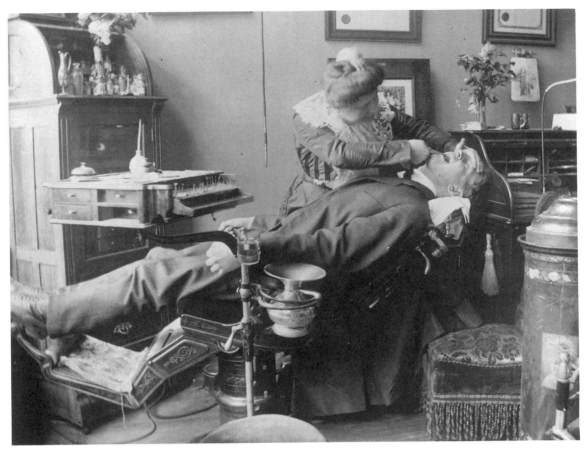

Although few women followed her example, Dr. Olga A. Lentz works as a dentist in St. Paul in 1910. The first known female dentist was also a midwesterner: Dr. Lucy Hobbs practiced in Iowa prior to the Civil War. Minnesota Historical Center; original photo by Albert Munson, courtesy of Chester Munson

State of Washington win a referendum on suffrage by a large margin. Washington is the first state to be added to the suffrage column since 1896, when Idaho granted the vote to women in a similarly low-profile campaign.

Meanwhile, Wyoming becomes the third state to elect women to its legislature when Mary G. Bellemy joins the House of Representatives. A Democrat in a Republican state, "Mollie" Bellemy votes to raise taxes for education and writes probate law that ensures equity for women.

✦ The 20,000-member Equality League organized by Harriot Stanton Blatch changes its name to Women's Political Union. Unlike National

American Woman Suffrage Association affiliates, it concentrates on lobbying the New York legislature and provies the opportunity for working-class women to testify to legislators. The women organize by precinct, hold outdoor rallies, and actively participate in legislative campaigns. They garner the most attention, however, by holding the first giant suffrage parade. While the reaction to this unladylike behavior initially is hostile, the parade proves successful enough that one will herald every New York spring until suffrage is a reality.

At the same time, Rachel Foster Avery, who was Susan Anthony's confidante for most of three decades, is among several longtime NAWSA members who resign because they are discontented with the leadership of the Reverend Dr. Anna Howard Shaw. With Anthony's niece, Lucy E. Anthony, Avery forms a separate Pennsylvania organization and works for state passage. Similar splinter groups appear from Baltimore to San Francisco as women become dissatisfied with their slow progress in obtaining the vote.

✦ In New York, a Men's League begins. It grows quickly and becomes an affiliate of the National American Woman Suffrage Association. James Lee Laidlow, "a banker and public-spirited man of New York City," will serve as president until the final victory in 1920, and many who join are congressmen and other public officials. They maintain a lower profile than the women in the movement, but participate in parades, send delegates to annual conventions, and offer valuable credibility.

In Florida, for example, the first Men's League begins before there are women's organizations in many cities—and its president is the mayor of Orlando. Soon chapters of the Men's League are formed in 25 states, from Maine to California and from Texas to North Dakota.

✦ Congress passes the Mann Act, which prohibits taking women across state or national boundaries for "immoral purposes." It makes prostitution a federal as well as a state crime if any interstate transportation—even mail—is involved.

The act will be vigorously enforced by several agencies, including the post office, which is particularly likely to read mail to and from France for tips on "the trade." Many women lobby for the act in an attempt to prevent what they call "white slavery," but other women find themselves falsely accused and their free movement hampered.

✦ Yale University honors Jane Addams with its first honorary degree granted to a woman. Nevertheless, Yale will not open to female students for many more decades. Addams—whose Illinois family rejected her desire to go to Smith College —is a graduate of Rockford Female Seminary.

Also this year, Adams publishes *Twenty Years at Hull House*. Her autobiographical story of the settlement house movement is a sales phenomenon and becomes an American classic. She has published several books in social and political science since 1902.

✦ Sociologist Margaret Byington publishes *Homestead: The Households of a Mill Town*, a study of the immigrant women, usually Slavic, who live in the steel town of Homestead, Pennsylvania. Byington will go on to write a dozen more books of sociology prior to 1941.

✦ The National Education Association, organized in 1870, elects its first female president, Chicago school superintendent Ella Flagg Young.

✦ A survey of 107 "non-Negro" colleges finds just 114 black female graduates—and half are products of Ohio's Oberlin College, even though its African-American enrollment has never exceeded 5%.

Other studies indicate that only two black women in the entire United States are practicing attorneys.

✦ Dr. Alice Hamilton heads the Illinois Occupational Disease Commission, the first such body in the world. A toxicologist, she is pioneering the field of industrial health through investigation of problems caused by noxious chemicals.

✦ The Reverend Annis Ford Eastman gives the funeral oration for Mark Twain, her former neighbor in Elmira, New York. Her first sermon was for a small Congregational church that was initially hostile. She turned them around by using as her text, "And the Lord sent Moses and Aaron and Miriam."

The Reverend Eastman is also the mother of Crystal Eastman, who will soon be a Woman's Party leader, and of Max Eastman, one of the era's best-known liberal writers.

✦ A first novel by California author Kathleen Norris is a best-seller; called *Mother*, it is based on the experience of Irish immigrant women. Norris' husband is her agent, and she will go on to sell over 10 million copies of 80 books.

Women authors hold the top-selling position during five of the past 10 years. In addition to

Norris, they are Florence Barclay, Mary Johnston, Frances Little, and Mrs. Humphry Ward.

◆ *New Idea Women's Magazine* asserts that "almost 1,000,000 women in the United States are either farmers or farm laborers."

◆ Women have worked as matrons in jails and prisons for decades, but this year Los Angeles is the first city to hire a woman for the job of "policewoman." She is Alice Stebbins Wells.

◆ When an October fire rages through the virgin forests of Lake of the Woods County, Minnesota, two families of nine and several smaller families cannot outrun it. Hundreds of thousands of acres burn, and this sparsely populated area sees 43 children, women, and men die.

At the same time, the Camp Fire Girls is formed to offer outdoor recreational opportunities to urbanized girls and their female leaders.

◆ Young Fanny Brice accidentally discovers that her talent lies in comedy rather than in singing and becomes an immense hit on vaudeville stages. When radio develops in the 1920s and 1930s, she delights audiences all over the nation; her "Baby Snooks" character is especially popular.

◆ Two decades before sound movies become available, Lois Weber and her husband, Wendell Phillips Smalley, are experimenting with techniques of matching sound to film. She will go on to a long career in Hollywood after her 1922 divorce and directs films for such prestigious studios as Paramount, DeMille, and especially Universal. Weber produces literally hundreds of motion pictures, writing or substantially rewriting the screenplays for most of them. When she dies in 1938, Lois Weber is well known as the most significant female director in Hollywood.

◆ In the fall, Chicago garment workers spontaneously emulate the New York strike. It begins when Bessie Abramowitz—who emigrated from Russia five years earlier and works for the elite men's clothing company of Hart, Schaffner and Marx—objects to a cut in the pay rate for buttonsewing from 4 cents to 3½ cents per garment. She organizes other young women, and although the

men of the United Garment Workers walk through their picket lines, some 18,000 women are on strike within a few weeks.

At a mass meeting, the women shout down the male union leader who proposes settling without recognizing a union for the women, and on October 27, almost 40,000 workers strike Chicago's factories. They meet in 16 different union halls to accommodate the different languages spoken by the workers, and experienced Women's Trade Union League leadership arrives from New York to assist. The strike lasts for 16 weeks, with Jane Addams playing a strong role in getting Hart, Schaffner and Marx to settle. It will take years, however, to achieve true union recognition, primarily because the male American Federation of Labor refuses to include women.

◆ On November 7, the first woman is commissioned in the National Guard. The circumstances, however, are uncommon. When the secretary to the governor of Wyoming resigns late in the governor's term, he appoints his daughter—and according to state law, "the Governor's Secretary shall have the rank of Major." Jean Willard Brooks is thus sworn in as a major; she has been educated in the East and will competently perform the duties of acting governor when both her father and the secretary of state go out of state at the same time.

1911 On Saturday, March 25, a fire in New York's Triangle Shirtwaist Factory kills 146. When flames destroy the elevator and the staircase, some women jump to their death, for the city's fire ladders do not reach the ninth-floor factory. Other dead women are found in a heap behind doors that management kept locked.

Most of the dead are young immigrant women, usually Jews from Russia or eastern Europe, with a minority of Italians. Because Triangle is a nonunion sweatshop that refused to settle in last year's strike, almost all of their workers are new arrivals. They are working on a Saturday, when other factories are closed, because most of these women support not only themselves but also whole families abroad. Many families will not know of the tragedy that befell their daughters for months, if ever. While some mourners search the city morgue in a vain attempt to determine which of over 50 unrecognizably charred bodies is their loved one, other bodies in better condition go unclaimed.

In December, factory owners Harris and Blanck will be acquitted of manslaughter charges by an all-male jury. One of the jurors justifies the verdict by saying that "the girls, who undoubtedly have not as much intelligence as others might have in other walks of life, were inclined to fly into a panic."

+ The labor committee that investigates the Triangle Fire is headed by Leonora O'Reilly, an organizer for the United Garment Workers who was until recently herself a garment worker. The committee works aggressively, and its recommendations are added to those of the official state commission on which Mary Drier serves as the only woman.

As a result, New York enacts legislation that will prevent future tragedies by ending many unsafe practices. Both O'Reilly and Drier go on to a lifetime of similar work; O'Reilly testifies before Congress on national labor needs, while Drier heads both the Women's Trade Union League and the Woman Suffrage Party in New York City.

+ Innovative Mary McDowell of the University of Chicago's settlement house spends the summer studying European methods of garbage disposal. Poor families in Chicago, as in other great cities, often live with garbage in the streets—which attracts vermin and causes disease.

+ The Society of American Indians is organized at Ohio State University, with members required to be of Native American ancestry. Within a few years, Gertrude Simmons Bonnin, a South Dakota Sioux called "Red Bird," will emerge as an organization leader. She moves to Washington, D.C., with her husband, where she lobbies, lectures, and edits the *American Indian Magazine*. An accomplished woman, she studied violin at the Boston Conservatory of Music and per-

formed in Europe; she has also lived among the Ute in Utah and, in 1901, published *Old Indian Legends.*

+ In south Texas, Jovita Idar de Jaurez forms the Mexican Feminist League. It not only advocates equality for women but also—like black women's organizations—takes the lead in opposing lynching. The previous year, she had organized the White Cross to bring aid to refugees of the Mexican Revolution.

+ During a famine in China, Baptist missionary Lottie Moon starves herself to feed others. Church authorities finally realize the missionary's condition and send her home, but the 72-year-old Virginian dies en route, near Kobe, Japan.

+ The International Woman Suffrage Alliance meets in Stockholm. Among its highlights is a sermon in "the ancient state church of Gusta Vasa," by the Reverend Dr. Anna Howard Shaw, who began preaching in 1870. She is supported by a women's choir and a female organist/composer, and the church is "crowded to the last inch."

The National Men's League for Woman Suffrage sends delegates to this convention, and the alliance expands into an international group. In Britain, the leaders include several members of the nobility, and future international meetings will feature participants from the Men's Leagues of Hungary, the Netherlands, and elsewhere.

When the Stockholm convention ends, President Carrie Chapman Catt begins a world tour on behalf of women; between 1911 and 1913, she will visit every continent except Antarctica.

+ At the World Congress of Races in London, men from Africa and other continents "eagerly" listen to a speech by Dr. Susan Maria (Smith) Steward, a black woman who has practiced medicine in New York and Ohio for more than 40 years.

+ A suffrage parade down Fifth Avenue features the Reverend Antoinette Brown Blackwell, who was ordained in 1853. She is currently pastor emeritus of All Souls Unitarian Church in Elizabeth, New Jersey.

◆ The National Council of Women Voters is organized this year in an attempt to unite women who are eligible to vote. The idea does not come to genuine fruition until a decade later, however, with the formation of the League of Women Voters. The chief problem is that the women who can vote are in the West, while the political and economic reforms that make up the council's platform are better suited to the industrial states of the East.

◆ The U.S. Senate issues an investigative report, *Importation and Harboring of Women for Immoral Purposes*. It contains letters confiscated from men who write of buying and selling women as chattel, often at prices similar to those paid for black slaves a few decades earlier.

At the same time, *The Social Evil in Chicago* is published by the city's Vice Commission; it is an almost salaciously detailed study of prostitution. It finds that—at a time when most women earn around $5 a week—streetwalkers make an average of $25, while women in a high-class house of prostitution may bring in as much as $400.

◆ Edith Wharton publishes *Ethan Frome* in French. Although this work quickly becomes an American classic, Wharton will live abroad after 1910. *The Age of Innocence* in 1920 adds to her acclaim, and she will return to accept an honorary degree from Yale in 1923—but when she dies in 1937, she will be buried at Versailles.

◆ Frances Hodgson Burnett, whose 1886 *Little Lord Fauntleroy* continues to sell, sees similar success with *The Secret Garden*. Burnett will publish some 50 books prior to her 1924 death, but *The Secret Garden* lives on long after its author is dead; it will be produced as a movie in 1949 and 1987, and is again popular as a 1991 musical.

◆ In a tremendously sophisticated campaign, California women gain the vote—without much help from national suffrage organizations. The advertising they use includes billboards, and they draw crowds with free entertainment; a railroad car of campaigners is especially effective at small-town whistlestops.

The effort put into the rural areas pays off as the vote is counted, for women win by a tiny statewide margin of one vote per precinct. Liquor interests again believe that they can control the election by controlling the urban vote—and especially in the San Francisco area, ballots have to be guarded to prevent fraud that would cancel the rural vote.

Again, the importance of pioneer heritage is demonstrated, as the rural West is better at securing women's rights than the supposedly cosmopolitan urban East.

◆ In November, the National Association Opposed to Woman Suffrage organizes in New York, where its headquarters will remain until 1918. The officers are all from the Northeast, and Mrs. Arthur M. Dodge will serve as president for most of the group's existence. Next year, they begin publishing *Woman's Protest*; the paper's name will be modified to the more politically acceptable *Woman Patriot* in 1918.

The women in the association are almost entirely the beneficiaries of inherited wealth, and although they have a presence in several campaigns, suffragists never see them as a genuine threat. Their numbers remain small, and many are so clearly a front for the political ends of their husbands that they actually rouse some middle-class women to join the suffrage cause.

◆ Astronomer Henrietta Leavitt dies at age 53, leaving a scientific legacy that few recognize. Since beginning work at the Harvard Observatory in 1895, she has discovered some 2,400 variable stars—or about half of all those known to exist. In addition, she made important advances in techniques for measuring the brightness, magnitudes, and distances of stars. Her complex work was beyond the comprehension of most, however, and her quiet personality never brought the fame she earned.

◆ Eight years after the Wright Brothers barely got their plane off the ground, a woman flies solo. She is 25-year-old Blanche Stuart Scott, and although she does not become as famous as some later female pilots, she will spend a lifetime in aviation.

Called the "Tomboy of the Air," she flies in the highly dangerous barnstorming shows that become popular in the 1920s and 1930s, and as late as 1956, she will work as an aviation consultant at Ohio's Wright Patterson Air Force Base.

1912 The mills of Lawrence, Massachusetts —where conditions are so bad that one-third of the textile spinners die before they work a decade—erupt in a massive strike. Although the era is prosperous, the city's mill owners impose a wage reduction, and approximately 20,000 workers, at least half of whom are female, walk off the job in January. The mostly immigrant workers lack a formal union and speak some 40 languages, but they parade and picket, and when militia fire into a demonstration, Annie LoPizzo is killed.

Her death brings national media attention, and Margaret Sanger is among those who come to evacuate the city's cold and hungry children, whose parents cannot buy coal or food. Officials try to prevent this embarrassing situation with force, and on February 24, police attack women who are boarding 150 children onto a train: They beat both women and children and then arrest 35 distraught mothers for "child neglect." Labor organizer Elizabeth Gurley Flynn will call this "a day without parallel . . . which literally shook America."

A congressional inquiry begins, and some 50 strikers testify in Washington; by mid-March, management rescinds the pay cut. National labor leaders credit women with winning the strike.

✦ The Lawrence strike is covered by Mary Heaton Vorse, a recent widow who is trying to support her family as a freelance writer. The strike establishes her as a labor specialist, and Vorse leaves her children with a governess while she travels the country covering labor stories. For several decades, she is perhaps the most knowledgeable journalist in the United States on these issues, and she gives particular attention to working women.

✦ Less attention goes to a strike by New York hotel and restaurant workers, despite the fact that work stoppages in service industries are far more un-usual than in manufacturing. In this strike, Rose Pastor Stokes emerges as a spokeswoman; a former Jewish immigrant cigarmaker who is published in magazines such as the *Century* and *Everybody's*, her 1905 marriage to a leftist philanthropist has helped make her activism possible.

✦ In the spring, New York's suffrage parade draws thousands of spectators, most of whom are awed by the marchers. They include women in academic robes, female physicians, attorneys, and architects, as well as women representing the seven western states in which women can vote. A monument to female solidarity, the parade includes women of every economic level from sweatshop worker to multimillionaire.

✦ Illustrator Laura Foster promotes suffrage with cartoons. One that she draws this year is titled "Make Way!" It shows a group of suffragists standing at the top of a globe and using their placards to push men off; among their banners is one reading "We Can Think."

✦ The National Association of Colored Women, which organized in 1896, finally endorses the vote for women. Although its president has been active in the suffrage movement, much of the membership echoed the conservatism of their husbands and subordinated their feminist interests to their racial ones.

From the beginning, however, NACW members demonstrate assertiveness: they campaign against lynching and against the leasing of prisoners' labor, and they call for boycotts of businesses that discriminate against blacks. Those traveling on trains to the annual conventions especially object to the railroads' refusal to sell them first-class tickets.

✦ Harriet Quimby, the first American woman licensed to fly, is killed in Boston harbor while attempting to land. Quimby had received her license less than a year earlier, on August 1, 1911, and she won $600 in a cross-country race only days later. After sailing to Europe the following spring, she became the first woman to pilot a plane across the English Channel.

The June crash probably was caused when her heavier male passenger shifted his weight; both were thrown out of the open plane and into the water, while the plane itself glided in with little damage.

◆ Julia Lathrop is the first woman appointed to a federal position that requires Senate confirmation. An 1880 Vassar graduate, she has been associated with Hull House and the University of Chicago for 20 years.

Republican President William Howard Taft appoints her chief of the newly created Children's Bureau, and when Taft loses his election this fall, Democratic President Woodrow Wilson will reappoint Lathrop. In office, she focuses on abolition of child labor, but also works for mothers' pensions and reduction in maternal deaths.

◆ When the National Child Labor Conference is held in Jacksonville, Florida, its well-known New York leader, Florence Kelley, takes time to speak to the newly formed local suffragist group. She discovers that neither the Board of Trade, which routinely hosts political speakers, nor the city's Woman's Club, at which she has appeared previously, is willing to rent space for a speech on suffrage.

◆ The question of mothers' pensions—or aid to women who get no support from their children's fathers—begins to be debated as guardianship laws change so that women increasingly get custody of children. At the same time, desertion rates are soaring. One study asserts that instead of being known as "a poor man's divorce," desertion should be called "a poor man's vacation," for most deserters eventually return to their wives, usually when the men are ill or unemployed. Meanwhile, most charities either refuse to assist deserted families or grant them less than widows receive.

◆ The best-selling nonfiction book of the year is *The Promised Land*, by Russian Jewish immigrant Mary Antin. She retained that name after her 1901 marriage to a German geologist who teaches at Columbia University. Their marriage is unhappy, however, and Antin is in both financial and emotional need of returning to the publishing success that she enjoyed as a teenager.

◆ Hadassah, which will become the largest organization of Jewish women in the world, is founded by Henrietta Szold, a longtime Baltimore leader. "Hadassah" is the Hebrew name for the ancient Queen Esther, a powerful leader of her people, and the group quickly exhibits similar ability. The women send nurses to Palestine within the year and sponsor more than 40 dentists, doctors, engineers, and other professionals there by the end of World War I.

Szold will travel the world spreading the Zionist message and raising funds for humanitarian efforts. Originally a Baltimore teacher, she has also enjoyed a career as a translator of Hebrew literature and as the editor of an annual directory, the *American Jewish Year Book*.

◆ The Girl Scouts begin in the South, when Juliette Gordon Low founds a Savannah, Georgia, troop and her friend Jessamine Flowers Link follows with a troop in Tampa, Florida. Both are modeled on the Girl Guides that Low has worked with during long visits to Scotland. At age 52, she is looking for meaning in her life. She is a childless widow whose husband was so deeply attached to another woman that he left most of his estate to her; Low recovered the property only after a long court case.

◆ In Calgary, Montana, Fannie Sperry wins the bucking horse contest, which makes her the state's champion bronco rider. From 1907 to 1925, she is a draw on the professional rodeo circuit; after her 1913 marriage, she is Fannie Sperry-Steele.

◆ Miami hosts the nation's first Miss America contest. The winner is Miss Georgia, Annie Laurie Kilpatrick.

◆ Lillian Gish makes her first film, *An Unseen Enemy*, for Hollywood pioneer D.W. Griffith, who cannot be bothered with learning her name and calls her "Blue" for the color of her hair ribbon. The $50 a week that he pays, however, is a fortune for 19-year-old Gish, who has been acting since age five to help support her family after their father deserted them.

Work will remain the center of her long life. When she dies at age 99 in 1993, Lillian Gish starred in 105 movies, plays, and television dramas. She never marries, lives with her mother, and makes her last film at age 94.

✦ Young African-American composer Helen Hagan earns a music degree from Yale University; although she goes on to additional study in France and at Columbia, she will never obtain a position commensurate with her credentials.

✦ Willa Cather, managing editor of the popular *McClure's Magazine*, publishes her first novel. She retires to full-time writing, and the following year, at age 40, issues *O Pioneers*. The theme of change, whether in the virgin prairie or in its immigrant settlers, makes it and *My Ántonia* (1918) into classics of Americana.

✦ In the same year that strikes convulse the Lowell, Massachusetts, area where her family has long held economic and political power, middle-age Amy Lowell publishes her first book of poetry. Her work is so good that she is not dismissed as another privileged poetess, and she goes on to international acclaim.

✦ Oregon grants women the right to vote—six years after the state's suffragists split from the national organization and adopted an independent political strategy. They lost referenda in 1908 and 1910, but their third attempt is successful, primarily because male voters are convinced that Oregon's women do not share the prohibitionist views of many eastern suffragists.

Longtime leader Abigail Scott Duniway directs the campaign from her wheelchair; her animosity against eastern suffrage leadership is so great that she has threatened to have the Reverend Dr. Anna Howard Shaw arrested if Shaw crosses the Oregon state line.

The success of the recent Washington and California campaigns, in which the national suffrage leadership was not very visible, makes credible Duniway's theory that male voters resent these outsiders—especially because the eastern women do not undertake campaigns in their own states.

✦ The year features six referenda on suffrage—as many as were held in all the years between 1896 and 1910. All are in the West or Midwest; in addition to Oregon, a relatively quiet Arizona campaign is successful, while Kansas—which has offered limited voting rights to women since 1861—finally grants full suffrage. The midwestern campaigns all go down to defeat, although women may have actually won in Michigan. The ballot-counting takes weeks, and the results from many precincts are so suspicious that even the governor accuses liquor lobbyists of election fraud.

✦ A number of women who lack the vote nonetheless campaign in the fall's three-candidate election for president. New York Democratic Party activist Daisy Harriman works for Woodrow Wilson, and he later appoints her to the Federal Industrial Relations Commission, where she will serve as the only woman from 1913 to 1916. Birth control advocate Mary Ware Dennett also supports Wilson and is rewarded by a position with the National Democratic Committee.

Progressive Party candidate and former president Theodore Roosevelt wants to return to the White House, and, in a historic move, he reaches out to Jane Addams, a National American Woman Suffrage Association vice president, to second his nomination at the new party's convention. Many other women also work for him, including popular author and immigration expert Mary Antin. Alice Roosevelt Longworth supports her father, splitting from her husband's Republican Party.

Incumbent president and Republican nominee William Howard Taft draws the least support from women, and Republicans lose the White House for the first time in two decades.

✦ Also in November, Congress admits the Alaska Territory. Although its government is restricted in many ways that governments of earlier territories were not, the first act of the new territory's legislators is the passage of a bill granting women the vote.

♦ In December, five women associated with Harriot Stanton Blatch's Equality League brave the winter cold to publicize suffrage by walking from New York City to Albany. The trip takes 13 days, during which time they speak to any crowd they can assemble.

1913 Washington, D.C., sees its first giant suffrage parade, as some 8,000 suffragists time their march from the Capitol to the White House to coincide with the press coverage scheduled for President Woodrow Wilson's inauguration.

The incoming president—the first Democrat in 20 years—also is a target. He explains his neutrality by pointing out that the president has no role in constitutional amendments, which are passed solely by Congress and state legislatures. Feminists, however, find Wilson's indifference especially frustrating because the new first family is overwhelmingly female, being composed of his wife and three daughters.

The marchers are led by Alice Paul, a young Philadelphian with Quaker roots who studied in England and was much influenced by its political model. Paul, who earned a Ph.D. from the University of Pennsylvania in 1912 and who will go on to obtain three law degrees in the future, has formed the Congressional Union as an offshoot of the National American Woman Suffrage Association.

The CU's parade signals a change of tactics to controversial political visibility. Because the NAWSA had never engaged in such unladylike behavior, city police misjudge the likely response and fail to protect the marchers from jeering men who attack the women. The result is a swell of public sympathy; the police chief loses his job, and the suffrage cause is energized.

♦ Some marchers bring attention to the parade even before it begins by walking from New York to Washington, D.C. A *Cleveland Plain Dealer* cartoonist admires their dedication and, in an analogy to George Washington, draws them crossing the Delaware. On the other hand, the *Jacksonville*

Floridian writes: "For several weeks the American people have been nauseated by that disgusting escapade of a horde of vulgar women who have started out to walk from New York to Washington in the interest of 'Votes for Women.'"

♦ The Congressional Union continues its activism after the March parade; it creates a "Suffrage School" in Washington to educate potential members and conduct "an uninterrupted series of indoor and outdoor meetings, numbering frequently from five to ten a day." Its newspaper, *The Suffragist*, begins in November, and within three years, it will replace the venerable old *Woman's Journal*.

♦ Along with Alice Paul, Lucy Burns is a top Congressional Union leader. A Vassar alumna who did graduate study in linguistics at Yale, Oxford, and two Germany universities, she became active with militant suffragists while at Oxford and then worked as a paid speaker in Scotland for two years. In January, she and Paul open an office in Washington, D.C., and after the March inaugural parade, Burns begins deliberately to seek publicized arrests for defacing property with suffragist graffiti. Eventually she is proud of her record as the suffragist who served the most jail time.

Other initial officers are Crystal Eastman, a fiery speaker who has law and sociology degrees from prestigious universities and is the author of a book on industrial accidents, and Mary Beard, who later evolves into perhaps the most important women's historian of the century.

♦ In addition to the Congressional Union, a less-noticed splinter group also begins to disassociate itself from the National American Woman Suffrage Association: Kate Gordon of New Orleans, who served as NAWSA corresponding secretary from 1901 to 1909, organizes the Southern States Woman Suffrage Conference. The group's approach is the opposite of the CU's. It emphasizes state campaigns, rather than a federal amendment, because it wants to enable southern states to craft legislation that will limit the vote to white women.

MADAM, WHO KEEPS YOUR HOUSE?

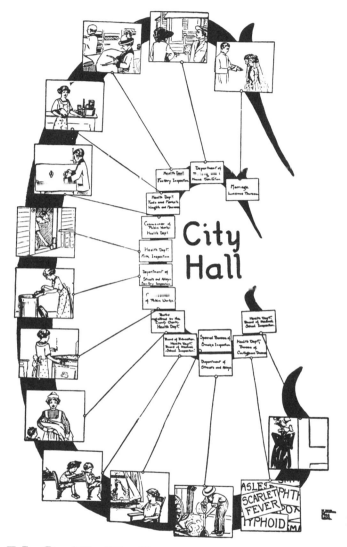

Who issues your license to marry?

Who gives you permission to build your home?

Who guarantees the quality of your furnishings, the purity of your food, your water— even your baby's milk?

Upon whom do you rely for the removal of your garbage? For your heat and fuel supply? For the protection of yourself and children from fire and contagious disease? For clean streets and unpolluted air?

Who is responsible if these matters are not properly looked after and disease or death results?

Read the answer in the picture.

Yet you say "you don't care to meddle with politics."

Madam, if you want your house well kept, you MUST meddle with politics, because politics has already meddled with you.

☞ **Be an efficient, modern housekeeper and demand**

VOTES FOR WOMEN!

NATIONAL AMERICAN WOMAN SUFFRAGE ASSOCIATION
505 FIFTH AVENUE　　　　　　　　　　**NEW YORK CITY**

The National American Woman Suffrage Association placed this and similar thoughtful advertisements in newspapers throughout the United States. This one was distributed as a handbill by the Minnesota Woman Suffrage Association, where women's voting rights were limited to elections on schools and libraries—but all of the issues that the ad raises must be addressed at other levels of government. Minnesota Historical Society

+ The International Woman Suffrage Alliance meets this year in Budapest. Carrie Chapman Catt presides, as she has for every biannual session since the organization's 1904 start. This, however, will be the last such meeting. World War I will dissolve feminist international action, and especially German women will lose the organizational gains they had made.

+ Colorado is the second state to elect a woman to its state senate, with the victory of Helen Ring Robinson. Four years later, Senator Agnes Riddle will make Colorado the first state to have elected two women to this position.

   Meanwhile, Illinois comes up with a new variation on partial enfranchisement. Women are granted the right to vote for president but no other offices. This halfway measure is nonetheless the first major victory for suffrage in a state east of the Mississippi.

+ Telephone operators conduct a major strike in New England, while retail clerks in Buffalo and Indiana walk off the job. Women in Michigan use violence in the strike of their copper-mining men. An aide to the governor complains, "Women continually resort to rock throwing. . . . Soldiers were assaulted with brooms, which . . . had been dipped with human excrement."

+ At the age of 83, "Mother" Mary Jones is sentenced to 20 years in prison for alleged illegal activity in organizing West Virginia miners. When the governor pardons her, she returns to the coal fields of Colorado, where she is on the scene for the Ludlow Massacre the following year.

+ A study of women who make artificial flowers on home contract shows the standard pay rate to be a dime a gross—or 144 flowers for just 10 cents. Families of four or more workers put in 12-hour days to make a dozen gross; at $1.20 a day, each worker averages 30 cents a day. Most are recent immigrants, especially from Italy; almost all are mothers and daughters in large families.

+ Under the aegis of the U.S. Senate, the last of 19 volumes in *Report on the Condition of Woman and Child Wage-Earners in the United States* is published. Among the women studied are those in the textile and garment industries and those in laundries and stores. Two volumes contain unusual information on the history of women in industry and in unions.

   The preconceived ideas of some—but not all—of the report's writers are demonstrated by the titles of two of the volumes: *Infant Mortality and Its Relation to the Employment of Mothers* and *Relation between Occupation and Criminality of Women.*

+ The post office refuses to deliver *The Call* because the magazine contains an article on syphilis. Its author, Margaret Sanger, is threatened with arrest.

+ Columbia University sociologist Elsie Clews Parsons uses the pseudonym John Main when she publishes *Religious Chastity,* a book on variations of sexuality in different religions. Dr. Parsons, the mother of six and wife of a congressman, feels that she cannot reveal her true identity—in part because of opposition to her 1906 book, which asserted that many gender distinctions are the artificial result of treating boys and girls differently.

+ *Woman's Share in Social Culture* by Anna Garlin Spencer is feminist theory that reviews the vital role of women in the evolution of civilizing societal structures. Spencer, who is also an ordained Unitarian minister, will publish some 70 articles in such prestigious journals as the *American Journal of Sociology* and the *International Journal of Ethics.*

+ "Pollyanna" enters the language as a useful common noun after the publication of Eleanor Hodgman Porter's *Pollyanna.*

+ Mary Pickford, already a stage veteran at age 15, acts in her first film. Called "America's Sweetheart" during the next three decades, she is at the center of the era's creation of "movie stars," while the new "moving pictures" profoundly change American culture.

+ Ch'ing-ling Soong graduates from Wesleyan Female College in Macon, Georgia; she will return to China, marry Sun Yet-sen, and help overthrow the Manchu dynasty. Her sister Mei-ling, who also studies at the Georgia school before graduating from Wellesley College, will become a formidable Chinese power after World War II. As Madame Chiang Kai-shek, she is internationally visible on behalf of the Nationalists in China's civil war with the Communists.

✦ Harriet Tubman is buried with military honors in Auburn, New York, where she had begun a Home for Indigent Aged Negroes soon after the Civil War. She supported it through the sale of *Harriet Tubman: The Moses of Her People* (1869), which was written for her by a white woman, Sarah Bradford, because Tubman remained illiterate.

She was honored with an 1897 reception by the National American Woman Suffrage Association, and her funeral includes eulogies by Frederick Douglass and Booker T. Washington, who acknowledge that no black man had done as much for "our people."

✦ Another reminder of the Civil War this year is the publication of *A Confederate Girl's Diary* by Sarah Morgan Dawson. Critics deem it "one of the most remarkable diaries penned by an American," and it will be reprinted throughout the century.

The author died in 1909, after a long life in New Orleans, Charleston, and France. As Sarah Fowler, she lived in Louisiana during the war with her widowed mother and two sisters; they endured the deaths of all but one male member of their large family.

✦ In December, some 2,000 Chicago women successfully rally when Ella Flagg Young's position as superintendent of schools is threatened. The male school board is upset by her progressive policies, which include a more relevant curriculum and—until the board cancels it—sex education. Two years later, at age 70, Young resigns.

1914 The Congressional Union's activism during President Wilson's first year proves successful in getting the constitutional amendment on suffrage out of committee, where it has lan-

guished for decades. On March 19, for the first time since 1887, the Senate votes on it—but because constitutional amendments require a 2/3 majority, the 34–35 margin by which it loses is not as close as it appears.

Also in March, Ruth Hanna McCormick, lobbying head of the National American Woman Suffrage Association, succeeds in getting a bill known as the Shafroth-Palmer Amendment introduced into the Senate. Her brainchild would require states to hold referenda on women's suffrage if 8% of the voters in the previous election sign a petition calling for such.

It is designed to counter the arguments of congressmen who say they favor women's right to vote but refuse to support an amendment to the federal constitution because of their reverence for states' rights. Such arguments are likely to be specious for several reasons, the most obvious of which is that many of these same congressmen are perfectly willing to support the proposed amendment on prohibition—a much greater invasion of states' rights to make decisions about their internal policies. "States' rights" is also a catchphrase for racism. Many congressmen (and other white people) do not want a federal amendment that would apply equally to black women—although, again, the 15th Amendment long ago set the precedent for the rights of individual voters over those of states.

Because the Shafroth-Palmer plan does not address the genuine political problems and especially because its proposed petition drives and referenda would be costly to implement, the legislation gains little support. Even most NAWSA members are unenthusiastic about their leader's amendment, and it further divides the NAWSA from the Congressional Union.

Some southern suffragists, meanwhile, become increasingly insistent that only state governments be targeted. Their hidden agenda is often racism, for they wish to write amendments to state constitutions that would exclude black women. Legislation introduced in Florida, for example, stripped the vote from those who were "ineligible on January 1, 1867" and from their "lineal descendants."

At the same time that these southern women begin insisting on state strategies, the more aggressive members of the CU demand attention solely to the federal amendment. The NAWSA's majority will ignore both sets of extremists to take the mainstream, pragmatic path of working on both state and national campaigns.

✦ Unknown Chicagoan Margaret Anderson begins *Little Review* and makes it a literary success from the first issue, which features Vachel Lindsay. The young publisher demonstrates amazing prescience: among the writers she introduces are Sherwood Anderson, Hart Crane, T. S. Eliot, Robert Frost, Emma Goldman, Ernest Hemingway, Amy Lowell, Ezra Pound, and Gertrude Stein.

✦ A strike by coal miners in Ludlow, Colorado, turns violent on April 20. Militia spray the tent colony where mining families live with machine-gun fire and then set fire to the rude homes. The bodies of 11 children and two women are burned beyond recognition. Like the Lawrence strike two years earlier, the Ludlow Massacre shocks the nation. Some of those who witnessed the incident, including a woman who lost three children, go to Washington and successfully lobby President Wilson to intervene.

✦ Margaret Sanger is arrested for writing about birth control in her publication *The Woman Rebel*. When she is indicted by an all-male grand jury, Sanger flees to Europe.

Her crusade for contraception is directly motivated by two things: she grew up after her Irish Catholic mother's death was hastened by 18 pregnancies; and she worked as a nurse in New York's Lower East Side, where the death of a patient, Sadie Sacks, made a profound impression on Sanger. A Jewish immigrant and the married mother of needy children, Sacks died from complications of a self-induced abortion, after physicians refused to give her information on preventing pregnancy.

✦ Congress passes the Smith-Lever Act, which provides federal funds for vocational education, especially in farm areas. Home economics is included in its provisions, and the bill thus is one of the first federal appropriations of money to be used primarily by women.

The act also subsidizes Home Demonstration Clubs, in which trained home economists teach women safe methods of food preservation, the use of new electrical appliances, and the like. The clubs also elect officers and use parliamentary procedure for meetings; they provide the first exposure that many rural women have to such activity.

✦ Minnesota women, under the leadership of Clara Ueland, organize a 2,000-member march for suffrage that energizes the Midwest on this issue. At the same time, African-American women in Minneapolis begin the Everywoman Suffrage Club.

✦ Katharine Anthony, who is Susan Anthony's niece, publishes a study of working mothers in Philadelphia. Among her findings is that the 370 women have suffered the deaths of 437 babies—or more than one case of infant mortality per woman.

✦ Despite being fatally ill, Wellesley College economist Dr. Katherine Coman spends the summer in Europe studying the social insurance programs in England, Sweden, Denmark, and Spain. She dies the following year, but decades later, her ideas will live on in Social Security.

✦ Publisher Mrs. Frank Leslie dies and leaves $2 million to Carrie Chapman Catt to be used to obtain the vote for women. The bequest is delayed by probate and ultimately is reduced to $1 million, but the money pays for three successful state campaigns in 1918 and endows the International Woman Suffrage Alliance. Much of Catt's willingness to adopt sophisticated public relations techniques is due to her knowledge that the bills can be paid from the Leslie bequest. At the peak of the suffrage campaign, she will employ some 200 full-time organizers.

✦ Elizabeth Arden expands her chain of beauty salons from New York to Washington. She hires chemists to create new cosmetics and eventually builds 100 salons that attract the world's wealthiest women. When makeup becomes more acceptable in the Roaring '20s, she will sell some 300 cosmetic items to the masses and become a multimillionaire.

◆ The lives of many American Indian women remain much the same as those of their foremothers. A drawing made this year of a Hidatsa woman called Goodbird shows her cooking over an open flame outside of her tepee, while a rack of animal hides dries in the sun.

◆ One of the greatest of silent movies features a young woman who overcomes a multitude of adversities: *The Perils of Pauline*, starring Pearl White, attracts huge crowds and spawns a number of sequels. An obvious imitation, *The Exploits of Elaine*, is less well known, but even it is popular enough to call for *The New Exploits of Elaine* and other follow-ups.

◆ As coeducation becomes increasingly common, Delaware is the last state to build a wholly separate public college for women.

◆ As president of the California Democratic Women's Club, young attorney Annette Adams campaigned hard for President Wilson in 1912, and this October, she is sworn in as the nation's first female assistant attorney general—over the objections of Attorney General James McReynolds, who finally gives in to lobbying by her California colleagues. Adams successfully prosecutes several cases in her San Francisco district.

◆ For the fall's midterm elections, the Congressional Union plans to demonstrate women's strength by campaigning in the nine states (all in the West) where women have the vote. A radical strategy is adopted: congressmen will be supported or opposed based on the British model of pressuring the party that holds the executive branch. Thus, the CU plans to work against all Democratic candidates because the president is a Democrat, regardless of whether these incumbents support suffrage or not. The National American Woman Suffrage Association strongly

objects, but CU members traverse the nation with highly visible advertising techniques such as railroad cars placarded with banners—and succeed in defeating 20 Democrats who support suffrage.

Meanwhile, the NAWSA conducts referenda in seven western and midwestern states, losing five; only Nevada and Montana extend the vote to women.

1915 On January 12—before the new Congress is sworn in—the House of Representatives takes its first vote ever on the proposed suffrage amendment to the Constitution, but it is far from a victory: The margin of 204 to 174 makes it a much larger loss than that in the Senate last March.

Incumbent congressmen doubtless are displaying their resentment of the Congressional Union's controversial political strategy during last fall's election—and yet the fact that the House cast a vote on the issue at all is historic.

◆ Also in January the Woman's Peace Party is founded by Jane Addams, Grace Abbott, Emily Balch, Carrie Chapman Catt, Alice Hamilton, Charlotte Perkins Gilman, Lucia Ames Mead, and others opposed to the war that began in Europe last August. Risking U-boat attack, they lead a group of 42 American women across the Atlantic in April for an International Congress of Women at the Hague.

Addams presides, and at the meeting's end, delegates work for peace throughout Europe. Balch, for example, travels to Denmark, Norway, Sweden, and Russia, where she meets with foreign ministers and other officials. Upon returning to the United States, she briefs President Wilson on her conferences.

In December, a second group of women makes a similar peace voyage on a ship funded by industrialist Henry Ford. They are led by former International Council of Women president May Wright Sewall of Indianapolis; during the summer, she convenes a women's peace conference in conjunction with the Panama-Pacific Exposition held in San Francisco.

Also in the international news is the fact that women in Denmark and Iceland win full suffrage this year.

✦ Young Vassar graduate Inez Milholland, who became a press star during the 1912 New York suffrage parade, is forced to leave her job as a war correspondent in Italy when the government there expels her because of her pacifism.

Milholland will return to the United States, work for suffrage during the 1916 presidential campaign, and die at age 30 of pernicious anemia. Her beauty and intense personality caused her 1913 marriage to a Dutch man to be considered worthy of front-page attention in the *New York Times.*

✦ The Fellsmere town charter, which includes woman suffrage, sneaks past the Florida legislature. In the next two biannual sessions, 22 other towns will emulate Fellsmere and pass local bills through the legislature that grant women the vote in municipal elections.

In the 1913 session, the legislature listened to speeches from several suffragists, including the National American Woman Suffrage Association organizer and future Montana congresswoman Jeanette Rankin; its 1917 session will feature a lengthy oration on behalf of suffrage by Mary Baird Bryan, wife of popular Democratic official William Jennings Bryan. While several votes are close, Florida never passes any form of suffrage except these municipal bills.

✦ Millionaire Alva Belmont subsidizes the 50,000 member Congressional Union. Belmont, who paid for an entire floor of Fifth Avenue office space for the NAWSA just a few years earlier, has transferred her support to the more militant group. Strategy is thought out at her Newport mansion, and when the CU transforms itself into the National Woman's Party, she will serve on the executive board, finance a tour of British suffragists, and even coauthor a fund-raising operetta.

The CU also sponsors a cross-country car convoy of women who hold rallies on their way from San Francisco's Panama-Pacific Expo to Washington, and on May 9, they march on the

Capitol to deliver another half-million suffrage petition signatures.

✦ Also at the Panama-Pacific Exposition, sculptor Gertrude Vanderbilt Whitney wins a bronze medal for a fountain that she carved; after volunteering in French hospitals during World War I, she will specialize in statues that commemorate soldiers.

✦ Whitney's prize-winning fountain may have been seen by future author Laura Ingalls Wilder, who attends the fair while visiting her daughter in San Francisco. Although already middle age, Wilder is still decades away from fame; much later, the journal she keeps on the fair will be published.

✦ Lillian Moller Gilbreth earns a doctorate in psychology from Brown University while she bears 12 children in 17 years. Last year, she published her first book, *Psychology of Management*; she will go on to write another half-dozen books, some with her business consultant husband, Frank Gilbreth.

They establish innovative management theories through careful time-motion analyses, including the use of film to observe workers. As a widow, Gilbreth will become a professor of management at Purdue University and be honored by the Society of Industrial Engineers. Her adult children later use her household as the model for a hit comedy, *Cheaper by the Dozen.*

✦ A Chicago directory of immigrants from Bohemia lists 36 male and 19 female physicians.

✦ Katharine Anthony publishes *Feminism in Germany and Scandinavia* and then embarks on biographies of women. She writes on Catherine the Great, Elizabeth I, and Marie Antoinette as well as Americans Louisa May Alcott, Margaret Fuller, Dolley Madison, Mercy Otis Warren, and her aunt, Susan B. Anthony. The last will be published in 1958, when she is 81.

✦ A contrasting publication is *Philosophy of Anti-Suffrage* by Tessie Jones, a highly theoretical treatise that emphasizes the priority of "natural rights" over "equal rights." Jones is active in the Minneapolis Association Opposed to the Further

Extension of Suffrage to Women. "Further extension" refers to the group's apparent approval of the right of Minnesota women to vote in school elections, which they have had since 1907.

✦ In off-year elections, four hard-fought referenda to give eastern women their first voting rights go down to defeat. The men of Massachusetts, New Jersey, Pennsylvania, and New York all firmly deny the vote to the women of their states.

In Massachusetts, where the margin of loss is greatest, there is the first strong evidence of organized opposition from the Catholic church as well as from the National Association Opposed to Woman Suffrage.

Shocked by the year's elections and by the militant action of Alice Paul's rival faction, the annual National American Woman Suffrage Association convention, meeting in December, replaces the Reverend Dr. Anna Howard Shaw with Carrie Chapman Catt, who was Susan Anthony's original choice as her successor.

Catt will demonstrate excellent political skills and remain president for the rest of the NAWSA's existence. She formulates a secret "Winning Plan" that draws skepticism both in and out of the suffrage movement—but only five years later, its promise will be fulfilled.

Catt hires Ida Husted Harper to handle publicity, and using remarkably sophisticated techniques, Harper will telegraph hundreds of press releases to newspapers. She succeeds in getting the feminist message reprinted in even small-town newspapers throughout the nation.

1916 Adopting the slogan "Every child a wanted child," Margaret Sanger and her sister-in-law, Ethel Byrne, open a birth control clinic in Brooklyn. Both are trained nurses, and almost 500 women visit the clinic in the 10 days it operates before police close it down.

Charged with creating a public nuisance, Sanger and Byrne are imprisoned for 30 days after an all-male jury returns a verdict of guilty. They will win a partial victory on appeal in 1918; meanwhile, the publicity results in tremendous growth for the newly founded National Birth-Control League.

✦ Russian-American anarchist Emma Goldman is also arrested and jailed for 15 days in the birth control controversy, although her offense is not overt action but simple free speech. The government also shuts down *Mother Earth*, which she has published for a decade, under wartime censorship policies.

At the same time, labor orator Elizabeth Gurley Flynn is arrested for alleged violation of the Espionage Act. The charges against her are dropped, but as a result, she helps found the American Civil Liberties Union.

✦ In June, the Congressional Union transforms itself into the National Woman's Party in Chicago, formally breaking its ties to the National American Woman Suffrage Association. Under the leadership of Alice Paul, the party will continue the strategy used in the 1914 election, aiming to influence the presidential election in the states in which women can vote.

The keynote speech at the party's founding is made by Californian Maud Younger, who is known as "the millionaire waitress" for her 1908 role in establishing a union of restaurant workers in San Francisco. Despite personal wealth, she served as president and as the union's delegate to the city's Central Labor Council; the union became the basis of a Wage Earners League that Younger founded for California's successful suffrage election in 1911.

✦ Up for reelection, President Woodrow Wilson sees that for political, if not constitutional, reasons he has to take a stand for suffrage. He responds to Carrie Chapman Catt's careful lobbying of him and sends her a June letter promising to "join my fellow-Democrats in recommending to the several States that they extend the Suffrage to women."

✦ The nation's third order of African-American nuns, the Franciscan Handmaidens of Mary, is founded in Savannah, Georgia. They encounter so much resistance there, however, that they move to Harlem in New York City in 1922.

◆ Federally subsidized Household Arts Training Schools are established, especially in southern cities. Motivated in part by successful models created by Floridian Blanche Armwood, these schools provide many black women with an opportunity to learn in scientifically designed home economics laboratories. At the same time, gas and electric companies begin to employ home economists to teach customers the use of new appliances.

◆ The International Ladies' Garment Workers' Union, which has about 100,000 members, wins a 14-week strike for better pay and working conditions. The ILGWU also sets an important precedent with union-sponsored health care centers.

◆ Financier Hetty Robinson Green dies. Much feared on Wall Street, she has increased the $5 million that she inherited in 1865 to more than $100 million—but even though her Chicago real estate alone is valued at over $5 million, she has lived like a pauper in a small apartment in the industrial town of Hoboken, New Jersey. Not always this eccentric, she enjoyed an 1867 honeymoon trip to Europe and brought up her two children with reasonable indulgence; she refused, however, to cover her husband's bankruptcy when he speculated on the market. After her death, tales of her miserliness become legendary.

◆ Sisters Adeline and Augusta Van Buren ride their motorcycles from New York to San Francisco. By this precedent they intend to demonstrate women's potential in a wartime motor corps.

◆ Painter Georgia O'Keeffe has her first exhibit in New York. Her lifestyle is as avant garde as her work, and her 1924 open marriage to photographer Alfred Stieglitz as well as bisexual affairs will make O'Keeffe a source of controversy during the next several decades. After she begins living in the Southwest in 1929, her work will feature bright color and desert themes that make it distinctively American.

◆ Landscape architect Beatrix Jones Farrand expands from private estates to public institutions. Specializing in college campuses, she becomes sufficiently respected that she receives commissions from Yale, Princeton, Vassar, and several midwestern colleges, including the University of Chicago. Perhaps her best work will be done at Dumbarton Oaks in Washington, where, in 1944, world leaders, surrounded by her beautiful landscaping, will make the first plans for the United Nations.

◆ In November, the first woman is elected to Congress: Montana elects Jeanette Rankin, an unabashed pacifist and an officer in the National American Woman Suffrage Association.

◆ When President Wilson speaks to Congress in December, National Woman's Party members score another coup by unfurling a banner from the House gallery—and are ready with press releases publicizing their action.

The national network of the Woman's Party can be seen with this 1916 photograph of a Connecticut woman and a New Jersey woman who are picketing in Illinois. The object of their attention was William Jennings Bryan, a former Democratic nominee who was campaigning for President Woodrow Wilson in Bloomington. After Bryan retired to Miami, his wife, Mary Baird Bryan—who was admitted to the Nebraska bar in 1888—lobbied for suffrage in Florida; his daughter, Ruth Bryan Owen, became the first woman elected to Congress from the South. Woman's Party Corporation/Sewall-Belmont House, Washington, D.C.

1917 On January 10, Woman's Party members begin holding banners outside of the White House, a visibility technique that they will maintain until suffrage passes—even though congressional action is needed to amend the Constitution.

Picketing the president's home is a new political tactic, but despite this radicalism, all goes well for the first six months. After the nation goes to war in April, however, the protestors will become more threatening to a security-minded administration, and even though most of the members of Woodrow Wilson's cabinet support suffrage, the women begin to be arrested for "obstructing the sidewalk."

✦ In March, Arkansas becomes the first southern state to grant women voting rights. The legislature's partial suffrage plan is limited to primaries, which are the only elections that matter in a solidly Democratic state. The exclusion from the general election is doubtless intended to prevent black women from voting; the few southern blacks who dare to vote invariably think of themselves as Republican, "the party of Lincoln."

When the 19th Amendment that grants full suffrage is finally taken up in the House in 1918, Arkansas will be the only southern state whose entire delegation is supportive. Florida's delegation will be the only other southern state to cast some—but not all—of its votes for suffrage.

✦ The legislatures of six other states emulate Illinois and grant women the right to vote for president, but in no other races. Except for Rhode Island, all of these are midwestern states. Presumably legislators are more liberal than the electorate, for suffrage referenda had been voted down in these places; Maine men also vote down a referendum in September.

✦ Senator John Shafroth of Colorado—whose female constituents have voted since 1893—introduces a bill granting voting rights to women in the Territory of Hawaii. It passes both Houses and is signed by President Wilson, but Hawaii's legislature fails to implement it.

✦ The United States enters the European war in April, less than a month after Woodrow Wilson is inaugurated for a second term. Because the 1916 campaign centered on a platform of "He Kept Us Out of War," many feel betrayed.

The anti-Wilson National Woman's Party becomes more militant, and during the next months, over 200 suffragists will be arrested while demonstrating in front of the White House. Almost half are jailed and go on hunger strikes. Except for Sundays, as many as 1,000 demonstrators "of all races and religions" picket "in rain and in sleet" throughout the year. None of the men who both verbally and physically attack the women is ever arrested.

✦ Representative Jeanette Rankin joins more than 50 male House members in voting against the declaration of war. The war will become more popular, however, and when it ends in the fall of 1918 at election time, Rankin will be defeated.

During her term in Congress, Rankin is the ranking Republican on a committee to draft a constitutional amendment for enfranchising women. She also sponsors a maternal health program that will pass after her tenure. Her first major speech after taking office is at Carnegie Hall, and she uses the opportunity to press for electoral reform, including the direct election of the president—a goal still unachieved near the end of the 20th century.

✦ Russia drops out of the war when the Communists overthrow the West's last monarch who claims a divine right to rule, Czar Nicholas II. Few notice that the new constitution of the Soviet Union gives women there the right to vote that most American women still lack.

✦ Mary Ware Dennett, who broke with many of her suffragist friends to campaign for Woodrow Wilson, resigns her prestigious position with the Democratic National Committee after Wilson reneges on his promise to keep the nation out of war.

Even well-respected Jane Addams suffers bitter criticism for her antiwar position. Donations to Hull House fall, and the Daughters of the

American Revolution expel her from the organization.

✦ Most women come to support the war, and tens of thousands volunteer for the Red Cross, the National League for Women's Services, and other organizations that are set up for war relief. Existing women's clubs also join in rolling bandages, selling liberty bonds, and supporting food and clothing drives for European refugees.

Women replace men in such occupations as streetcar drivers and postal workers, while others work at dangerous munitions plants. Over 1,000 women serve in Europe as civilian contract employees of the army, as translators, telephone operators, and ambulance drivers for the American Expeditionary Forces. At 75 sites in France, 233 bilingual American women recruited by AT&T handle the phone calls linking French and English military leaders.

✦ When the war begins, there are 403 nurses on active duty with the Army Nurse Corps; by its end, 21,480 have enlisted. In addition to service in the United States and the primary war zone of northern Europe, army nurses work in such far-flung places as Siberia, Serbia, Hawaii, and Puerto Rico. More than 200 ANC members will die, some of them from breathing the lethal mustard gas introduced in this war.

✦ The Navy Nurse Corps grows less dramatically than its army counterpart—from 406 to 1,386—but another 10,000 nurses work under the aegis of the American Red Cross; they are officially civilians. Approximately 10,000 women from all of these sources serve abroad. They work in field hospitals on the Continent, tend convalescents in England, and staff hospital ships taking men home. According to army records, nurses in combat areas "don gas masks, dig out of rubble, and provide exceptional care under the most austere circumstances." They will be honored at the end of the war with precedent-setting awards: Three women receive the Distinguished Service Cross, while 23 earn the Distinguished Service Medal.

✦ The YWCA, the Salvation Army, and other organizations also sponsor women to go overseas. More than 100 Salvation Army women provide services to the troops that range from banking to baking. The YWCA sends almost 3,500 women, some of whom specialize in the complex legal and economic problems of refugees; several YWCA volunteers earn France's Croix de Guerre.

The American Women's Hospitals are European institutions financed and operated by American women, and they are staffed by 350 female physicians from the United States. In New York, the War Department asks pioneer diphtheria researcher Dr. Anna Wessels Williams to train medical laboratory workers.

✦ Although she was a founder of the Woman's Peace Party, Carrie Chapman Catt, who presides over the National American Woman Suffrage Association, astutely decides that support of the war can make the crucial difference for the suffrage issue. She accepts an appointment to the Woman's Committee of the Council of National Defense, and her judgment proves correct: suffragists who support the war are increasingly seen as mainstream citizens who deserve the vote.

✦ Democratic activist Daisy Harriman chairs the government's Committee on Women in Industry. She also helps to create the Red Cross Motor Corps, which is made up of women unconventional enough to drive, and she goes to France in 1918 to supervise the Corps' 500 ambulance drivers.

✦ Sisters Katherine and Marjorie Stinson attempt to use their aviation ability to help the war effort but are rebuffed. Katherine, the second American woman to be licensed as a pilot, followed Harriet Quimby in 1912; Marjorie got her license in 1913, and with their mother, they have been running a Texas aviation school. When it is forced to close because of wartime shortages, Katherine joins the Red Cross ambulance service, while Marjorie works in the Washington offices of the navy's aeronautical division.

✦ Emma Goldman is arrested again because of her exercise of free speech. This time she is urging men to resist the draft, and wartime law allows a much harsher sentence than in previous cases.

After serving two years in federal prison, "Red Emma" is deported to Russia. She will be allowed to visit the United States only once, in 1934, but she remains active as a writer and speaker in Europe until her death in 1940.

✦ As wartime inflation brings higher prices, increasing numbers of workers go on strike for higher wages. Textile mill protests in Columbus, Georgia, turn violent this year, and next year, even such traditionally unorganized workers as office scrubwomen go on strike. A major strike by the International Ladies' Garment Workers at war's end will achieve a 44-hour week.

✦ Rheta Dorr is a war correspondent for the syndicate headed by the *New York Evening Mail*. When the war ends, she will continue to write syndicated articles on foreign affairs from Prague. Also an active suffragist, Dorr publishes a number of feminist books, including a biography of Susan Anthony.

✦ Crime reporter Dorothy Dix switches to writing an advice column that will appear in some 300 newspapers within a decade. With the sales of her books, she is estimated to earn $100,000 annually by the 1940s.

Dix receives an average of 500 letters a day; at the same time, *Ladies' Home Journal* averages almost a million letters to the editor annually.

✦ Pulitzer Prizes begin to be awarded this year, and women sweep the category for biography. The winning book is *Julia Ward Howe*, written in two volumes by her daughters Laura E. Richards and Maude Howe Elliott, assisted by their sister Florence Howe Hall. Both Richards and Elliott have established reputations as authors independent of their mother's history.

The precedent will not be repeated until near the end of the 20th century. Although a few women will win prizes for biographies of men and a few men will win for biographies of women, no other woman writing on a woman wins a Pulitzer.

✦ Fifteen women who are barred from membership in the all-male Booksellers League form their own organization. Near the end of the 20th century,

the Women's National Book Association is still extant.

✦ The National Park Service hires its first female guides—sisters Esther and Elizabeth Burnell, homesteaders near Estes Park, Colorado. Elizabeth, who earlier headed the math and physics department at an Ohio college, is an especially adept mountain climber; she goes on to write books and establish programs in nature studies.

✦ Even though Smith College is a women's school, its trustees refuse to give Ada Louise Comstock the title of acting president during a year between male presidents in which she performs the duties of this office. The first female administrator at the University of Minnesota, Comstock will serve from 1923 to 1943 as president of Radcliffe College.

✦ Cornell Medical College has a woman at the top of its graduating class—but although Dr. Connie Guion will develop a distinguished career both practicing and teaching medicine in New York, she does not receive a full professorship until her career is almost over, in 1946.

✦ China's first school for blind girls is opened by Mary Grace Knapp, who is sightless herself. She attended Boston's famous coeducational Perkins School for the Blind and then graduated with honors from Wellesley two years ago. As in most foreign cultures, the Chinese will not allow girls to learn along with boys.

✦ Altrusa Clubs begin with business and professional women who wish to positively affect civic life. Altrusa members raise money for libraries, playgrounds, and similar projects while also gaining a personal networking opportunity.

✦ Delaware establishes a Mothers' Pension Fund to aid "morally fit but destitute widows with children."

✦ A Detroit study shows the standard midwife fee for a home delivery is $7 to $10, and she visits daily for at least five days; physicians come once, and charge $10 to $30.

Midwives not only are cost efficient but also may offer superior safety. No less a personage than the president of the American Medical Association criticizes his colleagues and praises these women. His reports show that midwives are more likely than physicians to follow regulations and use silver nitrate, which prevents syphilis-caused blindness in newborns. He concludes that by this standard, "the doctors should be replaced by midwives."

✦ In October, New Yorkers see what will turn out to be their last annual suffrage parade—this one is organized by Carrie Chapman Catt and focuses on women's contributions to the war. It includes a petition for the vote that is signed by 1 million women who are working in the war effort. The public responds well to this focus, for many are impressed by the women working overseas and in munitions plants. Male voters who argued that only men should vote because only men serve in war are forced to reevaluate.

✦ The parade signals changed attitudes, and the East finally has its first victory when New York women win full suffrage in the off-year November election.

A postelection map of the states clearly reveals the advanced status of western women: full voting rights are in effect in 12 states, 11 of which are in the West. In other eastern states, women lose rights that they had gained: partial suffrage is reversed in Indiana, where a court declares the legislative grant unconstitutional, and in Vermont, where the governor vetoes the legislature's bill. Suffragists are especially chagrined to discover that on the same day as the New York victory, an Ohio referendum cancels out the partial suffrage that the legislature had granted.

✦ Also in November, Lucy Burns leads the National Woman's Party in emulating the British technique of hunger strikes. After being arrested during still another demonstration for the vote in front of the White House, she goes without food for almost three weeks; only then is she so weak that jailers succeed in force-feeding her. Her story and that of other hunger strikers make daily

headlines, and the depth of these women's commitment to political equality makes a profound national impression.

✦ In an attempt to upgrade the value of military medals, Congress rescinds many of the honors it has awarded in the past. Dr. Mary Walker loses the Congressional Medal of Honor she earned in 1865 for her work as a Civil War physician. Grieving, frustrated, and lacking support, even from feminists, the 84-year-old Walker dies after falling on the Capitol steps.

1918 On January 9, President Woodrow Wilson issues a formal statement in support of federal suffrage, and on January 10, the House passes "the Susan B. Anthony" amendment to the Constitution, which assures all women the right to vote in all elections.

The "ayes" are just exactly enough to meet the requisite two-thirds majority. The margin is so close and the scene on the floor so chaotic that the roll call is repeated three times to determine that the 274 to 136 count is accurate. Several representatives make extraordinary efforts to be there, including one who stayed in Washington to vote and then went home to his wife's funeral.

The Senate, however, does not follow suit. Finally, in September, President Wilson appeals in person to the Senate. He announces that a million women have entered the labor force since 1915 and strongly urges passage of the suffrage amendment, calling it "a necessary war measure." The Senate vote, taken the following day, is 62 to 34, two votes short of the necessary two-thirds majority.

The opposition is led by Republican Henry Cabot Lodge of Massachusetts, and 28 of the 34 opposing votes are cast by East Coast senators. The National Woman's Party newspaper calls the East "notoriously conservative"—but despite Republican opposition to suffrage and Democrat Wilson's leadership on its behalf, the Woman's Party continues to picket the White House and to target Democrats for electoral defeat.

✦ In March, Rose Pastor Stokes, who has not been nearly as visible in antiwar activity as many others,

The Political Equality Club of Cayuga County, New York, on the day that New York women won full suffrage. The president of this group, Emily Howland, is second from left. She endowed some 30 schools in the South, mostly for blacks, and played a key role in making Cornell University coeducational. Cayuga County Archives and the Cayuga Museum, Auburn, New York

is indicted for violation of the Espionage Act. It may be her status as a Jewish socialist that is the most important factor in her arrest for writing in a letter to the editor of the *Kansas City Star*: "I am for the people, while the Government is for the profiteers."

The trial judge virtually instructs the jury to find Stokes guilty and sentences her to 10 years in prison. An appellate court will reverse his ruling in 1920, but the experience further radicalizes her. Instead of writing for mainstream magazines as she has in the past, she will join the Communist Party and write for *Pravda* and the *Daily Worker*. When she dies at age 53 in 1933, some believe that her death is due to an earlier police beating.

✦ Also in March, another court behaves far differently: the District of Columbia Court of Appeals dismisses both the arrests and the convictions of women who have been picketing the White House. There simply is no constitutional grounds for arrest.

✦ Congress passes the Chamberlain-Kahn Act in response to a soaring rate of venereal disease among soldiers. The law disregards the civil rights of women: It calls for "mandatory examination" of any woman suspected of prostitution, and in some areas near military posts, women have a 9:00 P.M. curfew. Women there must carry written documentation of the propriety of their relationship with a male escort.

By the War Department's estimate, some 15,000 women are jailed under the law, while many more are detained and subjected to questioning. Women's organizations make no objections, for some—especially the YWCA—see the law as protecting chastity and as an opportunity to rehabilitate prostitutes.

The venereal disease issue is also addressed by *Poems of Passion* author Ella Wheeler Wilcox. Now a widow, she reads her poetry to soldiers in France and admonishes them to "come home clean."

✦ The navy, suffering from a lack of qualified clerical workers, researches the law and finds no legal barrier to enlisting women. On August 13, Opha Mae Johnson, formerly a civilian employee, is the first woman sworn into the United States military for a purpose other than nursing.

Some 12,500 women termed "yeomen (female)" will join the navy during the war, while the Marine Corps enlists 305 "Marinettes." Most serve in Washington, D.C., and virtually all do clerical work, but they are provided with uniforms and perform parade drills like the men. So eager are women to enlist that 2,000 line up in New York to apply for just five positions. None becomes an officer, and all are dismissed after the war ends.

Fifty-seven Yeomen (F) will die while in service, mostly from Spanish influenza spread by returning troops.

✦ Julia Stimson, a Vassar graduate and member of the Army Nurse Corps, is detached from the military to become chief nurse of the civilian women who serve with the American Red Cross

Women who enlisted in the navy during World War I were termed Yeomen (F), with the initial intended to make it clear that these yeomen were female. Those pictured were assigned to the Portsmouth, New Hampshire, Navy Yard. Women In Military Service Memorial; original photograph from the U.S. Naval Historical Center

in France. At the end of war, Stimson will be honored with the Distinguished Service Medal, one of the highest awards that the military grants.

It is the Red Cross's Jane Delano who is primarily responsible for recruiting some 20,000 professional nurses into the war effort. According to the Red Cross, 296 of these nurses die during their service, and Delano herself is one of the casualties; she will die in France next year, a victim of the horrific postwar influenza epidemic. Because Red Cross nurses are officially civilians, their families are not entitled to any federal insurance or funeral benefits.

Thirty-six Navy Nurse Corps members die during the war, and three are posthumously awarded the Navy Cross.

◆ The Red Cross also sets a precedent when, in its role as a quasi-official part of the military, it certifies some 1,800 African-American women as wartime nurses after the nurses emphatically insist on serving. They are segregated from white nurses and assigned to care for black men only.

A second milestone is the nation's first black women in the military: Eighteen are admitted to the Army Nurse Corps this year. They actually go on duty after the war is over, however, and will be released next August. The 18 serve at two posts in Illinois and Ohio, caring for African-American men and German prisoners of war.

◆ While the military claims there is a tremendous need for trained medical assistance, it turns down both black nurses and female physicians. When Dr. Nellie Barsness, a 1902 University of Minnesota Medical School graduate, is rejected by the Army Medical Corps, she serves for the French. An ophthalmologist, she specializes in restoring sight to soldiers blinded by poison gases.

◆ Among the women who find validation of their worth in wartime volunteerism is young Eleanor Roosevelt, who went to Washington when President Wilson appointed her husband an assistant secretary of the navy. The move from her New York City home enables her to get away from dominating matriarchs on both sides of the

The Red Cross certified African-American women as nurses for the first time during World War I, and the Army Nurse Corps also admitted its first black women near the war's end. These serve at Camp Sherman, Ohio. Women In Military Service Memorial; original photograph from the American Red Cross

Roosevelt family, who have long made her feel insecure.

◆ The National Birth Control League changes its name to the Voluntary Parenthood League. In the absence of Margaret Sanger, who is studying contraceptive issues in Europe, the organization is led by Mary Ware Dennett. In time, the two will see each other as rivals, for they are remarkably similar: both women have artistic experience, are divorced from architects, and bore three children, each suffering the death of one child.

◆ The American Philosophical Association elects Mary Calkins as its president; in 1909, she was chosen president of the American Psychological Association. The only other person to be similarly honored with the presidencies of these two prestigious organizations is the famous John Dewey.

Calkins, who has taught at Wellesley College since 1886, also risks her position by adopting leftist political positions, including opposition to the war.

◆ New Jersey at last develops public college for women, largely because of lobbying directed by the president of the College Women's Club of

New Jersey, Mabel Smith Douglass. Like other New Jersey women, she is a graduate of an out-of-state college, and she pressures the Rutgers University board of trustees to make this public institution coeducational. They are obdurate, but after almost a decade of lobbying, they finally charter a women's college offering gender-segregated courses near Rutgers.

The New Jersey College for Women opens in New Brunswick with Mabel Douglass as dean —and, in effect, as president, for she will make every decision affecting the young institution for more than a decade. Her only educational credential is her 1899 degree from Barnard.

◆ The American Bar Association finally admits women as members—decades after the first women were admitted to state bars.

◆ Student law Mary Donlon is editor in chief of the *Cornell Law Quarterly*. She will go on to a career as an attorney specializing in industrial relations and, in 1955, becomes a federal judge.

◆ Louise Boyer is hired by Metro as a screenwriter. In addition to pioneer moviemaking, she and her artist sister, Helen Boyer King, also develop innovative printmaking styles.

Next year, Dorothy Arzner will join Boyer as a Hollywood screenwriter. Arzner goes on to a career as a director; she develops a portable microphone for sound movies, and from 1927 to 1943, she will direct such stars as Katharine Hepburn.

◆ That women's wartime roles have improved their political status is clear in the midterm elections, which occur only a few days before the end of the war. Women win three of four suffrage referenda, losing by a close margin only in Louisiana. The three victorious states are all in the Midwest— South Dakota, Oklahoma, and Michigan. The National American Woman Suffrage Association spent $20,000 in Oklahoma, more than in any state thus far.

◆ The first woman to run for the U.S. Senate is Anne Henrietta Martin, whose independent candidacy gets 20% of the vote in Nevada. Martin's credentials include earning a master's degree from Stanford University, founding the history department at the University of Nevada, and leadership in the suffrage movement in both Britain and the United States. Under her presidency of the Nevada Equal Franchise, Nevada women won the vote in 1914, but relatively few women reward her with their vote. After a 1920 race has similar results, Martin will move to California and become a leader in the Woman's Party and the Women's International League for Peace and Freedom.

◆ On November 11, an armistice ends what is called the Great War until the advent of World War II makes it known as World War I. This four-year war (in which the United States was involved for less than two years) changes women's roles more than in any other period in the nation's history. Women not only make significant gains in political power, but they also enter new employment fields, and—without any organized leadership —begin to adopt more practical clothing.

◆ The war's end also brings the right to vote to women in Austria, Canada, Ireland, Poland, and the United Kingdom of England and Scotland, where so much recent suffrage attention has focused. Next year, they will be joined by Germany, Luxembourg, and the Netherlands. In all these countries, suffrage campaigns lasted a much shorter time than in the United States.

When the full enfranchisement of American women finally does pass in 1920, Carrie Chapman Catt will write that her "rejoicing was sadly tempered by the humiliating knowledge that 26 other countries had outdistanced America in bestowing political liberty upon their women."

1919 In January, the 18th Amendment to the Constitution reaches final ratification, prohibiting "the manufacture, sale or transportation of intoxicating liquors." The Women's Christian Temperance Union thus achieves its goal before the suffragists reach theirs, and prohibition is established by voters who are overwhelmingly male. The liquor industry nonetheless will continue to lobby against voting rights for women.

✦ Also in January, the House passes the proposed 19th Amendment that would grant women the vote, but the outgoing Senate defeats it by one vote. Nine senators who vote against it ignore resolutions from their state legislatures requesting the opposite position.

Many legislatures are in session meanwhile, and six more emulate the "Illinois plan" of allowing women to vote for president. Except for Maine, all are in the Midwest: Iowa, Minnesota, Missouri, Ohio, and Wisconsin.

Because it is actually the electoral vote, not the popular, that elects the president, these victories may be more apparent than real; nonetheless, women in 20 states will be eligible to vote in the 1920 presidential election, and no politician can ignore that fact.

✦ In March, the Texas legislature emulates Arkansas in granting women the right to vote in primaries —the only elections that matter in this virtually all-Democratic state. The margin of victory makes it clear that suffrage is no longer considered radical even in conservative areas of the country; the bill passes the Texas Senate with 17 ayes and 4 nays.

Texas women lobbied the legislature from a headquarters set up in a fashionable Austin hotel and ran a remarkable campaign. A Dallas lawmaker, for example, thought that he had dismissed them by requesting 5,000 signatures from his constituents, but they returned with 10,000 just four days later.

✦ When the new Congress takes office in March, the results of the 1918 election finally provide the

Bilingual telephone operators contracted with the Army Signal Corps to smooth communications between the Allies fighting World War I. These work out of the Crillon Hotel during peace negotiations in Paris. The seated supervisor, Merle Egan, later fought for veterans' status for her workers, who were known as "Hello Girls." Women In Military Service Memorial crucial vote count, and on May 21, the House of Representatives, by a margin of 304 to 90, approves the proposed 19th Amendment to the U.S. Constitution. The June 4 Senate vote is closer, just two votes over what is necessary for the two-thirds majority.

The proposed amendment reads:

The right of citizens of the United States to vote shall not be denied or abridged by the United States or by any State on account of sex.

The Congress shall have power, by appropriate legislation, to enforce the provisions of this article.

✦ Membership in the National American Woman Suffrage Association soars to 2 million, as women begin the campaigns to secure the amendment's approval in the legislatures of the 36 states that are necessary to meet the Constitution's requirement for ratification by three-quarters of the states.

Illinois and Wisconsin race each other to be first to ratify the amendment. Texas is the ninth state and the first southern state; the western states where women had the vote longest prove to be slow in granting their approval.

The National Woman's Party sends out a railroad car of women who have served time for suffrage in jail. Led by Lucy Burns, who has recovered from her hunger strike starvation, they campaign across the nation.

✦ Although they must be "householders" over 30, British women are enfranchised before American women—and the first woman to enter Parliament is American by birth. Nancy Langhorne Astor of Virginia has been a British citizen since her 1906 marriage. She serves in the House of Commons while her husband is in the House of Lords; Lady Astor devotes her major efforts to issues concerning women and children and is continually reelected until her 1945 retirement.

✦ Mary White Ovington becomes chairman of the board of the National Association for the Advancement of Colored People. A white woman, she will serve in this position until 1932, when she steps down to treasurer. Ovington excels at getting people of both sexes and races to work together in the NAACP, but her requests that suffragist leadership include black women in the campaign for the vote meet with little success.

✦ In April, Kansan Kate O'Hare, the mother of four, enters a Missouri prison to serve a five-year sentence for violation of the Espionage Act. No one accuses her of any spying activity; instead, like the far better known Emma Goldman, O'Hare was arrested because of an antiwar speech she made in North Dakota in 1917—which was basically the same populist, isolationist oration that had drawn midwestern audiences to her since 1902.

Also an author, O'Hare ran for Congress on the Socialist ticket in 1910. Her sentence will be commuted in 1920, and after the war hysteria subsides, she is pardoned by Republican President Calvin Coolidge.

✦ The Reverend Dr. Anna Howard Shaw, former president of the National American Woman Suffrage Association, is honored for her work in organizing women during the war with the Distinguished Service Medal, the highest military honor given to civilians. She dies soon afterward, worn out by a speaking tour on behalf of the proposed League of Nations.

✦ Due to women's entry into the workforce during the war, the Women's Bureau of the Department of Labor is created. It is initially headed by Mary Van Kleeck, an expert in women's employment issues who advised the Army Ordnance Department and served on the War Labor Policies Board.

Van Kleeck soon resigns in favor of her friend Mary Anderson, a Swedish immigrant who worked in the garment industry until age 39, when she was hired by the Women's Trade Union League to enforce the hard-won contract of the 1909 strike. Anderson has risen through labor's ranks and is a perfect choice to head the new bureau.

✦ After more than two decades at Wellesley College, Emily Balch has introduced new curricula, chaired her department, served in both appointed and elected positions in numerous associations, and done extensive research in several languages to write a classic book on immigration—but she is "not reappointed" because of her opposition to the war. At age 52, she loses her pension as well as her job.

✦ Dr. Alice Hamilton, who is also a leading suffragist and pacifist, becomes the first woman on the staff of Harvard Medical School; all of her students, of course, are male. She has pioneered the field of toxicology, and her research will lead to worker compensation programs for those injured by industrial hazards. Her reputation becomes international when she delivers a report to a Brussels conference in 1921.

✦ Grace E. Coates is the Labor Department's investigator during a strike of Tampa cigar workers. After interviewing the mayor, she concludes that even though city officials have an "autocratic spirit" and have actively promoted "lawless violence" against workers, the cigarmakers—many of whom are Hispanic women—are "not conquered."

✦ Wesleyan Female College in Macon, Georgia, drops "female" from its name, although it continues to be a single-sex institution. Founded in 1836 as Georgia Female College, it will survive through the 20th century as Wesleyan College— arguably the oldest women's college in the world.

✦ In coastal South Carolina, African-American teacher Septima Poinsette Clark gathers 10,000 signatures on petitions for better educational opportunity; the legislature, in a positive mood because of black contributions to wartime victory, responds with more money. Clark and her assistant are paid $35 and $25 a month to teach 132 students; a white teacher across the street in a better building is paid $85 for teaching three students.

✦ Jessie Redmon Fauset becomes literary editor of *The Crisis*, the publication of the National Association for the Advancement of Colored People. In this role, Fauset publishes some of the early works of writers who will go to fame as members of the Harlem Renaissance. She is extremely well credentialed: Fauset is a 1905 graduate of Cornell University, where she may have been the first black woman in the world to earn Phi Beta Kappa membership, and she did postgraduate work at the University of Pennsylvania and the Sorbonne. A significant author in her own right, she will be especially known for *The Chinaberry Tree* (1931). Historian Mary Beard includes Fauset's *Comedy: American Style* (1934) on a list of important books.

✦ Having growing up in both America and France, Sylvia Beach uses an inheritance from her mother to start Shakespeare & Company, a Paris bookstore that becomes a landmark for Americans abroad for the rest of the century. During the next decade, Beach's bookstore provides a home away from home to Katherine Anne Porter and other young writers, including Ernest Hemingway and F. Scott Fitzgerald.

✦ Architect Julia Morgan has several California buildings to her credit when William Randolph Hearst hires her to design Hearst Castle at San Simeon. It eventually will sprawl into a 165-room mansion, one of the costliest homes ever built.

Morgan's early career was advanced by Hearst's mother (who also was interested in architecture), but Morgan has long had independent success. She practices from 1904 until after World War II, sometimes supervising dozens of workers, and becomes especially known for YWCA buildings, including one in Hawaii.

An 1894 graduate of the University of California at Berkeley, Morgan was the first woman to study engineering there; she went on to the École des Beaux-Arts in Paris, where she was the first woman to graduate from the architecture program. Unlike Hearst, Morgan avoids publicity throughout her life.

✦ Anita Loos retains her maiden name when she marries a Hollywood colleague, for she is the well-paid author of some 200 scripts for silent movies. They will write two books on film production together, while Loos maintains her independent career.

✦ Worn out by the war and especially by his international speaking tours on behalf of the proposed League of Nations, President Woodrow Wilson suffers a stroke in October. Until his term ends more than a year later, many believe that his wife, Edith Bolling Wilson, is running the country. She keeps him hidden from public view as much as possible, excludes the vice president from the White House, and comes to be seen as the person actually making the decisions that she attributes to the president. The secretary of state will be forced to resign when he holds unauthorized cabinet meetings.

She is, incidentally, Wilson's second wife; he married her in 1915, after Ellen Axson Wilson died in 1914. The first Mrs. Wilson found politics so distasteful that she refused to hold an inauguration ball; instead she was quietly but deeply involved in charity, including working for better housing for Washington's black residents. Edith Wilson is a descendent of Pocahontas, and her Virginia family was devastated by the Civil War; although she became affluent with her first marriage, she is not known for generosity.

✦ It is a year for new beginnings, as several major organizations are founded that will endure through the century: the League of Women Voters, the National Federation of Business and Professional Women's Clubs, and the Women's International League for Peace and Freedom.

The League of Women Voters begins as victory for the vote is in sight. Carrie Chapman Catt, who has worked for suffrage virtually fulltime from age 31 to 61, is named honorary president for life, while longtime suffrage lobbyist Maud Wood Park becomes the league's president. Park, who was widowed young, established a very modern second marriage in 1908; she neither took her husband's name nor lived with him.

The league's first official convention will be held next February, when the National American Woman Suffrage Association hosts its "Victory Convention." Only about one of every 10 NAWSA members, however, will transfer her dues to the league when the suffrage group dissolves. Similarly, although the league's initial legislative agenda includes 38 items, just two (the Sheppard-Towner Act and the Cable Act) will come to fruition in the political conservatism of the next decade.

The National Federation of Business and Professional Women's Clubs also begins this year. It differs from the league in that its emphasis is on economic opportunity, but it quickly becomes a lobbying force for women that is in many ways more feminist than the league. BPW will be particularly influential during the Roosevelt years, when it establishes "talent banks" of qualified women who are available for governmental appointments. The name of their publication, *Independent Woman,* also provides an interesting contrast to the league's *Voter.*

The Women's Peace Party transforms itself into the Women's International League for Peace and Freedom, with Jane Addams as president. Both she and Emily Balch—whose antiwar stance cost her a college professorship—will be lifelong officers. Although its founders are women from old and wealthy families, the Women's International League for Peace and Freedom will be viewed as radical throughout the century.

1920 When legislatures in West Virginia and Washington provide the 34th and 35th votes approving the 19th Amendment, all of the expected states have ratified. The final vote must come from the South or New England: when the legislatures of Connecticut, Vermont, and Delaware fail to ratify, attention focuses on the border state of Tennessee, whose technical requirements for ratification recently were ruled unconstitutional by the Supreme Court.

In June, President Woodrow Wilson pressures Tennessee's Democratic governor to bring the legislature into session. The governor somewhat reluctantly calls a special session beginning August 9, and lobbyists on both sides of the issue pour into Nashville. Democratic Party leaders urge legislators, most of whom are Democrats, to vote for suffrage, arguing that their party will suffer in the coming presidential election if ratification fails. The Tennessee Senate promptly approves it by a wide margin.

Members of the Woman's Party "Prison Special" arrive in Chicago in 1919. All of these women had served time in jail for suffrage demonstrations in Washington, D.C. Using sophisticated public relations skills, they then traveled around the nation by train to bring media attention to their cause. Women's Party Corporation/Sewall-Belmont House, Washington, D.C.

The House of Representatives, however, panders to the lobbyists opposed to suffrage, who use everything from liquor to threats of kidnapping to change votes and delay action. When the vote is finally cast on August 18, initial parliamentary moves bring a 48 to 48 tie. The deciding vote then comes from 24-year-old Harry Burn, who has been voting with the opposition but who had promised his mother that he would vote for suffrage in the case of a tie. "Help Mrs. Catt put the rat in ratification," her letter to him urges.

Unwilling to acknowledge defeat, the opposition uses up another week making various moves for reconsideration and attempting to prevent the governor from signing and the secretary of state from enrolling the bill. What it is finally, formally signed on August 26, the long-suffering labor of suffrage is over at last.

✦ To the members of the National American Woman Suffrage Association, one of the most painful aspects of the Tennessee showdown is the desertion of Laura Clay and Kate Gordon: both were NAWSA officials under Susan Anthony's leadership, and they join the opposition in Nashville. Former presidents of suffrage associations in Kentucky and Louisiana respectively, they make the "states' rights" argument against the federal amendment and are candid about their distaste for enfranchising black women.

Another antisuffragist, Alice Wadsworth, is widely quoted when she says that granting women the vote "would enshrine nagging as national policy."

+ At age 93, Charlotte Woodward Pierce is the only woman who attended the 1848 Seneca Falls Women's Rights Convention and lived to vote in a national election.

Carrie Chapman Catt sums up the effort made since 1848: she counts 480 campaigns in state legislatures; 56 referenda to male voters; 47 attempts to add suffrage planks during revisions of state constitutions; 277 campaigns at state party conventions and 30 at national conventions; and 19 biannual campaigns in 19 different Congresses.

+ Among those most pleased to be enfranchised is the Reverend Antoinette Brown Blackwell, who attended her first suffrage meetings in the 1850s. She will die next year, and she preached her last sermon five years ago at age 90. The Reverend Olympia Brown, whom Blackwell mentored more than 50 years earlier, also lives to vote in this historic year. She is 85 and will take her first trip to Europe in 1926, when she is past 90. She dies in Baltimore a few months later.

+ The women of Colorado, who have been voting for 27 years, issue a report pointing out their spectacular progress with political offices controlling the state's educational system: "The office of State Superintendent of Public Instruction has been filled by a woman since 1894 and no man has been nominated for it."

Among the seven women who have held the office is Mary Bradford, who was also elected president of the National Education Association after Ella Flagg Young set that precedent in 1910. Colorado currently has some 600 women serving on school boards.

+ Wyoming women have been voting longer than any, and in this year's municipal elections, an all-female slate takes office in Jackson Hole. The mayor, the city council, and the city's executive offices are held by women, and they concentrate on paving roads and building a city park.

+ In this year of full enfranchisement for most American women, a total of 18 women have served in Utah's legislature. Since 1913, there has not been an election without at least one woman winning a legislative race.

+ President Wilson names Helen Hamilton Gardener to the Civil Service Commission, the highest such position yet granted a woman in the federal government. He makes the appointment in April, while the 19th Amendment is still an issue; he thus takes a genuine political risk, for some may still remember that Gardener published an openly atheistic book in 1884.

In private life, she is Helen Chenowith Day; her second husband is a retired military officer who brought her into contact with Washington's most powerful people. Indeed, suffragists credit her with favorably influencing both Wilson and her neighbor, the Speaker of the House. Probably because of these friendships, the appointment is not controversial, and Gardener serves with distinction on this body that governs federal employees for five years.

+ During this last year of President Wilson's tenure, Californian Annette Adams moves from her Justice Department assignment in San Francisco to its Washington, D.C., headquarters. Attorney General Mitchell Palmer values her political skills as highly as her legal ability, and she promotes his candidacy for the presidency. He does not receive the nomination, but she wins one token vote on the Democratic convention's 37th ballot.

+ The American Civil Liberties Union, with Jane Addams as a founder, is formed in response to serious infringements on free speech during World War I. Addams will be even more harshly criticized for her defense of free speech than for her pacifism—but she has long experience with criticism, for she jeopardized Hull House funding in its earliest days by defending the "anarchists" of the 1886 Chicago Haymarket Square riot.

+ The Army Reorganization Act grants "relative rank" to the women who make up the Army and Navy Nurse Corps. The rank does not include full benefits, and even though they may have a lifelong career, almost all nurses are limited to the Army ranks of lieutenant and captain.

World War I veteran Julia Stimson, recently named director of the Army Nurse Corps, is appointed a major—and she will hold that rank until six weeks prior to her death in 1948, when she is finally promoted to colonel. No other corps head has so low a rank.

✦ Over 80 women sail on the *Lapland* to the World's Christian Temperance Union convention in London. Some make a side trip to France and Belgium, where they visit cemeteries for American soldiers killed during World War I.

✦ The end of the war brings a serious rise in the number of divorce cases filed, and as the decade begins, there are 3.4 divorces per 1,000 married people—up from 0.8 divorces 50 years earlier. One factor is the return of soldiers who spread venereal disease to their wives, thus making their wartime infidelity obvious. Divorce rates will soar still higher with the liberation of the Roaring '20s.

✦ Photographer Jessie Tarbox Beals holds her 50th birthday party at her fashionable New York studio, a location formerly occupied by Louis Tiffany. As cameras become more common, however, her fortunes will decline; relocations to California and Florida are unsuccessful, and in 1942, her life ends in a Bellevue charity ward.

✦ Pioneer aviator Neta Snook Southern operates Kinner Airfield in Los Angeles. Among the flying students who save their money to take lessons from her is young Amelia Earhart.

✦ A Brooklyn store opened by Frieda Loehmann features discounts on clothes that failed to sell during the brief New York fashion season. Loehmann's concept proves successful, and stores bearing her name continue to expand throughout the nation long after her 1962 death.

✦ As white women find work in fields other than domestic service, the percentage of black women thus employed rises from 24% in 1890 to 40% in 1920. To some extent, this shift may also be indicative of the migration of many black families from the South to the North during World War I; these women found jobs as cooks and cleaners in urban homes that had been unavailable in their southern agricultural communities.

The Irish are the other large group serving the households of the urban Northeast: even after 80 years of steady immigration and upward mobility, Irish women still account for 43% of the nation's domestic servants.

✦ Educator Mary McLeod Bethune begins registering African Americans as soon as Florida women have the right to vote. Despite the terror of a night attack by the Ku Klux Klan, she urges them to vote for improved education. Perhaps because Bethune has been astute enough to ask such wintertime Floridians as John D. Rockefeller Jr. to serve on her board of directors, her school is never bothered by the Klan again.

✦ A study indicates profound gender stereotyping in black communities: Less than one-half of 1 percent of the nation's 3,855 black physicians are women.

✦ Republican presidential candidate Warren Harding employs Blanche Armwood, a home economics pioneer who has networks among African-American women throughout the South, to retain those voters for the "Party of Lincoln." A naturally gifted woman, Armwood was educated by nuns and passed Florida's teacher examination at age 12. She goes on to become the first black superintendent of Tampa's schools for blacks, but premature death will prevent the use of a law degree she earns in 1937.

✦ The wife of the Republican nominee, Florence Harding, actively campaigns among women, calling herself a suffragist and noting her background as a journalist—although neither of these was evident prior to the race. Meanwhile, Eleanor Roosevelt, wife of the Democrat's vice presidential nominee and mother of five, considers it improper to campaign.

✦ New York's Democratic Party includes a woman on its statewide slate, as Harriet May Mills is the nominee for secretary of state. She does not win, but sets a precedent as the first female candidate in a major state nominated by a major party.

◆ In November, Alice Mary Robertson, Republican of Oklahoma, defeats the Democratic incumbent to become the second woman elected to Congress. Robertson, who was born to missionaries in the pre–Civil War Indian Territory, had set an earlier precedent by joining the Washington Office of Indian Affairs in 1873. She then obtained a postmaster's appointment and ran a dairy farm, but despite this feminist lifestyle, she disassociates herself from suffragists and opposes the agenda of the League of Women Voters. Too conservative for even the Daughters of the American Revolution, she will be defeated in the next election—after establishing another precedent as the first woman to preside over the House of Representatives.

Approximately 8 million women cast their first ballots in this historic election, but Democrats are not rewarded for their key roles in ratification of the 19th Amendment. The political pendulum swings back to conservatism, and Republicans win more than 60 House seats and the next three presidential elections.

No active suffragists are elected, for although the cause of women's rights has triumphed, the public rarely values those whose radicalism creates such major change.

8

The Flapper and Beyond

1921–1939

1921　As their organizations disband, suffrage leaders dedicate a monument in the U.S. Capitol. On February 15, they celebrate Susan Anthony's birthday by unveiling a statue financed by the National Woman's Party and carved by Washingtonian Adelaide Johnson. It depicts Anthony between Elizabeth Cady Stanton and Lucretia Mott, the two women who led the call for the first Women's Rights Convention in 1848. A mass of uncarved stone behind the women is Johnson's vision of those who follow in the continuing struggle for full equality.

✦ Mary Ware Dennett believes that she is scheduled to speak on birth control at the National Woman's Party annual convention, and when the program omits her speech, she assumes that it is accidental and contacts president Alice Paul—who has a secretary write a reply that Dennett's speech is canceled. "The reasons being precisely the same as [those] used a decade ago for not listening to *suffrage*," Dennett fumes. "'Too controversial,' 'so much difference of opinion among our most valued members,' etc."

✦ Sculptor Mary Eberle, who has won prizes for her work since 1904, is elected to the National Academy of Design. She is especially known for her 1913 sculpture "White Slavery."

✦ Congress passes the Sheppard-Towner Act, which appropriates up to $1 million annually for states that provide matching funds to build maternity clinics aimed at lowering infant mortality rates. Approximately 3,000 prenatal/pediatric clinics are opened during the decade, and most of the physicians employed in them are women.

Even though the act will be repealed in 1929, it not only delivers health care to a significant number of women but also offers a valuable model for New Deal programs that follow in the next decade. The fact that it passes a year after all women are eligible to vote is considered a great victory for the newly formed League of Women Voters—but it will be the league's only significant legislative victory before a politically reactionary mood overtakes Washington.

✦ The Sheppard-Towner Act is implemented under the direction of social scientist Grace Abbott, director of the federal Children's Bureau.

Abbott has twice been thwarted in similar efforts. After a highly successful decade heading Chicago's Immigrants Protective League, she moved to Washington, D.C., in 1917 to enforce the ban on child labor that Congress passed the previous year—but the Supreme Court struck down the law in 1918. She returned home to head the new Illinois State Immigrants' Commission, only to see a new governor abolish it.

✦ Julia Lathrop leaves the Children's Bureau after shepherding it through its first decade, but does not fully retire. She concentrates on placing children orphaned by World War I, for which she will be honored by the governments of Poland and Czechoslovakia.

✦ Evangelist Aimee Semple McPherson, who was ordained by Chicago's Full Gospel Assembly when she was still a teenager, buys a Los Angeles radio station and begins construction on her extravagant 5,000-seat Angelus Temple. The mother of four, she retains the name of her second husband when they divorce, and wearing distinctive white robes, she preaches to large audiences as far away as Australia. She also builds a Bible college for several thousand students in Los Angeles and establishes such innovations as telephone counseling.

✦ "Downhearted Blues" is composed and recorded by young African American Alberta Hunter—but it will be Bessie Smith who makes the song famous. Hunter never achieves lasting fame, although she will star in the Broadway run of Oscar Hammerstein's *Show Boat* in 1927 and cuts an album more than 50 years later, in 1982.

✦ Postal authorities confiscate and burn four issues of Margaret Anderson's *Little Review* because she has violated their ban of James Joyce's *Ulysses* by serializing the novel. She is convicted of obscenity charges and fined, and the magazine, always on the verse of bankruptcy, is never published regularly again. Like others of the "Lost Generation" of writers and artists who exiled themselves to

Europe after World War I, she will move to Paris the following year; she does not return home until the Nazis overrun France in 1940.

◆ Edith Wharton is the first woman to win the Pulitzer Prize in literature for *Age of Innocence*. The winner of the drama prize is less well known: Zona Gale wins for *Miss Lulu Bett*. Gale writes of her native Wisconsin and has published numerous novels and stories with characters based in the small-town Midwest. She is also a political activist for progressive causes and counts Jane Addams among her friends.

◆ Faith Baldwin uses her maiden name when she publishes her first novel; she is immediately popular and will write more than 100 books prior to her death in 1978. In 1936 alone, four of her stories, which center on life among the wealthy, are made into movies.

◆ At Baltimore's Goucher College, Mary Wilhelmine Williams begins what may be the first college course devoted to the history of American women.

◆ During the summer, Bryn Mawr opens its lovely suburban Philadelphia campus to women who have had no other opportunity for advanced education. The Bryn Mawr Summer School for Working Women proves a model for several other colleges that reach out to blue-collar workers.

◆ General Mills creates Betty Crocker as an ideal homemaker image to feminize the flour industry for its customers, and she becomes a century-long marketing icon. She is the brainchild of General Mills home economist Marjorie Child Husted, who goes on to appreciable success as a business executive. Betty Crocker is drawn by New York illustrator Neysa McMein, who has illustrated the covers of national magazines; she also will create patriotic posters during World War II.

◆ When the Republicans take office, assistant attorney general Annette Adams, an active Democrat, is replaced by another, younger Californian, Mabel Willebrandt. After almost a decade with the Justice Department, Willebrandt will set another

precedent in 1928 by becoming the first woman to chair a committee at a Republican convention.

Meanwhile, Adams returns to California, practices law, and begins her assent in the judiciary; by 1942, she is a state appellate judge.

◆ The third woman elected to the House is Winnifred Mason Huck. Although she replaces her recently dead father, this is no courtesy appointment: even the Illinois Republican Women's Club endorses a man, and she must defeat challengers from both parties.

That she serves only four months is explained by Representative Huck's exceptional activism, for she even takes up the controversial cause of imprisoned men who spoke against World War I. She loses the next Republican primary to a man who apparently exceeds Illinois' $100,000 campaign limit, but her calls for an investigation go unheeded. When her liberal views bring defeat in the next election, she leaves the Republicans to become a Woman's Party activist.

◆ Alice Paul steps down from the chairmanship of the National Woman's Party and is succeeded by millionaire Alva Belmont. She buys a historic Capitol Hill mansion for the party's headquarters in 1926, and it will remain in the party's ownership throughout the century.

Meanwhile, both major political parties reach out to women through auxiliaries: Daisy Harriman—like Belmont, a millionaire with decades of experience in progressive causes—will serve throughout the decade as national president of the Democratic Women's Clubs. The Republican Party also organizes auxiliaries of women, but real power will remain with the virtually all-male county executive committees of both parties.

After completing her term with the National Woman's Party, Alva Belmont spends most of the rest of her life in France and returns to her early interest in architecture. She is internationally recognized for her restoration of a 15th-century castle and becomes one of the few women elected to the American Institute of Architects.

The Advisory Council of the National Woman's Party meets at Alva Belmont's Port Washington, New York, home in 1921. Belmont is in the center wearing a light-colored dress; she stands between Alice Paul on the left and Harriet Stanton Blatch on the right. Two other notable women are Lucy Burns, cofounder of the party with Paul, to the left behind Paul, and former congresswoman Jeanette Rankin, second from the right at the back. Woman's Party Corporation/Sewall-Belmont House, Washington, D.C.

✦ In off-year elections, Richmond banker Maggie Walker runs for Superintendent of Instruction of Virginia on the "Black Lily" ticket. While she does not come close to winning, she makes it clear that black women will exercise their new political rights.

✦ In an attempt to increase the tourist trade, New Jersey's Atlantic City begins the Miss America pageant. States send the winner of their beauty contests, and, with the exception of the Great Depression years of 1928 to 1935, this late-summer tradition will last through the century.

After protests from feminists in the 1960s and 1970s, sponsors will advertise the pageant more as a talent and scholarship competition, but during this early era, the swimsuit and evening gown components highlight an unambiguous contest to choose the most beautiful young woman in the United States.

The swimsuit competition, in fact, is a visible demonstration of the era's hallmark change in dress. Unlike the "bloomer" stage of dress reform in the 19th century, this transformation is not based on any feminist ideals; it is simply the effort of millions of young women to be fashionable. Feminine appearance, however, causes literally millions of family fights, as young women wish to adopt styles that their families (especially immigrant families) often find risqué.

During the few years between the end of World War I and the establishment of what is known as the Roaring Twenties, however, the image of women in the Western world is completely changed. "Flappers" in both Britain and America "bob" the long hair that women historically had worn piled heavily on their heads; the new, short, straight style is easily cared for and very liberating for sports and other activity. They also adopt skirts that rise first above the ankle and then, within a very short time, scandalously above the knee. They paint their faces with cosmetics, while petticoats, hats, high-top shoes, and especially corsets are tossed on the heap of fashion history.

In addition to these changes in dress, flappers pride themselves on the adoption of male habits in smoking, drinking, and driving cars. They dance suggestively to revolutionary jazz, and they crowd the moving picture shows that offer a new, romantic view of life. Without any visible leadership, without any organized political change, young American women liberate themselves from centuries of social history that in a very real, highly visible way had restrained them.

1922 The revolutionary change in women's image and activities is upsetting to many, and some remain so thoroughly opposed to the vote for women that two cases reach the Supreme Court arguing that the 19th Amendment was not legally added to the Constitution, even though millions of women have already cast ballots under its provisions. On February 27, the Court rules against these conservatives, pointing out that similar federal amendments have overruled "states' rights" for "half a century."

✦ Congress passes the Cable Act, which repealed previous legalisms that put a woman's citizenship in jeopardy when she married a noncitizen. The act is a reflection of women's independent political power now that they have the vote, for it begins to end the common-law principle that a married woman and man are one, and that one is the man.

There is one notable exception: a female citizen who marries an "alien ineligible to citizenship" continues to surrender her personal rights upon marriage. The language is aimed at Asians, who were barred from citizenship beginning in 1882, with the passage of the Chinese Exclusion Act. Thus, a woman born in the United States of Asian parentage loses her citizenship if she marries a man from Asia. This inequity will not be corrected until 1931.

✦ Another indication of the increased political power of women now that they have the vote is that Congress finally grants benefits to nurses who served more than two decades ago in the Spanish-American War. To receive their pension, nurses must prove that they served at least 90 days under contract with the armed forces.

✦ Washington residents are embarrassed by the Children's Crusade—a march of children whose parents are still in prison because of their opposition to World War I.

✦ "The Sex Side of Life" is banned by postal authorities, even though this sex education manual is used by the YMCA and was published in the *Medical Review of Reviews* in 1918. Originally written by Mary Ware Dennett for her teenage sons, some 25,000 copies of the article have been distributed by Dennett's Voluntary Parenthood League. The post office's ban begins a decade of legal battles for Dennett.

✦ Oklahoma Seminole Indians choose Alice Brown Davis as their first female chief. Davis is an educator who supports policies of integration with surrounding whites while also working for Seminole decision-making authority.

✦ Newlyweds DeWitt and Lila Bell Acheson Wallace, both Minnesotans who have moved to New York, found *Reader's Digest*. He recently has been fired from his job, and they use her savings to create the magazine's first issue in the basement of their Greenwich Village apartment. An active publisher all of her life, Lila Wallace will also collect art, design the magazine's offices, and promote philanthropies.

✦ Playwright Anne Nichols sets a record for the era's longest-running play with *Abie's Wild Rose*. The story of romance between a Jewish man and an Irish woman, her script uses deft comedy to deal with religious prejudice; its theme and characterization will be repeated in several future film and television plots.

✦ After almost two decades of writing in a wide variety of other genres, Emily Post publishes *Etiquette*. Her elite upbringing makes her a natural authority on the subject, while her 1905 divorce means that she has to work for a living.

The topic turns out to be one in which millions of Americans—especially women—are interested, for standards of behavior will change rapidly during the Roaring Twenties. She revises the book regularly for the rest of her life, in addition to writing a newspaper column after 1932. *Etiquette* lives on after Emily Post's 1960 death and has been reprinted more than 100 times.

◆ Writer Gene Stratton-Porter—who changed her name from Geneva at the suggestion of her husband—develops a film company for her prescient ecologically oriented novels, but when she dies two years later, her ideas die with her.

Although she will be largely forgotten, Stratton-Porter is extremely popular in her lifetime. Her first book, *Freckles* (1904), sells 1,400,000 copies, and, according to biographer Beatrice Hofstadter, the total sales of her 19 works make her work "second only to the novels of Scott and Dickens in their day." Eight books are made into films, and she has a worldwide audience estimated at 50 million. Her northern Indiana home will be preserved by the state.

◆ Willa Cather—who won no major awards for what became classics of the American prairie, *O Pioneers!* (1913) and *My Ántonia* (1918)—wins the Pulitzer Prize for *One of Ours*, a poignant story of World War I.

◆ On her 25th birthday, Amelia Earhart buys a plane with money she earned working as a telephone operator. She spends most of the rest of the decade teaching English to immigrants in a Boston settlement house, using her earnings to support her aviation hobby.

◆ Although Washington, D.C.'s Howard University has existed since the Civil War ended, only now is the first dean of women appointed. She is Lucy Slowe, a longtime area educator and civic activist.

◆ Ida Husted Harper publishes the last of *The History of Woman Suffrage*. Volumes 5 and 6 cover the period from 1900 to final victory in 1920 and are financed by a bequest from publisher Miriam Leslie. While more systematically organized than earlier tomes, the bias in favor of Susan Anthony's organization is clear, and the

contributions of groups not affiliated with the National American Woman Suffrage Association are excluded. The work ends with a report on the status of women in more than 30 nations.

◆ Margaret Sanger retains that name when she marries a millionaire who will support her work. His funds underwrite her new Birth Control Clinical Research Bureau in Manhattan.

◆ The first woman to serve on a supreme court is Florence Allen, who is elected in Ohio just two years after becoming a judge.

A graduate of Western Reserve University's College for Women, Allen spent the decade between 1904 and 1914 in music and in settlement house work; after being rejected by several law schools, she graduated from New York University Law School and passed the Ohio bar in 1914.

Five years later, she became Cleveland's first female prosecutor, and the following year—as soon as women could vote—she successfully ran for a local judgeship. Her network of suffragist friends then organized and took the first opportunity to elect her to the Ohio Supreme Court, winning by some 350,000 votes. Six years later, she will be reelected by a wide margin.

◆ Allen's case is unusual, and the rapid dissolution of suffragist networks is seen in the relatively disappointing number of women who run for office in this first good election opportunity after passage of the 19th Amendment. Wisconsin Democrats set a precedent by nominating longtime suffragist Jessie Jack Hooper for the U.S. Senate—but the honor is that of a sacrificial lamb, for she must run against the popular incumbent, liberal Republican Robert M. La Follette, and she loses in a landslide. She does win the Democratic stronghold of Milwaukee, despite her opposition to the sale of beer that is the city's economic base.

While no women win congressional seats, a number are added to state legislatures. Minnesota is exceptional in electing four: Myrtle Cain, Sue Dickey Hough, and Mabeth Paige all represent Minneapolis, while Hannah Kempfer wins in rural Otter Tail County. Only Paige develops a full political career. Within seven years, she is arguably the most powerful female legislator in the country, for she chairs the Committee on Public Welfare and Social Legislation. She will be reelected continually until 1944.

+ At age 87, Rebecca Felton of Georgia becomes the first female U.S. senator, although she holds that office very briefly. Felton's advice has been sought by male politicians since she managed her husband's first political campaign in 1874; a longtime columnist for the *Atlanta Journal*, she is recognized as a national women's leader.

When the incumbent dies during the fall campaign, Georgia's governor decides to honor Felton with the Senate appointment. The election's winner agrees to take office a day late, and Felton travels to Washington, where on November 21, she is sworn in as the first female U.S. Senator. The next day she makes a short speech, resigns, and returns to Georgia, where she will write her column for another seven years before dying at age 94.

1923 In a January election, Mae Ella Nolan becomes the fourth woman elected to the House; she is the first to fit the stereotype that many historians later assign to early congresswomen, in that she is the widow of a congressman.

Even so, she has to defeat three other candidates in her San Francisco district. In December, she takes over the Committee on Expenditures in the post office and becomes the first woman to chair a congressional committee. Nolan will decline to run in 1924.

+ In rural Sussex County, Delaware, Mrs. Wilmer Steele begins what will later be seen as an agricultural revolution: She raises and sells 500 chickens faster than is standard, and when her methodology is followed by others, she is credited with beginning the modern broiler industry.

+ The increased political conservatism of the 1920s is indicated by *Adkins v. Children's Hospital*, a Supreme Court ruling that strikes down a 1918 minimum-wage law for female workers. In its governing role for the District of Columbia, Congress had passed a minimum-wage standard for women working there; in striking it down, the Court nullifies all such laws as unconstitutional limitations on employers.

+ A proposed Equal Rights Amendment to the Constitution is introduced in Congress by supporters of the National Woman's Party. Drafted by suffrage leader Alice Paul, it proclaims: "Equality of rights under the law shall not be denied or abridged by the United States or by any State on account of sex."

The purpose is to end legislation that discriminates against women—but many former suffragists have worked hard to pass labor laws and other beneficial legislation for women, and they oppose the ERA because it would nullify such special protection. As a result, the amendment languishes in committee for decades; no woman in Congress will sign on as a cosponsor until 1943.

+ The federal government establishes the Bureau of Home Economics under the aegis of the Agriculture Department.

+ When Dr. Josephine Baker retires from the New York City Bureau of Child Hygiene, which she has headed from its inception, the statistics prove that she has achieved her goal: the city's rate of infant mortality is the best of any major city in the world. Dr. Baker has achieved this primarily by educating women—most of them immigrants, who required extra diligence and creativity to reach.

+ After a lifetime of studying the needs of workers and consumers in various industries for the progressive Consumers League, Josephine Goldmark issues what is considered her most important work, *Nursing and Nursing Education in the United States*. She has surveyed more than 70 nursing schools, and her study causes major changes in the profession. Nursing schools traditionally have been associated with hospitals, which often exploit the students as unpaid labor. Now a number of nursing schools follow Goldmark's recommendations that they affiliate with prestigious universities, seek endowments, and improve their academic standards.

+ Yale University awards a Ph.D. to Florence Seibert, who spent her graduate student days developing a method of eliminating contaminants from distilled water, which is a necessary step in the invention of intravenous therapy. Although she will wear leg braces all of her life, Dr. Seibert overcame childhood polio and earned an undergraduate degree in chemistry from Baltimore's all-woman Goucher College.

  With a picture of Marie Curie on her desk for inspiration, she ignores hostility from male students, for undergraduate education at Yale will remain closed to women for many more decades.

+ *Ladies' Home Journal* offers a $50,000 prize for the best plan to promote international peace, and more than 22,000 respond, including prominent statesmen and educators. When the top prize is awarded to a man who proposes greater use of the new World Court, the women who serve on the judging committee are criticized as both naive dupes and traitorous Communists. One woman is Eleanor Roosevelt; she is recruited by a more experienced internationalist, Esther Everett Lape, who also promotes the cause of national health care.

+ Rosewood, Florida, a town populated mostly by blacks, is completely destroyed during a week of pillaging by whites that leaves eight dead, including two black women. Survivors abandon their property and Rosewood disappears from maps; in 1994, the Florida legislature will compensate the families of the victims.

+ Mississippi is one of the first southern states to elect a woman to its legislature, as Nellie Nugent Somerville, who had been an active suffragist, enters the statehouse. Less than a decade later, her daughter, Lucy Somerville Howorth, will also be elected to the House; Howorth will go on to a government career when Franklin Roosevelt makes her one of the women who implement his New Deal.

+ DuPont Chemical names Elinore Herrick the production manager of a new factory near Nashville, Tennessee. While supporting her family as a factory worker in New York, Herrick has invented several labor-saving and safety devices—the first of which was motivated when her hands were injured by an unsafe machine.

  After earning an economics degree at age 34, Herrick will move on to be the only woman heading a regional office of the National Labor Relations Board during the Great Depression.

+ Baltimore's Rebecca Kohut is elected president of the World Congress of Jewish Women. Since her childhood immigration from Hungary in 1867, she has spent a lifetime in Jewish leadership and is especially recognized for World War I refugee work.

+ Anzia Yezierska publishes *Children of Loneliness*, an autobiographical novel about the children of immigrants. A Jew born in Poland, Yezierska won a prize for the best short story of the year in 1919, and she will go on to considerable fame with other novels in the same genre.

+ At age 31, Edna St. Vincent Millay is the first female poet to win the Pulitzer Prize; it is awarded for her third volume, *The Harp-Weaver and Other Poems*. She will publish more poetry and even a well-received opera libretto, but as her work becomes more political, she is less acclaimed.

+ Clara Bow signs her first film contract and soars to mercurial success. She becomes one of the first movie stars to be idolized by millions, many of whom emulate her short, easy hairstyle. Ultimately, her influence in lessening the time and effort that women spent on maintaining long, heavy hair is more important than Bow's acting career, which is over in a decade.

+ Bessie Smith's first record, "Down Hearted Blues," is a huge success, selling more than 2 million copies. She will go on to sing with the era's great jazz bands, working with both white and black musicians.

+ President Warren Harding, who has a long history of extramarital affairs, dies suddenly in Alaska after eating salmon that is allegedly spoiled. When no one else is sickened and he is buried without an autopsy, some suspect that his wife, Florence Harding, poisoned him. Upon her return to the

White House, she removes and burns many of his papers; she dies the following year at age 64.

1924 Astronomer Annie Jump Cannon, who has been affiliated with the Harvard Observatory since 1884, publishes her observations on 225,000 stars. Unfortunately, the nine volumes are titled the *Henry Draper Catalog*, at the request of the widow who endowed the project.

◆ The University of Chicago begins its School of Social Service Administration, the nation's first such graduate program, with Dr. Edith Abbott as dean. Abbott has particular expertise on immigration; she has published academic books and developed personal experience with Chicago's massive immigrant population. Her students will implement many of the school's progressive ideas in the next decade, when they are among Roosevelt's New Deal reformers. In 1927, *Social Service Review* begins publication with Abbott and Dr. Sophonisba Breckinridge as editors.

◆ Jessie Daniels Ames, who was founding president of the Texas League of Women Voters in 1919, begins a crusade against lynching. She is employed by the Atlanta-based Commission on Interracial Cooperation, and she will travel the South for the next decade, arguing with newspaper editors and public officials about preventing violence and assuring fair trials. It is lonely, dangerous work, and she is often attacked.

◆ The Pulitzer Prize in literature goes to Margaret Wilson for *The Able McLaughlin*. She joins Willa Cather, who won it the previous year, and Edith Wharton, who received the 1921 prize; Edna Ferber will win the following year. More women than men have won the prestigious award since its 1918 beginning: Ernest Poole got the very first award; Booth Tarkington received it twice; and no prize was awarded in 1920.

◆ St. Louis crowds are stunned by Marie Meyer, who stands on the wings of a plane as her husband, Charlie Fowler, pilots between downtown office towers. As Marie Meyer's Flying Circus, she performs daredevil acts, especially at midwest-

ern state fairs, until 1928, when her husband insists that they retire before they die.

◆ At the Olympics, tennis champ Hazel Hotchkiss Wightman wins gold medals for both doubles and mixed doubles. Dubbed the Queen Mother of Tennis, she won her first national tournament in 1909; the last will be in 1954, at age 67. Her record of 44 national championships stands for most of the century.

A graduate of the University of California at Berkeley, she lives most of her life in Massachusetts —where, next year, she will bear the last of five children.

◆ After her husband is crippled by polio and his nascent political career is in jeopardy, Eleanor Roosevelt begins building a network of women who ultimately will vote for him. Among her activities is participation in the League of Women Voters and the Democratic Women's Clubs, both of which are relatively new organizations that she helps develop. In this year's New York gubernatorial election, she organizes women throughout the state for Democrat Al Smith—against her cousin, Republican nominee Theodore Roosevelt Jr.

◆ The first woman to be nominated for national office by a major political party is Marie C. Brehm, a 65-year-old lifelong lecturer for the Women's Christian Temperance Union. She is nominated for vice president of the United States by the Prohibition Party—but because prohibition is national policy since the 1919 passage of the 18th Amendment, the party has no real platform and does not attract as many voters as it has in the past.

◆ At the Republican convention, one of the speakers is Hallie Q. Brown, who is finishing a four-year term as president of the National Association of Colored Women. At age 74 and single all of her life, Brown has been active in integrated organizations, including the Women's Christian Temperance Union and the International Council of Women. She will write the last of several books two years from now, when she publishes a biographical dictionary of black women, *Homespun Heroines and Other Women of Distinction* (1926).

+ In November, New Jersey Democrat Mary T. Norton sets precedents as the first woman elected to Congress from an eastern state, the first Democratic woman, and the first married woman. Her husband stays in New Jersey while she commutes to Washington, D.C., and when he dies a decade later, many of her colleagues are surprised to discover that she was married.

+ In this first presidential election year in which women in all states can run for office, two women—both Democrats—are elected governor: Nellie Tayloe Ross becomes governor of Wyoming and Miriam "Ma" Ferguson is elected in Texas.

Ross wins 20 of 23 counties, and her victory is even more impressive because Wyoming has a strong Republican majority. Many voters clearly ignore party affiliation to vote for her. Termed "the first woman governor" because she is sworn in two weeks earlier than Ferguson, Ross will serve in the state legislature after losing her reelection bid; she loses by less than 1,400 votes, as the electorate returns to party lines.

Ferguson is seen as a surrogate for her husband, a former governor barred from office after a 1917 conviction for corruption. Nonetheless she has to campaign hard and defeats eight male candidates. Because Texas is by far the biggest state to elect a woman, Ferguson will long hold the record as the woman receiving the largest total vote.

+ Republican Edith Nourse Rogers of Massachusetts is chosen secretary of the Electoral College, and she therefore becomes the first woman to announce an official vote for president. After her husband dies the following year, she will take his House seat and go on to establish a record for female longevity in Congress.

1925 After spending her adult life as principal of Washington, D.C.'s most prestigious high school for blacks, Anna Julia Cooper earns a doctorate from the Sorbonne. Born in slavery—probably fathered by her master—she is doubtless the world's best-educated black woman.

Widowed in her youth, she went on to educate herself at Oberlin, Columbia, and finally France's most prestigious university. She has been associated with Washington's public schools most of her life, but Cooper was forced out in the early 20th century, when she went to teach at a black college in Missouri rather than submit to the weakened curriculum that the District of Columbia's board of education proposed for black students.

Her dissertation at the Sorbonne is on French racial attitudes, especially as they played out in the revolt of Haitian slaves against French colonists in the era of Napoleon. The dusty Parisian archives in which she does her research motivate her to publish two other historical works in French.

Dr. Cooper will live on long after retirement. Like her Washington contemporary, Mary Church Terrell, Cooper witnesses the modern civil rights movement, dying in 1964 at age 105.

+ The *New York Times* makes Anne O'Hare McCormick a permanent columnist on politics, where she will write famous profiles on Adolf Hitler, Joseph Stalin, Benito Mussolini, and Winston Churchill that predict the rise of World War II. In 1936, she will become first woman on the *Times* editorial board, and the following year, she is the first female correspondent to win the Pulitzer Prize for journalism.

Liberal Republican Florence Kahn of San Francisco wins a special February election to replace her recently dead husband in Congress; she will go on to win five future elections. The first woman appointed to prestigious committees, including Military Affairs and Appropriations, she is extremely influential in bringing the naval installations to San Francisco Bay that prove vital during World War II. She is the first Jewish woman in Congress, and her first campaign centers on her opposition to prohibition.

+ Although Hawaiian women held powerful governing positions prior to the arrival of whites in the last century, only now is the first woman elected to modern Hawaii's legislature. She is Rosalie Keliinoi, and she concentrates on such activity as the passage of a bill allowing women to retain control of their property after marriage.

✦ Mexican American Ynes Mexia, who has lived most of her 55 years in the Northeast and Canada, goes to Mexico in search of rare plants. During the dozen years of her life that remain, she will develop a solid reputation as a botanist. She travels in dangerous locations from Alaska to the Amazon, returning with thousands of field specimens.

While she specializes in botany, leading ornithologists are also impressed by the new birds that she finds and manages to preserve under difficult tropical conditions. Department of Agriculture and university officials are sufficiently impressed by the work of this aging woman, who lacks a college degree, that they underwrite her explorations, and Harvard's herbarium names a genus for Mexia.

✦ Smith College professor Annie Abel, who earned her Ph.D. at Yale University in 1905, publishes the last of a three-volume study, *The Slaveholding Indians.* Her work is carefully documented though controversial, and it plays a key role in establishing Native American history as an academic field.

✦ The first woman invited to membership in the National Academy of Science is Florence Sabin, a Johns Hopkins professor of medicine since 1902; last year, she was elected as the first female president of the American Association of Anatomists. Dr. Sabin is the discoverer of numerous medical advances, especially in histology and the lymphatic system.

An 1893 Smith College graduate, she published a popular text, *An Atlas of the Medulla and Midbrain* (1901), while still a medical student. Dr. Sabin will "retire" to her childhood home of Colorado in 1938, where she successfully leads a public health crusade. She is active until her death at age 81, and she becomes, for Colorado, one of the two people that each state is allowed to honor with a statue in the nation's capital.

✦ Mary Ware Dennett resigns in protest from the Voluntary Parenthood League after Margaret

Sanger persuades the membership to adopt a more conservative lobbying strategy. Sanger urges the league to lobby for passage of state laws that permit the distribution of information on birth control by physicians only. She argues that this will finally end the organization's struggles with the post office over obscenity, but Dennett strongly believes that it is a step backward from their original feminist and free speech goals.

During the congressional session, Dennett stays at Washington D.C.'s Grace Dodge Hotel and uses the hotel's stationery to write for an appointment with first lady Grace Coolidge. She appeals in personal tones: "Like you, I have a New England background of Republican, Congregational, intellectual ancestry. I went to Miss Capen's school in Northampton"—but her efforts are in vain.

✦ Cartoonist Helen Hokinson is published in the *New Yorker* during the first year of its existence. Her befuddled characters gently satirize the affluent, and she is popular enough to remain with the chic magazine until her 1949 death in a plane crash. Three posthumous volumes of Hokinson's cartoons are then published.

✦ Edna Ferber, who has written historically based novels since 1910, wins the Pulitzer Prize with *So Big*; she follows up with best-sellers *Show Boat* (1926) and *Cimmarron* (1930). *Show Boat* will remain in continuous production as a play throughout the century.

✦ Lulu Hunt Peters sets a precedent by holding the top selling position for a nonfiction title during two consecutive years: *Diet and Health* is the most popular book for both 1924 and 1925.

✦ High infant mortality rates continue to indicate that many mothers are underfed and overworked. In an immigrant area near industrial Pittsburgh, one of every three babies dies; similar rates in the deep South are caused by medical neglect of both black women and poor whites.

✦ The Sisters of the Blessed Sacrament for Indians and Colored People establish Xavier University in

New Orleans. It is the nation's only Catholic college for blacks.

♦ Of 1,688 accredited schools of nursing in the United States, only 54 accept African-American students. Not surprisingly, most of those are affiliated with hospitals serving black communities; Chicago's Provident Hospital and Washington's Freedman's Hospital are especially known for training black nurses.

La Revue Nègre brings African-American dancers to Paris; although the company fails, Josephine Baker of St. Louis goes on to singular success. Known simply as Josephine, she dances with the Folies-Bergère, poses for Picasso, and is celebrated for seminude performances to new jazz sounds.

♦ Pearl Buck, who has lived most of her life in China with her missionary parents, is surprised but pleased to sell her first work to *Asia Magazine*. She is the young mother of a retarded daughter and is in an unhappy marriage; she wrote the article because she was desperate for a new coat. Two years later, the manuscript of her first novel will be destroyed during Chinese rioting against foreigners.

♦ At age 41, Alice Roosevelt Longworth bears her only child. The daughter of Theodore Roosevelt, she has been married almost 20 years. Her 56-year-old husband, a Republican, is now Speaker of the House, and Washington buzzes with rumors that the child cannot possibly be his.

♦ Poet Amy Lowell dies suddenly, only 15 years after the publication of her first sonnet. Called "the leading exponent of the modernist movement" in American poetry, her work is unabashedly that of a woman. Three more volumes of Lowell poetry will be issued posthumously; early this year, she established herself in a new genre with publication of a controversial biography on English poet John Keats.

Lowell's *What's O'Clock* wins the 1926 Pulitzer Prize for poetry after her death. The 1927 honoree is contrastingly obscure: Leonora Speyer will win next year for *Fiddler's Farewell*. Though

Speyer's credentials include the presidency of the Poetry Society of America, she never becomes well known to the public.

1926 Seattle, Washington, is the first major city to elect a woman as mayor. Republican Bertha Landes was elected to City Council in 1921 with the backing of suffragist friends, and while serving as acting mayor in 1924, she fired the police chief. Her victorious campaign for mayor is based on the need to clean up a corrupt police force that ignores vice in exchange for bribes.

♦ The first black female attorney admitted to practice before the U.S. Supreme Court is Violette Neatly Anderson—almost 50 years after the first black male was accorded this privilege in 1880.

Anderson is a graduate of the Chicago Law School, and in 1922, she became the first woman employed as an assistant prosecutor in Chicago. Her colleagues have so much respect for her that she will be elected vice president of the Cook County (Illinois) Bar Association.

♦ Aviator Bessie Coleman, who went to France in 1921 because no flight school in the United States would admit her, is killed in Florida while performing an upside-down stunt. Her French license was the first granted to a black aviator of either gender.

Born in 1892 in east Texas, she grew up with little schooling; her sharecropper mother also took in laundry for a living. In 1915, she went to Chicago, where—like another famous aviator, Jackie Cochran—she trained as a beautician. She saved her money, went to France, and received her license just a decade after the first white women did—and two years prior to Amelia Earhart.

Called Queen Bess, Coleman flew in shows all over the nation, always insisting that airfield audiences be integrated. She moved to Orlando last year, and she is rehearsing for a show sponsored by the Negro Welfare League of Jacksonville when she is killed. Like Harriet Quimby in 1912, Coleman literally falls to her death from the cockpit of her open plane. She is buried in Chicago and largely forgotten until 1995, when the post office issues a stamp in her honor.

+ Selena Sloan Butler founds the National Congress of Colored Parents and Teachers in Atlanta. White and black PTA units do not fully merge until 1970.

+ Interest in the Society of American Indians has dwindled, so Yankton Dakota writer and reformer Gertrude Bonnin organizes a replacement group, the National Council of American Indians. She has succeeded in persuading the General Federation of Women's Clubs to establish an Indian Welfare Committee, but the Great Depression will soon extinguish any hope for profound improvement in life on the nation's reservations. President of the council until her 1938 death, Bonnin is honored with burial in Arlington National Cemetery.

+ Philadelphia artist Cecilia Beaux wins the Gold Medal of the American Academy of Arts and Letters. While most of Beaux's work is portraits, her most famous painting is "The Dancing School." New York's Metropolitan Museum bought one of her portraits in 1915, and by the time of her 1942 death, she is widely exhibited.

+ The American Institute of Architects honors Theodate Pope Riddle with election as a fellow. Riddle practices in Connecticut and New York and is especially known for her restoration of the New York City house where Theodore Roosevelt was born.

+ American Katharine Blodgett is the first woman to earn a doctorate from England's ancient Cambridge University. She will go on to a career with General Electric, and in 1933, her molecular research becomes the basis for the development of nonreflective glass.

+ At age 20, Gertrude Ederle becomes the first woman to swim across the English Channel—and sets a record for speed, besting the male record by almost two hours. A member of America's 1924 Gold Medal Olympic team, Ederle once broke seven swim records in one day.

+ Irita Van Doren, a 1908 graduate of Florida State College for Women, becomes editor of the two-year-old book review supplement of the *New York Herald-Tribune*. In this position, she will influence the opinions of the nation's opinion makers until 1963.

Van Doren is recruited to the paper by Helen Rogers Reid. A Wisconsin native and 1903 Barnard College graduate, Reid worked as a social secretary and then married her employer's son—which eventually will allow her to inherit the *Herald-Tribune*. From 1918 to 1955, Reid actively works at the paper: She not only changes its format to carry more news of interest to women, but also will encourage Dorothy Thompson, Marguerite Higgins, and other outstanding female journalists. When Reid becomes publisher after her husband's 1947 death, the *Herald-Tribune* has more women in significant jobs than any other major newspaper.

+ Cartoonist Fanny Young Cory drops her married name of Cooney when she begins national syndication. Her strips, "Little Miss Muffett" and "Sonnysayings," will run in newspapers until 1956, while she publishes other cartoons in such magazines as *Life* and *Harper's Bazaar*.

+ Dorothy Parker's first book, *Enough Rope*, is a best-selling volume of witty verse with a cynical viewpoint seldom seen among women. She will join the *New Yorker* the following year, where her caustic commentary proves very popular. She also wins the O. Henry short story prize in 1929.

+ Mae West stars in a play that she wrote, daringly titled *Sex*. West will go on to become the first actor to earn $1 million in the movie business, reaching the height of her celebrity after she is 40.

+ *Gentlemen Prefer Blondes* is a tremendous hit for playwright Anita Loos, who becomes so popular that she earns as much as $2,500 a week even during the Great Depression of the next decade.

The play's title is said to be based on Loos' experience with literary critic H.L. Mencken, who joined his male friends in ignoring Loos—a successful writer of screenplays—to focus on an inane blonde.

✦ Theodore Dreiser's *An American Tragedy*, published this year, tracks almost exactly the facts of an actual 1906 case: the body of Grace Brown was dragged from an upstate New York lake that summer, after an overturned boat and the floating straw hat of a man drew attention to a presumed accident. No man's body was found, and an autopsy showed that Brown was pregnant and died from blows to the head, not drowning. Her killer was executed in 1907.

✦ Scarcely a day goes by during the second half of the year that the newspapers do not speak of radio evangelist Aimee Semple McPherson. Age 36, she vanishes from a California beach and, after a monthlong nationally publicized search, surfaces in Mexico claiming that she was kidnapped. No evidence of the alleged criminals can be found, however, and after six months of investigation, Los Angeles officials charge her with filing a false report. A grand jury adds charges of suborning perjury, but just before the case is to be heard, the prosecution drops the charges.

✦ Many women who were active pacifists during the war are now involved in the founding of the American Arbitration Association. As chief executive, Frances Kellor writes an ethical code for arbitrators and educates the public on the use of formal arbitration as a settlement procedure for disputes ranging from the labor/management level to wars between nations.

✦ The Daughters of the American Revolution reinter the bones of Revolutionary War hero Margaret Corbin in honor ceremonies at the U.S. Army's famous West Point Academy.

✦ At age 99, abolitionist teacher Emily Howland receives an honorary degree from the University of the State of New York. During her youth in the 1840s, her family insisted that she return to her rural home from school in Philadelphia because "it was not the thing for a girl to become over-educated."

✦ This congressional election year features Ruth Bryan Owen, daughter of former Democratic presidential nominee William Jennings Bryan, who runs from Florida's east coast. A young widow with four children, Owen had nursed in Egypt during World War I; after her English husband was badly wounded, she took her family to live with her parents in Miami, where both her husband and father soon die.

Her mother plots campaign strategy, and Owen attracts much attention by driving her car through the 500-mile district. Although she loses this race, she will become the first congresswoman from the South in 1928.

✦ In the decade between 1916 and 1926, eight women have been elected to the House of Representatives, only one of whom is a Democrat. With the election this year of Republican Katherine Langley of Kentucky, four women currently serve.

1927　Dancer Isadora Duncan dies in a freak accident in France: when the long scarf that she characteristically wears is caught in the wheel of an open car, her neck is broken.

She recently had given an acclaimed performance in Paris, but her personal life continued to be tragic. After losing three children, she married for the first time at age 44—and her Russian poet husband killed himself soon after. The 1922 tour of Russia on which she met him also brought her much criticism in the United States: even though Russia is known for dance and even though it was an ally in World War I, she toured during the height of America's "Red Scare."

✦ Aviator Blanche Hill, age 25, founds Avion Corporation with John K. Northrup. Their company builds the first all-metal aircraft, an important transformation from the Wright Brothers' wooden model. In 1933, Hill will become the founding president of Northill, an aviation development company that combines her name with Northrup's. An aircraft executive all of her life, she also serves as the founding president of Aeronautical Industry Technical Institute, which is one of the first schools to train aircraft workers.

✦ Twenty-one-year-old Louise Thaden wins the first Woman's Air Derby. Within the decade, she will hold international records for altitude, speed, and endurance, and the public regards her as highly at this time as Amelia Earhart.

✦ The American Mathematical Society invites Bryn Mawr professor Anna Wheeler to present a series of lectures on her research. Dr. Wheeler, who has been widowed twice, is the daughter of Swedish immigrants; she graduated from the University of South Dakota in 1903 and then studied at increasingly prestigious schools, including Germany's Gottingen University, before earning her 1910 doctorate at the University of Chicago.

She lectures on biorthogonal systems of function and their application to integral equations. Far into the 20th century, she will remain the only female mathematician so honored by the American Mathematical Society.

✦ Girl Scout founder Juliette Gordon Low dies. Both Low's executive ability and the popularity of physical activity for young women can be seen in the fact that, in just a decade, the Scouts have grown into an organization with troops in every state.

✦ In far-off Turkey, retired University of Chicago dean Marion Talbot serves the first of two terms as acting president of Constantinople Woman's College. Talbot received two of the earliest degrees granted women at prestigious universities, a B.A. from Boston University in 1880 and a B.S. from MIT in 1888.

✦ Lorena Hickok, whose journalistic credentials include the Sunday editorship of the *Minneapolis Tribune*, is hired by the Associated Press to do political reporting. This eventually leads to a close relationship with Eleanor Roosevelt; Hickok will leave the AP when Franklin Roosevelt takes office because she fears that she cannot report objectively.

Although some women have worked as political reporters since Civil War days, political reporting is still seen as an inappropriate job for a woman. An Associated Press official arrives in Austin intent on congratulating a reporter on his coverage of the Texas legislature—but when he discovers that "R. Baldwin Cowan" is Ruth Baldwin Cowan, he promptly fires her.

✦ Journalist Dorothy Day, a pacifist in World War I who has worked for socialist publications such as *The Call* and *The Masses*, surprises her friends by joining the Catholic church. She does not see this as incompatible with socialism, and will combine the two in an advocacy career that lasts through the Vietnam War.

✦ As jazz and blues become popular with white audiences, an all-black cast featuring Ethel Waters does a Broadway show, *Africana*. Waters had begun singing "St. Louis Blues" in a Baltimore nightclub during World War I; age 17 at the time, she called herself Sweet Mama Stringbean.

✦ Victoria Woodhull, the notorious presidential candidate of 1872, dies at her English estate, where she has lived in luxury since leaving the United States in 1877. She never abandoned her radical ideas, incorporating them into three books and publishing *Humanitarian* magazine from 1892 to 1910.

1928 Amelia Earhart is dubbed "Lady Lindy" when—as logkeeper and standby pilot—she flies with two men from Newfoundland to Wales. Their trip follows that of Charles Lindbergh by a year; Earhart becomes vice president of a new airline company and, at age 31, is globally popular.

✦ When Norwegian explorer Roald Amundsen disappears in the Arctic, Louise Boyd organizes an exhibition to search for him. He is never found by her or any other explorer, but Boyd will be honored by the governments of Norway and France. She will conduct regular Arctic expeditions throughout the 1930s, and in 1955, she again makes the news by flying over the North Pole at age 68.

✦ Although the time to begin a Frontier Nursing Service would seem to be over, people in the Appalachian Mountains still live without electricity, cars, or adequate medical facilities. Mary Breckinridge, a member of a politically historic family who grew up in Washington, D.C., while her father was a congressman from Arkansas, founds the nursing service in Kentucky. After enduring the deaths of both of her children, Breckinridge (who retained her family name despite two marriages) is determined to lower infant mortality rates. The medical network she develops does that within a decade, and it also serves as the impetus for the formation of the American Association of Nurse-Midwives.

✦ The new president of the Society of American Bacteriologists is Alice Evans, a Department of Agriculture employee. The honor is especially meaningful to Evans because she had been greeted with hostility a decade earlier, when she announced her findings on connections between disease in cattle and in humans. Her insistence on the need for pasteurization of milk is an important factor in making that a standard health requirement.

✦ Only three years after graduation from the University of Chicago, educator Eleanor Johnson pitches her idea for *My Weekly Reader* to American Educational Press. The newspaper for elementary schoolchildren is immediately popular, with some 100,000 students reading it in the first year, and it is eventually adopted by almost every school system in the country. Johnson goes on to a lifetime of educational consultantships and becomes the author of dozens of elementary textbooks.

✦ Although she has performed with the New York Philharmonic Orchestra, Philadelphia's Marian Anderson finds most concert halls closed to her because she is African-American. She goes abroad and is soon acclaimed: during the next decade, she will sing at Europe's most famous music festivals and appear before the royalty of several nations, while composer Jean Sibelius writes especially for her voice.

✦ Alice Stone Blackwell publishes the biography of her mother on which she has toiled for four decades, *Lucy Stone, Pioneer of Women's Rights*. Blackwell's political views become more radical with age, and she is an active socialist during this

depression era. She lives on until 1950, still mentally alert at age 93.

✦ The Berkshire History Conference is begun by women who feel excluded in the American Historical Association. While meetings are not necessarily held in the Berkshires, the conference will promote historical scholarship by women throughout the century.

✦ *Bad Girl*, a first book by Vina Delmar, is a big seller, and the next year, she has similar success with *Kept Woman* and *Loose Ladies*. Despite the cynicism of her 1932 title, *Women Live Too Long*, Delmar works well into the 1950s, writing plays and screenplays as well as novels that are issued by prominent publishing houses.

✦ The first Academy Award for Best Actress ever granted goes to 21-year-old Janet Gaynor.

✦ African American Margorite Joyner invents the permanent wave machine, which she uses to curl the hair of white women and to straighten hair for black women. Millions of women will use her invention, and Joyner enjoys appreciable wealth as a result.

✦ Seattle mayor Bertha Landes is endorsed by labor and by the newspapers; her efficient administration has improved the city's coffers and cleaned up corruption—but although prohibition is the law of the land, voters do not truly want a moralist as mayor, and she loses her reelection bid.

✦ While her husband runs successfully for governor of New York, Eleanor Roosevelt heads the national Democratic campaign among women.

✦ Three additional women are elected to Congress this fall, all of whom happen to be named Ruth. Republican Ruth Hanna McCormick, whose youngest child is just four, wins the race to take her recently deceased husband's seat in Congress. After just two months in the House, she announces her candidacy for Illinois' Senate seat in the 1930 election—but she appears far too ambitious to voters and will be swamped by the Democratic nominee.

The election of Republican Ruth Pratt of Manhattan attracts less attention but is more significant: Pratt is only the second woman elected to Congress from the East Coast, and although she married, her political career is not dependent on her husband. As a reform alderman of New York City, she had pushed the building of the Triborough Bridge and the East River tunnel, and in Congress she will adopt such liberal positions as voting against the sugar tariff because farmworkers will not share in the industry's increased profits. She will be reelected in 1930 but loses in the Democratic landslide of 1932.

Ruth Bryan Owen of Miami wins the seat for the East Coast of Florida. She will sponsor two particularly innovative pieces of legislation during her four years in the House: Owen tries to preserve Florida's Everglades from development, and, as a widow and mother of four, she attempts to translate the paeans that her male colleagues regularly make to motherhood into action by creating a cabinet-level Department of Home and Child. Neither will pass.

1929 When Congress convenes, Nebraska-born Ruth Bryan Owen has to argue for her right to be seated, even though her election opponent concedes that she won their Florida race. He belatedly charges that Owen was not eligible to run because, as a woman, she had forfeited her citizenship when she married a noncitizen. Even though her husband is dead and even though this particular injustice against women had been rectified with the 1922 Cable Act, he creatively claims that the seven-year waiting period for citizenship eligibility was not yet over when she filed to run. The House Elections Committee accepts his challenge, but Owen counters his legalisms with an impassioned plea for fairness and democracy and, amid national publicity, is seated. She will be the first Democratic congresswoman to serve on a major committee, Foreign Affairs.

✦ Seven years after postal authorities focused on Mary Ware Dennett's "Sex Side of Life," she is finally prosecuted. She is convicted but refuses to

Jane Addams, who led the founding of the Woman's Peace Party in 1915, continues her efforts for internationalism with this 1923 visit to Japan. Although viewed as a popular goodwill ambassador in the 1920s, Addams had been widely reviled during World War I; donations to Hull House fell dramatically because of her opposition to the war. In 1931, Jane Addams became the first American woman to win the Nobel Peace Prize. University of Illinois at Chicago; The University Library; Jane Addams Memorial Collection

pay the fine, and next year an appellate court upholds her position. The trial gives her efforts in sex education and birth control a great deal of positive coverage, as newspapers throughout the nation argue for her right to free speech. Dennett summarizes her long legal battle with a 1930 book, *Who's Obscene?*

✦ The textile mills of Gastonia, North Carolina, explode into one of the century's most tumultuous strikes, complicated by racism and politics. Women lead the picket lines, and Ella May Wiggins, a mill leader and mother of nine, is killed when vigilantes fire at unarmed strikers.

✦ First lady Lou Henry Hoover creates an international news fracas when she invites Mrs. Oscar De Priest, the wife of a black congressman from

Chicago, to a tea for congressional wives. Although De Priest has every right to be included and although Hoover has carefully selected a subgroup of these wives who would not be offended by the presence of a black woman, there is a huge uproar.

A Washington editorial denounces Hoover for "defiling the White House," and a Mobile paper deems it "an arrogant insult to the South and to the nation" that "has harmed Mr. Hoover to a serious extent." For the first time in history, a state legislature passes a resolution condemning a first lady: several other southern states follow the precedent set in Texas, and even in the North, the New Jersey Senate joins the clamor. In contrast, the Women's International League for Peace and Freedom issues a statement praising Hoover's precedent.

The uproar continues until the president makes a point of backing his wife by inviting a black educator from Alabama's Tuskegee Institute for lunch. Both Hoovers have traveled throughout the world and know people of many races, but the incident causes Lou Henry Hoover to shy away from further publicity. She does, however, establish another first when she makes a radio broadcast from the White House. A longtime Girl Scout activist, her speech emphasizes the importance of both physical and mental activity for girls.

✦ When the National Education Association meets in Atlanta, former Montana congresswoman Jeanette Rankin presents a speech entitled "Teachers and World Peace." She has spent much of her time in Georgia since 1924, when she bought a farm near Athens. Rankin's pacifist activism, however, has brought such negative attention that last year she sued the *Macon Evening News* for libel; she won a $1,000 judgment and a printed retraction.

✦ At age 35, Bess Furman joins the Associated Press and becomes the first woman to report on the House of Representatives for a news syndicate. Retaining her maiden name when she marries, she will pause her career only briefly after bearing twins at age 41. In 1943, she signs on with the *New York Times* and remains in their Washington Bureau for almost 20 years before her 1961 retirement.

✦ As the economy worsens, Maggie Mitchell Walker absorbs several financial institutions serving African Americans into her Richmond Consolidated Bank & Trust. A self-made woman who also built an insurance business, a newspaper, and a retail "emporium," Walker's bank will be one of relatively few black-owned businesses to survive the Great Depression.

✦ A study of 1,500 women who have earned Ph.D.s since 1877 shows generally pessimistic attitudes. Most women have been affected by routine quotas on the number of female professors that colleges hire, and those who do have jobs cite an overload of classes that limits their research and keeps them at lower job titles.

✦ The Sheppard-Towner Act that provides federal funds for maternity clinics is repealed after less than a decade. Male physicians, worried about this competition with their private practices, call the program "Bolshevik," and even some feminists object to the emphasis that the clinics place on infant, rather than maternal, health. Margaret Sanger assails the clinics for teaching "a poor woman how to have her seventh child, when what she wants to know is how to avoid . . . her eighth." The Sheppard-Towner Act will stand as the federal government's only experience with preventive health care for most of the century.

✦ The Ninety-Nines Club, named for its 99 initial members, is made up of women who are licensed pilots. Its first president is Amelia Earhart. By the end of the century, the group will have grown from 99 to some 7,000; it sponsors educational programs on aviation and especially encourages girls to fly.

✦ One of the era's most flamboyant aviators is Californian Pancho Barnes, who changed her name from Florence. This year, she does impressive air stunts in a daringly named movie, *Hell's Angels*; next year, she will set a women's air speed record of almost 200 miles an hour.

◆ At age 28, Margaret Mead earns a doctorate from Columbia, which is the most prestigious university in her field, anthropology. Her *Coming of Age in Samoa*, published the previous year, is on its way to becoming a classic; although she will be widely seen as a genuine leader in her field, she will never receive an academic position equivalent to her credentials. The American Museum of Natural History in New York City finally will give her full curator status in 1964, the same year that Columbia hires her—as an adjunct professor.

◆ Rose Knox of Knox Gelatine Company is the first woman elected to the board of directors of the Grocery Manufacturers' Association. She will head her company until age 90, and her employees demonstrate such loyalty that by 1937, 85% of them have worked there more than 25 years.

◆ Dorothy Eustis has spent the decade breeding German shepherds for intelligence and patience, and she now opens a Nashville school to teach sightless people and the dogs to work together. Emulating a Swiss model, her "seeing eye" school is the nation's first, and it will continue in Morristown, New Jersey, throughout the century.

◆ South Carolinian Julia Peterkin wins the Pulitzer Prize for her third novel, *Scarlet Sister Mary*. Critic H.L. Mencken thinks she is insufficiently grateful for his mentoring, however, and she never recovers from a lack of promotion during the Great Depression. Margaret Ayer Barnes, who wins the 1931 Pulitzer, will suffer the same fate—in contrast to the 1932 winner, Pearl Buck.

◆ Robert and Helen Lynd publish *Middletown*, a study of small-town lifestyles and values that will be a landmark of sociology for decades. Unlike other husband-wife writing teams, both of the Lynds are recognized for their work.

◆ The Daughters of the American Revolution open Constitutional Hall, a magnificent Washington, D.C., headquarters with a 4,000-seat auditorium. Since its 1890 founding, the DAR has been accumulating an unparalleled library of early American writings; eventually it will own over 60,000 books and manuscripts written prior to 1830. With chapters throughout the nation that are named for colonial women, the DAR is an early preserver of women's history.

◆ Standard Oil heir Frances Bolton endows the school of nursing at Western Reserve University with over $2 million. Nursing traditionally was not seen as a subject worthy of university academics, but Bolton has been impressed by nurses since her volunteerism during World War I.

◆ In addition to doing her own prize-winning sculptures during the last two decades, Gertrude Vanderbilt Whitney has also provided studio space for and purchased the work of artists less wealthy than she. This year, she offers to donate the entire collection—as well as a wing in which to house it—to the Metropolitan Museum of Art, which rejects the offer.

Two years later, despite the onset of the Great Depression, she begins the Whitney Museum of American Art in New York. Within the decade, she will also win the last of four honorary degrees from prestigious universities.

◆ An estimated 150 women work in New York City as professional photographers during this decade. Several are employed by major newspapers as staff photographers: Ella Barnett, for example, greets arriving ships to shoot debarking celebrities, while Florence Van Damm specializes in the theater news.

◆ Although women have been riding in rodeos for decades, when Bonnie McCarrol is thrown from a bucking Oregon bronc, breaks her neck, and dies, the public outcry is so great that other western exhibitions begin to refuse to allow women to participate. The coming of the Great Depression further restricts women from such competition.

◆ The stock market crashes in October, sending millions of overextended Americans into bankruptcy. Women will be seriously hurt as the Great Depression sets in, for most Americans agree that available jobs naturally should go to heads of households, who are assumed to be male. Some also believe that the entrance of women into the labor force caused the crash because they took away men's jobs. For the next decade, married women will be fired routinely.

✦ One woman who escapes the fate of many of her male colleagues in the stock market is Rosalind W. Alcott, who began her Wall Street career as a secretary. By disguising her telephone voice to sound male and signing her letters with initials, she played the market to become a millionaire. She sold her portfolio in September, and she will hold on to her money through the Great Depression. After 50 years of retirement in Los Angeles, Alcott is still a millionaire when she dies in 1990 at 104.

1930 The long-term devastation that the Great Depression wreaks on women's economic position can be seen in the fact that the number of women in college faculty/administrative positions peaks this year, at 32%. By 1960, the figure will have dropped to 19%.

✦ The number of women currently serving in the House of Representatives reaches a high of nine. Two are from Arkansas: Pearl Oldfield represents northeast Arkansas while Effiegene Wingo serves the southwest part. Both replace husbands in office but also win elections in their own right. They concentrate on capital projects for their rural districts in an era of both economic depression and natural disaster.

✦ Jessie Daniels Ames leads 26 other white women in founding the Association of Southern Women for the Prevention of Lynching. The ASWPL eventually is endorsed by a dozen Protestant and Jewish groups, and with particular support from Methodist women, it circulates petitions signed by more than 40,000 women and 1,300 law enforcement officials.

Because lynching is closely tied to rape in the minds of most southerners, Ames cites studies showing that only in about one-third of all lynchings is there even an accusation of rape. She tells her audiences that such male violence is not a defense of innocent womanhood but instead fascist political control of both men and women through fear.

✦ One of Ames' associates in the antilynching cause is author Georgia Madden Martin—a married woman who has called herself George since her first publication, in *Harper's Weekly* in 1895. A white woman who lives in Louisville, Martin also works, in vain, to promote the teaching of black history in Kentucky schools. At the same time, she takes other seemingly conservative positions: she opposes legislation such as the Sheppard-Towner Act because she does not want women to depend on the federal government.

✦ With an opening speech by New York Labor Commissioner Frances Perkins, 14 students begin the Vineyard Shore School for Women Workers in Industry, located on the Hudson River about 80 miles north of New York.

Perkins is consistently one of the nation's highest-ranking female governmental officials during her career—but she nonetheless has a running battle with the Mount Holyoke alumni office, which for years tries to "correct" her listing into "Mrs. Paul Wilson."

✦ At age 63, Edith Hamilton publishes her first book. *The Greek Way* examines the contrasts and parallels between life in the modern world and in ancient Greece, and it is widely discussed by people searching for eternal truths in a time of economic disaster. Hamilton will write more books on ancient history, publishing her last at age 90. Acclaimed by both critics and laypeople, her work continues to sell decades after her death.

✦ Gracie Allen and her husband, George Burns, perform their first radio comedy; while his name comes first in "Burns and Allen," it is Gracie who gets the laughs, while George has the straight lines. They are such a hit that CBS gives them their own show two years later, and within a decade, they have 45 million regular listeners and are earning $9,000 a week. Unlike much of the era's comedy, Gracie Allen does not get her laughs at the expense of any minority, and the two provide the nation with comic relief through the depression and the war years beyond.

✦ Gwen Bristow publishes what is later termed "the first real mystery novel," *The Invisible Host*. It grows out of fanciful conversations she and her husband have had about killing a neighbor whose radio is too loud.

✦ When the first of the *Nancy Drew* adventure series aimed at girls is published this year, the author uses the pseudonym Carolyn Keene. Not until late in the century will she reveal her true identity: she is Mildred Augustine Wirt Benson, whose name has changed with two marriages and subsequent widowhood in her native Iowa. At age 87 in 1993, she will still consider herself a working professional writer—she has published more than 120 books—but "so sick of Nancy Drew I could vomit!"

In addition to 30 Nancy Drew books, she does another series this decade called *Ruth Darrow Flying Stories*. They are modeled on amateur aviator Ruth Elder, who, as a 1927 passenger, was the first woman to fly across the Atlantic. The more popular Nancy Drew character, however, grows wholly out of the author's imagination of how, ideally, a girl would want to behave. Despite the immense popularity of her books for decades into the future, the Strantemeyer Syndicate for which she works uses the Great Depression as its justification for paying her a flat rate of only $150 per book.

✦ Cissy Patterson, a member of a publishing family, gives up the life of a socialite and buys the *Washington Herald*, a newspaper that appears moribund in this first year of the Great Depression. In part because she hires female reporters and assigns topics that women find interesting, circulation soars.

Within a decade, Patterson will take over the competing Hearst papers, and by World War II, her *Times-Herald* boasts the largest audience in this most newswise of cities. She multiplies her inherited wealth at least 16 times, and some call her "the most powerful woman in America."

✦ Although the depression makes it extremely difficult for most women to get jobs in academia, Radcliffe graduate Doris Zemurray Stone begins working as an archaeologist and ethnologist with Tulane University's Middle America Research Institute. She remains there until 1941, when she will join the staff of Harvard's Peabody Museum as an expert on prehistoric Central America.

✦ Composer Ruth Crawford wins a Guggenheim Fellowship, a prize that began just five years ago, which enables her to study classical music in Europe. She has been composing since 1923 and completed her master's degree at the American Conservatory in Chicago last year. After her 1932 marriage, she will be known as Ruth Crawford-Seeger; she lives in the Washington, D.C., area and develops a specialty in American folk music with the Library of Congress. Although she continues her classical work and writes *Suite for Wind Quintet* just a year prior to her 1953 death, Crawford-Seeger will be remembered for folk music, especially after her stepson, Pete Seeger, becomes a famous folk singer.

✦ South Dakota's secretary of state, Republican Gladys Pyle, runs unsuccessfully for governor.

✦ One of the most bizarre election situations ever occurs this year: When Republican Katherine Langley won election to Congress in 1926, she replaced her husband—who had been convicted of violation of federal liquor laws. Reelected in 1928, she managed to get President Calvin Coolidge to pardon her husband in exchange for his promise never to run for office again. Without telling her, he violates his word and announces his intention to run for the seat that his wife holds. She refuses to remove her name from the ballot, and both lose to the Democratic nominee.

1931 Democrat Hattie Caraway of Arkansas is the first woman to serve in the U.S. Senate when her husband dies in office and she is appointed to the vacancy. She will, however, go on to establish an independent political career: she will win two close elections and serve in the Senate through the depression and World War II.

✦ Jane Addams is the first American woman to win the Nobel Peace Prize. She donates her prize money—more than $16,000—to the Women's

International League for Peace and Freedom, of which she is president for the remainder of her life.

✦ As Americans become increasingly disillusioned with the results of World War I, the League of Women Voters sends 6,000 petitions to the International Disarmament Conference.

✦ Pearl Buck's second book, *The Good Earth*, sets success records. It wins the Pulitzer Prize, is translated into dozens of languages, and is made into an award-winning film. Immediately famous, Buck writes almost a book a year for the rest of the decade, while also divorcing her husband and marrying her publisher. All of her work is based in Asia, where she travels extensively because she fears that foreigners will soon be banned.

✦ Dorothy Thompson, a young journalist on assignment in Europe, interviews Adolf Hitler; she publishes a book warning of the danger he represents and is expelled from Germany as a result. By the end of the decade, over 170 newspapers will publish Thompson's columns, which are syndicated by the *New York Herald-Tribune*. Her reputation will be eclipsed, however, by that of her second husband, Nobel novelist Sinclair Lewis—while his alcoholism and debts distract her from her own work.

✦ Historian Mary Beard publishes the first of three uncommon books in this decade: *Understanding Women* (1931), *America Through Women's Eyes* (1933), and *Laughing Their Way: Women's Humor in America* (1934). She also works on creating a World Center for Women's Archives, but meets with little success during this depression era.

✦ Although they never become as famous as Fannie Farmer and Julia Child, the mother-daughter team of Irma Starkloff Rombauer and Marion Rombauer Becker rank as giants of American culinary history. Their *Joy of Cooking*, first issued this year, will sell millions of copies; it remains in print throughout the century.

✦ The National Air Race opens to women—but when Phoebe Omlie wins $12,000 and a new car for her first-place finish, women soon will be declared ineligible again. Omlie is already the two-time winner of the Powder Puff Derby, which began in 1929 and will continue throughout the century.

✦ African-American teenager Billie Holiday is dancing in a nightclub to support her sickly mother when she discovers that she can earn more tips by singing. She will cut her first records in 1933, and after her debut at Harlem's famed Apollo Theater, she becomes the era's outstanding female jazz singer.

✦ Although African-American blues pioneer Bessie Smith has made 150 records, some of which have sold as many as 100,000 copies a week, Columbia Records does not renew her contract, allegedly because of her alcoholism.

✦ Congress officially adopts "The Star-Spangled Banner" as the national anthem, over objections from those who prefer Katherine Bates' "America the Beautiful."

"God Bless America" becomes synonymous with Kate Smith, who this year sings the first of some 15,000 radio shows that make her one of the most popular figures of the 1930s and 1940s.

✦ The 27 Broadway producers who turned down *The Barretts of Wimpole Street* are chagrined when the play, which is based on the life of English poet Elizabeth Barrett, earns a healthy profit for producer Katherine Cornell, who also performs the leading role. More than a decade later, the play is popular enough to tour for soldiers in World War II.

1932 Democrat Hattie Caraway of Arkansas becomes the first woman to preside over the U.S. Senate, and she uses the occasion to announce her intention to run for a full term. Many scoff at her chances for winning, but in the fall, she defeats seven men, including a former governor and a former senator.

Her campaign stresses her support for the proposed New Deal reforms, and she also receives strong support from World War I veterans who appreciate the help she gave them when the

Hoover administration sent troops to oppose a veterans' demonstration in Washington.

Representative Pearl Oldfield still serves in the House, and Arkansas thus becomes the first state to have women in both branches of Congress.

+ Amelia Earhart reaches the height of fame when she becomes the first woman to solo across the Atlantic. She flies a Lockheed monoplane, and her trip from Newfoundland to Ireland takes 15 hours during the night of May 21 and 22. Congress honors her with the Distinguished Flying Cross, and France gives her its Legion of Honor.

+ Far less attention is given to Ruth Rowland Nichols, who becomes the first female pilot of a regularly scheduled airline. She flies between New England and New York.

+ In June, Willa Eslick of Tennessee is listening to her husband's speech when he falls and dies on the House floor. She defeats three men to replace him in Congress, but legal technicalities prevent her from running for a full term.

+ At age 65, Laura Ingalls Wilder publishes *The Little House in the Big Woods*, the first of a series of books based on her youth during the pioneer days of the Midwest. It touches the heartstrings of readers who remember simpler times and sells extremely well, although it comes out at the depression's low point. Wilder goes on to write a half-dozen more books in the series, the most popular of which is *Little House on the Prairie* (1935).

+ Ellen Browning Scripps dies. An active writer and publisher, she also invested wisely: Her original inheritance multiplied more than 40 times during the building of the newspaper chain that retains her family name today. Among the projects she endowed is Scripps College, founded in 1925 as a liberal arts institute for women in the college town of Claremont, California.

+ Americans are cheered by the success of 19-year-old swimmer Helene Madison at the Olympics, where she wins three gold medals. She also sets an astonishing number of other sports records this year, including winning all of the world's freestyle swimming categories for women.

+ Katharine Hepburn wins her first Academy Award for her performance in *Morning Glory;* she will make at least a movie a year during the rest of the depression decade. The women she portrays include a number of historical figures, and in 1936, she stars in *A Woman Rebels*, which features a Victorian girl who grows up to join the English women's rights movement.

+ The Chicago Symphony Orchestra sets a precedent by being the first major symphony to perform a work written by a black women. *Symphony in E Minor* is a prize-winning composition by Florence Price, a 1906 graduate of the New England Conservatory of Music. Price grew up in Arkansas and began to compose after marriage and motherhood. Her works will be performed frequently in this decade and the next, and she is considered the first successful black female composer of classical music. She also writes songs; one suite, "Songs to a Dark Virgin," is especially popularized by Marian Anderson.

+ German psychiatrist Karen Horney immigrates to the United States. She has practiced psychiatry since receiving her medical degree from the University of Berlin in 1911, and Dr. Horney presciently foresees the danger of fascism to intellectuals. Especially with her *New Ways in Psychoanalysis* (1939), she will become the first prominent psychiatrist to challenge Freudian ideas on women.

+ Republican Alice Roosevelt Longworth unsuccessfully campaigns against her distant cousin Franklin Roosevelt. She is a first cousin of Eleanor Roosevelt and has considered her a rival since childhood, when the orphaned and painfully lonely Eleanor drew sympathy from their mutual relatives.

Both women lost their mothers when they were young, but they developed very different personalities and political ideas. While Eleanor will become the era's most serious crusader for the dispossessed, Alice enjoys decades of popularity with caustic newspaper editors who count on her for witty but cutting quotes on anyone or anything unfashionable.

✦ Women play their first major roles at significant internal levels of presidential campaigning, as the Roosevelt team includes such experienced New York politicos as Molly Dewson and Frances Perkins. Eleanor Roosevelt campaigns nationwide for her husband, whose paralyzed legs limit his mobility. Republican denial about the depth of the depression results in great Democratic victory, and the landslide will be further validated in the 1936, when Roosevelt loses only 8 of 531 electoral votes.

✦ Miriam "Ma" Ferguson is again elected governor of Texas, after losing her 1926 reelection bid. The state Supreme Court sides with her when the incumbent challenges the vote count, and her second term will be considered a success. Among other accomplishments, she convinces the legislature to pass a tax on oil for the benefit of schools. Feeling that she finally has overcome the charges of corruption that have plagued the populist Fergusons all of their political lives, she does not seek reelection.

✦ While many women are pressured into surrendering their jobs to men in the nadir of the Great Depression, others are able to win the political plums of congressional seats against male candidates. Isabella Greenway of Arizona, a lifelong friend of Eleanor Roosevelt, wins at the same time that Franklin Roosevelt does; Kathryn O'Laughlin defeats a Kansas incumbent; and Virginia Jenckes of Indiana outruns two incumbents. All of the women are Democrats.

1933   Frances Perkins takes the oath of office as secretary of labor on the same day that Franklin Roosevelt is sworn in as president. The first female member of the cabinet, she will be one of just two cabinet members to serve during Roosevelt's entire presidency; she will lead the nation's working class through the Great Depression and World War II.

Perkins becomes one of the most important cabinet members of all time, for under her leadership, the nation gains the basics of the modern economy: Social Security, minimum wages and maximum hours, unemployment compensation, and the abolition of child labor are among the major changes she implements. Given organized labor's resistance to having a woman in its top position and her private difficulties with her mentally ill husband, Frances Perkins' political and economic success will be little short of spectacular.

✦ Franklin Roosevelt grants more high positions to women than any previous president, and many of the appointments come via recommendations from Molly Dewson. The first female political party operative with genuine White House access, she managed aspects of both Roosevelt's gubernatorial campaign and Al Smith's 1928 presidential campaign.

From the Democratic Party's headquarters, Dewson will implement campaign seminars that are taken by some 100,000 women. She successfully pushes for the "equal division" principle that brings both men and women as delegates to nominating conventions, and mandates that they share chairman/vice chairmanships in the local party units.

✦ Ruth Bryan Owen makes diplomatic history when she is appointed by President Roosevelt as minister to Denmark. When she marries a Dane in 1936, however, the State Department belatedly discovers that Danish law will not allow a woman married to a Danish citizen to retain the position.

✦ Nellie Tayloe Ross, former governor of Wyoming, becomes the first woman to head the U.S. Mint. She is a Democrat in a Republican state, and Roosevelt thus promotes her career. Ross heads the mint through the Great Depression, World War II, and beyond, when President Truman reappoints her. She will oversee the construction of the Fort Knox gold vault and deal with a serious paper shortage during the war.

✦ Dr. Grace Langdon is appointed Child Care Director of the Works Projects Administration, and during the next few years, she conducts the bureaucratic miracle of setting up some 2,000 publicly funded child care centers, with at least one in every state. The aim is to allow poor women to work at the low wages that the depressed economy offers, without having to bear additional expense for child care.

◆ President Roosevelt appoints Mary Anderson, the longtime head of the Women's Bureau of the Department of Labor, as head of the U.S. delegation to the International Labor Organization, over the objections of Labor Secretary Frances Perkins.

◆ Driving an old jalopy, former journalist Lorena Hickok roams through the country for the next three years, anonymously checking on the delivery of New Deal services for the Roosevelt administration. She pays particular notice to unemployed professionals, who find themselves in the embarrassing position of having to accept government aid. Long after Hickok is dead, her letters to Washington will be published as *One Third of a Nation: Lorena Hickok Reports on the Great Depression* (1981).

◆ The Women's Work Division of the Federal Emergency Relief Administration is headed by Ellen Woodward, who daily receives some of the thousands of letters Eleanor Roosevelt gets from women desperate for employment.

◆ The first lady receives unprecedented amounts of mail, much of it in response to the fact that Eleanor Roosevelt is the first to conduct regular press conferences—these are a real boon to female journalists, who often scoop their male competitors on White House stories.

Eleanor Roosevelt also receives more hate mail than any previous first lady—but even that gets a polite response. Roosevelt's empathy for blacks, whose plight she publicizes, is often the impetus for the hate mail. She risks the Democrats' "Solid South" by inviting blacks to the White House, and later causes a national stir when she sits in the middle of the aisle in a segregated Birmingham hall rather than choose between the white and black sides.

◆ Washington educator Nannie Burroughs writes candidly of the inferior position of black women: "Stop making slaves and servants of our women. . . . The Negro mother is doing it all. The women are carrying the burden. . . . The men ought to get down on their knees to the Negro women. They've made possible all we have. . . ."

◆ The monthly *Catholic Worker* begins with socialist Dorothy Day as editor and publisher. Despite depression poverty, 150,000 subscriptions are sold within the first three years.

◆ Gertrude Stein, an American who has lived in France since 1902, publishes the most famous of her cleverly abstract and deceptively titled books, *The Autobiography of Alice B. Toklas*. Toklas, also an American, is Stein's lesbian companion; the two remain in France through both world wars, where their salon provides an important network for avant garde painters and writers.

◆ At age 69, Frances Benjamin Johnston wins a Carnegie grant to photographically record southern architecture. The 7,000 pictures in this series will be just part of the treasure that Johnston donates to the Library of Congress prior to her death in New Orleans in 1952. She began her great American photo album in the 1880s.

◆ When her novel *The Promenade Deck* is a success, Ishbel Ross retires from the *New York Herald-Tribune*, where she has been a reporter since 1918. She soon switches from fiction to biography, and her name will become especially familiar to students of women's history. Ishbel Ross will publish more than 20 nonfiction books, most of them biographies of first ladies or of women such as Elizabeth Blackwell and Clara Barton. She also writes widely in popular magazines, and she will still be writing when she dies in 1975 at age 79.

◆ Hollywood's best-known female producer is Dorothy Arzner. The drama she produces this year, *Christopher Strong*, features Katharine Hepburn as a determined aviator. It will come to be seen as a feminist classic, but the depths of the

Great Depression is not a propitious time for Arzner's innovative ideas.

✦ The times are right for nostalgic remembrance of the sturdy virtues of an earlier era, and Rose Wilder Lane publishes her most successful book, *Let the Hurricane Roar*, which is based on her pioneer Dakota childhood. She is the daughter of Laura Ingalls Wilder, whose reminiscence of frontier Wisconsin, *Little House in the Big Woods*, was published last year. The mother's work will sell better than the daughter's, and Lane will act as Wilder's agent as the popular *Little House* series continues.

✦ Six months after resigning from New Jersey College for Women—where she has served as the founding president in all but title—Mabel Smith Douglass rows out on a lake and never returns. A widow who has lost a son to suicide, she is 56.

In 1955, New Jersey will rename the college for her, and in 1963, her body is finally discovered. It appears that her death was also a suicide.

✦ Prize-winning poet Sara Teasdale commits suicide by drug overdose after a long depression. Her critically acclaimed *Strange Victory* is published posthumously.

✦ The Institute for Advanced Study, where Albert Einstein and other great thinkers will work, opens in Princeton, New Jersey, with an endowment from Carrie Frank Fuld. She and her family built a successful retail chain that they sold to Macy's just before the depression hit.

✦ Divorce rates fall during the Great Depression. Although the era is more politically liberal than the Roaring '20s, it is socially more conservative. In addition, couples simply cannot afford the court costs of divorce.

At the same time, the effectiveness of Margaret Sanger, Mary Ware Dennett, and other birth control crusaders is evident in the birth rate, which falls steadily throughout the depression. As economic conditions make having large families more difficult, women are clearly exercising control over their reproductive functions.

A longtime donor to Sanger's birth control crusade, incidentally, is Katharine Houghton Hepburn, the mother of Katharine Hepburn. Both grew up in the central New York town of Corning at the same time, but they did not know each other then: Sanger was one of 11 children in the poor Irish Higgins family, and they lived across the tracks from the Houghtons, who owned Corning Glass.

✦ In December, the final steps are taken to repeal the Prohibition amendment to the Constitution that was adopted in January, 1920. Although millions of voteless women supported this amendment in the 19th and early 20th centuries, it is clear that "The Great Experiment" has failed, and few women use their new voting rights to oppose repeal.

1934 President Franklin Roosevelt's appointment of Ohio's Justice Florence Allen to the U.S. Court of Appeals is the highest-ranking judicial appointment yet granted to a woman. Allen will serve at this level, which is just below the Supreme Court, until retirement.

✦ In contrast, Roosevelt's attorney general, Homer S. Cummins, rules that government agencies may exclude women by classifying particular federal jobs as suitable for men only. Beyond that, Section 213 of the National Economy Act provides for the actual firing of female federal employees if they are married. Much of the public supports this view, as during the Great Depression jobs—especially government jobs—are increasingly seen as a sort of charity to be dispensed on the basis of need, not merit.

The national convention of the League of Women Voters, meeting in Boston, strongly disagrees. Legislative chair Marguerite Wells of Minneapolis says: "Women fully qualified for specific work have been dismissed for the sole reason that they were married. We believe that merit is the . . . principal qualification for government service, and that marital status should have no weight in the dismissal of persons. . . . A man is never dismissed from a position for which he is qualified as soon as he takes the marriage vows."

No stamp related to women has been issued since 1907. This year's tribute is "Mothers of America," which features James Whistler's famous yet much lampooned portrait of his mother.

Photographer Dorothea Lange mounts an exhibition on the unemployed, and the traumatized expressions on the faces of white-collar men draw particular attention. Lange is hired by the federal Farm Security Administration to document the condition of farmworkers, and the photographs she produces join with John Steinbeck's *Grapes of Wrath* to shock the nation's conscience.

Although she does not become as famous as Lange, young Esther Bubley will also take dramatic pictures for the Farm Security Administration and its bureaucratic successor, the Office of War Information. Like Margaret Bourke-White, Bubley also goes on to shoot for *Life* magazine. She turns the mundane into the lively; when assigned to Standard Oil sites in Texas, for example, she takes empathetic pictures of the forlorn lives of oilworkers' wives.

News stories headline the May 23 shootout in rural Louisiana that kills Bonnie and Clyde, an unmarried couple who have terrorized Texas during recent years.

Bonnie Parker was a Dallas waitress when she met Clyde Barrow. Declaring herself to be "bored crapless," she helped him escape from a Waco jail, and they took off on a spree of bank robberies in which a number of people, including law enforcement officials, have been killed. Bonnie ensured publicity by sending newspaper editors pictures of herself in brazen poses as well as sentimental poems that she wrote. At age 23, she is dead.

Reporter Genevieve Forbes Herrick, whose stories—including an exclusive interview with gangster Al Capone—have been featured by *Chicago Tribune* since she joined the paper in 1918, is forced to resign. The strongly anti-Roosevelt *Tribune* does not approve of her friendship with Eleanor Roosevelt, and no other paper values this contact enough to offer her a comparable job. Herrick struggles until World War II, when she heads the magazine and book division of the Office of War Information.

President Roosevelt appoints Grace Abbott to the Council on Economic Security, where she helps plan the implementation of Social Security; in 1935, he will appoint her as a representative to the International Labor Organization.

The director of the federal Children's Bureau since 1921, Abbott also was president of the National Conference of Social Work, and, despite America's failure to join the League of Nations, she served as an unofficial member of the league's Advisory Committee on Traffic in Women and Children.

The American Association of Schools of Social Work elects Sophonisba Breckinridge president. During her three decades as a University of Chicago social scientist, Dr. Breckinridge has trained many of those who implement Franklin Roosevelt's New Deal.

Anne Morrow Lindbergh is awarded the National Geographic Society's Gold Medal. She has co-piloted with her aviator husband, Charles Lindbergh, on a six-month trip that took them over the North Pole; her book on this, *North to the Orient*, will be a best-seller next year. A published author at age 23 while still single, Lindbergh will continue to write the rest of her life.

In Paris, the Legion d'Honneur is conferred on Therese Bonney for her work on cultural exchange between the United States and France, and especially for the exhibition she does this year to commemorate the 100 years since the death of American Revolutionary War hero the marquis de Lafayette.

A native of Syracuse, New York, Bonney studied at the University of California, Harvard, and Columbia before earning her doctorate at the Sorbonne. She runs an innovative news project in Paris called the Bonney Service, which distributes American press items to more than 30 foreign countries. This is the first of the honors she will win.

◆ Evangeline Booth, who became an American citizen in 1923, ousts her brother to be elected commanding general of the Salvation Army throughout the world. She moves back to London to direct the organization's activities in 80 countries but will retire to suburban New York five years later.

◆ Columbia University anthropologist Ruth Benedict publishes *Patterns of Culture*, which introduces the public to cultural relativism. Translated into more than a dozen languages, the book become a classic social science text. It marks only the beginning of Benedict's contributions to modern anthropology.

◆ Lillian Hellman's first play, *The Children's Hour*, is a tremendous success, winning the annual Drama Critics Circle award only three weeks after opening. Much reproduced since, it will be made into a film titled *Dark Angel*. Hellman's subject is a daring one, for the play, based on an actual case, shows how two teachers are destroyed by insinuations of lesbianism.

◆ The Pulitzer Prize goes to Caroline Miller for *Lamb in His Bosom*, a novel about pioneer life in South Georgia. A decade will pass before her second novel, *Lebanon* (1944), comes out; although she lives more than 50 years longer, Caroline Miller Ray never publishes again.

◆ Fannie Hurst's *Imitation of Life* is made into a movie; a second version in 1959 is even more successful. It is the story of a young biracial woman who passes for white, and especially the poignant scenes with her black mother cause many to think seriously about racism.

Hurst, who also befriends young African-American writer Zora Neale Hurston, will go on to be considered the nation's highest-paid writer in the next decade. She writes both fiction and nonfiction, features women, and sells well.

◆ Edith Wharton, the author of more than 50 books of fiction and nonfiction, is elected to the American Academy of Arts and Letters. She has lived in France since 1910.

◆ *Tender Is the Night* is F. Scott Fitzgerald's fictionalization of his wife's mental illness, literally based on Zelda Fitzgerald's hospital file. In the 1920s, Scott and Zelda—widely known by their first names—styled themselves as the personification of the indulgent Jazz Age. Although a probable genius in her own right, Zelda subordinated her work to his, and when the sophisticated world of the Lost Generation gives way to the realities of the Great Depression, both suffer from alcoholism and mental breakdown. Scott will die in 1940, and Zelda's life ends tragically in a 1947 fire at a North Carolina sanitarium.

◆ Thirty-five years after her graduation from Woman's Medical College of Pennsylvania, Lillie Rosa Minoka-Hill receives her medical license from Wisconsin. The daughter of a Mohawk mother and a Quaker physician and the widow of an Oneida man, she bore six children in nine years after her 1905 marriage, and then supported the family by practicing medicine after her husband's 1916 death. While she ministers especially to poor Oneida living on reservation land, Minoka-Hill is so respected by other physicians that some advance her the $100 fee to take the state licensing examination, which will enable her patients to obtain reimbursement from Federal Relief funds.

◆ Mine worker organizer Mother Jones dies six months after being honored on her 100th birthday. She is buried with miners after a requiem mass, for despite her political radicalism, she maintained many of the conservatisms of her Irish Catholic heritage. Her 1925 autobiography made it clear that she believes men should earn enough to maintain women in their proper place at home.

◆ In the fall elections, Eleanor Roosevelt campaigns for her friend Carolyn O'Day, who defeats 10 others to win New York City's at-large congressional seat. O'Day has a long history of labor and feminist leadership and has chaired the school board in Rye, New York. She will serve in Congress until shortly before her 1943 death, actively pushing New Deal reforms.

1935 The first high-level government position for a black woman goes to Florida's Mary McLeod Bethune, whom President Franklin Roosevelt appoints to head the Office of Minority Affairs of the National Youth Administration.

The depression-era agency specializes in job training and job creation, and Bethune will travel around the nation working not only for young African Americans but also for Mexican and Native Americans. Her home becomes the gathering place for Roosevelt's unofficial "Black Cabinet," most members of which are male.

✦ Several organizations merge into the National Council of Negro Women; they elect Mary McLeod Bethune president and she serves until 1949. With a Washington, D.C., headquarters, the NCNW soon has some 800,000 members who focus on job opportunity during the depression. Other goals include ending the poll tax, passing fair employment laws, and ensuring a place for black women in the military.

✦ "Ma" Barker is killed in a machine-gun shootout with federal authorities while hiding in Oklawaha, Florida. The acknowledged brains behind a $3 million series of bank robberies in the Midwest, Barker dominates her three adult sons. Besides sending them to rob banks, she insists that they attend church. To the public, such criminal behavior in a woman is so unusual that she is featured in the media for years.

✦ Dorothy and DuBose Heyward turn their stage play into a libretto for George Gershwin's uniquely American folk opera, *Porgy and Bess*.

✦ Bette Davis wins her first Academy Award for *Dangerous*; she will receive a second three years later with *Jezebel*.

✦ Newspapers are filled with the story of the custody fight over little Gloria Vanderbilt. Her aunt, famed sculptor and art patron Gertrude Vanderbilt Whitney, denounces her mother, Gloria Morgan Vanderbilt, as an unfit parent. Because Whitney has lived all of her life in the art world, which is perceived as hedonistic, the court is inclined to take her charges of immorality especially seriously, and the mother loses her child.

✦ Photographer Berenice Abbott does a series of pictures of New York that brings her fame and adds to the identification of photography as an art form; her project is funded by the New Deal's Works Progress Administration. In the 1940s, she teaches photography to Diane Arbus, who becomes known for avant garde work later in the century.

✦ The year's Pulitzer Prize for poetry goes to Audrey Wurdemann; the honoree for 1937, Marya Zaturenska, will be equally unpublicized. Between them will be Robert Frost, who will win the third of his four Pulitzers.

✦ The Federal Writers' Project is a depression-era agency that offers work and vital hope to unemployed writers. One of the few states in which this agency is headed by a woman is Florida, where Carita Doggett Corse does an exceptionally good job of using the project to document minority history. Her writers conduct numerous interviews with elderly blacks who lived in slavery, thus creating invaluable histories of illiterate people.

A native of the Jacksonville area and a 1909 Vassar graduate, Corse will direct the state's Planned Parenthood when the depression ends.

✦ With her gender disguised as "S.F. Porter," Sylvia Feldman Porter begins a column on financial issues that eventually reaches 40 million readers a day. Not yet 22, she will write her column for more than a half-century; when she dies in 1993, she is still writing for 450 newspapers and has published 30 books on money management.

A native New Yorker, she married a year prior to her 1932 graduation from Hunter College, where she switched from English to finance, in part because of "an overwhelming curiosity" about the causes of the Great Depression. She persuades the *New York Post* to give her a chance at writing a column by "S.F. Porter"—because, as she says, "I wanted to prevent any readers from knowing a girl was writing [on] finance."

✦ A month prior to her death, retired president M. Carey Thomas speaks at the 50th anniversary of the founding of Bryn Mawr. She reminds students of her youth: "I had never known a woman who had gone to college nor seen anyone who had seen a woman who had gone to college."

1936   The U.S. Post Office issues its first stamp that honors an American woman of genuine achievement. Susan B. Anthony is recognized with a stamp on the 30th anniversary of her death.

The 3-cent stamp is a commonly used denomination that will be reissued in 1955.

✦ For the year between January 1936 and January 1937, the nation has two women in the U.S. Senate, as Rose McConnell Long of Louisiana joins Hattie Caraway of Arkansas. Long is appointed to the vacancy created by the assassination of her husband, Huey Long, and she goes on to win a special election in April. Unlike Caraway, however, Long will decline to establish a political career and does not run for a full term.

As many as 2,000 people an hour filed past the casket of Jane Addams during a two-day memorial at Chicago's Hull House. Although Addams is remembered largely as the founder of the immigrant settlement house movement, she was also the lifelong president of an organization still seen as radical near the century's end, the Women's International League for Peace and Freedom.   University of Illinois at Chicago; The University Library; Jane Addams Memorial Collection; Wallace Kirkland Papers

◆ Margaret Sanger finally wins a long series of court cases with a ruling that says, in effect, that birth control and obscenity are not synonymous and that bans on obscenity do not imply bans on pregnancy prevention. Physicians in most states begin to import contraceptive materials and prescribe their use.

◆ *Gone with the Wind* is published, despite second thoughts by its author, Atlanta socialite Margaret Mitchell, who had changed her mind after allowing a Macmillan publisher see her incomplete, much-rewritten, nine-year-old manuscript. Neither its daunting 1,000-plus pages nor Great Depression poverty prevents the book from setting a number of best-seller records, including the most books sold in a single day.

Mitchell will win the Pulitzer Prize for fiction next year. Her long-term success will present a sharp contrast to last year's winner, Josephine Johnson, who quickly becomes obscure.

◆ A new magazine named *Life* appears that soon takes photojournalism to unprecedented heights —and the picture on its first cover is by young Margaret Bourke-White, who fashioned that name by combining her maiden name with her mother's maiden name. A 1927 Cornell graduate, Bourke-White quickly became recognized as an industrial photographer; she was hired by *Fortune* magazine in 1929 and published a 1931 photo book on the Soviet Union. Next year, she will publish the most famous of several books that she does with writer Erskine Caldwell; *Have You Seen Their Faces?* photographically documents the pain of the Great Depression.

◆ Flying a light plane, geographer Gloria Hollister Anable finds 43 previously unmapped waterfalls, including some of the world's highest, in the South American country of British Guiana. A fellow of the New York Zoological Society, she set the woman's record for depth of descent in the ocean in 1931.

◆ Publisher Blanche Knopf predicts the cultural consequences of rising fascism. "There is not a German writer left in Germany who is worth thinking about," she says. "The gifted writers and enterprising publishers" are leaving, and she welcomes many to her publishing house. Her astuteness leads to such profitable acquisitions as William L. Shirer's *Berlin Diary* (1941), which earns the house $1,500,000 in its first year. She also recruits the work of Nobel winners Sigrid Undset and Simone de Beauvoir.

◆ The French award the Legion d'Honneur to American-born bibliophile Sylvia Beach. The medal is primarily for her courageous 1922 publication of James Joyce's *Ulysses*, which had been banned as obscene. Beach painstakingly edited his nearly unreadable manuscript and printed the first volumes at her own expense; for many years, the book was available only at her Paris bookstore.

In 1941, Beach will close the store and hide its books rather than risk Nazi confiscation—but she is arrested anyway and imprisoned for much of 1943.

◆ Democrat Franklin Roosevelt appoints Eleanor Dulles as director of financial research for the Social Security Board, despite her prominent Republican family. Herself a Republican and a 1917 Bryn Mawr graduate, she has earned a 1926 Ph.D. in economics from Harvard/Radcliffe, published five books on international finance, and taught at the prestigious Wharton School of Economics.

◆ The League of Women Voters broadcasts its Cincinnati convention on radio. Hundreds of simultaneous meetings are held, and leaguers circulate a half-million petition cards for equity in civil service jobs.

◆ *The Women* by playwright Clare Booth Luce is too feminist for depression-era stages; it will do better decades later, after a 1973 revival. Luce, however, already has other literary achievements, for even prior to her 1935 marriage to Time-Life publisher Henry Luce, she was an author and held top editorial positions with *Vogue* and *Vanity Fair* magazines.

◆ Although western states accounted for three of the first five women in Congress, the region has been slow to add to that record. Democrat Nan

Wood Honeyman of Oregon defeats Republican and Independent men to win this year, but she will lose a close reelection race. Representative Honeyman attended finishing school with Eleanor Roosevelt, and her constituents vacillate between appreciating and resenting this connection.

✦ When President Roosevelt opens the Inter-American Conference for Maintenance of Peace in December, the only woman in the delegation to Buenos Aires is Elise Furer Musser. She is an officer of the Democratic Women's Clubs and a former Utah state senator. Like many other Utah women, she was born abroad and emigrated after converting to Mormonism; Senator Musser moved to the United States in 1897 from Switzerland, which makes her a particularly apt choice for peace negotiations.

✦ The world is stunned when British King Edward VIII gives up the throne in December to, as he says, "marry the woman I love." Baltimore socialite Wallis Warfield Simpson cannot become queen because she has divorced twice. Except for World War II, when they go to the Bahamas, they will enjoy a leisurely life in France as the Duke and Duchess of Windsor.

1937 Amelia Earhart disappears. In her "Flying Laboratory," she had set out from Miami on June 1, accompanied by one man on a highly publicized flight around the world. All goes well for the first month, but on July 2, radio contact ceases while they fly a 2,500-mile leg between New Guinea and a tiny Pacific island where Earhart planned to land. No compelling evidence of what happened is ever found, and the Amelia Earhart mystery becomes part of American lore.

✦ Representative Mary T. Norton of New Jersey chairs the House Labor Committee and thus plays a strong role in the New Deal employment legislation that becomes the basis of the modern economy. By World War II, when defense industry labor proves vital to victory, she is a key member of Congress. Norton also provides leadership for working women: she sponsors an equal

pay bill and works for government-funded child care.

✦ Alabama's governor is widely criticized when he appoints his wife, Dixie Bibb Graves, to a vacancy in the U.S. Senate. Senator Graves is herself criticized when she speaks against an antilynching bill as an invasion of states' rights. Hers is not a minority opinion, however, and the proposed federal law to ban lynching does not pass.

✦ In Fairfield, Connecticut, 32-year-old Margaret Rudkin begins Pepperidge Farms, specializing in bread that she sells at more than twice the standard price. Its quality is so extraordinary that demand is instant, and she hires a staff of female bakers. Like Rose Knox of the gelatin business, Rudkin not only sets the standard for her field, but also demonstrates the efficacy of paying good wages, benefits, and bonuses. Her multimillion-dollar success makes her a perfect model for Harvard Business School, where Rudkin lectures occasionally until her death 30 years later.

✦ Freda Kirchwey rises to publisher at *The Nation*, where she will shape the opinions of national leaders until 1955. A visionary who runs about a decade ahead of political trends, she is especially influential with the liberal policy makers who serve under President Franklin Roosevelt—and she will make a point of waiting to retire until the crisis of McCarthyism is over.

✦ When the Japanese bomb Canton as World War II begins in the Pacific, one of those who organizes refugee aid is American citizen Rose Hum Lee, who has been working as a businesswoman in China for the last decade. A native of Montana, she will go on to appreciable success after returning to the United States and earning a doctorate in sociology at the University of Chicago. The first Chinese American woman to head a university department, Dr. Lee will publish a pioneering study, *The Chinese in the United States of America* (1960).

✦ Floridian Zora Neale Hurston publishes *Their Eyes Were Watching God*, which will be considered her most significant novel. The first black student at Barnard College, Hurston has studied with anthropological pioneer Franz Boas; she becomes adept at ferreting out folk stories, even using the new technology of film to record black life. This unconventional subject matter and her use of dialect make her books and plays both original and controversial.

+ Disillusioned by a return trip to segregated America, famous Paris dancer Josephine Baker becomes a French citizen. When France falls to the Nazis three years later, she travels in the Middle East and North Africa, entertaining troops and gathering intelligence for the French resistance. At the war's end, she is honored with three medals, including the French Croix de Guerre.

+ Blues singer Bessie Smith dies after a Tennessee car accident; rumors grow that she bled to death after she was refused admission to a segregated hospital, but no documentation confirms this.

+ Eleanor Roosevelt publishes her first book, *This Is My Story*; she will write many others prior to her final autobiography in 1961. She also writes a syndicated newspaper column, "My Day," and does regular pieces for *Ladies' Home Journal* and *McCall's*, as well as other magazines. She joins the American Newspaper Guild and, ignoring those who ridicule her voice, also speaks on radio.

By putting her ideas, including such innovations as subsidized child care and health care into writing, Roosevelt forgoes the usual politician's dodge of claiming to be misquoted.

+ Another wife/husband team takes over *Ladies' Home Journal*, trying to combat a decline in circulation in this depression decade. Like original publishers Louisa and Cyrus Curtis, Beatrice Gould and her husband, Bruce, succeed in returning readers to the magazine by focusing on women's changing roles: Especially during World War II, the venerable old *Ladies' Home Journal* will publish more progressive articles than magazines that are considered more liberal.

+ Marguerite Tjader Harris begins *Direction*, a literary journal that will publish such writers as John Dos Passos and Langston Hughes. With support

from novelist Theodore Dreiser, the journal endures through World War II.

+ After decades without any female figures on stamps, the post office issues the third in four years. It is dedicated to Virginia Dare, who in 1587 was the first English child born in America. Her mother, Elenor White Dare, who courageously sailed to an unknown land in the last stages of pregnancy, is not mentioned.

The 350th anniversary of Virginia Dare's birth also marks the beginning of a pageant on the site of the nation's first English settlement, North Carolina's Roanoke Island. "The Lost Colony" will be presented every summer throughout the century and becomes America's longest-running outdoor drama.

+ A hundred years after collegiate coeducation began, the nation has 451 coeducational institutes of higher education, 80 men's colleges, and 120 women's colleges. The president of Oberlin College estimates that during the past century, a million women have received the bachelor of arts degree—following the example of the first four who matriculated at Oberlin in 1837.

1938 Pearl Buck wins the Nobel Prize for Literature just eight years after publication of her first book. She will remain the only American woman honored with this prize for 50 years, and only a half-dozen women of any nationality receive it.

+ Author Willa Cather is elected to the Academy of Arts and Letters less than a decade before her death. Among her many other accolades is the first honorary degree that Princeton University granted to a woman.

+ *The Yearling*, a short novel about a boy's love for a deer, achieves the status of a classic almost immediately after publication. It wins the 1939 Pulitzer Prize, and author Marjorie Kinnan Rawlings goes on to great success while continuing to live in backwoods Florida.

+ In the summer, Britain's newly crowned king and queen visit America, and the media has a field day about the fact that the first lady serves them hot dogs. Some portray this as gauche and insulting to the royalty, while others defend hot dogs as a democratic American tradition.

When Roosevelt publishes her reminiscences, she will point out that she not only "corralled two friends to cook hot dogs on an outdoor fireplace" at her Hyde Park summer home but also served several other items that "Their Majesties had not tasted before," including smoked turkey, "several kinds of ham cured in different ways from different parts of the country," and strawberry shortcake.

◆ Harvard finally gives astronomer Annie Jump Cannon the rank of professor—after she has been affiliated with its observatory for almost 50 years and has cataloged some 350,000 stars. No other astronomer or group of astronomers will equal this record, which includes some 300 rare variable stars and five nova. Although she was honored by the Royal Astronomical Society in 1914 and by Oxford University in 1925, Cannon's full professorship is granted just two years prior to her retirement.

◆ Composer Amy Beach, who has been writing music for more than four decades, issues her Opus #150, a piece for piano, violin, and cello. In addition to classical and sacred music, she has published more than 150 popular songs. When she dies at age 77 in 1944, just three of her hundreds of musical compositions remain unpublished. All of this is particularly exceptional in view of the fact that she was almost entirely self-taught—she had only one brief course in harmony as a teenager and never formally studied composition.

◆ *Snow White and the Seven Dwarfs* is translated and illustrated by Wanda Gág, who grew up speaking German in Minnesota. Two years earlier, she did the same for *Tales from Grimm*, and both works become classics of children's literature. Also, a Gág print is chosen as one of just three by Americans in a Museum of Modern Art show entitled "Art in Our Time."

◆ Baroness Maria von Trapp flees the Nazi occupation of Austria. She settles in Vermont with her husband and the seven children from his first marriage whose lives later are featured in an extremely popular stage and screen show, *The Sound of Music*. The family, which includes three more children born after the von Trapps 1927 marriage, will support themselves with national singing tours.

◆ German-born Anna Marie Hahn is executed in Ohio for the murders of at least five men. Newspapers describe her as a blond, beautiful 32-years-old who lives with her husband and child in Cincinnati and advertises herself as a care provider for "gentlemen in poor health." After officials discover arsenic in the body of one man who died in her home, others are exhumed and poison is found in them, too. She has inherited property from a number of men, and some believe she may have killed as many as 15. A jury of 11 women and one man sentences Hahn to the electric chair.

◆ Aviator Jacqueline Cochran beats a field of men to win the transcontinental Bendix Air Race. Cochran is one of the few participants in this expensive activity who grew up underprivileged; she began work in a Georgia textile mill at age eight and earned the money to fly by creating her own cosmetic sales line. She retained her maiden name when she married.

◆ Beatrice Fox Auerbach takes over management of Hartford's G. Fox & Co., the nation's largest privately owned department store, and when she retires in 1965, business has multiplied 10 times. She introduces such innovations as toll-free ordering and is particularly known for progressive personnel policies, including interest-free loans to employees.

◆ Journalist Agnes Smedley publishes *China Fights Back: An American Woman with the . . . Army*. It is based on the decade that she has spent sharing the sufferings of Mao Tse-tung, Chou En-lai, and other Chinese during The Long March.

◆ Japanese planes attack Shanghai, killing some 1,300 civilians in the first day. Among the Americans there at the time is Eleanor B. Roosevelt, who only coincidentally shares the first lady's name; she is married to Theodore Roosevelt Jr., which makes her a cousin by marriage to the first family.

She lived in France during World War I, which she describes as "a child's tea party" compared with the Shanghai bombing. Because she knows both China's Madame Chiang Kai-Shek and the Japanese premier, Prince Konoye, she sends them telegrams, pleading that they arrange a cease-fire to enable neutral parties to leave. The next day, 410 Americans, "practically all women and children," crowd onto a small boat, and with shells and sniper bullets barely missing them, they make the dangerous 12-mile trip down the Whangpoo River to a waiting ship of the U.S. Navy.

A more perilous evacuation from Shanghai is that of Mrs. Lester Petersen, her physician husband, and two other men who escape in a 36-foot boat. Evading warships and enduring storms, they sail 5,000 miles in 85 days and set a record for Pacific crossing.

✦ The fall elections bring a milestone: the first black woman in a state legislature is Crystal Bird Fauset of Pennsylvania. A graduate of the prestigious Teachers College of Columbia University, she has been employed by the YWCA and by American Friends Service Committee, a Quaker organization. It is through these connections that the Democratic Party recruits her to run in an overwhelmingly white district of Philadelphia. White women organize a phone bank—then a new technique—and she wins the election.

There are 27 white women legislators in the nation, and the Pennsylvania legislature has five African-American men. Fauset is unique in combining the two, but she disappoints her supporters by resigning less than a year later for "a broader opportunity" as an assistant director with the depression-era Works Progress Administration.

✦ South Carolina becomes the second state to have two women in the U.S. House of Representatives simultaneously. Both Elizabeth Gasque and Clara McMillan are elected to replace their husbands; Gasque serves only four months, but

McMillan has a full term and goes on to a Washington career with three major agencies. Arkansas was the first state to have two women in the House; all four women are Democrats.

✦ The first Republican woman is elected to the U.S. Senate but is never sworn in. Gladys Pyle, a South Dakota suffragist who has served in the legislature and as secretary of state, is elected to serve out a two-month vacancy, but the Senate does not go into session during her time in office.

✦ In the nation's first close, bitter race between a woman and a man for the U.S. Senate, incumbent Hattie Caraway barely defeats Representative John McClellan, whose slogan is "Arkansas needs another man in the Senate." Arkansas women organize and campaign hard for Caraway; they are joined by men from labor and veterans' organizations.

1939 In January, a New Jersey Republican introduces a House resolution calling for the impeachment of Labor Secretary Frances Perkins because she refuses to deport a California labor activist, Harry Bridges. Perkins endures hate mail encouraged by right-wingers who call her a Communist, and even a *New York Times* editorial blithely dismisses her monumental economic achievements with "Shall we save this woman? Or ruin her?"

Perkins testifies before the House Judiciary Committee, which votes against any further investigation—but the press writes little about this, and the personal attacks continue for years.

✦ When the Daughters of the American Revolution refuse to rent their Washington hall to African-American singer Marian Anderson, a civil rights milestone results. Among the hundreds of white Washingtonians who sign petitions objecting to the DAR's action are two Supreme Court justices and several Cabinet members; Eleanor Roosevelt resigns her honorary DAR membership; and Representative Carolyn O'Day heads a committee to make the concert a success. In the appropriate setting of the Lincoln Memorial, Anderson's powerful voice reaches out to national attention.

Agricultural workers—almost always families of women and children as well as men—represented the nadir of Great Depression poverty. These lived in a temporary camp in Butler County, Missouri, after their eviction from a plantation where they had been sharecroppers. Library of Congress, U.S. Department of Agriculture Farm Security Administration; photo by Arthur Rothstein

The first lady's intervention on behalf of Anderson is entirely typical, for Eleanor Roosevelt is a consummate networker. Even some in the administration disapprove of her energetic promotion of women's careers: Joseph Kennedy, father of a future president and current ambassador to England, complains, "She's always sending me a note to have some little Suzie Glotz to tea at the Embassy."

✦ Anthropologist Ruth Benedict introduces a second fundamental of 20th century thought when she coins the word "racism" in her *Race: Science and Politics*. Given the rise of nazism in Europe, the book is both timely and courageous, for many respected scholars argue for the inherent supe-

riority of northern Europeans and their American descendants.

✦ Dorothy Schiff becomes the major shareholder of the *New York Post*. During the next three decades, she will serve as both publisher and editor-in-chief, guiding this major metropolitan newspaper through strikes and the advent of competing television. Although she marries four times and is the mother of three, she retains her maiden name; calling herself a "crusading liberal," Schiff's editorials speak for "honest unionism, social reform and humane government."

✦ Her time in prison because of her opposition to World War I has made Kate O'Hare Cunningham aware of the need for penal reform. This year the governor appoints her assistant director of the California Department of Penology. She fires corrupt officials, separates juvenile boys from adult male prisoners, and otherwise improves notorious conditions at San Quentin and other prisons. Her work is so respected that future Governor Earl Warren, a Republican, requests input from this avowed socialist.

◆ Clara Adams makes aviation history by piloting a Pan American Clipper around the world. She flies between Port Washington, New York, and Newark, New Jersey, in 16 days, 19 hours, and 4 minutes.

◆ The movie version of *Gone with the Wind* premieres in Atlanta with unmatched extravagance. People across the nation will stand in line to see it, and after winning several Academy Awards, it becomes Hollywood's all-time most valuable property. After Margaret Mitchell realizes that she will not share equitably in its profits, she pursues court cases that set important precedents for authors in intellectual property rights and taxation.

◆ The movie also makes Hattie McDaniel a household name, when she becomes the first African-American actor to win an Academy Award. At age 44, she is a veteran of the entertainment industry, having won her first award for a dramatic presentation to the Denver Women's Christian Temperance Union as a teenager. Although she now has some 50 bit parts in movies to her credit, she is usually stereotyped as a servant. Musically talented as well, McDaniel has both composed and recorded songs—but nevertheless was forced to work as a maid during the depressed economy of the last decade.

◆ The work of a Vermont farmwoman who becomes known as Grandma Moses is exhibited at New York's Museum of Modern Art. Anna Robertson Moses had taken up painting when arthritis made needlework impossible at age 77; by 80, she is a national celebrity. During the two decades that remain of her life, she will complete as many as 1,500 paintings, do interviews on national television, and be recognized as the artistic world's leading primitivist.

◆ The only commissioned work by a black artist at the World's Fair in New York is that of Augusta Savage. A Florida native, Savage moved to New York to study art and became part of the Harlem Renaissance. With encouragement from the New Deal's Federal Art Project, she developed a successful career as a sculptor.

◆ Washington sculptor Adelaide Johnson calls in reporters to witness her destruction of her feminist artwork because she believes she has received insufficient financial support from women. The media will feature her in other stories—many of them centered on inconsistently dated "birthdays" at which she claims to be more than 100—until her 1955 death at age 94.

◆ The official state paleontologist of New York is Winifred Goldring. She holds this position until 1954, and her colleagues elect her to major office in the national organizations for both geologists and paleontologists.

◆ In September, when Europe erupts into World War II, popular CBS radio newsman Edward R. Murrow puts Kentuckian Mary Martin Breckinridge on the air to describe the London scene as Germany attacks. Breckinridge, who has been a photojournalist in Europe during the last decade, is such a hit that CBS features her regularly. By the end of the year, she is reporting from the Continent, including Berlin.

◆ "On a hunch," photographic journalist Therese Bonney goes to Finland just before the Soviets attack. She hides in forests and snowbanks while planes drop bombs, creating a unique photographic record. The Finnish government will bestow the White Rose on her, an honor seldom granted to a woman.

Next year, she will shoot pictures of refugees at the Franco-Belgian front. The only correspondent at the battle of the Meuse, Bonney then exhibits her photos at the Museum of Modern Art in New York and at the Library of Congress.

She features children and titles the exhibit "To Whom the Wars Are Done."

+ Lillian Hellman's *Little Foxes* gives Tallulah Bankhead what she believes is her all-time best role. An Alabama accent combined with a baritone voice and blonde beauty has made Bankhead a stage and screen sensation since 1925, but although she will win the New York Film Critics 1944 award for best actress and is popular with audiences, her career is marked by critical scorn.

+ The three-decade career of comedian Fanny Brice is recounted in a movie, *Rose of Washington Square*. In the 1960s and 1970s, it will be redone as the Broadway hit and award-winning movie *Funny Girl* and its sequel, *Funny Lady*.

+ Country singer Patsy Montana is the first woman to record a song that sells more than a million copies. The song is "I Want to Be a Cowboy's Sweetheart."

+ The end of the decade marks a publishing precedent that will not be matched by any man during the century: Pearl Buck's *The Good Earth* and Margaret Mitchell's *Gone with the Wind* each have held top-selling status for two years of the decade.

+ Dorothea Lange's photographs in *American Exodus: A Record of Human Erosion* spell out the conditions that made some depression years the only time in American history when more people emigrated out of the country than entered.

+ Ten women have been elected to the House of Representatives during the 1930s; all but two are Democrats. In contrast, 9 of the 12 elected in the 1920s were Republicans. The fears of those who opposed suffrage as a wild political unknown are thus proved wrong, for women, like men, are part of the current national trend.

+ After women have voted for two decades, it is evident that the Northeast, where most suffragist activism was based, is not more likely to elect women to Congress. The 22 women elected to the House have come from 16 states: New Jersey and Massachusetts each have had one and New York, three.

The southern states of Arkansas and South Carolina have elected three and two respectively, while Tennessee, Kentucky, and Florida each chose one. Women from four western states (Montana, California, Arizona, and Oregon) and four midwestern states (Oklahoma, Kansas, Illinois, and Indiana) make up the rest of the female House membership. California is the only one of the western and midwestern states to have twice elected a woman.

Four women, all southerners, have been sworn into the Senate, but only one (from Arkansas) had significant tenure.

9

Women in the
War and Postwar

1940–1960

1940 Daisy Harriman, who was appointed minister to Norway by Franklin Roosevelt in 1937, becomes a true hero of diplomatic history when, at age 70, she endures several Nazi air raids while helping Americans and others escape the German invasion. She continues to provide diplomatic assistance to refugees from neutral Sweden before finally escorting Norwegian royalty to the United States.

✦ Radio reporter Mary Martin Breckinridge heads CBS's Amsterdam office. When the Netherlands falls to the Germans, she takes the last train to Paris, and when that city falls, she goes on to broadcast from Italy.

Helen Kirkpatrick has a similar role in print media. She has worked as a freelance journalist in Europe since her 1931 graduation from Smith College and is able to use her personal contacts to predict the German invasion of Belgium eight days before it happens.

✦ When Dr. Tilly Edinger escapes Nazi Germany, she is welcomed by the director of Harvard's Museum of Comparative Zoology. There she does pathbreaking work, such as tracing the evolution of the human brain, and, in 1963, her colleagues will elect her president of the Society of Vertebrate Paleontology.

✦ The work of the Association of Southern Women for the Prevention of Lynching can be deemed a success: for the first year ever, there are no lynchings in the United States. Two years later, the organization will dissolve.

✦ For the first time, the U.S. Post Office honors more than one woman in its annual new stamp issues. Three significant women are featured: author Louisa May Alcott, temperance and suffrage leader Frances Willard, and Nobel Peace Prize winner Jane Addams.

✦ Alicia Patterson, the daughter and granddaughter of publishers of the *Chicago Tribune* and the *New York Daily News*, begins *Newsday* on Long Island. She targets suburban readers, many of whom are housewives, and defies expert advice in using an unconventional format of smaller-size

pages. When Patterson brings the paper to profitability within six years, she earns the rare distinction of founding a major metropolitan paper at a time when many newspapers are going bankrupt.

✦ After the death of her husband, Jesse Vann becomes publisher of the *Pittsburgh Courier*, a nationally circulated weekly newspaper that is a must-read for African-American leaders throughout the nation. Mary McLeod Bethune is among its regularly featured columnists, and Vann will be the active business head for more than two decades. By 1945, the paper will gross about $2 million annually, making her perhaps the wealthiest black woman in America. Before Vann retires in 1963, her paper will cover such milestone stories as the integration of the armed forces and the 1954 school Supreme Court decision on school desegregation.

✦ The American Radium Society honors Edith Quimby for her pioneer research in nuclear medicine. Quimby works on medical applications of radioactive isotopes in cancer treatment, and she also has developed and publicized safe techniques for personnel administering radiation. The next year, Quimby will be honored with the Gold Medal of the Radiological Society of North America; it is only the second time that this medal is awarded to a woman—the first went to the famous French discoverer of radium, Marie Curie.

✦ Social scientist Elsie Clews Parsons caps a lifetime of achievement with the presidency of the American Anthropological Association. She also has been elected president of the American Folklore Society (1918–20) and the American Ethnological Association (1923–25).

✦ Novelist Ellen Glasgow, who has written of life in the changing South for almost 50 years, is chosen for membership in the American Academy of Arts and Letters; she will win the Pulitzer Prize the following year. Her personal life is an apt symbol of her literary theme, for she lives alone in the family mansion while Richmond industrializes around her.

Glasgow's Pulitzer will be the last that a woman wins in the literature category for almost two decades: At this point in the award's history, 12 women and 10 men have won; there will be no women winners through the rest of the 1940s and the 1950s.

✦ Bertha M. Bower dies; using male pseudonyms, she has authored 57 westerns, many of which were made into movies.

✦ Harriot Stanton Blatch, daughter of Elizabeth Cady Stanton, publishes her autobiography and dies at age 83. Blatch also published a number of feminist works, including a book on her mother that she coauthored with a brother. They were the only two of Stanton's seven children to carry on her activism.

✦ Incumbents who are being renominated traditionally do not attend party conventions until their acceptance speech, and so Eleanor Roosevelt precedes Franklin to the Democratic convention, where she again demonstrates her great political skill. She mediates a serious split over the vice presidency: incumbent Texan John Nance Garner refuses to join Franklin Roosevelt in running for an unprecedented third term, at least in part because FDR has given little power to him. FDR wishes to replace him with Agriculture Secretary Henry A. Wallace of Iowa, but many southern Democrats consider Wallace too radical. Eleanor Roosevelt manages to mollify them, and Wallace becomes her husband's vice president—until 1944, when he is displaced by Harry Truman. Eleanor Roosevelt will retain the respect of both the Wallace and Truman factions.

✦ In October, Mary Margaret McBride goes from a New York regional market to a national network of radio stations, setting the standard for talk shows aimed at women. Although originally hired to do household hints, McBride quickly switched her format to one of broader interest and became so popular that advertisers plead to sponsor her.

A native of Missouri, she is a 1919 graduate of the University of Missouri's School of Journalism and already has enjoyed a long career in print news. She also has written almost a book a year since 1926; the best-known, *How Dear to My Heart*, comes out this year.

✦ Los Angeles teacher Elizabeth Rider (later Montgomery) creates the characters of Dick and Jane, who will be used in elementary school reading books far into the future. Millions of children love Dick and Jane, despite their gender stereotypes and the unreality of the fact that their mother does her housework wearing heels.

✦ In the fall elections, Representative Frances Bolton, Republican of Ohio, retains the seat that she won in February when her husband died in office, despite the opposition of party leaders who expect her to step down. She organizes Cleveland women, wins the campaign, and is appointed to the prestigious House Foreign Affairs Committee. Within three years, she is one of six Republicans to draft the party's platform on foreign policy.

✦ Republican Jeanette Rankin, who was the first woman elected to the U.S. House in 1916, runs again and is elected once more on a pacifist platform. Her personal history will repeat itself: when she keeps her campaign promise and is the only member of Congress to vote against World War II, her Montana constituents punish her with defeat in the next election.

1941 With the United States still neutral in the war, aviator Jacqueline Cochran—who holds five national and international speed records—flies a bomber from Canada to England and signs on as a captain in the British Air Transport Authority. She recruits other American women for the ATA, and they go on to pilot 120 types of planes over Britain's dangerous skies.

✦ In March, Eleanor Roosevelt flies with black male pilots at an air base in Tuskegee, Alabama, to help them prove their claims of competence. Ten days later, their program is funded and they go on to shoot down some 400 Nazi planes. Jackie Cochran has already appealed to Roosevelt for help with female pilots, but the first lady finds the military unresponsive on this.

◆ In May, Representative Edith Nourse Rogers introduces a bill to establish the Women's Army Auxiliary Corps; on Christmas Eve, after the Japanese surprise attack on Pearl Harbor and the declaration of war, the secretary of war grants approval. After "acrid debate" in which one congressman brands it "the silliest piece of legislation" he has ever seen, the bill will pass the following spring. The induction of women other than nurses into the army is a historic change in the status of women, and the final 249 to 86 margin is a mark of the esteem in which Rogers is held by her colleagues.

◆ When the Germans break their treaty and invade the Soviet Union in June, Margaret Bourke-White is the only foreign photographer there. She is the first woman to receive credentials from the U.S. Army as a war correspondent when the United States enters the war in December, and she covers combat in North Africa, Italy, and Germany. She survives the torpedoing of her ship and, at the war's end, photographs General George Patton's troops entering Germany. Millions see the pictures she sends back to *Life*.

◆ Photographs by Dorothea Lange are also featured in *Life*, and she becomes the first female photographer to receive a prestigious Guggenheim Fellowship. During the war, she will document the conditions of Japanese Americans who are forced into desert camps; when the War Relocation Authority finds her photographs too sympathetic, she leaves that agency to work with the Office of War Information.

◆ The government of unoccupied France awards the Croix de Guerre to photojournalist Therese Bonney. She also records the bombing of Britain this year; next year, she will return to Finland as a "lone wolf" correspondent for *Collier's*.

The pictures she takes will be issued as *Europe's Children* in 1943—at her own expense, after a dozen publishers turn her down. Critics call them "unforgettable" and say that no one else has done work "so sharply moving, so overwhelming heartbreaking." Not surprisingly, when her privately printed run quickly sells out,

a major publisher will take over the book in 1944. By that year, Bonney has crossed the Atlantic 104 times.

◆ On a stormy night in late June, the Germans torpedo the Dutch ship *Maasdam*, with 17 American Red Cross nurses aboard. They maintain their composure under attack, and all but two survive their lifeboat trips to England.

A few days later, however, a second vessel is torpedoed and eight American women are killed. The German submarine surfaces after the attack and offers to take female survivors aboard, but the women prefer to take their chances on the sea rather than become prisoners of war. One group drifts in a lifeboat for 12 days with only a little food and water; another boat that includes women from New York and New Jersey is adrift 19 days. The women are semiconscious when rescued, and two Englishmen on board are dead.

A veil of military secrecy often covers such incidents, however, and few Americans become aware of these heroic women who volunteer before U.S. involvement in the war is official. Other wartime changes in women's roles are publicized, however, and this new image is doubtless responsible for the long-running popularity that greets two new comic strips: "Wonder Woman" begins in July, and "Brenda Starr," a crusading news reporter, debuted last year. Both features are drawn by men, and both will have national audiences for decades.

◆ Author Pearl S. Buck founds the East and West Association in an attempt to foster international harmony. She personalizes her commitment to ending racism by adopting several racially mixed children and writing extensively of Asian culture in popular magazines. Her work helps intensify the sympathy that Americans have for the Chinese, who are under wartime attack by the Japanese.

◆ Twenty-four-year-old Georgian Carson McCullers issues *Reflections in a Golden Eye*, following up on her success the previous year with *The Heart Is a Lonely Hunter*. She goes on to be called "*the young writer*" of the decade, winning both the

Drama Critics Circle Award and the O. Henry short story prize.

Many will consider *The Member of the Wedding* (1946) her best work, and she will be elected to the National Institute of Arts and Letters in 1952, despite complex health problems that keep her in a wheelchair for much of her 50-year life.

✦ Wellesley professor Ola E. Winslow wins the Pulitzer Prize for biography with her study of 18th-century evangelist Jonathan Edwards.

✦ Ruth Frankel subordinates her scholarly career to her husband's when she marries Daniel Boorstin. Although for the next 50 years, she works on every one of the dozens of books that eventually make him a much-honored historian and head of the Library of Congress, her name never appears with his.

✦ At age 41, Russian-born sculptor Louise Nevelson has her first exhibit. In her long career, she becomes known for wooden wall mountings that include seemingly out-of-place objects. Her 1967 exhibit at New York's Whitney Museum will feature metal and plastic, and she will be honored by the American Academy of Arts and Letters prior to her 1988 death.

✦ Dr. Karen Horney, who challenges Freudian assumptions on "normal" female behavior, is barred from the New York Psychoanalytic Institute. No official explanation is made, and almost half of the men present abstain from voting. In response, she and several colleagues of both genders form the Association for the Advancement of Psychoanalysis.

✦ Virtually all opposition to U.S. entrance into the war stops after the December 7 bombing of Hawaii's Pearl Harbor by the Japanese, but the leftist *Catholic Worker*, under the editor Dorothy Day, continues its pacifist position. It is exceptional, for most of the tiny minority who oppose U.S. entrance into World War II are right-wingers. A half-dozen such organizations use the word "mother" to attract women—usually from the upper class—to their anti-Roosevelt, anti-Semitic, and pro-fascist views.

Most are centered in the isolationist Midwest, and although some of these women picket the White House to demonstrate their opposition to entering the war, the organizations quickly lose membership when the Japanese bomb U.S. bases in the Pacific without warning. Germany and the other European Axis nations immediately follow with declarations of war against the United States, and almost all Americans then unite to support the British, who have faced the fascists alone for more than a year.

✦ On Christmas Day, women in the Army Nurse Corps are among those bombed when the Japanese attack the Philippines. Some evacuate to Australia, but most go on to serve for months in the jungles of Bataan, a name that becomes synonymous with starvation and death. One army nurse will later describe herself as "always hungry, always frightened" during her time there. Women, like men, eat rats, snakes, and monkeys to survive; they dig foxholes to hide from dive bombers, and they attempt to run "hospitals" equipped with as little as a single teaspoon. With virtually no medical supplies, they attempt to treat nearly 1,000 wounded men per day.

1942 The army nurses on Bataan hold out until April 9, when U.S. commander Douglas MacArthur leads a retreat to Australia. He leaves some of his forces behind, however, including nurses who serve a crowded hospital in a cave under the giant rock of Corregidor. On April 29, when the Japanese celebrate their emperor's birthday, the bombing begins at 7:30 A.M. and continues all day, with as many as 100 explosions per minute reverberating through the rock. "Several times the power plant was hit," says one later, and "we would be in total darkness."

Twenty-one nurses manage to escape to Australia, and in the summer, they will be honored with a ceremony at the White House. Others are not so lucky: 88 ANC women become prisoners of war; along with American and British civilians who are in the area, a total of some 500 women will be confined to a Manila prison camp for the next three years. Although women have long been warned that the Japanese brutally rape Chinese, Korean, and other Asian women, the Japanese are surprised to find Western women in the Pacific, and treat them better than was expected. Nonetheless, the women will endure near-starvation conditions in captivity.

✦ Eight bills are introduced in Congress on the subject of drafting women for war industries—something that both enemies and allies abroad are doing. Attention centers on the National War Service Act, sponsored by Vermont Senator Warren Austin, which calls for the compulsory registration of women 18 to 50, who would then be required to serve in whatever industrial or agricultural job they were assigned.

All of the bills are sponsored by Republicans or conservative southern Democrats; the Roosevelt administration generally opposes the idea—not because it is necessarily opposed to the concept of registering and drafting women, but rather because it believes the labor shortages, which are local, not national, can best be solved by volunteerism rather than compulsion.

Nonetheless, more than two-thirds of Americans consistently tell pollsters that they approve of the concept of drafting women for defense industries if necessary.

✦ When troops pour into the beachheads of North Africa, over 200 U.S. women in the nurse corps move with them. At Oran and Arzew, they wade ashore, bullets and bombs exploding around them, and set up their life-saving hospitals. For a week, the nurses work round the clock, sleeping only in brief naps. In February, several units are caught behind German lines; First Lieutenant Mary Ann Sullivan earns the Legion of Merit for her valor in getting out of the Kasserine Pass with Germans both ahead of and behind her.

✦ The dangerous conditions to which nurses abroad are exposed cause serious changes in their preparations back home. Their traditional white dresses are discarded for camouflage pants, and training centers in the United States require them to hike 20 miles while carrying a 30-pound pack. Women learn other combat techniques, including dealing with chemical warfare; they chlorinate their water and put out incendiaries. Their final test features a 75-yard infiltration course, in which nurses crawl on their stomachs through what a *New York Times* reporter calls a "no-man's land of trenches and barbed wire with charges of dynamite going off . . . and machine-gun bullets singing a few inches over their heads." Men complete the same obstacle course, and at Camp Young, Arizona, a woman sets the speed record.

✦ Wartime rationing begins on May 5 with sugar. Because ships are converted to war use and the needs of the military take priority over the needs of civilians, many other items will be rationed before the war ends. Housewives learn to cope with limited supplies of food and clothing; no appliances or cars are built during the war, and all items based on petroleum, rubber, and metal are in short supply. Women lead conservation drives and donate everything from dishpans to wedding rings for military uses.

✦ The Women's Auxiliary Army Corps is officially established on May 15; modified to Women's Army Corps in 1943, it will enlist approximately 100,000 women by the war's end. Commanded from Washington, D.C., by Oveta Culp Hobby of Texas, WACs will train at bases in Iowa, Florida, and Georgia.

Black women are included from the beginning, as National Council of Negro Women president Mary McLeod Bethune serves on the Corps' Advisory Board. WACs will perform in hundreds of occupational specialties and serve all over the globe. Although those who work closely with them—including Supreme Allied Commander Dwight D. Eisenhower—will testify to the exceptional abilities of many WACs, they are plagued throughout the war by a range of false charges centered on sexuality.

✦ Congress authorizes the U.S. Navy to form the WAVES, an acronym for Women Accepted for Volunteer Emergency Service. The word "volunteer" is intended only in contrast to men who are drafted; like the army's WACs, WAVES are paid, wear uniforms, hold rank, and are subject to military discipline. They are commanded by Mildred McAfee, who takes leave from the presidency of Wellesley College. WAVES generally will be college-educated, often in scientific and technical areas. Unlike the WACs, WAVES do not serve overseas, nor are black women accepted until late in the war.

✦ Forty highly qualified female pilots form the Women's Air Ferrying Squadron. They serve under 28-year-old Nancy Harkness Love, who flew bombers to the Canadian border while the United States was neutral. The shortest-lived of the wartime women's units, the WAFS will merge with the Women's Air Service Pilots (WASPs) a year later. Jacqueline Cochran forms the WASPs after returning from service with the British Air Transport Authority when the United States enters the war.

✦ In November, the Coast Guard begins its SPARS, which—like the Coast Guard itself—will be the smallest of the wartime military units for women. SPARS officers set a precedent when they train with Coast Guard cadets at the prestigious U.S. Coast Guard Academy in New London, Connecticut. Lieutenant Commander Dorothy C. Stratton heads the SPARS.

✦ By the war's end, more than 400,000 women will have served the nation in the military units established for women. They work in almost all noncombat "MOS" (military occupational status) categories, including over 400 of the army's 625 job slots. While most are in various clerical capacities, women also pack parachutes, print photographs of combat sites, direct air traffic, compute artillery distances, translate messages, repair and refuel planes, and, especially, instruct men. Women teach all-male classes in celestial navigation, instrument flying, gunnery, and many other topics. They also work as chemists, cartographers, electricians, weather forecasters, and even dog and pigeon trainers. They operate teletypes, send up balloons, sort mail, spot enemy aircraft, run motor pools, play in bands, and literally perform hundreds of tasks beyond the kitchen and laundry

African Americans in the Women's Army Corps work as mechanics at Fort Huachuca, Arizona. Many women became mechanics in the military; the navy's WAVES and the army's Air WACs were especially likely to be trained for such work. Women In Military Service Memorial

duty to which many military men originally intended to assign them.

✦ As war casualties soar, the National Nursing Council for War Service aims to locate the 100,000 women who have graduated from nursing schools but abandoned the profession, while the Office of Civilian Defense pleads for another 100,000 volunteers to become aides in local hospitals.

✦ While the media cries for nurses, the services of female physicians are underutilized. Again, Congress is more liberal than the military, and congressional intervention is necessary to make the military use what is available to them. Female physicians are commissioned only after Congress specifically authorizes them next year. Even then, fewer than 100 female physicians will be accepted into the Medical Corps during the war.

Meanwhile, medical schools continue to maintain quotas on the number of applications from female students that they will accept—and the women fortunate enough to be admitted find further barricades when they are ready to serve their residencies. In this first full year of the war, just 105 of the 712 hospitals that are approved by the American Medical Association for internships will accept applications from women.

+ Following models developed in England and Canada, the Women's Land Army provides as many as 60% of the agricultural workers in Oregon during this first summer of the war. There is a tremendous need for farm labor because even though farmers are exempt from the draft, many young men who traditionally held these jobs prefer to join the service—just as America is expected to feed the wartorn world.

Next year, Congress will make the Women's Land Army an official subdivision of the Department of Agriculture; with Florence Hall as its head, millions of women will be recruited to harvest crops throughout the nation. Usually young women from cities, they are often college students on summer break. They wear uniforms, live in camps, and are paid the standard low wages of agricultural laborers. Initially many farmers are skeptical about using women—especially college-educated ones—for this kind of hard work, but most soon see that the women are eager to demonstrate both their ability and their patriotism.

+ Despite its name, the War Manpower Commission addresses all of the nation's labor needs, including—and even especially—the need for women to enter the job market. Its Women's Advisory Committee is chaired by Margaret A. Hickey, the successful owner of a St. Louis business school, who also will serve as national president of the Business and Professional Women's Clubs.

+ Australian nurse Elizabeth Kenny establishes the Sister Kenny Institute in Minneapolis, which offers innovative muscular techniques for the treatment of polio. Physicians denounce her as uncredentialed and simplistic, but as thousands of patients testify to the healing powers of heat and exercise, her methodology is widely adopted.

+ Women frequent the movie theaters in unprecedented numbers during the war. Many go primarily to see the newsreels, for, prior to television, this is the most effective way of getting graphic coverage of the battlefronts.

+ *Woman of the Year* is a success for Katharine Hepburn and Spencer Tracy, and they go on to make several more films featuring smart women. In *Adam's Rib* (1949), Hepburn and Tracy are lawyers on opposite sides in a murder case, and in *Desk Set* (1957), she is a librarian who consistently outperforms Tracy's new computer.

+ After Agnes DeMille choreographs Aaron Copland's *Rodeo* for a Russian ballet company, she goes on to become Broadway's leading choreographer in the next two decades. She wins particular acclaim for *Oklahoma!* the following year.

+ Susanne Langer publishes *Philosophy in a New Key*, an abstract work on the philosophical subdivision of aesthetics that is nevertheless sufficiently readable to sell more than half a million copies.

+ *Crusader in Crinoline*, a study of Harriet Beecher Stowe by Forrest Wilson, wins the Pulitzer Prize for biography.

+ The war presumably changes attitudes on women to such a degree that women win two Pulitzer Prizes for history, the first since the award began in 1917. Margaret Leech wins this year for *Reveille in Washington*, a social history of the capital during the Civil War, and Esther Forbes will win next year for *Paul Revere and the World He Lived In*. No woman is similarly honored with this prize until 1960, when Leech wins a second time.

+ The most featured November election race is that of sophisticated playwright Clare Booth Luce, wife of Time-Life publisher Henry Luce, who is elected from an affluent Connecticut suburb of New York. The Republican Party quickly promotes her; she is assigned to the prestigious Military Affairs Committee and will deliver the keynote speech at the 1944 Republican convention.

After four years in Congress, Representative Luce will not run for reelection in 1946; she retires from politics until the Republicans retake the White House in 1953.

1943 With the formation of the Women Marines in January, all military branches have units for women. Some 20,000 women will serve in 225 Marine military specialties, but the majority do clerical work; they make up 85% of enlisted personnel at Marine Corps Headquarters in Washington, D.C..

The Women Marines are commanded by Ruth Cheney Streeter, who receives the same rank of colonel that is awarded to Army director Hobby—but Hobby not only created the military model for women, she also commands more than five times as many recruits.

◆ Codenamed "Rover" for security purposes, Eleanor Roosevelt continues to be Franklin's "eyes and ears," as she travels tens of thousands of miles during the war. She has been especially prescient about the situation of Jews in Europe, long ago warning her husband to pay more heed.

◆ Congress passes the Bolton Bill, which is intended to bring more women into nursing to meet the wartime need. Representative Frances Bolton has already secured more than $1 million in assistance to nursing schools, but this bill sets up a Cadet Nurse Corps and grants aid directly to students. As a result, about 125,000 women train in 1,225 schools. It sets a congressional precedent for the appropriation of funds to women.

◆ When Colonel Julia A. Flikke retires, the Army Nurse Corps is headed by Florence Blanchfield; both women were veterans of World War I. They command almost 60,000 women all over the globe, many of whom are killed or taken as prisoners of war. Despite this responsibility, neither is promoted beyond colonel—a rank often given men who command 500.

◆ The depression's Works Projects Administration is no longer needed, and its Child Care division also is abolished—despite a crying need for day care at a time when millions of mothers work in defense plants. Instead, other agencies set up several new plans to meet this need. Dr. Grace Langdon, who had a decade of successful experience in building 2,000 WPA centers, is passed over; these better-funded positions to go to inexperienced men.

◆ In Elkton, Maryland, a May explosion at a munitions plant kills 15 and injures 54, most of them women. This industry has long been dominated by women, including many black women; employers say that they prefer to hire women because the manufacture of ammunition allows no bravado, and women, they believe, are less likely to engage in reckless behaviors.

The work is nonetheless inherently dangerous. Elkton has another explosion later this year, while the arsenal at Pine Bluff, Arkansas, also has two fires in one year. A black woman, Anne Marie Young, will receive the highest civilian award that the War Department gives for her courage in rescuing coworkers there.

Munitions plants are deliberately built in rural areas where explosions will be less dangerous. Thousands of women are thus recruited to small towns where few services are available, the cost of living is artificially high, and many residents are clear about their hostility to these newcomers—who spend their days or nights packing deadly chemicals into bullets and bombs. These "production soldiers" are vital to victory, but few recognize their valor.

◆ Families with members in the service post blue stars in their windows as a symbol, while women who have lost children in the war are honored as Gold Star Mothers. One of the war's most poignant cases of bereaved motherhood takes place this year when the USS *Juneau* goes down in the Pacific, killing all five sons of Iowa's Sullivan family. Mrs. Sullivan and her daughter-in-law, Katherine Mary, are then recruited by the Navy to make speeches intended to encourage production in defense plants. They point out that such employment is excellent mental therapy as well as beneficial for the war effort; housework alone, Mrs. Sullivan says, allows "your grief to remain very sharp, for there is nothing else for you to think about."

◆ Doris Fleeson, who began working as a political reporter for the *New York Daily News* in 1926, joins *Woman's Home Companion* and does serious war reporting for this mostly female audience. She writes from European battle scenes and does incognito reporting on black markets of rationed goods. After the war, she will make the difficult transition to newspaper syndication. With initial promises from only the *Boston Globe* and Washington's *Evening Star*, she soon will have more than 100 papers carrying her daily column with the United Features Syndicate. Fleeson covers the Truman, Eisenhower, Kennedy, and Johnson administrations, and she is the first woman to be recognized as a political commentator with a national audience.

✦ Reporter Inez Robb, who works for the International News Service, returns from Tunisia, where she has covered the African war front. In reporting that morale is high, she also makes it clear that these combat veterans trust her: "Every soldier you meet—whether he's a flier, an engineer, an infantrymen—takes you aside and earnestly informs you that his outfit is the best darn outfit over there and the one that's winning the war."

✦ Radcliffe students are permitted to enroll in Harvard classes because so many male students have gone to war.

At the same time, Radcliffe begins the Arthur and Elizabeth Schlesinger Library on the History of Women in America. The project is inspired by the donation of the papers of Maud Wood Park, the first president of the League of Women Voters. Schlesinger Library soon becomes the nation's most extensive archival source for women's history.

✦ *Out of the Kitchen—Into the War* is published by Susan B. Anthony II, niece of the famous suffragist. A journalist for the Associated Press and one of the first women hired by the *Washington Star*, Anthony eventually authors eight books.

✦ *Ladies' Home Journal* feminist editor Dorothy Thompson writes a monthly column explicating the war's effect on women and astutely predicts women's postwar world.

✦ Elinore Herrick, herself a former factory worker, is personnel director of Todd Shipyards, which employs over 140,000 women and men in 10 port cities. After the war is over, she will write on labor issues for the *New York Herald Tribune* —the newspaper that also features Dorothy Thompson on its editorial pages.

✦ Sculptor Selma Burke, a member of the artistic movement known as the Harlem Renaissance, has a 45-minute private meeting with President Franklin Roosevelt, after which she does a bust. Her profile of Roosevelt will appear on dimes coined after his death.

✦ The O. Henry Memorial Award goes to Margarita (Rita) G. Smith, sister to better-known writer Carson McCullers.

✦ Mary Woodard Lasker becomes a "driving force" of the American Cancer Society, which she co-founds this year. Prior to her death in 1994, she and her husband will endow prestigious medical research awards.

✦ Well into her retirement after four decades of teaching at Bryn Mawr, Dr. Nellie Neilson is elected president of the American Historical Association. She is the first woman to hold this position—and will be the last for another for four decades.

✦ At age 25, African-American singer Ella Fitzgerald is the youngest person ever admitted to the American Society of Composers, Authors, and Publishers. She will work with famous whites such as George Gershwin and Irving Berlin, as well as black talents such as Louis Armstrong and Duke Ellington. The winner of many awards, she becomes known as the era's great female jazz singer.

✦ Nashville's Ryman Auditorium—which has featured artists ranging from Isadora Duncan to Katharine Hepburn since its 1892 construction —becomes home to the Grand Ole Opry. Women not only are an integral part of country music, but they also retain their popularity as they age; in particular, Mother Maybelle Carter will influence dozens of female stars who appear on this stage in the future. Comedian Minnie Pearl is a weekly regular on Opry broadcasts, which reach isolated mountain women listening on battery-powered radios every Saturday night.

1944 While carefully deleting details that would be helpful to the Nazis, Collier's publishes the story of "thirteen nurses and seventeen men of the American Army Air Forces" whose plane was shot down in the mountains of German-occupied Albania last November. Two Detroit nurses, Lieutenants Lillian J. Tacina and Eugenia H. Rutkowski, tell the story of the 60 days the group spent dodging bullets in several German raids, while they crossed 850 miles of rough Balkan terrain to reach a rescue ship on the Adriatic. They walked almost the entire way, wearing out their shoes and enduring dysentery, pneumonia, and jaundice in blizzard conditions.

The nurses give much credit to Albanians who not only risked their lives to help with their escape but also shared their meager food supply. "All we talked about was food," said one nurse of these near-starvation weeks. They also note the condition of Albanian women at the farmhouses where they rested: "The barefoot women did all the work and kept in the background, while the men, who had shoes, did the fighting and the talking."

The women are part of a unit assigned to Bari, Italy, where each "cares for a planeload of litter cases, and each [male] sergeant cares for a planeload of patients who can still walk." The particular plane on which they were flying when shot down got lost in bad weather—but the fog

Members of the Women's Army Corps march past the Arc de Triomphe after U.S. forces liberated Paris in 1944. WACs served throughout the world, from Australia to Alaska, working in hundreds of military occupational specialties. Women In Military Service Memorial

obscured the Germans' vision just enough to allow for evasion and a relatively safe landing.

+ Young reporter Marguerite Higgins persuades the *New York Herald Tribune's* publisher to overrule her editors and send her to cover the invasion of Europe. Bilingual because of her French mother, Higgins moves with the Army through France, and in 1945, she will enter Berlin with the Allied victory over the Nazis. At age 25, Maggie Higgins will fill front-page space all over the nation as she writes on the horrors of the concentration camps and the resulting Nuremberg trials.

+ Representative Frances Bolton arrives in Paris two days after its liberation from the Nazis. She has paid her own way to Europe to check on the conditions of Army and Navy nurses, for her colleagues in Congress see her as their authority on these two corps. She also is in England during raids by the first guided missiles; in June alone, these German V-1 rockets ("buzz bombs") kill over 2,700 London civilians. The French will award Bolton with their Legion d'Honneur in 1956.

+ Mabel K. Staupers of the National Association of Colored Graduate Nurses leads lobbying efforts that eventually force the Army and Navy Nurse Corps to accept the services of black nurses. Ironically, although these two corps need trained women more desperately than any other of the women's military units, the Army Nurse Corps will maintain a strict quota of black nurses until next January, and the Navy Nurse Corps admits none at all.

+ When 80% of all resignations from the Navy Nurse Corps are because of regulations that require nurses to be single, the Navy finally permits NNC members to wed. This applies only to women already in the Corps, however, and qualified married nurses still are not allowed to enlist.

+ In a jesting analogy to the "nine old men" on the Supreme Court, the lieutenant colonels in the Women's Army Corps call themselves the "Nine Old Women."

The oldest, just 44 years of age, is Katherine Ralston Goodwin, who is director of WACs in the Army Service Forces; the youngest is 30-year-old Emily Claire Davis, director of WACs in the Ground Forces. Perhaps the most visible is Betty Bandel, who meets with exceptional success in recruiting women for her command, the Army Air Forces. Elizabeth Strayhorn is the only woman to command an Army training center; she inherited the command at Fort Oglethorpe, Georgia, when the male commandant was transferred.

The other most significant commands are held by Anna "Tony" Wilson for the European Theater of Operations, Westray Battle Boyce for the Mediterranean, and Mary-Agnes Brown for the Pacific. The two remaining women are Florence Newsome and Jessie Rice, who serve in Washington, D.C.

+ Because the Allies' wartime alliance with the Soviet Union means there is a demand for courses in Russian and because no qualified men are available to teach it, Princeton University hires its first woman. Ludmilla B. Turkevich, who has a Columbia doctorate in Russian, will remain with Princeton for the rest of her life—but for 17 years, she will hold the low rank of lecturer and her contract must be renewed annually.

+ A slight rewording of the Woman's Party's proposed Equal Rights Amendment to the Constitution makes little change in its prospects for passage. Although both major political parties begin to include the ERA as a low-profile part of their platforms, the amendment remains locked in congressional committee. Most female Roosevelt administration insiders oppose the ERA; they have spent their lives creating legislative protections for women, and they fear that this progress will be lost by passage of a constitutional amendment that would allow no special consideration for women.

+ The year's best-seller is *Strange Fruit*, a story of interracial love, by Lillian Smith, a white woman who lives in rural Georgia. The book is immensely controversial; it is banned in Boston, and the post office lifts its censorship only after intervention by Eleanor Roosevelt.

Smith demonstrates tremendous bravery by continuing to write about the destructiveness of racism, including *Killers of the Dream* (1949) and *One House* (1959), which she thinks is her best work. Not merely an intellectual, she also works in civil rights organizations and befriends young Martin Luther King Jr. Twice her home and manuscripts are torched by arsonists.

✦ The University of Minnesota publishes Alice Tyler's *Freedom's Ferment,* which will set a new standard for social history. The book explores the expansion of democratic ideals among the masses, and it inspires many historians to write on aspects of American life beyond the political and military—which leads to the inclusion of women.

✦ Dr. Barbara McClintock is elected president of the Genetics Society of America. Like many women in nontraditional areas, the war provides her first monetary research support.

✦ Nearly a decade after her retirement from Harvard Medical School, pioneer toxicologist Dr. Alice Hamilton is listed in *Men of Science*. Still later—in 1995—Hamilton will be honored with a stamp issued by the U.S. Post Office.

✦ Texan Sarah McClendon gets her Washington press credentials, but initially she is afraid to speak at the era's rather formal press conferences. In time, she will play a major role in moving that format to a fairer, more democratic style, and presidents of both parties will defer to her sometimes unusual questions from the front row. When McClendon celebrates her 50th anniversary as a reporter in 1994, the U.S. Senate will give her a standing ovation.

✦ Ira Jarrell is the first woman to become superintendent of schools for Atlanta. Her achievement is even more remarkable because, during her long teaching career, she also rose to the presidency of the local union, an affiliate of the American Federation of Teachers—something that ordinarily would blacklist a teacher in antiunion Georgia.

A superb administrator, she will maintain this top position through the controversies of racial integration, until retirement in 1960. One of her chief accomplishments is the introduction of male principals in elementary schools.

✦ Radio preacher Aimee Semple McPherson dies from an overdose of sleeping pills at age 53. Her life has been on a downward course since much of her audience lost faith in her after her mysterious 1926 disappearance. The politically conservative views she preached not only did not fit the New Deal era, but especially after her second divorce, they also contrasted with her personal life. She died estranged from most of her family, including her mother, who had served as McPherson's financial manager during her most successful years.

✦ After 25 years as head of the Women's Bureau of the Department of Labor, 72-year-old Mary Anderson resigns. Her reason is only partially a readiness to retire: Anderson feels that her boss, Labor Secretary Frances Perkins, is not sufficiently committed to the Women's Bureau.

Perkins, in turn, can reasonably argue that the profound problems of the Great Depression and World War II have demanded greater attention and that as the first woman on the cabinet, she cannot risk alienating powerful men.

✦ Eleanor Roosevelt speaks at a luncheon honoring Dorothy Jacobs Bellanca, who has been a garment worker organizer since she was a child laborer in Baltimore at the turn of the century. A Jew from Latvia, she gave up her vice presidency in the United Garment Workers when she married a Sicilian who also was a UGW vice president.

An interesting comparison is Rose Pesotta, who refuses to run for reelection as a vice president of the International Ladies' Garment Workers' Union this year. On the convention floor, she accuses the union's male leadership of maintaining a quota of only one woman on its executive board—despite the fact that 85% of the 300,000 ILGWU members are women. Pesotta (who was born Peisoty in Russia) says she is tired of being a token and returns to work as a sewing machine operator.

◆ After 23 years with the Internal Revenue Service, Anne Scheiber retires; although she has a 1924 degree from Washington's National University Law School, the IRS has never promoted her or permitted her to use her legal training.

Scheiber takes her $5,000 in savings and begins investing in the stock market, and when she dies in 1995 at 101, she is worth $22 million. She leaves the money to Yeshiva University for the use of Jewish female students, cleverly writing her will so that the IRS—which discriminated against her —will not be able to collect a dime of her bequest.

◆ When Franklin Roosevelt is nominated for an unprecedented third term at this year's Democratic convention, another precedent also begins: Dorothy Bush calls the roll of the states, something that she will do for the next 40 years. As the party's national secretary, she handles the vote count for 10 conventions; she is never opposed for reelection and retires in 1988.

◆ Crystal Bird Fauset, who in 1938 became the first black woman elected to a state legislature, makes a disastrous political move. After her Works Progress Administration position ended when that depression agency closed, the Roosevelt administration provided her with a job for the Democratic Party—but shortly before the election, she endorses Roosevelt's opponent, Thomas Dewey.

Roosevelt defeats Dewey, and Faucet is abandoned by the Republicans who recruited her. She spends the rest of her life lecturing on race relations; her appeals for an African diplomatic post after the Republicans regain the White House are in vain.

◆ Women's Army Corps commander Oveta Culp Hobby keeps secret the fact that she is hospitalized several times for exhaustion. Charged with creating a military unit comparable to nothing extant, Hobby managed to recruit, train, and supervise some 100,000 women assigned to posts all over the globe—but at great cost to herself. The mother of two and still in her 30s, she routinely works 14 hours a day, seven days a week.

When she resigns in July of 1945, after the European war is over, Hobby will be rewarded with the Army's Distinguished Service Medal. Although the DSM had been awarded to more than 20 women in World War I, historical records on women are so poorly preserved that many believe this is a precedent. Indeed, a number of publications erroneously cite both Hobby and other women as the first to receive this medal.

◆ The Women's Air Service Pilots is disbanded by Christmas, even though the war is not yet over. Until the Battle of the Bulge brings a major setback, people believe that victory is around the corner—and male pilots now want the positions held by these quasi-military women. Some 2,000 WASPs have flown more than 30 million miles in 77 types of aircraft for various military purposes. A monument at their home base in Sweetwater, Texas, will bear witness to the 38 WASPs who lost their lives in service to their country.

◆ Army nurses at the Battle of the Bulge spend their Christmas season moving patients and hospital equipment at night, so that the roads are available to the troops in the day. They do this, of course, under blackout rules, which allow not even the light of a cigarette, and in one of the coldest winters Europe has ever seen. When they finally settle into semipermanent quarters in France, the small detachment of nurses in the 57th Field Hospital discover that they have been supporting 24 battalions of men, many of whom are in critical condition.

One woman will remember "being surrounded by German troops during the battle and shielding critically wounded patients under the operating table when the hospital was strafed." Another tells of her unit in Belgium, which performed 388 operations in 80 hours: "Everyone worked until they were on the verge of collapse." When the Germans attack, this 107th Evacuation Hospital moves out 400 patients in 10 minutes and loses none. Several days later, a 107th nurse sees a German POW wearing the pajamas she left behind.

"Flight nurses" begin operations in the remote terrain of Burma and other areas of the South Pacific this year. Usually one woman flies alone on planes that—because they carry weapons into war zones—are not marked with the Red Cross and thus are exposed to all the dangers of combat. They will establish an amazing record of success: During the 13 months that remain of the war, these young women move out 37,000 men and lose just one patient.

Often they perform a doctor's duty, for they see men in emergency conditions with faces half blown away or with gaping chest and stomach wounds. They administer oxygen and plasma, adjust medications to match the plane's altitude, and handle shell-shocked psychiatric cases without assistance. Trained at Kentucky's Bowman Field, these women not only learn specialized medicine but also become familiar with parachuting, dodging machine-gun fire, and swimming fully clad.

1945 Because "the need is too pressing to await the outcome of further efforts at recruiting," President Franklin Roosevelt in his State of the Union speech calls for an amendment of the Selective Service Act to "provide for the induction of nurses into the Armed Forces."

A poll shows that 73% of Americans support the president on this, and, for the first time in American history, Congress debates drafting women. Although votes on amendments are close, the final version of the Nurses Selective Service Act is approved by the House by an overwhelming 347 to 42 in March.

In early April, it is reported out favorably by the Senate Military Affairs Committee, the only important amendment being to strike the exemption that the House had given to married women. In early May, however, the Army enters Berlin, the war in Europe is over, and the bill dies when the need is no longer urgent. The precedent for drafting women is not set, but it comes very close —and very few congressmen argue against this historic change in the status of women.

When Congress convenes, the nation is without a female presence in the U.S. Senate for the first time since 1931, when Hattie Caraway of Arkansas joined the Senate. Although she had previously withstood close races against conservative men, Caraway lost last fall's election to liberal William Fulbright. President Roosevelt appoints Caraway to a commission on federal employment, and she lives the rest of her life in Washington, D.C.

Under the command of Major Charity Adams of the Women's Army Corps, the 6888th Central Postal Directory is the first unit of black WACs sent overseas. They demonstrate their value by setting speed records in sorting an enormous backlog of mail for soldiers.

Letters from home are extremely precious to those on war duty, and millions of women write every day. Post office advertisements encourage this—but although the mail load is greatly increased and although military women are efficient in handling it, relatively few civilian women are hired for postal jobs.

Two months before the European war ends, Hadassah founder Henrietta Szold dies in Jerusalem. Past 80, she has spent the last decade assisting Jews who flee from the Nazis. On her 70th birthday, she was the first woman granted an honorary Doctor of Hebrew Letters by the Jewish Institute of Religion, and last year, Boston University gave her an honorary degree for her lifetime of humanitarian service. With the world still at war and civilian travel banned, she listened to the ceremony by radio.

NBC radio reporter Helen Hiett broadcasts the news when Italians hang Mussolini. She had earlier scoops in the war too: Hiett was one of the last to broadcast from occupied France, sending her reports via shortwave radio before the Vichy government forced her to flee to Switzerland. From there, she went to neutral Spain, where her broadcast about the bombing of Gibraltar won the National Headliners Award—a first for women.

A 1934 graduate of the University of Chicago, she will continue a radio and television career after marriage and motherhood; when she dies in 1961, while climbing in the French Alps, her name is Helen Hiett Waller.

◆ When the Germans surrender and the concentration camp at Buchenwald is liberated, Margaret Bourke-White takes graphic photos of the horrors there. *Life*'s editorial board debates whether to publish them, for the unwritten journalistic rule has been that the public is shielded from viewing the true scenes. The editors decide to adopt Bourke-White's view that the reality of fascism will never be understood unless the pictures are realistic, and her compelling photos are unveiled to the world.

◆ General Dwight D. Eisenhower awards the first Medal of Freedom to a foreign woman: Charlene Chable Rotondo, who will die in New Hampshire in 1990, is honored for saving the lives of 32 American pilots captured in Nazi-occupied France. Herself taken prisoner by the Germans, she escaped to carry on her work.

◆ Captain Sue Dauser, who headed the Navy Nurse Corps throughout the war, is honored with the Distinguished Service Medal. As superintendent of the NNC from 1939 to 1946, she also was the first woman promoted to captain.

Mildred McAfee, who commanded the Navy's WAVES, returns to the presidency of Wellesley College in December. Although she set policy in a new institution and commanded 100,000 women during the war, she never rose above captain—a rank given men who command as few as 500. The same is true for WAC commander Oveta Culp Hobby, who had no rank at all until 1943, when she was made a colonel. Although congressional leaders discussed granting the generalship that Hobby was due, the promotion never materialized.

The leader of the Women's Air Service Pilots, internationally famous Jacqueline Cochran, is not granted military rank at all prior to the disbandment of the WASP, but she does receive the Distinguished Service Medal this year.

◆ The Labor Department announces that 7 million women have joined the workforce since 1941, as defense industries prove so desperate for labor that many hire more women than men. Women surprise the skeptical by performing well in aircraft plants, shipyards, and dangerous munitions factories, and they find new opportunities in nontraditional jobs ranging from taxi driver to department store Santa Clauses. Many "white-collar" jobs formerly held by men become forever "pink collar," as women take over such occupational slots as bank tellers, train ticket agents, and retail clerks. Women make up about 35% of the labor force during the war, or more than one of every three workers.

◆ Political reporter May Craig, who began writing for Gannett newspapers in 1931, is not successful in her attempt to attend an all-male dinner of the White House Press Conference Association, but she does succeed in getting rest room facilities for female journalists at the Capitol's press galleries. The 1943 president of the Women's National Press Club, Craig obtained credentials as a war correspondent last year and reported from both the European and Asian fronts. She will go on to specialize in electronic media, becoming especially associated with the television interview show *Meet the Press* in the 1950s and 1960s.

◆ An unprecedented number of divorce cases fills the nation's courts, as couples find that war has changed them and as new prosperity provides the money to file suit. Nowhere in the nation, however, may couples divorce by mutual consent. Many states allow divorce only on the grounds of proven adultery or long-term desertion, while South Carolina law has no provision at all for divorce.

Nevada is the most prominent of a handful of states that have developed divorce laws to create a cottage industry attracting revenue from divorce seekers: one marital partner goes to a "divorce mill" state, establishes six weeks of residency, and obtains the decree. The Supreme Court rules this year that states must recognize divorces granted by any other state as legal.

◆ The war offers historic opportunities to women in science. Among them are botanist Fanny-Fern Davis, an employee of the U.S. Golf Association, whose herbicide is demonstrated on the White House lawn. Herbicides are useful in warfare because pilots can see targets better if forests are defoliated. At the same time, Davis works with her husband, also a botanist, on the hydroponic growing of vegetables, which is aimed at getting fresh produce to troops in combat areas.

Dr. Eloise Gerry, a recognized specialist in forestry since World War I, uses her abilities to determine the habitat of foreign wood. Similarly, geologist Julia Ann Gardner, who earned her doctorate from Johns Hopkins in 1911, is so astute that she can study the sand used as ballast in Japanese weaponry to tell the military from what beach in Japan it came.

The woman who will receive the most postwar attention for her scientific work is WAVE Ensign Grace Hopper, who has a Yale doctorate and who programs the nation's first large-scale digital computer in a basement at Harvard. Among the common assignments given to WAVES is the calculation of ordnance ranges, and Hopper uses this early computer to figure target distances for the D-Day invasion. After her husband is killed in combat, she stays on with the postwar Navy; eventually she will be termed "the Grand Old Lady of Software."

◆ The war's most significant clerical job may be that of Pearl Noble, who is the nation's official engrosser of treaties. She serves in the State Department under both the Roosevelt and Truman administrations and is responsible for ensuring that complex documents in various languages are perfect. Among others, she prepares the agreements that set up the United Nations headquarters and the North Atlantic Treaty Organization —and in a time of manual typewriters, carbon paper, and erasers, Noble is proud that she once typed 50 pages without an error.

◆ As the war winds down, one indication of the general attempt to return women to their traditional roles is the formation of the Future Homemakers of America. FHA membership will become a virtual requirement for girls in many high schools during the next few decades, especially among southern whites.

◆ Like blacks in the South, Alaskan natives frequently encounter discrimination; businesses even post signs saying that they do not want Indian customers. When Alaska's territorial legislature holds hearings on a proposed civil rights bill, Elizabeth Peratrovich gives such moving testimony on the injustices she has encountered that the legislature overwhelmingly passes a bill assuring natives access to public accommodations and the right to live in the neighborhood of their choice.

◆ The last of some 1,800 poems left by Emily Dickinson when she died in 1886 are finally published. Much of the delay was because Dickinson's only brother, who was also her executor, had an adulterous relationship with Mabel Loomis Todd, a family friend who prepared the handwritten poems for publication.

Todd (a descendant of Plymouth pioneer Priscilla Alden) took these poems with her when she left Massachusetts after Emily's sister, Lavinia

WAVES run the air traffic control tower at the Naval Air Station in Anacostia, near the capital. Although many women proved their competence in such jobs during the war, few were able to continue in these well-paid positions after the war ended. Women In Military Service Memorial and the U.S. Navy

Dickinson, successfully sued to recover property that her brother had given to Todd.

◆ After a lifetime of scholarship on women, 70-year-old Mary Beard publishes *Woman as a Force in History*. Her famous husband is no longer alive to protect her from hostile reviewers, however, and they attack her viciously, despite Beard's careful research and unusual insight.

◆ In the last year of the war, Jessamyn West finds success writing fiction based on the moral dilemma of pacifist Quakers during the Civil War. *The Friendly Persuasion* is popular enough to be the basis of a major movie and hit song in the next decade.

◆ The year's best-selling book is *Forever Amber* by Kathleen Winsor. Despite its setting of 17th-century England, the candid sexuality of its female protagonist makes it very controversial. While banned in Boston, millions elsewhere buy the book and stand in lines two years later to see the movie.

◆ "Little Lulu" begins what will soon be a starring role in Dell's comic books. Drawn by Marjorie Henderson Buell—who signs herself simply "Marge"—"Little Lulu" has been featured in the pages of *Saturday Evening Post* since 1935. An adventurous girl often seen skipping school and playing practical jokes, she is also the target of mischievous behavior from boys—especially after the author retires and the strip is written by men. Not only do Lulu's male friends run the standard "No Girls Allowed" clubhouse, they also practice a "Mumday," on which they speak to no females, including their mothers.

◆ The Pulitzer Prize for drama goes to Mary Chase, whose *Harvey* is the delightful story of an invisible rabbit. The movie version also enjoys long-term popularity, with television reruns for the rest of the century.

◆ After the death of Susan Anthony's sister Mary, with whom Anthony lived for many years, her longtime home at 17 Madison Street in Rochester is in danger of being lost to history. A group of local women, mostly elderly, manage to incorporate themselves, buy the property, and turn it into a National Landmark.

◆ Because she is fluent in Chinese, the State Department sends Camilla Biggerstaff to China; as Camilla Mills, she was a missionary there in the 1920s. During the war, she worked for the Office of Strategic Services, the forerunner of the modern Central Intelligence Agency (CIA). She can remain in China only a year, however, before Communist victories there force Americans to leave.

◆ A number of women are involved in the formation of the United Nations:

New York Times columnist Anne O'Hare McCormick serves on a secret advisory committee to President Roosevelt that formulates postwar policy, and this leads to her appointment as a delegate to UN formative meetings. FDR also appoints former congresswoman Ruth Bryan Owen to a special assignment at the State Department, where she assists in drafting the charter. She will go on to chair the UN's research committee in 1948. At the same time, Virginia Gildersleeve, who has headed Barnard College since 1911, is the only woman in the delegation to the February planning conference.

After President Roosevelt's death in April, President Harry S Truman appoints fellow Southerner Mary McLeod Bethune, and when the charter is finalized in San Francisco in the summer, Bethune is the only woman of color in the world to have official status at the birth of the United Nations. Dr. Edna Fluegel also serves as a "special assistant" at this meeting; she later donates related papers to Georgetown University. Woman's Party attorney Alice Paul also plays a key role in the specific use of feminine nouns in human rights documents.

Finally, President Truman insists that former first lady Eleanor Roosevelt accept a leading role in the UN. Despite her comments to reporters after FDR's death that "the story is over" and she is a "nobody," New Year's Eve will find her headed to London for the first full meeting of this unprecedented organization.

1946 Emily Balch wins the Nobel Peace Prize. After being fired from Wellesley College for her opposition to World War I, Balch has worked for the Women's International League for Peace and Freedom from its Geneva headquarters. She is equally concerned with the "freedom" portion of the league's agenda and early recognized the dangers of fascism, speaking out on such prewar signals as aggression in Manchuria, Ethiopia, and Spain. During the war, Balch worked for Japanese Americans interned in the West and for Jewish refugees; at age 79, she is internationally honored.

✦ State Department men initially doubt the diplomatic ability of Eleanor Roosevelt, the only female delegate to the United Nations, but she soon proves them wrong. During two years of tedious meetings in Geneva, Paris, and New York, she uses her fluent French to chair the Human Rights Committee in endless debates on such important matters as the rights of refugees from the Soviet Union. Although the subject matter is vital, the meetings are procedural nightmares of trivial motions and objections intended to obstruct the agenda's completion.

✦ As the head of the Women's Action Committee for Victory and Lasting Peace, Vera Whitehouse pressures Eleanor Roosevelt on the details of United Nations administration. Whitehouse works for an atomic energy control mechanism, an effective international court system, and other specifics of new global organization, but her biggest behind-the-scenes success is the creation of the United Nations Educational, Scientific and Cultural Organization (UNESCO).

✦ Strikes were banned during the war (although a few occured, including one by black women in North Carolina cigarette plants), and labor protests therefore erupt at its end. The largest strike by women in American history begins when 230,000 telephone operators walk off the job. A 23-year-old "girl" in San Francisco is knocked unconscious, and women are arrested in New Jersey and Chicago, but the phone workers win a wage increase.

✦ The domestic worker as a regular part of middle-class homes vanishes during the war. A half-million women—many of them black—leave these jobs for the better opportunities available during the war, and they never return.

Wages remain high in the postwar economy, and women no longer are limited to cooking and cleaning for others, as had been the case in the 1930s. At the same time, the availability of many new appliances in the postwar world makes a maid less necessary, and middle-class couples who had talked of "the servant problem" during the war begin instead to cherish the privacy of the servantless home.

✦ The return of veterans brings widespread fears of unemployment, and despite the wartime experience of women in the workforce, a Gallup Poll finds that fundamental attitudes on female employment have not changed since the Great Depression. Both in 1936 and 1946, more than 80% of Americans believe that a woman should not work if her husband has a job. Even three-quarters of the women polled agree.

✦ Congress passes the War Brides Act to provide for the immigration of women who married American men overseas. While these immigrants receive the automatic citizenship of their husbands, both they and their new families frequently have to make difficult adjustments—especially German and Japanese women, who were so recently enemies. Many Women's Army Corps members who serve as escorts on ships of war brides also make it clear that they resent this assignment.

✦ Among the women who found life-expanding opportunity during the war was Smith College graduate Julia McWilliams, who went to Ceylon with the Office of Strategic Services—the forerunner of the modern CIA. She was introduced to exotic food there, and after her marriage this year to foreign service officer Paul Child, she will go to Paris, where as Julia Child, she becomes famous for her culinary skill.

✦ One of the year's best-sellers is *The Chrysanthemum and the Sword*, a study of Japanese culture by anthropologist Ruth Benedict. The Office of

War Information had employed Benedict for advice on dealing with enemy peoples during the war, and she will receive a grant from the Office of Naval Research for a major study of Asian and European values.

Dr. Benedict also edited *The Journal of American Folklore* for 15 years and, in 1947, will be elected president of the American Anthropological Association. Columbia University finally will grant her a full professorship in 1948, shortly before her sudden death at age 61.

+ Frances Xavier Cabrini is the first American citizen to be declared a saint. Canonized less than a century after her birth in Italy, Mother Cabrini led the church's work with Italians in America after her 1889 immigration. She became a U.S. citizen in 1909, and the Missionary Sisters of the Sacred Heart of Jesus that she founded had over 1,500 members in 67 convents throughout the world when she died in 1917.

+ Margaret Mitchell dies after being hit by a car. *Gone with the Wind*, which has sold 8 million copies in the decade since publication, enjoys a sales renewal in postwar Europe. The Nazis had banned it, presumably because of Mitchell's assertive heroine and intelligent African Americans.

+ Estée Lauder begins a cosmetic company. When her family finally takes the business public in 1995, its annual sales will be almost $3 billion.

+ The Republicans win control of the House of Representatives in the fall election, and because Edith Nourse Rogers is the most senior member of Veterans Affairs, she chairs the committee. Rogers therefore is extremely influential in drafting the historic GI Bill that provides college education, homeownership, and other assistance to millions of veterans.

+ Republican Representative Frances Bolton moves up to the chairmanship of the subcommittee on the Near East and Africa for the House Foreign Affairs committee. The previous year, Bolton met with the pope, and the following year, she will be the first woman received by the king of Saudi Arabia.

1947 Biochemist Gerty Radnitz Cori shares the Nobel Prize in Medicine with her husband, Carl Cori. They are honored for their discoveries in glucose enzymes and glycogen metabolism, which grew out of work on malignant tumors. During the course of this research, Dr. Cori was told more than once that her presence in the laboratory was detrimental to her husband's career.

Both earned their medical degrees in their native Prague, and the newly married couple immigrated to the United States in 1922. After a few years in Buffalo, they spend their careers at Washington University in St. Louis—but it is only after this year's prize that the university offers her a full faculty position.

Dr. Cori is the first female physician to win the Nobel Prize in Medicine since the global competition began in 1901. She leaps from underpaid obscurity to international honors, and President Truman will appoint her as an official of the new National Science Foundation.

+ The Navy Nurse Corps, which has existed since 1908, is "regularized," with its rank and other benefits made comparable to those of navy men. When the Army Nurse Corps, which is a decade older, is also regularized, wartime commander Colonel Florence Blanchfield is the first woman sworn into the regular army—but she is demoted from full colonel to lieutenant colonel in the process.

+ Author and folklorist Zora Neale Hurston, who published her autobiographical *Dust Tracks on the Road* (1942) at the height of her success, is arrested for child molestation. Although the charge is eventually dismissed because it is clearly false, Harlem newspapers exploit and embellish the story until her reputation is ruined. She returns to Florida from New York, and while she will sell occasional written works, Hurston—the first black graduate of prestigious Barnard College—will work at menial jobs until her 1960 death in a welfare institution.

+ Academy Award winner Hattie McDaniel stars in the very popular radio show *Beulah*. She refuses to use stereotyped black dialect, insists on a contract that allows her to change any script she finds distasteful, and earns $2,000 a week.

During the war, McDaniel headed the Hollywood Victory Committee's work among black soldiers, and she also successfully sues against housing discrimination. She continues the integration cause even in death, for in 1952, Hattie McDaniel will be the first African American buried in Los Angeles' Rosewood Cemetery.

+ The Tony Awards for achievement in live theater are named for actor/producer Antoinette Perry Frueauff. Best known as Tony Perry, she died last year at age 59; she directed her first major play in 1928. Among her most successful Broadway productions was *Harvey*, which won a Pulitzer Prize for playwright Mary Chase.

+ Reader's Digest Condensed Books begins with Agnes Rogers Allen as a founding editor. She remains with this project until retirement, while also writing her own books, including *Women Are Here to Stay* (1949). She endows a New York Public Library room for the use of writers, which is dedicated to her husband, author Fredrick Lewis Allen.

+ The publication of *Let's Cook It Right* begins a career in nutritional advice for Adelle Davis, who will also go on to sell millions of copies of books on physical fitness.

+ Marjory Stoneman Douglas, who has published fiction and nonfiction in national magazines since 1924, writes *River of Grass* about Florida's Everglades. It becomes a classic of environmental literature, and although attempts to drain the unique wetland continue to be made for another three decades, Douglas' message is eventually heeded.

+ Novelist Willa Cather dies. She has been much honored since her 1922 Pulitzer Prize, including election to the American Academy of Arts and Letters in 1938 and several honorary degrees. While her most famous work is set in frontier locales, Cather has lived in New York City since 1904.

1948 In recognition of the 100 years that have passed since the first Women's Rights Convention in Seneca Falls, the post office issues a stamp featuring three great leaders: Elizabeth Cady Stanton and Lucretia Mott, who convened the event, and Carrie Chapman Catt, who led the completion of the 1848 goal of enfranchisement. Susan Anthony, who did not attend the Seneca Falls meeting, already has been honored with a stamp that was issued in 1936 for the 30th anniversary of her death.

Several other stamps for women are issued this year. The individuals are Red Cross founder Clara Barton, Girl Scout founder Juliette Gordon Low, and—more obscurely—Moina Mitchell, who began the American Legion's tradition of selling paper red poppies as a fund raiser for disabled veterans. Gold Star Mothers, the designation given to women who lost children in World War II, are also honored. All five stamps are of the most commonly used 3-cent type.

+ The Women's Armed Services Integration Act formalizes the position of WACs, WAVES, and other non-Nurse Corps military women. The air force is separated from the army, and its female unit is dubbed the WAF—Women's Air Force. Mary Hallaren, who commanded army women overseas during the war, is the first of these to be commissioned into the regular army; she became WAC director last year and remains at the relatively low rank of colonel.

The bill is a compromise that provides a place for women, but it not only limits their rank, benefits, and occupational categories, it also holds them to a quota of 2% of the total forces. Nevertheless, it is an important milestone, marking the first inclusion of nonnursing women in the peacetime military.

+ The American Nurse Association begins admitting African-American members, although several affiliated state organizations still bar them. At the same time, Mary Church Terrell sues the Washington, D.C., chapter of the American Association of University Women for membership; when she wins, most of the white women ostracize her and form another chapter.

+ For the first time since 1917, a woman wins the Pulitzer Prize for biography. Margaret Clapp is honored for *Forgotten First Citizen: John Bigelow*, about a 19th-century New York writer and diplomat. Three years later, Margaret Louise Colt will win the prize for a book on a less obscure figure, *John C. Calhoun.*

+ The United Cerebral Palsy Fund is founded by Isabelle Goldenson and her husband, Leonard, a movie and television executive whose celebrity contacts enable her to raise funds for medical research. Their daughter was born with the disease when Isabelle Goldenson contracted rubella while pregnant in 1943; the child dies in 1973, never having learned to walk or talk. After interviewing "more than 100 doctors without gleaning much information" on the disease, Goldenson is motivated to fund research. She will also play a role in the establishment of reserved parking spaces for the disabled.

+ Michigan lawyer Anne Ruth Davidow Seeger files suit to overturn a state law that bans a woman from working as a bartender in any bar not owned by her father or husband. She loses the case.

+ The Ladies Professional Golf Association has its beginnings in a Miami hotel room. While all-time great athlete "Babe" Zaharias gives the LPGA public visibility, Minnesotan Patty Berg is its first president. Berg goes on a lifetime of professional golf, and in 1995, she will be the first woman honored by the male Professional Golf Association with its Distinguished Service Award.

+ Alice Cunningham is the first African-American woman to earn an Olympic award; she wins a medal for the high jump.

+ A nine-month prison term for narcotics violations does not matter to fans of Billie Holiday, who pack Carnegie Hall to hear her sing upon release. She will be arrested again in 1949 and 1956 but remains popular, especially in Europe. Her autobiography, *Lady Sings the Blues,* is published three years prior to her 1959 death. Many acclaim her as the greatest jazz singer of all time.

+ In November, Maine elects Margaret Chase Smith to the U.S. Senate, thus making her the first woman to serve in both the Senate and the House, to which she had been elected in 1940. A Republican who votes with the Democratic Party more often than many Democrats, Smith is especially interested in maritime issues and is known as "the mother of the Navy's WAVES."

+ Dorothy McCullough Lee is elected mayor of Portland, Oregon. She is the first woman chosen to lead a major city since Bertha Landes became mayor of Seattle in 1926.

+ Although Utah has elected more than 50 women to its legislature, this year marks its first election of a woman to Congress. Reva Beck Bosone, a Democrat from a largely Republican state, is a graduate of the University of California at Berkeley and a former judge; her voting record will be fairly liberal, and in 1952, she is defeated as being "soft on communism." As Mormons become more conservative in the second half of the century, no other Utah woman follows Bosone to Congress.

+ On December 10, the United Nations adopts the Universal Declaration of Human Rights, and Eleanor Roosevelt, who chairs the Human Rights Committee, receives a standing ovation. The document has been thrashed out during two years of debates between governments that have vastly different views of the rights of women and other minorities, but the ultimate statement is more liberal than any similar American document. Roosevelt has assisted the women's caucus in making sure that the language used is gender-neutral.

+ Gladys Vandenberg, who is married to the air force's chief of staff, notices burials in Arlington National Cemetery that are not attended by any family or friends. She organizes the Arlington Ladies so that no soldier or sailor will be buried unmourned.

The group continues through the century, and some of its veterans attend thousands of funerals. They witness the burials of military women, too, and volunteer comfort to their survivors.

1949   Having surprised the pundits by winning election in his own right, Democrat Harry S Truman begins his first full term as president and appoints a number of women to office.

Paper money has a feminine name on it for the first time when Georgia Neese Clark becomes United States Treasurer. A small-town Kansas banker, she is appointed by Truman because she was one of very few in her profession to believe that he could win the 1948 election.

Truman also is considered the first president to have a woman in a top position on his innermost staff. She is Beth Campbell Short of Oklahoma, and she is in charge of White House correspondence.

✦ In July, President Truman names Democratic Party fund-raiser Pearl Mesta as ambassador to Luxembourg. Hers is the third major diplomatic appointment granted to a woman, following Ruth Bryan Owen and Daisy Harriman under President Roosevelt. Although Mesta inherited her wealth, she is acknowledged to be an exceptionally good businesswoman who actually increased her fortune during the Great Depression. She points out that Luxembourg, although one of the smallest countries in the world, is its seventh largest producer of steel, and she tells reporters that she has visited those steel mills on business trips. Once active in Alice Paul's National Woman's Party, she learned her way around Washington by lobbying for the Equal Rights Amendment.

After the Republicans take office and Mesta loses her appointment, she returns to Washington, where invitations to her gatherings are much prized; she is long known as "the hostess with the mostest."

✦ President Truman also appoints Minnesota's Eugenie Moore Anderson as ambassador to Denmark, where her signature on a commercial treaty sets a precedent for women. She will go on to serve as minister to Bulgaria under President John Kennedy.

✦ As Nobel Prize winner Pearl Buck has long predicted, the Chinese civil war ends with a Communist victory. While politicians argue viciously over "who lost China," Buck joins with lesser-known writer Eslanda Robeson in *An American Argument*, a dialogue on racism. During this era, Robeson, the wife of African-American singer Paul Robeson, also is called before the House Un-American Activities Committee, which considers her commitment to racial equality communistic. Buck is too popular to be thus interrogated, but she uses a male pseudonym for several books published during this time of endangered free speech.

✦ The first blacks are admitted to the Women Marines, one of the few service units that saw no integration during World War II. At the same time, the Navy has its first female admiral when Lucile P. Leone, who is assigned to the Public Health Service, is promoted to rear admiral.

✦ Representative Frances Bolton, Republican millionaire from Ohio, writes an article for *American Magazine* bluntly titled "Women Should be Drafted." She finds "gallantry sadly out of date and rather stupid."

✦ Mildred Gillars, who broadcast for the Nazis during the war, is convicted of treason in Washington, D.C. "Axis Sally," age 49, will spend the next 12 years in a West Virginia federal prison for women. A native of Maine, she was recruited to work for the Nazis by her German lover. Gillars began broadcasting in 1940, before the United States entered the war, and continued until its very last day of May 8, 1945. Specializing in persuading American soldiers to surrender, she was the highest-paid radio personality in Germany.

"Tokyo Rose" was at least as infamous on the Pacific front, and one of several English-speaking women who broadcast under that name—34-year-old UCLA graduate Iva Toguri D'Aquino —is convicted of treason in San Francisco. Despite evidence that she was forced into this work when she was captured in Japan at the war's outbreak, D'Aquino will spend more than six years in prison.

- Sportswriters name "Babe" Didrikson Zaharias the outstanding female athlete of the century. Despite the fact that half of the 20th century remains when this proclamation is made, no one will touch Zaharias' record for success in many areas: the 1932 winner of three Olympic medals, she also wins prizes for track, basketball, baseball, diving, bowling, and tennis. A native of Texas, she is married to a Greek immigrant who promotes her career. Also a founder of the Ladies Professional Golf Association, she is the first woman to earn $1 million by playing golf.

- Massachusetts Republican Representative Edith Nourse Rogers is named in the divorce suit filed by the wife of her longtime campaign manager. Rogers continues her relationship with the man, and although they never marry, she wills her Maine vacation home to him when she dies in 1960. This personal situation does not affect her political career.

- At age 88, advice columnist Dorothy Dix retires. She has been published in newspapers for more than a half-century, and her column is the longest-running by the same author. She is read by 30 million people on three continents.

- Anthropologist Margaret Mead publishes a precursor to much modern feminist thought with *Male and Female: A Study of the Sexes in a Changing World*. A popular personality in the media, Mead has a tremendous impact on American thought, especially through her introduction of the alternative family structures and peaceful lifestyles she discovered among prewar Pacific island cultures.

  A similar book comes out in France this year, and after it is translated, Simone de Beauvoir's *The Second Sex* has global influence. It powerfully points out the inherently inferior position assigned women in virtually all societal institutions. Ironically, de Beauvoir herself is an excellent example of the secondary roles her book decries: although she is a well-credentialed philosopher, both Europeans and Americans see her as an appendage to her longtime lover, philosopher Jean-Paul Sartre.

1950 President Harry S Truman appoints the only woman ever to have served as assistant secretary of defense. Personnel expert Anna Rosenberg is chosen at the special request of Defense Secretary George C. Marshall, who had observed her work on soldier morale during World War II.

Credited with "knowing more Army privates than anyone else," Rosenberg had eaten GI rations and slept on the ground during observation trips for President Roosevelt, and in 1945, she became the first woman to receive the Medal of Freedom.

- For the first time in American history, women are "called involuntarily to military service along with men," when thirteen platoons of Women Marine Reserves are mobilized for the Korean War in June.

  During the next five years, 120,000 women will serve in all branches of the military. The majority stay in the United States, but 540 members of the Army Nurse Corps are among the first Americans to arrive in Pusan. They set up hospitals in combat zones, while Navy nurses serve on hospital ships and Air Force nurses fly with Air Evacuation units.

- Journalist Agnes Smedley, who long ago correctly predicted a Communist victory in the Chinese civil war, dies in England. At her request, her ashes are returned to China, where the government buries them with honors for this "Friend of the Chinese Revolution."

- Senator Margaret Chase Smith electrifies the nation by denouncing her fellow Republican Senator Joseph McCarthy for his abuse of civil liberties; her speech to the Senate, "A Declaration of Conscience," will become an important historical document. When McCarthy tries to take revenge by endorsing her Republican primary opponent, Smith trounces him with an amazing 82% of the vote.

- The Women's Trade Union League, which reached the height of its success 40 years earlier in the garment strike of 1909–10, formally disbands when Rose Schneiderman, at age 68, is appointed secretary of labor for the state of New

York. To some extent, it is a victim of its success, for after Schneiderman became union president in 1926 and her friend Franklin Roosevelt was elected president in 1932, much of the protective legislation that the WTUL advocated was passed as part of the New Deal. With the new legislation, as well as the ascension of rightists both in and out of labor circles after World War II, the WTUL disbands.

◆ Susan B. Anthony is added the Hall of Fame for Great Americans. Counting Anthony, the hall features 8 women and 89 men, including such obscure ones as James Buchanan Eads, William Thomas Green Morton, Augustus Saint Gaudens, Matthew Fontaine Maury, and Simon Newcomb.

◆ The Pulitzer Prize for poetry goes to Chicagoan Gwendolyn Brooks for *Annie Alley.* She is the first African-American woman to win, and she will go on to many other books and honors.

◆ Lucille Ball becomes an "overnight success" after three decades of seeking her fortune. She modeled in the 1920s under the pseudonym Diane Belmont; in the 1930s, she made several unsuccessful movies; and after her 1940 marriage to Cuban Desi Arnaz, she continued to seek acting jobs while waiting for him to return home from road trips with his band. This year, they form Desilu Productions, go into television, and *I Love Lucy* brings laughter to millions.

◆ Blues singer Ethel Waters achieves celebrity in another field: She earns the New York Drama Critics Circle Award for her performance in Carson McCullers' play *A Member of the Wedding.* Waters' autobiography, *His Eye is on the Sparrow,* is published next year to best-selling response.

◆ After starring this year in *All About Eve*—Bette Davis will sue Hollywood studios several times during the next decade for better acting roles.

◆ The November election features the first large-state U.S. Senate race between a man and a woman, as Republican Richard Nixon beats Democrat Helen Gahagan Douglas in a bitter election.

During her three terms in the House, Douglas strongly supported Presidents Roosevelt and Truman, and as Truman's appointee, she played a role in the development of the United Nations. It is this role that Nixon terms "communistic"; with other personal attacks on her and her Jewish movie star husband, Melvyn Douglas, he defeats her—and earns himself a reputation for dirty tricks.

So vicious is the campaign that other women are deterred from running in major races, and Democratic woman does not win a Senate seat until 1960.

1951 On a January morning, Captain Anna McGoff Robie, who serves in the 14th Field Hospital in Korea, is "awakened by a loud thumping sound." She sees "thousands of North Korean and Chinese prisoners marching by" and within a month, her hospital treats "30,000 patients, all very dirty and full of lice." Like other nurses, she goes three months without a shower—but is sprayed twice a week with the pesticide DDT.

◆ Hannah Arendt publishes *The Origins of Totalitarianism* and becomes a U.S. citizen at the same time. After earning her doctorate under some of the greatest German philosophers, she escaped from the Nazis after they jailed her in 1933. She fled to Paris, where she was again arrested and imprisoned after that city fell to the Nazis.

Her book is the first systematic analysis of the political philosophy that led to World War II, and she will continue to write similarly acclaimed—yet controversial—works until her death in 1975.

◆ The National Association of Colored Graduate Nurses disbands, with its leadership saying that because "the doors have been opened," there is no longer a need for a separate nursing organization based on race.

◆ Marianne Moore's seventh book wins her the Pulitzer Prize for poetry. A recognized part of New York's avant garde since 1915, Moore has lived with her mother and taught Sunday school most of her life. She will win the National Book Award the next year and be elected to the pres-

The housekeeping staff at Northwestern Hospital in Minneapolis on strike for union representation in 1951. Almost 50 years later, most similar women workers are still unorganized. Minnesota Historical Center

tigious American Academy of Arts and Letters in 1955.

The decade's other female winner in poetry is Moore's friend Elizabeth Bishop, who will win in 1956 for *Poems North and South*. Bishop's life is seemingly more sophisticated than Moore's: she divides her time between New York and the Florida Keys, teaches at Harvard, and consults for the Library of Congress.

✦ Reporter Marguerite Higgins wins the Pulitzer Prize for journalism. She is the Far East bureau chief for the *New York Herald Tribune* and covers the Korean War—despite objections from military men, who are overruled by General Douglas MacArthur. Taking the first plane to Korea when war broke out, she witnessed the first soldier's death and endured combat conditions to report on the fall of the capital city of Seoul.

✦ *The Chicago Defender* has long been one of the few national publications aimed at African Americans, and this year Ethel Payne begins a career there that ultimately brings her a reputation as the nation's preeminent black female journalist. Specializing in politics, she will report from every

inhabited continent except Australia. She covers warfare from Nigeria to Vietnam and will be the only black correspondent at a 1956 international conference in Indonesia.

✦ As chief historian for the Army Ordnance Corps, Constance McLaughlin Green writes a history of World War II for the Department of Defense.

✦ Democratic Party leader India Edwards, who has successfully urged President Truman to appoint more women to high office, turns down his offer of the national party chairmanship. She is unwilling to battle the men of the proverbial smoke-filled room.

✦ Lillian Vernon begins a mail-order business in her home. Within four decades, she will be shipping her catalog to almost half of the households in the United States.

Rose Totino bakes a pizza for the Minneapolis banker who is considering her loan application because he does not know what pizza is. She begins her business in a small kitchen, and two decades later, when she turns it over to Pillsbury for $22 million, her frozen pizza is the nation's top seller.

A third business innovation this year is that of Marion Donovan: she earns the gratitude of parents far into the future when she patents the disposable diaper. Her model is fashioned from a cut-up shower curtain and absorbent padding, but manufacturers turn her down, saying that production would not be cost efficient. When she personally sells them in department stores and —as any mother would predict—meets with instant success, she sells the business for $1 million.

1952 The House Un-American Activities Committee targets playwright Lillian Hellman for visiting the Soviet Union—which she did in a 1945 goodwill tour on an American plane flown by a Soviet crew, at a time when the two nations were allies against Germany and Japan.

Some suspect that the right-wingers' true complaint is the feminist challenge that Hellman's successful plays pose to the status quo, regardless, her work is blacklisted in Hollywood and on Broadway.

✦ During the war, Margaret Sanger's Voluntary Parenthood League (which was the National Birth Control League earlier in the century) changed its name once more: the new, more politically advantageous name is the Planned Parenthood Association, and this year, it expands into the International Planned Parenthood Association. Sanger travels throughout Asia promoting the cause, while she also raises money to finance research on a birth control pill.

✦ The post office perpetuates a national myth when it issues a stamp honoring Betsy Ross, but this is balanced by another stamp issued this year: "Women in Our Armed Services" depicts women in their uniforms for the Army, Navy, Marines, and Coast Guard during World War II.

✦ Dr. Florence Seibert testifies to the World Health Organization on behalf of the skin test that she has developed for diagnosing tuberculosis. Her test will become standard, and tuberculosis—a leading cause of death in the previous century—will be largely eradicated in modern cultures. Choosing not to profit from human misery, she does not patent this or any other of her significant medical inventions.

✦ The Women's Bureau of the Department of Labor reports that there are some 12,000 female physicians in the nation compared with approximately 200,000 male ones.

✦ Aside from her political and educational career, Mary McLeod Bethune has had a lifelong interest in a life insurance company that she helped develop early in the century when blacks could not get coverage elsewhere. All 13 of the men who cofounded Central Life Insurance with her have now died, and Bethune becomes the only female president of an insurance company in the United States.

In the same year, President Truman appoints her as an emissary to Liberia.

✦ At age 67, Edna Ferber enjoys renewed best-seller status with *Giant*, a Texas-based novel that

becomes a hit movie and song. *Ice Palace* (1958) follows up this success with the story of the nation's last frontier, Alaska. Single all of her life, Ferber is one of America's wealthiest authors when she dies in 1968. Ferber is the only woman to have a best-seller in this decade, and only one woman will do so in the next; in contrast, during the century between 1852 and 1952, women topped the best-seller list on an average of one in every three years.

✦ Experimental photographer Elizabeth Austen is "discovered," crippled and penniless, in a Staten Island home for paupers. More than 50 years earlier, she had taken some 5,000 photos of upper-class society; the glass plates that she preserved re-create a world long gone.

✦ A precedent is set in the fall elections when Oliver Payne Bolton wins an Ohio seat adjacent to that of his mother and joins her in Congress. The headlines feature him telling his mother to "stay the hell out of my district," but his political career will be much less successful than hers. While she never loses an election in 29 years, he is in and out for a decade. Near the end of the century, they remain the only mother-son team to have served in Congress.

✦ Leonor K. Sullivan, Democrat of St. Louis, defeats an incumbent congressman; she will go on to win reelection 12 times. The author of the food stamp program, she finally succeeds in passing that bill in 1964, and in 1968, she leads the floor fight for truth-in-lending credit reform.

✦ The presidential election sees the Republicans take control of the White House for the first time in 20 years. Popular Army General Dwight D. Eisenhower defeats Illinois Governor Adlai Stevenson; while Eleanor Roosevelt leads women in campaigning for Stevenson, a former New Deal administrator and United Nations diplomat, Eisenhower is backed by women who appreciate the support that he gave to women in the wartime military.

1953 Among those called before the House Un-American Activities Committee is 70-year old labor expert Mary Van Kleeck, whose American heritage dates back to colonial New York. Her patriotism is questioned because she writes sympathetically of the working class and because she traveled to the Soviet Union, America's ally in World War II, after the war ended.

◆ Ethel Rosenberg, the only woman in American history to be executed for espionage, dies with her husband, Julius, in the electric chair at New York's Sing Sing prison on June 19—the day following their 14th wedding anniversary. The mother of two young children and a former secretary, the evidence against her is slim, and the case is an international cause célèbre throughout the decade.

Like Mary Surratt, who was wrongly executed because her son and boarders in her rooming house were involved in the assassination of Abraham Lincoln, Rosenberg's case is one of guilt by association during an era of similar hysteria. Her Jewish heritage is also a factor, for many people seem inexplicably to resent Jewish Americans as Holocaust horrors are revealed.

◆ The first female diplomatic appointment outside of northern Europe goes to former Republican congresswoman Clare Luce Booth, whom President Eisenhower appoints as ambassador to Italy. Because Booth's political connections are augmented by the fact that she is married to the publisher of America's most well-read magazines, the appointment of Frances Willis as ambassador to Switzerland is an even more significant milestone. Willis is the first woman to rise through the ranks at the State Department to achieve such a prestigious position.

◆ Eisenhower appoints a man to replace Democrat Nellie Taylor Ross as director of the U.S. Mint; Ross, who was the nation's first female governor, has headed the mint for two decades, since Franklin Roosevelt appointed her in 1933.

However, Eisenhower is careful to replace U.S. Treasurer Georgia Neese Clark with another woman, Republican activist Ivy Baker Priest. Women will hold that largely ceremonial post for decades into the future.

◆ President Eisenhower, who worked with Oveta Culp Hobby when she headed the Women's Army Corps, gives her the second Cabinet appointment made to a woman: she becomes head of the newly created Department of Health, Education and Welfare. The agency itself is controversial, and Hobby—who is from Texas—draws additional right-wing attacks when she appoints Jane M. Spaulding, an officer in the National Association of Colored Women, as her chief assistant.

◆ Aviator Jacqueline Cochran becomes the first woman to break the sound barrier. She has been experimenting with jet planes since the Air Force belatedly granted her military rank in 1948, and Cochran will go on to set several more records in the next decade, when she is over 50 years old. In 1959, her colleagues will honor her with election as the first female president of the Fédération Aéronautique Internationale.

◆ NBC Television hires Pauline Fredrick to cover the United Nations, and she develops a national following as the first woman reporting serious television news. A foreign correspondent during World War II, Fredrick covered the Nuremberg trials of Nazi officials, and she will report on the

Women who served in the Korean War lived and worked in primitive, dangerous conditions. The war set a precedent when Women Marine Reserves were called up for involuntary service, and members of the Army Nurse Corps were among the first to arrive in Korea. Women in Military Service Memorial

Korean War, revolutions in Africa and the Middle East, and the 1962 Cuban missile crisis. After more than two decades with NBC, in 1976, she will become the first woman to moderate a presidential debate.

+ At nearly age 90, Mary Church Terrell, who has grown impatient with the slow progress of civil rights since her first turn-of-the-century activity, finally wins a Supreme Court victory. The case developed out of her leadership in some of the nation's first integration actions, when she led other blacks in a sit-in at a Washington restaurant. They were refused service, and when she sues on the basis of never-repealed Reconstruction laws, the Court is forced to concede her case.

Even more creatively, Terrell surreptitiously buys up theater tickets that she distributes to African Americans, thus forcing management to either admit them or play to an empty house.

+ Dorothy Parker, whose 20-plus screenplays include *A Star Is Born* (1937) and Lillian Hellman's *Little Foxes* (1941), writes a stage play, *Ladies of the Corridor*. Its portrayal of women's lives is too honest for the era, however, and at the end of her life, Parker will feel that she is a failure.

1954　Dr. Virginia Apgar, whose Columbia University anesthesiology professorship set several precedents in the past two decades, develops a system for measuring the health of newborns at delivery. The Apgar Score is used in hospitals throughout the world for the rest of the century.

+ Ella Baker is elected president of the New York City branch of the National Association for the Advancement of Colored People, and as a sign of her belief in grass-roots organizing, she moves the office from downtown to Harlem. Baker has worked in various civil rights capacities in the North since 1927; in 1957, she will return to her native South to become executive secretary of the newly formed Southern Christian Leadership Conference. There she puts her decades of experience to work for young Martin Luther King.

+ For years to come, national life will revolve around the decision that the Supreme Court

hands down just before its summer recess. In *Brown v. Topeka Board of Education*, it rules that the city of Topeka, Kansas, may not send black children to segregated schools when a neighborhood school is available for white children. School integration will absorb public attention for decades to come, as many systems resist the court's ruling.

This vital precedent for racial equality is set in the name of Linda Brown, one of 20 black children whose parents sued on their behalf in 1950. Like the others, she lives in a white neighborhood but was forced to travel past nearer schools to attend an elementary school for blacks.

+ Former teacher and congressional employee Nancy Dickerson becomes associate producer of CBS's *Face the Nation*. Her ambition is to be an on-air television reporter, however, and she works for that goal by obtaining newsworthy interviews from contacts she made as a staffer of the Senate Foreign Relations Committee. In 1960, she becomes the network's first female correspondent—at the same time that she begins a five-minute radio show called *One Woman's Washington*.

+ The top graduate at Yale Law School is Ellen A. Peters—and not one law firm offers her a job. She teaches and, a decade later, becomes the law school's first tenured female professor. She continues to benefit from the revived feminist movement and, in 1984, Peters will rise to chief justice of the Connecticut Supreme Court.

+ Amy Vanderbilt begins writing a syndicated column on etiquette that challenges Emily Post's dominance of this field. The women are from two of America's wealthiest families, and their entrance into public life signifies an end to the upper-class notion that ladies may not work for money. The rules of polite society undergo rapid adjustment in this postwar era of increased democratization and greater informality; the disappearance of servants and the entrance of middle-class women into the work force are just two factors that call for change in social rituals.

◆ Philadelphian Grace Kelly wins the Academy Award for Best Actress only two years after making her first major movie. She will marry Prince Rainier III of Monaco in a fairy-tale wedding in 1956 and will live the rest of her life abroad. Although her film career is extremely short, the Princess Grace image will remain one of Hollywood's benchmarks for women.

◆ The Pulitzer Prize in spot news photography goes to "Mrs. Walter M. Schau, Amateur."

◆ While no postage stamp has yet honored a black woman, the second one with a Native American woman is issued this year. It depicts Sacajawea, a Shoshoni who breast-fed her infant as she scouted for the Lewis and Clark expedition in 1805. The stamp, which reads 1804–1954, is in honor of the expedition's 150th anniversary. The post office opts for the variant spelling of "Sacagawea" and shows her in a canoe with men under the heading of "Lewis and Clark Expedition."

◆ In the November election, Minnesota Democrat Coya Gjesdal Knutson, the daughter of Norwegian immigrant farmers, defeats an incumbent Republican. She will become the first woman on the House Agriculture Committee, an assignment of tremendous importance to her constituents. She will also obtain the first funding for cystic fibrosis research and will propose ideas that are later adopted, including student loans and the income tax checkoff to fund presidential campaigns.

1955 Tranquilizers go on the market, and within five years, 1.15 million pounds are sold annually, mostly to women.

◆ Although few social commentators notice, the postwar culture sees a dramatic rise in out-of-wedlock births: the number of babies placed for adoption is up 80% from a decade ago.

◆ Leftist orator Elizabeth Gurley Flynn spends her 65th and 66th birthdays in a West Virginia federal prison. Like many discontented depression-era intellectuals, she joined the Communist Party in 1937, thereby violating the Smith Act—passed in 1940.

Although Flynn actively supported the government during World War II, she was retroactively targeted by McCarthy-era prosecutors and convicted in a nine-month trial. Refusing the option of deportation to the Soviet Union, she publishes two books while imprisoned.

◆ Oveta Culp Hobby resigns from her cabinet position because her husband is critically ill. She had overseen the startup and success of both the Women's Army Corps and the Department of Health, Education and Welfare, but she is nonetheless criticized for various problems with the new polio vaccine.

◆ President Eisenhower appoints Mary Donlon, a New York attorney who specializes in industrial issues, to the U.S. Customs Court. She is the first woman to serve on this branch of the federal judiciary.

◆ Eisenhower does not reappoint Eugenie Anderson, who represented the United States in Denmark under Truman. In a speech summarizing her experience, Anderson predicts that the 20th century will not be known for either fascist or Communist dictatorship, and that what distinguishes the century "won't even be the rise of Asia. It will be the triumph of the western democracies—the real emergence of a real community . . . of free nations."

◆ Gwendolyn Carter, a professor at Smith College, publishes *The Politics of Equality*, a farsighted view of South African apartheid. In the next decade, Dr. Carter, who is white, will be one of the founders of the new academic field of African studies.

◆ The American College of Nurse-Midwives is founded in Washington, D.C., at a time when the use of midwives is at a historic low point.

◆ Anne Morrow Lindbergh's *Gifts from the Sea* is a best-seller; some of it presages future commentary on the status of women.

◆ A New York theater is renamed for Helen Hayes in honor of her half century of Broadway acting. Hayes works both on stage and screen, and her career is far from over. She will win a second Academy Award in 1970; her first was in 1932.

Among the historically important women she depicts during this long career are Cleopatra, Harriet Beecher Stowe, and Mary of Scotland in a play written especially for her. Her portrayal of Queen Victoria requires her to age 80 years during two hours.

✦ Using the pseudonym Ann Landers, Esther Friedman Lederer begins writing an advice column for the *Chicago Sun-Times*. Only a month later, her twin sister, Pauline Friedman Phillips, begins a similar feature for *San Francisco Chronicle* as Abigail van Buren, or "Dear Abby." Both are popularly syndicated, and the twins keep their relationship secret from their millions of readers for years.

✦ On December 1, in Montgomery, Alabama, seamstress Rosa Parks is tired after a long day of work and refuses to give up her bus seat to a white man. "I had enough," she explains later. "I wanted to be treated like a human being." She is arrested and jailed, and her action gives Martin Luther King, Jr., the catalyst for a boycott that begins the nation's first successful massive resistance to segregation.

1956 Long before James Meredith's more famous university integration, Autherine Lucy sets the precedent at the University of Alabama. Soon after the 1954 court decision that required tax-supported schools to accept students without regard to race, Lucy successfully filed suit in federal court to study library science at Alabama. Her February 3 attempt to enroll is greeted by a mob of 1,000, who threaten her as she rides to class with the dean of women. Intimidated by the violence, the university suspends her just three days after admission.

Despite threats to her life, Lucy goes back to court to have the order enforced, and with future Supreme Court justice Thurgood Marshall, the lawyer assigned her by the National Association for the Advancement of Colored People, she again wins. In March, however, the university trumps up a technical violation of school rules

and again expels her. Neither Marshall nor the NAACP pursues this obvious miscarriage of justice, and Lucy's case dies.

✦ Resistance to the Supreme Court's ruling on school desegregation is so strong that South Carolina passes a law forbidding government employees from membership in civil rights organizations. Septima Poinsette Clark—who has taught in Charleston area black schools for 40 years—is fired when she refuses to deny her membership in the NAACP.

✦ No women have ever won a Pulitzer Prize for news reporting. Two years ago, the Pulitzer committee began a category for "Local General Reporting," and this year, it is won by a woman. Caro Brown of the Alice, Texas, *Daily Record* shares the prize with a male reporter from another small-town Texas paper. Their work has been dangerous, for the story they break succeeds in ending the career of a man who had political control of this area near the Mexican border.

✦ *McCall's* has its highest single-issue sales ever with a cover story titled "The Mother Who Ran Away."

✦ The median annual income for women is $2,179 annually, while the analogous figure for men is $4,466. For nonwhite women, the number plummets to $970.

✦ Divorced, a mother, and lacking a high school education, Bette Graham takes one of the few jobs always open to women and becomes a typist, even though she is unskilled at this, too. In attempting to use white paint to cover her mistakes, she invents Liquid Paper—and within a decade has a $1 million business.

✦ On the other end of the scale is businesswoman Josephine Bay, chairman of the board of American Export Lines, who inherits enough stock in the prestigious brokerage firm of A.M. Kidder to be elected chairman and president. She is the first woman to head a New York Stock Exchange brokerage house.

◆ Designer Hattie Carnegie dies a multimillionaire, having achieved a dream that began when, as a young Austrian immigrant, she so admired financier Andrew Carnegie that she changed her name from Henrietta Koningeiser. She opened a New York dress shop in 1909, where she specialized in hats and in the "little Carnegie suit" that became a staple of fashionable wardrobes. Her third marriage, which lasted 30 years, was a commuter one: her husband lived on the West Coast, while she remained in New York and Paris.

◆ Women continue to dominate the garment trade, but they still lack proper representation in their own unions. Although the 626,000 women who belong to the International Ladies' Garment Workers' Union and the Amalgamated Clothing Workers make up about 75% of the total membership, only four of 35 seats on the unions' governing boards are held by women.

◆ Maria Callas, who was born Maria Kalogeropoulos in New York, returns from Greece to debut with the New York Metropolitan Opera. In the 1970s, her name will be linked with that of Aristotle Onassis, the husband of former first lady Jacqueline Kennedy Onassis.

◆ The La Leche League is founded to promote breast-feeding, which has become uncommon during the past several decades. Most physicians believe that bottle-feeding is more scientific, and as most babies are delivered in hospitals after World War II, women's breasts are routinely bound to stop the flow of milk.

◆ Tenley Albright becomes an international media star after winning the gold medal for figure skating. Unlike most young athletes, however, she will go on to distinguish herself by graduating from Harvard Medical School in 1961; she practices medicine the rest of her life.

◆ For the first time since the passage of the 19th Amendment 36 years ago, the number of men and women who cast ballots in the presidential election is approximately equal. Many older women never became accustomed to voting and have been unwilling to defy disapproving husbands.

1957 Columbia University announces that the law of parity, which had governed modern physics, has been disproved by Dr. Chien Shiung Wu, a Manhattan Project physicist who worked on producing fissionable uranium for the atomic bomb. She was born in China in 1912 and earned her doctorate in physics at the University of California.

◆ Evelyn Wood is nearly 50 when she begins the career that makes her a household name. She teaches speed reading at the University of Utah (where she had earned an English degree almost three decades earlier), and the class is so popular that she will open her own school just two years later.

The Evelyn Wood Reading Dynamic Institute is based in Washington, D.C., where people in government have a particular need to comprehend masses of information quickly. Her success is ensured when President Kennedy takes office in 1961—just four years after Wood taught her first class—and sends his staff to learn her method. She will sell her business and retire less than a decade later, in 1966; at the height of enrollment, in 1978, there are 150 Evelyn Wood reading schools throughout the nation.

◆ Betty Friedan surveys Smith College alumnae and finds great dissatisfaction among her peers. After spending the next several years testing and refining her thesis, she publishes the results as *The Feminine Mystique* (1963). The book will ignite a revitalized women's movement.

◆ Congress establishes the Civil Rights Commission, but the agency is seen as intended for blacks. More than a decade will pass before women's rights begin to be viewed as civil rights that are enforceable by the commission.

◆ Daisy Bates, who was elected president of the Arkansas chapter of the National Association for the Advancement of Colored People a year prior to *Brown v. Topeka*, draws international attention in the fall, when she begins to integrate Little

Rock's Central High School. Her action is the first in the South. She will endure arrest, the bankruptcy of the newspaper that she and her husband publish, and assault by rocks and bullets for years afterward.

She has recruited six girls and three boys who attempt to integrate the school, but Governor Orval Faubus calls out the National Guard to side with whites who block them. After rioting breaks out, President Eisenhower sends federal troops to replace the Guard, and the school system slowly integrates. It is the lead story in the media for most of the year.

+ In an effort to overcome an image of racism abroad, the State Department sponsors African-American singer Marian Anderson on a 12-nation tour. The following year, she is named a delegate to the United Nations.

+ Dorothy I. Height becomes president of the National Council of Negro Women, a position she will hold for more than three decades. A social work graduate of New York University, she rose to executive positions with the YWCA after beginning her career there in 1938. Height moved to New York from her native Richmond in hopes of attending Barnard, but was told that the college already had two blacks.

+ Althea Gibson is the first black American to play tennis in England's famous Wimbledon tournament. A recent graduate of Florida Agricultural and Mechanical University, she has held the National Negro Women's Championship since 1948. In 1958, she will win the American Tennis Association's women's championship and the U.S. national singles' title; she is named Woman Athlete of the Year by the Associated Press.

+ *Atlas Shrugged* adds to the stature of Russian-born author Ayn Rand. Like her earlier best-seller, *The Fountainhead* (1943), Rand's novel is a paean to unrestrained capitalism and individualism.

+ A contrasting book is *Peyton Place*, a discussion-maker of huge proportions among women, which becomes a hit movie starring Lana Turner

and Hope Lange this year. Its author, Grace Metalious, is condemned from pulpits for her scandalous portrayal of the internal life of a seemingly upright New England town.

1958 Mary Roebling joins the 32-member board of governors of the American Stock Exchange, the first woman to hold such a position. Since 1937, she has been president of a New Jersey bank, which she will lead to over $1 billion in assets by her 1994 death. A feminist, Roebling also chairs the board of Denver's Women's Bank in 1978.

+ In record cold, some 13,000 African Americans turn out for Lincoln Day dinners in 22 southern cities. This kickoff of a campaign to double the number of registered black voters is headed by Southern Christian Leadership Conference executive secretary Ella Baker.

+ Seventy-four-year-old Ethel Percy Andrus is the founding president of the American Association of Retired Persons. An experienced organizer, she has already founded the National Retired Teachers Association and successfully fought for health care benefits for former educators. Andrus also edits *Modern Maturity*, the AARP's publication, and when she dies in 1967, it will be on its way to eventual status as the nation's highest-circulation magazine.

+ Mary Valasquez Riley is the first woman elected to the council of the Arizona Apache tribe. She is 50 years old and will spend the next two decades building businesses intended to make her tribe economically independent.

+ Joyce Chen, a native of Beijing, opens a Mandarin restaurant in Boston, where gourmets James Beard and Julia Child will become regular patrons. Chen goes on to write cookbooks and popularize Chinese cooking on public television.

+ The Childbirth Without Pain Education Association begins to educate women on the French Lamaze techniques for labor and delivery. Their aim is to end the era's use of heavy sedation during childbirth and to give women more understanding and control of their bodies.

✦ The fall election is devastating to Democratic Representative Coya Knutson: "Coya, Come Home," a letter allegedly written by her husband, is widely publicized by Minnesota Republicans, and after four successful years in Congress, she is defeated. Postelection investigation by a House subcommittee reveals that her husband is a hopeless alcoholic and that the letter's charges of romantic involvement with a staff member were false, but no one is punished for this slander.

1959 Lorraine H. Hansberry becomes the first African American to win the New York Drama Critics Circle Award for *A Raisin in the Sun*. The play is a long-running success, but Hansberry dies just six years later, at age 35.

✦ Mary Lou Werner of the *Washington Evening Star* is the first woman at a major metropolitan newspaper to win the Pulitzer Prize for reporting. The same newspaper will have a second winner the following year, when Miriam Offenberg is honored with this prize.

Jean Schneider shares in the Pulitzer Prize for history when the winning book's author, the University of Chicago's Leonard White, gives her credit for a lifetime of work. "She has contributed so much" to not only this book but also to his others, he says, "that it is just to acknowledge my obligation on the title page." Schneider, however, never publishes anything under her own name.

✦ At age 41, Phyllis Diller appears on Jack Paar's popular late-night television show and instantly becomes the most famous female stand-up comedian of her era. Just four years earlier she had been a bankrupt California housewife facing eviction after her husband was fired from his job. When "the power company threatened to turn off the electricity," Diller found a job, self-confidence, and soon, a new life.

Her husband convinced her to try stand-up comedy; her first appearance, two years ago in San Francisco, was a hit, and now she goes national with a new style that appeals especially to women. Diller's jokes revolve around her life as a suburban housewife with five children, and millions of women can identify with her frequently black—but never profane—sense of humor.

✦ Thousands of workers strike against New York City hospitals; as with factory women in the past, they endure arrests and violence, but their successful union will soon be emulated elsewhere.

✦ President Eisenhower appoints Clare Booth Luce, who served as ambassador to Italy for three years before her 1956 resignation, as ambassador to Brazil. Her Senate confirmation is controversial because Luce has become increasingly right wing—and only a month after winning the vote, she retires permanently.

✦ At age 75, Eleanor Roosevelt begins teaching at Brandeis University, a new institution established by post-Holocaust Jews. She has spent the last decade demonstrating her characteristic energy and continues to write both books and periodical pieces.

✦ A study shows that women earn 34% of all bachelor's degrees, 32% of the master's, and just 11% of the doctorates awarded.

✦ The Massachusetts legislature provides for a statue in memory of the 300th anniversary of the death of Mary Dyer, a Quaker missionary hanged by Puritans for her religious ideas.

1960 The birth control pill receives federal approval and goes on the market. When Margaret Sanger dies six years later, millions of American women will be using oral contraceptives. More than any other single factor, the birth control pill—which was initially researched with funds raised largely by Sanger—will provide women unprecedented freedom in their personal lives.

✦ Two days before the March filing deadline for his reelection, Oregon's Democratic U.S. senator—the state's first in 40 years—dies. Widow Maurine Brown Neuberger files in his place and goes on to defeat not only other Democratic candidates but also the Republican nominee, an ex-governor.

A former state legislator in her own right, Senator Neuberger will work for the creation of the President's Commission on the Status of Women, amend the tax code to make it easier to deduct child care expenses, and support other reform. She will not run for reelection in 1966.

+ Republican Representative Edith Nourse Rogers of Massachusetts dies in office at age 79, having never lost an election during a 45-year political career.

With Roger's death, Frances Bolton of Ohio becomes "Dean of the Women in Congress," for her 20-year tenure is now the longest. The ranking Republican on the Foreign Affairs Committee, she is sometimes disparagingly called "the African Queen" because of her interest in that continent—but this white woman, who is probably the wealthiest member of Congress, is praised in black publications.

+ The Student Nonviolent Coordinating Committee (SNCC) begins in Atlanta and soon leads integration of public facilities throughout the South. Civil rights leader Ella Baker mentors the young people involved. A few years later, a well-known white male political scientist terms Baker "the most tireless, the most modest, and the wisest activist I know."

+ First-class postage rises from 34¢ to 44¢, and the first 4-cent stamp dedicated to women is an all-purpose item titled "The American Woman." A mother and daughter are at the center, and to the sides are symbols for "Civic Affairs," "Education," and "Arts and Society."

A second stamp this year honors the 50th anniversary of the Camp Fire Girls. The larger Girl Scouts of America will receive a 4-cent stamp two years later.

+ Leontyne Price debuts with the Metropolitan Opera; she is the first African-American woman to achieve widespread fame as a diva. Born in Mississippi, she moved from the historic black Central Stage College in Wilberforce, Ohio, to Julliard School of Music in New York City. Price is so talented that major compositions are written for her, and she will go on to a 25-year career with the Met.

+ *Look* magazine features Floridian Betty Skelton, who has set speed records both in planes and in race cars. She held the World Light Plane altitude record in 1949 and 1951, and she continues to break records on the ground: By 1965, she will be a four-time winner of the Land Speed Record for Women, with a top speed of 315.72 mph.

As Betty Skelton Frankman, she will be the first woman inducted into the NASCAR International Automotive Hall of Fame when it begins in 1983, and in 1985, the Smithsonian Air and Space Museum will display her airplane.

+ Pilot Sue Synder sets a civilian record for round-the-world flight. Her trip, which begins and ends in Chicago, lasts one minute less than 63 hours.

+ After 20 years of marriage and 10 years of success, comics Lucille Ball and Desi Arnaz divorce. She replaces him as president of Desilu Productions, stars in *The Lucy Show*, and will be inducted into the Television Hall of Fame in 1984.

+ "Migrant Mother" by Dorothea Lange is chosen as one of the century's 50 best photos. Lange also will be honored with the first exhibit of a female photographer's work, at New York's Museum of Modern Art; the show is held shortly after her 1965 death.

+ In the fall, the first race between two women for the U.S. Senate occurs when Democrat Lucia Cormier runs against Republican Margaret Chase Smith in Maine. Smith, the incumbent since 1948, wins.

+ The last of the Shakers, the religious sect founded by Mother Ann Lee in 1774, die during the counterculture decade of the 1960s. Their farms in several states will be turned into museums.

10

The Counterculture Years and the Revival of Feminism

1961–1980

1961 African Americans Marian Anderson and Mahalia Jackson sing for President John F. Kennedy's inauguration. Anderson will be awarded the Medal of Freedom by President Johnson three years later, while Jackson, who made her first recording in 1923, continues her tradition of sold-out annual Carnegie Hall concerts. Jackson refuses to sing anything other than sacred music, and her Christmas carols are especially popular in Europe.

✦ In response to lobbying by Esther Peterson, President Kennedy's choice to head the Women's Bureau of the Department of Labor, he appoints the nation's first Commission on the Status of Women. It is chaired by Eleanor Roosevelt, and her chief priority is the equal-pay legislation that Congress will pass soon after her death. The commission will issue its first major report in 1963, the year of Kennedy's assassination, but Lyndon Johnson and succeeding presidents will continue the tradition in some form for 20 years.

✦ At age 59, Dr. Janet Travell is the first female physician officially in charge of a president's health. A specialist in pain, she has taught John Kennedy relaxation techniques to help him cope with his chronic backaches since 1955.

✦ When first lady Jacqueline Bouvier Kennedy speaks perfect French to cheering Parisians, the president follows with "I'm the man who brought Jackie Kennedy to Paris." Educated at the exclusive Miss Porter's School and at Vassar, as well as at George Washington University, she is the most sophisticated first lady the nation has known—but she also worked as a photojournalist for the *Washington Times-Herald* prior to marriage, and, much later, she will work as an editor at Doubleday. Between 1960 and her 1994 death, Jacqueline Kennedy never falls from the Gallup Poll's top-ten list of most admired women.

✦ Elite Princeton University begins making exceptions to its exclusion of women and admits a few to some graduate programs. The academic world does not collapse, and in 1968, the university opens all graduate departments to women. The

following year, women will be admitted to the historic undergraduate college.

✦ A year prior to the highly publicized admission of African American James Meredith to the University of Mississippi, young Charlayne Hunter (later Hunter-Gault) quietly integrates the University of Georgia. She goes on to a career in both print and broadcast journalism, including heading the *New York Times*' Harlem bureau from 1968 to 1977.

✦ The Southern Christian Leadership Conference sets up "folk" schools to teach blacks who never became literate under segregation. Many are conducted by women and are held in places such as beauty parlors. Students are also encouraged to register to vote.

✦ Eula Johnson leads the integration of south Florida's beaches with a swim-in at Fort Lauderdale. She also files suit to desegregate the local schools.

✦ Her time in federal prison has moved Elizabeth Gurley Flynn further to the left, and, at age 71, she becomes the first woman elected president of the Communist Party USA. Flynn dies three years later and is buried with honors in Moscow's Red Square.

✦ *McCall's* magazine publishes a story by one of the 26 women who, during the past two years, have undergone the same grueling examinations administered to male astronauts. Although half of the women pass—a percentage comparable to men—the National Aeronautics and Space Administration cancels the women's program without explanation. Few notice the article, and there is no organized protest by women.

✦ The Supreme Court upholds a Florida law that automatically exempts women from jury duty; to be included on potential juror lists, a woman must take the initiative of volunteering. Eighteen other states have versions of this law, while three—Alabama, Mississippi, and South Carolina—still bar women from juries completely. Such conditions not only make it impossible for a female defendant to be tried by her peers but also make it more difficult for female attorneys to practice.

◆ Although women won Pulitzer Prizes at rates similar to those of men for the first decades of the prize's existence, no woman has won the literature prize in 19 years. This year, it goes to Harper Lee (whose true name is Nell Harper Lee) for *To Kill a Mockingbird*. The book and its award-winning movie version bring widespread discussion of rape and racism.

The story is based on an actual case in the author's hometown of Monroeville, Alabama. Like Margaret Mitchell, she lives the rest of her life in her native area and never writes another similar book.

◆ The Pulitzer Prize for poetry also goes to a woman this year: Phyllis McGinley wins for *Times Three: Selected Verses from Three Decades*.

◆ Ariel Durant's name begins to appear with that of her husband, Will Durant, on the best-selling history and philosophy books they publish. A 1967 volume of their series, *The Story of Civilization*, wins the Pulitzer Prize.

◆ Julia Child, Simone Beck, and Louisette Bertholle publish volume 1 of *Mastering the Art of French Cooking*, which will become a classic in the field. Two years later, Julia Child's Boston public television show, *The French Chef*, is syndicated to national popularity.

◆ On November 1, some 50,000 participate in Women's Strike for Peace. They push for a nuclear test ban and march with banners that read "End the Arms Race—Not the Human Race." Some WSP members are called before the House Un-American Activities Committee the following year, where their rational argumentation does much to diminish the committee's fading credibility.

One WSP founder is New Yorker Bella Abzug, a 1945 Columbia Law School graduate who will be elected to the House in 1970.

◆ Women in Ellisville, Illinois, organize a ballot write-in that they keep secret from the town's men, and they elect women to all of the town's offices. After serving two terms and achieving their goals of new capital projects in water, sewers, and roads, the women will leave office jointly in 1969.

1962 Although women have served in the House of Representatives for almost a half-century, only now is the first woman appointed to the powerful Ways and Means Committee, which writes tax law. She is Democrat Martha Griffiths, an attorney, former legislator, and judge from Michigan, who was initially elected to Congress in 1954.

◆ *Silent Spring* becomes the foundation of the modern environmental movement. Rachel Carson's book about the dangers of chemical overuse and especially the pesticide known as DDT will stir the wrath of the chemical and agriculture industries, but it inspires national debate. President Kennedy appoints an investigating committee, and DDT eventually is banned. Meanwhile, Carson endures great hostility from much of the business and scientific communities. Prior to publication of books on oceanography in the fifties, she supported her family by working as a biologist for the Fish and Wildlife Service; she writes *Silent Spring* while dying of cancer.

◆ Katherine Anne Porter's *Ship of Fools* is a bestseller—almost two decades after the 72-year-old author copyrighted the manuscript because she could not find a publisher. Although her first story had been published in 1923, success eludes Porter until old age: *Ship of Fools* belatedly wins the National Book Award and other honors. She will publish her last book just three years before her death at age 90.

◆ Mississippi sharecropper Fannie Lou Hamer, who was the 20th child in her family when she was born in 1917, leads a group of black men and women to register to vote. Local officials refuse to register them, and Hamer loses her job and home. When she continues her crusade, she is repeatedly arrested and beaten.

◆ African American Daisy Bates is greeted by the Ku Klux Klan when she returns to Little Rock after delivering her memoirs to a New York publisher. She and her husband remain in Little Rock, however, and they eventually return to successful publication of their newspaper. Two years earlier, the Supreme Court reversed her conviction for violating state law when she refused to release membership lists of the National Association for the Advancement of Colored People.

+ Dolores Huerta is a cofounder of the United Farm Workers, a union for agricultural workers— most of whom are migrant families in which everyone works; the women, with double responsibilities at home and in the fields, work hardest of all.

+ *Sex and the Single Girl* is a huge seller for Helen Gurley Brown, a California advertising agent who was born in Arkansas 40 years earlier. She follows up with *Sex and the Office* (1964); both books discuss the unmarried state with an attitude of candid liberation.

+ In her 50s, Bette Davis is once again a box-office draw with *Whatever Happened to Baby Jane?* She will repeat this success with *Hush, Hush Sweet Charlotte* (1964); both movies feature chillingly macabre women.

+ Marilyn Monroe, the sex symbol of a generation, dies at age 36. Clearly depressed, she takes an overdose of sleeping pills at her Los Angeles home in August; in June, Twentieth Century-Fox fired her when she reported for work just five days of a seven-week period. As a child named Norma Jean, she lived with 12 foster families; the first of her three marriages was at age 16.

+ In western New York, Ruth Colvin begins the Literacy Volunteers of America to teach illiterate adults to read.

+ Dr. Frances Oldham Kelsey, who administers the New Drug Division of the Food and Drug Administration, is honored with the Distinguished Service Medal for her role in keeping thalidomide off of the U.S. market. Because of Dr. Kelsey's cautious attitudes, American women have been largely spared the horrific experience of European women, who gave birth to thousands of malformed babies because their doctors prescribed this tranquilizer during their pregnancies.

+ More attention focuses on Sherri Finkbine, a pregnant Arizona woman who finds it necessary to go to Sweden for an abortion when she fears that thalidomide has caused her fetus to be badly deformed. Her husband had brought the pills home from England, and Finkbine was unknowingly exposed during her second month of pregnancy.

Already the mother of four, Sherri Finkbine uses the professional name of Sherri Chessen as star of a daily Phoenix television show for children, *Romper Room*. Her physician advises ending the pregnancy, but their appeals for a legal abortion in Arizona are futile. She, the physician, and the hospital are threatened with prosecution if they proceed.

+ President Kennedy honors Mary Anderson on her 90th birthday. A Swedish immigrant who once worked as a servant, Anderson headed the Women's Bureau of the Department of Labor for the first quarter-century of its existence.

+ The United Auto Workers honors journalist Mary Heaton Vorse, who has written on labor issues since 1912. Although invariably sympathetic to workers, Vorse did not shrink from writing candid exposés on union corruption during the 1950s.

+ Economist Eleanor Dulles retires after a career with the federal government that is longer than those of her famous brothers, Secretary of State John Foster Dulles and CIA director Allen Dulles. After working on the implementation of Social Security, she went on to the State Department during World War II, where she played a major role in the reconstruction of postwar Germany.

Despite these extraordinary credentials, her highest position was when President Eisenhower granted her "personal rank" as minister when she set out on a 60-country tour of underdeveloped nations. At retirement, she asserts her belief that the State Department exploited her well-known name while offering her little reward. "This place," she says, "is riddled with prejudices. If you are a woman in government service you just have to work ten times as hard."

Indeed it is only now, under the Kennedy administration, that a woman rises to deputy assistant secretary—the highest position yet achieved at the State Department's Foggy Bottom headquarters. Moreover, this is a political appointment that takes place over the heads of the career service men: Kennedy names Katie Louchheim, a Washington power-behind-the-scenes who was vice chairwoman of the Democratic National Committee when he was elected.

◆ Eleanor Roosevelt dies a few weeks after her 78th birthday party, to which she invited only children. Although she served in the first seven sessions of the United Nations General Assembly, she does not receive the Nobel Peace Prize for which President Kennedy nominated her—but she has earned countless other honors and a lifetime of love from millions who mourn her as "the mother of a generation."

1963 Congress passes the Equal Pay Act, which several members had proposed two decades earlier. At that time, although the nation was in desperate need of labor for World War II defense plants, women were routinely paid much less than men for identical tasks. The law, however, will prove difficult to enforce, for slight distinctions in job descriptions are used to negate its "equal work, equal pay" principle.

◆ Representative Martha Griffiths of Michigan leads public hearings that show the inequity of women's wages, and the hearings reveal further discrimination in credit, insurance, education, and other areas of the economy. As a result, Griffiths sponsors legislation to establish equity for women in Social Security payments and (less successfully) an adequate system of health care.

◆ President Kennedy's Commission on the Status of Women has taken a leadership role on these issues, and this year he urges the states to form similar bodies. Some governors have already begun to emulate the national action: Michigan led the way last year, soon followed by Washington

state. Next year, the National Conference of Governors' Commissions on the Status of Women will convene—but because most depend on a governor's goodwill, some go out of existence under new administrations; others consist of honorary appointments and exist mostly on paper. By the end of the next decade, however, 30 states and 140 localities have such commissions.

◆ The first Harvard diplomas are granted to women. Previously they had received Radcliffe degrees even if they had actually done their course work at Harvard. It is not until the next decade, however, that coeducation is complete, when all Harvard libraries are finally opened to women, joint commencements are held, and quotas limiting female admissions are abolished. At the time, Harvard is more than 300 years old.

◆ Dr. Maria Goeppert Mayer is the first woman to win the Nobel Prize for theoretical physics—after a lifetime of largely unpaid jobs.

A native of Germany, she married an American physicist and moved to the United States in 1930. She wrote an outstanding Ph.D. dissertation that same year; in the next decade, while mothering two children, she coauthored a widely used textbook with her husband and published her own research monographs, but nepotism rules prevented Mayer from working at the prestigious eastern universities that employed her husband.

Like many other female scientists, World War II offered her first opportunity, as Mayer joined her friend, Enrico Fermi, on the Manhattan Project that developed the atomic bomb. After the war, the University of Chicago gave her a position as a full professor—but without a salary. Her first genuine academic job came almost three decades after her Ph.D., when the University of California hired both Mayers in 1959—just five years prior to the Nobel for her brilliant research on nuclear structure. Her husband, who consistently encouraged her to publish, never won the prize.

◆ Dr. Rita Levi-Montalcini of Washington University in St. Louis is honored by the United Cerebral Palsy Association for developing techniques to selectively grow parts of the nervous system in animals. Her research is cited as "among the most imaginative in neuroembryology."

+ President Kennedy honors Frances Perkins, the innovator of Social Security, unemployment insurance, and other fundamentals of modern economics, at a dinner celebrating the Labor Department's 50th anniversary. At age 83, Perkins is teaching in a Cornell University labor studies program.

+ Historian Barbara Tuchman wins the Pulitzer Prize for general nonfiction in the second year after this category begins. Her book is *The Guns of August*, an exploration of the causes of World War I.

   This year's prize in the history category also goes to a woman: Constance McLaughlin Green wins for *Washington, Village and Capitol, 1800–1878*—but almost 30 years will pass before another woman wins the Pulitzer Prize for history.

+ *The American Way of Death* by British-born Jessica Mitford comes out at the same time as Ruth Mulvey Harmer's *The High Cost of Dying*. Their confrontation of the funeral industry causes widespread public discussion and some reform—but death rituals in America will continue to be an almost exclusively male field, in contrast to most ancient cultures in which women prepared bodies for their final end.

+ The Supreme Court rules that school-sponsored prayer and Bible reading are unconstitutional violations of students' individual freedom of religion. The suit has been brought by Texas atheist Madalyn Murray O'Hair on behalf of her son; as an adult, he will join her in heading the American Atheist movement, which continues to operate out of Austin. Madalyn Murray O'Hair is the object of hatred and ridicule for decades.

+ Hull House, which Jane Addams and Ellen Gates Starr began in Chicago in 1889, finally ceases operation. A decade later, the original house on Halstead Street and the stately adjacent dining hall will open as a museum and learning center.

+ Twenty-six years after she disappeared over the Pacific, aviator Amelia Earhart is honored with an 8-cent airmail stamp. Eleanor Roosevelt's death last year is commemorated with a first-class 5-cent stamp, which will be issued again in 1984.

+ The first Weight Watchers office opens in New York City, but entrepreneur Jean Nidetech has to have her husband sign the lease. Two years ago the five-foot seven-inch Nidetech weighed 214 pounds; she began turning her life around when she realized that sharing her weight problems with similar women gave them mutual encouragement. She will franchise her idea and, 15 years later, will sell Weight Watchers for $72 million. She keeps a framed copy of her 1961 bank balance of $1.59.

+ Mary Kay Ash has a similar business success story: after resigning from her position as a sales executive because the company refuses to give her the clerical assistance that men receive, she fills a legal pad with her observations on the inequities and inefficiencies of the business world. "Before I realized it," she says, "I'd put on paper a marketing plan that would give women a truly equal opportunity."

   She buys a skin care formula from an acquaintance and, with nine friends, begins Mary Kay Cosmetics. Within three decades, she has a $1 billion business, with 325,000 people she is careful to call "sales associates" or "consultants" rather than "employees."

+ Poet Sylvia Plath commits suicide in London. The gifted young mother of two had suffered from depression since her college days, and despite some literary success, she has lost her identity to her more recognized husband, Ted Hughes, also a poet. Her best work will be published after her death, and especially *The Bell Jar*—which her estate initially publishes under a pseudonym—will become immensely popular among feminists in the decade ahead.

+ Katherine Dunham, who specialized in black dance traditions when she earned a 1936 master's degree in anthropology from the University of Chicago, reaches the acme of her career and choreographs *Aida* for the Metropolitan Opera.

In 1966, she will advise the State Department on the World Festival of Negro Arts in Senegal.

◆ After 21 years with the *New York Herald Tribune*, famed war correspondent Marguerite Higgins joins *Newsday*, the Long Island newspaper founded by Alicia Patterson Higgins' column is syndicated three times a week in 90 papers—but she contacts a rare tropical disease in Vietnam and dies a painfully slow death in 1966, leaving behind two children under 10.

◆ Jacqueline Kennedy is the only first lady in modern times young enough to be pregnant in the White House. In August, her fourth and last delivery ends tragically as Patrick Bouvier Kennedy dies soon after his birth at Cape Cod's Otis Air Force Base.

◆ A century after the Emancipation Proclamation, the largest civil rights march ever takes place at the Lincoln Memorial in August. It moves President Kennedy to propose legislation, but Congress will not act prior to his assassination in November.

◆ African-American dancer Josephine Baker, now a French citizen, returns home for the civil rights march. With her third husband, she has adopted a "rainbow tribe" of a dozen children of different nationalities—but in 1968, her French estate will be sold to pay her debts. Princess Grace of Monaco offers Baker a home, and she continues to dance; she gives her last performance at age 69, two days before her 1975 death.

◆ On Sunday, September 15, dynamite hidden by racists explodes in a Birmingham Sunday school, and four black girls are killed: 14-year-old Addie Mae Collins, Cynthia Wesley, and Carole Robertson; and 11-year-old Denise McNair. No one will be convicted for their murder until 1977.

◆ The November assassination of President Kennedy leads to the first regular female presence on the national television news, as Nancy Dickerson—who had been assigned the presumably dead-end job of covering the vice president—now becomes highly visible. After switching from CBS to NBC earlier in the year, she now has her own daily news show and appears regularly on other newscasts.

◆ Betty Friedan publishes *The Feminine Mystique*, which almost instantly turns her into the Susan Anthony of a newly revitalized women's movement. She graduated from Smith College in 1942 as psychology major Betty Goldstein, and the book is based on her methodological surveys of Smith alumnae. When she discovers that almost all of these well-educated women feel the same disillusion and lack of purpose that she does, she writes a powerful thesis with which millions of quietly desperate women identify. Friedan goes from obscure suburban housewife to controversial television guest, and her thoughts set in motion the formation of the feminist organizations that transform the rest of the century.

1964 Texan Lyndon B. Johnson pushes the 1964 Civil Rights Act through a reluctant Congress soon after he assumes the presidency. The law assures federal support to victims of discrimination, whether the discrimination is based on race, religion, or other factors—but the word "sex" is added as an afterthought by the bill's opponents because they think it highlights what they view as the absurdity of the legislation.

The Equal Employment Opportunity Commission that is created to implement the act lacks effective enforcement powers, and Congress will repeatedly resist administration efforts to strengthen it. Nonetheless, the law will prove crucial to the rising status of women in the next decades.

◆ Republican Senator Margaret Chase Smith of Maine declares herself a candidate for the presidency and runs in the primaries of several states. She will receive some token votes on the first ballot of the convention that nominates Barry Goldwater.

◆ President Johnson tells the Women's National Press Club that he is making an effort to include women in his administration and announces the appointment of Virginia Mae Brown of West Virginia to the Interstate Commerce Commission. The announcement comes as a surprise to Brown, who has not yet been consulted. She is the nation's first female state commissioner of insurance and was also West Virginia's first female assistant attorney general.

He also appoints Esther Peterson as special assistant to the President for Consumer Affairs. The newly created position is termed "the first official woman adviser to the President in U.S. history." Peterson's first work is aimed at holding down food prices.

Finally, President Johnson continues a tradition begun by his ideological mentor, Franklin Roosevelt, when he names Marjorie Jay Tibbets as ambassador to Norway.

+ After a lifetime of proving that severe disabilities can be overcome, Helen Keller is awarded the Medal of Freedom by President Johnson. She has been employed by the American Foundation for the Blind since 1924 and was especially effective during World War II—in her 60s then, her hospital tours offered hope to soldiers whose injuries paled in comparison with being both deaf and blind since childhood. Keller's life also served as the basis of a 1955 Academy Award-winning movie and a 1960 Pulitzer Prize-winning play.

+ The Medal of Freedom is also awarded to Dr. Helen Brook Taussig, a pediatrician and surgeon who earned her honors degree from Johns Hopkins after becoming deaf. Dr. Taussig developed surgical techniques to treat the congenital heart defect that causes "blue babies"—and, to make this research possible, she also did pioneer work on the fluoroscope. Last year, she was elected president of the American Heart Association.

+ The post office recognizes the 50th anniversary of the Smith-Lever Act that funded home economics and other vocational education, but nothing in the design of the 5-cent stamp issued this year indicates that. Instead, it is a paean to "Homemakers," with a picture of a rural house.

+ Despite physical assault, African American Fannie Lou Hamer files to run for Congress from Mississippi. Although the district's population is 68% black, less than 8% of them manage to overcome the literacy test obstacle to voter registration, and she loses the June primary.

In August, Hamer leads the Mississippi Freedom Democratic Party to the Democratic National Convention in Atlantic City, where they challenge the state's whites-only delegation. The convention is disrupted for days when the credentials committee offers a compromise that satisfies neither faction.

+ Former Army commander and Cabinet member Oveta Culp Hobby becomes sole publisher of the *Houston Post* when her publisher husband dies. She has held various titles at the newspaper since the 1920s and added to the communications network with a string of television stations in the 1950s.

+ Catholics begin canonization proceedings for Katherine Drexel, who gave up an inheritance of millions to found the Sisters of the Blessed Sacrament for Indians and Colored People.

+ The Pearl S. Buck Foundation begins; it will continue Buck's long advocacy for children, especially the mentally retarded and Eurasians—the unwanted babies of American fathers and Asian mothers who are born as a result of the Korean and Vietnam wars.

+ Negatively impressed by the pollution of Lake Erie, which is so bad that the water literally catches fire, Lady Bird Johnson uses her position as first lady to emphasize what becomes known as "beautification." Among other things, she oversees the planting of a million daffodils along Washington's Potomac River.

+ *Hello, Dolly!* is a tremendous stage hit for 41-year-old Carol Channing, who wins the Tony Award for her performance. Three years later, she wins the Golden Globe for the movie *Thoroughly Modern Millie*.

+ A weekly newspaper in suburban Ohio begins publishing humor columns by Erma Bombeck—for $3 each.

+ Hazel Brannon Smith of Lexington, Mississippi, is the first female newspaper editor to win a

Pulitzer Prize. She is honored more for her courage than for literary merit: her editorial support for racial integration has forced her to withstand boycotts from the state's White Citizen Council for a decade. Smith, who is white, bought her first paper during the Great Depression; she now owns three, and the one in Jackson will be bombed this year by segregationists.

◆ The nation is horrified by the brutal murder of young Kitty Genovese on a New York City street. At least 37 people later acknowledge hearing her screams, but no one comes to her rescue. Some explain away their refusal to get involved by saying that they thought she was being beaten by her husband.

◆ Patsy Mink is the first Hawaiian-American woman elected to Congress. Born Patsy Matsu Takemoto, she earned a law degree from the University of Chicago in 1951 and has served in both houses of the Hawaii legislature.

Representative Mink will prove a strong national leader on women's issues during the next decade. She is one of the first to argue against the Vietnam War as an unwise diversion of revenue from domestic needs.

1965 On March 25, Viola Gregg Liuzzo is shot dead by Alabama racists. A white, 38-year-old Michigan mother of five, she went South to participate in Martin Luther King Jr.'s civil rights march from Selma to Montgomery. The 25,000 marchers were headed back home when the car that Liuzzo drove is attacked; she dies instantly.

The next day, President Lyndon Johnson announces on national television that four white men have been arrested, but their two trials in state courts bring only acquittal. In December, a federal jury in Montgomery sentences three Ku Klux Klansmen to 10 years in prison—not for murder, but for violation of Liuzzo's civil rights under an 1870 Reconstruction law.

◆ The Supreme Court, citing several sections of the Constitution, rules in *Griswold v. Connecticut* that states may not ban the distribution of contraceptives to married people. The case was brought by Estelle Griswold, head of the state's birth control forces, who opened a clinic designed to bring about her arrest.

Although the law banning contraceptives was passed in 1879, the fact that it is still enforced is a reflection of Connecticut's large Catholic population. The case is thus a victory for freedom of religion as well as a triumph of individual liberty over state power.

◆ President Johnson appoints Patricia Roberts Harris ambassador to Luxembourg. A civil rights attorney and Howard University educator, Harris was a 36-year-old married woman when she graduated at the top of her George Washington University Law School class in 1960. She becomes the first African-American woman to represent the nation abroad.

◆ The Commission on the Status of Women established by President Kennedy issues *American Women*, with an introduction by anthropologist Margaret Mead. The report is almost 300 pages, compared with the commission's first report in 1963, which was only 75 pages. Commonly known as "the Peterson report" for Labor Department Women's Bureau chief Esther Peterson, it details the status of American women in such areas as education, employment, and the legal system.

◆ The year is a high point for enrollment in Catholic parochial schools, with 3,500,000 students. The decline that will begin this year is due in part to an increasing scarcity of women willing to enter teaching sisterhoods.

◆ *Cosmopolitan*, a family magazine founded in 1886, teeters on the edge of bankruptcy when Helen Gurley Brown is hired as editor. She transforms it into a magazine aimed at the emerging liberated woman who will come into her own during the next decade, and *Cosmo*, as it becomes known, soars to unprecedented sales as this previously untapped market reveals itself.

Shirley Ann Grau wins the Pulitzer Prize for *The Keepers of the House* (1964). A young Tulane University literature professor, Grau lives in Metarie, Louisiana, with her husband and two children. She will continue to publish a number of novels during the next decades, but despite her Pulitzer, none is a best-seller.

+ African American Septima Poinsette Clark, who was fired from the Charleston, South Carolina, school system less than a decade earlier because of her membership in the National Association for the Advancement of Colored People, is elected to its school board. The previous year, she had accompanied Martin Luther King, Jr., when he accepted the Nobel Peace Prize, and in 1979, she will be honored at the White House by President Jimmy Carter.

1966 In January, President Lyndon Johnson appoints Constance Baker Motley as a judge for the district court of Manhattan, making her the first black woman on the federal judiciary. Born in 1921 to Caribbean immigrant parents in New Haven, Connecticut, she earned degrees from New York University and Columbia University Law School. She began the practice of law under the best of mentors: NAACP lawyer Thurgood Marshall, who next year will become the first African American on the Supreme Court.

Motley had another milestone two years ago, when she became the first black woman elected to the New York State Senate. She was the only woman among 58 men.

+ A career employee of the State Department since 1948, Carol Laise is named ambassador to Nepal. She sets another precedent the following year by marrying Ellsworth Bunker, America's ambassador to Vietnam. When the two resume their careers in Washington, Carol Laise Bunker is the first female assistant secretary of state.

+ Lurleen Wallace is elected governor of Alabama by a wide margin; age 39, she is married to incumbent George Wallace, who is ineligible to run for reelection. She becomes the first woman elected governor since 1924, and Alabama joins Texas and Wyoming as a state that is, at least ostensibly, headed by a woman.

+ The Department of Justice files the first suit implementing the 1964 Civil Rights Act, but it is aimed at racial, not gender, discrimination. St. Louis construction unions are taken to court, but even though they exclude women as well as racial minorities from apprenticeship programs, the Justice Department targets equity only for black men.

+ Despite the passage of the Equal Pay Act, full-time female workers average just 58% of the earnings that men receive. Only 7% of the nation's physicians and fewer than 4% of its attorneys are women. Only about one in every five elementary school principals is a woman, while women account for just 4% of high school principals.

+ After three decades, the United Auto Workers finally has a woman on its board of directors—Detroit's Olga Marie Madar, who has worked for Chrysler since 1933 when she was hired for the talent she brought to the corporate softball team. In 1970, Madar will become the UAW's first female international vice president, and she is the founding president of the Coalition of Labor Union Women in 1974.

+ In July, the nation is shocked by the cold-blooded murder of eight nursing students in their Chicago dormitory by intruder Richard Speck. Much discussion centers on the passivity of the young women, whose behavioral training has ranked politeness over survival.

A month later, Charles Whitman climbs a tower at the University of Texas and randomly kills 12 people, including a pregnant woman, while injuring more than 30. He had killed his wife and mother the previous night so that they would not be "embarrassed" by his plans.

In September, Valerie Percy, the 21-year-old daughter of a leading Illinois politician, is stabbed to death in her home.

Directly emulating the mass murderers, an Arizona high school senior with a desire to "make a name for himself" enters a Mesa beauty shop in November, forces the women to lie on the floor, and then methodically shoots them; five die.

+ Sex researchers Virginia E. Johnson and William H. Masters issue their clinically detailed study, *Human Sexual Response*. Masters and Johnson will become household names, as both the scholarly and the prurient are fascinated by their innovative methodology, which includes measuring physiological reactions of couples who make love in their laboratory.

✦ When the president's daughter Luci Baines Johnson weds in August, Washington, D.C., sees its most publicized wedding since that of Alice Roosevelt in 1906. The following year, Lynda Bird Johnson also becomes a White House bride.

✦ Advertising executive Mary Wells is the talk of Madison Avenue when she begins her own firm and has accounts worth $25 million in six months. Wells began work at Macy's in 1950 and headed the department store's fashion advertising by age 23.

✦ Novelist Mary McCarthy, who has a 30-year career as a distinguished writer in periodicals and books, publishes *The Group*. This story of the postgraduate experience of Vassar women receives both critical and popular acclaim.

✦ At age 69, Catherine Drinker Bowen publishes *Miracle at Philadelphia*, which becomes a classic study of the writing of the Constitution. Although she grew up in the tradition of upper-class women who were only informally educated, she developed a long writing career in a number of literary forms; she is best known as a biographer, but her early publications are on music.

✦ Regional writer Mari Sandoz dies at age 65. Like the better-known Willa Cather, she writes of the Nebraska plains; *Old Jules* (1935), the story of her tyrannical father, is especially adept at showing the hardships women faced in this isolated setting.

National obituaries also note the death of California cartoonist Gladys Parker, 56, who drew the comic strip "Mopsy."

✦ The 75th anniversary of the General Federation of Women's Clubs is honored with a 5-cent stamp. It is the first such stamp for an organization of women, although two girls' organizations have been honored.

Also this year, the first stamp for a female artist is designed: it honors Mary Cassatt and features one of her mother-child paintings.

✦ When cosmetics businesswoman Elizabeth Arden dies, she leaves her $60 million self-made estate to female relatives and longtime employees. Born Florence Nightingale Graham sometime between 1878 and 1884, she has obscured her birth records to hide her true age.

✦ Young mother Anne Moore begins a business when she patents the "Snugli," a device to carry a baby on one's back, much like Native American women traditionally did. The idea quickly catches on and makes Moore a millionaire.

✦ In October, the National Organization for Women is founded at a meeting attended by 300. To some extent, the concept of NOW has grown out of discussions between women who serve on status-of-women commissions, who are keenly aware of women's needs and yet cannot take the political action necessary to achieve their goals because they function under apolitical government regulation.

NOW's first chairwoman, University of Wisconsin professor Kathryn Clarenbach, is such a woman—but it is best-selling author Betty Friedan who is seen as the mother of NOW; Friedan serves as president until 1970.

✦ Barbara Jordan, a 30-year-old lawyer, becomes the only woman and the only African American in the Texas Senate. She began her political activism with Texan Lyndon Johnson's campaign for vice president, and she advises him on the era's civil rights legislation.

1967 The National Education Association elects the first African-American president in its 106-year history, North Carolina teacher Elizabeth Koontz. Her election not only marks the breaking of a color barrier but also is indicative of an organizational revolt by teachers against administrators.

After her presidency, Koontz will head the Women's Bureau of the Department of Labor and serve as a delegate to the United Nations Commission on the Status of Women.

+ Congress removes limitations on the rank of women in the military, but several years will pass before the Pentagon takes advantage of the law and begins promoting women to top positions.

+ One of the National Organization for Women's first goals is ending newspapers' practice of separating classified advertising by gender. In New York, Miami, and other cities, NOW members draw attention to the issue, and newspapers soon respond with categories such as "Clerical" and "Sales" rather than the traditional "Help Wanted —Men" and "Help Wanted—Women."

+ A group calling itself Mothers for Adequate Welfare chain themselves inside a Boston welfare office. When police eject them, more than 50 people, including police, are injured. A similar number is arrested for property destruction in rioting that continues for several days.

+ African American Dr. Jane Wright becomes dean of Harlem Hospital, the first woman to hold this position. She also serves on the President's Commission on Heart Disease, Cancer and Stroke.

+ Public television begins broadcasting *Making Things Grow* with Boston's Thalassa Cruso, a British-born gardener who soon has a large audience. Cruso's offbeat approach to horticulture also makes her a popular guest on late-night commercial television, and she follows up with several books.

+ Greece's ruling military junta deprives entertainer Melina Mercouri of her citizenship and property in Greece because of her alleged "antinational activities" in the United States. In exile, she encourages other Greeks to overthrow the dictatorship in their homeland; because of her celebrity image, her speeches attract global attention.

+ Television reporter Betty Furness replaces retiring Esther Peterson as President Johnson's advisor on consumer issues.

+ At age 38, Anne Sexton wins the Pulitzer Prize for poetry. Neither this nor her 1963 nomination for the National Book Award will be enough to help her overcome the depression that hospitalizes her several times, and in 1974, Sexton, the mother of two, kills herself.

+ Shirley Temple Black finds that her childhood stardom is not enough for California Republicans to nominate her to Congress; she loses the primary to an "unknown" male trial lawyer.

+ Boston school board member Louise Day Hicks, an avowed segregationist, leads a field of 10 in the nonpartisan race for mayor, but she loses the runoff to moderate Kevin White.

1968 One of the nation's most tumultuous of election years begins when President Lyndon Johnson fails to win a majority in the New Hampshire primary, and he responds by announcing that he will not run for reelection.

In April, Coretta Scott King offers a model of brave mourning when her husband, Dr. Martin Luther King, Jr., is assassinated, and in May, she opens the Poor People's Campaign by speaking to 50,000 people in front of the Lincoln Memorial. Ethel Kennedy shows the same valor when Senator Robert Kennedy, who is running for president, is assassinated in June, leaving her pregnant with her 11th child.

In August, riots in black sections of Miami greet delegates to the Republican convention, while at the Democratic convention, Chicago policemen assault both Vietnam War protestors and television reporters covering the event. In the words of an official report issued in December, both men and women are victims of "indiscriminate police violence . . . inflicted on persons who had broken no law."

+ Shortly before eliminating himself from candidacy, Lyndon Johnson sends Congress the first presidential message in the nation's history that deals exclusively with the needs of American Indians. Also this year, Congress passes the 1968 Civil Rights Act, which is primarily intended to ensure racial equity in housing and public facilities but also benefits women.

The Consumer Credit Protection Act is the most important piece of new legislation for women; it assures women of the right to obtain loans in their own names and to maintain credit histories separate from those of their husbands.

◆ The only member of Congress to have voted against both world wars, 88-year-old Jeanette Rankin leads some 5,000 women in a Capitol Hill protest against the Vietnam War.

◆ Pope Paul VI issues a lengthy encyclical that reaffirms Catholic opposition to any form of birth control other than the abstinence involved in the "rhythm method" of avoiding sex during a woman's fertile period. Because many women find it impossible to determine when they are fertile, millions of Catholics begin to use birth control pills despite the canon. One-third of the congregation at Washington's St. Matthew's Cathedral walks out during the reading of the encyclical; a Gallup Poll shows that 58% of Catholics oppose the official view; and even a survey by the *National Catholic Reporter* says that priests are evenly split on the birth control issue.

The church loses the support of others still when it opposes the marriage of Jacqueline Kennedy to Aristotle Onassis because Onassis has been divorced.

◆ Muriel Siebert, who began her finance career as a $65-a-week trainee in 1950, spends $445,000 to become the first woman to purchase a seat on the 176-year-old New York Stock Exchange. Siebert will remain the only woman among more than 1,300 male stock exchange members for a decade, and she senses so much hostility that she waits two years before using the dining room privileges to which she is entitled.

Also this year, Mimi Randolph is the first woman to be a floor clerk in the 98-year history of the New York Cotton Exchange. A multi-talented woman, Randolph also starred in *Fiddler on the Roof*.

◆ Federally Employed Women is founded in Washington, D.C., by women who work for the national government. Their primary aim is to end gender-based discrimination in civil service jobs, and within two decades, FEW will have 200 chapters nationwide.

◆ Decades after the precedent was set by Franklin Roosevelt in 1934, President Johnson appoints the nation's second woman as a federal appellate judge. She is Colorado native Shirley Mount Hufstedler, who is a 1949 graduate of Stanford law school. She continued to practice after marriage and motherhood in the 1950s and was appointed to the Superior Court of Los Angeles County in 1961 and to the state appellate level in 1966.

◆ Despite Ellen Richards' pioneer work at the Massachusetts Institute of Technology almost a century ago, only now is tenure granted to the first woman in the engineering department. She is Mildred S. Dresselhaus, who overcomes not only the handicap of her gender but also of being a mother. She hid her pregnancies and returned to work only a day or two after delivery—and, she says, "the guys didn't even notice there was a change."

◆ Diahann Carroll is the first African American to star in a regular television series. *Julia* is the story of a woman who supports her family as a professional nurse after her husband dies in Vietnam.

◆ African-American entertainer Eartha Kitt receives much negative publicity for the candid views she gives at a White House luncheon that honors women active in civic causes. When Kitt, who has been working with young people in Washington, D.C., states her belief that the Vietnam War is a factor in urban riots, most media assail her for this violation of decorum. In 1975, it will be revealed that the CIA, FBI, and other agencies had kept her under surveillance since 1956 and probably spread misinformation that damaged her career.

◆ Another African-American woman, Marian Wright Edelman, founds the Children's Defense Fund, which she will push into a nationally recognized force for good. She is a graduate of Atlanta's Spelman College and of Yale Law School, and she will model the Washington-based children's project on her experience as a lawyer for the National Association for the Advancement of Colored People in Mississippi, where she implemented civil rights and antipoverty programs.

+ Curtis Publishing sells *Ladies' Home Journal*, its financial base for 85 years, because circulation has dropped under male editorship. Feminist staffers revolt against this corporate insensitivity two years later, and with articles that display more understanding of its audience, the magazine revives.

+ *New York Times* crossword puzzle editor Margaret Farrar retires; the first person to hold this position, she began the newspaper's reputation for erudite puzzles.

+ The Library of Congress celebrates the centennial of *Little Women* with an exhibit on Louisa May Alcott. The post office also honors 19th-century feminist Lucy Stone, but with an infrequently used 50-cent stamp.

+ Katharine Hepburn becomes the first woman to earn three Academy Awards for best actress. This award is for *The Lion in Winter*, in which she plays Eleanor of Aquitaine, who married the king of England after divorcing the king of France.

+ *Tell Me You Love Me, Junie Moon*, a first novel by Marjorie Kellogg, sells to the movies for "an astronomical sum," despite its unconventional subject matter of disfigurement.

+ When feminists picket the Miss America contest in Atlantic City, New Jersey, they draw the most attention that the media has given to the new National Organization for Women. Although many of the press reports negatively focus on alleged bra-burners, millions of women hear of NOW for the first time.

+ Yale University announces that for the first time since its 1718 formation, it will admit women at the undergraduate level. The change is more striking than that at some other Ivy League institutions: because Connecticut never developed a Seven Sister college, Yale had less opportunity to absorb female students gradually, as was the case at Harvard and Columbia.

President Kingman Brewster accelerated his plans for coeducation after students invited some 700 young women from 22 eastern colleges, who came and spent a week. According to *Time*, Yale offered "to go steady with its old friend Vassar"—in Poughkeepsie, New York—but "was turned down."

+ Massive strikes by teachers, many of whom are women, take place from New York to New Mexico. The most unconventional action may be in Florida, where some 35,000 striking teachers pack a rally at the Orange Bowl. They are in violation of state law and some are jailed, but eventually they win improved salaries.

National Education Association president Elizabeth Koontz presciently says: "The schools in the big cities of this country are being strangled by bureaucracy. They are dying from an elephantiasis of school board and central office control."

+ The nation also begins to face a shortage of nurses, as women become dissatisfied with traditional jobs. Of 821 hospital nursing schools in the United States, 60 announce that they are closing because of low enrollments. One-third of all registered nurses no longer work in this field.

+ The Communist Party USA has not nominated anyone for president since 1940. This year, it nominates 38-year-old African American Charlene Mitchell.

+ The fall election sets a major precedent when Shirley Chisholm of New York is the first black woman elected to Congress. She defeats the Tammany Hall establishment in the Democratic primary as well as a popular black man who runs on a Republican-Liberal coalition ticket in the general election.

+ Representative Frances Bolton, who has been more involved with African issues that almost anyone in Congress, is defeated. At age 83, she is an easy target during this tumultuous election year, and she loses her Ohio seat for the first time in 29 years.

1969 California adopts the nation's first "no fault" divorce law. The concept enables couples to divorce by mutual consent, without having to provide "grounds" for the dissolution of the marriage by proving that one partner or the other is at fault.

Other states emulate the model so quickly that divorce reform, an initial goal of the revived feminist movement, almost immediately disappears from its agenda.

✦ Virginia Mae Brown moves up to the chairmanship of the Interstate Commerce Commission, making her the first woman to head an independent administrative agency of the federal government. She has a personal history of unconventionalities: her mother was president of a West Virginia bank, and after marrying a man also named Brown at age 36, she continued her career while bearing two children. As ICC chairman, she sets such precedents as forbidding employees to accept gifts from those doing business with the agency; nevertheless, Richard Nixon does not reappoint her when her term expires.

✦ Navy officer Marguerite Chang, who was born in China, invents a device for triggering explosives in underground nuclear test sites. Much of Chang's work will remain classified.

✦ Air Force Reserve Officer Training programs become coeducational. At the same time, women students are among those who protest the Vietnam War on college campuses throughout the nation. At Duke University, tear gas is used against them; at the University of Wisconsin, the National Guard aims fixed bayonets at students; at Harvard, almost 200 students are arrested for sit-ins at administrative offices; and City College of New York is closed down by mostly black and Puerto Rican demonstrators. In October, Women's Strike for Peace is among the organizers of almost a half-million marchers who go to Washington and San Francisco for Vietnam Moratorium Day.

✦ Hospital workers in Charleston, South Carolina, many of whom are African-American women, go on strike. Their picket lines are attacked, and the

Anna Mae Hayes, chief of the Army Nurse Corps, commanded most of the 7,500 military women who served in Southeast Asia during the Vietnam War. On June 11, 1970, Hayes became the first woman in American history to be promoted to the rank of general. Women In Military Service Memorial

National Guard is called in to restore order. Although their union is not recognized, they win substantial wage increases.

✦ Public television begins broadcasting *Sesame Street*, the brainchild of producer Joan Ganz Cooney. The show sweeps the next year's awards, receiving an Emmy and a Peabody in its first year of production. Cooney's nonsexist scripts become a model for other educational media.

✦ Margaret Bourke-White retires after 33 years with *Life* magazine. Besides covering the depression and World War II, she reported on the end of colonialism in India and Africa and put a human face on the Korean War by specializing in families split between the north and south. She continued to work after developing Parkinson's disease, publishing a number of books of photos.

✦ Judy Garland dies at age 47, burdened with addictions and unable to return to the fame she achieved as a 17-year-old. Millions mourn her with her most famous song, "Somewhere Over the Rainbow." Olympic skater Sonja Henie, also a Hollywood star, dies in a plane crash.

✦ The nation is absorbed in the story of how Senator Edward Kennedy's car plunged off a darkened Martha's Vineyard bridge, killing young campaign worker Mary Jo Kopechne.

✦ American women see an exciting international scene this year: Golda Meir, who emigrated from Kiev, Russia, to the United States in 1906 and grew up in Milwaukee, is sworn in as premier of Israel. At the same time, Indira Gandhi is prime minister of India; 21-year-old Bernadette Devlin is elected to the House of Commons from Northern Ireland; and Liberia's Angie Brooks is president of the 24th Assembly of the United Nations.

✦ The National Association for the Repeal of Abortion Laws forms in New York. The group expects a long struggle of state-by-state legislative reform, but within four years, the Supreme Court will dramatically ease NARAL's task.

✦ The National Women's Hall of Fame is established in Seneca Falls, New York, where the first women's rights meeting was held in 1848. The privately run museum will continue to admit both living and dead women of historic importance in annual ceremonies throughout the century. Those honored range alphabetically from Abigail Adams to "Babe" Zaharias.

✦ The post office honors its second female artist when popular primitivist Grandma Moses is recognized just eight years after her death at age 101. The stamp features her "July Fourth" painting.

1970 Philadelphia's historic Woman's Medical College of Pennsylvania, which more than a century ago offered women their first systematic opportunity to study medicine, admits men and changes its name to Medical College of Pennsylvania.

✦ After congressional hearings reveal the barriers that women face as medical students, the Women's Equity Action League files a class action suit against the nation's medical schools. In response, schools begin to drop the quotas on women that have been routine, and the number of first-year female students rises. From 504 in 1959, it will climb to 3,647 in 1975.

✦ Women are involved in the environmentalist movement that has been emerging since Rachel Carson's *Silent Spring*, and two significant events occur this year: The nation's first Earth Day, celebrated in April, is a rousing success, as almost 20 million people participate, and activists headed by Marjory Stoneman Douglas defeat plans for a Miami airport that would negatively affect the Everglades.

✦ After President Richard Nixon acknowledges that the Vietnam War has secretly been expanded to Cambodia, protests erupt throughout the nation. At Ohio's Kent State University, National Guardsmen fire into a crowd, killing 8 and injuring 12, including young women. The most poignant picture of this sad era is of a horror-struck girl at Kent State who is kneeling over a body; she is not a student, but one of many teenagers who have run away from affluent homes in a time of tremendous generational conflict.

Ten days after the Kent State massacre, police in Jackson, Mississippi, spray a women's dormitory with at least 140 rounds of ammunition after an alleged rock-and-bottle-throwing incident. This event has a racial context rather than an antiwar one, but the two cause nationwide campus protests. Some 400 colleges and universities close down during May, and many cancel the remainder of the academic year.

✦ "Greetings, fellow bums," cries film star Jane Fonda when students and other young people again assemble in Washington, D.C., to protest the war in Vietnam. Fonda—who won the esteemed New York Film Critics Award earlier in the year—is referring to President Nixon's labeling of war protestors as "bums."

She is arrested at least three times this year: after assisting Indians in the Seattle area with their militant takeover of a historic fort; at Fort Hood, Texas, during an antiwar rally at that military post; and when returning from Canada, where she encourages draft evaders—this time she has allegedly assaulted a police officer.

✦ On June 11, the military finally has its first women of top rank, as Anna Mae Hayes, chief of the Army Nurse Corps—which has existed since 1901—and Elizabeth P. Hoisington, director of the Women's Army Corps, are promoted to brigadier general in the same ceremony. General Hays and General Hoisington have their stars pinned on by controversial Vietnam War commander William C. Westmoreland.

Gender bias is presumably greater than racial bias in the military, for there are already three black, male generals.

✦ The Justice Department files its first case that uses the 1964 Civil Rights Act against gender—as opposed to racial—discrimination. Libbey-Owens-Ford, a glass manufacturer based in Toledo, Ohio, is sued for discriminating against women in its hiring practices. Six months later, the company settles out of court and adopts new employment policies.

In October, the Civil Rights Commission issues a lengthy report charging federal agencies with failing to enforce laws designed to overcome historic inequities. The Equal Employment Opportunity Commission also reports that about 25% of its caseload concerns discrimination against women, even though women constitute by far the largest segment of the applicable population.

✦ New York State passes a liberalized abortion law on July 1, and almost immediately hospitals are swamped with out-of-state women seeking legal abortions. Physicians are unfamiliar with techniques, equipment is not in stock, and many women endure frustrating and costly delays.

✦ To commemorate the 50th anniversary of the ratification of the 19th Amendment that ensured women's right to vote, NOW promotes a one-day strike by women on August 26. Under the leadership of its second president, Wilma Scott-Heide, NOW's primary aim in the decade ahead will be ratification of the Equal Rights Amendment, which was initially introduced in Congress in 1923. Additional NOW goals include ending employment discrimination; making 24-hour, low-cost child care available to mothers; and reforming the educational system, especially in the expansion of female athletics and in revision of textbooks to reflect women's varied lives.

The August 26 date is termed Women's Equality Day, and some 10,000 New Yorkers join in a march that, for the first time in the history of women's rights parades, includes openly homosexual women. In Los Angeles on August 29, the first major demonstration by Chicano men and women is held.

The post office recognizes the 50th anniversary with a stamp unveiled at Adams, Massachusetts, where Susan Anthony was born in 1816. The 6-cent stamp features a late-era suffrage scene with an automobile as well as a contemporary woman moving the levers on a voting machine.

✦ Nurse veterans of Vietnam contend with favoritism shown to male paramedics: the nurses have had to pay for their own education before they join the military, whereas the paramedics are trained at government expense. Back in civilian life, the paramedics are often hired at salaries that are higher than those paid to better-credentialed nurses.

✦ Kansas City, Missouri's Dorothy Bradford writes as many as 250 letters a week to soldiers serving in Vietnam. By the war's end, she has sent some 10,000 gifts.

✦ After introducing the concept of modern dance to the public during 50 years as an innovative choreographer, Martha Graham retires—but she continues to direct Martha Graham Center of Contemporary Dance. Among her most famous productions are several that featured historically significant women, including Medea, Clytemnestra, Emily Brontë, and Emily Dickinson.

✦ Several books on the women's liberation movement are published this year, and the best-seller among them is *Sexual Politics* by Kate Millett. *The Sensuous Woman*, a book that celebrates female sexuality in what some see as an antifeminist way, is also a best-seller. Meanwhile, Erma Bombeck tops humor sales with *I Lost Everything in the Post Natal Depression*. Her irreverent view of motherhood will bring other best-sellers, and her column, "At Wit's End," is syndicated in some 800 newspapers.

✦ In the first year that a Pulitzer Prize is awarded for journalistic commentary, one of the two winners is a woman. She is Ada Louise Huxtable of the *New York Times*; Emily Genauer of *Newsday* and Mary McGrory of the *Washington Star* will receive this honor in 1974 and 1975.

The Pulitzer Prize for literature goes to Jean Stafford for *Collected Stories*. Stafford, who grew up in Colorado, will die on Long Island in 1979 at age 64.

✦ Popular rock singer Janis Joplin dies of a heroin overdose at age 27. Her brief but stellar career took her from Texas to Hollywood, where she was dubbed "queen of the white blues." She was especially known for drinking from a bottle of Southern Comfort on stage, and her death prompts countless discussions of the era's use of drugs and alcohol.

✦ In the fall elections, attention focuses on ardent feminist and pacifist Bella Abzug, who unseats an incumbent Democrat in the primary and then wins the general election for a congressional seat from New York City. On her first day in the House, she will introduce a resolution demanding immediate withdrawal from the Vietnam War.

✦ Republican Lenore Romney loses a U.S. Senate bid in Michigan against Democratic incumbent Phillip Hart by an overwhelming margin. The vote is especially significant because Romney's husband is a former governor and a current member of the cabinet, while Senator Hart must overcome the political liabilities incurred by his wife's antiwar activism. Jane Hart, a student at George Washington University who will earn her college degree in 1972 at age 48, is an increasingly visible protestor against the Vietnam War.

1971 The January issue of *Art News* focuses on "Women's Liberation, Women Artists, and Art History." The cover features a painting traditionally considered to be the work of Jacques-Louis David, which is now attributed to one of his female students.

✦ Much of the public is astonished to realize that Swiss women still lack the right to vote that most European and American women have enjoyed for decades. In February, male voters in Switzerland finally pass the suffrage referendum; in October, eight women are elected to the parliament. In a few conservative areas, however, women may not vote in municipal elections.

✦ Oklahoma City joins Portland and Seattle as sizeable cities that have chosen women for their top job: Patience Latting, a former city council member and League of Women Voters activist, becomes mayor in April.

✦ The Civil Service Commission rules that references to gender must be removed from federal job descriptions, except for a few cases, such as guards in women's prisons.

✦ For the first time since its 1942 inception, a woman wins the Pulitzer Prize for national reporting. Lucinda Franks of United Press International shares the prize with a male colleague.

✦ Congress passes a comprehensive child care bill expanding on the highly successful Head Start program that was implemented a few years earlier as part of Lyndon Johnson's antipoverty programs. This bill reflects lobbying by middle-class women, however, who need greater access to well-run child care. It offers subsidies to private and nonprofit child care providers.

The Senate also swears in its first female pages this year.

✦ The U.S. Marine Corps marks two milestones this year: barracks are gender-integrated and the first female marines are allowed to continue on duty through pregnancy. Meanwhile, the air force names its first female general: she is Jeanne Holm, director of the Women's Air Force, and she found youthful inspiration in her aunt, Claudia Holm, who served with the American Expeditionary Forces in Europe during World War I. Two years later, Jeanne Holm will become the first woman to wear two stars, when she is promoted to major general.

+ The National Women's Political Caucus begins in July with a press conference intended to influence the next presidential election. Among its founders are Representatives Bella Abzug and Shirley Chisholm, NOW founder Betty Friedan, and journalist Gloria Steinem. The Caucus' formation receives far more attention in the mainstream media than was the case when NOW began just five years earlier.

+ Representative Chisholm, incidentally, says that when she served in the New York legislature, "I had not been in favor of repealing all abortion laws." But after "heavy thinking," especially about women she knew whose health was permanently damaged because they lacked access to safe abortions, she switched her position. She adds that this is a greater political risk for her than for a white politician "because there is a deep and angry suspicion among many blacks that even birth control clinics are a plot by the white power structure to keep down the number of blacks."

African American Mary Frances Berry publishes *Black Resistance, White Law: A History of Constitutional Racism*. It is the first in a series of scholarly works on how the law has failed to offer equal protection not only for racial minorities but also for women and children. Berry uses vernacular language in her popular lectures on these issues, however, and therefore is not seen so much as a scholar but rather as a political radical. Later in the decade, President Jimmy Carter will risk the disapproval of conservatives when he appoints Berry to the Civil Rights Commission and as an assistant secretary of education.

+ Billie Jean King attracts millions to televised tennis games, and this year she becomes the first female athlete to earn more than $100,000 annually. Once she breaks the precedent, others quickly follow. In the next two years, tennis stars Chris Evert and Margaret Court each earn more than $200,000.

+ At age 51, Gerda Lerner publishes *Woman in American History*, and next year, she adds *Black*

Women in White America: A Documentary History. Based at the University of Wisconsin, Lerner will pioneer a new approach to the history of American women during the next two decades. From *Female Experience: An American Documentary* (1977) to *The Creation of Feminist Consciousness* (1993), her works become basic to the new field of women's studies.

+ With growing recognition of the need to integrate women into the study of history, Radcliffe College sponsors the publication of a three-volume biographical dictionary, *Notable American Women*, by Harvard University Press. A fourth on modern women will be added in 1980.

+ Elizabeth Janeway, a successful author since 1943, launches a string of thoughtful feminist books: *Man's World; Woman's Place* (1971), *Women; Their Changing Roles* (1973), and *Between Myth and Morning; Women's Awakening* (1974). All serve to revitalize the women's movement.

+ Australian Germaine Greer, author of *The Female Eunuch*, is featured on a number of television talk shows. Dr. Greer teaches literature in England, but spends a year promoting her thesis that women have been taught to repress their sexuality in ways that make them analogous to powerless eunuchs.

+ Pearl Buck, whose work since the 1930s has dealt with such issues as abortion, prostitution, and forced marriage, publishes *Of Men and Women* (1971). Other titles that reflect her awareness of the era's growing feminism are *To My Daughters, With Love* (1967) and *The Kennedy Women: A Personal Appraisal* (1970). Buck is still writing when she dies two years later at age 81, the esteemed author of 100 books and many more shorter works.

+ *The Complete Stories of Flannery O'Connor* appears several years after her 1964 death from lupus. O'Connor's writing career lasted only about a decade, for the first of her two novels was published in 1953, but her literary reputation will grow rather than decline. Her forlorn characters bear a similarity to those of Carson McCullers, a fellow Georgian who also suffered from long-term illness.

✦ Though the post office has been issuing stamps dedicated to women for nine decades, this year marks the first for a female poet. The honor naturally goes to Emily Dickinson.

✦ At age 48, photographer Diane Arbus commits suicide, despite her success. She won two Guggenheim Fellowships in the 1960s, has been published in national magazines, and had a 1967 exhibit at the Museum of Modern Art—but displayed only a few dozen of her most innovative works. She will become internationally famous after the Museum of Modern Art does a posthumous show of her unconventional photographs of various eccentrics. Arbus' obsessions range from circus sideshows to drug addicts to twins who marry twins.

✦ Houston restaurateur Sybil Leek claims to be a 560-year-old witch and says there are at least 400 covens of witches in the United States. Louise Huebner deems herself the "official witch" of Los Angeles; she not only writes on witchcraft but also sells recorded chants to cast spells. Occult bookstores, many of them run by women, have doubled their sales in the past three years, while the mass public exhibits its interest in the supernatural by packing the movie theaters to see *Rosemary's Baby* and *The Exorcist*.

1972 In March, Congress passes the Equal Rights Amendment to the Constitution. Although it had languished in committee since

Members of the Women's Strike for Peace picket the White House on a cold March day in 1970. A larger group of women assembled on the Capitol steps to present Congress with petitions against the use of tax dollars to continue the warfare in Southeast Asia. Library of Congress

1923, the spirit of the times is such that both the House and Senate provide the necessary two-thirds vote without significant debate.

Hawaii is the first state to begin the ratification mandated by the Constitution, which calls for approval by three-quarters of the states.

Congress also passes legislation aimed at correcting historical discrimination against girls and women in educational institutions. Particular attention will focus on what becomes known simply as Title IX, the portion of the act that bans schools from spending more money on athletics for men and boys—a practice that has long been traditional in almost all schools.

◆ Women's Equity Action League, led by Dr. Bernice Sadler, immediately uses the legislation to file charges against some 250 institutions of higher education. WEAL has gathered a tremendous amount of documentation on discriminatory practices that are routine in academia. Among other examples, Sadler points out that women hold less than one-fourth of all faculty positions and female students are often limited by quotas in medical and other professional schools.

◆ Representative Shirley Chisholm runs in the spring presidential primaries, and when the Democratic convention is held in the summer, she receives 151 first-ballot votes, or 29% of the convention's delegates. Hers is the first credible national campaign by a black female candidate.

◆ The Supreme Court, in *Reed v. Reed*, rules that an Idaho law granting automatic preference to men over women as the executors of estates is unconstitutional.

A second decision is equally significant: In *Eisenstadt v. Baird*, the Court expands its 1965 *Griswold v. Connecticut* decision and makes birth control available without regard to the marital status of the purchaser. The plaintiff is Bill Baird, a Massachusetts man who sued to strike down a law that—in accordance with the Court's 1965 decision—allowed only married couples to purchase contraceptives.

◆ Pope Paul VI hands down a decree barring women from even the smallest of formal roles traditionally assigned to priests. On the other hand, the University of Notre Dame, a Catholic institution, accepts undergraduate women for the first time in its 130-year history.

At the annual convention of the United Methodists, a women's caucus protests the fact that women compose 54% of the church's members but have only 13% representation in its governing body.

◆ Little notice is given to the fact that Arizona elects the first female state senate majority leader. A Republican, she is future Supreme Court justice Sandra Day O'Connor.

◆ In contrast, the Ohio ordination of Sally Priesand as the nation's first female rabbi attracts much media attention. At age 25, she is a graduate of the Hebrew Union College-Jewish Institute of Religion in Cincinnati.

◆ Women at the *New York Times* begin the battle that will absorb them most of the decade. Armed with statistics showing that less than 10% of the paper's reporters are women—and many of those are assigned to the traditional women's pages

This nurse working in Vietnam probably outranks the men pictured. Military nurses traditionally have been college-educated officers, while male medics were primarily enlisted men who received their training at government expense in the military. Yet, as civilians after their service, many male paramedics got better-paid hospital jobs. Women in Military Service Memorial

—they confront the paper's all-male executives. When years of negotiations produce little change, the women file a class action suit, which is settled out of court in 1978. The *Times* sets up hiring and promotion goals and pays a $350,000 settlement, a niggardly amount when divided among the 550 women who are parties to the suit.

✦ *Washington Post* publisher Katharine Graham encourages coverage of the story behind the story when burglars break into the Democratic Party headquarters in June. The Watergate investigation (named for the office complex in which the burglary took place) eventually reveals criminal activity at the highest level of government. The *Post*'s coverage is reprinted throughout the nation, and ultimately President Richard Nixon will be forced to resign.

Graham also accepted serious personal risk last year, when she published the classified "Pentagon Papers" that revealed the dark side of the Vietnam War. Her colleagues reward her commitment to the truth by making Katharine Graham the first female president of the American Newspaper Publishers Association and the first female board member for the Associated Press.

✦ Martha Mitchell, wife of Attorney General John Mitchell, makes surreptitious phone calls to reporters (especially United Press International's Helen Thomas), in which she alleges that she is held against her will by guards whose orders are to prevent her from telling what she knows about the Watergate scandal.

Mitchell's husband is forced to resign as Richard Nixon's campaign manager, but most politicians and journalists dismiss her as an alcoholic. As the full story develops the following year, she receives somewhat more respect, but she is never called as a witness in the impeachment hearings that eventually send her husband to prison. Martha Mitchell will die in 1976, shortly before John Mitchell loses his final appeal to the Supreme Court.

✦ With a major donation from Katharine Graham, *Ms.* magazine begins under the editorship of Gloria Steinem and other feminist journalists. To the surprise of the publishing world, it is soon profitable.

No professional in the field would predict what soon happens: the audience for *Ms.* is large enough that its editors can afford the luxury of refusing to accept advertising demeaning to women, while *Life*, one of the most popular magazines of the century, goes bankrupt next year.

✦ The navy emulates the army and air force and promotes a woman to its highest rank: Alene B. Duerk, head of the Navy Nurse Corps, which was established in 1908, becomes a rear admiral in April. Although she is aware that her possible promotion has been debated (and resisted) at the Pentagon since the first army women were promoted to top rank two years ago, no one informs Duerk that it is imminent. She learns of it while driving down the Ohio Turnpike, listening to the radio news.

The navy also sets a precedent this year by using a male/female crew on the hospital ship, USS *Sanctuary*. Nurses, of course, have long worked aboard hospital ships, but the presence of female sailors in the crew is new.

✦ A New York nun, Sister Elizabeth McAlister, is convicted of smuggling letters to and from antiwar prisoners who allegedly conspired to kidnap Secretary of State Henry Kissinger. In an 11-week trial of eight Catholic peace advocates, she is one of just two convicted.

✦ Twenty-eight-year-old black student leader Angela Davis is acquitted of complicity in a San Francisco political kidnapping plot; she had already been fired from her teaching position at the University of California.

✦ The draft ends this year, and women benefit in several ways from new rules aimed at increased recruitment. Women no longer have to meet higher standards than males for enlistment, and for the first time, the dependents of women in the military become eligible for benefits. Women also become eligible for ROTC (Reserve Officer Training Corps) programs, which pay college students while they train part time.

In general, however, the funding of male and female college students continues to be highly inequitable, for the most lucrative of athletic scholarships remain closed to women.

◆ Historian Barbara Tuchman wins her second nonfiction Pulitzer Prize for *Stilwell and the American Experience in China, 1911–45.* General Joseph W. Stilwell, also known as "Vinegar Joe," commanded American troops in Southeast Asia during World War II.

◆ The American Psychological Association chooses Anne Anatasi as its president, the first women since Mary Calkins was elected 50 years earlier. Anatasi is known primarily for her work on mental testing: she has developed tests used by the military and by college entrance boards, and her *Psychological Testing* (1954) has been reissued many times.

◆ After the death of 77-year-old J. Edgar Hoover, who headed the Federal Bureau of Investigation since 1924, the FBI finally begins hiring women in capacities other than clerical.

◆ Clerical workers on the staff of the National Education Association go on strike, emulating striking teachers, whose dues pay their salaries, and the organization's management quickly concedes.

◆ Former beauty queen Bess Myerson serves as New York's commissioner of consumer affairs; she is highly successful in curbing exploitative business practices.

◆ A California Chevrolet dealership makes headlines by hiring women as "salesmen"; young Joy Kennedy breaks records by averaging 12 car sales a month.

◆ Film star Jane Fonda, who won an Oscar last year for her portrayal of a prostitute in *Klute,* becomes more controversial when she goes to Hanoi. She has been involved in antiwar activity for years, but many see this trip into enemy territory as a particular betrayal of American soldiers. Next year, Fonda will marry antiwar activist Tom Haydn; together they become successful left-wing politi-

cal leaders, while her acting career will continue to rank at the top for many years.

◆ Helen Gurley Brown's *Cosmopolitan* becomes the first major magazine to features a nude centerfold of a man.

◆ After 30 years without losing an election, 74-year-old Republican Margaret Chase Smith of Maine is defeated. The U.S. Senate becomes all-male for the first time since the four-year period between Hattie Caraway's 1944 loss and Smith's 1948 election.

The House gains a woman who will become its most valuable member on feminist questions during the next crucial decades. Democrat Pat Schroder of Colorado wins a narrow victory on an antiwar platform, and she will become the most powerful woman on the House Armed Services Committee. A graduate of the University of Minnesota and of Harvard Law School, she and her husband bring their two small children to Washington; Schroder eventually becomes the most senior congresswoman in the House.

◆ The first woman to receive a vote in the electoral college is Tonie Nathan, the vice presidential nominee of the Libertarian Party. The vote is cast by a Republican man who deserts his official duty to vote for winner Richard Nixon.

◆ In December, the United Nations General Assembly passes a resolution proclaiming 1975 as International Women's Year.

1973 When Congress convenes in January, two more African-American women join Shirley Chisholm in the U.S. House: Barbara Jordan of Houston and Yvonne Brathwaite Burke of Los Angeles: In June, Cardiss Collins of Chicago wins a special election after her husband dies in a plane crash.

Jordan is the first black congresswoman from the South, and she quickly becomes a celebrity with her incisive questioning during the Judiciary Committee's hearings on the impeachment of President Richard Nixon. Burke sets a different precedent later this year, when she is the first congresswoman to bear a child while in office.

Collins ultimately sets the record as the longest-serving black congresswoman.

Corrine Claiborne "Lindy" Boggs of Louisiana joins the U.S. House in March, when she wins an election to replace her husband; Hale Boggs is presumed dead in an Alaskan plane crash that took place during the previous fall's presidential campaign. Lindy Boggs will go on to almost two decades of service in Congress, and she when retires in 1990, she is the only white member representing a black-majority district—but more people know her as the mother of popular political commentator Cokie Roberts.

◆ On January 22, an all-male Supreme Court, by a 7 to 2 vote, hands down a decision that impacts women more than any other single ruling in its history, for it has the effect of legalizing abortion throughout the United States.

It is based on two appeals on which the Court rules simultaneously: *Roe v. Wade*, a Texas case, and *Doe v. Bolton*, a Georgia case. In each, women who sought abortions used anonymous identities to sue state law enforcement officials; *Roe v. Wade* becomes the public focus because the Texas law was more severe.

Young, female attorneys play major roles in both cases: Margie Pitts Hames argues against Georgia's statute, while Sarah Weddington becomes famous for her victory in the Texas case. She is just 27, and even though her previous legal experience was limited to wills and uncontested divorces, the highly experienced men of the Supreme Court requested that this young woman present the second argumentation after they had heard her once.

In striking down both states' laws, the Court declares that American women have a right under the Constitution's personal liberty clauses to decide whether they will be pregnant, and government may not interfere with patient/physician privacy.

It is truly the year of the Supreme Court, as it hands two other major victories to women. In *Frontiero v. Richardson*, the Court rules 8 to 1 that spouses of male and female military members are entitled to equal benefits, thus ending years of discrimination against military women whose husbands do not receive benefits akin to those of wives of military men. Four justices volunteer that they view any such gender-based distinction as "immediately suspect"—an opinion that some legal experts see as eliminating the need for the Equal Rights Amendment, if only one more justice had joined to create a majority.

◆ The National Women's Political Caucus meets in Houston and bills the gathering as the first political convention of women since Victoria Woodhull's 1872 event. The caucus is headed by Frances Farenthold, a recent Texas gubernatorial candidate who received some votes for vice president at the last Democratic Party convention.

◆ President Nixon appoints Elizabeth Hanford to the Federal Trade Commission. A North Carolina native and 1965 graduate of Harvard Law School, she will marry divorced Kansas senator Robert Dole two years later and continue to serve in appointed governmental positions as Elizabeth Dole.

◆ Without acknowledging that it is guilty of discrimination, American Telephone and Telegraph and its Bell System affiliates pay out $38 million to 15,000 female and minority employees who brought a class action suit for promotions to job classifications previously closed to them. It is the largest such settlement yet, and the victory is won without participation from the Communications Workers of America, the union that ostensibly represents these workers.

◆ *Newsweek* signs an agreement with female employees who filed a discrimination case against the magazine three years ago; the corporation promises to increase the number of women writers to at least one-third of the total.

◆ Less than 4% of the nation's veterinarians are women, and more than half of those began their practice in the last decade.

◆ Opportunities for women in higher education administration remain very rare: the National Association of State Universities and Land Grant Colleges reports that just three women are presidents of such public institutions, at the University of Texas Nursing School, the Regional Campus Administration of Indiana, and New York's Hunter College. The same report points out that throughout the nation, women's average college grades are higher than those of men.

- Michigan Representative Martha Griffiths leads another round of investigations into working women's lives, a decade after her first study. The Joint Economic Committee that she chairs reports discrimination in virtually every aspect of public and private employment; in addition to job discrimination, women also are handicapped in educational opportunity, credit rights, social security, insurance, and pensions.

- Despite what a journalist terms an "astonishing furor," Colonel Mary E. Bane of California's Camp Pendleton becomes the first woman to command a nearly all-male Marine Corps battalion.

    At the same time, women are finally regularized into the Coast Guard. The first to be sworn in is Alice Jefferson; in San Francisco two years later, Eleanor L'Ecuyer will be the first woman to head a Coast Guard division.

- The post office honors author Willa Cather, who was born a century ago, with a first-class, 8-cent stamp.

    An 18-cent stamp dedicated to physician Elizabeth Blackwell is not connected to any particular anniversary, but it marks the first stamp to recognize the scientific achievements of a woman.

- Young Frances Fitzgerald receives both a National Book Award and a Pulitzer Prize for *Fire in the Lake*, a study of the Vietnam War in the context of Asia's cultural history. Because most American policy makers are ignorant of this history, Fitzgerald is immediately controversial, despite her years of research in and out of Vietnam.

    The insider positions occupied by Fitzgerald's parents adds further fuel to the fire; her late father was a deputy director of the CIA, while her mother, Marietta Peabody Tree, served in various United Nations positions in the Kennedy and Johnson administrations.

- Erica Jong becomes a household name with *Fear of Flying*. Her novel about female sexuality is so candid that some condemn it as pornography, but Jong continues to publish at a furious rate. She will be the author of a dozen books, including feminist theory and poetry, when she is elected by her peers to the presidency of the prestigious Authors Guild in 1992.

- Although Margaret Truman published a 1956 memoir of her life in the White House as a young woman, she now begins a highly successful publishing career with a biography of her father. She follows up with biographies of her mother and other women, soon dropping the use of her married name. In 1980, she will switch genres with *Murder in the White House*; it proves very popular, and she will write mysteries with Washington settings almost annually.

- The Pulitzer Prize for poetry goes to Maxine Winokur Kumin for *Up Country*. She is also the author of some two dozen books for children, four of which she wrote with the more famous Anne Sexton. In 1981, Kumin will be honored with a consultantship in poetry at the Library of Congress.

- *Deeper into Movies* wins a National Book Award for Pauline Kael. Since joining the *New Yorker* in 1968, she has been a leader in establishing film criticism as an intellectual discipline.

- American Airlines hires Floridian Bonnie Tiburzi as the first female pilot to fly Boeing's 727 jet plane. She is 25 years old and has been flying since she was 12.

- On September 20, women across the country are heartened when Billie Jean King soundly defeats Bobby Riggs in a televised Houston Astrodome tennis match. Both Riggs and most sports experts have denigrated King's ability and bragged that a woman cannot beat a man, but she trounces him 6–4, 6–3, 6–3.

- Althea Gibson, the 1960 winner of the World Professional Tennis Championship, announces her return to professional tennis at age 45. Soon afterward, she will become one of relatively few women inducted into the Black Sports Hall of Fame.

- New York's Whitney Museum (which is named for artist Gertrude Whitney) features the work of Lee Krasner, whose art has been neglected compared with that of her husband, Jackson Pollack. Critics agree that her style is fresh and completely different from his.

- By the end of the year, 30 of the 38 necessary states have ratified the proposed Equal Rights Amendment to the Constitution.

1974   In the first full year after *Roe v. Wade*, 28% of all pregnancies end in abortion. The rate will remain substantially the same throughout the next two decades.

- Congress passes the Women's Educational Equity Act, which is intended to help fund the 1972 legislation that corrected past discrimination in schools. The act appropriates $20 million for new programs aimed at girls and women, especially in athletics, vocational education, math and science, and other areas in which schools traditionally concentrated on male students to the exclusion of females.

  Later in the year, President Gerald Ford signs a bill opening Little League to girls. This change is in response to feminist agitation over statistics such as one released at the beginning of the decade by the high school sports federation: while 3.7 million boys participated in sports, only 300,000 girls did.

- The Supreme Court strikes down school board rules in Cleveland that impose unpaid leaves and other restrictions on pregnant teachers, without regard to their personal medical conditions. The Court also offers a practical benefit to Florida widows when it upholds a tax break that the legislature has granted them; but although the Court is careful to say that the benefit is fair because widows have a "disproportionally heavy burden" compared with widowers, the decision becomes still another argument against the Equal Rights Amendment. Many who oppose the ERA do so because they fear women will lose such benefits if the Constitution requires all legislation to treat men and women equally.

- Four Episcopalian bishops ignore their church's edicts and ordain 11 women on July 29 in Philadelphia. By a 129 to 9 vote, the House of Bishops overwhelmingly declares their ordination invalid, but the women see it as the beginning of vital change.

- Asian and other Third World women have replaced the eastern Europeans who were exploited by clothing manufacturers at the beginning of the century, and this year, 128 Chinese women go on strike against Espirit de Corp. With assistance from the International Ladies' Garment Workers' Union, they carry their case through the courts for almost a decade before finally winning a judgment against the manufacturer's violation of labor and health laws.

  On the other hand, as the decade nears its completion, women will make up approximately 75% of the membership of the ILGWU—but there are just two on its 18-member executive board.

- The Coalition of Labor Union Women forms under the aegis of the AFL-CIO, with aims similar to those of the Women's Trade Union League early in the century. When AFL-CIO president George Meany is aloof, the women hotly inform him that they "did not come to swap recipes."

- As some women come to believe that economic equality is an impossibility, feminist banks and credit unions open. Nor are they limited to major metropolitan areas; even midsize cities such as Denver, Miami, and this year, New Haven, Connecticut, develop such institutions. Most, however, remain undercapitalized and do not succeed in the long run.

- Several groundbreaking exhibitions on art by women are held this year; while most feature current works, "The Pennsylvania Academy and

Its Women, 1850–1920" explores forgotten women from the past.

◆ Headlines focus on the kidnapping case of Patricia Hearst, the 20-year-old daughter of a powerful publishing family. She is held captive for almost two months by a radical group that calls itself the Symbionese Liberation Army. Two years later, however, much of the public believes that she was a willing accomplice, and a California jury, which has a majority of women, will convict Hearst of assisting her captors in an armed bank robbery.

◆ Army 2nd Lieutenant Sally D. Murphy is the first woman in the military to pilot a helicopter. At the same time, Lieutenant (JG) Barbara Allen becomes the first navy aviator; unfortunately, as Barbara Rainey, she will be killed in a 1982 Alabama plane crash.

◆ In the same year that the League of Women Voters extends membership to men, girls are allowed to participate in Little League baseball. The following year, a girl is the winner of the National Soap Box Derby for the first time.

◆ Most would consider Lauren Hutton, age 31, to be nearing the end of her modeling career. Instead, when she notices that a baseball player has successfully argued for a million-dollar contract because his industry is youth-oriented, Hutton makes the same point—models, like baseball players, have limited working years. She refuses to accept bookings, tells photographers that she wants an exclusive contract, and ends up with an assignment for Revlon that is so well paid she can afford to work just 20 days a year and still be the highest-paid model in history.

Hutton, whose all-American good looks developed while she grew up playing with snakes in the swamps of Mississippi and Florida, wants the free time to indulge in her first love of exploring the far corners of the globe. *Time* and *Newsweek* put her on their covers, the term "supermodel" is coined for her, and her calculated unavailability becomes a factor in continuing a stellar career beyond age 50.

◆ Science fiction writer Ursula Le Guin repeats her 1969 triumph and again sweeps the awards for the year's best book in her genre. Unlike most technologically oriented science fiction, her stories deal with the gender complexities of the future.

◆ Congress designates Washington's Sewall-Belmont House as a National Historic Site. The house, built by Robert Sewall in 1800 at the top of Capitol Hill, was bought by Alva Belmont in 1929 to serve as the headquarters of the Woman's Party.

◆ Mary Louise Smith is elected chairman of the Republican National Committee, the first woman to hold this position.

◆ In the 50th anniversary of the first national election in which women can vote, Connecticut elects the first female governor whose political career is independent of any male relative. Democrat Ella Tambussi Grasso, the daughter of Italian immigrants, is a Mount Holyoke graduate who was elected to the state legislature in 1952. She honed her political skills, was elected to Congress in 1970, and this year defeats a Republican congressman for the governorship.

◆ At age 64, liberal Republican Millicent Fenwick is elected to Congress from Princeton, New Jersey. The divorced mother of two, she has held editorial positions with *Vogue* and other chic magazines since 1938. Her opposition to the Vietnam War and her emphasis on ethics after the Republican scandal of Watergate make her the model role for the fictional Representative Lacey Davenport of "Doonesbury" comic-strip celebrity.

1975   Carla Anderson Hills, a 41-year-old attorney with the Justice Department, is chosen by President Gerald Ford to be Secretary of the Department of Housing and Urban Development. She is just the third woman to serve on the Cabinet level, following Frances Perkins in 1933 and Oveta Culp Hobby in 1953. Two decades have passed between each of these three appointments, but that slow pattern will soon end.

◆ President Ford also sets a precedent by appointing the first woman to the National Labor Relations Board. She is Betty Southard Murphy, an attorney who has specialized in wages and hours for the Department of Labor.

◆ The last American woman to die in the Vietnam War is air force flight nurse Captain Mary T. Klinker, who is evacuating Vietnamese orphans when their plane crashes during takeoff.

When the military withdraws from Vietnam, some 11,000 military women have served in the combat zones of the Southeast Asia; eight were killed. Another 20 women with the Red Cross, United Service Organizations, and other quasi-military assignments also have died during the long years of the war.

Most military women are nurses, although some serve as physicians, physical therapists, air traffic controllers, intelligence officers, and in other specialties. A total of 265,000 women serve during the Vietnam era, many of them on hospital ships and at stations in Japan, the Philippines, Guam, and Hawaii.

◆ Almost a century after the first International Congress of Women, the United Nations hosts its first conference that focuses exclusively on women's issues. It is held in Mexico City, and more than 6,000 attend from all over the globe. The official 1,300 representatives of more than 100 countries approve a plan of action for the next decade that includes improving women's economic position and promoting political participation by women. Another 5,000 women attend the Women's Tribune, which offers a more exciting, but unofficial, agenda. Some tribune participants fight over control of the microphone, while the official convocation is staid in comparison.

◆ While the United Nations has proclaimed this International Women's Year, it is also one of the Holy Years conducted by the Catholic church every 25 years. This year, six new saints are canonized, including Elizabeth Ann Bayley Seton, the founder of the Sisters of Charity. She is the first American-born saint.

◆ Fifteen years after the birth control pill went on the market, a Princeton University study shows that 79% of all married white women of childbearing age use some form of contraception. Moreover, in one-third of such couples, one of the partners has opted for voluntary sterilization.

◆ The Gridiron Club, a prestigious group for Washington, D.C., journalists, begins admitting women. The first is Helen Thomas, a longtime reporter with United Press International who is known for her perceptive questions at presidential press conferences.

◆ The Supreme Court finally strikes down the jury service exemptions for women that are still routine in many states. It rules that these violate the Sixth Amendment, which grants defendants an impartial jury. The decision, *Taylor v. Louisiana*, is in direct opposition to the Court's ruling only a little more than a decade earlier, when, in *Hoyt v. Florida*, it upheld the automatic exclusion of women from juries.

The Court also extends the equal rights principle by ruling that Social Security death benefits may not be limited to widows; otherwise, a working woman pays into a fund that will not benefit her survivors. The opinion even spells out that the Court cannot "justify the denigration of the efforts of women who . . . work."

These decision, plus 1971's *Reed v. Reed* and 1973's *Frontiero v. Richardson*, also have the ironic effect of making the Equal Rights Amendment less of a legal necessity. Had the Court chosen to make these rulings earlier, the factious debate over ERA might have been avoided, but as it is, feminists argue that future Courts may not continue this trend and that the ERA is of itself an important symbol. Only one state, North Dakota, ratifies the amendment this year.

◆ The Court makes a number of other significant decisions this year. In one case, it rules that monetary payments for violations of fair employment law should be "the rule, not the exception"; in another case, it rules that a state cannot prohibit newspaper advertisements for legally available abortions. The Court also stops communities from banning the popular rock musical *Hair*, which contains a scene in which both men and women are nude.

+ The Indian Health Service, a unit of the U.S. Interior Department, concedes that it has been sterilizing women without their knowledge or consent.

+ The House Un-American Activities Committee, which has subpoenaed many women and men during three decades of interrogations into private lives and public activism, especially for peace, is finally abolished.

+ Congress overrides President Ford's veto of a health care bill that contains funds for family planning and rape prevention.

+ Feminists successfully push reform of rape laws in state legislatures. The law passed by Minnesota this year is typical: it makes rape cases easier to prosecute by legislating that the victim need not provide either a witness or physical evidence of resistance, and that the defense may pursue only limited questioning of her previous sexual history.

+ In a highly publicized North Carolina trial, a jury of six whites and six blacks finds 21-year-old African American Joan Little not guilty of killing her 62-year-old white jailer. She was in prison for breaking and entering when, she says, he sexually assaulted her. Hundreds of women, black and white, march in support of her self-defense claim, and the jury agrees.

+ A Pennsylvania court rules that girls may participate in all high school sports, including football and wrestling.

+ Rose Kushner publishes *Why Me? What Every Woman Should Know About Breast Cancer to Save Her Life*. Although initially her work is scorned by physicians, Kushner will see medical practices change by the time the disease kills her in 1990. Her work results in an emphasis on prevention and on treatment by methods other than radical mastectomies.

+ *The War Against the Jews* is published by Lucy Dawidowicz, an American who was studying in Poland when World War II began. She survived the Holocaust to become an expert on it, while also rebuilding Jewish archives in Poland after the war.

+ Annie Dillard wins the Pulitzer Prize for general nonfiction with her autobiographical *Pilgrim at Tinker Creek*.

+ *Alice Doesn't Live Here Anymore*, starring Ellen Burstyn, reflects the effect of the women's movement on films. One of several television shows featuring liberated women is *Rhoda*; its wedding episode sets a television audience record and its star, Valerie Harper, actively campaigns for the Equal Rights Amendment.

+ Opera impresario and musicologist Sarah Caldwell, an Arkansas native, conducts the New York Philharmonic. A few months later, she marks a lifetime achievement by becoming the first woman to conduct the Metropolitan Opera.

+ A Philadelphia exhibit entitled "Women in Photography, an Historical Survey," includes photographs by women "throughout the 130 years of the history of the medium."

+ In Hereford, Texas, near Amarillo, the National Cowgirl Hall of Fame begins. Two decades later, it will be in sound fiscal condition and successfully draws attention to the importance of women in western heritage. In addition to well-known figures such as Sacajawea, Narcissa Whitman, and Wilma Mankiller, the hall also will feature more obscure women, such as Arizona's Alice Greenough Orr, whose long career included rodeo riding in the 1920s and acting in television westerns in the 1990s.

1976　The nation celebrates its second centennial, and, for women, it is a great contrast to the first. Instead of being excluded, as Susan Anthony and others were when they tried to participate in 1876, women are so much a part of the celebration that most people do not even notice that Congress' Joint Committee on Bicentennial Arrangements is chaired by a woman, Representative Lindy Boggs of Louisiana. The House recognizes Boggs' historical expertise, and she will serve in similar capacities for future events.

+ The post office issued a stamp last year in honor of Sybil Ludington, whose Revolutionary War ride was longer than that of Paul Revere. No more women of that era are acknowledged in this bicentennial year, however; the post office instead takes note of the Spanish-American War of 1898. It issues a stamp commemorating nurse Clara Maass, who died in 1901 from experiments to discover the cause of yellow fever.

+ After intense lobbying by networks of women's organizations, Congress requires the military to open its prestigious academies to women. Female cadets will join young men at the army's historic West Point, the Naval Academy at Annapolis, and the newer Air Force Academy in Colorado Springs. The following year, women will join the crews of two Coast Guard ships, and in 1978, the Coast Guard becomes the first service to open all assignments to women.

+ Congress refines earlier legislation on credit rights for women, insisting that loan applications ask no questions of women that they do not ask of men and that women's income be included when a married couple applies for a mortgage—something that is still not routine.

The Senate Select Committee on Intelligence conducts hearings on abuses of power by the CIA and FBI, which have targeted members of women's liberation groups for surveillance.

The Senate also follows up on the recommendations of last year's Mexico City meeting and at last ratifies the 1948 and 1953 United Nations conventions on Political Rights of Women. They assure women of such rights as the vote, elective office, and "all public functions . . . on equal terms with men, without any discrimination."

+ Anne Armstrong, a Texan who cochaired the Republican National Committee from 1971 to 1973, receives the most prestigious diplomatic appointment yet granted to a woman—the ambassadorship to Great Britain. A 1949 graduate of Vassar, like other Republicans of this era, she supports the Equal Rights Amendment.

+ In *Planned Parenthood of Central Missouri v. Danforth*, the Supreme Court strikes down a clause in state law that requires a married woman to obtain her husband's consent prior to an abortion, and—by a bare majority—another clause that mandates a minor female to obtain her parent's permission. Because many girls who seek abortions are incest victims, the latter is especially troubling to Planned Parenthood Workers.

Congress restricts Medicaid funds for poor women's abortions, allowing it only in the case of rape or endangerment to the mother's life or health. Feminists file suit and receive an immediate injunction that stops implementation of the bill.

+ The National Organization for Women asks the Internal Revenue Service to audit the Roman Catholic Church to see if "tax-exempt dollars" are funding the "enormous political machine" that seeks to overturn *Roe v. Wade*. The call for an audit is closely tied to public shock at the revelation that a mail solicitation for the needy by the Pallottine Fathers of Baltimore has spent only about a half-million of some $20 million raised on the alleged cause; the rest has gone to luxury apartments and other real estate.

+ Headlines throughout the year are absorbed with Karen Ann Quinlan, a 21-year-old New Jersey woman who has been in an irreversible coma from a drug overdose since April 1975. Her parents appeal to the courts to force the hospital to disconnect her respirator, but when that is done, she surprises most observers by continuing to breathe. Quinlan is artificially fed and will remain comatose for more than a decade, until finally dying in 1985. The case generates much discussion on the right to die, and California responds with the first law allowing patients to restrict hospitals from taking extraordinary measures to prolong life.

+ Alice Olson wins a $750,000 settlement from the CIA when the spy agency acknowledges that it caused the 1953 death of her husband, Frank

Olson, by using him to experiment with the hallucinogenic drug LSD.

Olson was rearing the couple's three children in Washington's Maryland suburbs when her husband plunged to his death from the window of a New York hotel room. His CIA colleagues told her that he had killed himself, and only recently did she discover—in a newspaper article —that he had been the unwitting object of hallucinogenic experimentation. President Gerald Ford apologizes to her on behalf of the United States.

◆ The Justice Department files the first gender-based suit under the 1968 Fair Housing Law, charging mortgage institutions in New Jersey and Utah with asking questions of women that they do not ask of men or married couples.

◆ The Census Bureau issues a report on the changing status of women over the past 25 years. Since 1950, women have risen from 6% to 19% of all college graduates; they constitute 44% of current student bodies. The number of employed women has doubled since 1950, and many more of them are mothers who must combine parenting with employment: 37% of women with preschool children are now in the labor force, compared with 12% in 1950. Divorced women have risen from 2.5% to 6.8% of the total population.

◆ A New York Times survey shows that during the past decade, the number of women enrolling in theological seminaries has risen from 3% to 35% of all students. Their presence is forcing major change in the nature of religious ministry and in the schools' curricula. Episcopalians are still debating the status of 15 women who have been unofficially ordained during the past two years, and although many other Protestant denominations now ordain women, the vast majority of them work as assistants to men.

◆ The increase in female journalists causes sex scandals in Congress to receive widespread publicity this year; as long as most journalists were men, such activity went unreported. Two congressmen are charged with using public funds to pay women who do no congressional work this year,

and one of them, Wayne Hayes of Ohio, is forced to resign. Representative Allan Howe of Utah is convicted of soliciting sex from a prostitute.

◆ North Carolina executes 52-year-old Velma Barfield by lethal injection for the poisoning death of her lover. Two decades will pass before the next woman is executed.

◆ Newswoman Barbara Walters sets a precedent when she negotiates a $5 million contract with ABC Television to anchor the nightly news— which is a milestone in itself. Walters specializes in interviews and is highly successful at asking tough questions in a polite way. Her candor has extended to first ladies: She asked Mamie Eisenhower about her alleged alcoholism and queried Lady Bird Johnson about the president's attraction to other women.

◆ NBC hires popular New York television journalist Betty Furness for the morning news show Today. Furness has built a local reputation for taking her cameras out to publicize consumer ripoffs, and she continues this nationally for the next 16 years, while in her 60s and 70s.

◆ Both Walters and Furness owe a debt to Mary Margaret McBride, who dies this year at age 77 in New York. A native of Missouri, McBride pioneered the concept of a radio talk show aimed at women. She expanded from the Midwest to national recognition, exposing her kitchen-based audience to the wider world.

◆ Editor/publisher Dorothy Schiff retires, leaving intact the New York Post's record of continuous publication since Alexander Hamilton founded it in 1801. She has led the paper for almost four decades, and those who buy it from her will not have nearly her record of success. One key to attracting readership was her publication of an uncommon number of female columnists, including Doris Fleeson, Sylvia Porter, and Eleanor Roosevelt.

◆ Boston Globe columnist Ellen Goodman begins national syndication. Her writing is exceptional in its clear feminist positions on the issues discussed in the op-ed pages of newspapers. Her unusual insights soon prove popular, and within two decades, she is published in some 440 newspapers.

◆ No woman has won a Pulitzer Prize for biography since 1951, but a woman is the subject of this year's winner: Richard W. B. Lewis wins for a book on Edith Wharton. In 1972, Joseph Lash won for *Eleanor and Franklin*, which profiled the Roosevelts.

◆ In the summer, Representative Barbara Jordan of Texas becomes the first black and the first woman to deliver a keynote address at a national nominating convention. She takes the stage at a Democratic convention chaired by Representative Lindy Boggs of Louisiana, which is another first for women.

◆ President Ford honors Catherine Filene Shouse with the Presidential Medal of Freedom, primarily for her efforts in founding the Wolf Trap Park for the Performing Arts in Virginia.

◆ *for colored girls who have considered suicide when the rainbow is enuf* is an award-winning Broadway hit for writer Ntozake Shange, a 1970 Barnard graduate.

◆ *Roots* is the publishing phenomenon of the decade, and author Alex Haley has spent some of his 12 years of research in the seemingly incongruous setting of the Washington headquarters of the Daughters of the American Revolution. Although that organization is well known for a racist past, it also has preserved many original documents that Haley finds helpful in tracing the history of his family in slavery.

◆ The National Women's Political Caucus charges both major parties with lowering their female participation instead of raising it: the delegates to this year's Democratic convention were 31% women, compared with 40% in 1972; the Republican figure dropped from 30% to 28%.

◆ After speaking of her experience with forced retirement at the White House Conference on Aging, senior citizen activist Maggie Kuhn forms the Grey Panthers to work against age discrimination.

Two years ago, she appeared on Johnny Carson's popular *Tonight* show, where she lambasted Carson for his "Aunt Blabby" character.

◆ Liz Claiborne uses $200,000 in loans from family and friends to begin her clothing company, which is worth $117 million when it goes public just five years later. At age 47, she has a long career as a clothing designer, and she markets her own label to the masses of women entering the work force.

◆ The November election for president is a close one, as women divide on party lines because both incumbent Republican Gerald Ford and Democratic challenger Jimmy Carter support the Equal Rights Amendment and other feminist causes. Rosalyn Carter proves an effective campaigner in Carter's narrow victory.

◆ Scientist Dixy Lee Ray wins the governorship of Washington. She runs as a Democrat, despite the fact that Republican President Richard Nixon appointed her to the Atomic Energy Commission in 1972. Her margin of victory surprises pundits, for she is seen as a politically inexperienced college professor. This "outsider" image, however, makes her tenure difficult; she also alienates environmentalists and will lose the next Democratic primary.

In New York, Bella Abzug gives up her House seat to run for the Senate and loses. The House also will miss the leadership of Hawaii's Patsy Mink, who also—like Abzug—is defeated in the Democratic primary of her Senate quest. President Carter will appoint Mink as assistant secretary of state for environmental and scientific affairs.

1977 When Dixy Lee Ray is inaugurated as governor of Washington, she joins Connecticut's Ella Grasso—who took office two years ago—as the first women to serve simultaneously as governors since the 1925 inaugurations of Nellie Tayloe Ross in Wyoming and Miriam Ferguson in Texas. Unlike Ross and Ferguson, Grasso and Ray are both unmarried women who built their own careers. That more than 50 years have passed since the nation had two women as governors is a reflection of the slow progress women have made since the 1920s.

- Jimmy Carter is the first president to appoint two women to his Cabinet and to appoint an African-American woman. Even prior to taking office, he names Juanita Kreps as secretary of commerce—an unconventional slot for a woman. Kreps, an economist at Duke University, also set a precedent by being the first woman on the governing board of the New York Stock Exchange.

  African-American attorney Patricia Roberts Harris, who served as ambassador to Luxembourg under Democrat Lyndon Johnson, fulfills two roles in the Carter administration: she will head the Department of Housing and Urban Development until 1979, when she takes over another Cabinet-level position, Health and Human Services.

- Lillian Carter, the president's mother, proves an exceptional role model for older women. She will travel extensively during his administration, often speaking on her experience of joining the Peace Corps as a 68-year-old widow and working in India.

- When they leave the White House, Gerald and Betty Ford sign separate contracts for their memoirs. When her comes out in 1978, it reveals that the first lady has suffered from addictions to both alcohol and drugs, beginning with prescription painkillers for arthritis. In 1982, she will cofound the Betty Ford Clinic in Rancho Mirage, California, which attracts many celebrities seeking to break addictions.

- During the late winter and spring legislative sessions, Indiana becomes the 35th of the 38 states necessary to ratify the Equal Rights Amendment, but the amendment is rejected in Virginia, Nevada, North Carolina, and Florida. Some of the votes are close: in Florida, for example, it passes the House and loses narrowly in the Senate. At the same time, however, Idaho joins Nebraska and Tennessee in rescinding its previous ratification—a situation so uncommon that legal experts cannot agree on its effect. Even the best interpre-

tation, however, still leaves the ERA three states short of final approval.

ERAmerica, a coalition of labor, religious, and women's groups formed the previous year, conducts extensive campaigns in an attempt for ratification by another three states. Many celebrities join in the effort; among the most popular speakers is humorist Erma Bombeck. In the end, however, Indiana's ratification will be the last.

- Some opposition to the ERA arises because it is increasingly tied to the issue of sexual orientation. When Florida's Dade County, which includes Miami, passes an ordinance banning discrimination against homosexuals in January, the forces for repeal are led by Anita Bryant. A former Miss Oklahoma who placed third in the 1958 Miss America contest, she is a popular television spokesperson for orange juice and thus has an immediate national audience. Her faction wins the June repeal, but the crusade does long-term harm to her singing career.

- The Supreme Court continues to make decisions that obviate the need for the Equal Rights Amendment: it strikes down an Oklahoma law that set differing ages for women and men to buy beer, and in Alabama, it voids minimum height and weight requirements for prison guards as inherently discriminatory toward women. In the Oklahoma case, it was men who were the target of the unfair legislation.

  On the other hand, in cases involving three different states, the Court rules that governments do not have to expend funds for the elective abortions of poor women. In New York City, the Health Department reports almost as many abortions as live births.

- President Carter appoints former Representative Bella Abzug to cochair his National Advisory Committee on Women. Her political style continues to be controversial, however, and he soon asks for her resignation. Abzug subsequently loses elections for Congress and for mayor of New York City.

- African American Eleanor Holmes Norton, a 1964 Yale Law School graduate, is President

Women march in Washington on August 26, 1977, with a banner bearing the text of the Equal Rights Amendment. Many wear white with purple sashes, colors associated with the suffragist movement of the early century. This celebration of the anniversary of the 19th Amendment is another conscious feminist effort to link women with their history. Library of Congress

Carter's choice to head the Equal Employment Opportunity Commission. She will go on to become the District of Columbia's representative in Congress in 1990, despite publicity concerning her failure to pay local income taxes.

✦ Eleanor Smeal is elected president of NOW and becomes its first salaried officer. After her NOW presidency, she will found a political action committee, the Fund for a Feminist Majority.

✦ A torch that will be carried by more than 1,000 female runners is lighted at the historic birthplace of the women's movement in Seneca Falls, New York, and is borne to Houston, where national symposia following up on International Women's Year takes place.

The Houston event is organized largely by Kathryn Clarenbach, who served from 1970 to 1972 as the first president of the National Association of Commissions for Women.

✦ In response to lobbying from feminists, Congress restores the Congressional Medal of Honor that was taken from Civil War physician Mary Walker in 1917. Walker, of course, is long since dead.

✦ Congress also finally grants veterans' benefits to women who served with the American Expeditionary Forces in World War I—six decades after the women could have used them.

✦ Outraged Wisconsin women force a recall election that removes a male judge from the bench and replaces him with a woman. The judge had sentenced a rapist to just a year of probation, while criticizing the victim for wearing "provocative" clothing.

◆ An anonymous Seattle woman sues an insurance company that refuses to sell more than $50,000 worth of life insurance to housewives. Companies defend this common industry policy by arguing that because a housewife produces no income, her life cannot be worth much. The state court rules in the woman's favor.

◆ The Census Bureau reports great change in family structure: The number of households in which one person lives alone or with unrelated people has risen 40% during the decade. The trend causes the Department of Housing and Urban Development to adopt a definition of "family" that is not dependent on marital status.

◆ The post office issues its second stamp intended to honor the women of the American Revolution. Part of a series entitled "Skilled Hands for Independence," it depicts a seamstress.

◆ Female artists sponsor several exhibitions this year, but the one that receives most attention is "Women Artists: 1550–1950," at the Los Angeles County Museum of Art. Although very few people have heard of any of these artists, critics applaud their high-quality work.

◆ President Jimmy Carter gives painter Georgia O'Keeffe, who was elected to the American Academy of Arts and Letters in 1969, a Medal of Freedom. Afterward, O'Keeffe returns to her remote New Mexico home, where she will continue to paint almost until her death at age 98.

◆ New York radiologist Dr. Rosalyn Sussman Yalow wins the Nobel Prize for Medicine. Age 56, her life's work is in nuclear medicine and immunology, and she wins for her role in developing tests capable of measuring tiny amounts of enzymes, hormones, and other biological content. She is the married mother of two and is the nation's first woman to win this prize.

At the same time, Dr. Ruth Sager is elected to the National Academy of Sciences for her outstanding work in genetics. Both are role models for young women, as the nation's medical schools announce that their female students have increased 700% since 1959.

◆ A Marine Corps study reports that "even with time off for maternity leave . . . servicewomen lost much less time than men because of their lower incidence of absence without leave, desertion, and drug- and alcohol-related problems."

Other barriers fall when the first joint basic training classes of men and women are conducted and the first women are assigned to the elite Fleet Marine Force.

◆ The first woman to qualify for the Indianapolis 500 is Janet Gutherie, a 39-year-old New York City physicist who endures much hostility to fulfill her desire to race. Fuel pump failure forces her out of this year's contest after 27 laps.

Shirley Muldowny, however, has an excellent year. She beats more than 100 men to win top place in the National Hot Rod Association's drag races. Muldowny also twice breaks world records at other events; she wins significant prize money and summarizes, "I think I've proven I'm no female side show."

◆ Just 21, Californian Debbi Fields borrows $50,000 to open a shop specializing in her chocolate chip cookies, and Mrs. Fields' Cookies quickly becomes a multimillion-dollar business.

◆ Virginian Mary Lee Settle wins the National Book Award for fiction for *Blood Tie*. An accomplished writer, Settle's memoir of serving in the British military prior to U.S. entry into World War II, *All the Brave Promises* (1966), is the record of her extraordinary dedication to the defeat of fascism.

◆ *The Women's Room*, a first novel by Marilyn French, breaks precedent as a feminist treatise that also is tremendously popular with mainstream readers. French, an English professor with a Harvard Ph.D. and the divorced mother of two, not only will repeat this year's success with other future novels, but also will write serious feminist theory. *The War Against Women* (1992), for example, explores systematic oppression ranging from such cultural practices as female infanticide to violence in the home.

◆ When Wyoming's Nellie Tayloe Ross dies in the same year as Elvis Presley, few take note of the passing of the nation's first female governor. She is 101 and has lived in Washington, D.C., more than four decades, since her retirement after the Roosevelt administration, in which she served as U.S. Treasurer.

Her counterpart in the Truman administration, U.S. Treasurer Georgia Neese Clark, lives on as Georgia Neese Gray until 1995, when she dies at age 95.

1978 After issuing nearly 50 stamps related to women, the post office acknowledges African-American women. The first-class, 13-cent stamp goes to the brilliant and courageous Harriet Tubman.

It is the last stamp honoring women to be issued this decade; nine were released, while the 1960s featured 10.

+ Six years after the army, navy, and air force have set the precedent, the marines appoint a woman to their highest rank. Margaret A. Brewer is promoted to general in May; ironically, she has the same surname as Lucy Brewer, the legendary first female Marine, who served in the War of 1812 disguised as a man.

The navy also has its first African-American female captain this year, when Joan C. Bynum, a member of the Nurse Corps, is promoted to that rank.

Most significantly, the army abolishes its 35-year-old WAC (Women's Army Corps) and integrates women into the mainstream of the service. Army women will now belong to the corps that is appropriate to their training rather than to their gender.

+ Illinois, the only major northern state that has not ratified the Equal Rights Amendment, votes it down despite a strong campaign. The coalition of organizations supporting the ERA begins boycotting states that have not ratified; national conventions of major organizations are moved from places such as New Orleans, meaning the loss of millions of dollars in revenue to those states. In July, the National Organization for Women conducts a giant march in Washington, D.C., urging

Congress to extend the ratification deadline, which is next March.

+ Illinois' defeat of the ERA causes some to point out that it is the home state of Phyllis Schlafly, whom both its advocates and the media deem the ERA's most effective opponent. Schlafly, who ran unsuccessfully for Congress in 1952, 1960, and 1970, also lost a 1967 bid for the presidency of the National Federation of Republican Women. After that defeat, she formed the right-wing Eagle Forum, which she will head for decades.

Although too conservative to win elections, Schlafly has greater success as a lecturer and author—especially with her self-published *A Choice Not an Echo* (1964), which supported Republican nominee Barry Goldwater and sold some 3 million copies.

+ Eighteen women currently serve in the U.S. House, but none hold elective positions in the Senate. Two women become senators this year, however, when both Muriel Humphrey of Minnesota and Maryon Allen of Alabama are appointed to the seats held by their recently dead husbands. Both are Democrats, and Humphrey was well known as the nation's "second lady" when her husband was vice president under Lyndon Johnson.

+ The Supreme Court refuses to consider an appeal from a Pueblo woman who wishes to bring sex discrimination charges against her tribe, which bars tribal membership to children whose fathers are not Pueblo. The Court does not speak to the gender issue but rather to the separate governance of Native Americans.

+ Meg Greenfield of the *Washington Post* becomes the first woman working for a major metropolitan newspaper to win the Pulitzer Prize for editorial writing. The *Post*'s publisher is Katharine Graham, and next year, she will promote Greenfield to editor of the editorial page.

+ The first female governor of the Federal Reserve Board is economist Nancy H. Teeters, a 1952 Oberlin graduate who had not considered a career until her in-laws offered to pay for her education.

+ Midge Constanza, who has been one of the most visible women inside the White House, resigns this year; politico Anne Wexler joins the staff. Both specialize in dealing with business, labor, and other interest groups that want access to the president.

+ In the last 15 years, the percentage of female students in schools of veterinary medicine has risen from 5% to 37%.

+ Janet Gutherie comes in eighth at the Indianapolis 500—despite driving her race car with a broken wrist that she hides from officials.

+ President Carter invites feminist poet Eve Merriam to read her work at the White House. At New York University in 1965, Merriam taught what she believes was the nation's first college course in women's studies; she also wrote *We, the Women*, a pioneer feminist documentary broadcast on CBS.

+ Novelist Joyce Carol Oates is elected to the American Academy of Arts and Letters, just 15 years after publishing her first book of short stories. She won the 1970 National Book Award with *Them*, a novel featuring a lower-class female protagonist whose life is beset by violence.

Contrasting characters fill the novels of Judith Krantz, whose *Scruples* is the first of a series featuring affluent, sophisticated women. Although dismissed by critics, her books sell extremely well, and within a few years, Krantz is making more money than any novelist in the world.

+ In New York, Mary Anne Krupsak, who defeated Mario Cuomo to win the Democratic nomination for lieutenant governor in 1974, now challenges the governor under whom she serves. Voters consider this disloyal, and Governor Hugh Carey overwhelmingly defeats her, effectively ending her career.

At the same time, Hawaii elects its first woman as lieutenant governor. She is former state senator Jean King.

+ Nancy Kassebaum, the daughter of 1936 Republican presidential nominee Alf Landon and recently divorced mother of four, is elected to the U.S. Senate from Kansas. Her father and other politicos are surprised when Kassebaum—whose previous political experience was limited to a small-town school board—defeats eight men in the Republican primary and carries 56% of the vote in the general election.

More than 50 years after women started voting, she is the first woman in the Senate who did not have a husband preceding her in Congress.

1979 When a January storm dumps 20 inches of snow on Chicago, Mayor Michael Bilandic, who inherited the office after the death of the city's nearly omnipotent Mayor Richard J. Daley, seems powerless to clean the streets. Jane Byrne, also a Daley protégée who headed his consumer department, takes on the incumbent—who had fired her—and beats him in the primary by a margin that stuns party operatives. Her general election margin is the greatest of any mayoral candidate in a large city since 1901.

Byrne is the nation's first female mayor of a megalopolis, and women throughout the nation take pride in her achievement. She bills herself as a reformer, takes on the city's unions, and drastically cuts budgets. The result, however, is turmoil and endless backstabbing, for even though all of the players are Democrats, Byrne is unable to unite them behind her. She will lose her 1983 reelection, and eventually Richard M. Daley—a bitter enemy to Byrne—succeeds his father in office.

+ Some 60,000 abortion-rights opponents mark the sixth anniversary of *Roe v. Wade* with a "March for Life." Shortly afterward, the Department of Health, Education and Welfare announces that Medicaid funding of abortions has plummeted by 99% in the year since the Supreme Court approved congressional restrictions.

On the other hand, the Court again affirms the right of even young women to abortions: in *Bellotti v. Baird*, it strikes down a Massachusetts law requiring unmarried minors to obtain the consent of both parents or a judge. The case is another victory for Bill Baird, whose crusade for reproductive rights also brought a 1972 milestone when the Court ruled that the sale of birth control pills could not be limited to married people.

✦ President Jimmy Carter proclaims the week of March 8, which includes the United Nation's International Women's Day, as National Women's History Week. During the next decade, the entire month of March will evolve as Women's History Month, largely through the tremendous efforts of the California-based National Women's History Project.

✦ The U.S. Mint honors Susan B. Anthony by profiling her on the only major new coin issued in the century, but it is an immediate flop. Even feminists are disappointed with the Susan Anthony dollar, which is so like a quarter that it causes confusion and people refuse to use it. Nevertheless, the mother of the suffrage movement is the first woman to be depicted on a U.S. coin.

✦ The issue of spousal abuse begins to be broadly discussed this year when three cases set precedents. In California, Idalia Mejia is acquitted of killing her husband after she testifies to his record of extreme brutality. The other cases set even more important precedents, and especially the Oregon case of John and Greta Rideout holds headlines for months.

Eventually he is acquitted of raping her—but the fact that a court accepts the premise that a husband can be guilty of raping his wife is a major milestone. Much of the public finds the precedent almost inconceivable, but its importance is soon clear, for a few months later, a Massachusetts man goes to prison for the rape of his estranged wife. Within the next five years, more than 20 states will pass laws eliminating marriage as a defense against rape charges.

✦ When the pope visits the National Shrine of the Immaculate Conception in Washington, D.C., Sister M. Theresa Kane uses her platform position to urge him to provide "the possibility of women as persons being included in all ministries of our

church." Fifty-three of the 5,000 nuns attending stand in silent protest while the pope speaks.

✦ Hazel Johnson-Brown is the first African-American woman to reach top military rank. She is promoted to brigadier general with the command of the Army Nurse Corps, the military's oldest unit for women.

At the same time, Lieutenant (JG) Beverly Kelley becomes the first woman to command a military vessel, when she takes over the Coast Guard's *Cape Newagen*.

✦ Corporals Vicki L. Gagilia and Betty Jo Rankin are praised for their courage when the American embassy in Pakistan that they guard is attacked by a mob of 10,000. Despite agreement that they performed well, women are pulled from embassy assignments for several years.

✦ The female pilots of World War II finally receive some benefits, primarily because of the efforts of Senator Barry Goldwater, who had flown with WASPs and rated them "equal to or better than their male counterparts."

✦ About 80 women fly in the cockpits of major airlines, but they remain a tiny fraction of the nation's 70,000 pilots. Moreover, most of them are assigned the secondary work of navigation.

✦ Although Congress has exempted itself from equal employment legislation, the Supreme Court rules in favor of a woman who was fired by a Louisiana representative. In *Davis v. Passman*, Shirley Davis avers that Representative Otto Passman told her that he wanted a man in the job slot, and the Court says she has a constitutional right to sue him for sex discrimination.

✦ Feminist attention focuses on Utah, where Sonia Johnson is ex-communicated from the Church of Jesus Christ of the Latter-Day Saints. Johnson, a former missionary with a Ph.D. and four children, has campaigned for the Equal Rights Amendment, an activity the Mormon leadership deems "seditious." She goes on the lecture circuit and a decade later publishes a best-seller on her experience, *From Housewife to Heretic* (1982).

The church's position stands in great historical contrast to its politics in the early century: not only were Utah women the first in the nation to vote, but the Mormons also supported the national suffrage movement by funding an official liaison. Moreover, after years of controversy, the church accepted its first black men as priests last year, but the question of women's ordination is not even discussed.

✦ Historian Barbara Tuchman is the first woman elected president of the American Academy of Arts and Letters. Her books are acclaimed by both the public and scholars—although it is significant that her two Pulitzer Prizes were awarded for general nonfiction, not for history. Last year's book, *A Distant Mirror: The Calamitous 14th Century*, will be widely discussed. Its topic, the devastation of the medieval plague, is increasingly timely as the AIDS epidemic grows in the next decade.

✦ Two unusual movies explore the lives of low-income, white southern women. *Coal Miner's Daughter* stars young Sissy Spacek as Loretta Lynn, who rose from West Virginia poverty to superstardom as a country singer.

Norma Rae is a film about grim factory life and union organizing; despite the seemingly unlikely topic, it is popular with both critics and audiences and wins a Best Actress Oscar for Sally Field. In 1984, Field will win again for *Places in the Heart*, the story of a young widow who works with a black escaped prisoner to make a success of her cotton farm.

✦ Congress extends the period for ratification of the Equal Rights Amendment from seven years to nine years, thus giving feminists until June of 1982 to get three more states to approve the amendment.

Much opposition has exploited the decade's antiwar sentiment by arguing that the amendment would subject women to the draft for the first time—ignoring the fact that with the Nurses Selective Service Act of 1945, Congress assumed that it had the right to draft women.

✦ As satellites reveal the surface of Venus, the International Astronomical Union announces that cartographers will use only female names for geographical features there. Volcanoes and large craters will be named for historical women; smaller ones will be given female first names from various cultures; valleys will be variants of "Venus" in different languages, and other features will be named for female mythological figures.

✦ The prestigious *New York Times* names 33-year-old Le Anne Schreiber as sports editor, where she will supervise a 55-member, mostly male staff. Her promotion is not unrelated to the fact that the *Times* settled a sex discrimination suit by its female employees last month, and part of the settlement was a promise to fill 25% of its senior news positions with women. The paper's executive editor says, "She knows a lot about sports, she has good news judgment, and she taught English at Harvard. I'm kind of tickled about that third qualification." Schreiber, on the other hand, says that her "glory day" came at Rice University in Texas, when she made a 50-yard run for a touchdown in Powder Puff football.

One of the decade's hottest topics in sports is the admission of female reporters into locker rooms. *Sports Illustrated* reporter Melissa Ludtke files suit this year against the baseball commissioner and the New York Yankees for refusing her admittance, but the milestone has been passed in other sports, including the rough world of hockey. *New York Daily News* reporter Lawrie Mifflin says of the Knickerbockers' dressing room, "It's so grubby and smelly that it's totally asexual."

✦ Democrat Dianne Feinstein, who has been on San Francisco's Board of Supervisors since 1970, is elected mayor. Challenged by gun control opponents in a 1983 recall election, she will win an amazing 80% of the vote.

✦ The Democratic Governors' Conference elects Connecticut's Ella Grasso as its chair. Sadly, Grasso will have to resign her governorship the following year because of illness; she dies just five weeks later.

✦ An element of President Carter's 1976 campaign platform was the separation of education from the Department of Health, Education and Welfare. After Congress narrowly passes enabling legislation early in the year, HEW splits into two Cabinet-level agencies, Health and Human Resources and Education. In December, the president appoints Shirley Hufstedler as head of the new Department of Education. She has risen through California's judiciary to the highest levels, but initially professional educators are leery of her ability to understand their profession. She soon wins them over and successfully supervises some 17,000 employees and a $14 billion budget.

✦ *The Brethren: Inside the Supreme Court* by Watergate investigative journalist Bob Woodward reveals that a chief reason why the male justices are reluctant to have a woman on the Court is that they routinely watch pornographic movies when ruling on obscenity cases. Although they consider this a necessary part of their jobs, they expect to feel uncomfortable about showing films that degrade women to a female colleague.

1980 As the decade begins, women are twice as likely as men to fall beneath the government's official poverty line. Half of the nation's poor families are headed by women.

✦ For the first time in America's history, manufacturing slips to second place as an employer of women. It is displaced by the secretarial/clerical category.

Ironically, at a time when fewer women are working in traditionally union-organized, blue-collar jobs, the AFL-CIO finally includes the first woman on its Executive Council. She is Joyce Dannen Miller, the president of the Coalition of Labor Union Women.

✦ As a result of assiduous lobbying during the last decade, the military's ancient academies have female graduates this spring. The honor of being the first woman at the U.S. Naval Academy goes Elizabeth Belzer, while Andrea Hollen is the army's first at West Point. At the Air Force Academy, there are 97 women in a class of 887; the

Coast Guard has 14 women among 156 graduates; the navy has 55 of 947; and the army, 61 of 870. The marines have none, while the air force continues its comparatively progressive policies and has the highest percentage of female cadets.

Also, after ignoring the issue for most of four decades, the Department of Defense extends veteran status to women who served in World War II's Women's Army Auxiliary Corps during the 1942–43 period before the "Auxiliary" was dropped and it became the Women's Army Corps.

Most significantly, the House Armed Service Committee—prodded by Colorado Representative Patricia Schroeder—holds hearings on sexual harassment in the military. In August, however, the Navy begins discharge procedures against a number of women accused of homosexual activity.

✦ After years of lobbying by women's groups, the Equal Employment Opportunity Commission declares sexual harassment to be an unlawful employment practice that falls under the EEOC's purview.

✦ No states ratify the Equal Rights Amendment this year, and several vote it down—in the case of Illinois, for the seventh time. Other states raise questions of constitutional law by attempting to revoke their previous approval. For the first time since ratification of the ERA was added to its platform in 1940, the Republican Party excludes it.

✦ The Supreme Court, in a 5 to 4 decision, upholds a congressional ban on the use of Medicaid funds to pay for abortions. The ban is called the Hyde Amendment for its sponsor, Representative Henry Hyde, Republican of Illinois. The Court also upholds an Illinois ban on using state funds for most abortions. The election of Ronald Reagan at year's end confirms rising conservatism on this issue.

✦ The Supreme Court continues to create the equal rights principle by ruling against state worker's compensation plans that automatically grant benefits to the survivors of male workers but not to widowers who have lost their working wives.

Three federal judges in Pennsylvania go even further in their argument for the ERA principle when they rule that applying military draft registration to men only is unconstitutional. The Supreme Court stays this decision and will overturn it next year; the Selective Service law continues to affect only men.

✦ Female professors in Georgia win two court precedents: the Board of Regents is ordered to pay $86,500 to six women who suffered discrimination at Georgia Southwestern College; and in a University of Georgia case, the same judge sends a male professor to jail after he refuses to divulge how he voted when a faculty committee denied tenure to a woman.

Meanwhile, the University of Minnesota settles out of court and awards $100,000 to a woman who was not granted a tenure track position by the chemistry department.

A larger award—$16 million—goes to female employees of the Government Printing Office in Washington, who prove a history of discrimination in a class-action suit.

✦ Female students at the University of California at Berkeley insist on a grievance procedure to handle complaints against professors who harass students by demanding sex for grades. They organize a demonstration when a sociology professor is only mildly reprimanded for his sexual advances to female students.

✦ Chicago is scandalized by the revelation that almost 200 women have been strip-searched when arrested for traffic violations and similar minor offenses.

The city pays $69,500 to settle this case, but the problem remains. In 1984, the Supreme Court will condemn Chicago police procedure that subjects women, but not men, to strip-searches when they enter jail.

✦ Californian Candy Lightner founds Mothers Against Drunk Drivers (MADD) after her daughter is killed by a man who, despite three drunken drinking convictions, has served just two days in jail. Saying that law enforcement's attitude toward manslaughter by the intoxicated makes it "the only socially accepted form of homicide," she begins a national crusade. Just two years later, Congress will pass legislation in direct response to Lightner's efforts.

✦ The nation's first in-vitro fertilization clinic opens in Norfolk, Virginia. The Georgeanna and Howard Jones Institute for Reproductive Medicine has 3,000 applications from infertile couples on the day it opens, and it will have its first success with a baby born next year.

On the opposite side of the reproductive question, the Census Bureau announces a "striking increase" in the number of women who are delaying childbirth and/or choosing not to bear children at all. The number of married women in their early 20s who are childless has soared from 24% in 1960—when the birth control pill was introduced—to 41% last year.

✦ A study by Dr. Ann Barnes at Massachusetts General Hospital confirms that drugs prescribed in pregnancy can have effects reaching far into the next generation: Women whose mothers took diethylstilbestrol in the 1940s run twice the risk of problem pregnancies as women whose mothers were not exposed to DES.

✦ The American Cancer Society issues a recommendation that women over 50 obtain annual mammograms, while those over 35 should use this new technology that X-rays the breast with "periodic discretion."

✦ When internal division brings multiple resignations among male executives at 20th-Century Fox, the studio turns to 36-year-old Sherry Lansing, who becomes the first female CEO of a major Hollywood studio—even though she has been in the film business just over a decade.

A 1966 graduate of Chicago's Northwestern University, Lansing initially went to Los Angeles to teach high school in the notorious Watts ghetto, but her love of film lead to her first Hollywood acting job in 1970. From there, she rose to the ranks of script reader, story analyst, and executive editor to the vice president of creative affairs. Two of her movies, *Kramer v.*

Kramer and *The China Syndrome*, are current successes with both critics and audiences.

✦ The award-winning *Kramer v. Kramer* stars Meryl Streep, a 1971 Vassar graduate, as a mother who leaves her husband and young son because of the emptiness of her life as an urban housewife. It explores issues of divorce and especially of the responsibilities and joys of fatherhood at a time when some feminists are beginning to rue the divorce law reforms of the past few decades.

Due to laws that make divorce easy to obtain, more and more women are finding their living standards drop dramatically after divorce while men's rise. Alimony is rarely granted except in high-income families, while "deadbeat dad" enters the language to describe the routine flounting of child support orders.

✦ The Reverend Marjorie S. Matthew of Michigan is elected as a bishop of the United Methodist Church. She thus becomes the nation's first woman to sit on the governing body of a major religious denomination.

✦ The post office begins a decade of restoring women to history with five stamps issued this year. They honor Dolley Madison, first lady and 1814 wartime hero; Edith Wharton, who won the first Pulitzer Prize in literature granted to a woman; Blanche Stuart Scott, the first woman to fly solo; and Frances Perkins, the first in the cabinet. The great communicator Helen Keller, who was both deaf and bind, shares a stamp with her innovative teacher, Anne Sullivan.

All except Scott receive the first-class, 15-cent stamp; Scott is featured on a 28-cent airmail stamp.

✦ At age 80, Taylor Caldwell publishes *Answer as a Man*, which will be her last book. She has written an average of almost a novel a year since 1938, many of which were made into movies. In addition to the *nom de plume* by which she is known, she also wrote under two masculine pseudonyms.

✦ Two women from the *Boston Globe* win the Pulitzer Prize: Ellen Goodman for commentary and

Joan Vennochi for special local reporting. The other female winners are both Floridians; Bette Orsini of the *St. Petersburg Times* wins for national reporting, while the *Miami Herald*'s Madeleine Blais gets the feature writing award.

✦ President Jimmy Carter loses his reelection bid to former California Governor Ronald Reagan. He and Nancy Reagan are the nation's first actors to occupy the White House, and the election also make it clear that the nation now tolerates divorce at the highest levels. Although Reagan is the first divorced man to be elected president, there is virtually no discussion of this precedent in the campaign.

✦ The election is termed the Reagan revolution, as the Republicans win control of the U.S. Senate for the first time since 1954. One of the women who benefits from Reagan's coattails is Paula Hawkins, who becomes Florida's first female U.S. senator. A self-described "Maitland housewife," Hawkins previously won a position on the state's public utilities commission and is seen as a consumer advocate. She will seriously harm that image, however, when her most visible early action in Congress is a press luncheon to decry food stamp fraud—at which steak and expensive out-of-season asparagus is served.

✦ The four years of the Carter administration pass without any vacancy occurring on the Supreme Court, and the promise to appoint a woman at the next opportunity becomes a campaign issue. Carter has appointed a historic number of women at lower levels: 40 of his 262 appointments to federal judgeships have been women.

✦ In December, the 34th Assembly of the United Nations approves a Convention on the Elimination of All Forms of Discrimination Against Women. It is the result of a Copenhagen conference earlier in the year that marked the halfway point of a decade dedicated to rights of women. Thus, the target period for "elimination of all forms of discrimination" is an unlikely five years.

11

A Multiplicity of Women in Modern America

1981–1995

1981 President Ronald Reagan does not continue the tradition established by President Kennedy's 1961 creation of the Commission on the Status of Women. Although some 250 local commissions have emulated it, the national body dies when Reagan takes office.

✦ The Reagan inauguration motivates former Republican congresswoman and ambassador Clare Booth Luce, age 78, to return to Washington from her Hawaiian retirement. She has focused on anticommunism since the 1950s, and Reagan appoints her to his Foreign Intelligence Advisory Board; he further honors her with the Presidential Medal of Freedom in 1983.

✦ Georgetown University professor Jeane Kirkpatrick is Reagan's appointee as United Nations ambassador. She is the first woman to hold this position, and although a registered Democrat, she has drawn favorable attention from conservatives for her academic articles on foreign affairs.

✦ Sandra Day O'Connor of Arizona becomes the first woman on the Supreme Court on July 7. When she is appointed, 101 men have served during the Court's 191-year history. Public impatience at last to have a woman in this position is clear in the Senate's 99 to 0 confirmation vote. O'Connor reveals that after graduating from law school in 1951, the only jobs she was offered were secretarial.

✦ The Labor Department confirms the dwindling of full-time housewives when it announces that more than half of all women are employed outside the home: 52.4% of females over age 16 are in the labor market. The age segment in which there is the greatest rate of increase—25 to 34—is also the age group most likely to have young children at home.

More than one in every three women works in a clerical job, which leads the prestigious Katherine Gibbs Secretarial School to predict a 45% increased demand for secretaries by 1990. The predictors do not anticipate the rise of personal computers, however; by the end of the decade, the Katherine Gibbs enterprise will be fighting off bankruptcy. As millions of professional people

Sandra Day O'Connor of Arizona testifies at Senate confirmation hearings on her appointment to the Supreme Court in July 1981. Although women have served in Congress since 1917 and in the cabinet since 1933, O'Connor is the first at the top level of the judicial branch of government. Library of Congress

discover that they can type on a computer, there is far less demand for personal secretaries.

✦ An uncommon situation in San Jose, California, becomes the focus of those concerned with improving the status of women. The city has a woman as mayor and a female majority on its city council, but its female employees must go on strike to gain attention for the principle of "comparable worth." Feminists have discussed this concept for several years, and now labor unions —especially the American Federation of State, County, and Municipal Employees—join in the cause.

An independent study reveals what most people already know about the relative worth of job titles: they relate more to gender than to credentials, for an assistant mechanic employed by the city earns an annual salary that is more than $9,000 higher than that of a graduate nurse with life-and-death responsibilities.

After a nine-day strike, the San Jose women win an appropriation of $1.5 million to begin funding salary increases for jobs traditionally held by women.

◆ "Palimony" entered the language last year when Michelle Triola, who uses the last name Marvin, sued actor Lee Marvin for alimony at the end of their six-year cohabitation. Even though the two had never married, a California court ordered him to pay her more than $100,000; this year, two higher courts overturn the ruling.

◆ The public is fascinated by the murder trial of Jean Harris, headmistress of an exclusive Virginia finishing school. She is convicted of killing her longtime lover, Herman Tarnower, a New York physician and the author of a best-selling diet book, because he is interested in a younger woman.

◆ The effect of last year's election is demonstrated in midsummer, when a Senate Judiciary subcommittee holds highly controversial hearings on a bill that would, in effect, ban all abortions and possibly even contraceptives. It votes 3 to 2 to recommend that the full Senate pass legislation declaring that "the Congress finds that the life of each human being begins at conception." Many physicians, scientists, and theologians join feminists in arguing that politicians do not have sufficient expertise to legislate in the complex question of when life begins.

◆ The most effective treatment of breast cancer continues to be controversial as additional studies this year indicate that surgeons have been too willing to perform radical mastectomies. Less traumatic surgery combined with chemotherapy results in better survival rates, and some feminists accuse physicians of thoughtlessly practicing obsolete but financially rewarding medicine.

◆ Another medical milestone is the first successful prenatal surgery, performed this year at the medical school of the University of California at San Francisco. Rosa Skinner, who is pregnant with fraternal twins, allows the surgery after an ultrasound examination reveals a urinary blockage in her unborn son.

◆ Pat Carbine, whose magazine career includes top positions at *Look* and *Ms.*, becomes the first woman to chair the Advertising Council.

◆ Postage stamps honor poet Edna St. Vincent Millay, biologist Rachel Carson, and, in the first to a female athlete, "Babe" Didrickson Zaharias. Next year a stamp will be issued for Civil War physician Mary Walker.

◆ Janet Cooke of the *Washington Post*, a 26-year-old African American, wins the Pulitzer Prize for feature writing but loses both the prize and her job when it is revealed that her report on a youthful drug addict is a "composite," rather than an actual case. The prize is then awarded to Teresa Carpenter of New York's *Village Voice*.

◆ Kathy Whitmire, a 35-year-old accountant and childless widow, defeats the incumbent to become mayor of Houston. An early member of the National Women's Political Caucus, Whitmire became Houston's comptroller in 1977 and used this position to criticize the mayor's patronage spending. She defeats both him and the county sheriff by a wide margin. A stunning administrative and political success, she will be reelected four times, garnering as much as 73% of the vote. In 1988—when Houston is the nation's fourth-largest city—she will appoint Elizabeth Watson as its first female police chief.

1982   As the year begins, over 900 women hold positions as state legislators—compared with 344 just a decade earlier.

◆ President Ronald Reagan is forced to withdraw his nomination of William C. Bell as head of the Equal Employment Opportunity Commission after civil rights groups point out his lack of qualifications. Instead, African-American conservative Clarence Thomas is appointed and confirmed by the Senate; no women are considered for this and other civil rights positions.

◆ The Equal Rights Amendment—first introduced in Congress in 1923—dies on June 30. With 35 of the 38 necessary states having approved it, the ERA has passed the lower body in several state legislatures, while their senates have blocked it. The last state to vote is Florida, where the House passes it, but the Senate votes it down by 21–19, with one senator deserting his campaign pledge to support it. Eight days later, the ratification period and the proposed amendment dies.

◆ The Supreme Court expands the meaning of Title IX of the 1972 equal educational access legislation by ruling that it applies to female employees as well as to students. At the same time, the Court rules that a public university nursing program in Mississippi must accept men as students.

◆ Minnesota does a comparable worth study and begins increasing the salary levels of the state's female employees. Some $22 million will be appropriated for more than 8,000 women in such historically underpaid job categories as social work. The appropriation requires no tax increase, and the example will be used by feminists in other states to counter hysterical arguments on the cost of equity.

◆ Although their numbers are declining, American Catholic sisterhoods still count more than 120,000 members. They have a controlling interest in over 1,600 hospitals, orphanages, and nursing homes, and they teach more than 3 million students in Catholic educational institutions.

◆ Kateri (or Catherine) Tekakwitha becomes the first Native American to be canonized by the Catholic church. She lived in the area that is now upper New York State, near the Canadian border, and escaped from her tribe to live among Christians in 1677.

◆ When fall enrollment figures are collected, the United Church of Christ sets a milestone: it is the nation's first denomination to have a female majority among its seminary students.

◆ The Pulitzer Prize in history goes to C. Vann Woodward for his edition of an authoritative version of Mary Chesnut's Civil War diary, which at last offers readers access to the insights that Chesnut recorded more than 120 years earlier.

The year's prize for poetry is awarded to *Collected Poems* by Sylvia Plath, almost two decades after her suicide.

◆ *On Golden Pond* wins 72-year-old Katharine Hepburn an unprecedented fourth Academy Award for best actress; she has been nominated for nine others during her 50-year career.

◆ The September death of Academy Award winner Grace Kelly shocks the public. Her daughter was driving when their car plunged off a Côte d'Azur hill; the daughter survives, but Princess Grace of Monaco dies at 52.

◆ The nation suffers its most severe economic conditions since the Great Depression: Business failures are double what they were three years earlier and more than 10% of the labor force is unemployed in October. The layoff rates are markedly worse for men than for women, and more and more women begin assuming a larger share of family income responsibility.

Male voters do not blame their declining economic position on the Reagan administration, however, as what will become a long-term gender gap appears clearly this year. Men are more likely than women to support the Republican administration: while women vote for Democratic candidates by a margin of 59% to 38%; the male margin is a smaller 53% to 43%.

◆ Republican Millicent Fenwick of New Jersey gives up her safe House seat to run for the Senate, which the Republicans control. In an exception to the "Reagan revolution," however, she loses a close race to Democrat Frank Lautenberg. The "Doonesbury" cartoons that are based on her nonetheless continue to feature Lacey Davenport as a congresswoman.

◆ Democrat Shirley Chisholm of New York, who became the first black woman elected to Congress in 1968, is defeated in the rising conservative tide. She is also hurt by redistricting after the 1980 census.

◆ Another prominent African American, Patricia Roberts Harris, also loses an election this year. The first black woman to serve as a U.S. ambassador and the first to hold two cabinet positions, she loses the Washington, D.C., mayoral race to Marion Barry. Harris will die at age 61, just three years after losing this election to a man who later will be convicted as a drug felon.

Voter registration lists in Washington are in complete disarray, and among 20,000 people who are told that they are not registered to vote is *Washington Post* publisher Katharine Graham.

✦ Two women win Democratic nominations for governor, but both Vermont's Madeline Kunin and Iowa's Roxanne Conlin lose to Republican men in the general election.

✦ On Veterans' Day, a monument to the soldiers of the Vietnam War is dedicated in Washington, D.C.—but not without controversy. A competition to design the memorial had been announced in 1980, and when Maya Ying Lin came in first among 1,421 anonymous entries, the eight male judges were shocked to discover that they had chosen a 21-year-old, Chinese-American Yale undergraduate.

Lin's plan for a long, black granite wall chronologically listing each soldier who died in Vietnam quickly becomes a target for criticism, especially by veterans' groups—some of whom are financed by Texas billionaire Ross Perot. They will succeed in placing a traditional statue of soldiers nearby; the commission paid to its male sculptor remains secret, but Lin estimates it to be about 20 times what she earned.

During the next decade, however, most of the public will come to agree that Lin's simple wall makes a compelling statement. Many travel thousands of miles to see it, and her innovative design inspires people to place flowers, notes, and other remembrances beneath the names of loved ones.

✦ On December 16, for the first time in history, the House cites a Cabinet-level official for contempt: The 259 to 105 vote is aimed at Environmental Protection Administration chief Anne Burford. An attorney and former Colorado state representative, she is following White House orders when she refuses to release records on the EPA's

management of its $1.6 billion "superfund" for hazardous waste clean-up.

As Anne Gorsuch after her February marriage, she will be forced to resign by the Reagan administration next March. When the documents are finally released to Congress, the contempt charge will be dropped.

1983 Rita M. Lavelle, the head of the Environmental Protection Administration's solid waste division, precedes her boss, Anne Gorsuch, into final disgrace. The Reagan administration fires Lavelle in February, after news stories reveal that she has harassed environmental engineers who report hazardous waste, while enjoying luxuries provided by the industries she is charged with regulating.

Interior Secretary James Watt, whose actions also have been widely criticized by environmentalists, is similarly forced to resign after the most recent of several media uproars: Watt defends the diversity of his office by saying that he has "a black, a woman, two Jews, and a cripple."

✦ On a pool table in a New Bedford, Massachusetts, bar, a woman is raped by four men; none of the bars' patrons rallies to her defense. All involved are Portuguese, and when a trial in nearby Fall River results in convictions for the men, most of the Portuguese community protests the sentences as anti-immigrant, while the victim is vilified for filing charges.

When the Supreme Court upholds the convictions next year, the decision is hailed nationally as a major milestone for viewing rape as a serious crime. The justices also castigate the news media and lower courts for allowing the victim's identity to be so clearly spelled out that she is forced to move.

✦ Pioneer geneticist Dr. Barbara McClintock wins the Nobel Prize. Only the third unshared Nobel in science given to a woman, it is the first to an American woman. At age 81, she is recognized for her work on "jumping genes," or the discovery that genes are capable of moving within a chromosome.

McClintock tells interviewers that when she earned her Cornell doctorate in 1927, no one would hire her. She struggled on part-time pay for a decade, until she finally got an assistant professorship in Missouri. Her "jumping genes" theory also initially met with ridicule.

+ Ten-year-old Samantha Smith becomes an international celebrity when she writes a letter to Soviet leader Yuri Andropov urging world peace. He is so moved that he funds a trip to the Soviet Union for her Maine family.

+ The media focus tremendous attention on the lawsuit of one of their own: Kansas City television reporter Christine Craft sues Metromedia after she was fired for being "too old" and "not deferential enough to men." When a tape is played in which a station-hired consultant calls Craft a "mutt" and invites a focus group to rate her poorly, a federal jury determines that she suffered from a discriminatory standard that does not apply to men. They award her a $500,000 judgment, but the judge reverses the jury and orders a new trial.

+ The Supreme Court strikes down an Akron, Ohio, city ordinance that requires hospitalization for first-trimester abortions. The decision is 6 to 3, and Justice Sandra Day O'Connor votes with the minority.

Two weeks later, Congress takes its first vote on the abortion issue, and a constitutional amendment supported by the Reagan administration loses by a surprising margin. It would have begun overturning the *Roe v. Wade* decision by declaring that "a right to abortion is not secured by this Constitution."

+ The Reagan administration is further alienated from women's rights groups when one of its appointees, Barbara Honegger, resigns from the Justice Department and denounces the antidiscrimination project to which she was assigned as a "sham." The White House responds by calling Honegger "a low-level Munchkin" and implies that her only role in the administration was to dress as a bunny for the annual Easter egg roll.

Not surprisingly, polls show the gender gap widening. The Republican Party deals with this by hiring the president's daughter, Maureen Reagan, to work on improving his image with women.

+ A happy contrast is the smooth appointment of two women with public service histories to the cabinet, where each replaces a man. Former Massachusetts congresswoman Margaret Heckler is named to Health and Human Services, while Elizabeth Hanford Dole moves from the White House staff to become head of the Department of Transportation.

+ On June 18, Sally Ride becomes the first American woman in outer space when she spends six days aboard the *Challenger*. She launches two communication satellites and serves as flight engineer during the trip.

This achievement—for which she outplaced some 8,000 applicants—comes just a decade after Ride's graduation from Stanford. She earned a doctorate in physics there in 1978, the same year in which she was selected as a NASA astronaut candidate. Ride retained her maiden name when she married another astronaut last year.

Two Soviet women preceded her in space—the first one 20 years ago.

+ The public barely notices what may be the largest strike by women in history. Although some 675,000 telephone workers strike against the Bell System, so many phone calls are now fully automated that their action has little public effect.

+ The future of working women is significantly assured when the Supreme Court rules that retirement plans may not make smaller payments to women than to men simply because women as a class live longer. The decision is 5 to 4, and Justice Sandra Day O'Connor straddles the issue: she votes with the majority, but prevails upon her male colleagues to limit the decision to future retirement plans, instead of applying it retroactively to current payouts. The case was filed by Nathalie Norris of Arizona and won her young lawyer, Amy Gittler.

✦ When Catholic bishops issue a pastoral letter on peace, they credit socialist journalist Dorothy Day for moving the church in this direction. The *Catholic Worker*, which Day edited for almost 50 years until her 1980 death, opposed every war during that time, including World War II.

✦ New York's Yeshiva University sponsors the first Holocaust seminar to focus explicitly on the experience of women.

✦ A task force of the United Methodist Church urges that male nouns such as "Lord" and "King" not be used for God, but the general body rejects modification of nomenclature.

✦ For the first time since its 1943 inception, a woman receives the Pulitzer Prize for musical composition: Ellen T. Zwilich wins for *Three Movements for Orchestra*. A graduate of Florida State University, in 1975 Zwilich became the first woman to earn a doctorate from the famed Juilliard School of Music. Two years after winning the Pulitzer, she will be honored with the newly created composer's chair at Carnegie Hall. "I have moved heaven and Earth," she says, "to make sure that my life revolves around composing."

✦ This year's Pulitzer Prize for general nonfiction is awarded to Susan Sheehan for her study of mental illness, *Is There No Place on Earth for Me?* A similar subject brings the drama prize to Marsha Norman, who wins for *'Night, Mother*. Her unconventional exploration of the mother-daughter relationship revolves around the daughter's determination to kill herself.

Another somber view of women's lives wins both the literature Pulitzer and the American Book Award for Alice Walker. *The Color Purple* is the story of a black woman brutalized first by her father and then by her husband; it goes on to box-office success as a movie starring Whoopi Goldberg. Walker, who was born in rural Georgia in 1944, is the first African-American woman to win the Pulitzer Prize for Letters since the competition began in 1918.

✦ A black woman wins the annual Miss America contest for the first time. She is Vanessa Williams, Miss New York and a student at Syracuse University. Disgrace will soon follow her joy, for Williams is stripped of her crown when it is revealed that she posed for nude photos. As it turns out, however, the first runner-up is also an African American, and New Jersey's Suzette Charles replaces Williams.

✦ A rock singer by the name of Madonna bursts on the pop culture scene. Within a very short time, millions of young women imitate her appearance, which includes crucifixes and other religious symbolism adorning extremely revealing clothing. The furor rises next year with the release of an album entitled *Like a Virgin*.

✦ Female soldiers are among those deployed to Grenada this year, and Colleen Nevius becomes the navy's first female test pilot.

✦ The post office commemorates 19th-century mental health reformer Dorothea Dix with a 1-cent stamp, while Nobel Prize–winning author Pearl Buck receives a 5-cent stamp. Next year, industrial engineer Lillian M. Gilbreth will be recognized with a 40-cent stamp.

✦ Near Austin, Texas, Lady Bird Johnson donates land and money to fund the National Wildflower Research Center. The former first lady advocates greater use of native plants both because that is ecologically sound and because "I want our regions to look like themselves."

✦ Popular singer Karen Carpenter dies at age 32 from complications arising from the eating disorder anorexia nervosa. Her death focuses attention on excessive dieting, a danger almost exclusive to women.

The deaths of two young television personalities are also widely mourned. Jessica Savitch, a popular 35-year-old NBC anchor, is killed in a Pennsylvania car accident, while Catherine Mackin dies at age 42. A Washington correspondent for ABC and NBC, Mackin became the first woman to televise from the floor of both parties' national conventions in 1972.

+ *USA Today* begins publication with Cathleen P. Black as president and later publisher. Although many are initially skeptical of a newspaper that lacks a geographical identity, it soon proves a perfect fit in an increasingly mobile society. In 1992, Black's colleagues will demonstrate their esteem for her creativity by making her the first female head of the Newspaper Association of America.

1984   When former American Federation of Teachers official Linda Chavez becomes head of the Civil Rights Commission in January, she sets aside many of the goals held by her erstwhile colleagues in the AFL-CIO to adopt the conservative agenda of a presidential nominee. The Civil Rights Commission begins backing off its historic support of affirmation action, bilingual education, and other programs. Chavez terms the concept of comparable worth unacceptably "radical."

Her comments relate to an ongoing case in Washington, where, later this year, a federal judge will order the state to end its pattern of discrimination against some 15,000 female employees. A study done several years earlier revealed, for example, that mechanics earned almost twice as much as medical records analysts, and the average monthly salary of carpenters was $1,654, while social workers averaged $961. The responsibilities involved in the stereotypically women's jobs, the judge rules, are at least comparable to those of jobs in which men are paid much more.

+ Minnesota nurses go on strike. Women from the National Education Association, which is holding its annual convention in Minneapolis, join the picket lines.

+ The Democratic Party convenes in July, and Geraldine Ferraro becomes the first woman on a major presidential ticket when nominee Walter Mondale chooses her as his running mate.

Ferraro, whose father immigrated from Italy, earned her law degree in 1960 and retained her maiden name when she married John Zaccaro. The mother of three, she was elected to Congress in 1978—just six years before her nomination for the vice presidency. Mondale is committed to the idea of a woman at the top of the ticket, and among others he considers are San Francisco mayor Dianne Feinstein and Kentucky governor Martha Layne Collins.

Women all over the nation hold spontaneous parties when the convention nominates Ferraro, but the euphoria begins to dissipate when ethics charges are filed against her soon after the nomination. Broad campaign issues are lost in a haze of complex financial accusations brought against her and her husband.

A Catholic, Ferraro also is criticized for being personally opposed to abortion while supporting the principle of choice for other women. Although this is the same position held by many popular male politicians who are Catholic, church officials condemn Ferraro much more harshly. In the fall, the Mondale/Ferraro candidacy is soundly defeated by incumbents Reagan/Bush.

+ The Supreme Court rules that an Atlanta law firm may not exclude a woman from becoming a partner merely because she is a woman. It also asserts that marrying a man of another race is an insufficient reason to take away a woman's custody of her children. Although these are giant victories in the history of women's rights, they are scarcely noted in modern society.

Much more attention goes to a decision in which the Court approves of state laws that compel Jaycee clubs to admit women. Because these clubs originated as the Junior Chamber of Commerce, the court declares them to be business organizations that cannot exclude women. With no dissenting votes, the justices recognize the validity of the feminist point that forcing women into the Jaycette auxiliary does not offer equal commercial access to businesswomen.

+ In another case, the Court does not heed feminist argumentation. Its decision in *Grove City College v. Bell* cuts back on the meaning of Title IX of the 1972 Education Act: The Court rules that enforcement of equity principles can apply only to specific programs, not to an entire educational institution. Women's rights groups fear that the ruling will mean, for example, that a physical education department may discriminate against female students without endangering the school's federal funds.

The House immediately votes to negate the decision by clarifying congressional intention in Title IX, but after months of lobbying, the Senate kills the bill. Senators are persuaded that the Court ruling applies only to the narrow case of the small, private Pennsylvania college that brought the suit.

◆ The Labor Department announces that for the first time in the nation's history, white males are a minority of the labor force.

◆ Congress shows unusual unanimity in targeting "deadbeat dads." Without a single dissenting vote, both houses pass requirements that states set up systems for collecting child support from wages and other sources. Although the law applies to noncustodial parents whose children are on welfare as well as to those who are not, the problem will remain essentially unsolved a decade later. A large number of single mothers will continue to support their children without significant financial aid from fathers.

◆ Census Bureau statistics make clear the fact that many women are returning to school to improve their chances of supporting their children decently: the number of women age 25 to 44 who are enrolled in college has more than tripled since 1970. Women now constitute a majority of college students in this age group.

◆ The public becomes aware of acquired immune deficiency syndrome, or AIDS. Scientists are unsure, but believe the disease is caused by sexual contact and that it usually is fatal. At the same time, the Center for Disease Control reminds the public that other venereal disease rates are rising and that women are at greater risk because their symptoms are usually less obvious than those of men.

◆ Ethel Merman, a favorite musical comedy star for half a century, dies at age 75. Born Ethel Zimmerman, she first captured the nation's heart in the 1930 George Gershwin show *Girl Crazy*.

◆ "Dr. Ruth" becomes a household name as sex therapist Ruth Westheimer enjoys great popularity on radio and television talk shows. The contrast between her appearance and her candor on sexual matters is part of her appeal, for she looks and sounds like a conventional German-Jewish mother.

◆ Kentuckians Sallie Bingham and Eleanor Bingham Miller are ousted from the board of the Louisville *Courier-Journal* when they challenge their brother's control of the family business. Sallie Bingham turns down a $26.3 million offer for her stock, and five years later, publishes an exposé on her powerful family.

◆ The publishing phenomenon of the year is *And the Ladies of the Club*. Not only is it a massive tome of almost 1,200 pages, it is by an 88-year-old author. For 50 years, Helen Santmyer has written her saga, based on a small-town Ohio women's club in the 19th and early 20th centuries. A 1918 Wellesley graduate, Santmyer studied at Oxford prior to spending most of her life as an Ohio English professor and librarian. She greets national success from a nursing home.

◆ In October, Kathryn Sullivan is the first American woman to walk in space. She works on refining methodologies for refueling satellites, while veteran astronaut Sally Ride continues her work on this eight-day *Challenger* mission.

Two other women, Judith A. Resnick and Anna L. Fisher, are among the crew of *Discovery* shuttle flights in August and November.

◆ Traditionally Republican Vermont ignores the Reagan revolution to elect Democrat Madeline Kunin; she is the state's first female and first Jewish governor. Kunin erases a deficit, increases the education budget, passes strong environmental legislation, and is twice reelected.

1985 Each January anniversary of *Roe v. Wade* is marked by increasingly large protests against the decision. After some 70,000 join the "March for Life" this year, the Reagan administration responds with a promise to go to court to overturn the decision.

- Soon after President Ronald Reagan's second inaugural, Jeane Kirkpatrick resigns as his ambassador to the United Nations. She obtains a $900,000 book advance and later reveals that she felt excluded by Washington foreign policy decision makers.

- The Cherokee Nation chooses Wilma Mankiller as its first female chief. Mankiller, a divorced mother of two daughters, is elected by America's second-largest tribe because she has built a solid record of achievement in economic development for the 150,000-member tribe. She governs with a budget of about $70 million from the capital of Tahlequah, Oklahoma, and she will be reelected for another decade.

  Mankiller's mother, incidentally, "does not have one drop of Indian blood," but her life "centered around [the] Cherokee family." Although the new chief was born in Oklahoma, she grew up in San Francisco after her father relocated the family as part of a federal program to urbanize Indians. In 1969, she participated in the occupation of Alcatraz Island with a group of Native Americans and Berkeley students, and then spent a decade unhappily married to a wealthy Ecuadorean before returning to Oklahoma in 1977.

- Although women have headed post offices since colonial days, Deputy Postmaster General Jackie Strange is the first woman to reach that rank. Such positions were political appointees during most of the nation's history, but after the post office was restructured as a quasi-private corporation in 1971, no woman was appointed to the nine-member board of governors until 1980.

- Another female Reagan appointee resigns under pressure: Marianne Hall leaves her copyright position when a House subcommittee investigates complaints that a book she wrote reveals her racism.

- The year brings fatal setbacks for the concept of comparable worth, which will be largely laid aside as a feminist goal during the next decade. The Civil Rights Commission continues to reject calls for reevaluating public service jobs on the basis of their inherent skills rather the traditional standard of the gender of most jobholders; belying the original aim of a civil rights body, it argues simply that correcting these injustices would be too costly for governments.

  The Justice Department adds to the irony when it intervenes on the side of the State of Illinois against nurses who are suing for increased pay. Not only is such intervention unconventional, but the federal attorney also argues that the free market is inviolable and that judges should not make decisions on wage issues—something that, of course, judges have been doing on minimum wage and similar cases for a century.

  Finally, an appelate court throws out the decision of the judge who ordered raises for women in Washington State last year, and even San Francisco mayor Dianne Feinstein vetoes an $8 million appropriation to increase the pay scales of women and minorities.

  There is one hopeful sign this year: Los Angeles agrees to an employee contract that brings librarians' wages up to the level of maintenance men.

- The United Nations marks the end of the decade dedicated to women's issues that began in Mexico City in 1975. Some 17,000 people—about three times the number of Mexico City participants—from 157 nations attend a conference in Nairobi. As was the case before, most attend the unofficial nongovernmental organizations forum, where women from all over the globe exchange ideas on improving their status. This conference does not attract nearly the media attention it garnered in the more feminist 1970s—nor what it will have a decade later, when it is held in Beijing in 1995.

- When a summit meeting between American leader Ronald Reagan and Soviet leader Mikhail Gorbachev ends, Roxanne L. Ridgway of the State Department drafts the statement of their achievements. She is a diplomatic veteran, having served as ambassador to Finland and to East Germany before rising to assistant secretary of state for European Affairs.

- The second African-American woman honored with a first-class postal stamp is Mary McLeod Bethune. In addition to other achievements, Bethune was president of the National Association of Colored Women, the National Association of Teachers in Colored Schools, and the Association for the Study of Negro Life and History; she was a vice president of the National Association for the Advancement of Colored People and served on the board of Planned Parenthood and other national organizations. Throughout her busy life, Bethune also found time to write for black publications, including weekly columns for the *Pittsburgh Courier* and the *Chicago Defender*.

  The post office also reaches back into the nation's early history to honor first lady Abigail Adams, whose thoughtful writing still shines after more than 200 years.

- The Pulitzer Prize for letters goes to Alison Lurie for *Foreign Affairs*. For both this year and the last one, the winners of the poetry category remain unknown to the general public: Mary Oliver wins in 1984 for *American Primitive* and Carolyn Kizer wins this year for *Yin*.

- Libby Riddles is the first woman to win Alaska's demanding dog sled race, the Iditarod. When other racers stop for a blizzard, she goes on alone and gains a decisive lead in her 17-day trek. The reward is $50,000.

- Californian Patti Frustaci sets a national record for the largest multiple birth, but three of the six children she bears in May die soon after delivery.

- After years of annual debate, the Conservative Rabbinical Assembly finally admits female rabbis as members. Amy Eilberg, who graduated earlier in the year from Jewish Theological Seminary, is the first woman ordained as a Conservative rabbi.

1986 A *Challenger* rocket explodes over the Atlantic after blasting off from NASA's Florida launch site on the exceptionally cold morning of January 28. It is the first space launch to include two women, and both are killed. Among the seven passengers on the fatal flight are veteran astronaut Judith Resnick and science teacher Christa McAuliffe, ages 36 and 37, respectively. The public especially identifies with McAuliffe, who last year won a fierce competition to be the first "ordinary citizen" to soar into space.

- "Amazing Grace" Hopper, who has written computer programs for the navy since 1944, retires at the rank of rear admiral. She is the author of several computer languages, including the widely used COBAL, and is credited with coining the word "bug" in reference to computer problems.

  Age 79 when she finally leaves her work, Admiral Hopper has been so highly valued by the Navy that she has been granted annual extensions since "mandatory" retirement at 62. The nation's oldest military officer, she is honored on its oldest ship, the USS *Constitution*, with the Distinguished Service Medal.

- In *Thornburgh v. American College of Obstetricians and Gynecologists*, the Supreme Court strikes down a Pennsylvania law designed to discourage abortions by making them more difficult to obtain. The vote, however, is a bare 5 to 4, as Reagan appointees to the Court begin to make their mark.

  In several pornography cases, the Court offers mixed opinions on the validity of local regulations. Feminists too disagree on this issue. While many see a direct link between pornography and violence against women, others argue for free expression.

  The Supreme Court hands down a landmark decision when it hears its first sexual harassment case. In unambiguous language, it declares demands for sexual favors on the job to be a violation of the 1964 Civil Rights Act.

- In New York City, a federal judge cites Catholic officials for contempt, saying they refuse to release subpoenaed documents and "willfully misled" him. The case is brought by abortion rights groups that question the church's tax-exempt status when it takes political positions and endorses antiabortion candidates.

- Congressional liberals join with conservatives to almost halve the budget of the Civil Rights Commission. The liberals are distressed by the failures of this agency and of the Equal Employment Opportunity Commission, both of which are headed by black men. The EEOC has a burgeoning backlog of cases and its chief, Clarence Thomas, is candid about his unwillingness to support the affirmative action goals for which the EEOC was created.

✦ Ann Bancroft is the first woman to explore the North Pole. She will focus on the opposite end of the globe in 1992, when she leads an all-woman team in Antarctica; their only method of transportation is skis.

✦ Postage stamps honor three women: abolitionist and feminist Sojourner Truth; Belva Lockwood, the nation's first female practicing attorney; and Pulitzer Prize-winning author Margaret Mitchell. Incidentally, while American Legion fund-raiser Moina Mitchell was honored in 1948, no stamp has yet been issued for astronomer Maria Mitchell, who discovered a comet in 1847.

✦ Only a few female journalists won the Pulitzer Prize since its 1917 beginning, but the impact of the revived women's movement is clearly demonstrated in a review of recent winners: they include *Boston Globe* reporters Anne De Santis (1972) and Joan Vennochi (1980), Margo Huston of the *Milwaukee Journal* (1977), Loretta Tofani of the *Washington Post* (1983), Lucy Morgan of the *St. Petersburg Times* (1985), and Edna Buchanan of the *Miami Herald* (1986).

✦ The end-of-the-year headline grabber is the case of Mary Beth Whitehead, a married New Jersey woman who signed a contract and accepted $10,000 to bear a child for William and Elizabeth Stern. Elizabeth Stern cannot have children, and Whitehead was artificially inseminated with William's sperm—but when the baby was born in March, Whitehead reneged on the contract. She fled to Florida, and when authorities find her, they return "Baby M" to New Jersey and the custody of the Sterns. The case adds new complexities to reproductive ethics, and the legal questions involved are without precedent.

✦ Kentucky Governor Martha Layne Collins, who is not up for reelection this year, is criticized because an excessive number of her husband's business associates have gotten state appointments.

In California, Supreme Court Chief Justice Rose Bird loses a merit retention referendum. For the first time in the state's history, voters reject three sitting justices; one of the two men thrown out with Bird is Hispanic.

Florida Senator Paula Hawkins is trounced by Democratic Governor Bob Graham; because he is pro-choice, many women support him. Hawkins also has been in poor health since a stage screen fell on her during a television interview.

✦ Two women run in a closely watched U.S. Senate race in Maryland: Congresswoman Barbara Mikulski, who began her career on the Baltimore City Council in 1971, defeats the controversial former head of the Civil Rights Commission, Linda Chavez. Mikulski is the first Democratic woman elected to a full Senate term since 1960.

Pollster Celinda Lake will later call this midterm election the "best example" of the growing gender gap, which shows women voting increasingly for Democrats, while men are apt to support Republicans. Women's votes return control of the Senate to Democrats this year; Republicans had won a majority of Senate seats with the 1980 Reagan election.

1987 A New Jersey judge allows Elizabeth Stern to adopt her husband's child, thus enforcing the contract that surrogate mother Mary Beth Whitehead made with the Sterns. Many believe that this is in the best interest of the child: publicity on the case has made it clear that the Stern home is more stable than that of Whitehead, who leaves her husband and is pregnant with another man's baby by the end of the year.

A group of women who have served as surrogate mothers without publicity comes forward to speak to this choice as humane and child-centered. They reveal that some 500 childbirths since 1978 have involved a surrogate mother, either as an ova donor or as a full-term gestational carrier.

The Vatican responds with a proclamation denouncing surrogate motherhood and in-vitro fertilization, along with abortion, contraception, and other technologies aimed at reproductive control.

◆ A Pentagon report criticizes the navy and the Marine Corps for ignoring sexual harassment and discrimination against female personnel in the Pacific command.

◆ The "marriage pool"—the number of eligible, employed men—available to black women on Chicago's South Side is just 18 men for every 100 women.

◆ An analysis of *Time* magazine shows that since 1923, when it began, women have been featured on 482 of 3,386 covers, or about 14%. Worse, the current situation is deteriorating, for women appeared more frequently in the 1970s than in the 1980s.

◆ The American Historical Association honors Oklahoman Angie Debo a few months prior to her death at age 98. Without any academic support, Debo has been writing midwestern history for 40 years. In particular, her *And Still the Waters Run* (1966) is a classic study of the Five Civilized Tribes.

◆ A California case honors motherhood, for the court agrees that a state may require employers to provide pregnant women with job security and maternity leave.

A second California case is a setback for the Reagan administration's view on affirmative action: the court upholds a plan in which a woman was promoted over a man whose credentials are arguably better.

Finally, a ruling on Rotary Club membership is an exact rerun of the issue decided in 1984 on the Jaycees. After this second decision comes down, the Lions and Kiwanis clubs voluntarily begin admitting women.

◆ Joan Rivers, a huge success in stand-up comedy as well as in talk-show television and humor-book authorship, faces a crisis with the suicide of her husband, Edgar Rosenberg—the butt of many of her jokes during the past two decades.

In 1994, when she is 60, Rivers will turn to drama to explore this painful, personal issue; she joins her daughter in a television production on how they coped. Arguing that the topic "is not dealt with, not discussed," she will point out that "suicide hits one family in six."

◆ Rita Dove wins the Pulitzer Prize for *Thomas and Beulah*, poems inspired by her grandparents. In 1993, she will become the nation's first black and its youngest poet laureate. An Akron, Ohio, native who teaches at the University of Virginia, she will accept this appointment with the Library of Congress at age 41.

◆ The National Museum of Women in the Arts opens in Washington, D.C., with an exhibit titled "American Women Artists, 1830–1930." The driving force behind the museum is Wilhelmina Cole Holladay, who has been collecting work by female artists for almost three decades. Holladay, who grew up in the same western New York area that was home to Susan Anthony and other early feminists, donates works by some 150 women throughout the world, dating back as far as the Renaissance.

◆ The last two postage stamps of the decade in honor of women go to two of the 19th century's most influential people, educator Mary Lyon and author Julia Ward Howe.

1988 Chemist Gertrude Elion wins the Nobel Prize in medicine. She is honored for a lifetime of work on developing synthetic DNA, which can disrupt the reproductive cycles of viruses and bacteria. Her research made possible drugs that are used in treating leukemia, malaria, and other diseases; it also played a crucial role in overcoming tissue rejection in organ transplants.

A New York native and a 1937 Hunter College graduate in chemistry, Elion was told that she was "too cute" to work in a lab. Like countless other women, initially she was forced to enroll in secretarial school, despite her college degree. She earned a 1941 master's degree from New York

University, and after futilely seeking work in her field, was finally hired when so many men had gone to war that laboratory jobs opened to women. She joined the pharmaceutical firm of Burroughs Wellcome in 1944 and remained there the rest of her career.

A North Carolina resident since 1970, Elion retired from Burroughs Wellcome in 1983 and began teaching at Duke University and the University of North Carolina. Although she never earned a doctorate, she will be the recipient of 14 honorary doctorates by 1993.

+ The Supreme Court upholds the use of statistical data to demonstrate patterns of employment discrimination. Although this practice has been used to show the reality of bias in an objective way for more than a decade, some affirmative action opponents continue to press the issue, and next year the Court will begin to reverse itself.

With one member not voting, the Court splits evenly on an Illinois law mandating that girls under 18 obtain parental or judicial permission for abortions; the effect of the tie vote is to uphold a lower court's nullification of the law. Feminists oppose such laws not only as a limitation on the lives of young women, but especially because such underage pregnancies are particularly apt to involve incest.

+ A survey of federal employees finds more than four of every 10 women report themselves as victims of sexual harassment at some point in their careers. The worst statistics come from the State Department.

+ Congress overrides President Reagan's veto of legislation that reverses the Supreme Court's 1984 decision in *Grove City College v. Bell*. The law now makes it clear that federal funds may be withheld from an educational institution when any part of the institution engages in gender discrimination.

A Senate filibuster, however, kills other legislation opposed by the Reagan administration. Bills to establish a right to unpaid parental job leave and to subsidize child care remain on the calendar when Congress adjourns.

+ Coretta Scott King, the widow of slain civil rights leader Martin Luther King, Jr., leads a demonstration at the Lincoln Memorial to mark the 25th anniversary of her husband's famous March on Washington.

+ African-American sisters-in-law Jackie Joyner-Kersee and Florence Griffith Joyner are the talk of the Olympics. They win a total of five gold medals in running and jumping events.

+ The Reverend Barbara Clementine Harris of Philadelphia becomes the first female bishop of the Episcopal church. Elected in the diocese of Massachusetts, she is the first woman in the world to hold this position. Harris, a 58-year-old black woman, will be installed in internationally publicized ceremonies in Boston next year. Many are openly critical of Harris' election, and some separate from the church because of it.

+ Sacred Heart Sister Rose Philippine Duchesne, who pioneered Catholicism in the early 19th-century Midwest, is canonized by Pope John Paul II on July 3. Four American women have now been declared saints. A few months later, however, the Pope issues another apostolic letter limiting the status of women in the church.

+ Toni Morrison's *Beloved* sweeps the literary scene and wins the Pulitzer Prize. Her *Song of Solomon* won an award from book critics in 1978, and last year, a group of African-American authors signed a nationally publicized letter when Morrison's *Beloved* failed to win the National Book Award.

+ Democratic presidential nominee Michael Dukakis creates a milestone when he chooses Massachusetts political scientist Susan Estrich as his campaign manager. Although he loses by a wide margin to incumbent vice president George Bush, Democrats increase their numbers in Congress and in state legislatures; again, a gender gap is evident, with women more likely to support Dukakis, while men are apt to vote for Bush. The media widely criticize Dukakis for what they see as his unemotional response to a debate question on the theoretical rape and murder of his wife.

1989 Women deploy with military units that invade Panama, and Army Captain Linda L. Bray leads an infantry unit engaged in a firefight against Panamanian Defense Forces. Three women are nominated for Air Medals when the helicopters they pilot encounter heavy enemy fire.

✦ In San Francisco, federal judge Marilyn Hall Patel throws out the comparable worth case that would benefit female employees of the State of California.

At the Supreme Court level, accountant Ann Hopkins wins a mixed victory in her employment discrimination suit. The media gives great coverage to at least one aspect of the case: Price Waterhouse rejected her for partnership because she was allegedly unladylike; she was told to wear jewelry and attend charm school.

Most high court decisions, however, go against women, as the antiaffirmative action policies of recent presidents begin to affect the Court's membership. In the worst reverse for female employees, the Court disallows the long-accepted premise that statistical patterns of discrimination demonstrate personal bias.

✦ Media attention to the Missouri case of *Webster v. Reproductive Health Services* implies that the Supreme Court is on the verge of repealing its 1973 *Roe v. Wade* decision on abortion. The July ruling is not quite as dramatic as the public is led to believe: the Court confirms the right of states to regulate abortions in the interest of public health, which has been true all along. It does, however, add to public confusion on the issue, for in upholding Missouri's ban on abortions in public hospitals, the Court seems to contradict aspects of its 1986 Pennsylvania decision.

Nor does voting with the majority protect Sandra Day O'Connor, the only woman on the Court, from personal attack: Justice Antonin Scalia writes a separate opinion, which—in the words of objective observers—"ridicules" her.

While the case is being debated, hundreds of thousands of women participate in a march supporting abortion rights.

✦ Connie Chung leaves NBC to return to CBS, which offers her approximately $1.5 million per year. Chung, who grew up in Washington, D.C., was the only child in her family born in the United States; they escaped from Japanese-occupied China in 1944, and five of her nine siblings died during World War II.

✦ Women have run libraries since their inception, but only now does the American Library Association choose a woman as executive director—even though four out of every five ALA members is a woman. Linda Crismond of Los Angeles will direct the organization, which was founded in 1876.

✦ For the first time since 1965–66, women win the Pulitzer Prize for Letters in two consecutive years. Toni Morrison, the 1988 winner, is joined by Anne Tyler, who wins for *Breathing Lessons*. Tyler is the first white female winner in 16 years, since Eudora Welty won in 1973.

Two women are also consecutive-year winners of the Pulitzer Prize for editorial writing. Only a handful of women have won this category since it was established in 1917, but Lois Wille of the *Chicago Tribune* wins this year, while Jane Healy of the *Orlando Sentinel* won the previous year.

✦ Pulitzer Prize–winning historian Barbara Tuchman dies at age 77. Her first book was published when she was 44, and her last, *The First Salute*, a study of the American Revolution, came out last year. *The March of Folly* (1984), a history of warfare from Troy to Vietnam, was also a best-seller.

1990 Although women remain a distinct minority in most professional fields, they are making great strides: during the two decades since the revived women's movement of 1970, women have increased their numbers from 6% to 27% of lawyers and judges; from 16% to 38% of pharmacists; from 11% to 22% of physicians; from 13% to 30% of stockbrokers; and from 14% to 44% of economists.

This year also marks a milestone for female doctorates: the 36,027 awarded are the most ever. Women now earn 36% of all doctorates, up from 11% in 1960.

✦ A new term appears during the decade in the business world, as "mommy track" denotes women who are presumed to have chosen motherhood over executive success. Unlike earlier eras, these days new mothers generally are expected to return to work within six weeks of delivery, but because they must meet the demands of child rearing—without the state support common in European businesses—it is understood that they will be less available for weekend and evening work, and therefore not promotable.

✦ The decade also sees the expansion of cable television to almost all households, which has a tremendous cultural impact because it allows more programming aimed at small groups, rather than the mass marketing of broadcast television. Cable channels develop that are aimed at women, and women find much more opportunity to produce, direct, and perform other executive functions in these smaller markets.

Another profound change can be seen on comedy channels, which offer new access for female comedians. This phenomenon naturally spreads to nightclub performance, and the number of women starring in clubs soars from 2% at the beginning of the 1980s to 20% as the 1990s begin. Many female comedians display another important cultural transformation: like men, they use profanity and scatology in their routines—but with a uniquely feminine spin, discussing such previously forbidden topics as menstruation.

✦ Antonia Novello is the first woman to be appointed Surgeon General of the United States. Born in Puerto Rico in 1944, she was educated there and at Johns Hopkins University and the University of Michigan. A pediatrician, she works at the National Institutes of Health and teaches at Georgetown University.

Dr. Novello will add depth to public health concepts during her tenure as surgeon general, for she views violence as a national epidemic. She argues that violence in the home, workplace, and streets needs to be addressed with the same sort of educational campaign that has been mounted to end smoking and improve diets.

✦ Congress enacts an Indian Arts and Crafts Act that provides up to 15 years in prison and/or $1 million in fines for selling goods as Indian-made that are not certified by a recognized tribe. The act protects those who earn their living through needlework and other crafts, which is a particular benefit to women. In the same year, the census reveals that 1% of the nation's population is Native American.

✦ Dorothy Height, president of the National Council of Negro Women, speaks of the change between the problems faced by NCNW founder Mary McLeod Bethune and those Height confronts today. Inspired by Bethune when she began civil rights work in 1937, she now says, "The fundamental difference between kids of the civil rights generation and today . . . is that young people today haven't really known what downhard segregation was."

Instead, she sees the major problems as drug use and teenage pregnancy. She cites the NCNW's pregnancy prevention program, begun in 1982, as "the largest in the country outside of Planned Parenthood, and certainly the largest one for people of color."

✦ With the exception of 1951 cowinner Marguerite Higgins, no women won the Pulitzer Prize for international reporting during the first four decades of its existence. Four women achieve the award, however, during the decade just ended: Shirley Christian of the *Miami Herald* and Karen Eliot House of the *Wall Street Journal* win in 1981 and 1984, while Katherine Elison of the *San Jose Mercury News* and Sheryl WuDunn of the *New York Times* earn the 1986 and 1990 prizes.

✦ I. O. Sulzberger, the "matriarch of the *New York Times*," dies at age 98. Although her father passed his publishing position to her husband instead of to her, she played an active role with the paper, and newsman James Reston calls Sulzberger "the most remarkable woman our profession has seen in my lifetime."

✦ Environmentalist Marjory Stoneman Douglas speaks to the Florida legislature on her 100th birthday. She will survive Hurricane Andrew in 1992, and when President Bill Clinton honors her with the Medal of Freedom in 1993, Douglas will use the media opportunity to discuss the warfare in Bosnia. She offers insights based on her service there during World War I.

✦ NASA honors the women who, 50 years earlier, worked as "computers" for the National Advisory Committee for Aeronautics. Based at Virginia's Langley Field, the women did the necessary mathematics for flight experimentation in a time prior to calculators. Their calculations were virtually error-free—and faster than early computers.

✦ Two postage stamps recognize Olympic Gold Medal winners: Hazel Wightman, whose tennis career spanned 50 years, and Helene Madison, who held more than 60 swimming records in 1932.

The post office also releases two other stamps depicting award-winning poet Marianne Moore and antilynching journalist Ida B. Wells, who is also known as Ida Wells-Barnett. All are honored with first-class stamps, now worth 25 cents.

✦ When war breaks out in the fall, the largest deployment of women in military history goes to the Persian Gulf: more than 40,000 women will be deployed with Operation Desert Shield/Desert Storm. Like their male counterparts, women will die and will be taken as prisoners of war.

✦ African American Sharon Pratt Dixon is the first woman to be elected mayor of Washington, D.C. Many do not accept her tenure, however, and in 1994, the former mayor, convicted drug user Marion Barry, will oust her.

✦ Hawaii's Patsy Mink, a strong feminist leader in Congress more than a decade ago, returns to the House of Representatives that she left in 1976.

✦ In the most hotly contested fall election, Democrat Ann Richards becomes governor of Texas. The first woman elected state treasurer in 1982, she defeats a conservative Republican millionaire in a bitterly fought race to become governor. He makes an issue of her previous problems with alcohol.

In Kansas, Democrat Joan Finney upsets the incumbent Republican governor. Kansas thus becomes the first state to have women as both governor and as U.S. senator, a position held by Republican Nancy Kassebaum.

Texas also set a precedent with Richard's victory: it is the only state twice to elect a woman as governor. Since 1924, just seven states have elected women to their top position. In alphabetical order, they are: Alabama, Connecticut, Kentucky, Texas, Vermont, Washington, and Wyoming.

In contrast to the early women elected to Congress, most of whom were Republicans, all of the women elected to governorships have been Democrats.

1991 Major Marie Rossi is the most visible of 15 servicewomen who die on duty during Operation Desert Storm. She led dozens of missions into Iraq to deliver fuel and ammunition, and she is killed when her helicopter crashes in Saudi Arabia in March.

Truck driver Melissa Rathbun-Nealy and flight surgeon Rhoda Cornum draw media attention when they are taken prisoner by the Iraqis.

Women from all military branches served in the Arabian Peninsula during Operation Desert Shield/Desert Storm. They wear the heavy gear pictured not for warmth but to protect them from blowing sand.
Women In Military Service Memorial

Although the war brings attention to the lack of civil rights for Middle Eastern women, when it ends in April, the Kuwaiti monarch is restored to his throne, and even upper-class women on the Arabian penisula continue to live without the fundamental liberties that American women gained in the last century.

◆ The Senate confirms Dr. Bernadine Healy as head of the National Institutes of Health; presumably because she is Catholic, she does not face the "litmus test" of opposition to abortion that plagues other health appointees in this era.

Yet Dr. Healy says that her "heart and soul is feminist"—something that is not surprising in view of her life experience. At age 47, she is a divorced mother of two, and she reports sexist incidents at Harvard, where she earned her medical degree in 1970, and at Johns Hopkins, where she spent most of her career. Dr. Healy's tenure at NIH also will involve controversies, especially because of her outspoken policy change aimed at correcting the historic neglect of research on women's health.

◆ According to Washington, D.C.'s Joint Center for Political Studies, the number of black women in elective office increased from 131 in 1970 to 1,950 in 1990. In last year's election, almost half of the African Americans elected to state legislatures were female.

◆ In *Rust v. Sullivan*, the Supreme Court not only chips away at the right of privacy established by *Roe v. Wade* but also assails free speech by ruling that health professionals in clinics receiving government funds may not answer patients' questions on abortion except to discourage it.

The only woman on the Court, Sandra Day O'Connor, dissents from the 5 to 4 ruling. The case will be a strong factor for feminists in the 1992 election, who argue that the Republican appointees of the past decade are reversing the right to reproductive freedom.

At the same time, the Louisiana legislature passes a law that threatens physicians performing abortions with sentences of 10 years at hard labor.

◆ Two young women win Pulitzer Prizes in journalism: Susan Faludi, writing for the *Wall Street Journal*, wins in exploratory journalism, while Sheryl James of the *St. Petersburg Times* wins for feature writing. Faludi is better known as the author of *Backlash: The Undeclared War Against American Women* (1991). Her book warns that women lost during the 1980s some of the gains they made in the 1970s.

The Pulitzer award for Meritorious Public Service goes to Jane Schorer of the *Des Moines Register* for drawing attention to the issue of publishing the names of rape victims. News media have traditionally refrained from releasing the names of those victimized by this crime, but some feminists are beginning to urge change, for keeping the names secret implies shame.

Finally, this year marks the first time ever that a Pulitzer Prize for history is awarded to a woman for a book on women's history. Laurel Thatcher Ulrich wins for *A Midwife's Tale: The Life of Martha Ballard*, which is based on the diary Ballard kept from 1785 to 1812.

◆ The post office honors the first American woman licensed to fly: Harriet Quimby, killed in a 1912 plane crash, receives a 50-cent airmail stamp.

◆ Geologist Doris Malkin Curtis is elected president of the 17,000-member Geological Society of America—in the same year that she dies at age 77. An expert in petroleum reserves, Curtis spent much of her career exploring for Shell Oil.

◆ The National Academy of Sciences finally invites chemist Gertrude Elion to join—three years after she won the Nobel Prize. In addition to her many other credentials, Elion has also served as president of the American Association for Cancer Research.

◆ A report says that the median age of nuns in several cities is more than 65, and retirement funds are millions of dollars short. Only 21 women join the nation's 160 orders of Catholic sisters this year; while the number of priests has declined only slightly in the past 30 years, the number of women entering sisterhoods has plummeted.

✦ When National Organization for Women president Molly Yard suffers a stroke, attorney Patricia Ireland of Florida assumes the presidency. Yard, a 1933 Swarthmore graduate and social worker, developed her feminist attitudes as the daughter of missionary parents in China, where she witnessed the tragic effects that cultural bias against females can have. A longtime Pennsylvania NOW activist, she was elected national president in 1987, following Eleanor Smeal.

✦ University of Oklahoma law professor Anita Hill draws unprecedented attention to the Senate confirmation hearings of Clarence Thomas, whom President George Bush has nominated to replace Thurgood Marshall on the Supreme Court. Many citizens oppose Thomas because his legal experience is uncommonly slim for such a powerful position, but the masses focus on Hill's charges that Thomas sexually harassed her while he was her boss at two federal agencies. That both are African-American and that some of the harassment took place, ironically, while Thomas chaired the Equal Employment Opportunity Commission adds to the controversy. After protracted hearings, the Senate confirms Thomas by a vote of 52–48.

✦ A Las Vegas gathering of navy aviators, traditionally known as the Tailhook Convention, becomes extremely controversial when 27 Navy women later allege that they have been subjected to gross forms of lewdness in the hotel's halls. Lieutenant Paula Coughlin takes the lead in pushing for redress; congressional hearings are held and the secretary of the navy is forced to resign. In the end, however, Coughlin's career suffers at least as much as that of the males who misbehaved.

✦ A second, similar case also makes headlines throughout the year. In May, medical student William Kennedy Smith is arrested for rape at the Palm Beach home that has long belonged to his politically powerful maternal family. He argues that the sex was consensual, and in December, a jury finds him not guilty. Debate also centers on identifying victims in rape trials; after his acquittal, victim Patricia Bowman speaks out publicly.

1992 Women win all five of the gold medals won by Americans at the Winter Olympics.

✦ Dr. Mae C. Jemison becomes the first African-American woman in space when she is part of the *Endeavor* shuttle mission. Born in Alabama, she grew up in Chicago, earned a degree in chemical engineering at Stanford, and went on to medical school at Cornell. Her mission on the space shuttle is to study the relationship between gravity and ova.

✦ At age 83, Eudora Welty receives the National Book Foundation Medal for Distinguished Contribution to American Letters. She won the Pulitzer Prize in 1973 for *The Optimist's Daughter*, but her best-known book, *The Ponder Heart*, came out 20 years earlier, during the 1950s, when no woman won a Pulitzer. Welty is a lifelong resident of Jackson, Mississippi, and her humorous tales of Southern life have been compared favorably with Mark Twain.

✦ A first-class stamp is issued in honor of satirist Dorothy Parker.

✦ Although America's first published poet—in 1650—was a woman, the Library of Congress has filled the annual position of poet laureate with men since its 1985 creation. This year the first woman is named: Mona Van Duyn, who won the Pulitzer Prize for poetry last year for *Near Changes*. Age 71, Van Duyn grew up in Iowa and lives with her husband of 50 years, English professor Jarvis A. Thurston, in St. Louis.

✦ When Connecticut psychiatrist Dr. Helen Langner celebrates her 100th birthday, she is still practicing one day a week. Dr. Langner is the only surviving member of her 1922 medical school class at Yale; she was the only woman in the class, and the fourth to earn a medical degree there.

✦ Yale University professor Evelyn B. Man dies at 87. In a long career as a biochemist, she developed the first effective measurement of thyroid levels, an important step in preventing mental retardation caused by chemical imbalance.

After 14 years as head of Planned Parenthood, Faye Wattleton resigns to become a television journalist on women's issues. She has led the organization through the most difficult decade of preserving *Roe v. Wade*, and *Time* magazine calls her an "eloquent advocate" for reproductive freedom.

In an election called "The Year of the Woman," 24 women are elected to the House of Representatives. California becomes the first state to have two women simultaneously in the U.S. Senate, with the election of Dianne Feinstein and Barbara Boxer. Illinois is the first state to elect an African-American woman, Carol Mosely Braun. Patty Murray of Washington—whose average donor gives only $35—also joins incumbents Nancy Kassebaum and Barbara Mikulski. The Senate reaches a historic peak with six women among its 100 members; all but Kassebaum are Democrats.

It is not "The Year of the Woman" for former vice presidential nominee Geraldine Ferraro, who loses the Democratic primary in her New York U.S. senate race. Ferraro, who received a $1 million advance for her autobiography, *My Story* (1985), is hurt by family scandal: her husband was acquitted of extortion charges in 1987, while her son was convicted of drug violations in 1988.

Salem, Massachusetts, observes the 300th anniversary of its witch trials. A memorial garden lists the name of each victim, along with the date and method of execution. At the same time, the city's seal trivializes the tragedy with witches on broomsticks.

1993 African-American poet Maya Angelou greatly expands her audience when she reads a poem for the inauguration of her fellow Arkansan, Bill Clinton. Her autobiographical novel, *I Know Why the Caged Bird Sings* (1970), returns to best-seller status, with 3,500,000 copies in print by 1995.

In keeping with his campaign promises, President Clinton appoints more women to high office than ever in American history. Janet Reno of Florida becomes the highest-ranked female cabinet member in history when she is named attorney general. The Department of Energy is headed by Hazel O'Leary of Minnesota, and Donna Shalala of California takes over Health and Human Services.

Just below cabinet level are Carol Browner, who heads the Environmental Protection Agency, IRS Commissioner Margaret Richardson, Surgeon General Joycelyn Elders, and Jane Alexander, head of the National Endowment for the Arts. Heading the Women's Bureau of the Department of Labor is Karen Nussbaum, the innovative founder of the clerical workers' union, Nine-to-Five.

Within the White House, the budget director is Alice Rivlin, the chair of the President's Council of Economic Advisers is Laura D'Andrea, and the press secretary is Dee Dee Myers.

The most prestigious of all diplomatic appointments goes to a woman for the first time, when President Clinton names Pamela Harriman ambassador to France. Other ambassadorships include Madeleine Albright to the United Nations and Jean Kennedy Smith—who, as ambassador to Ireland—has the rare privilege of presenting her credentials to Ireland's first female president, Mary Robinson.

First lady Hillary Rodham Clinton, a graduate of Wellesley College and Yale Law School, has a respected reputation as an attorney and as a leader of the Children's Defense Fund. She will devote this year to reform of the nation's inadequate health care system.

Some of those whom President Clinton attempts to appoint to office fail to get sufficient support for congressional confirmation when their personal records on tax payments for household help are questioned—a subject that never arose in previous confirmations when the household head was assumed to be a man who bore no responsibility for his household help.

Dr. David Gunn, an Alabama physician who works in one of two Pensacola clinics that cannot attract Florida doctors because they are the target of antiabortion demonstrations, is shot to death on March 10. Michael Griffin, an unemployed chemical plant worker, believes his actions are divinely inspired and seems surprised when he is sentenced to life in prison.

- On April 28, the nation celebrates its first "Take Our Daughters to Work Day." Organized primarily through *Ms.* magazine, thousands of parents bring their daughters with them to their workplace. When critics wish to add boys to the scene, organizers respond that the point is not a career day, but rather an attempt to raise the self-esteem of girls and to introduce them to career realities.

- Also on April 28, Secretary of Defense Les Aspin announces that he has canceled the Pentagon's ban on women in combat aviation positions, effective immediately. He also recommends that Congress repeal legislation barring women from Navy combat ships. At the same press conference, the Air Force introduces three female pilots chosen for fighter pilot training. Also this year, women deploy with units assigned to Somalia and Bosnia.

  Another major precedent is set at the Pentagon when Sheila A. Widnall becomes secretary of the air force. A 55-year-old MIT professor who is recognized as an international expert on aerodynamics, she is the first female head of a military service.

- President Clinton appoints the second female member of the Supreme Court, Ruth Bader Ginsberg. He notes that because she had "experienced discrimination, she devoted the next 20 years of her career to fighting it." She won five of six cases that she argued before the Supreme Court as an American Civil Liberties Union lawyer in the 1970s, and in 1980, President Jimmy Carter appointed her to the federal bench. Even conservative Republicans call Ginsberg "brilliant" and "very careful, thoughtful, and bright."

  The first Jewish woman on the Court, she was also one of the first women admitted to Harvard Law School; she transferred to Columbia to be near her husband and, when she graduated in 1959, found that "not a law firm in the entire city of New York" would hire her as a lawyer. Despite her prestigious work on the law reviews at both schools, they considered her unqualified because she had children. Ginsberg initially was forced to work as a secretary.

- In a June special election, Texas adds Republican Kay Bailey Hutchinson to the women in the U.S. Senate, giving the nation a high of seven women among the 100 senators. She is the state's first woman in this position, and three jets carry 500 Texans who cheer when she is sworn in.

- When Congress passes the Clinton administration's proposed Family and Medical Leave Act, the difference between the perspective of men and women in elective office is clear: 87% of the congresswomen and 57% of the congressmen vote for the bill. Women also successfully push for greater appropriations for breast cancer research.

- Toni Morrison wins the Nobel Prize for literature. She is the first African-American woman to win and only the second American woman: it has been more than 50 years since Pearl Buck was the first in 1938.

  Educated at Howard and Cornell universities, Morrison became a senior editor at Random House in 1967; she encouraged other black writers there and in her teaching position at Princeton.

- Almost three decades after her death, another posthumous book by Lillian Smith is published. Like other work by this white Georgian who spent her life fighting racism, it is poignantly titled *How Am I to Be Heard?*

- Despite the famous contributions of women such as Williamina Fleming and Annie Jump Cannon from the earliest days of astronomy, women account for only 12% of the practicing members of that field. An American Astronomical Society conference addresses the problem and, among other things, reports on an experiment in which the same paper was distributed under the names of John McKay and Joan McKay. Few women were surprised to learn that "John" got better evaluations.

✦ The median earnings of women are 76% of that of men, up from 63% in 1979. Women earn more than $900 billion annually, four times the 1975 total.

✦ At a time when more women are in the workforce than ever before, the AFL-CIO has only one woman on its 33-member executive board—down from a high of three.

✦ Philadelphia's Marion Williams is the first singer to win a $374,000 MacArthur Foundation "genius" award. She specializes in gospel music and has turned down $100,000 to sing blues.

The 1993 election of Minneapolis mayor Sharon Sayles Belton is of particular significance, since African Americans make up a relatively small portion of that city's population. A city council member since 1983, she has also served as president of the National Coalition Against Sexual Assault. Mayor's Office, Minneapolis, Minnesota

✦ A woman now represents the United States in the United Nations, and that may be a factor in the historic decision at a Vienna meeting to declare wartime rape a crime.

Women from all over the world ignore their own governments to work together: they print petitions in 23 languages, demanding that "gender violence, a universal phenomenon which takes many forms across culture, race and class, be recognized as a violation of human rights."

✦ *Cosmopolitan* editor Helen Gurley Brown, who published her autobiography the previous year, writes *The Late Show: A Semiwild But Practical Survival Plan for Women Over 50.* She is 71 and still married to the man she wed at age 37.

✦ Julie Krone, who began horse racing in Florida in 1981, wins the Belmont Stakes, making her the first female jockey to win a Triple Crown race.

✦ The post office produces stamps in honor of blues singer Dinah Washington, country singer Patsy Cline, and film star Grace Kelly, who married the Prince of Monaco in 1956.

✦ Also in November, a poignant memorial near the Vietnam Wall in Washington is dedicated to the women who served in that war. Although the veteran's administration has not kept track, a volunteer effort called Sister Search believes that about 11,500 women were assigned to Vietnam, mostly as nurses. The names of the eight who were killed are inscribed on the nearby wall.

One of the leaders in creating the monument is Joan Furey, a Bronze Star Vietnam veteran, who now heads the women's division of the Department of Veterans Affairs.

✦ According to Colorado Representative Pat Schroeder, who has long taken the lead on feminist issues, the year is a milestone in congressional history: 30 bills on women's issues are enacted into law; the previous record was five. Next year's election, however, will bring a backlash.

✦ New Jersey has an off-year election for governor, and Republican Christine Todd Whitman defeats the incumbent Democrat with a promise to reduce taxes by 30%. She thus joins the three women currently serving as governor, bringing the total to a historic high of four of the 50 states. The others—all Democrats—are Joan Finney of Kansas, Barbara Roberts of Oregon, and Ann Richards of Texas.

1994 In Pensacola, antiabortion activist the Reverend Paul Hill shoots two men to death and injures a woman in his pro-life quest. Dr. John Byard Britton and Lieutenant Colonel James Barrett are killed. Britton traveled from Florida's Atlantic coast to serve the beleaguered Ladies Center, a gynecological clinic offering abortion services, near the Alabama border. Barrett was a 74-year-old retiree who volunteered his time to escort women from their cars into the clinic. June Barrett, also a retired military officer, is shot twice, but recovers quickly.

✦ The post office begins issuing stamps honoring women in far greater numbers than ever before: more than 20 will be introduced in the next two years, which is more than any decade thus far.

The entertainment series begun last year continues by honoring silent film stars Clara Bow, ZaSu Pitts, and Theda Bara; jazz singers Ma Rainey, Bessie Smith, Ethel Waters, and Billie Holiday; Broadway musical star Ethel Merman; and big-band radio vocalist Mildred Bailey.

A western series includes sharpshooter Annie Oakley and Arizona pioneer Nellie Cashman, as well as Shoshoni explorer Sacagawea, who had been honored with a stamp in 1954.

One of the most significant of the roles recognized by these stamps is that of pediatrician Virginia Apgar, whose "Apgar Score" for newborns is used throughout the world. While the entertainers and westerners are honored with first-class stamps that demonstrate their activities, Dr. Apgar's stamp is an odd-denomination 20-cent stamp; it shows the face of an elderly woman and says only "Virginia Apgar."

✦ Atlanta becomes the first major city to have an African-American woman as police chief when Mayor Bill Campbell appoints veteran policewoman Beverly Harvard.

✦ In an Alabama case, the Supreme Court rules that attorneys may no longer use their peremptory challenges in jury selection to exclude jurors solely on the basis of gender. The decision is based on a man's plea: he argues that he is unfairly excluded from a jury hearing a paternity suit.

✦ Vassar College, which has long viewed itself as a prominent leader on women's rights, is surprised to find itself guilty of discrimination against married women. Federal Judge Constance Baker Motley rules that the college must pay approximately $400,000 to biologist Cynthia Fisher, a married mother of two, whose promotions have not been equal to those of men or unmarried women with lesser credentials. In making her decision, Motley notes that Vassar has not granted tenure to a married woman in the "hard" sciences in the past 30 years.

✦ The 375,000-member American Bar Association chooses Roberta Cooper Ramo, a New Mexican of Native American descent, as its president-elect. She becomes the first woman to preside over this prestigious organization of attorneys.

Ramo, who could not get a job when she graduated from law school at the University of Chicago in 1967, says that her most satisfying court case involved freeing Martin Luther King, Jr.'s, civil rights workers from jail. She was so poor at the time that she had to borrow cab fare from her clients.

✦ The Ivy League has its first female president when Judith Rodin is named president of the University of Pennsylvania.

✦ *Failing at Fairness: How America's Schools Cheat Girls* is published by Myra and David Sadker, who are both professors of education at American University. The Sadkers spent a decade observing classroom behavior and documented a number of ways in which teachers unconsciously demonstrate that they take male students more seriously than females. It is a life's work for Myra Sadler, who dies the following year at age 52.

✦ Lieutenant Kara S. Hultgreen, one of the navy's first female combat pilots, dies when her plane dives into the ocean near her training site of the USS *Abraham Lincoln*. Some argue that this proves women are incapable of being pilots, but investigation shows that her death was due to the plane's mechanical failure.

Navy women also deploy on combat ships to Haiti and the Middle East this year, and women serve with United Nations forces in Rwanda.

◆ President Clinton appoints Mary Shapiro to head the federal Commodity Futures Trading Commission. After she turns down a request from the Chicago Board of Trade that she exempt pension and other institutional funds from federal regulation, the Board of Trade president says that he "won't be intimidated by some blonde, 5-foot-2 girl." Shapiro, who points out that she is 5 feet 5 inches and not a girl at 39, forces him to apologize.

◆ For the first time, more than half of the nation's largest companies have at least one woman on their boards—but women still account for only 6.9% of all corporate board seats. At the same time, just three of Fortune's top 1,000 companies have female chief executives.

◆ Jean Gannett Hawley dies at age 70. As publisher of Gannett Communications, she has overseen the operations of newspapers and television stations in seven states, ranging from Maine to California. .

◆ Congress passes the Violence Against Women Act, which makes it a federal crime to cross state lines in the assault of a spouse or domestic partner. A West Virginia man will be the first to be convicted under the act's provisions: he drives between Kentucky and West Virginia for most of a week, with his wife beaten into unconsciousness in the trunk of his car.

More than 1,500 shelters for battered women have been built in the two decades since feminists began drawing attention to the issue of violence in the home.

◆ The United Nations Conference on Population and Development in Cairo, Egypt, focuses on women as the key to success in these areas. American delegates stress the need for an improved status of women in the fundamentals of education and employment, but conservatives, especially from the Vatican, object to reproductive policies that empower women. Translators find the work difficult, for many languages have no equivalent terms for words such as "empower"; in Arabic, there is not even an acceptable translation for "sex."

◆ The controversial tenure of Dr. Joycelyn Elders, the nation's first black, female surgeon general, ends when she suggests that masturbation should be taught as part of sex education classes. President Clinton will leave the office vacant next year, after the Republican-controlled Senate rejects his nomination of Dr. Henry Foster, a black obstetrician who is condemned for having performed a handful of legal abortions during a long career primarily dedicated to teenage mothers.

◆ Someone phones in a false bomb threat when the aircraft carrier *Eisenhower* sails from its Norfolk, Virginia, naval base with 400 women among the 5,500 sailors. Its six-month sea mission will be the longest yet for female crew members serving on a warship. One of the women explains that she feels safer than on previous missions: "We can defend ourselves [better] than someone on a repair ship or resupply ship."

◆ The Pulitzer Prize for literature goes to Vermont's Annie Proulx for *The Shipping News*. Proulx, who published her first novel, *Postcards*, just two years ago at age 57, is also is the first woman to win the Faulkner Award of the writers' group PEN. "I've run out of being stunned," she says of this sudden recognition.

◆ The world's last major bastion of musicial male chauvinism falls when American Anne Manson conducts the distinguished Vienna Philharmonic during the famous Salzburg Festival.

◆ Bonnie Blair becomes the most decorated woman in U.S. Olympic history when she wins five gold medals for speed ice-skating. Her coach predicts that she will be remembered as "one of the greatest athletes in the history of our country."

♦ When Oklahoma legislator Betty Boyd takes the floor to talk about her struggle with breast cancer, "No one in the chamber moved. Then one by one, men rose to speak of the agony breast cancer inflicted on a wife, a mother, a sister." The legislature passes Boyd's proposed referendum to raise money for breast cancer research and prevention with a 1% tax on movies, concerts, and other entertainment. In November, however, voters reject the proposal.

♦ The midterm elections indicate something of a backlash against women. In the two highest-profile cases, Texas Governor Ann Richards loses to George Bush, Jr., son of the recently defeated president, and California Senator Dianne Feinstein barely holds on to her seat. The number of women holding seats in state legislatures drops slightly from 1,547 to 1,533. Women now make up 21% of all legislators; they are composed of 848 Democrats, 669 Republicans, and 16 others.

One woman is added to the U.S. Senate—long-time Republican House member Olympia Snowe of Maine—for a total of eight women, which is the most ever. The House has 48 women among 435 members.

♦ In December, the first sexual harassment suit against the United Nations is settled when American Catherine Claxton is awarded more than $210,000. The United States is the only sizable nation whose delegation is headed by a woman, and Ambassador Madeleine Albright empathizes with the needs of female UN staff members: "There is no question about it," she says, "this is a very male organization." Of 185 member nations, 75 have no women in professional positions.

1995 Air Force Lieutenant Colonel Eileen Collins is the first woman to pilot a spacecraft. The flight is also historic in that the spacecraft visits Russia's space station; it signals the end of the Cold War that ironically motivated much of the original NASA program.

Collins thoughtfully takes with her mementos from female aviation pioneers, including Bobbi Trout, whose pilot license was issued so early that it was signed by airplane inventor Orville Wright. Collins also carries remembrances from 13 women who passed the tests to become astronauts with NASA's Mercury program in 1961, only to find their entrance abruptly canceled because of gender. A woman flew in a spacecraft for the Soviet Union as early as 1963.

♦ The Justice Department reports that 58% of President Bill Clinton's judicial appointments have been women and minorities, compared with 13% in the Bush administration's first two years. During the comparable time in the Reagan administration, just 8% of appointments went to women and ethnic minorities.

♦ Business executive Myrlie Evers-Williams ousts the incumbent head of the National Association for the Advancement of Colored People by a 30 to 29 vote after a series of corruption charges against male NAACP directors, some of which center on sexual harassment. She is the first woman to head the civil rights organization, which is now nearly a century old.

Her first husband, Medgar Evers, was killed by a white racist in 1963; the guilty man has been convicted only recently. Her second husband, who strongly encouraged her to run and to pursue the case against Evers' killer, dies of cancer just days after her election.

♦ A bipartisan federal commission issues a three-year, 250-page study of the "glass ceiling," a term that began to be used in the late 1980s for the invisible limitations on women near the top of corporate structures. The report, which is based on 1990 census data, concludes that women have made far less progress than those who oppose affirmative action recognize: of the nation's senior management positions, 95% are held by white men, who constitute only 43% of the total workforce.

Funding for the Glass Ceiling Commission was sponsored by Republican Senator Robert Dole when his wife, Elizabeth Dole, was secretary of labor under President George Bush. After a lifetime of government positions, she moved from there to the private sector—where her

$200,000 salary as head of the Red Cross became controversial. Even though men who direct similar agencies receive such salaries, the Red Cross is identified in many minds with the selflessness of its American founder, Clara Barton.

✦ First lady Hillary Clinton and her 15-year-old daughter Chelsea spend Chelsea's spring break visiting Southeast Asia. The first lady highlights the importance of educating girls and investing in women's business and farming ventures. Her trip also draws international attention to such violence against women as the infanticide of girls and the killing of brides whose dowries are deemed insufficient.

Earlier in the year, at a United Nations meeting on women in Copenhagen, Hillary Clinton announced American commitment of funds aimed at empowering Third World women with small business loans. It is modeled on a successful project that her husband had established while governor of Arkansas: lending small amounts of money to women is proving a viable path to financial success.

✦ At commencement ceremonies at the nation's oldest military academy, the army's West Point, a woman graduates at the top of the class. Rebecca Marier is ranked first of 988 cadets in both academics and military leadership.

✦ Just a little more than two decades after women were fully integrated into the Coast Guard, an amazing 53% of this year's Officers Candidate School class is women.

On the down side, a Minneapolis survey of female veterans finds that 90% of those under age 50 have experienced sexual harassment. The Pentagon criticizes the study's methodology and says that "only" 64% of active-duty women report such problems.

✦ On June 22, ground is broken at Arlington Cemetery for a living memorial to the nation's military women. Organized by retired Air Force General Wilma Vaught, Women in Military Service to America plans an educational center that will feature computerized memories from every female veteran who can be located.

Two women who served in World War I attend the ceremony, along with dozens of dignitaries. Among them are the chief of Naval Personnel, who points out that almost 10,000 women currently are assigned to 87 ships, while his counterpart in the Air Force reports on 300 female pilots. President Clinton's speech recognizes that "women have been in our service since George Washington's troops" and that the memorial "makes a long overdue downpayment on a debt we will never fully repay."

✦ Women win two major sexual harassment lawsuits against the chief executive officers of large corporations. The CEO of W.R. Grace, a chemical business, is forced from his job in March because of his harassment of female employees; in August, cosmetic manufacturer Del Laboratories pays a record $1.2 million to 15 women mistreated by its chief. The latter case is especially significant because the women do not allege that he has insisted on sexual favors, but rather that he created a hostile work environment with verbal and physical insults.

✦ It is revealed that the death of 39-year-old *Boston Globe* health care columnist Betsy Lehman was a medical mistake. Despite being treated for breast cancer at one of the city's most prestigious hospitals and despite being married to a staff scientist, she was given four times the normal dose of chemotherapy.

✦ Texan Norma McCorvey, who as "Jane Roe" was the plaintiff in the 1973 case that secured abortion rights, holds a press conference to reveal her new association with the antichoice movement —even though she has been most recently employed as marketing director of a Texas abortion clinic.

At the same time, the Kaiser Family Foundation issues a directory of physicians willing to oversee the use of birth control pills as a "morning after" method of inducing a menstrual period. It is titled *Emergency Contraception: The Nation's Best Kept Secret*.

✦ The first black president of a Seven Sisters college is Ruth Simmons, who is inaugurated as president of Smith College. Her parents were sharecroppers.

✦ For the first time in Yale's 182-year history, women outnumber men in the entering medical school class. Of the nation's 126 medical schools, 18 have a majority of women—including the most prestigious Harvard and Johns Hopkins medical schools.

✦ To acknowledge the 75th anniversary of women's voting rights on August 26, the post office issues a first-class stamp that portrays two historic marches: the suffragist parade that coincided with President Woodrow Wilson's 1913 inauguration and a 1976 Illinois march in support of the Equal Rights Amendment. Neither of these dates correlates with the 75th anniversary year of 1920, when the 19th Amendment was ratified. Moreover, the inclusion of an ERA march in a stamp commemorating the 19th Amendment further confuses women's history, for many (perhaps even most) suffragists did not support the amendment.

A few days earlier, the post office honored Alice Paul, leader of the more militant wing of the suffrage movement, with a 78-cent stamp; Carrie Chapman Catt, the mainstream leader, had received a commemorative stamp much earlier.

Celebrations of the 19th Amendment are held throughout the nation on August 26, and a Washington march attracts women who wear 1913 dresses and walk the same route as the famous parade that year. The League of Women Voters sponsors a traveling exhibit, the National Archives opens a special exposition, and thousands of women's organizations throughout the country commemorate the day.

✦ In addition to the stamp for the 75th anniversary of suffrage, the post office joins Universal Studios in a June ceremony announcing a 32-cent stamp for Marilyn Monroe.

A first-class, 20-stamp Civil War series includes four women: nurses Phoebe Pember (for the Confederacy) and Clara Barton (for the Union), South Carolina diarist Mary Chesnut, and the courageous African-American emancipator Harriet Tubman.

A first-class stamp is produced for pioneer black aviator Bessie Coleman. Two other women are recognized on stamps with unusual denominations—anthropologist Ruth Benedict is depicted on a 46-cent stamp, and a 55-cent stamp honors industrial toxicologist Dr. Alice Hamilton. Unlike last year's stamp for Dr. Virginia Apgar, Hamilton's includes "M.D.," but neither shows these physicians in a work setting.

✦ Eunice Kennedy Shriver becomes the first living woman to be illustrated on a coin: the U.S. Mint issues a silver-dollar commemorative coin honoring her and her brother, President John F. Kennedy, for their work in creating the Special Olympics for retarded children.

✦ Millions of television viewers watch the year-long trial of O. J. Simpson, a football and media celebrity, for the murder of his ex-wife, Nicole Brown Simpson, and her male friend, Ronald Goldman. Domestic violence experts point to the case as a classic pattern of spousal abuse, but the jury acquits Simpson. Its majority is black women; Simpson is black and the victims are white.

Even though she loses the case, lead prosecutor Marcia Clark earns a $4.2 million book contract at the trial's end. It is the third-highest advance in publishing history—but a few days later, it is announced that assistant prosecutor Christopher Darden will receive slightly more for his book.

✦ In China, the United Nations hosts the last of the year's conferences on women's issues, and hundreds of American women attend the sessions held for nongovernmental organizations. Even though the 46-member official delegation includes such moderates as Thomas Kean, a former Republican governor of New Jersey, many conservatives object to U.S. participation. They cite China's poor human rights record, but few point out that similar conferences were held in Mexico City in 1975 and in Kenya in 1985—nations that also have no particular regard for human rights.

After much public debate on whether Hillary Clinton should attend, the first lady silences most critics by using the platform candidly to criticize China and other nations for their abuse of individual freedoms, especially those of women.

◆ Teenager Shannon Faulkner wins her court battle for admission to The Citadel, a South Carolina military school supported with tax dollars, but leaves after the first week, during which many of the school's young men have made their hostility clear. However, the Supreme Court's rejection of the school's last-minute appeal is applicable to other women, and as the year ends, several indicate their intention to apply for admission to this last bastion of publicly funded exclusionary education.

◆ Republican Robert Packwood of Oregon is forced to leave the U.S. Senate after almost two dozen women come forward to testify on his personal history of sexual harrassment. Packwood managed to persuade his constituents that the charges were baseless when he was reelected last fall, but finally gives up when his own diary entries speak to the truth of what the women have said.

◆ Representative Enid Waldholtz, Republican of Utah, marks two milestones this year: she was the first congressional freshman in 70 years to be appointed to the powerful Rules Committee, and she became the second woman in congressional history to give birth while in office.

In November, however, her dream world comes crashing down: federal investigators issue a warrant for her husband's arrest when he disappears rather than answer questions about his role as her campaign treasurer. Last year, she defeated Democratic incumbent Karen Shepherd with a last-minute huge infusion of advertising dollars.

◆ Democratic Representative Patricia Schroeder of Colorado announces that she will not seek reelection, and colleagues from both parties acknowledge that "every woman in this house is walking in her footsteps." Schroeder came to Congress when her children were preschoolers, and now they have graduated from college. "It's time," she says, "to tackle new challenges."

◆ The Labor Department estimates that, when the century ends, women will make up close to half of the workforce, or more than double the rate at the beginning of the century. Currently, more people are employed in businesses owned by women than by all Fortune 500 companies combined.

Selected Bibliography

BOOKS

Abbott, Edith. *Women in Industry*. New York: Appleton & Co., 1909.

Abzug, Bella. *Bella! Ms. Abzug Goes to Washington*. New York: Saturday Review Press, 1972.

Addams, Jane. *Twenty Years at Hull-house*, with autobiographical notes. New York: Macmillan, 1910.

Alexander, Alland. *Jessie Tarbox Beals*. Camera-graphic Press, 1978.

Allen, Agnes Rogers. *Women Are Here to Stay*. New York: Harper & Co., 1949.

Ames, Jessie Daniels. *Southern Women Look at Lynching*. Atlanta, Ga.: Association of Southern Women for the Preventation of Lynching, 1937.

Andrews, Matthew Page. *The Women of the South in War Times*. Baltimore: Norman Remington Co., 1923.

Anthony, Carl Sferrazza. *First Ladies*, 2 vols. New York: William Morrow, 1990.

Anthony, Katharine. *Susan B. Anthony: Her Personal History and Her Era*. New York: Doubleday, 1954.

Anthony, Susan B., and Ida Husted Harper. *History of Woman Suffrage*, volume 4. Rochester: privately printed, 1902; reprinted New York: Arno Press, 1969.

Balch, Emily. *Beyond Nationalism: The Social Thought of Emily Greene Balch*, edited by Mercedes M. Randall. New York: Twayne Publishers, 1972.

Banner, Lois W. *Women in Modern America: A Brief History*. New York: Harcourt Brace Jovanovich, 1974.

Barbour, Philip L. *The Three Worlds of Captain John Smith*. New York: Macmillan, 1964.

Bataille, Gretchen, ed. *Native American Women: A Biographical Dictionary*. New York: Garland Publishers, 1992.

Bates, Daisy. *The Long Shadow of Little Rock*. New York: David McKay Co., 1962.

Baxandall, Rosalyn, Linda Gordon, and Susan Reverby. *America's Working Women: A Documentary History, 1600 to the Present*. New York: Vintage Books, 1976.

Beach, Cora M., ed. *Women of Wyoming*. Casper: Wyoming Historical Society, 1927.

Beard, Charles A., and Mary Ritter Beard, revised by William Beard. *The Beard's New Basic History of the United States*. New York: Doubleday, 1968.

Beard, Mary Ritter. *Woman as a Force in History*. New York: Macmillan, 1945.

Beeton, Beverly. *Women Vote in the West: The Woman Suffrage Movement, 1869–1896*. New York: Garland Publishers, 1986.

Bennett, Ralph, ed. *Settlements in the Americas*. Newark: University of Delaware, 1993.

Berkin, Carol R., and Clara M. Lovett, eds. *Women, War and Revolution*. New York: Holmes & Meier, 1980.

Berkin, Carol. R., and Mary Beth Norton, eds. *Women of America: A History*. Boston: Houghton Mifflin, 1979.

Blackwell, Alice Stone. *Lucy Stone*. Boston: Little, Brown, 1930.

Blackwell, Elizabeth. *Pioneer Work in Opening the Medical Profession to Women*, edited by Dr. Mary Roth Walsh. New York: Schocken Books, 1977.

Blanchfield, Florence A. *The Army Nurse Corps in World War II* and *Organized Nursing and the Army in Three Wars*. Washington, D.C.: 1948 and 1950.

Blatch, Harriot Stanton, and Alma Lutz. *Challenging Years: The Memoirs of Harriot Stanton Blatch*. New York: G.P. Putnam's Sons, 1940.

Blumenthal, Walter Hart. *Women Camp Followers of the American Revolution*. Philadelphia: G.S. MacManus Co., 1952.

Boller, Paul F. *Presidential Wives*. New York: Oxford University Press, 1988.

Bradford, Sarah. *Scenes in the Life of Harriet Tubman*. Originally published 1869; reissued New York: Corinth Books, 1961.

Breckinridge, Sophonisba. *Women in the 20th Century: A Study of Their Political, Social, and Economic Activities*. New York: McGraw-Hill, 1933.

Brockett, L.P., and M.C. Vaughn. *Women's Work in the Civil War*. Philadelphia: Zeigler, McCurdy, 1867.

Bryant, Charles S., and Abel B. Murch. *A History of the Great Massacre by the Sioux Indians in Minnesota*. Cincinnati: Rickey and Carroll, 1864; reprinted in Germany, 1973.

Buck, Pearl. *My Several Worlds: A Personal Record*. New York: John Day Co., 1954.

Bullough, Vern. *The Subordinated Sex*. Athens, Ga.: University of Georgia, 1988.

Butler, Elizabeth Beardsley. "Women and the Trades." In Paul H. Kellogg, ed., *The Pittsburgh Survey: Findings in Six Volumes*. New York: Charities Publication Committee and the Russell Sage Foundation, 1909.

Campbell, D'Ann. *Women at War with America*. Cambridge, Mass.: Harvard University Press, 1984.

Campbell, Helen. *Prisoners of Poverty: Women Wage-Workers, Their Trades and Their Lives*. Boston: Roberts Brothers, 1895.

Catt, Carrie Chapman, and Nettie Rogers Schuler. *Woman Suffrage and Politics: The Inner Story of the Suffrage Movement*. New York: Charles Scribner's Sons, 1923.

Chafe, William H. *The American Woman, Her Changing Social, Economic and Political Roles, 1920–1970*. New York: Oxford University Press, 1972.

Chesnut, Mary Boykin. *Diary From Dixie*. Boston: Houghton Mifflin, 1949.

———. *Mary Chesnut's Civil War*, edited by C. Vann Woodward. New Haven, Conn.: Yale University Press, 1981.

———. *The Private Mary Chesnut: The Unpublished Diaries*, edited by C. Vann Woodward and Elisabeth Muhlenfeld. New York: Oxford University Press, 1984.

Child, Lydia Maria. *The History of the Condition of Women*. Boston: J. Allen & Co., 1835.

Chitwood, Oliver Perry. *A History of Colonial America*. New York: Harper & Brothers, 1948.

Clay, Jehu Curtis. *Annals of the Swedes on the Delaware*, 4th ed. Chicago: John Ericsson, 1938.

Commission on the Bicentenary of the U.S. House of Representatives. *Women in Congress, 1917–1990*. Washington, D.C.: U.S. Government Printing Office, 1991.

Congress of Women. *The Congress of Women Held in the Woman's Building, World's Columbian Exposition, Chicago, U.S.A., 1893*, edited by Mary Kavanaugh Oldham Eagle. Philadelphia: C.R. Parish, 1894.

Cott, Nancy F. *The Bonds of Womanhood: "Women's Sphere" in New England, 1780–1835*. New Haven, Conn.: Yale University Press, 1977.

Crapol, Edward P., ed. *Women and American Foreign Policy*, 2nd ed. Wilmington, Delaware: Scholarly Resources, 1992.

Crocheron, Augusta Joyce. *Representative Women of Deseret*. Salt Lake City, Utah: J.C. Graham & Co., 1884.

Croly, Jane Cunningham. *History of the Woman's Club Movement in America*. New York: H.G. Allen & Co., 1898.

Dannett, Sylvia. *She Rode with Generals*. New York: T. Nelson, 1960.

Daughters of Utah Pioneers. *An Enduring Legacy*. Salt Lake City, Utah: privately printed, 1978.

Dawson, Sarah Morgan. *A Confederate Girl's Diary*. Edited by James I. Robertson, Jr. Westport, Conn.: Greenwood Press, 1972; originally published by Indiana University Press, 1960.

Degler, Carl. *At Odds: Women and the Family in America*. New York: Oxford University Press, 1981.

Dennett, Mary Ware. *Birth Control Laws*. New York: F.H. Hitchcock, 1926.

DePauw, G. *Seafaring Women*. New York: Houghton Mifflin, 1982.

DeVries, Raymond. *Regulating Birth: Midwives, Medicine, and the Law*. Philadelphia: Temple University Press, 1985.

Dexter, Elisabeth A. *Colonial Women of Affairs*. Boston: Houghton Mifflin, 1924.

Dorr, Rheta Child. *Susan B. Anthony*. Originally published 1928; reissued New York: AMS Press, 1970.

Douglas, Helen Gahagan. *A Full Life*. New York: Doubleday, 1982.

DuBois, Ellen Carol. *Feminism and Suffrage: The Emergence of an Independent Women's Movement in America, 1848–1869*. Ithaca: Cornell University Press, 1978.

Duniway, Abigail Scott. *Pathbreaking: An Autobiographical History of the Equal Suffrage Movement in the Pacific Coast States*. Portland, Oreg.: James, Kerns, & Abbott Co., 1914.

Eaton, Clement. *A History of the Old South*. New York: Macmillan, 1949.

Ellet, Elizabeth F. *The Pioneer Women of the West*. Philadelphia: Henry T. Coates & Co., 1852.

Ellis, Edward Robb. *The Epic of New York City*. New York: Coward-McCann, 1966.

Evans, Sara M. *Born for Liberty: A History of Women in America*. New York: The Free Press, 1989.

Fairbanks, Carol. *Prairie Women*. New Haven, Conn.: Yale University Press, 1986.

Fischer, Christiane. *Let Them Speak for Themselves: Women in the American West, 1849–1900*. Hamden, Conn.: Archon Books, 1977.

Flexner, Eleanor. *Century of Struggle*. New York: Atheneum, 1974.

Flynn, Elizabeth Gurley. *Women Have a Date with Destiny*. New York: Workers Library Publishers, 1944.

Foner, Philip S. *Women and the American Labor Movement*. New York: Collier Macmillan, 1980.

Foster, Catherine. *Women For All Seasons: The Story of the Women's International League for Peace and Freedom*. Athens: University of Georgia Press, 1989.

Franklin, John Hope, and August Meier, eds. *Black Leaders of the Twentieth Century*. Urbana: University of Illinois Press, 1982.

Franzen, Monika, and Nancy Ethiel, with Nicole Hollander. *Make Way! 200 Years of American Women in Cartoons*. Chicago: Chicago Review Press, 1988.

Frey, Sylvia R., and Marian J. *New World, New Roles: A Documentary History of Women in Pre-Industrial America*. New York: Greenwood Press, 1986.

Friedan, Betty. *The Feminine Mystique*. New York: W.W. Norton, 1963.

Frost, Elizabeth, and Kathryn Cullen-Dupont. *Woman's Suffrage in America: An Eyewitness History*. New York: Facts On File, 1992.

Fuller, Margaret. *Woman in the Nineteenth Century*. Originally published 1855; reissued New York: W.W. Norton, 1971.

Gage, Matilda Joselyn. *Woman, Church and State*. Originally published 1893; reissued New York: Arno Press, 1972.

Gannon, Michael. *Florida: A Short History*. Gainesville: University Press of Florida, 1993.

George, Carol V.R., ed. *"Remember the Ladies": New Perspectives on Women in American History*. Syracuse, N.Y.: Syracuse University Press, 1975.

Gilman, Charlotte Perkins. *Women and Economics*. Boston: Small, Maynard & Co., 1899.

Gluck, Sherna B. *Rosie the Riveter Revisited: Women, the War and Social Change*. Boston: Twayne Publishers, 1987.

Golemba, Beverly E. *Lesser-Known Women: A Biographical Dictionary*. Boulder, Colo.: Lynne Rienner Publishers, 1992.

Goings, Kenneth W. *The NAACP Comes of Age*. Bloomington: Indiana University Press, 1990.

Gordon, Linda. *Woman's Body, Woman's Right: A Social History of Birth Control in America*. New York: Grossman, 1976.

Gray, Dorothy. *Women of the West*. Millbrae, Calif.: Les Femmes, 1976.

Green, Harry Clinton, and Mary Wolcott Green, under the aegis of the Daughters of the American Revolution. *The Pioneer Mothers of America*, 3 vols. New York: G.P. Putnam's Sons, 1912.

Grimké, Sarah Moore. *Letters on the Equality of the Sexes and the Condition of Women*. Originally published 1838; reissued New Haven, Conn.: Yale University Press, 1988.

Haber, Barbara. *Women in America: A Guide to Books*. New York: G.K. Hall, 1978.

Haber, Louis. *Women Pioneers of Science*. New York: Harcourt Brace Jovanovich, 1979.

Hale Sarah Josepha. *Woman's Record, or Sketches of Distinguished Women.* New York: Harper & Brothers; published in three editions, 1853, 1869 and 1876.

Harper, Ida Husted. *History of Woman Suffrage,* vols. 5 and 6. New York: National American Woman Suffrage Association, 1922.

————. *The Life and Work of Susan B. Anthony,* 3 vols. Indianapolis: Hollenbeck Press, 1898–1908.

Hartmann, Susan: *The Home Front and Beyond: American Women in the 1940's.* Boston: Twayne Publishers, 1982.

Hemenway, Robert E. *Zora Neale Hurston: A Literary Biography.* Urbana: University of Illinois Press, 1977.

Henderson, Ann, and Gary Mormino, eds. *Spanish Pathways in Florida.* Sarasota, Fla.: Pineapple Press, 1991.

Hewitt, Linda L. *Women Marines in World War I.* Washington, D.C.: U.S. Marine Corps, 1974.

Hewitt, Nancy A. *Women's Activism and Social Change: Rochester, New York, 1822–1872.* Ithaca: Cornell University Press, 1984.

Hill, Marilyn Wood. *Their Sisters' Keepers: Prostitution in New York City, 1830–1870.* Berkeley: University of California Press, 1993.

Hine, Darlene Clark, ed. *Black Women in United States History,* 16 vols. Brooklyn, N.Y.: Carlson Publishing, 1990.

Holt, Rachman. *Mary McLeod Bethune: A Biography.* New York: Doubleday, 1964.

Horan, James D. *Desperate Women.* New York: Putnam's, 1952.

Hosmer, Rev. William. *Appeal to Husbands and Wives in Favor of Female Physicians.* New York: George Gregory, 1858.

Howe, Julia Ward. *Reminiscences.* Boston: Houghton Mifflin, 1899.

Hughes, Gwendolyn Salisbury. *Mothers in Industry: Wage-Earning by Mothers in Philadelphia.* New York: New Republic, 1925.

Hutchinson, Emilie Josephine. *Women's Wages.* New York: Columbia University Press, 1919; reissued New York: AMS Press, 1968.

Hutchinson, Louise Daniel. *Voice from the South: Anna J. Cooper.* Washington, D.C.: Smithsonian Institution Press, 1981.

Irwin, Inez Haynes. *The Story of the Woman's Party.* New York: Harcourt Brace & Co., 1921.

James, Edward T., Janet Wilson James, and Paul S. Boyer, eds. *Notable American Women,* 3 vols. Cambridge, Mass.: Harvard University Press, 1971.

Janeway, Elizabeth. *Man's World; Woman's Place.* New York: William Morrow, 1971.

Jacobi, Mary Putnam. *"Common Sense" Applied to Woman Suffrage.* New York: G.P. Putnam's Sons, 1894.

Jeffrey, Julie Roy. *Frontier Women: The Trans-Mississippi West, 1840–1880.* New York: Hill and Wang, 1979.

Jolly, Ellen Ryan. *Nuns of the Battlefield.* Providence, R.I.: Providence Visitor Press, 1927.

Jones, Mary. *Autobiography of Mother Jones,* edited by Mary F. Parton. Originally published 1925; reissued New York: Arno Press, 1969.

Kammen, Carol. *Lives Passed: Biographical Sketches from Central New York.* Interlaken, N.Y.: Heart of the Lakes Publishing, 1984.

Karlsen, Carol. *Devil in the Shape of a Woman: Witchcraft in Colonial New England.* New York: Vintage, 1989.

Kass-Simon, G., and Patricia Farnes. *Women of Science: Righting the Record.* Bloomington: Indiana University Press, 1990.

Katz, Esther, and Anita Rapone, eds. *Women's Experience in America: An Historical Anthology.* New Brunswick, N.J.: Transaction Books, 1980.

Kearney, James R. *Anna Eleanor Roosevelt: The Evolution of a Reformer.* Boston: Houghton Mifflin, 1968.

Kennedy, Susan Estabrook. *If All We Did Was to Weep at Home: A History of White Working-Class Women in America.* Bloomington: Indiana University Press, 1979.

Kerber, Linda K. *Women of the Republic: Intellect and Ideology in Revolutionary America.* Chapel Hill: University of North Carolina, 1980.

Kerber, Linda, and Jane Sherron De Hart. *Women's America: Refocusing the Past*, 4th ed. New York: Oxford University Press, 1995.

Kessler-Harris, Alice. *Out to Work: A History of Wage-Earning in the United States*. New York: Oxford University Press, 1982.

Klaw, Spencer. *Without Sin: The Life and Death of the Oneida Community*. New York: Penguin Books, 1993.

Kneeland, George J. *Commercialized Prostitution in New York City*. New York: The Century Co., 1913.

Knight, Sarah Kemble. *The Journal of Madam Knight*. Originally published 1825; reissued Boston: Small, Maynard & Co., 1920.

Larcom, Lucy. *New England Girlhood*. Boston: Houghlin Mifflin, 1889.

Lash, Joseph. *Eleanor and Franklin*. New York: W.W. Norton, 1971.

———. *Eleanor: The Years Alone*. New York: W.W. Norton, 1972.

Lerner, Gerda. *Black Women in White America*. New York: Pantheon Books, 1972.

———. *The Woman in American History*. Menlo Park, Calif.: Addison-Wesley, 1971.

Livermore, Mary. *My Story of the War: A Woman's Narrative of Four Years' Personal Experience*. Hartford, Conn.: A.D. Worthington & Co., 1888.

Litoff, Judy Barrett, and Judith McDonnell, eds. *European Immigrant Women: A Biographical Dictionary*. New York: Garland Publishing, 1994.

Logan, Rayford W., and Michael R. Winston, eds. *Dictionary of American Negro Biography*. New York: W.W. Norton, 1982.

Lunardini, Christine A. *From Equal Suffrage to Equal Rights: Alice Paul and the National Woman's Party, 1910–1928*. New York: New York University Press, 1986.

Lutz, Alma. *Susan B. Anthony: Rebel, Crusader, Humanitarian*. Boston: Beacon Press, 1959.

MacKinnon, Janice R., and Stephen R. MacKinnon. *Agnes Smedley: The Life and Times of an American Radical*. Berkeley: University of California, 1988.

MacDonald, Anne L. *Feminine Ingenuity: Women and Invention in America*. New York: Ballantine Books, 1994.

Martin, George. *Madame Secretary: Frances Perkins*. Boston: Houghton Mifflin, 1976.

Martin, Theodora Penny. *The Sound of Their Own Voices: Women's Study Clubs, 1860–1910*. Boston: Beacon Press, 1987.

Marzolf, Marion. *Up From the Footnote: A History of Women Journalists*. New York: Hastings House, 1977.

Makower, Joel, ed. *The American History Sourcebook*. New York: Prentice-Hall, 1988.

McHenry, Robert ed. *Liberty's Women*. Springfield, Mass.: G. & C. Merriam, 1980.

McKerns, Joseph P., ed. *Biographical Dictionary of American Journalism*. New York: Greenwood Press, 1989.

McKinley, A.E. *Suffrage Franchise in the Thirteen Colonies*. New York: B. Franklin, 1969.

Mead, Margaret. *Male and Female: A Study of the Sexes in a Changing World*. New York: William Morrow, 1949.

Milanich, Jerald T., and Charles Hudson. *Hernando de Soto and the Indians of Florida*. Gainesville: University Press of Florida, 1993.

Miller, Page Putnam, ed. *Reclaiming the Past: Landmarks of Women's History*. Bloomington: Indiana University Press, 1992.

Mohr, James C. *Abortion in America*. New York: Oxford University Press, 1978.

Moore, Frank. *Women of the War*. Hartford, Conn.: S.S. Scranton & Co., 1866.

Morison, Samuel Eliot. *Admiral of the Ocean Sea: A Life of Christopher Columbus*. Boston: Little, Brown, 1942.

Mott, Frank Luther. *A History of American Magazines, 1741–1850*. Cambridge, Mass.: Harvard University Press, 1930.

Morello, Karen Berger. *The Invisible Bar: The Woman Lawyer in America, 1638 to the Present*. New York: Random House, 1986.

Murphy, Marjorie. *Blackboard Unions: The AFT and the NEA, 1900–1980*. Ithaca, N.Y.: Cornell University Press, 1990.

National Association of Commissions for Women. *Recollections of the Past Presidents,*

1970–1995. Greensboro, N.C.: Commission on the Status of Women, 1995.

Nelson, Randy F. *The Almanac of American Letters.* Los Altos, Calif: William Kaufman, 1981.

Newcomber, Mabel. *A Century of Higher Education.* New York: Harper & Brothers, 1959.

Norton, Mary Beth. *Liberty's Daughters: The Revolutionary Experience of American Women, 1750–1800.* Boston: Little, Brown, 1980.

Oakley, Ann. *Woman's Work.* New York: Vintage Books, 1976.

Ogilvie, Marilyn Bailey. *Women in Science.* Cambridge, Mass.: MIT Press, 1986.

O'Neill, Lois Decker. *Women's Book of World Records and Achievements.* Garden City, N.Y.: Anchor/Doubleday, 1979.

O'Neill, William L. *Everyone Was Brave: A History of Feminism in America.* Chicago: Quadrangle Books, 1971.

Parks, Maud Wood, ed. *Victory, How Women Won It: A Centennial Symposium, 1840–1940.* New York: H.W. Wilson, 1940.

Planck, Charles E. *Women With Wings.* New York: Harper & Brothers, 1942.

Pleck, Elizabeth, and Ellen K. Rothman. *The Legacies Book: A History of Women and the Family in America, 1607–1870.* Washington: The Annenberg/CPB Project, 1987.

Proceedings of the Woman's Rights Conventions Held at Seneca Falls and Rochester, New York, July and August, 1848. New York: Robert J. Johnston, 1870; reprinted New York: Arno Press, 1969.

Reckless, Walter C. *Vice in Chicago.* Chicago: University of Chicago, 1933; reissued Montclair, N.J.: Patterson Smith Publishing, 1969.

Read, Phyllis J. and Bernard L. Witlieb. *The Book of Women's Firsts.* New York: Random House, 1992.

Redfern, Bernice. *Women of Color in the U.S.* New York: Garland Publishers, 1989.

Report on the Condition of Women and Child Wage-Earners in the United States, Senate Document 645, 19 vols. Washington, D.C.: U.S. Government Printing Office, 1911–13.

Richardson, Marilyn. *Maria W. Stewart: America's First Black Woman Political Writer.* Bloomington: Indiana University Press, 1987.

Riley, Glenda. *Divorce: An American Tradition.* New York: Oxford University Press, 1991.

Roberts, Janet. *Those Magnificent Mountain Women.* Lincoln: University of Nebraska Press, 1990.

Roberts, Mary M. *American Nursing.* New York: Macmillan, 1954.

Robinson, William H., Jr. *Early Black American Poets.* Dubuque, Iowa: William C. Brown Publishers, 1969.

Roosevelt, Eleanor. *The Autobiography of Eleanor Roosevelt.* New York: Harper & Brothers, 1961.

Roosevelt, Eleanor, and Lorena Hickok. *Ladies of Courage.* New York: G.P. Putnam's Sons, 1954.

Rosenberg-Smith, Carroll. *Disorderly Conduct.* New York: Knopf, 1985.

Ross, Ishbel. *Ladies of the Press.* New York: Harper & Co., 1936.

Ross, Joyce. *J.E. Spingarn and the Rise of the NAACP.* New York: Atheneum, 1972.

Ross, Nancy. *Westward the Women.* Originally published 1944; reissued Freeport, N.Y.: Books for Libraries Press, 1970.

Rossiter, Margaret. *Women Scientists in America: Struggles and Strategies to 1940.* Baltimore: John Hopkins University Press, 1982.

Rothman, Barbara Katz. *In Labor: Women and Power in the Birthplace.* New York: W.W. Norton, 1982.

Rothman, Sheila M. *Woman's Proper Place: A History of Changing Ideals and Practices, 1870 to the Present.* New York: Basic Books, 1978.

Rowbotham, Sheila. *Women, Resistance and Revolution: A History of Women and Revolution in the Modern World.* New York: Pantheon, 1972.

Ryan, Mary P. *Womanhood in America: From Colonial Times to the Present,* 2nd ed. New York: New Viewpoints, 1979.

Salem, Dorothy C., ed. *African American Women: A Biographical Dictionary.* New York: Garland Publishing, 1992.

Salmon, Lucy Maynard. *Domestic Service*, 2nd ed. New York: Macmillan, 1901.

Sanger, Margaret. *My Fight for Birth Control.* New York: Farrar & Rinehart, 1931.

Scharf, Lois. *To Work and to Wed: Female Employment, Feminism, and the Great Depression.* Westport, Conn.: Greenwood Press, 1980.

Schlesinger, Arthur M. *New Viewpoints in American History.* New York: Macmillan, 1922.

Schneider, Dorothy and Carl J. *American Women in the Progressive Era.* New York: Facts On File, 1993.

Schwartz, Gerald. *A Woman Doctor's Civil War: Esther Hill Hawks' Diary.* Columbia: University of South Carolina Press, 1984.

Scott, Anne F., ed. *Unheard Voices: The First Historians of Southern Women.* Charlottesville: University Press of Virginia, 1993.

Scott, Anne F., and Andrew M. Scott. *One Half the People: The Fight for Woman Suffrage.* Philadelphia: J.B. Lippincott Company, 1975.

Shaw, Anna Howard. *The Story of a Pioneer.* Copyrighted by the author, 1915; reissued New York: Kraus Reprint Co., 1970.

Sherr, Lynn and Jurate Kazickas. *Susan Anthony Slept Here.* New York: Random House, 1994.

Sicherman, Barbara, and Carol Hurd Green, eds. *Notable American Women*, vol. 4. Cambridge, MA: Harvard University Press, 1980.

Sigaud, Louis A. *Belle Boyd: Confederate Spy.* Richmond, Va.: The Dietz Press, 1944.

Sinclair, Andrew. *The Better Half: The Emancipation of the American Woman.* New York: Harper & Row, 1965.

Smith, Jessie Carney, ed. *Notable Black American Women.* Detroit: Gale Research, 1992.

Smith, Page. *Daughters of the Promised Land: Women in American History.* Boston: Little, Brown, 1970.

Solomon, Barbara. *In the Company of Educated Women.* New Haven, Conn.: Yale University Press, 1985.

Spofford, Harriet Prescott. *The Servant Girl Question.* Boston: Houghton Mifflin Co., 1881; reprinted New York: Arno Press and the New York Times, 1977.

Spruill, Julia Cherry. *Women's Life and Work in the Southern Colonies.* New York: Russell & Russell, 1969.

Stage, Sarah. *Female Complaints: Lydia Pinkham and the Business of Women's Medicine.* New York: W.W. Norton, 1979.

Stanton, Elizabeth Cady. *Woman's Bible.* 2 vols. Originally published 1895 and 1898; reissued New York: Arno Press, 1972.

Stanton, Elizabeth Cady, Susan B. Anthony, and Matilda Joselyn Gage. *History of Woman Suffrage*, vols. 1–3. New York: Fowler & Wells, 1881–86; reprinted New York: Arno Press, 1969.

Steber, Rick. *Women of the West.* Prineville, Oreg.: Bonanza Publishing, 1988.

Sterling, Dorothy, ed. *Turning the World Upside Down: The Anti-Slavery Convention of American Women.* New York: Feminist Press, 1987.

———. *We Are Your Sisters: Black Women in the Nineteenth Century.* New York: W.W. Norton, 1984.

Stern, Philip Van Doren. *Secret Missions of the Civil War.* Chicago: Rand, McNally, 1960.

Stetler, Susan L. *Almanac of Famous People.* Detroit: Gale Research, 1989.

Stowe, Harriet Beecher. *Life of Harriet Beecher Stowe.* Boston: Houghton Mifflin, 1891.

Stremlow, Mary V. *A History of the Women Marines, 1946–77.* Washington, DC: U.S. Marine Corps, 1986.

Taylor, Susie King. *A Black Woman's Civil War Memoirs.* Privately printed, 1902; reprinted New York: Arno Press, 1968.

Tebbel, John William, and Mary Ellen Zuckerman. *The Magazine in America, 1741–1990.* New York: Oxford University Press, 1991.

Terrell, Mary Church. *A Colored Woman in a White World.* Washington, D.C.: Ransdell, 1940; reissued New York: Arno Press, 1980.

Thomas, Evangeline, ed. *Women Religious History Sources.* New York: R.R. Bowker Co., 1983.

Tierney, Helen. *Women's Studies Encyclopedia: Views from the Sciences.* New York: Greenwood, 1989.

Treadwell, Mattie E. *The Women's Army Corps.* Washington, D.C.: Office of the Chief of Military History, Department of the Army, 1954.

Truman, Margaret. *Women of Courage.* New York: William Morrow & Co., 1976.

Tyler, Alice. *Freedom's Ferment.* Minneapolis: University of Minnesota Press, 1944.

Underwood, John Levi. *The Women of the Confederacy.* New York: Neale Publishing Co., 1906.

U.S. Post Office. *Women on Stamps.* Washington, D.C.: Government Printing Office, 1995.

Van Kleeck, Mary. *Working Girls in Evening Schools.* New York: Survey Associates for The Russell Sage Foundation, 1914.

Veglahn, Nancy J. *Women Scientists.* New York: Facts On File, 1991.

Velazques, Loreta Janeta. *The Woman in Battle: A Narrative of the Exploits, Adventures, and Travels of Madame Loreta Janeta Valazquez.* Hartford, Conn.: T. Belknap, 1876; reissued New York: Arno Press, 1972.

Ware, Susan. *Holding Their Own: American Women in the 1930s.* Boston: Twayne Publishers, 1982.

Warren, Mercy Otis. *History of the Rise, Progress, and Termination of the American Revolution.* Boston: Manning and Loring, 1805.

Weatherford, Doris. *American Women and World War II.* New York: Facts On File, 1990.

———. *American Women's History: An A-Z of People, Organizations, Issues, and Events.* New York: Prentice-Hall, 1994.

———. *Foreign and Female: Immigrant Women in America, 1840–1930.* New York: Schocken, 1986; revised edition, New York: Facts On File, 1996.

Weimann, Jeanne Madeline. *The Fair Women.* Chicago: Academy, 1981.

Wells-Barnett, Ida. *Crusade for Justice: The Autobiography of Ida B. Wells,* edited by Alfreda M. Duster. Chicago: University of Chicago Press, 1970.

Wertheimer, Barbara Mayer. *We Were There: The Story of Working Women in America.* New York: Pantheon, 1977.

Wertz, Richard W. *Lying-In: A History of Childbirth in America.* New York: The Free Press, 1977.

Whiting, Lilian. *Women Who Have Ennobled Life.* Philadelphia: The Union Press, 1915.

Whitman, Alden. *The Obituary Book.* New York: Stein & Day, 1964.

Willard, Frances E., and Mary Livermore, eds. *A Woman of the Century: Leading American Women.* New York: Charles Wells Moulton, 1893; reissued Detroit: Gale Research, 1967.

Wilson, Dorothy Clarke. *Palace of Healing: The Story of Dr. Clara Swain.* New York: McGraw-Hill, 1968.

———. *Stranger and Traveler: The Story of Dorothea Dix, American Reformer.* Boston: Little, Brown, 1975.

Woody, Thomas. *History of Women's Education in the United States,* 2 vols. New York: Science Press, 1929.

Woolstein, Howard B. *Prostitution in the United States.* New York: The Century Co., 1921; reissued New York: Appleton-Century, 1969.

Worthington, C.J., ed. *The Woman in Battle.* Hartford, Conn.: T. Belknap, 1876.

Wortman, Marlene Stein. *Woman in American Law: From Colonial Times to the New Deal.* New York: Holmes & Meier, 1985.

Wright, Frances. *Views on Society and Manners in America.* London: Longman, Hurst, et al., 1821; reissued Cambridge, Mass.: Harvard University Press, 1963.

Wyoming Society of the Colonial Dames. *Brides on the Open Range, 1875–1887.* Cheyenne: privately printed, 1936.

Yost, Edna. *American Women of Science.* Philadelphia: Fredrick A. Stokes, 1943.

Zophy, Angela Howard, ed. *Handbook of American Women's History.* New York: Garland, 1990.

PERIODICAL ARTICLES

Anderson, M. "Negro Women on the Production Front." *Opportunity: Journal of Negro Life* (April 1943).

Bottome, P. "Woman After Two Wars." *Independent Woman* (February 1944).

Bourke-White, Margaret. "Women in Lifeboats." *Life*, February 22, 1943.

Brown, Patricia Leigh. "A Ghostwriter and Her Sleuth: 63 Years of Nancy Drew." *The New York Times*, Sunday, May 9, 1993.

Burroughs, Nannie Helen. "Chloroform Your Uncle Toms." *The Louisiana Weekly*, December 23, 1933.

Child, Richard. "The Industrial Revolt at Lawrence." *Collier's*, vol. 48, March 9, 1912.

Clarke, A.R. "Thirty-seven Months as Prisoners of War." *American Journal of Nursing* (May 1945).

Clephane, W.C. "Local Aspects of Slavery in the District of Columbia," *Records of the Columbia Historical Society* (1899).

Commetti, Elizabeth. "Women in the American Revolution." *New England Quarterly* (September 1947).

Eckhaus, Phyllis. "The Brief Life of a Passionate Feminist: Inez Milholland, 1886–1916," *Harvard Magazine* (Nov.-Dec. 1994).

Evans, Richard Xavier. "The Ladies Union Benevolent and Employment Society, 1850." *Records of the Columbia Historical Society* (1938).

Field, Vena Bernadette. "Constantia: A Study of the Life and Works of Judith Sargeant Murray." *University of Maine Studies* (February 1931).

Fleeson, D. "Within Sound of the Guns." *Woman's Home Companion* (January 1944).

Gildersleeve, Virginia C. "Women Must Help Stop Wars." *Woman's Home Companion* (May 1945).

Harris, Ted C. "Jeanette Rankin in Georgia." *Georgia Historical Society Quarterly* (Winter 1974).

"Heroic Nurses of Bataan and Corregidor." *American Journal of Nursing* (August 1942).

Huddleston, Sarah M. "Mrs. E.D.E.N. Southworth and Her Cottage." *Records of the Columbia Historical Society*, 1920.

Kellor, Frances A. "The Protection of Immigrant Women." *Atlantic* (February 1908).

Jorgenson, Chester E. "Gleanings from Judith Sargeant Murray." *American Literature* (March 1940).

Larsen, Arthur J. "Crusader and Feminist: Letters of Jane Grey Swisshelm." Minnesota Historical Society, *Narratives and Documents* (1934).

Lawson, Ellen N., and Marlene Merrill. "Antebellum Black Coeds at Oberlin College." *Oberlin Alumni Magazine* (Jan.-Feb., 1980).

Lee, Don L. "The Achievement of Gwendolyn Brooks." *Black Scholar* (Summer 1972).

Luce, Clare Booth. "Victory Is a Woman." *Woman's Home Companion* (November 1943).

Mayer, Dale C. "An Uncommon Woman: The Quiet Leadership Style of Lou Henry Hoover." *Presidential Studies Quarterly* (Fall 1990).

McAfee, Mildred. "Women's Reserves." *Annals of the American Academy of Political Science* (May 1943).

Merrill, Marlene D. "Daughters of America Rejoice: The Oberlin Experience." *TimeLine* (Oct.-Nov. 1987).

Oldham, Ellen M. "Early Women Printers of America." *Boston Public Library Quarterly* (Jan.-July 1958).

"One Hundred American Women Who Made a Difference." *Women's History* (in association with the National Women's History Project), vol. 1, no. 1 (March 1995).

Porter, Sarah. "Life and Times of Ann Royall." *Records of the Columbia Historical Society*, 1907.

Post, Robert C., ed. "1876: A Centennial Exhibition." *Smithsonian* (1976).

Proctor, John C. "Belva Ann Lockwood." *Records of the Columbia Historical Society* (1933).

Quarles, Benjamin. "Frederick Douglass and the Woman's Rights Movement." *Journal of Negro History* (June 1940).

"Records of Deborah Sampson Gannett, Woman Soldier of the American Revolution." *Prologue: The Journal of the National Archives* ( ).

Rector, Theresa A. "Black Nuns as Educators." *Journal of Negro Education*, 1982.

Reed, Helen L. "Women's Work at the Harvard Observatory." *New England Magazine* (April 1892).

"Role of the Black Mammy in the Plantation Household." *Journal of Negro History* (July 1938).

Selmon, Bertha. "History of Women in Medicine." *Medical Woman's Journal* (December 1947).

Spector, Bert. "The Great Salk Vaccine Mess," *Antioch Review* (1980)

Stone, Lucy. "Oberlin and Women." *Oberlin Jubilee* (1883).

Stuhler, Barbara. "Organizing for the Vote." *Minnesota History* (Fall 1995).

Sullivan, Mrs. Thomas. "I Lost Five Sons." *American Magazine* (March 1944).

Thompson, Dorothy. "New Woman in the New America." *Ladies' Home Journal* (January 1945)

———. "Women and the Coming World." *Ladies' Home Journal* (October 1943).

Tucker, David M. "Miss Ida B. Wells and Memphis Lynching." *Phylon: The Atlanta University Review of Race and Culture* (Summer 1971).

Turner, Edward R. "Women's Suffrage in New Jersey: 1790–1807," *Smith College Studies in History* (October 1915–July 1916).

Villard, Oswald Garrison. "Shall We Conscript Women?" *Christian Century*, August 4, 1943.

Vorse, Mary Heaton. "The Girls of Elkton, Maryland: Munitions Workers." *Harper's* (March 1943).

ARCHIVES CONSULTED

(Abigail) Adams National Historic Site
American Labor Museum
Arizona Historical Society
Boston Public Library Rare Book Department
Boston University Mugar Nursing Achives
Cayuga County [New York] Historical Society
Colorado Historical Society
Deerfield [Massachusetts] Historical Society

Dutch Settlers Society of Albany
General Federation of Women's Clubs, Washington
Georgetown University Special Collections
Historic New Orleans Collection
Holland Society of New York
Houghton Rare Books Library, Harvard University
Johnson Hall [New York] Historic Site
Library of Congress
Maryland Historical Society
Maryland State Archives
Metropolitan Historical Commission of Nashville, Tennessee
Minneapolis Public Library Special Collections
Minnesota Historical Society
Mogan Center for Lowell [Massachusetts] History
Mount Holyoke College
National Archives
National Park Service
New York Public Library
Ninety Nines, Inc./International Women Pilots, Oklahoma City
Oberlin College Archives
Rockefeller Archives Center
Schlesinger Library of Radcliffe College
Seneca Falls Historical Society
Sewall-Belmont House/National Woman's Party
Shaker Heritage Society, Watervliet, New York, and Harrodsburg, Kentucky
Smithsonian Institution
Sophia Smith Collection of Smith College
Susan B. Anthony House of Rochester
Temple University Urban Archives
Harriet Tubman Home, Auburn, New York
University of California Bancroft Library
University of Illinois at Chicago/Hull House
University of South Florida Special Collections
USS *Constitution*, Charlestown, Massachusetts
Maggie L. Walker National Historic Site
Emma Willard School, Troy, New York
Women's Hall of Fame, Seneca Falls, New York
[Woman's] Medical College of Pennsylvania Archives
Women in Memorial Service to America, Inc., Washington, D.C.
Women's Rights National Historical Park, Seneca Falls, New York

Index

Page numbers in *italics* indicate illustrations

INDEX FRANÇAIS